Toxic Torts

The U.S. tort, or personal injury law, cloaked behind increased judicial review of science, is changing before our eyes, except we cannot see it. U.S. Supreme Court decisions beginning with *Daubert v. Merrell Dow Pharmaceutical* altered how courts review scientific testimony and its foundation in the law. The complexity of both science and the law mask the overall social consequences of these decisions. Yet they are too important to remain hidden. Mistaken reviews of scientific evidence can decrease citizen access to the law, increase incentives for firms not to test their products, lower deterrence for wrongful conduct and harmful products, and decrease the possibility of justice for citizens injured by toxic substances. Even if courts review evidence well, greater judicial scrutiny increases litigation costs and attorney screening of clients and decreases citizens' access to the law. This book introduces these issues, reveals the relationships that can deny citizens just restitution for harms suffered, and shows how justice can be enhanced in toxic tort cases.

Carl F. Cranor is Professor of Philosophy at the University of California, Riverside. His work focuses on issues concerning the legal and scientific adjudication of risks from toxic substances and from the new genetic technologies. He has written *Regulating Toxic Substances: A Philosophy of Science and the Law* (1993), edited *Are Genes Us? The Social Consequences of the New Genetics* (1994), and coauthored the U.S. Congress' Office of Technology Assessment report, *Identifying and Regulating Carcinogens* (1987). His articles have appeared in diverse journals such as *The American Philosophical Quarterly, Ethics, Law and Contemporary Problems, Risk Analysis,* and the *American Journal of Public Health.* He is a Fellow of the American Association for the Advancement of Science and the Collegium Ramazzini and a member of the Center for Progressive Reform, a nonprofit think tank of legal scholars committed to protecting the public health and the environment.

Toxic Torts

Science, Law, and the Possibility of Justice

Carl F. Cranor

University of California, Riverside

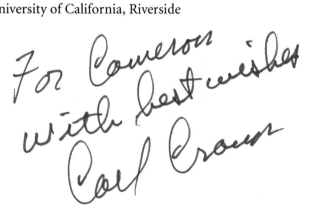

 CAMBRIDGE
UNIVERSITY PRESS

CAMBRIDGE UNIVERSITY PRESS
Cambridge, New York, Melbourne, Madrid, Cape Town,
Singapore, São Paulo, Delhi, Mexico City

Cambridge University Press
32 Avenue of the Americas, New York, NY 10013-2473, USA

www.cambridge.org
Information on this title: www.cambridge.org/9780521728409

First published 2006
First paperback edition 2007
Reprinted 2012

A catalog record for this publication is available from the British Library.

Library of Congress Cataloging in Publication Data

Cranor, Carl F.
Toxic torts : science, law, and the possibility of justice / Carl F. Cranor
    p. cm.
Includes bibliographical references and index.
ISBN 0-521-86182-9 (hardback : alk. paper)
1. Toxic torts – United States.   2. Hazardous substances – Law and legislation – United States.
3. Chemicals – Law and legislation – United States.   I. Title.
KF1299.H39C73   2006
346.7303′8 – dc22   2006015960

ISBN 978-0-521-86182-3 Hardback
ISBN 978-0-521-72840-9 Paperback

For Crystal, Chris, and Taylor

Contents

Preface

It is tempting to say that our tort, or personal injury, law is changing before our eyes, except we cannot see it. These modifications are occurring because of Supreme Court decisions that increased the screening of expert (largely scientific) testimony in the law, but it is difficult for all but the best informed to comprehend them. Some who understand them welcome them, some do not, and some will have more mixed assessments of them. However, most citizens cannot even have an opinion on the relevant issues because they are unaware of them and because the topics themselves are not easily accessible. The barriers to understanding this important legal institution are the result of subtleties most of us never think about – issues about scientific evidence and reasoning, and legal procedures that are complex and inaccessible to most of us.

The actual and potential transformations of this part of our legal system are too important, however, to remain hidden and too important for an informed citizenry to be left in the dark about them. Citizens risk having their realistic access to the tort law and the possibility of justice within it reduced and they will not know it. Judges and lawyers are at risk of being manipulated by slogans about "sound science," not realizing there are more scientifically accurate and legitimate ways to think about science, law, and the interaction between the two. There is even a risk to the legitimacy of the law itself, if mistaken scientific arguments are used to frustrate its aims. The issues posed by the potential changes in our legal system are not easy, however. In order to "see" and come to have a better appreciation of them, we must understand more about some of the procedures in the law that occur before trial, not something most of us are aware of. We also must understand some basics of the sciences that assist in revealing human harm from exposure to toxic substances. In addition, there are subtleties about these sciences and different evidentiary patterns of harm that must be appreciated. Too simplistic a view of the subjects will inadvertently skew the science, the law, and our protections under it.

This book seeks to make some progress on these issues. I have sought to introduce those not familiar with legal procedures to some of the basics of the law to locate the legal issues. I also have sought to introduce those not familiar with some of the basics in the relevant sciences to such information. However, in order to understand subtler points about law and science and their joint consequences for the law, the discussion must go further. Consequently, it is necessary to discuss details of legal procedure as well as legal decisions that have brought the changes or that have implemented them. We should understand what judges have said about science in adjudicating alleged personal injuries from exposure to toxic substances. However, to assess the impact of their decisions and the reasons they have given for reviewing the science as they did, we also need to appreciate some of the finer points about different kinds of scientific evidence, how it can be integrated to show harm, and how scientists utilize studies in order to arrive at judgments that a substance has contributed to harm. In short, one cannot shrink from grappling with some of the details of scientific evidence and reasoning. I have tried to address these issues, but in a way that provides the reader with an understanding of how the interaction between science and the tort law can profoundly affect our realistic access to the legal system, our possibilities of justice within it, and deterrence of wrongful behavior or harmful products.

In writing this book, I have learned and had various kinds of assistance from many. I will no doubt forget some whose comments, insights, contributions, or conversations have been of value, but I hope not. If I have, I hope they will forgive my faulty memory. Three people ably assisted research on and the preparation of the final manuscript. David Strauss provided excellent research assistance, including research on case reports (Chapter 4), many useful conversations, and fine editorial skills in earlier stages of the project. Richard Doan, Shannon Polchow, and Laura Lawrie gave excellent, detailed help in preparing the manuscript for publication. In the intellectual gestation that is needed for a project such as this, I received invitations to contribute to a variety of conferences, journals, or volumes that facilitated the development of some of the ideas that found their way into the book. Invitations from John Conley, Susan Haack, Sharon Lloyd, Michael Moore, Lee Tilson, David Shier, David Michaels, Celeste Monforton, Tom McGarity, Raphael Metzger, Wendy Wagner, and Rena Steinzor were particularly important. They provided quite helpful comments on drafts of earlier papers or on the book itself over the years. I also learned from Margaret Berger, Michael Green, Peter Graham, Paul Hoffman, Joe Sanders, Katherine Squibb, Vern Walker, Lauren Zeise, and numerous others. I had the opportunity to present much earlier versions of some of the chapters of the book (which would now be unrecognizable) to the Southern California Law and Philosophy Discussion Group. Comments by Gregory Keating, Larry Solum, Sharon Lloyd, Steve Munzer, Marshall Cohen, Aaron James, Cynthia Stark, and Chris Naticchia early on assisted the development of the ideas in the text.

I have had the good fortune to deepen my understanding of science, scientific reasoning, and aspects of the law as a result of several kinds of experiences.

Early research on risk assessment and an appointment as a Congressional Fellow in 1987, where I served at Congress's Office of Technology Assessment, provided important background. Service on California's Proposition 65 Science Panel in the early 1990s, a recent appointment to California's Electric and Magnetic Fields Science Advisory Panel (1999–2002), and membership on the University of California, Irvine's, Scholars Committee to Evaluate Perchlorate (2003–2004) gave me the opportunity to see up close numerous examples of scientific studies, scientific reasoning, interpretations of evidence, and even legitimate disagreements between well-respected scientists. I was a participant on these panels but also an observer of them. I gained much from both roles. Attendance at annual meetings of the Collegium Ramazzini and conversations with Fellows of the Collegium have kept me in touch with leading researchers and developments in cancer research. Considerable contact with members of the University of California scientific community also has been invaluable. Jerry Last, long-time director of the University of California's Toxic Substances Research and Teaching Program, should be mentioned, not so much for particular contributions to this project, but for enticing me down this path, trenchant comments along the way, and a good deal of financial and other support over the years. Raymond Neutra pointed me toward important methodological research that was ultimately quite valuable. I owe special thanks to David Eastmond, Chair of the Environmental Toxicology Program, a coauthor and collaborator. I could always call on him to provide examples or references, to make suggestions for extending the ideas, to read something I had written, and to ensure that I understood scientific points and had expressed them correctly. A joint research project with Dave funded by National Science Foundation Grant No. 99–10952 ("A Philosophic and Scientific Investigation of the Use of Scientific Evidence in Toxic Tort Law") together with grants from the University of California's Toxic Substances Research and Teaching Program greatly facilitated background research as well as work on the book itself. Intramural funds from the University of California, Riverside, assisted along the way. The writings of and many conversations with my colleague Larry Wright, a nearly career-long student of nondeductive inferences, have deepened my understanding of the forms of argument that are central to science.

Contacts with practicing lawyers and scientific witnesses and brief involvement in some litigation have provided more ground-level views of the law and some of the hurdles faced by lawyers and experts in presenting science in toxic tort cases. Many, many conversations with Joe Cecil over the years have challenged and clarified my thinking on these issues. Joe and several anonymous reviewers provided immensely valuable comments on the submitted version of the manuscript that greatly improved the final version. John Berger of Cambridge University Press has been a supportive and imaginative editor for this project. Although I have learned from many in working on this book, none of them is responsible for any errors or shortcomings in the final product. The love and support of my family – Crystal, Chris, and Taylor – have made the task much easier (although their patience with discussions of toxicants, law, or science may be approaching a limit).

I have tried to present some of the actual and potential transformations in toxic tort law as a result of recent legal decisions and how it could better incorporate and utilize complex scientific evidence in the future to achieve its goals. I hope this helps others to think further about the issues and to better understand this part of our legal system.

1

The Veil of Science over Tort Law Policy

INTRODUCTION

A significant, unseen revolution in the tort (personal injury) law is in progress. It is hidden from the public, except for those litigating toxic tort issues and well-informed researchers. These legal changes are difficult to discern because they are veiled behind a fabric of scientific complexity and detail, as well as arcane legal procedures that are not well known and are difficult to penetrate. Yet this veil must be lifted, the scientific and legal issues understood and put into perspective in order to appreciate the policy modifications in our legal system that can substantially affect the safety of ordinary citizens, both plaintiff and defense bars, corporate behavior, and fundamental legal relationships between citizens. This revolution involves science, law, and the possibility of justice for those who have been injured by the actions or products of others. What is the relationship among science, law, and the possibility of justice that it poses a problem?

Ordinarily, science has nothing to do with justice. Science provides one of the most reliable means for investigating empirical claims and producing comparatively objective evidence about them. Scientific research has resulted in considerable accumulation of knowledge about the world,[1] in a substantial track record of predicting observable events,[2] and as a consequence in "huge advances in human understanding [of the natural world and forces in it] . . . over the ages."[3] Scientific research greatly informs our understanding of human and animal biology, our environment and the larger world around us. Moreover, certain fields of science – epidemiology, toxicology, and clinical medicine, among others – are centrally needed to inform courts of whether and to what

---

[1] Philip Kitcher, *The Advancement of Science: Science without Legend, Objectivity without Illusions* (New York: Oxford University Press, 1993), 1.

[2] Alvin I. Goldman, *Knowledge in a Social World* (New York: Oxford University Press, 1999), 249.

[3] Larry Wright, *Critical Thinking* (New York: Oxford University Press, 2001), 233.

extent exposure to a product might have contributed to someone's injuries. Knowledge and understanding are the dominant virtues of scientific inquiry.

Justice, by contrast, provides normative guides for assessing our institutions, our laws and our relations to one another. It assists the design of laws or institutions when it is necessary to create new ones. Justice is the "first virtue of social institutions"[4] and the preeminent virtue of the law. A central principle of justice for the law is that if one person injures another without legitimate justification or excuse, the first should "put the matter right" with the injured party.[5] Putting the matter right might "require the harm-doer to restore something to the person harmed, or to repair a damaged object, or (when the unharmed position cannot be restored, as it usually cannot be) to compensate the harm-sufferer."[6] This is a matter of corrective or rectificatory justice. Matters must be set right between the parties because "the harm-doer and harm-sufferer are to be treated as equals, neither more deserving than the other . . . one is not entitled to become relatively better off by harming the other."[7]

Personal injury or tort law is one aspect of the law that provides a forum in which those who have been wrongly injured by the actions or products of others may seek redress for their injuries. It is largely concerned with implementing corrective or rectificatory justice.

The relationship among science, law, and justice has become a pressing issue because of recent decisions by the U.S. Supreme Court in *Daubert v. Merrell Dow Pharmaceutical* and its *sequelae, General Electric v. Joiner* and *Kumho Tire v. Carmichael*.[8] A variety of considerations probably moved the Court to rule on the issues in these cases, most of which I do not mention. However, among other things it sought to ensure that legal cases were not based on grossly mistaken science and that legal decisions better comported with the science needed in the cases at the bar.[9] The particular mechanism it used to ensure

---

4 John Rawls, *A Theory of Justice* (Cambridge, MA: The Belknap Press of Harvard University Press, 1971), 3.

5 Tony Honoré, "The Morality of Tort Law – Questions and Answers," in *Philosophical Foundations of Tort Law*, ed. David G. Owen (Oxford: Clarendon Press, 1995), 79.

6 Honoré, "The Morality of Tort Law," 79.

7 Honoré, "The Morality of Tort Law," 79.

8 *Daubert v. Merrell Dow Pharm., Inc.*, 509 U.S. 579 (1993); *General Elec. Co. v. Joiner*, 522 U.S. 136 (1997); *Kumho Tire Co. v. Carmichael*, 526 U.S. 137 (1999).

9 Justice Stephen Breyer, "Introduction," *Federal Reference Manual on Scientific Evidence*, 2nd ed. (Washington, DC: Federal Judicial Center, 2000), 3–4. Other motivations included how to handle different types of evidence in toxic tort litigation, a concern that too much "junk science" entered the courtroom, a desire to foster case-processing efficiency and economy. Perhaps they were even interested in changing the balance between plaintiffs and defendants (toward defendants) and shifting decision-making power from judges to juries. See Margaret A. Berger, "Upsetting the Balance Between Interests: The Impact of Supreme Court's Trilogy on Expert Testimony in Toxic Tort Litigation," *Law and Contemporary Problems* 64 (Summer 2001): 289–326, as well as Michael H. Gottesman, "From *Barefoot* to *Daubert* to *Joiner*: Triple Play or Double Error," *Arizona Law Review* 40 (1998): 753–780, for discussions of these points.

this was to impose on judges a heightened duty to review scientific testimony and its foundation before experts could testify in a trial (this is a review of the "admissibility" of evidence). These Supreme Court decisions have wide application, but two of them concerned toxic torts, or claims for personal injuries in which the plaintiffs alleged that toxic substances had harmed them. Moreover, adjudication of toxic torts centrally needs science to ensure justice between parties. Toxic torts, thus, are the focus of this book.

Concerns about the possibility of justice for wrongfully injured parties have developed as a result of the Supreme Court decisions and how courts have subsequently reviewed scientific testimony and its foundation. Judges have probably increased their scientific sophistication as a result of the trilogy of cases.[10] They may have further to go, however. If courts do not review scientific testimony and its foundation sufficiently well, they risk denying one of the parties at the bar the possibility of justice. Plaintiffs are the litigants at greatest risk, because they have the initial burden to produce evidence. However, even if courts review evidence well, the fact and perception of greater judicial scrutiny increases litigation costs and attorney screening of clients. These, too, decrease citizen access to the law and decrease the possibility of justice for those injured by toxic substances. Together these can threaten the legitimacy of torts as an institution committed to correcting wrongs inflicted on citizens.

As citizens we cannot "see," that is, understand, the institution and the subtle changes that are occurring without appreciating some of the details of science, law, and the science-law interaction. The subjects addressed in this book arise from the fact that we live in a scientific and technological society, but we have not yet fully developed sufficient institutional expertise, norms and procedures to ensure that science and the law will function well together and to give injured parties the realistic possibility of justice.

Aspects of our collective scientific understanding have resulted in products that are among the benefits of an advanced technological society. These include not only the products of an earlier period of industrialization but also the products of the chemical revolution that was born in the nineteenth century and grew to maturity following World War II. There is also the promise of social benefits from more recent developments that have yet to fully to mature in DNA and biotechnological research, as well as nanotechnology, the science and engineering of the vanishingly small.

However, the same products that provide benefits may also carry risks of harm themselves or in their manufacture, by-products, use or disposal. In some instances the products, the processes by which they are produced, their disposal, or other of their unanticipated features result in actual harm to those who are exposed to them. The law is the main institution that aims to provide protections from risks and any harms that might result if the risks materialize.

---

[10] Berger, "Upsetting the Balance Between Interests," 300, note 71.

Some legal institutions have the responsibility to try to prevent such harms from occurring in the first place – typically these are the *regulatory* or *administrative* institutions. Some administrative agencies, such as the Food and Drug Administration (FDA) or parts of the Environmental Protection Agency (EPA), have legal authority to screen some products or substances, for example, drugs, new food additives, cosmetics (under the FDA), or pesticides (under the EPA) *before* they enter commerce and there is substantial human exposure. Laws authorizing such interventions are so-called premarket laws. Premarket screening laws impose legally mandated testing, agency review, and some level of demonstrated safety before the products are permitted to enter commerce. Other agencies, such as the Occupational Safety and Health Administration (OSHA), the Consumer Product Safety Commission (CPSC), and parts of the FDA and EPA, operate under laws that authorize them to identify the risks of harm *after* the products are in commerce, but *in theory* might authorize the use of surrogate means to identify the risks before they materialize into actual human health and environmental harm (although this may not be carried out well in practice). These are so-called postmarket laws.

If these laws *function well*, risks to persons will largely be prevented in the first place under premarket laws or they will be identified and then reduced or eliminated under postmarket laws before they cause (too much?) harm. However, such laws in themselves or as administered too often do not catch the risks before harm occurs to the public, the workforce, or the environment. And, of course, any accidents that cause harms should be redressed as a matter of corrective justice.

If firms, regulatory agencies, and others miss toxic substances or otherwise fail to protect citizens from harm, the tort law offers the possibility of corrective justice, of post-facto setting right the matter of a victim's injuries. That is, the tort law in principle aims to provide post-injury compensation sufficient to restore the injured person to the condition he or she would have been in had the injury not occurred in the first place (this, of course, is an ideal that in many cases cannot be realized). In addition, the threat of tort suits for harmful behavior or products aims to provide deterrence, some motivation for those whose activities or substances pose risks to others to modify their behavior and products to reduce the risks.[11] Torts, thus, could serve as a kind of backup to other institutions, if it functioned well.

Postinjury compensation (or punishment in the criminal law) is a distant second to avoiding injuries in the first place; "An ounce of prevention is worth a pound of cure," for the victim, his or her family, and typically for society as a whole.

---

[11] In quite extreme cases, even the criminal law may be utilized to try to deter firms from acting in ways likely to injury and may be utilized to punish those who deliberately or recklessly cause harm. See, for example, *People v. O'Neill, Film Recovery Systems, et al.,* 550 N.E. 2d 1090 (1990).

At its best, the tort law has probably functioned imperfectly. Indeed, a number of researchers have pointed out that in order for torts to serve the aims of justice and deterrence better there should be much more claiming on behalf of injured parties than typically occurs.[12] How federal and state courts review the use of expert testimony and its scientific foundation in the aftermath of these decisions profoundly affects the possibility of justice for citizens injured without legitimate excuse or justification. I will argue that the Supreme Court decisions concerning the review of scientific testimony and its foundation have further hampered the functioning of torts.

It is difficult to overestimate the social and legal importance of *Daubert*, its progeny, and their implementation by lower courts, which pose substantial philosophic and social issues. For example, following this decision the percentage of cases ending in summary judgments before trial more than doubled with 90 percent of them going against plaintiffs.[13] The Federal Judicial Center surveyed federal judges and attorneys about expert testimony in 1991 and 1998. Although in 1991 75 percent of the judges reported admitting all proffered expert testimony, by 1998 59 percent indicated that they admitted all proffered expert testimony without limitation.[14] Significantly, what little research has been done suggests that when trial courts have excluded scientific experts and litigants appealed, federal appellate courts decided more cases against plaintiffs than against defendants. Appellate courts also tend to rule more against plaintiffs than did the trial courts of origin.[15]

Some courts' *implementation* of *Daubert* and its progeny have erected unreasonably high or scientifically mistaken barriers for admitting expert testimony based on scientific evidence into tort trials. Scientific evidence and reasoning appear to be more complex than judges were prepared for when the Supreme Court enhanced their responsibilities. Such decisions result in a factually inaccurate basis on which to base further legal proceedings and, thus may deny the victims of toxic exposures the possibility of a public trial for their claims of wrongfully inflicted injuries and the possibility of justice. More rarely, they can deny defendants a reasonable defense.[16] In many cases, courts are setting

---

[12] Michael J. Saks, "Do We Really Know Anything about the Behavior of the Tort Litigation System – and Why Not?" *Pennsylvania Law Review* 140 (1992): 1183–1190, 1284–1286; Clayton P. Gillette and James E. Krier, "Risk, Courts and Agencies," *University of Pennsylvania Law Review*, 38 (1999): 1077–1109.

[13] L. Dixon and B. Gill, *Changes in the Standards for Admitting Expert Evidence in Federal Civil Cases Since the Daubert Decision* (Santa Monica, CA: RAND Institute for Civil Justice, 2002).

[14] Molly Treadway Johnson, Carol Krafka, and Joe S. Cecil, *Expert Testimony in Federal Civil Trials: A Preliminary Analysis* (Federal Judicial Center ed., 2000).

[15] Kevin M. Clermont and Theodore Eisenberg, "Anti-Plaintiff Bias in the Federal Appellate Courts," *Judicature* 84 (2000): 128. (New research "reveals an unlevel appellate playing field: defendants succeed significantly more often than plaintiffs on appeal from civil trials – especially from jury trials" (128).)

[16] Recently, the City of Chicago was required to compensate a man for brain-stem injuries following an encounter with the police. The city was unable to mount a defense based on an

substantive policies in tort law but disguising it behind a veil of scientific rulings. How courts conduct evidentiary reviews also may threaten the constitutional right to a jury trial, if a trial judge overreaches his or her authority to review the scientific foundation of expert evidence and mistakenly keeps a plaintiff from receiving a jury trial.[17] Poor implementation of *Daubert* and its progeny will also decrease plaintiffs' access to the legal system, because of courts' dismissal of cases or attorneys' screening out all but the most winnable of cases.[18] As a result, there will be fewer settlements and fewer successful trials for deserving plaintiffs, further weakening any tort law deterrence to those who create use and distribute toxic products.[19] Poor implementation of *Daubert* may tempt firms to be less responsible than they might otherwise be in testing their products or to hide the results of studies showing adverse effects, lead to more toxic substances entering commerce, and drive good scientists from participating in the legal system, a task they are reluctant to undertake in any case. Of course, if courts admit too many experts who testify beyond the evidence or their expertise or, worse, are dishonest, this can lead to overdeterrence and keep beneficial products from the market or increase their costs. At a minimum, then, it is important for courts to be quite accurate in reviewing expert testimony in order to serve both sides of the bar and justice in torts.

However, even if judicial admissibility decisions were *implemented well* within the *Daubert* framework, there remains a concern about whether this would be adequate. Heightened judicial screening of scientific experts increases the pre-trial costs and procedural hurdles of bringing a case. This almost

alternative theory of injury because its expert's theory was judged "too speculative" and the expert was not admitted for trial. (Margaret Cronin Fisk, "Chicago Hope: A $28M Verdict," *National Law Journal*, 10 Nov. 1999, A10.)

17 Raphael Metzger, "The Demise Of *Daubert* In State Courts," Commentary for Lexis Nexis MEALEY'S Emerging Toxic Torts 14 (5) (June 3, 2005): located at http://www.mealeys.com. Some state and federal courts also have expressed such views: *Howerton v. Arai Helmet, Ltd.* (2004) 348 N.C. 440, 697 S.E.2d 674, 692 (Under the authority of *Daubert* courts "may unnecessarily encroach upon the constitutionally mandated function of the jury to decide issues of fact and to assess the weight of the evidence."); *Brasher v. Sandoz Pharmaceuticals Corp.* (N.D. Ala. 2001) 160 F. Supp. 2d 1291, 1295 (applying *Daubert*, but noting that "[f]or the trial court to overreach in the gatekeeping function and determine whether the opinion evidence is correct or worthy of credence is to usurp the jury's right to decide the facts of the case"); *Logerquist v. McVey*, 196 Ariz. 470, 488, 1 P.3d 113, 131 (2000) ("The Daubert/Joiner/Kumho trilogy of cases . . . puts the judge in the position of passing on the weight or credibility of the expert's testimony, something we believe crosses the line between the legal task of ruling on the foundation and relevance of evidence and the jury's function of whom to believe and why, whose testimony to accept, and on what basis."); *Bunting v. Jamieson*, 984 P.2d 467, 472 (Wyo. 1999) (adopting *Daubert*, but nonetheless expressing concern that "application of the Daubert approach to exclude evidence has been criticized as a misappropriation of the jury's responsibilities. . . . '[I]t is imperative that the jury retain its fact-finding function.'").

18 Gillette and Krier, "Risk, Courts and Agencies," 1077–1109.

19 Carl F. Cranor, "Scientific Reasoning in the Laboratory and the Law," *American Journal of Public Health*, Supplement 95:S1 (2004): S121–S128.

certainly reduces plaintiffs' *realistic* access to the law because of greater attorney and expert screening of the merit of victims' cases. Without access injured parties are denied the possibility of justice. It also is likely to exacerbate existing perverse incentives for defendants not to test and not to monitor their products. Finally, it does not adequately address more fundamental science-law problems. Within existing legal structures, there is insufficient legal concern with the safety of products before they enter commerce. There is too little legally required testing of products prior to commercialization and significant human exposure. Thus, too many products and substances enter commerce without adequate scientific understanding of their properties and consequences. Once products are in commerce there also appears to be too little monitoring of products for adverse effects. In addition, in the tort law, legally the burden of proof is on injured parties to show that the substances caused their harm, not an easy task. Moreover, scientific efforts to show such harm are hindered by the kinds of risks and harms involved, by human studies that too frequently fail to detect real adverse effects, by scientific procedures, and by the need to identify risks and harms on the frontiers of scientific disciplines. In many instances, the public and workforce, as well as the environment, become guinea pigs for determining which substances are harmful and which not.

Understanding these issues necessitates some understanding of details of two complex "institutions": science and the law. One must understand their procedures and practices, as well as how they can interact to produce such unfortunate outcomes and how they could interact better in order to provide reasonable protections against the risks and harms that can arise from the products of a modern technological society.

I sketch these issues and then develop them in the remainder of the book.

THE LEGAL ADMISSIBILITY OF EXPERT TESTIMONY AND SCIENTIFIC EVIDENCE

In establishing a legal case for compensating an injured party, the plaintiff must show that a defendant, who the plaintiff believed harmed her, had a legal duty to prevent harm, defendant breached that legal duty, plaintiff suffered a legally compensable injury, and defendant's action was the factual and legal cause of the injury in question. In many cases, the requisite legal action is in products liability, typically a strict liability body of law (in which defendant's negligence or carelessness need not be shown). However, it is critical that plaintiffs show that defendant's action or products *caused* or *contributed* to plaintiffs' injuries. In federal toxic tort cases, plaintiffs typically must establish that a defendant's substance "can cause" the adverse effect in question (so-called general causation) as well as that defendant's action or product "did cause" plaintiff's injury (so-called specific causation). Litigants seek to show such claims by means of scientific evidence and expert testimony, with experts testifying about what scientific studies show concerning alleged causal connections. However, for scientific experts to perform this function, they must be permitted to testify at trial; in legal argot, they must be "admitted" to give that testimony.

Before 1993, introducing scientific evidence and having experts admitted tended not to be overly difficult. If a litigant had well-qualified experts whose testimony was *relevant* to the scientific and technological issues, would assist a jury in understanding them, and was based on studies "generally accepted in the relevant scientific community," judges tended to admit them and let cross-examination during trial determine whose experts the jury believed.[20]

Since the 1993 *Daubert* decision, judges have conducted much more searching reviews of expert testimony and its foundation before trials commence. After initial complaint(s) and answer(s) have initiated a legal case, and after discovery (including depositions of the parties and experts involved), during *pretrial* hearings a judge hears from both parties and reviews whether the experts will be permitted to testify before a jury. If an expert critical to a litigant's case is not admitted, the litigant (typically the plaintiff) may be unable to establish factual premises needed for causation, in which case the judge would dismiss the attempted legal action because there would be no factual issue for the jury to decide.[21] (All of these issues are developed in more detail in Chapter 2.)

Thus, "preliminary" reviews of experts can result in dismissal of the case without a trial. Consequently, *how* and *how well* judges conduct their preliminary review of experts can determine the outcome of a legal action, affect the possibility of justice between parties and strongly influence wider social effects of the tort law.

The Need for Scientific Studies

The same scientific institutions, some of whose results have led to beneficial technological products, have developed investigative procedures, standards of proof, and research methods designed to produce comparatively objective knowledge that will stand the test of time. These are important features of the scientific enterprise and part of what provides its honorific standing among empirical inquiries. A subset of the health and biological sciences assists in identifying risks and harms to persons on which parties to litigation must rely

---

[20] David L. Faigman, David H. Kaye, Michael J. Saks, and Joseph Sanders, *Modern Scientific Evidence: The Law and Science of Expert Testimony* (St. Paul, MN: West Publishing Co., 2002), 7–8; Michael Gottesman, Georgetown Law Center, presentation at "Science, the Courts, and Protective Justice," February 27, 2003, sponsored by the Science and Environmental Health Network and Georgetown Environmental Law and Policy Institute.

[21] Fleming James, Jr. and Geoffrey C. Hazard, Jr., *Civil Procedure*, 2d ed. (Boston: Little, Brown and Company, 1977), 149. (Defendant is entitled to judgment as a matter of law, when there is no genuine issue of fact between the litigants.)

to argue for or defend against claims that a product has harmed someone. These include, *inter alia*, epidemiology, toxicology, genetic studies, and clinical medicine. Science is known for controlled studies (or studies which sufficiently mimic controlled studies) in which a variable in question is identified and studied in isolation from other effects to see if it makes a causal contribution to an effect. Ideally, such studies would involve large numbers of experimental and control subjects. Researchers seek to ensure that any results are not merely the result of accidental relationships but are appropriate representatives of more general features of substances and the affected population. Moreover, scientists take care to ensure that results are not mere artifacts of the studies themselves.

The careful design of studies, winnowing of data, and presentation of results that are the hallmark of scientific research transposed into the context of the tort law, perhaps surprisingly, can pose problems. There must be information available for study. There must be funding in order for studies to be conducted. Scientists must design sufficiently sensitive studies and have sufficient time to conduct them properly to detect the risk or harm in question. Procedures internal to science may slow the discovery of harm. Any scientific results to be utilized in a court case must be pertinent to the legal issues involved (but usually they are not designed for such purposes). There must be effective communication between scientists and judges, but conventions of science hinder this.

The preceding comments are merely an *abstract* statement of some of the problems concerning scientific studies needed for the tort law, but the practical use of them for a particular legal issue is often not straightforward; these conditions are not always easy to satisfy. Courts and many commentators may have underestimated these problems in toxic tort cases (issues I take up in Chapters 5 and 6).

Special Features of Toxic Substances

Properties of toxic substances exacerbate some of these problems, as well as stressing and straining the law. In order to show that exposure to toxic substances caused or contributed to human harm substantial, time-consuming, often long-term scientific studies are needed. Human epidemiological studies are among the best kinds of evidence of human harm from toxic exposure. However, these often have not been conducted on a substance or product at issue in a tort case. It is difficult to identify who has been exposed and how much exposure they received. The studies can be expensive to conduct. More seriously, judges and the larger public may not appreciate how insensitive they can be (that is, they do not detect comparatively rare diseases or subtle effects at all well). Regrettably, too frequently they cannot detect an adverse effect, even if it is present.

Scientists very often utilize studies in experimental animals, usually rats or mice, to provide evidence that substances cause or contribute to human harm. Although there is some disagreement about animal studies, most scientists, and especially toxicologists, view animal studies as quite good evidence for identifying toxicants and their adverse effects. The main reason is that the pathological development of tumors in other mammals is believed to resemble that in humans. Molecular, cellular, tissue and organ functions are believed to be similar between different species of mammals, including rodents and humans.[22] This is a feature of the "vertical integrity" of organisms.[23] Moreover, animal studies tend to have some advantages over human studies, as few epidemiological studies have been done and it is wrong deliberately to expose humans to toxicants to test for adverse effects.[24] However, animal studies are time-consuming and costly to conduct, taking at a minimum five years and costing $2 million to $5 million dollars.[25] In addition, often because of the rareness of disease effects, it is difficult to determine adverse effects at exposures to which humans are subject (exposures in animal research tend to be higher than human exposures to create studies sufficiently sensitive to detect diseases). As a result, extrapolation from adverse effects in animals to adverse effects in humans provides an opening for criticisms of them. Because of properties of toxicants, subtleties of their effects, and often rareness of diseases, there are enough needed scientific inferences to invite critiques. Animal studies (and other kinds of toxicological evidence) that can point to human harms are often denigrated and dismissed, although these kinds of evidence are better than many federal judges have said they are and usually much better than defendants will admit in court.

Any difficulties utilizing the different kinds of evidence for inferring causal relationships in the law are exacerbated by several specific features of typical biochemical risks that pose scientific difficulties. These problems in turn can

---

[22] D. P. Rall, M. D. Hogan, J. E. Huff, B. A. Schwetz, and R. W. Tennant, "Alternatives to Using Human Experience in Assessing Health Risks," *Annual Review of Public Health* 8 (1987): 355, 362–363 (noting that biological processes are quite similar from one species to another); James Huff and David P. Rall, "Relevance to Humans of Carcinogenesis Results from Laboratory Animal Toxicology Studies," in *Maxcy-Rosenau-Last Public Health & Preventive Medicine*, 12th ed., ed. John M. Last and Robert B. Wallace (Norwalk, CT: Appleton & Lange, 1992), 433, 439 (noting that significant scientific understanding of neural transmission, renal function, and cell replication and development of cancer have come from non-human species, often species far removed phylogenetically from humans [434]). James Huff makes somewhat stronger claims in "Chemicals and Cancer in Humans: First Evidence in Experimental Animals," *Environmental Health Perspectives* 100 (1993): 201, 204 (stating that the array and multiplicity of carcinogenic processes are virtually common among mammals, for instance between laboratory rodents and humans).

[23] Ellen K. Silbergeld, "The Role of Toxicology in Causation: A Scientific Perspective," *Courts, Health Science and the Law*, 1, 3 (1991): 374.

[24] Rall et al., "Alternatives to Using Human Experience in Assessing Health Risks," 362–63 (noting that for most chemicals, particularly environmental and occupational chemicals, epidemiologic data are insufficient to confirm the absence or presence of significant risk).

[25] Jerold Last, Director, University of California Toxic Substances Research and Teaching Program, personal communication, 18 Apr. 2004.

be exacerbated by the practices of scientific inquiry. The end result can stress and strain the legal system.

Carcinogens, reproductive toxicants, and neurotoxicants are invisible, undetectable intruders that can have long latency periods (e.g., from a few months to more than forty years for cancer[26]), rarely leave signature diseases, often operate by means of unknown, complex, subtle molecular mechanisms and, when they materialize into harm, injure humans in ways that researchers might not discover for years. The results can be catastrophic for affected individuals.[27] Understanding the properties of such substances and assessing any risks they pose, requires even more subtle scientific expertise and studies than for other areas of inquiry. And they usually must be conducted on the frontiers of existing scientific knowledge.[28]

The problems posed by the properties of molecular invaders are exacerbated by the effort, difficulties, costs, and time it takes to establish toxicity effects. Scientific studies for determining risks and harms can be comparatively insensitive (human epidemiological studies), not fully understood (animal studies used for inferring toxicity effects on humans), in their infancy (some short-term tests that hold some promise), or yet to be developed (molecular or DNA techniques that might aid etiological investigations).[29] Often researchers must assemble various kinds of evidence, most of which taken individually will not be decisive by itself, in order to identify a substance as toxic to humans. This can be subtle, arcane work, and some courts appear to have struggled to assess it.

These problems are aggravated in the circumstances of most toxic tort suits. Plaintiffs, needing to show that a substance causally contributed to a disease, often start at a substantial disadvantage for two reasons: first, in general little is known about the properties of potentially toxic substances, and, second, the tort law is in effect a post-market response to toxic injury. Consider these in turn.

There are about 100,000 chemical substances or their derivatives and metabolites registered for use in commerce. About one-third likely result in little exposure and another 23 percent are polymers, thus probably presenting only minimal risks (because they are large molecules).[30] Nonetheless, there remains substantial ignorance about this universe. The National Research Council in 1984 found that for the vast majority of substances there was no toxicity data

[26]   Carl F. Cranor and David A. Eastmond, "Scientific Ignorance and Reliable Patterns of Evidence in Toxic Tort Causation: Is There a Need for Liability Reform?" *Law and Contemporary Problems* 64 (2001): 6, 12–13.

[27]   Carl F. Cranor, *Regulating Toxic Substances* (New York: Oxford University Press, 1993), 3–5.

[28]   Cranor, *Regulating*, 12–48.

[29]   Cranor, *Regulating*, 12–48.

[30]   James Huff and David Hoel, "Perspective and Overview of the Concepts and Value of Hazard Identification as the Initial Phase of Risk Assessment for Cancer and Human Health," *Scandinavian Journal of Work Environment and Health* 18 (1992): 83–89.

in the public record.[31] In the early 1990s there was insufficient change in the data to justify updating the National Academy Report.[32] For the three thousand substances produced in the *highest volume*, there remained substantial knowledge-gaps for about 75 percent of them as recently as 1998 (only 7 percent had complete toxicity information) when the U.S. EPA entered into a voluntary agreement with the producers to close these gaps.[33] There were another one to twelve thousand high-production-volume substances for which extensive toxicological information would be quite important but that was not available.[34]

Thus, in general, the probability is that for any given substance little is likely to be known about it. Consequently, someone who alleges that they have been harmed by exposure to the substance must find experts who have studied or are aware of studies about such substances, but pertinent research may not have been done.

Secondly, the postmarket context of the tort law poses several issues. The law imposes the burden of proof on the plaintiff seeking to rectify the injuries from which she suffers. The plaintiff has the burden to produce enough evidence to justify a legal trial and the burden to persuade a jury that she more likely than not has been harmed by exposure to the substance. Equally or more important, however, plaintiff's experts may have to overcome implicit scientific burdens and standards of proof to establish that the substance in question can cause the harm that plaintiff suffered (scientific standards of proof tend to be much higher than legal standards of proof). This can be especially difficult for harms caused by molecules.

Moreover, plaintiffs are in a poor position to ferret out the evidence to toxicity and present it. The firms creating and using such substances are in a much better position to develop and investigate the properties of such substances. However, as the above generic data suggest, companies appear not to have done a good job of understanding and providing public information about the toxicity of their own products.[35] Thus, plaintiffs are substantially disadvantaged

[31] National Research Council, *Toxicity Testing: Strategies to Determine Needs and Priorities* (Washington, DC: U.S. Government Printing Office, 1984), 84.

[32] John C. Bailor, University of Chicago, and Eula Bingham, University of Cincinnati, members of the 1984 NRC Committee, personal communications at Collegium Ramazzini, Bologna, Italy, 2002.

[33] "EPA, EDF, CMA Agree on Testing Program Targeting 2,800 Chemicals," *Environmental Health Newsletter* (Business Publishers, Silver Spring, MD), 37 (Oct. 1998): 193; Elaine M. Faustman and Gilbert S. Omenn, "Risk Assessment," in *Casarett and Doull's Toxicology*, 6th ed., ed. Curtis D. Klaassen (New York: McGraw-Hill, 2001), 85–86.

[34] U.S. Congress, Office of Technology Assessment, *Screening and Testing Chemicals in Commerce* (Washington, DC: U.S. Government Printing Office, 1995), 3.

[35] See Cranor and Eastmond, "Scientific Ignorance," 14; Margaret A. Berger, "Eliminating General Causation: Notes Towards a New Theory of Justice and Toxic Torts," *Columbia Law Review* 97 (1997): 2135; Gerald Markowitz and David Rosner, *Deceit and Deception: The Deadly Politics of Industrial Pollution* (Berkeley: University of California Press, 2002);

as a result of factors beyond their control and often because of the failures of others.

In addition, with the exception of some products subject to pre-market testing, such as drugs, food additives and pesticides, most substances and products enter the marketplace without any *legally required* toxicity testing.[36] This almost ensures there will be poor data on the substance or product, about which plaintiffs then have the legal and scientific burdens to find and produce evidence. Because the regulation of suspect substances that enter the market without legally required testing will occur only if a governmental agency bears a burden of proof to show a *risk of harm* and a tort action will proceed only if a plaintiff shows *actual harm*, firms have incentives to resist testing their products and monitoring them for adverse effects and often they have not. (Governmental entities also have not always been forthcoming.[37])

The legal and scientific burdens and standards of proof in postmarket contexts can be exacerbated by inferential practices within science. In research for its own sake there is a standing temptation to do more research, gather more data, deepen understanding, and adopt standards of proof to ensure conclusions with greater certainty. If these are inappropriately or deliberately adopted by judges in reviewing expert testimony and scientific evidence, or exploited by those defending substances, this greatly increases already substantial barriers to tort law access and admissibility of experts.

INJURIES MAY LONG PRECEDE THE SCIENTIFIC UNDERSTANDING OF THE CAUSES OF INJURY

Ignorance about substances, corporate failure in assessing the toxicity of their products, some features of substances, and problems in establishing toxicity

Ricardo Alonso-Zaldivar & Davan Maharaj, "Tests Show Firestone 'Had to Know,' Probers Say," *Los Angeles Times*, 21 Sept. 2000, C1; "Safety: Congress Cites New Evidence Against Tire Maker as Sentiment Swings in Favor of Criminal Penalties in Such Cases," *Los Angeles Times*, 21 Sept. 2000, C1; Richard A. Oppel, Jr., "Environmental Tests 'Falsified,' U.S. Says," *New York Times*, 22 Sept. 2000, A14; Melody Petersen, "Settlement Is Approved in Diet Drug Case," *New York Times*, 29 Aug. 2000, C2; David Willman, "The Rise and Fall of the Killer Drug Rezulin; People Were Dying as Specialists Waged War Against Their FDA Superiors," *Los Angeles Times*, 4 June 2000, A1; David Willman, "Risk Was Known as FDA Ok'd Fatal Drug," *Los Angeles Times*, 11 March 2001, A1; and *In re: Phenylpropanolamine (PPA) Products Liability Litigation*, 289 F. Supp. 2d 1230 (2003) (W.D. Washington).

36 U.S. Congress, Office of Technology Assessment, *Identifying and Regulating Carcinogens* (Washington, DC: U.S. Government Printing Office, 1987), 126–127.

37 See, e.g., Gayle Greene, *The Woman Who Knew Too Much: Alice Stewart and the Secrets of Radiation* (Ann Arbor: University of Michigan Press, 1999) and Matthew L. Wald, "U.S. Acknowledges Radiation Killed Weapons, Workers," *New York Times*, 29 Jan. 2000, A1. The production of rocket fuel caused contamination in some of the nation's groundwater with perchlorate and other known toxicants (*In re: Redlands Tort Litigation* (2001), referenced in *Lockheed Martin Co. v. Superior Court*, 109 Cal. App.4th 24 (2003)).

effects together suggest that for any randomly selected substance it is unlikely that scientists will understand its toxicity properties well. Simply conducting the studies and accumulating the missing scientific information can be quite slow. As a consequence *injuries* from a substance might easily precede scientific understanding and documentation of that fact, and they might precede it by years, sometimes decades. Tort law compensation is retrospective. This poses a substantial problem: the possibility of justice for injured parties cannot be attained until there is sufficient legally recognized scientific evidence that exposure to a substance causes or contributes to disease. The comparatively sparse health and safety data about the vast majority of substances in the chemical universe substantially burdens the tort law in its aims of justice and deterrence.

However, there is a much deeper and more intractable issue: in many cases, it can take years to have clues that substances cause harm, and even longer to document the cause of damage. Whether scientists will ever have a full understanding of the toxicity of a given substance is an even more open issue (if they ever do). Consider benzene, an important industrial product and by now a well-known human carcinogen. Benzene was implicated in the 1890s of causing various blood diseases.[38] In the 1920s, it was reported to cause leukemia. By 1939 a number of investigators recommended substituting other products for benzene because of its known toxicity. In 1948 even the American Petroleum Institute "concluded that the only safe level from exposure to benzene was zero."[39] However, substantial regulation of benzene did not come for another sixty years. In 1974 the World Health Organization's International Agency for Research on Cancer, shortly after it was established in 1970, noted that it could only indicate that a relationship between benzene exposure and the development of leukemia was "suggested" by case reports and one case-control epidemiological study.[40] By 1982 the same organization judged that there was sufficient evidence that benzene was carcinogenic to man,[41] and by 1987 it found that benzene "*is* carcinogenic to man."[42] Surely people were

[38] R. Snyder, "The Benzene Problem in Perspective," *Fundamental and Applied Toxicology* 4 (1984): 692–699; H.G.S. van Raalte and P. Grasso, "Hematological, Myelotoxic, Clastogenic, Carcinogenic, and Leukemogenic Effects of Benzene," *Regulatory Toxicology and Pharmacology* 2 (1982): 153–176; *Casarett and Doull's Toxicology*, 4th ed., ed. Mary O. Amdur, John Doull, and Curtis D. Klaassen (New York: Pergamon Press, 1991), 686.

[39] European Environmental Agency, *Late Lessons from Early Warnings: The Precautionary Principle 1896–2000, Environmental Issue Report no.* 22 (Luxembourg: Office for Official Publication of the European Communities, 2001), 38–51, esp. 39.

[40] International Agency for Research on Cancer, "Benzene," *Monographs on the Evaluation of Carcinogenic Risks to Humans* 7 (1974): 203. Rev. 19 March 1998. Available: http://www-cie.iarc.fr/htdocs/monographs/vol07/benzene.html.

[41] *International Agency for Research on Cancer* 29 (1982): 93. Available: http//www-cie.iarc.fr/htdocs/monographs/htdocs/Vol29/Benzene.html.

[42] International Agency for Research on Cancer, "Benzene," *Monographs, Supplement 7* (1987): 120. Rev. 6 Feb. 1998. Available: http://www-cie.iarc.fr/htdocs/monographs/suppl7/benzene.html (visited November 19, 2000) (emphasis added).

contracting leukemia long before 1982 or 1987, and probably at higher rates than were seen in the 1970s and 1980s. However, until the last two decades there would have been limited scientific consensus on it. Thus, there would have been no compensation for anyone who contracted leukemia from benzene exposure until there was "appropriate" documentation of the injuries in question.[43]

Benzene is not an isolated case; similar problems have attended the scientific discovery of the adverse health effects of arsenic, dioxin, lead, asbestos, benzidine, and betanaphthalamine dyes and other substances.[44] (Often, the failure of the scientific community to understand the toxicity of substances is not accidental – firms who control much of the information have been known to stonewall for years or decades.[45])

The future might not be quite as bad as the past in this regard: scientists and the general public are more aware now than they were in the past that products can be toxic; there are now better scientific procedures available for identifying toxicants; and there are more scientists performing such studies. However, one should not be a Pollyanna on this issue, because, although there is little systematic evidence, benzene may be more representative than a substance such as Bendectin, which occasioned the Supreme Court's change in how scientific evidence in the tort law is treated. For Bendectin there was a relatively quick scientific evaluation of some of its effects, because alleged birth defects (shortened limbs) would appear at birth and there were good hospital and pharmaceutical records that facilitated the identification and quantification of exposure to Bendectin. Such good evidence is quite rare and different from most substances – those with long latency periods, subtle adverse effects, or for which human evidence is not readily available.[46] Thus, slow knowledge accumulation poses a serious barrier to the production of information needed

---

[43] For example, Marvin Sakol, a hematologist testified during the OSHA hearings on benzene that for one leukemia patient with an occupational history of benzene exposure the discharge diagnosis was changed from leukemia to aplastic anemia so his "widow would receive $10,000 in industrial compensation." "Occupational Exposure to Benzene; Proposed Rule and Notice Hearing," *Federal Register* 50, no. 239 (10 Dec. 1985), 50518–19.

[44] See, for example, Robert A. Goyer and Thomas W. Clarkson, "Toxic Effects of Metals," in *Casarett and Doull's Toxicology*, 6th ed., 818–821 (arsenic); Paul Brodeur, *Outrageous Misconduct* (New York: Pantheon Books, 1985) (asbestos); and David Michaels, "Waiting For The Body Count: Corporate Decision Making and Bladder Cancer in the U.S. Dye Industry," *Medical Anthropology Quarterly* 2 (1988): 215, 218–221 (on benzidine and beta-naphthalamine dyes).

[45] Markowitz and Rosner, *Deceit and Deception* (lead and vinyl chloride); Paul Brodeur, *Outrageous Misconduct* (asbestos).

[46] W. J. Nicholson, "IARC Evaluations in the Light of Limitations of Human Epidemiologic Data," *Annals of the New York Academy of Sciences* 534 (1988): 44–54 (showing for about 18 substances, exposure conditions or processes that are carcinogenic (and that have quite high relative risks), there has been evidence of their human carcinogenicity for many decades, but action on them occurred only recently).

for a tort suit. Statutes of limitation that require legal complaints about harms from exposures be filed in a timely manner only add to the problem.[47]

THE SCIENCE-LAW INTERACTION

The combined effects of harms caused by molecules and scientific complexity, as well as scientific and legal burdens and standards of proof can be ameliorated or exacerbated by how the law addresses and adjudicates the interests at stake concerning these issues.

Before *Daubert* there were concerns that sometimes courts were permitting plaintiffs' or defendants' experts who testified on the basis of obviously mistaken scientific views. When this involved plaintiffs' experts it may have resulted in mistaken verdicts or settlements for plaintiffs, some increased costs for companies and marginally higher costs for consumers of their products. Courts may still fail to exclude experts who testify too far beyond the evidence or who testify as their employers want.[48] Since the *Daubert* decision, however, some courts in more aggressive gatekeeping appear to be *preventing* experts from testifying for mistaken scientific reasons.[49] Some courts have demanded that experts base their testimony on particular kinds of evidence, even though scientists would not insist on such evidence in order to come to a conclusion about the toxicity of a substance, whereas other courts sometimes exclude evidence that scientists would typically rely on to draw inferences.[50] Some courts have utilized comparatively simple and constrained rules for reviewing scientific testimony and its foundation. Courts would do much better to recognize there are different explanatory paths and various patterns of evidence that can be assembled to understand toxicity.[51]

[47] Michael D. Green, *Bendectin and Birth Defects* (Philadelphia: University of Pennsylvania Press, 1996), 192, 208. Statutes of limitation "are ... legislative enactments [that] prescribe the periods within which action may be brought upon certain claims or within which certain rights may be enforced." (*Black's Law Dictionary* (Minneapolis, MN: West Publishing Co., 1968), 1077.)

[48] Joseph N. Gitlin, Leroy L. Cook, Otha W. Linton, and Elizabeth Garrett-Mayer, "Comparison of "B" Readers' Interpretations of Chest Radiographs for Asbestos Related Changes," *Academic Radiology* 11(2004): 843–856 (found highly significant differences between plaintiffs' experts' readings of chest radiographs compared with independent readers; plaintiffs' experts' positive readings suggesting lung impairment were much more frequent than independent readers; the differences are too substantial to be attributed to interobserver variability.). See also, Samual R. Gross, "Expert Evidence," *Wisconsin Law Review*, 1991 (1991): 1113–1232, who discusses a variety of structural incentives that result in or select for expert witnesses who will be amenable to their employers' goals.

[49] Cranor and Eastmond, "Scientific Ignorance," 28–34. Most examples are from federal jurisdictions, but one-third or more of the state courts are following *Daubert* or adopting more stringent standards. The remainder are not following *Daubert*, with some even explicitly rejecting it, for example, *Donaldson v. Central Illinois Public Service Co.,* 199 Ill. 2d 63 (2002).

[50] Cranor and Eastmond, "Scientific Ignorance," 28–34.

[51] Cranor and Eastmond, "Scientific Ignorance," 34–45.

Thus, some courts in implementing *Daubert* have frustrated the Supreme Court's aim to ensure legal results comport better with the pertinent science. Such judicial decisions also can have an abiding legal import through precedent or by "Following the Joneses" of sister courts.[52]

To the extent that courts make it more difficult for scientists to testify, plaintiffs are disadvantaged fourfold – by the law's ordinary burdens and standards of proof, by science's ordinary burdens and standards of proof, by a general legal structure that permits the vast majority of substances to enter commerce without adequate toxicity testing, and by courts' making choices that only enhance the difficulties faced by those alleging injuries from toxic exposures. Thus, poor implementation of *Daubert*'s recent requirements for screening expert testimony and its foundation can erect sometimes mistaken and often quite high barriers for plaintiffs seeking access to trials for their alleged injuries. The profound legal changes and larger social consequences that can result from such decisions have tended to be hidden from public view in pretrial hearings[53] and behind the complexities of science, precluding more open discussion of the issues. Citizens will now have even less understanding of their legal system and its consequences for their lives. Yet the tort law cannot avoid claims of harm caused by molecular invaders as a result of epistemic difficulties, because citizens have a right to compensation for harm wrongfully caused by others, provided the necessary requirements for tort compensation are satisfied.

In addressing these issues, I do not present a social science study that provides a comprehensive view of the legal system or even of federal decisions; that is neither my expertise nor easily done. Rather, I present a philosophic analysis of some decisions in which courts have screened experts and written opinions about their views. Moreover, this is an essay about institutions and how administrators of the law shape and mold it by their decisions. This is also not an essay that aims to assign blame. Quite the contrary, I hope to reveal aspects of the tort law by considering in some detail the law-science interactions suggested by the decisions of its administrators, the judges. The responsibilities the Supreme Court gave federal judges are complex and difficult, given their generic and typically nonscientific education. It does not prepare them well for such tasks. If they err, it seems that such mistakes could occur because of too little acquaintance with the relevant fields.

Inter alia, I examine courts' *reasons* for admitting or excluding evidence and compare these with consensus scientific committees' views of similar evidence and reasoning. The reasons judges give for their decisions provide a window into their assessment of scientific evidence and testimony. Some examples illustrate

---

52 *Casey v. Ohio Medical Products, Inc.*, 877 F. Supp. 1380 (N.D. Cal 1995), excluded case studies and its reasons have been repeated (not as legal precedents), probably resulting in the mistaken exclusion of case studies in other cases.

53 Carl F. Cranor, "*Daubert* and the Acceptability of Legal Decisions," *Law and Philosophy Newsletter* (Fall 2003): 127–131.

some of the pitfalls of judicially constructed guides for reviewing scientifically relevant evidence and subtle scientific arguments, illuminate some of subtleties of scientific evidence and inferences and suggest strategies that courts might follow to better review complex, more nuanced scientific arguments. Other examples show courts reviewing evidence and testimony very similar to how scientists themselves would. Courts too often utilize fairly simple heuristics for assessing the scientific foundation of expert testimony. These fail to do justice to the complexity and subtlety of that evidence and deprive the law of much of the evidence on which decisions should be made. Such scientific mistakes also can foreclose the possibility of justice for the parties whose experts are excluded (typically plaintiffs).

SOME SOCIAL IMPACTS OF THE SCIENCE-LAW INTERACTION

Although there are good generic institutional and philosophic reasons to be concerned about these law-science trends, there have been obvious effects on actual participants in litigation. These in turn send disturbing messages through the legal system and to other potential litigants.

Walter Allen

Walter Allen worked as a maintenance worker at Baton Rouge General Hospital for more than twenty years. As part of his duties he was sometimes required to replace cylinders containing ethylene oxide (ETO), a substance used to sterilize medical and surgical devices.[54] Walter Allen died of brain cancer. His widow and son filed suit against several defendants, including American Sterilizer Company, the manufacturer of ETO sterilizers, and Pennsylvania Engineering for wrongful death, alleging that Walter Allen's exposure to ETO caused or contributed to his brain cancer.

ETO is a direct-acting, potent mutagen and genotoxin. A mutagen causes mutations in the DNA of the cells of living organisms that are typically inherited from cell to cell or from generation to generation. The term "genotoxin" connotes a broader range of DNA damage that is not necessarily inherited as mutations are.[55] ETO is particularly potent, because it causes chromosomal and genetic damage in both humans and other mammals.[56] Moreover, it is a small molecule that acts "directly" on the genes. That is, it is small enough

[54]   *Allen v. Pennsylvania Engineering Corp.*, 102 F.3d 194, 195 (5th Cir. 1996).
[55]   R. Julian Preston and George R. Hoffmann, "Genetic Toxicology," in *Casarett and Doull's Toxicology*, 6th ed., 321–350, esp. 321–322.
[56]   International Agency for Research on Cancer, "Ethylene Oxide," *Monographs* 60 (1994): 73. Rev. 26 Aug. 1997. Available: http://www-cie.iarc.fr/htdocs/monographs/vol60/m60–02.htm (visited April 26, 2002).

that it can penetrate into the DNA of cells without needing to be reduced into smaller components by the body's metabolic processes. Finally, it is a known human carcinogen.[57]

But did ETO cause Mr. Allen's brain cancer? Because the Allens alleged that Walter's exposure to ETO caused or contributed to his brain cancer, they needed testimony from appropriate scientists to support their causation claims. The Allens' experts faced heightened post-*Daubert* scrutiny before they could testify at his trial. Moreover, because brain cancer is quite rare, there were only some small human studies suggesting that ETO caused or contributed to brain cancer and a meta-analysis showing that ETO did not contribute to brain cancer. (It is quite difficult for negative studies to show there is no toxic effect.) Consequently, for their testimony the Allens' experts had to piece together various other kinds of evidence that scientists frequently must utilize to infer conclusions about disease, but such evidence is less direct than very large, well-conducted, and sensitive human studies would have been.

In pretrial hearings, the federal district court judge reviewed the experts' testimony and the basis of their opinions. Without giving reasons she ruled that the Allens' experts, including one who had written a textbook chapter on ETO, were not qualified to be admitted into trial (she did not speak to their scientific arguments, only their qualifications). Because they were not, the Allens could not argue before a jury that Walter's exposure to ETO contributed to his brain cancer. Consequently, the trial court granted a judgment for the defendants. The "trial" was over at the stage of pretrial hearings. There likely was no larger public discussion of this case, Mr. Allen's exposure, his circumstances of employment, the distribution of risks involved, or the toxicity of ETO.

The Allens' attempt at compensation for his injuries was not quite at an end, however. They appealed the district court decision to the Fifth Circuit Court of Appeals in New Orleans. The appellate court noted that the district court's four-line opinion on the substance of the Allens' experts' qualifications was "cursory" and agreed to hear the appeal. However, the Allens fared no better with the appellate court than with the trial court, although the opinion was longer and contained reasons for rejecting their experts and the evidence on which they relied. The Fifth Circuit upheld the trial court's exclusion of the Allens' scientific evidence. It ruled that the Allens' expert testimony that ETO caused brain cancer "was not scientifically valid . . . and [that it] was not based on facts reasonably relied on by experts in the field."[58] It came to this *legal* conclusion because it found that no epidemiological study had established "a statistically significant link between ETO exposure and human brain cancer,"[59] that studies showing ETO causes brain cancer in rats are unreliable, and that

[57] *Allen v. Pennsylvania Engineering Corp.*, 102 F.3d. at 196.
[58] *Allen v. Pennsylvania Engineering Corp.*, 102 F.3d. at 194.
[59] *Allen v. Pennsylvania Engineering Corp.*, 102 F.3d. at 194.

cell studies showing that ETO has "mutagenic and genotoxic capabilities in living organisms... is the beginning, not the end of the scientific inquiry and proves nothing about causation without other scientific evidence."[60]

However, the evidence on which the plaintiffs' experts from Harvard's School of Public Health relied is typical of the evidence that scientists routinely utilize to judge the carcinogenicity of substances. They documented similar adverse effects in rats exposed to ETO, which they argued provided a reasonable model for human effects. They also relied on some suggestive but not decisive human studies and utilized important information about the structure and potent mutagenic biological activity of ETO itself. As respectable, conscientious scientists they assembled the best available evidence to assess whether ETO caused or contributed to Walter Allen's brain cancer.

Because the appellate court appeared not to have understood fully the scientific evidence and argument (or perhaps plaintiffs' attorneys and their experts could have explained the issues better), and because plaintiffs' principal experts were not permitted to testify, the Allens' case could not proceed beyond pretrial hearings. Thus, they could not even present their argument to a jury that defendants had wrongly harmed Mr. Allen. Their case was at an end.

Lisa Soldo

Lisa Soldo delivered her second child on December 26, 1990, but chose not to breastfeed her baby. Her treating physician prescribed a fifteen-day course of Parlodel, a lactation suppression drug, to decrease the production of breast milk. She used most or all of her prescription before discarding the drug on about January 16. However, she suffered a severe headache and ultimately a hemorrhagic stroke (bleeding in the brain that damaged brain tissue) on about January 18, 1991.[61]

Lisa Soldo brought a suit against Sandoz Pharmaceutical alleging that Parlodel caused her stroke, a quite rare event among women of childbearing age, but somewhat more common among those who have just given birth.[62]

After plaintiffs and defendants both identified their expert witnesses in this case and the other side deposed them (questioned what their testimony would be under oath), the district court judge appointed his own experts to assist him in assessing the expert testimony presented by the plaintiff's two leading experts. He appointed David A. Flockhart, a professor of medicine and pharmacology, William J. Powers, a neurologist, and David A. Savitz, an

---

60 *Allen v. Pennsylvania Engineering Corp.*, 102 F.3d. at 198.

61 *Soldo v. Sandoz Pharmaceuticals Corp.*, 244 F. Supp. 2d 434, at 446–448 (W.D. Pa., January 13, 2003).

62 Department of Health and Human Services, Food and Drug Administration, "Notice on Opportunity for a Hearing on a Proposal to Withdraw Approval of the Indication of Bromocriptine Mesylate (Parlodel) for the Prevention of Physiological Lactation," *Federal Register* 59 (August 23, 1994), 43347.

epidemiologist. These judicially retained experts were asked to address two questions about each expert to assist the judge – whether the methodology or technique employed by plaintiff's experts in judging that Parlodel *can cause stroke* were scientifically reliable and whether the methodology or technique employed by them can be applied to the facts of the case. The judge-appointed experts were then asked whether, even if they answered these questions in the negative, their own opinions were sufficiently open to dispute that there is "legitimate and responsible disagreement" within their profession about their assessment of plaintiff's experts.[63]

The neurologist argued that plaintiff's two experts did not utilize reliable scientific methodology in judging that Parlodel can cause strokes and that it did cause Lisa Soldo's stroke. In addition, he argued that even though Parlodel can and does cause peripheral vasoconstriction, it may not follow that a drug can have similar effects in the vascular system of the brain. Thus, he argued, plaintiff's experts relied upon an improper analogy. The epidemiologist argued that as there were no human epidemiological studies showing that Parlodel can cause strokes, even though plaintiff's experts "made reasonable and even perhaps the best possible use of the data at hand to assess whether Parlodel caused Ms. Soldo's intracerebral hemorrhage,"[64] they did not draw proper scientific conclusions. The pharmacologist argued that both plaintiff's experts used "acceptable methodology and technique in opining that Parlodel can cause stroke" and agreed with them. He also agreed with one plaintiff's expert that it was plausible that Parlodel did cause Lisa Soldo's stroke, given the information he had available. However, he could not agree with the other expert that Parlodel was the most likely cause of her stroke, because the second expert knew that she had taken the cold medicine Contac and the expert had not ruled this out as a possible cause of her stroke (the first plaintiff's expert seemed not to have had this information).

Thus, two independent experts argued that plaintiff's experts did not use reliable methodology in forming their arguments that Parlodel *can cause* strokes, whereas one argued that one of plaintiff's experts did use a reliable methodology in concluding that Parlodel *can cause* strokes. However, there was a legitimate dispute between experts about plaintiff's experts' testimony – is this sufficient to permit a jury to decide between litigants?

In a sharp, skeptical, scathing ninety-six-page opinion, the trial judge attacked plaintiff's experts and his own judicially appointed experts that argued that Parlodel could cause hemorrhagic strokes. Because he concluded that they could not have utilized reliable methodology to infer general causation,

---

[63] Expert reports in *Soldo vs. Sandoz Pharmaceuticals Corporation*, Civil Action No. 98–1712 (January 16, 2002).

[64] David a. Savitz, "Report to Court Concerning Federal Rule of Evidence 706" (in response to Judge Donald J. Lee's (Western District of Pennsylvania) order creating an expert panel to assess the methodology or techniques employed by plaintiffs' experts) (September 30, 2001), 4.

he then excluded the plaintiff's experts and issued a summary judgment for the defendants, since there was no factual issue for a jury to consider. The judge seemed to take sides in the scientific disagreements and settled views about which scientists reasonably disagreed. Lisa Soldo's case appeared to be at an end.

However, Lisa Soldo's story did not end there. Judge Lee's opinion was so sharp and harsh that plaintiffs considered appealing it to the Third Circuit Court of Appeals, one of the circuit courts that has reviewed scientific evidence sensitively. Surprisingly, plaintiffs and defendants both had incentives to settle at this point. Defendants perhaps did not wish to risk a written opinion reversing the district court's favorable exclusionary ruling, while plaintiffs may not have wanted additional litigation and costs. Consequently, the parties settled out of court.

Melissa Globetti

In 1993 Melissa Globetti, thirty-three, from Alabama gave birth to her sixth child and also took Parlodel to suppress lactation.

> Her health was good. She had no known risk factors for coronary disease; she had no family history of heart disease, was not a smoker, was not overweight, was relatively young, and had very low (indeed, "protective") cholesterol levels. . . . Neither during the pregnancy nor the delivery did she experience any hypertension, and she had no history of high blood pressure. After giving birth, she decided not to breast feed, so, pursuant to a standing order of her obstetrician for non-breast feeding mothers, she was given 2.5 mg of Parlodel, . . . twice daily for fourteen days, to suppress lactation. Mrs. Globetti had taken Parlodel before in connection with some or all of her five prior deliveries.
>
> On the fifth or sixth day after delivery, Mrs. Globetti began to experience chest pain and was rushed to the emergency room of the local hospital in Talladega. Ultimately it was found that she had suffered an acute myocardial infarction of the anterior wall of her left ventricle. Angiography failed to reveal any thrombus, dissection, or occlusion of the coronary artery that could explain the AMI, and her initial cardiologist, Dr. Watford, concluded that it had been caused by a spasm of the coronary artery. Although Dr. Watford noted the possible association between Parlodel and the AMI and advised her to avoid it and other medications known to have vasoconstrictive effects, he expressed the opinion that the spasm was simply spontaneous. Mrs. Globetti's current treating cardiologists, Drs. Finney and Cox, as well as plaintiff's retained experts, Drs. Waller and Kulig, all now express the opinion that the Parlodel caused or contributed to the arterial spasm that caused her AMI.[65]

---

[65] *Globetti v. Sandoz Pharmaceuticals Corp.*, 111 F. Supp. 2d 1174, 1175–1176 (N.D. Ala., September 6, 2000).

After considering expert reports and other data in support of her case, the judge admitted her experts. (I return to this later.)

Ruby Quinn

Ruby Quinn delivered a baby by Caesarean section in August 1991. After initially choosing to breastfeed, she changed her mind when she was admitted to the hospital with stomach pains six days later. She was given a prescription for Parlodel. About September 14, approximately three weeks after the birth, she developed headaches she initially attributed to dental work. On September 21 she "developed paralysis on her left side and experienced slurred speech."[66] With blood pressure at 180/90 she was taken to the hospital, where she was diagnosed with a cerebral infarction (blockage). She had "suffered an ischemic stroke due to the blockage of blood flow to the brain through the right middle cerebral artery."[67] A forty-year-old African American who was somewhat overweight or obese and mildly hyperlipidemic, she had no personal or family history of stroke. Plaintiff's scientists argued on the basis of evidence similar to that used in Soldo's and Globetti's cases that Parlodel caused her stroke.

Lisa Soldo, Melissa Globetti, and Ruby Quinn appear to have had nothing in common other than giving birth to a child and taking Parlodel to suppress lactation. One suffered a hemorrhagic (bleeding) stroke, one a heart attack, and one an ischemic (blockage) stroke that all alleged had been caused by taking Parlodel. In the three cases in pretrial hearings to review expert testimony and the scientific basis of their claims, Sandoz Pharmaceuticals moved to exclude plaintiffs' experts and preclude the trial from going forward.

In Lisa Soldo's case, the judge concluded that plaintiff's experts failed to demonstrate general causation – that Parlodel could cause hemorrhagic strokes – and were thus excluded.[68]

---

[66] *Brasher v. Sandoz Pharmaceuticals Corp.*, and *Quinn v. Sandoz Pharmaceuticals Corp.*, 160 F. Supp. 2d 1291, at 1293.

[67] *Brasher v. Sandoz Pharmaceuticals Corp.*, and *Quinn v. Sandoz Pharmaceuticals Corp.*, 160 F. Supp. 2d at 1293.

[68] *Soldo v. Sandoz Pharmaceuticals Corp.*, 244 F. Supp. 2d 434, at 557–558 ("The Court concludes [contrary to Dr. Flockart], as did Dr. Powers and Dr. Savitz, that the existing data regarding Parlodel and stroke are simply insufficient both in terms of quantity and type to reliably support the testimony of Drs. Kulig and Petro").

"Although the Court recognizes that courts in other Parlodel cases have been willing to lower the bar of sufficiency to conform to the lack of informative data, see, for example, *Globetti v. Sandoz Pharm. Corp.*, 111 F. Supp. 2d 1174, 1179 (N.D. Ala., 2000) (allowing testimony of Drs. Kulig and Petro because they made best use of available evidence), this Court concludes that adoption of such a shifting standard would strip Rule 702 and Daubert of their objective anchors by lowering the admissibility standard to meet whatever evidence happens to be available, regardless of its scientific unreliability.")

Melissa Globetti's and Sally Quinn's cases had different outcomes at the district court level. Chief United States Magistrate Judge Putnam ruled that Melissa Globetti's experts' opinions were "scientifically reliable and, consequently, [Sandoz Pharmaceutical's] motion for summary judgment on the ground that plaintiffs cannot establish the necessary causal link between the acute myocardial infarction (AMI) and Parlodel is due to be denied."[69] He also ruled against Sandoz in the Quinn case. Globetti's and Quinn's cases, based on scientific evidence very similar to Lisa Soldo's, were permitted to proceed to a jury trial by the same judge. Although both proceeded, the issues concerning the admissibility of scientific evidence could still be appealed at a later date, which they have not been to the author's knowledge.

However, in *Globetti* Judge Putnam felt the need

> to explain [why he reached] a conclusion about the admissibility of this scientific testimony different from that reached in [other Parlodel] cases. . . . The court believes that in those cases the *Daubert* standard [for admitting expert testimony] was applied incorrectly, creating *much too high a standard of admissibility*. [The earlier Parlodel] cases seem to equate *Daubert's* reliability standard with *scientific certainty*, which is far from what the Supreme Court intended in *Daubert*. Science, like many other human endeavors, draws conclusions from *circumstantial evidence* when other, better forms of evidence is not available. As already noted above, one cannot practically conduct an epidemiological study of the association of Parlodel with postpartum AMI. Moreover, one cannot ethically experiment on human beings, exposing them to the near certainty of some number of deaths, simply to satisfy some evidentiary standard. *Hollander* and *Brumbaugh* [earlier Parlodel cases] failed to recognize that *Daubert* does not require, or even allow, the trial court to determine the scientific "correctness" or certainty of the evidence, but only that the facts from which the opinion is *inferred* are themselves scientifically reliable. [Emphasis added]

Two particularly striking kinds of evidence that Globetti, Quinn, and Soldo all had were (1) data from the FDA and its regulatory action and (2) a particularly persuasive case study from France showing that Parlodel indeed narrowed the coronary arteries within a short period after administration.

The U.S. Food and Drug Administration, after several years of trying to get label instructions changed, and an additional five- to six-year struggle trying to get the company to withdraw the drug, finally issued a rule to withdraw approval for Parlodel as a lactation suppression drug in 1994, because it was "not shown to be safe for use under the conditions of use upon the basis of which the application was approved."[70] The FDA had received adverse reaction reports

---

[69]   *Globetti v. Sandoz Pharmaceuticals, Corp.*, 111 F. Supp. 2d 1175.
[70]   Dept. of Health and Human Services, *Federal Register* 59 (1994), 43347.

of seizures, hypertension, strokes and heart attacks (some leading to deaths) beginning as early as 1983 "in a small but significant number of patients," and had a possible biological mode of action.[71] Moreover, it believed "that the number of women experiencing such adverse experiences may well be greater than those reported to FDA."[72]

In addition, there were some particularly vivid case studies; consider one. A French woman, who had suffered a heart attack after taking Parlodel following birth of her child, had been asked by her (ethically insensitive?) physicians if she would agree to undergo a "rechallenge," essentially an experimental re-administration of the drug under controlled conditions in which physicians could see if she had the same reaction to Parlodel a second time. She agreed. The rechallenge resulted in compelling evidence that the drug narrowed the coronary arteries within a short time after the rechallenge was begun. The *Globetti* court found this evidence pertinent to plaintiff's scientific case because Ms. Globetti suffered precisely the same adverse effect. The same judge also found this evidence provided scientific support for Ruby Quinn's cerebral stroke. The *Soldo* court did not find the evidence particularly helpful for Lisa Soldo's ischemic stroke.

All three courts were presented with animal evidence of Parlodel's vasoconstrictive effect but with different endpoints than the women who suffered adverse effects. They also were presented with medical textbooks noting the vasoconstrictive features of this class of drugs.

We will revisit the Parlodel cases and their evidence later, but the point to notice is that the courts disagreed on whether to admit essentially the same kind of evidence and same kinds of experts. Moreover, both district and appellate courts are disagreeing about whether to admit expert testimony and the supporting scientific evidence that Parlodel has the potential for strokes and heart attacks. There also can be disagreements between courts on the proper reasons for not admitting experts and scientific evidence. It is likely to occur in other cases.

Robert Joiner

Robert Joiner was an electrician in Thomasville, Georgia. During the course of his work he was required to work with the city's electrical transformers, which used a mineral-based fluid as a coolant, which was contaminated with PCBs, furans, dioxins, and other organic substances. Mr. Joiner alleged that in the course of his work repairing and cleaning PCB-insulated capacitors his exposure to polychlorinated biphenyls (PCBs), furans, dioxins, and other

---

[71]   Dept. of Health and Human Services, *Federal Register* 59, 43351.
[72]   Dept. of Health and Human Services, *Federal Register* 59, 43351.

organic substances (several of which were known carcinogens) contributed to his lung cancer.

> Joiner testified that dielectric fluid got all over him at times, that he would swallow a small amount of dielectric fluid when it splashed into his mouth, and that dielectric fluid had splashed into his eyes on several occasions.[73]

He often inhaled smoke from burning PCBs. Mr. Joiner had also been a smoker for about eight years, but had stopped smoking ten years earlier (and ten years before he was diagnosed with lung cancer) after marrying a born-again Christian woman concerned about his lifestyle.[74]

The district court judge following *Daubert* excluded plaintiff's experts from testifying. *Inter alia* the court ruled that because their reasoning and methodology was based upon studies in baby mice and epidemiological studies that suffered from various imperfections, it was not "reliable." The judge held the infant mice studies were flawed because (a) there were only two, (b) the mice were exposed to "massive doses of PCBs," (c) the kinds of tumors seen in the mice were not the kinds of cancer tumors Joiner had, and (d) when plaintiff's experts were given an opportunity to explain the use of such studies, they only argued that animal studies were commonly relied upon by the scientific community to identify human hazards, but did not explain why the particular studies were persuasive in this case.[75] In addition, the court held that each epidemiological study relied on by plaintiff's experts suffered from sufficient difficulties that it did not assist plaintiff's case. In short, "the studies simply do not support the experts' position that PCBs *more probably than not* promoted Joiner's lung cancer. That is, the court was not persuaded by a preponderance of proof that the studies support the "knowledge" the experts purport to have (i.e., that PCBs, "to a 'reasonable degree of medical certainty,'" promote small cell lung cancer in humans).[76] Defendants had argued that the particular kind of lung cancer from which Joiner suffered would not have been caused by PCB and cigarette smoke exposures.

The judge ruled that because plaintiff's experts' testimony did not rise above "subjective belief or unsupported speculation," it was inadmissible, thus rendering his evidence of disease causation insufficient to present a "material issue of fact" for a jury. The judge dismissed the suit. Because the experts could not testify, the Joiners' trial was at an end except for appeals. They appealed, and appellate opinions based on these facts helped to create the law on admissibility of evidence, which I consider in Chapters 2, 3, and 7.

---

73   *Joiner v. General Electric Co.*, 78 F.3d 524, at 528 (11th Cir. 1996).
74   Daniel Teitelbaum, one of Joiner's experts, personal communication, Feb. 2003.
75   *Joiner v. General Electric Company*, 864 F. Supp. 1310, at 1324.
76   *Joiner v. General Electric Company*, 864 F. Supp. 1310, at 1326 (citing *Wells v. Ortho Pharmaceutical Corp.*, 615 F. Supp. 262, 295 (N.D. Ga. 1985).

Several larger points emerge from the *Allen, Globetti, Quinn, Soldo,* and *Joiner* cases. In *Allen,* the court did not permit experts to testify because there were no "statistically significant" epidemiological studies showing that ETO caused or contributed to brain cancer, even though there was some suggestive human data. Also, because the court reasoned that because studies showing that ETO caused brain cancer in rats were not replicated in mice, the rat studies could not contribute scientifically to a claim that ETO caused or contributed to brain cancer in humans. Both the court's demand for human epidemiological studies in support of expert testimony and its rejection of the particular animal studies are scientifically problematic, which we will consider later. Should experts not be permitted to testify if they cannot support their scientific opinion with statistically significant human epidemiological studies? Should animal studies be permitted to support a scientific judgment that a substance can cause cancer or other diseases in humans? What is the relevance of animal studies since animals are not humans, but both are mammals? Can such evidence be responsibly combined with other kinds of evidence to support an inference that a substances causes or contributes to human harm? In *Joiner,* the infant mice studies, a critical part of plaintiff's case, were especially difficult to address, and it is a reasonable speculation that they appeared to be such implausible evidence that this might have significantly colored the judge's decision (but it was not the only issue).

In *Soldo,* there were other issues: the FDA data, the evidentiary value of case studies, and structure-activity evidence. What does a judge do when epidemiological studies cannot be ethically conducted or are likely much too insensitive to detect the adverse effect in question? Moreover, two judges disagreed concerning the same evidence – the *Soldo* judge excluded Soldo's experts who would testify that Parlodel probably caused her hemorrhagic stroke, whereas the *Globetti* and *Quinn* judge permitted the same experts to testify that Parlodel probably caused Globetti's heart attack and Quinn's ischemic stroke. What accounts for the differences between these cases? The evidence was identical or virtually identical, the experts were the same, the product was the same, although there was some differences in the injuries allegedly caused.[77]

If reasonable experts can and do disagree about whether scientific evidence supports a conclusion and a scientist testifies within this range of views, should that be sufficient to show that an expert has a "reliable methodology?" Or must experts have near certainty for their views or must there be near unanimity for the conclusions the experts assert? Must scientists testifying support their

---

[77] The adverse effects in the Parlodel cases may have influenced different judicial rulings. Tort actions for coronary occlusions and ischemic strokes (occlusions or spasms in cranial arteries) allegedly caused by Parlodel appear to have been more successful than hemorrhagic stroke (cranial bleeding) cases. Whether these differences should make a scientific or legal difference is less clear, but I do not pursue this point.

testimony by particular kinds of evidence, or should they be permitted to testify based on the kinds of studies they would routinely use for such purposes? Should judges even be assessing experts' conclusions or are these something that largely should be left to juries to consider? The book that follows addresses these issues.

SUMMARY

Chapter 2 ("Legal Background") reviews some of the principal legal procedures of a typical tort case, locating at which step in these procedures federal judges play such a crucial role in reviewing scientific evidence that supports expert testimony. Next, it summarizes how the Bendectin litigation began as well as how the particular *Daubert* case arose. It then presents the other two cases in the trilogy that focus mainly on procedural issues. Finally, it discusses some of the aftermath of the Bendectin litigation and considers recent amendments to the Federal Rules of Evidence concerning expert testimony.

Chapter 3 ("Institutional Concerns about the Supreme Court's Trilogy") briefly reviews some of the lessons from the leading Supreme Court cases that resulted in the legal changes and then considers some more troubling issues that have been raised by these decisions. The more serious concerns will be revisited in subsequent chapters once there is a better background for understanding the scientific issues and the science-law interaction.

Chapter 4 ("Studies of Toxicity and Scientific Reasoning") rehearses some of the kinds of scientific evidence that might be offered for the claims that substances cause harm to humans. Next, it more extensively presents less common kinds of evidence. A greater focus is to consider in more detail some features of scientific (nondeductive) reasoning and its implications, because it appears that courts and others may not fully understand it. The nature of scientific reasoning has substantial consequences for some recommendations about how scientific evidence should be reviewed, for some principles proposed to guide the activity and for the ease with which well-qualified respectable experts can disagree with one another.

Next, because it is typically difficult to have the best evidence to present in legal cases, Chapter 5 ("Excellent Evidence Can Make Bad Law: Pragmatic Barriers to the Scientific Discovery of Harm and Fair Admissibility Decisions") addresses some of the pragmatic barriers that make acquisition of evidence of harm more difficult than it would be if the best evidence were immediately available. For example, the creation of products that could potentially cause harms to humans or the environment appears to be out of control of the legal institutions that could offer some protections. At present the scientific community appears to have little understanding of the toxicity properties of most of these substances. Moreover, as a society we may not have the scientific resources, and appear reluctant to provide funding, to remedy the most pressing problems quickly. More seriously, these difficulties are exacerbated by a variety of less well-known features of substances and aspects of scientific research that will hinder the quick identification of toxicants for tort law purposes. These pragmatic barriers should serve as cautions to those who might insist on the best kinds of scientific evidence, high degrees of certainty or the quick production of evidence of human harm in toxic tort cases – in most cases, it simply will not be available.

Chapter 6 ("Science and Law in Conflict") brings science and legal decisions together. It first briefly reviews some differences between science and the law and some of the critical tensions that jeopardize their functioning well together. It next discusses instances in which courts have required or excluded scientific evidence for reasons that are contrary to the views of consensus scientific committees. Some courts are reviewing scientific evidence and expert testimony based on overly restrictive heuristics that are at odds with how most scientists would address similar issues. This both frustrates the aim of the *Daubert* trilogy to have the law more closely comport with the needed scientific information and puts justice at risk between the parties. Thus, some judges have substituted constrained heuristics (or even rules) for more subtle assessments that would recognize good and reasonable science that the scientific community recognizes.

Chapters 7 ("Enhancing the Possibility of Justice Under *Daubert*") and 8 ("Is *Daubert* the Solution?") considers some different solutions to the problems raised in the book: Is there a way the tort law can maintain fidelity to science within existing causes of action without depriving wrongfully injured plaintiffs the possibility of justice? Or should courts find alternative doctrines of liability to provide compensation for those exposed to toxicants and to provide some deterrence for wrongful invasion of interests in the future?

Chapter 7 suggests a procedure judges could follow in reviewing scientific evidence, building on some suggestions in *Kumho Tire* and cases from the Third Circuit Court of Appeals, whose understanding and review of scientific evidence is close to that of the scientific community. It also considers some complex evidentiary patterns (not relying mainly on human evidence), largely using carcinogens as examples, of how different kinds of evidence can support a scientific case for causation. Courts must learn to review a wider range of evidence with greater sensitivity and sophistication than many have to date in order to serve law, science, and justice much better.

However, even subtle reviews of scientific evidence in toxic tort cases within existing federal rules may fall short of a more comprehensive need to bring the science of our technological society more fully into the law to guide institutional decisions. *Daubert* and its implementation have no doubt improved the scientific sophistication of judges, as well as making more legal decisions compatible with the pertinent science and increasing the acceptability of legal decisions by the scientific community. However, these developments have had some adverse consequences as well. To the extent that courts do not review the science well, this will undermine the aims of the decisions. It also appears that there will remain too little institutional concern with the uncertainties concerning the safety of products before they enter commerce and following them once they are in commerce. Even worse, under the procedures of *Daubert* there are temptations for litigants defending their actions to utilize uncertainty to slow regulation or frustrate tort suits, and to construct a view of science for courts that is at odds with most working scientists, creating an "insidious science" with a patina of respectability to it. Similar incentives can motivate litigants to distort scientific studies and the literature for legal purposes. These consequences can corrupt the science and our (and judges') view of it.

Decisions about the science needed to assess risks and harms in the tort law can adversely affect institutional structures that already appear not to work well and to fall well short of reasonable goals. Chapter 8 argues that the *Daubert* trilogy and its implementation create structural incentives to decrease testing for risks from products. It creates motivations to reduce scientific and institutional understanding of the potential toxicity of products in our midst. Apart from a major overhaul of our legal structure on the regulatory side (for which there likely is little political will), courts could take some steps toward addressing these issues by modifying their reviews of expert testimony within a law that has a causation requirement. Or, they could modify tort law liability rules themselves in order to provide greater incentives to test products for adverse consequences and to monitor products once they are in commerce. Will we as a society go beyond the current half measures that have several counterproductive consequences? Will we stay with the status quo, in which there is too little legal concern with uncertainties concerning the safety of products before they enter commerce, creating incentives that increase risks to the safety of the public, the workforce, and the environment? This remains to be seen.

2

Legal Background

INTRODUCTION

The law is one of the complex institutions that must be understood in order to identify the science-law issues, to see why they are so critical to the functioning of the legal system and to understand why mistaken decisions about the admission of expert testimony can be of wider social concern. Moreover, for both historical and ongoing disputes, it is important to understand why some of the legal changes have occurred.

This chapter first provides some institutional background about the tort law, including some specific steps in civil procedure, in order to identify the stage at which courts consider the admissibility of evidence. This reveals why admissibility decisions at this point in the timeline leading to a trial can be so crucial to the litigants (mainly the plaintiffs), to the law, and to society more generally. Second, it sketches the context in which the U.S. Supreme Court decided to take the legal admissibility of scientific evidence. Finally, it considers three recent U.S. Supreme Court cases and how these have modified the admissibility of expert testimony and its scientific basis, and some recent amendments to the Federal Rules of Evidence subsequent to the Court cases.

THE TORT LAW

The legal actions that are of concern arise in the *tort* or *personal injury* law. Tort law is that

> body of law which is directed toward the compensation of individuals, rather than the public, for losses which they have suffered within the scope of their legally recognized interests generally, rather than one interest only [such as contracts], where the law considers that compensation is required.[1]

[1] *Prosser and Keeton on the Law of Torts*, 5th ed., ed. W. Page Keeton (St. Paul, MN: West Publishing Co., 1984), 5–6.

Tort law is often contrasted with criminal law, which, as a common account describes it, is typically "concerned with the protection of interests common to the public at large, as they are represented by the entity which we call the state; often it accomplishes its ends by exacting a penalty from the wrongdoer."[2] It is also contrasted with contract law, which imposes liability "for the protection of a single, limited interest, that of having the promises of others performed," and with quasi-contractual liability that has been "created for the prevention of unjust enrichment of one person at the expense of another, and the restitution of benefits which in good conscience belong to the plaintiff."[3] The tort law is concerned with compensation for injuries a person has suffered that were intentionally or negligently inflicted by others, or inflicted "without fault" for which a person can recover under strict liability laws.[4]

The conception of justice on which the tort law rests is historically traceable to Aristotle's principle of rectificatory justice: it seeks to rectify wrongs – make matters right – that have been done to persons and to restore them to the condition they were in before the injury occurred.[5] The tort law is one part of a legal system concerned with citizens' failure to comply with the law.[6] In a perfect world there might be little or no use for the tort law – if citizens conformed to the law, were extremely careful about how their activities affected others, and voluntarily and immediately compensated those harmed by any inevitable accidents. Alas, we do not live in such a world. Not all carefully conform to the law; not all are as careful as they should be; injuries inevitably occur (and even in a perfect world, it might be difficult to avoid them). In addition, of course, when people should be compensated is a contentious issue usually requiring an authoritative body to adjudicate the issues, to determine when compensation is owed and to ensure that it is paid. Consequently, there is a need for an institution that permits citizens injured by others to bring a legal action to rectify those harms and to compel compensation.

Moreover, as I noted in the first chapter, if other legal institutions functioned impeccably to identify and remove risks from chemical products before they materialized into harm, there would be a lesser need for torts. However, neither premarket laws, such as drug or pesticide laws, nor postmarket laws that seek to reduce risks of products in commerce before they materialize into harm appear to work well (as I consider later).

The tort law is privately enforced by those who believe they have been injured by others (contrasted with the criminal law that is publicly enforced

---

2 *Prosser and Keeton,* 5.
3 *Prosser and Keeton,* 5.
4 *Prosser and Keeton,* 32.
5 Aristotle, *Nicomachean Ethics,* trans. Terence Irwin (Indianapolis: Hackett Publishing Company, 1985), 125.
6 Rawls, *A Theory of Justice,* 246, 351 (the tort and criminal laws are part of imperfect compliance with principles of justice (351)).

by an agency of the state). Plaintiffs who have been exposed to substances that they believe harmed them may file suits seeking compensation for the injuries suffered in order to restore them to the status quo ante.

I have introduced this generic conception of the tort law to place it within the legal landscape. However, the specific issues of concern in this book and their importance are revealed by locating them within legal procedures.

A LEGAL CASE IN OUTLINE

How does a person bring a legal action in torts? Suppose that as in the case of Walter Allen, his wife believes that he was exposed to a toxic substance (which he was) and that as a result of that exposure he contracted brain cancer and died. What are some of the legal steps she or her legal representative must take in order to have a jury trial on the issue and, ultimately, to recover damages for injuries she might have suffered?

Complaint and Answer

Mrs. Allen would typically secure a lawyer, preferably quite a good one. The lawyer would determine whether she has a plausible theory of liability for Walter Allen's injuries, and in what legal jurisdiction her case should be heard. Her lawyer would then draft and file a "complaint" with the court in question. This complaint would "allege facts showing the defendant's primary duty toward him, defendant's breach of that duty, and (in many cases but not all) actual injury and a causal relation between defendant's breach of duty and that injury"[7] for which plaintiff is entitled to legal relief.[8] Because the *Allen* case involved the product ethylene oxide and was subject to product liability law,[9] she has only to show that the product injured her husband, that she suffered legally compensable injuries and that she should be compensated for the injuries.

The party(ies) named as defendant(s), in this case, American Sterilizer and Pennsylvania Engineering, would have an opportunity to respond by means of an "answer." Defendant's answer would normally deny the factual allegations on which the case rested and might even deny that there was a substantive theory of liability under which plaintiff could receive legal relief, even if the facts were as she alleged. That is, the defendants might deny that plaintiff was exposed to the substances in question, and might go on to claim that the substances

---

[7] Fleming James, Jr. and Geoffrey C. Hazard, Jr. *Civil Procedure* (Boston: Little, Brown and Company, 1977), 77.

[8] This particular style of a complaint is chosen as fairly representative, although in an earlier time complaints had to be both more stylized and in some ways more specific. The Federal Rules of Civil Procedure only require "a short and plain statement of the claim showing that the pleader is entitled to relief" (*Federal Rules of Civil Procedure* 8(a) (2)).

[9] *Allen v. Pennsylvania Engineering Corp.*, 102 F.3d 194.

alleged were not toxic, that even if exposure had occurred, the concentrations of the substance were not harmful, and that, even if plaintiff were exposed to the substances in concentrations which were toxic, plaintiff was not entitled to legal relief under the substantive law of the jurisdiction. Such responses are one of the rituals of the law.[10]

Discovery

Next, the two sides would engage in a discovery process. These are official procedures that are made available so that litigants can discover the "facts and possible evidence in the case, and at least ascertain in part what detailed fact issues may arise for trial, as well as the opponent's positions concerning factual matters."[11] Each party may address written interrogatories to the opponent, seek documents from the other side, orally examine witnesses under oath who have filed depositions, as well as examining anyone who may have some knowledge of the subject matter of the suit.[12]

Pretrial Conferences

Once discovery is completed, there is a pretrial conference (or conferences) to address issues between parties. Following that, the trial begins.

However, it is at this point, during the pretrial hearings, that plaintiffs face some of the issues that arise concerning the admissibility of scientific testimony and evidence. In particular, the plaintiff has the "burden of producing evidence" or the "burden of production."[13]

> Our system [of law] leaves it to the parties to [investigate the case or furnish the evidence upon which they are to be decided]. If, now, neither party offers any evidence at the trial, what will happen? The answer is that one party loses. He may, therefore, be said to bear the risk of this consequence of nonproduction of evidence. Or as we more often say, he bears the burden of producing at least some evidence.[14]

---

[10] The last part of defendants' answer is only the first of many instances in which plaintiffs may face motions by defendants aiming to end a case. Roughly, a defendant claims that even assuming the correctness of the evidence that plaintiffs have alleged (in the complaint in this case), or discovered prior to trial or established at trial, such evidence is insufficient as a matter of law to establish a basis for legal recovery for alleged harm suffered. These are all legal devices by which one party or the other might seek to have a judge rule as a matter of law that the legal theory or the evidence (as the case may be) on the other side of the issue was so lacking that the legal process should be terminated. Typically, plaintiff faces these issues more than defendant because the plaintiff has the initial burden of showing that there is some reason to change the legal status quo and the burden of producing enough evidence to justify the legal process continuing.

[11] *McCormick on Evidence*, sec. 3 (2nd ed., ed. John W. Strong, 1972), 3.

[12] *McCormick on Evidence*, 3.

[13] James and Hazard, *Civil Procedure*, 245.

[14] James and Hazard, *Civil Procedure*, 245.

In a toxic tort suit, the plaintiff must introduce sufficient evidence that she was exposed to a potentially toxic substance and that it more likely than not caused her injuries (along with other evidence about defendant's responsibility, and so on). Typically, because of the scientific nature of the required evidence, plaintiffs must rely upon both scientific studies and the testimony of expert witnesses. It is these that have become the focus of debates in light of the Supreme Court's decision in *Daubert*.

Before or during pretrial conferences, plaintiffs may face a variety of motions petitioning the judge legally to review experts to evaluate whether they should be "admitted" to testify in the case and these are likely to be accompanied by a motion to dismiss the case. In particular defendants may file a variety of motions concerning expert testimony plus a motion for summary judgment. Rule 26 of the Federal Rules of Civil Procedure "requires the disclosure of not only the full opinions to be offered by certain experts, but also the bases for the opinions."[15] At this point, an opponent may challenge the admissibility of one or more expert witnesses. Such challenges may take the form of a motion to strike the evidence or a motion for an *in liminie* hearing (a motion to have evidence or expert testimony reviewed by the judge in a specific hearing before trial).[16] That is, a court can issue a decision based on papers the litigants have submitted or hold a hearing where "issues in the case can be more fully explored."[17] Some courts have required hearings in certain instances, but in general there appears to be considerable flexibility on how expert testimony is reviewed.[18] Although the judge has authority to "require parties to present objections to expert testimony at any point during the case," typically such objections would be made "shortly after the close of expert discovery" or "shortly before trial."[19]

At the time experts are challenged, opponents may file a motion for a summary judgment. This would allege that based on plaintiffs' "pleadings, depositions, answers to interrogatories, and admissions on file, together with the affidavits [by experts and others], if any . . . " plaintiffs' case lacked an adequate evidentiary basis to establish all the elements needed for their theory of liability.[20] If critical experts have not been admitted to testify, opponents may succeed in ending the case at this point.

Once plaintiff and defendants have passed any pretrial motions or hurdles they might face, including the adequacy of the scientific basis of their claims, the case proceeds to trial.

---

15 *Federal Rules of Civil Procedure* 26(a)(2).
16 *Federal Rules of Civil Procedure* 104 (a) and *Black's Law Dictionary,* 8th ed., (St. Paul, MN: West Publishing Co., 2004), 803.
17 *Manual for Complex Litigation,* section 23.353, 509–510.
18 *Manual for Complex Litigation,* section 23.352, 510 (citing *Oddi v. Ford Motor Co.,* 234 F.3d 143, 154 (3d Cir. 2000)).
19 *Manual for Complex Litigation,* section 23.352, 508.
20 *Federal Rules of Evidence* 56(c).

Plaintiff's Case-in-Chief

Plaintiff presents her case first, because she has a general burden to show that there is some reason to change the legal status quo and because she has a burden to produce evidence, the burden of production. That is, plaintiff must present legal theories and sufficient evidence to justify "a finding in [her] favor . . ."[21] Plaintiff presents her evidence and experts, subject, of course, to cross-examination. At the end of this presentation, her case-in-chief, she might once again face a motion from defendants seeking to end the legal proceedings on the grounds there is not a legally adequate evidentiary basis for a reasonable jury to find for her or that there was no legal theory under which she could was entitled to recover compensation. That is, defendants might well move for a "directed verdict."[22] If this motion is denied, then the presentation shifts to the defense.

Defendant's Case-in-Chief

Next, the defense presents its case-in-chief – legal theories and evidence to counter plaintiff's claims on the issues in question. Following this presentation, defendants might move for a directed verdict in their favor on the grounds that plaintiff's evidence, taking it in the sense most favorable to her, when compared with defendant's evidence does not present a substantial issue of fact to go to a jury.[23] If this fails, the sides proceed to closing arguments.

Closing Arguments and Proposed Jury Instructions

After both sides have made their concluding arguments, each submits proposed jury instructions. These are proposals about how the judge should instruct the jury on factual and legal issues. The judge reviews them, decides what instructions should be used, and then instructs the jury.

Plaintiff's Burden of Persuasion

When the case goes to the jury, the plaintiff faces a second burden of proof, the "burden of persuasion."

> If . . . the trier [of fact – the jury] is operating under a system which requires him to decide the question one way or the other, then to avoid caprice that system must furnish him with a rule for deciding the question when he finds his mind in this kind of doubt or equipoise. Where the parties to a civil action are in dispute over a material issue of fact, then that party who will lose if the

---

[21] James and Hazard, *Civil Procedure*, 268.
[22] *Federal Rules of Evidence* 50(a)(1), and James and Hazard, 280–288.
[23] James and Hazard, *Civil Procedure*, 280–288.

trier's mind is in equipoise may be said to bear the risk that the trier will not be affirmatively persuaded or the risk of nonpersuasion upon that issue.[24]

In less convoluted prose, if the plaintiff does not establish her factual and legal claims to the required standard of proof, plaintiff loses. Moreover, it is the members of the jury who must be persuaded; "the judge is not directly concerned in solving the problem."[25]

Plaintiff's Standard of Proof

The burden of persuasion is one thing (concerning *who* must establish a factual or legal issue), how difficult it is to lift or carry the burden is another – that is the "standard of proof." The standard of proof is the *degree of certainty* to which a litigant must make her claims to the satisfaction of a fact finder (typically the jury) in order to prevail on an issue. In the criminal law, the state has the burden of proof to establish the necessary elements of a crime in order to obtain a conviction of an accused. It must establish its factual and legal claims "beyond a reasonable doubt" to the satisfaction of a jury. The standard of proof needed to establish legal claims can and do differ from one area of the law to another.

In most areas of the tort law the plaintiff must establish her case by a *preponderance of evidence* to the satisfaction of a jury.[26] Equivalent formulations are that she must establish her claims by a "greater weight of the evidence" or that she must establish the required claim by showing that it is "more likely than not true." Carrying this burden to the required standard refers "not to the number of witnesses or quantity of evidence but to the *convincing force* of the evidence"[27] (emphasis added).

If plaintiff has persuaded the jury that her claims are more likely than not true, the jury will find in her favor. If not, the jury will find for the defendant. Once a jury decision has been reached, the trial judge may review it and if he agrees, enters a judgment for the winning party. However, jury verdicts are subject to postjury reviews by the judge and, of course, subject to appeal to higher courts.

SUBSTANTIVE ISSUES IN THE TORT LAW

In addition to these generic issues of civil procedure, a plaintiff must establish the *substantive elements* required of tort law in order to obtain legal relief for injuries suffered. In particular a plaintiff must show (1) that defendant had a

---

[24] James and Hazard, *Civil Procedure*, 241.
[25] James and Hazard, *Civil Procedure*, 242.
[26] James and Hazard, *Civil Procedure*, 243.
[27] James and Hazard, *Civil Procedure*, 245, referring to Maguire, *Evidence, Common Sense and Common Law* 180 (1947).

legal duty toward the plaintiff which was breached, (2) that this violation *caused* (and was the proximate cause of) plaintiff's injury, and (3) that the injury is compensable under the law or in some other way that justifies legal relief.[28]

Causation in Toxic Tort Suits

The element of concern for our discussion is that plaintiff must show by appropriate evidence that defendant *caused* plaintiff's harm. In toxic tort cases in federal jurisdictions, this showing typically breaks into two distinct causation claims that must be established (although as we will see in Chapter 8, sometimes this rigid distinction can be misleading and has been rejected by some states). First, plaintiff must show *general causation*: that defendant's substance *can cause* or is capable of causing harms of the kind from which plaintiff suffered. Second, she must show causation specific to that plaintiff or *specific causation*: that defendant's action or product caused or contributed to plaintiff's disease. That is, if a plaintiff complains that ETO caused her husband's injuries, she must show that it is more likely than not that ETO can cause the kinds of injuries from which he suffered and that it is more likely than not that defendant's ETO (and not something else) caused or contributed to the injuries. Such bifurcation of causation is not needed in more ordinary tort cases, such as car accidents, because it will be obvious that a five-thousand-pound car traveling at moderate to high rates of speed *can* cause considerable physical damage to many objects.

Because most diseases have multiple causes, to meet the specific causation requirement litigants must rule out other significant possible contributors to plaintiff's condition. Litigants might use epidemiological studies to establish that in a general population of people exposed to the substance suspected of causing the harm there was a sufficiently elevated rate of disease to satisfy the burdens and standards of proof on general causation. They can and do also utilize animal and other toxicological studies to provide compelling evidence that a substance *can* cause a certain adverse effect in humans, for example, that the anticancer drug CCNU (1-(2-chloroethyl)-3-cyclohexyl-1-nitrosourea) can cause cancer in humans.[29] In order to establish that plaintiff's exposure in question likely caused or contributed to her disease, plaintiff's expert must infer this conclusion from the general studies and from more particular information about plaintiff's exposure and circumstances.

Plaintiff must establish both general and specific causation by a *preponderance of the evidence*; she must show that it is more likely than not that defendant's substance is capable of causing injuries of the kind from which plaintiff suffered and that it is more likely than not that defendant's substance caused her specific

---

[28] James and Hazard, *Civil Procedure*, 98.
[29] See IARC, "Chloroethyl Nitrosoureas," *Monograph Series, Supplement 7* (1987): 150. Available: http://www-cie.iarc.fr/htdocs/monographs/suppl7/chloroethylnitrosoureas.html.

injuries. Thus, to return to our example, Mrs. Allen must show that it is more likely than not that exposure to ETO is capable of causing brain cancer and that it is more likely than not that ETO (rather than something else) contributed to her husband's brain cancer.

The Role of Scientific Evidence and Expert Witnesses in Establishing Causation

In order for the plaintiff to establish both general and specific causation required in toxic tort cases, she must present evidence admissible in court that is sufficient to persuade a jury that her injuries more likely than not were caused by exposure to defendant's substance. In toxic tort cases, this evidence is often established in large part by introducing expert testimony based on appropriate scientific studies. Scientific evidence is typically provided by any studies that have been done concerning the toxicity of substances to which plaintiff was exposed (although it is usually difficult to provide this data) or by the exposure of others to the substance or by other kinds of toxicologic evidence, in order to show that the substance more likely than not *can* cause such injuries like those the plaintiff suffered. For specific causation plaintiffs must show that there was sufficient exposure and other evidence to support the claim that defendant's substance more likely than not *did cause* plaintiff's injuries.

To understand this idea and some of the evidentiary requirements for establishing scientific claims in toxic torts, we need to place the use of scientific evidence in the tort law within a broader framework. First, as some of the treatises put it, the common law insists "upon the most reliable sources of information."[30] For example, witnesses to an event such as an automobile accident that causes injury may testify to that fact, provided that they have firsthand knowledge of the event or transaction at issue. However, even for witnesses to testify to events that can be perceived by the senses, they "must have had an opportunity to observe, and must have actually observed the fact."[31] By contrast

[t]he expert has something different to contribute. This is the power to draw inferences from the facts, which a jury would not be competent to draw. To warrant the use of expert testimony two general elements are required. First, some courts state that the subject of inference must be so distinctively related to some science, profession, business or occupation as to be beyond the ken of laymen. . . . Second, the witnesses must have sufficient skill, knowledge, or experience in or related to the pertinent field or calling as to make it appear that his opinion or inference will probably aid the trier in the search for the truth.[32]

---

[30] *McCormick on Evidence*, sec. 340 (ed. John W. Strong, 4th ed., 1992).
[31] *McCormick on Evidence*, sec. 10 (ed. John W. Strong, 4th ed., 1992).
[32] *McCormick on Evidence*, sec. 10 (ed. John W. Strong, 4th ed., 1992).

That is, a person who seeks to testify as an expert must first be admitted as appropriately qualified and then may testify to the science or technical matter at issue.[33]

Thus, scientific expert opinion may be used in support of general or specific causation claims provided the expert is appropriately qualified, the expert's testimony has an appropriate scientific basis, the testimony is appropriately relevant to the factual issues in dispute, and it will assist the jury in coming to conclusions. In a toxic tort case the plaintiff's scientific witnesses must present opinions regarding a causal relationship between exposure to the toxic product and the injury that are appropriately grounded in science.

The Admissibility of Evidence

Courts consider several issues in assessing expert testimony. The first is whether any proffered evidence, including expert testimony, is *admissible*. Trials proceed according to rules and procedures "that make it clear when proof has been presented so that [evidence] is officially introduced and thereupon [may] be considered" by the jury."[34] Thus, such evidence must be officially "admitted" to be considered by a jury. Moreover, an expert cannot testify regarding any matter he or she chooses. An expert's credentials typically would be reviewed to ensure that he or she has the appropriate qualifications, experience and education to testify to the issues in the case. In addition, the scientific foundation of his or her testimony would be reviewed to ensure that the testimony is appropriately grounded in scientific research and methodology.

Before 1993, introducing scientific evidence and having experts admitted tended not to be difficult: if a litigant had well-qualified experts whose testimony was *relevant* to the scientific and technological issues, would assist a jury in understanding them, and their methodology was not based on "novel" techniques or studies, judges tended to admit them and let cross-examination during trial guide the jury in deciding the weight to accord the testimony and whose experts to believe.[35] Most courts utilized the *Frye* test. This was a principle for judging the underlying basis of expert testimony that had been created when a defendant in a murder case had sought to introduce a precursor of

---

[33]   At the time the Federal Rules of Evidence stated that

> If scientific, technical, or other specialized knowledge will assist the trier of fact to understand the evidence or to determine a fact in issue, a witness qualified as an expert by knowledge, skill, experience, training or education, may testify thereto in the form or an opinion or otherwise. (*Federal Rules of Evidence*, section 702 (1988).)

Subsequently, the Rules of Evidence have been amended to reflect recent legal developments.

[34]   *McCormick on Evidence*, sec. 51 (ed. Edward W. Cleary, 3rd ed., 1984).

[35]   Faigman *et. al., Modern Scientific Evidence*, 7–8; Michael Gottesman, Georgetown Law Center, presentation at "Science, the Courts, and Protective Justice," 27 Feb. 2003, sponsored by the Science and Environmental Health Network and Georgetown Environmental Law and Policy Institute.

lie detector tests, a "systolic blood pressure detection test."[36] The pertinent language was

> Just when a scientific principle or discovery crosses the line between the experimental and demonstrable stages is difficult to define. Somewhere in this twilight zone the evidential force of the principle must be recognized, and while the courts will go a long way in admitting expert testimony deduced from a well-recognized scientific principle or discovery, the thing from which the deduction is made must be sufficiently established to have gained general acceptance in the particular field in which it belongs.[37]

The *Frye* test required that the generic kinds of studies, tests, or techniques on which an expert might rest expert testimony must be "generally accepted in the pertinent field." The systolic blood pressure test had not been "generally accepted" at the time of *Frye* so the defense expert in that case was not permitted to testify. It was "easy to apply and required little scientific sophistication on the part of judges," and "if one were a card carrying member of a recognized occupation or profession, one's proffered expert testimony was admitted and the validity of the underlying knowledge was assumed [especially as along as one was not relying on a "novel" study or technique]."[38]

The U.S. Supreme Court did not require such detailed scrutiny of scientific testimony as recently as 1983 in *Barefoot v. Estelle*, a capital murder case.[39] In this case, an expert for a criminal defendant was permitted to testify, even though his own profession had taken a strong public stand against the position he argued and the Court indicated it was "unreliable." The Court held that contrary testimony and cross-examination could correct any mistaken views he might articulate.[40] Since the 1993 *Daubert* and related decisions, judges have conducted much more searching reviews of expert testimony and its foundation before trials commence, which we discuss later in this chapter.

Summary Judgment

A second issue concerning a litigant's evidence is that even if a particular expert's testimony is *admissible*, it *may not be adequate* to support each element of plaintiffs' legal theory. If not, there is no legal issue for a jury to decide and the case can end right there. For example, if plaintiffs' evidence only supports a claim that defendants' substance might *possibly cause* the disease in question, there would be "no genuine issue as to [that fact] and the moving party would be entitled to a judgment [in its favor] as a matter of law."[41] If there is not

---

36 *Frye v. U.S.*, 293 F. 1013 (D.C. Cir. 1923).
37 293 F. at 1014.
38 Faigman *et al., Modern Scientific Evidence*, 7–8.
39 *Barefoot v. Estelle*, 463 U.S. 880 (1983).
40 *Barefoot v. Estelle*, 463 U.S. at 899 (1983).
41 *Federal Rules of Evidence* 56(c).

scientifically valid and reliable evidence to support each element of a litigant's case, a judge may find that there is no issue for a jury to consider and issue a decision for the opposing side, a so-called summary judgment.[42]

Judgment as a Matter of Law

A third major issue concerns whether, during a trial, a party to a legal dispute has presented a "sufficient evidentiary basis for a reasonable jury to find for that party on that issue . . . "[43] This finding and accompanying judgment as a matter of law would be made after plaintiffs have presented their case-in-chief or after both sides have presented evidence in support of their respective views, but before the case goes to the jury. Such a review would typically involve a comparative assessment of a party's evidence versus the opposing party's evidence.[44] If a court finds one side's evidence so overwhelms the evidence by the opposing party such that no reasonable jury could find for the opposing party, he or she may issue a decision for the first without having a jury decide the case. Or, for a judgment notwithstanding the verdict, if a jury decided, say for the plaintiff, but a judge found that no reasonable jury could come to such a conclusion, he or she can overturn the verdict.

Some Procedural Puzzles

Some of the distinctions indicated earlier between the admissibility of evidence, a summary judgment and a judgment as a matter of law appear to have been conflated in litigation concerning Bendectin. I need not settle these issues, but it is important to note them. Some courts ruling on the evidence in the Bendectin cases had a full trial record on which to base their assessment of evidence. Thus, they could properly engage in a comparative assessment of plaintiffs' versus defendants' evidence and issue a judgment as a matter of law that plaintiffs'

---

[42] A motion for summary judgment is "typically supported by affidavits of witnesses who would be competent to testify at trial – affidavits containing statements of fact which would be admissible at trial if made by these witnesses. The movant's opponent then has the charge to submit counter-affidavits of similarly competent witnesses. Both sides may also use the products of discovery – depositions and interrogatories that establish uncontested facts, admissions made upon requests to admit, etc. If the opponent does not controvert the proofs offered in support of the motion, and the movant's affidavits show without contradiction facts which would entitle him to judgment as a matter of law, then summary judgment may be granted. If, on the other hand, the proofs fail to exclude all bases on which judgment might be rendered in favor of the person against whom the motion is made, summary judgment must be denied." James and Hazard, *Civil Procedure*, 220–221. See also, *Federal Rules of Evidence* 56(c).

[43] *Federal Rules of Evidence* 50(a).

[44] After only one side has presented evidence it might be so insufficient that a reasonable jury could not find for the plaintiff. After both parties have presented evidence, this finding would be explicitly comparative with the judgment that one party's evidence so overwhelms the other party's evidence that there is no factual issue for a jury to decide.

evidence was insufficient for a jury verdict.[45] Other courts not having a trial record, but facing experts prepared to testify that Bendectin caused birth defects, ruled the experts' testimony inadmissible and, then, because there was too little evidence on plaintiffs' side to support their cause of action issued a summary judgment. Whether they should have ruled such evidence inadmissible is controversial. Faced with pressures not to go through other trials when at the end they would in all likelihood have to rule for defendants, they sought to save time and money by declaring plaintiffs' evidence inadmissible before trial rather than later comparing plaintiffs' and defendants' evidence during or after trial. Their actions, however, tended to blur the "line between admissibility and sufficiency" (or judgment as a matter of law in above terminology) in these cases.[46] In the Supreme Court *Daubert* decision (considered below) the Court seemed to endorse this procedure, inviting both summary judgments and judgments as a matter of law as a way of addressing inadequate scientific evidence.[47]

The qualification of experts, whether they can testify, and what constitutes an appropriate basis or foundation for their testimony are some of the issues that have arisen in several recent Supreme Court cases and that provide the background for the treatment of litigants in toxic tort cases. Focusing on these arcane legal and scientific issues is needed to locate the use of scientific evidence in the tort law and to address some of the tensions between science and the law.

Recent developments require judges to review proposed expert testimony very early in the legal process. The Federal Rules of Civil Procedure were amended in 1993 to

> require a party, independently of any discovery request, to disclose the identity of all expert witnesses expected to testify at trial; to provide, among other things, the experts' written signed reports stating all opinions to be offered and support for opinions; and to make the expert available for deposition after the report is submitted.[48]

---

[45] Joseph Sanders, "Scientific Validity, Admissibility and Mass Torts after *Daubert*," *Minnesota Law Review* 38 (1994): 1387, 1433 (citing *Richardson v. Richarson-Merrell Inc.* (D.C. Cir. 1988), *cert. denied*, 493 U.S. 882 (1989), *Brock v. Merrell Dow Pharmaceuticals, Inc.*, 884 F.2d 166 (5th Cir. 1989), *modified*, 884 F.2d 166 (5th Cir. 1989), *cert. denied*, 494 U.S. 1046 (1990), and *Ealy v. Richardson-Merrell, Inc.*, 897 F.2d 159 (D.C. Cir.), *cert. denied*, 498 U.S. 950 (1990)).

[46] Margaret A. Berger, "Procedural Paradigms for Applying the Daubert Test," *Minnesota Law Review*, 78 (1994): 1335–1386; Sanders, "Scientific Validity, Admissibility and Mass Torts," 1434. See also, Joseph Sanders, *Bendectin on Trial: A Study of Mass Tort Litigation* (Ann Arbor: University of Michigan Press, 2001), 155–156 (arguing that some Bendectin courts mistakenly ruled plaintiffs' evidence inadmissible and then issued a summary judgment that because plaintiffs could "present no competent evidence on the causal question" their evidence was insufficient).

[47] *Daubert v. Merrell Dow Pharmaceuticals*, 509 U.S. 579, at 596 (citing both *Federal Rules of Civil Procedure* 56 and 50(a)).

[48] Margaret A. Berger, "Evidentiary Framework," *Reference Manual on Scientific Evidence* (Washington, DC: Federal Judicial Center, 1994), 49.

These requirements are triggered by the date of trial,[49] but the controlling *Daubert* decision "suggests that in civil litigation, issues concerning the admissibility or sufficiency of expert testimony *should be raised before trial.*"[50]

Thus, in the outline of a legal case discussed earlier, judicial and litigant review of expert witnesses typically occurs *after discovery* but *before a jury is empanelled and before a trial proper begins.* This review has become very important and might be "outcome determinative" as some courts have noted.[51] (Whether or not there is an actual hearing on expert witnesses is a separate issue, but there need not be.)[52]

If a litigant, either plaintiff or defendant, fails to have all the necessary experts *admitted* to testify in a trial, his or her case may be at an end. This was the fate of Walter Allen's widow and son in *Allen v. Pennsylvania Engineering* and Lisa Soldo. In each instance, the plaintiffs were not permitted to present their case to a jury and in effect *had no legal case* because the judge decided a critical expert's testimony was not admissible and the scientific basis for causation needed for a tort cause of action could not be presented at trial. Consequently, because they could not offer evidence to establish their legal claims, there was no factual issue for the jury to decide.[53] The judges issued summary judgments legally ending plaintiffs' cases without a public jury trial of the issues involved.

Less frequently, similar exclusions could occur on the defense side. Recently, the City of Chicago was required to compensate a man for brain-stem injuries following an encounter with the police. The city was unable to mount a defense based on an alternative theory of injury because its expert's theory was judged "too speculative" and the expert was not admitted for trial.[54] The City was limited in the defense it could present and lost a jury verdict. Exclusion of defendants' experts might arise once plaintiffs have met their burden of production or perhaps when defendants are put in the position of testifying against well-established research, for example, concerning the effects of asbestos or tobacco smoke.

To summarize: Decisions about the admissibility of experts occurs early in the sequence of legal events leading to a trial before the trial proper in front of a jury ever begins. If a litigant's experts are not admitted to testify in a trial, that party's case may end at that point, unless there is some other way to establish the claims (there typically is not in toxic tort cases).

---

[49] Berger, "Evidentiary Framework," 50.
[50] Berger, "Evidentiary Framework," 50.
[51] *General Electric Company v. Joiner,* 113 S.Ct. 512, 517 (1997).
[52] Faigman *et al., Modern Scientific Evidence,* 14–15; *Manual for Complex Litigation,* section 23.353, 509–510; *Kumho Tire Company, LT., v. Carmichael,* 526 U.S. 137, 152 (1999).
[53] *Federal Rules of Evidence* 56(c).
[54] Margaret Cronin Fisk, "Chicago Hope: A $28M Verdict," *National Law Journal,* 10 Nov. 1999, A10.

RECENT DEVELOPMENTS IN THE ADMISSIBILITY
OF EXPERT TESTIMONY

The Bendectin Litigation and Related Cases

The legal issues that have modified the law and exacerbated problems for plaintiffs arose with an antinausea drug for pregnant women with the trade name, "Bendectin."[55]

Specifically, the social-legal events leading to this litigation began with David Mekdeci, who was born in 1975 with a shortened right forearm, missing two fingers from his malformed right hand with limited use of the other two fingers. He was missing pectoral muscles in his chest, limiting his ability to move his right arm. He was anticipated later in life to have a "congenital heart defect."[56] Over time his distressed mother, reflecting on drugs she had taken during her pregnancy with David, inquired about the etiological role those drugs might have had in his birth defects. The family brought suit against Merrell National Laboratories, the manufacturer of Bendectin, that she believed (and there was some evidence suggesting that it) could have contributed to David's malformed limbs. "The day before David's fifth birthday, . . . a jury in a federal court in Orlando [Florida] awarded Michael and Betty Mekdeci [David's parents] $20,000 in their lawsuit," an amount hopelessly inadequate to compensate plaintiffs or even to pay their lawyers.[57] This verdict was unsatisfactory in a number of ways, was overturned by the trial judge, and the case was unsuccessful on retrial. The Mekdecis not only received nothing, but Merrell, playing hardball, requested over $200,000 in legal expenses from them. The trial judge reduced this to $6,000, which became a lien on their middle-class house (which they were not required to pay).[58]

The personal and legal saga that began with the Mekdecis directly affected not only the thousands of people affected by Bendectin (approximately 2000 cases were filed), but the consequences of that litigation are still reverberating through the legal system today as a result of several U.S. Supreme Court decisions (as well as appellate and district court decisions implementing the Supreme Court's decisions) that arose directly or indirectly from the Bendectin litigation.

Concerns about the Companies

Bendectin had been created, manufactured, and distributed in the United States beginning in the late 1950s by Richardson-Merrell Pharmaceutical. This was

---

[55]   Much of the following discussion concerning the context of this litigation is based upon Green, *Bendectin and Birth Defects*, 1996).

[56]   Green, *Bendectin*, 1.

[57]   Green, *Bendectin*, 3, 121–158.

[58]   Green, *Bendectin*, 3, 121–158.

was the same company that had been licensed in 1956 to distribute thalidomide, the drug that ultimately caused eight to twelve thousand birth defects in Europe and about forty in the United States.[59] In addition, about the same time Merrell had also developed Mer/29, one of the early anticholesterol drugs. Mer/29 caused adverse side effects, such as cataracts, lost or thinned hair, and mild to severe skin reactions. Data presumably showing the safety of MER/29 were "faked."[60] Litigation in the U.S. concerning thalidomide and Mer/29 cost Merrell about $100,000,000 in tort damages and settlements.[61] Moreover, according to the judge in the Mer/29 litigation Merrell acted in "reckless disregard of the possibility it would visit serious injury upon persons using it," falsified test data, withheld data from the FDA, misrepresented the safety of the drug to the medical profession, all of which could lead a jury to conclude that Richardson-Merrell acted "with wanton disregard for the safety of all who might use the drug."[62] This background created an atmosphere of suspicion within the FDA and was well known to the plaintiffs' bar, both of which added to the firm's problems when there were concerns that Bendectin could cause birth defects.

Moreover, the discovery process in the early Bendectin litigation revealed that animal studies conducted by Merrell suggesting that Bendectin was a teratogen were not followed up, and Merrell delayed sending the results to the FDA for three years. There had also been extensive behind-the-scenes efforts to manage, even manipulate, the reporting of birth defects in patients whose mothers had taken Bendectin and any potentially adverse news stories that threatened to break about the drug and its effects.[63]

Other firms probably added to this skepticism. For example, Michael Green notes that so much evidence appeared in the Dalkon Shield cases of "corporate wrongdoing and fraud" that it led to routine "multi-million dollar punitive damages."[64]

Perception of a Tort Law Crisis

If the FDA and others were suspicious of Richardson-Merrell Pharmaceutical, some were also concerned about the tort law – the institution that in principle provides redress for wrongly inflicted injuries. The Bendectin litigation occurred during a period in which there was a widespread perception and discussion of a crisis in the tort law. Critics of the tort law pointed to an earlier expansion of liability for defendants, alleged overlitigiousness by Americans, increasing damage awards, an increase in punitive damages, and

---

[59] Philip J. Hilts, *Protecting America's Health: The FDA, Business, and One Hundred Years of Regulation* (New York: Alfred K. Knopf, 2003), 158.
[60] Green, *Bendectin*, 146.
[61] Green, *Bendectin*, 89.
[62] Green, *Bendectin*, 88 (quoting the federal judge in *Toole v. Richardson-Merrell, Inc.*).
[63] Green, *Bendectin*, 129.
[64] Green, *Bendectin*, 15.

"an uncertainty about where it all would end."[65] Also, there was concern that expert witnesses could be found to opine on nearly any issue with the result that judges and juries could be misled and that the system was "biased in favor of plaintiffs, whom sympathetic jurors favor."[66] According to this view, the result was *overdeterrence* – useful technologies would be driven from the market and U.S. industry rendered less competitive in international markets, as it has been alleged that physicians have been driven from medical practice by increased malpractice insurance premiums caused by malpractice suits. Indeed, it was claimed that the tort law could be a substantial drag on the economy. For some the Bendectin litigation became almost an exemplar of the ills of the tort law. Whether such claims were true is another issue to which we briefly return at the end of the chapter.

There also may be a story yet to be fully investigated about how the perception of a tort law crisis was created or arose. There has been the suggestion that a concerted public relations campaign on the part of the National Chamber of Commerce, major firms, their industry groups, supporters, and politically associated think tanks created or significantly contributed to the perception.[67]

The Supreme Court Daubert Litigation

Daubert v. Merrell Dow Pharmaceuticals, Inc.: The specific events leading to the Supreme Court decision began when Jason Daubert and Eric Schuller were born with serious birth defects.[68] Their mothers and others suspected that Bendectin was a contributor to their injuries.[69]

Their cases came fourteen years into this litigation and after a number of epidemiological studies had finally been done on the relationship between

---

[65] Green, *Bendectin*, 19.

[66] Green, *Bendectin*, 20.

[67] See, for example, the National Chamber Litigation Center Web page that credits a mid-1970s memorandum from F. Lewis Powell, later a Supreme Court Justice, with triggering a concerted Chamber of Commerce effort to litigate cases favorable to business interests and in general to create an "advocacy program [that] has grown to include all aspects of employment relations, environmental regulation and enforcement, government contracts, as well as other cutting-edge legal issues in the areas of class action reform, product liability, toxic torts, and punitive damages." (Located at: http://www.uschamber.com/nclc/about/anniversary.html. [visited September 2004].) There is considerable anecdotal evidence about many additional activities, but no extensive scholarly work on the subject to my knowledge.

More recently, the Republican Contract with America advocates "commonsense legal reforms" that seek to restrain plaintiffs' attorneys and recovery for certain kinds of damages. (Located at: http://www.house.gov/house/Contract/CONTRACT.html [visited September 2004].)

Finally, "tort reform" is the object of a number of organizations that seek to protect their economic interests by reducing lawsuits. See, for example, John Micklethwait and Adrian Wooldridge, *The Right Nation: Conservative Power in America* (New York: The Penguin Press, 2004), esp. 110, 158, 176.

[68] See *Daubert*, 509 U.S. 579, 582 (1993).

[69] 509 U.S. at 582.

exposure to Bendectin and birth defects. Merrell Dow's expert submitted an affidavit that stated that no published study had found Bendectin to be a human teratogen and that therefore claimed that use of Bendectin during the first trimester of pregnancy had not been shown to increase the risk of birth defects.[70] Plaintiffs' experts concluded that Bendectin could cause birth defects, basing their conclusion on: (1) test tube and animal studies linking Bendectin and malformations; (2) studies showing similarities between the molecular structure of Bendectin and other teratogens; and (3) a reanalysis of published epidemiological studies.[71]

The trial court, likely confusing the admissibility of evidence with its legal sufficiency,[72] agreed with defendants and excluded plaintiffs' experts. It then granted a summary judgment for defendants before trial.[73] The court held that, because there was a plethora of epidemiological evidence regarding Bendectin, plaintiffs' substantial nonepidemiological evidence was not sufficient to create a material issue of fact and defeat the summary judgment motion.[74] The trial court relied on the *Frye* general acceptance test from a 1923 criminal case.

The *Frye* rule for the admissibility of scientific evidence was formulated in a criminal case in which a defendant tried to introduce a precursor of lie detector tests. That court held that novel scientific evidence or methodology on which an expert relied to testify had to have "general acceptance" in the relevant scientific community to be admitted for consideration at criminal trial.[75] The original test applied to generic "tests," studies or technological devices, not to opinion testimony (although this appeared to change over time in some jurisdictions, but not others, such as California[76]).

The Ninth Circuit Court of Appeals affirmed the trial court's exclusion of evidence,[77] also following the *Frye* general acceptance test.[78] The court apparently gave great weight to the fact that other appellate courts had not admitted reanalyses of epidemiological studies regarding the teratogenicity of Bendectin that had never been published nor peer-reviewed.[79] Furthermore, it noted that the large number of published studies opposing plaintiffs' position that Bendectin could cause birth defects undermined the efficacy of re-analyses that

---

[70] See 509 U.S. at 582.
[71] See 509 U.S. at 583.
[72] Sanders, "Scientific Validity, Admissibility and Mass Torts," 1387.
[73] See *Daubert v. Merrell Dow Pharm., Inc.*, 727 F. Supp. 570, 575 (S.D. Cal. 1989), *aff'd*, 951 F.2d 1128 (9th Cir. 1991), *vacated*, 509 U.S. 579 (1993).
[74] See *Daubert v. Merrell Dow Pharm., Inc.*, 727 F. Supp. 570, 575.
[75] See *Frye v. U.S.*, 293 F. 1013 (D.C. Cir. 1923).
[76] *Roberti v. Andy's Termite & Pest Control, Inc.*, 6 Cal. Rptr. 3d 827 (2003).
[77] See *Daubert v. Merrell Dow Pharm., Inc.*, 951 F.2d 1128, 1131 (9th Cir. 1991), *vacated*, 509 U.S. 579 (1993).
[78] See 951 F.2d at 1129–30.
[79] See 951 F.2d at 1130.

reached the opposite conclusion.[80] The plaintiffs petitioned the U.S. Supreme Court to hear the case and it did so.

The Supreme Court, seemingly granting a victory to plaintiffs, vacated the Ninth Circuit's decision because it had been based on the *Frye* rule, not the Federal Rules of Evidence that had been legislated in full knowledge of the existence of the *Frye* rule. It then remanded the case for reconsideration under its newly articulated standard for admissibility of scientific opinion evidence.[81]

On remand, the Ninth Circuit Court of Appeals in a controversial opinion decided against the Dauberts without returning the case to the district court of origin. It reasoned that there was no reason to return it to the trial court, "If as a matter of law, the proffered evidence would have to be excluded at trial."[82] The expert testimony would have to be excluded, the court concluded, because plaintiffs could not show that exposure to Bendectin more likely than not doubled their risk of birth defects according to the court.[83] This last point is scientifically and legally controversial.[84] We return to both points in Chapter 6.

The *Frye* "general acceptance" test had posed several concerns. Some argued that *Frye* was too *conservative*, "for it imposes a protracted waiting period that valid scientific evidence and techniques must endure before gaining legal acceptance."[85] On this view it would keep perfectly good, but not yet broadly accepted cutting-edge science (e.g., DNA analysis) or testimony from the courtroom.[86] It could also be seen as vague about what constituted the "general acceptance" of a particular kind of study or test.[87] And, it may be difficult to determine in which *particular field* a kind of scientific study should be generally accepted.[88] At the same time, it also has been criticized for being quite liberal; "the more narrowly a court defines the pertinent field, the more agreement it is likely to find."[89] Perhaps in the extreme, any expert might conceivably be permitted to testify as long as there was some appropriate self-vouching community of experts who would support the principles and methods of expert testimony, for example, in astrology or necromancy.

Ultimately, on statutory grounds the Supreme Court held that the Congressional adoption of the Federal Rules of Evidence had superseded the *Frye*

[80] See 951 F.2d at 1130.
[81] See *Daubert,* 509 U.S. at 597–98.
[82] *Daubert v. Merrell Dow Pharm., Inc.,* 43 F.3d 1311, 1315 (1995).
[83] *Daubert v. Merrell Dow Pharm., Inc.,* 43 F.3d 1311 (1995).
[84] Carl Cranor, John G. Fischer, and David A. Eastmond, "Judicial Boundary Drawing and the Need for Context-Sensitive Science in Toxic Torts after *Daubert v. Merrell Dow Pharmaceuticals, Inc.,*" *Virginia Environmental Law Journal* 16 (1996): 1–77, 37–40.
[85] Faigman *et al., Modern Scientific Evidence,* 8.
[86] *Wright & Miller Treatise,* 29 Fed. Prac. & Proc. Evid. §6266 at note 13.
[87] Faigman *et al., Modern Scientific Evidence,* 9.
[88] Faigman *et al., Modern Scientific Evidence,* 9
[89] Faigman *et al., Modern Scientific Evidence,* 9

rule.[90] In developing a view that supported greater court review of expert testimony, the Court used a policy argument. It noted that the law typically requires *firsthand* knowledge of the facts as evidence on legal issues.[91] Expert testimony is an exception to this general requirement, because an expert does not necessarily have firsthand knowledge of material to which he or she might testify.[92] However, the relaxation of the firsthand knowledge requirement with its "insistence upon 'the most *reliable sources of information,*' . . . is premised on an assumption that the expert's opinion will have a reliable basis in the knowledge and experience of his discipline."[93] Consequently, expert opinion must satisfy *some indicators* of reliability.

Another way to think about these issues is that the *Daubert* decision sought to ensure that expert testimony is based on appropriate science pertinent to a legal decision. Thus its aim might be seen as winnowing expert testimony so that a jury decision, which is ultimately based in part on either plaintiffs' or defendants' experts' accounts of the science, will be within the bounds of respectable scientific views about the issue involved or at least not beyond the boundaries where reasonable scientific experts might disagree. Consequently, it might have sought to ensure that whatever a jury decides will not be beyond respectable scientific reasoning on that issue and will be (broadly) *scientifically acceptable* (within the boundaries of science that the scientific community itself would not find unacceptable). This does not ensure that the overall verdict will be acceptable, but an important aspect of it will be.[94]

Because judges were now more involved arbiters of the reliability of expert testimony and its foundation (contrary to the *Frye* doctrine), the Court held that a judge must review the testimony of a scientific expert to ensure that it is grounded "in the methods and procedures of science," which "connotes more than subjective belief or unsupported speculation,"[95] although "the subject of scientific testimony [need not] be 'known' to a certainty . . ."[96] Consequently,

> the trial judge must . . . [conduct] . . . a *preliminary assessment* of whether the *reasoning or methodology underlying the testimony is scientifically valid* and of whether that *reasoning or methodology properly can be applied to the facts in issue.* (emphasis added)[97]

90   See *Daubert*, 509 U.S. at 588–589.
91   *Daubert*, 509 U.S. at 588–589.
92   *McCormick on Evidence*, (ed. Edwin W. Cleary et al., 3rd ed., St. Paul, MN: West Publishing Co., 1992), 909–911 and *Daubert*, 509 U.S. at 592.
93   *Daubert*, 509 U.S. at 592. Whether firsthand knowledge is a reliable analogy for scientific "reliability" is a separate and more difficult issue.
94   Cranor, "*Daubert* and the Acceptability of Legal Decisions," 127–131. There are deeper issues here to which I will return in later chapters (especially Chapter 8).
95   509 U.S. at 590.
96   509 U.S. at 590.
97   *Daubert*, 509 U.S. at 592–593. In *dicta* the Court outlined several nonexclusive, nonnecessary factors for courts to consider in evaluating experts' reasoning and methodology: (1) the falsifiability, or testability, of the theory guiding the technique used to reach the offered

The assessment must be a *preliminary* one,[98] because too intrusive a judicial review can usurp a jury's role and threaten the Seventh Amendment right to a jury trial.[99] And the Court envisioned a flexible inquiry that "must be solely *on principles and methodology, not on the conclusions* that they generate."[100] If an expert's testimony fails on either reliability or relevance, she may be excluded from testifying at trial. As we have discussed, if a litigant loses a critical witness, the case may be legally dismissed.

Finally, Court recognized the "'liberal' thrust of the Federal Rules and their 'general approach of relaxing the traditional barriers to 'opinion' testimony . . .'" suggesting that this was an improvement over the *Frye* "general acceptance" test.[101]

In seeking to clarify its views, in a somewhat puzzling section, the Court addressed some concerns of the parties and *amici* on both sides of the case. It first dismissed the suggestion that abandonment of the general acceptance test would lead to a flood of "junk science" that would confuse juries. The Court noted: "Vigorous cross-examination, presentation of contrary evidence and careful instruction on the burden of proof are the traditional and appropriate means of attacking shaky but admissible evidence."[102] In addition to this traditional protection, if the proffered evidence were truly of dubious value the court could admit it but grant a summary judgment prior to trial, or direct a verdict after jury trial, if plaintiffs' evidence were so obviously overwhelmed by defendants' evidence that no reasonable jury could decide for plaintiffs.[103]

The Court then considered the worry that gatekeeping judges, shackled by the chains of "scientific orthodoxy," would somehow stifle the search for truth.[104] Surprisingly, the Court noted the differences between the search for truth in the legal context and in the scientific context, but seemed to get it backward.[105] The Court, with a significant bow to the philosopher of science, Karl Popper[106] (much of whose work has long been outdated) pointed out that incorrect hypotheses are very useful in advancing scientific knowledge,

conclusion; (2) publication and peer review of the theory; (3) any known or potential rate of error of the technique; and (4) general acceptance within the relevant scientific community (593–594).

98   *Daubert*, 509 U.S. at 588 (quoting *The Federal Rules of Evidence*, section 702).
99   Justice Stephen Breyer, "Introduction," *Federal Reference Manual on Scientific Evidence*, 2nd ed. (Washington, DC: Federal Judicial Center, 2000), 4.
100   *Daubert*, 509 U.S. at 594–595 (emphasis added).
101   509 U.S. at 588.
102   509 U.S. at 596.
103   509 U.S. at 596 (citing both Federal Rules of Civil Procedure 56 and 50(a)).
104   509 U.S. at 596–97.
105   509 U.S. at 596–97.
106   There are substantial problems with the implicit Popperian view of science, as I briefly consider in Chapter 3. See, for example, G. Edmond and D. Mercer, "Recognizing Daubert: What Judges Should Know about Falsificationism," *Expert Evidence*, 5 (1996): 29, and James Woodward and David Goodstein, "Conduct, Misconduct, and the Structure of Science," *American Scientist*, 84 (1996): 479.

particularly when their incorrectness is shown.[107] However, incorrect hypotheses are of little use in the much quicker and more final context of a particular legal case.[108] The Court strangely seemed to suggest that the scientific basis of expert testimony and a legal decision should be on even firmer ground than a result in the scientific field itself. The Court acknowledged that a judge will occasionally incorrectly exclude valid scientific methodologies, but that such exclusion is part of the balance to be struck in the legal context where the admission of an erroneous technique can have grave and irreparable consequences to the parties involved in an adversarial case.[109] Thus, the court seemed to reverse the roles of science and the law because it seemed to suggest that it was of greater importance that the science admitted into legal cases should be more certain than the scientific studies that provide the foundation for future scientific developments. This is even more odd when we recall that often legal cases are brought at a time when the relevant science is "on the frontiers of scientific knowledge" and unlikely to be established with great certainty.[110] The suggestions contained in this part of the court's opinion are particularly troublesome as we will see in Chapter 7 (especially given the Court's views in *Kumho Tire* and the fact of reasonable scientific disagreements).

Joiner v. General Electric *and* Kumho Tire v. Carmichael: The *Daubert* case was quickly followed by *General Electric v. Joiner* (1997) and by *Kumho Tire v. Carmichael* (1999), two Supreme Court decisions focusing primarily on procedural issues.[111] The Daubert Court had not addressed the standard of review that should be applied by appellate courts in reviewing trial court decisions on the admission of expert testimony. Subsequent to *Daubert* most circuits held that an "abuse of discretion standard" applies, which means that a trial judge's ruling on the admissibility of scientific evidence must be "manifestly erroneous" or "clearly erroneous" before it can be overturned.[112] The

---

[107] 509 U.S. at 597.

[108] 509 U.S. at 597.

[109] See 509 U.S. at 597. One implicit message indicated in this passage is that it is a permissible social cost for courts to mistakenly exclude "valid scientific methodologies." This contributes to a false negative mistake on scientific grounds. It also has irreparable consequences to the parties involved, if they have been wrongly harmed by others and have no possibility for corrective justice.

[110] There is a further issue concerning whether judges in their admissibility decisions ought to be even-handed in protecting against factual false positives or factual false negatives. I argue in later chapters that they should.

[111] *General Elec. Co. v. Joiner,* 522 U.S. 136 (1997); *Kumho Tire Co. v. Carmichael,* 526 U.S. 137 (1999).

[112] See, e.g., *American & Foreign Ins. Co. v. General Elec. Co.,* 45 F.3d 135, 139 (6th Cir. 1995) (lower court exclusion of expert testimony on circuit breaker design must be clearly erroneous to show abuse of discretion); *United States v. Dorsey,* 45 F.3d 809, 815–16 (4th Cir. 1995) (applying abuse of discretion standard to lower court ruling on admissibility of forensic anthropologist's testimony); *Bradley v. Brown,* 42 F.3d 434, 436–37 (7th Cir. 1994) (holding that lower court's findings regarding doctors' testimony will not be overturned "unless they are manifestly erroneous").

Third[113] and Eleventh[114] Circuits took somewhat different views because admissibility decisions could be so decisive in determining the outcome of legal cases. The Supreme Court considered these issues in the second of the trilogy of cases to address expert testimony: *Joiner v. General Electric*.[115]

Recall (from Chapter 1) that Robert Joiner worked as an electrician for the city of Thomasville, Georgia, *inter alia*, repairing and cleaning the city's electrical transformers, which used a mineral-based fluid as a coolant. Mr. Joiner alleged that his exposure to polychlorinated biphenyls (PCBs), furans, dioxins and other organic substances (several of which were known carcinogens) contributed to his lung cancer. He and his wife brought suit on these issues at a district court in Georgia.

The district court judge following *Daubert* excluded plaintiffs' experts from testifying, because the testimony did not rise above "subjective belief or unsupported speculation," thus rendering it inadequate to present a "material issue of fact" for a jury. The judge granted a motion for a summary judgment and dismissed the suit. Because the experts could not testify, the Joiners' case was at an end.[116]

Plaintiffs appealed to the Eleventh Circuit Court of Appeals, which took a careful look at the District Court Judge's exclusion of plaintiff's expert witnesses. The Eleventh Circuit Court of Appeals found that the trial court had misunderstood plaintiffs' experts' methodology and ruled that when exclusion of evidence had such an "outcome determinative" effect on a trial, an appellate court should more carefully review admissibility decisions.[117] It held that the District Court Judge had abused her discretion in excluding evidence. The Eleventh Circuit, thus, reversed the trial court. However, defendants sought review of the Circuit Court's decision in the Supreme Court, which decided on the appropriate standard of appellate review of a district court's admissibility ruling.

The Supreme Court overturned the Eleventh Circuit's procedural ruling, holding that "abuse of discretion" is the proper standard for reviewing trial court decisions concerning the admissibility of evidence and holding that federal appellate courts may invalidate such rulings only if the lower court "abuses its discretion."[118] A trial judge has not abused her discretion if, "[w]here there are two permissible views of the evidence, the choice between them cannot be clearly erroneous."[119] Thus, if a judge admits or excludes an expert critical to a case, she cannot be overturned on appeal unless the decision was clearly

113 See *Paoli*, 35 F.3d at 741–52.
114 *Joiner v. General Electric Co.*, 78 F.3d 524 (11th Cir. 1996).
115 *General Elec. Co. v. Joiner*, 522 U.S. 136 (1997).
116 *Joiner v. General Electric Co.*, 864 F.Supp. 1310 (N.D. Georgia 1994).
117 *Joiner v. General Electric Co.*, 78 F.3d 524 (11th Cir. 1996).
118 *General Elec. Co. v. Joiner*, 522 U.S. 136, 139 (1997).
119 *Cooter & Gell v. Hartmarx Corp.*, 496 U.S. 384 at 400 (1989) quoting *Anderson v. Bessemer City*, 470 U.S. 564, 573–574 (1985).

mistaken. This is not an impossible appellate hurdle to overcome but a very difficult one. A litigant could fail to have a critical witness admitted, have the case dismissed as a consequence, and not prevail on the admissibility decision on appeal.[120]

In addition, a majority of eight judges,[121] excluding Justice Stevens, then proceeded to do something it had not done in *Daubert* – examine the details of the scientific record. In a surprisingly elaborate discussion of plaintiff's expert's evidence, the court applied the newly articulated standard for appellate review of evidence and upheld the District Court's review of expert testimony and its foundation as not being an abuse of discretion. It held that the district court had not abused her discretion in rejecting *each piece* of evidence relied on by Joiners' experts as inadequate to support the conclusions that he contracted lung cancer from exposure to PCBs. It found that plaintiffs' reliance on studies of infant mice exposed to PCBs failed to support the conclusion that PCBs caused lung cancer.[122] The Court also concluded that the District court ruled properly in excluding individually each of the epidemiological studies as providing a reasonable foundation for expert testimony.[123]

Respondent Joiner had argued, contra the district court, that the weight of the evidence methodology was reliable and that this court's review had violated the *Daubert* principle that "the focus, of course, must be solely on the principles, not on the conclusions they generate." To this a majority of the Supreme Court responded:

> He claims that because the District Court's disagreement was with the conclusion that the experts drew from the studies, the District Court committed legal error and was properly reversed by the Court of appeals. But conclusions and methodology are not entirely distinct from one another. Trained experts commonly extrapolate from existing data. But nothing in either *Daubert* or the Federal Rules of Evidence requires a district court to admit opinion evidence which is connected to existing data only by the *ipse dixit* of the expert. A court may conclude that there is simply too great an analytical gap between the data and the opinion proffered . . .[124]

---

120   If we take the language seriously – where there are two permissible views of the evidence, the choice between them cannot be erroneous – this poses a difficult problem for a judge faced with testimony that is on the frontiers of scientific research, precisely where legitimate scientific disagreements are highly likely. The abuse of discretion standard suggests that judges' admissibility decisions would not be reviewed no matter which choice was made, even if they consistently decided one way only, for example, always for plaintiffs or always for defendants. If both views are respectable, a judge should not choose between them.

121   *General Elec. Co. v. Joiner*, 522 U.S. at 143–147.

122   *General Elec. Co. v. Joiner*, 522 U.S. at 143–147.

123   *General Elec. Co. v. Joiner*, 522 U.S. at 143–147.

124   *General Elec. Co. v. Joiner*, 522 U.S. at 146–147. The phrase "ipse dixit" means "He himself said it; a bare assertion resting on the authority of an individual" (*Black's Law Dictionary*, 961 (St. Paul, MN: West Publishing Co., 1968)).

Justice Stevens was sufficiently concerned about this section of the ruling that he dissented. He would have left review of the admissibility decision to the appellate court, which is closer to the evidence. In addition, he pointed out that the Supreme Court's ruling did not remain faithful to *Daubert*'s insistence that the focus be "solely on principles and methodology, not on the conclusions they generate."[125] Moreover, because Joiner's experts utilized a "weight of the evidence" methodology to support their conclusions, "[t]hey did not suggest that any one study provided adequate support for their conclusions, but instead relied on all the studies taken together (along with their interviews of Joiner and their review of his medical records)."[126] Because the focus of the trial court's ruling "was on the separate studies and the conclusions of the experts, not on the experts' methodology ("Defendants . . . persuade the court that Plaintiffs' expert testimony would not be admissible . . . by attacking the conclusions that Plaintiffs' experts draw from the studies they cite"), the evidence assessment by the court of appeal was "persuasive."[127] Moreover, Stevens argued, both defendants and federal agencies utilize similar methodologies in drawing inferences from studies about the carcinogenicity of substances. Finally, "using this methodology, it would seem that an expert could reasonably have concluded that the study of workers at an Italian capacitor plant, coupled with data from Monsanto's study and other studies, raises an inference that PCBs promote lung cancer."[128]

The final Supreme Court case developing new law was *Kumho Tire v. Carmichael*. The admissibility issue concerned an engineer who, by training and experience, claimed to be able to determine, by inspection and a methodology he developed, after the fact of a tire failure whether a tire that had shredded and caused a car accident had been defective. The trial court excluded the engineer's testimony but the Eleventh Circuit Court of Appeals overturned the trial court.[129] The Supreme Court in turn reversed the Eleventh Circuit, holding that the *Daubert* factors may apply to all expert testimony, and that the abuse-of-discretion standard "applies *as much to the trial court's decisions about how to determine [scientific] reliability as to its ultimate conclusion.*"[130] Thus, the Court held that a judge has discretion both to decide how to conduct an admissibility review as well as *making the actual admissibility judgment* with both subjected to the abuse of discretion standard of review.

Interestingly, the unanimous court, perhaps aware that district courts might be overly zealous in their review of evidence, noted that trial courts need

125 *General Elec. Co. v. Joiner*, 522 U.S. at 152 (citing *Daubert v. Merrell Dow Pharmaceuticals*, 509 U.S. at 595).
126 *General Elec. Co. v. Joiner*, at 152–153.
127 *General Elec. Co. v. Joiner*, at 152.
128 *General Elec. Co. v. Joiner*, at 152.
129 *Carmichael v. Samyang Tire, Inc.*, 131 F.3d 1433 (1997).
130 *Kumho Tire Co. v. Carmichael*, 526 U.S. 137, 152 (1999).

discretionary authority "to avoid unnecessary 'reliability' proceedings in ordinary cases where the reliability of an expert's methods is properly taken for granted ... as well as to avoid 'unjustifiable expense' and delay as part of their search for 'truth' and the 'jus[t] determin[ation]' of proceedings."[131]

The *Kumho* Court noted that the aim of admissibility should be to ensure "that an expert ..., employs in the courtroom the same level of intellectual rigor that characterizes the practice of an expert in the relevant field."[132] A judge may exclude expert testimony that falls "outside the range where experts might reasonably differ, and where the jury must decide among the conflicting views of different experts, even though the evidence is 'shaky.'"[133] I return to this guidance in Chapter 7.

The Admissibility Picture after the *Daubert* Trilogy

The picture of how trial court judges should review expert testimony following this trilogy of cases seems to be the following. Trial judges have a heightened duty to review expert testimony and its scientific foundation to determine whether "the *reasoning or methodology underlying the testimony is scientifically valid* and ... whether that *reasoning or methodology properly can be applied to the facts in issue*" (emphasis added).[134]

Moreover, the Court seemed to have endorsed the view that the newly articulated admissibility rules were more liberal (would result in admitting a wider range of evidence) than the rejected *Frye* rules,[135] but this has been put into doubt by the implementation of the decisions by other courts. Trial courts must focus on the reasoning and methodology of an expert, not her conclusions, unless there is too great a "gap" between the methodology and conclusion as *Joiner* reasoned. Judges are authorized to review all experts under their heightened duty of review, but have considerable discretion to decide both how to review their testimony and how to determine its admissibility. A trial judge has not abused her discretion, if "[w]here there are two permissible views of the evidence, the choice between them cannot be clearly erroneous."[136] Thus, if a judge admits or excludes an expert critical to a case, she cannot be overturned on appeal unless the decision was clearly mistaken. This discretion is needed to ensure that courts can avoid both unnecessary delay as well as unjustifiable expense in conducting these proceedings.

---

[131] *Kumho Tire Co. v. Carmichael*, 526 U.S. at 153 (Justices Scalia, O'Connor, and Thomas joined the majority, but also issued a concurring opinion cautioning courts not to perform admissibility reviews "inadequately" (526 U.S. at 159).

[132] *Kumho Tire Co. v. Carmichael*, 526 U.S. at 152.

[133] *Kumho Tire Co. v. Carmichael*, 526 U.S. at 153.

[134] *Daubert*, 509 U.S. at 592–593.

[135] *Daubert*, 509 U.S. at 589

[136] *Cooter & Gell v. Hartmarx Corp.*, 496 U.S. 384, at 400 (1989) quoting *Anderson v. Bessemer City*, 470 U.S. 564, 573–574.

Finally, a trial judge should seek to assure that an expert "employs in the courtroom the same level of intellectual rigor that characterizes the practice of an expert in the relevant field,[137] and may exclude expert testimony that falls "outside the range where experts might reasonably differ, and where the jury must decide among the conflicting views of different experts, even though the evidence is 'shaky.'"[138] That is, although there is an emphasis on experts evaluating evidence and reasoning about it in the courtroom as they would in their own fields, this decision suggests that trial and appellate judges also should be alert to admitting experts whose testimony is within "the range where experts might reasonably differ."[139]

Subsequent to these decisions, the Federal Rules of Evidence have been amended to reflect the decisions and codify the changes. Rule 702 now reads

> If scientific, technical, or other specialized knowledge will assist the trier of fact to understand the evidence or to determine a fact in issue, a witness qualified as an expert by knowledge, skill, experience, training, or education, may testify thereto in the form of an opinion or otherwise, if (1) the testimony is based upon sufficient facts or data, (2) the testimony is the product of reliable principles and methods, and (3) the witness has applied the principles and methods reliably to the facts of the case.[140]

The proposed rule requires that expert testimony must be "based upon *sufficient* facts or data," the testimony itself should be the product of "reliable principles and methods," and the expert should apply the principles and methods "reliably" to the facts of the case. In some respects the amended Rule 702 more clearly separates issues for courts to consider, distinguishing between the facts or data, the testimony based on them and the application of the testimony to the facts of the case. (There may be difficulty in finding "reliable principles and methods" for expert inferences, as I consider in later chapters.)

Comments on the amended Rule also indicate various "factors" to assist judges in reviewing testimony for reliability (building on the original *Daubert* decision).[141] There is some ambiguity as to *what* these "*Daubert* factors" should

---

137   *Kumho Tire Co. v. Carmichael*, 526 U.S. at 152.

138   *Kumho Tire Co. v. Carmichael*, 526 U.S. at 153.

139   *Kumho Tire Co. v. Carmichael*, 526 U.S. at 153.

140   Advisory Committee on Evidence Rules, "Proposed Amendment: Rule 702" (December 2000) (emphases in original and indicate new material).

141   Additional considerations are referenced in Advisory Committee on Evidence Rules, "Proposed Amendment: Rule 702" (December 2000). (1) Whether experts are "proposing to testify about matters growing naturally and directly out of research they have conducted independent of the litigation, or whether they have developed their opinions expressly for purposes of testifying." *Daubert v. Merrell Dow Pharmaceuticals, Inc.*, 43 F.3d 1311, 1317 (9th Cir. 1995). (2) Whether the expert has unjustifiably extrapolated from an accepted premise to an unfounded conclusion. See *General Elec. Co. v. Joiner*, 522 U.S. 136, 146 (1997) (in some cases a trial court "may conclude that there is simply too great an analytical gap between the data and the opinion proffered"). (3) Whether the expert has adequately accounted for obvious alternative explanations. See *Claar v. Burlington N.R.R.*, 29 F.3d 499

be applied: the testimony itself, studies on which the testimony is based, or inferences experts make from underlying studies. These are each different. Some of them seem to apply most naturally to studies or tests on which expert testimony is based and less well to expert inferences. Others are more general admonitions.

Several observations by the Committee are of interest. The Committee found that, while the rejection of expert testimony is "the exception rather than the rule ... 'the trial court's role as gatekeeper is not intended to serve as a replacement for the adversary system.'"[142] It also reiterated the *Daubert* Court's admonition about the importance of "vigorous cross-examination, presentation of contrary evidence, and careful instruction on the burden of proof" as means to attacking "shaky but admissible evidence."[143] Finally, following the Third Circuit Court of Appeals, it notes that proponents

> do not have to demonstrate to the judge by a preponderance of the evidence that the assessments of their experts are correct, they only have to demonstrate by a preponderance of evidence that their opinions are reliable. ... The evidentiary requirement of reliability is lower than the merits standard of correctness.[144]

All this is salutary, as I argue in Chapter 7. However, there remain some issues in understanding the change in law and in how courts are applying the decisions from *Daubert* as I consider in what follows.

THE AFTERMATH OF THE BENDECTIN LITIGATION

Critiques

Although in *Daubert* the Supreme Court held for plaintiffs, they lost on remand in the Ninth Circuit Court of Appeals, and so did virtually every other Bendectin

(9th Cir. 1994) (testimony excluded where the expert failed to consider other obvious causes for the plaintiff's condition). Compare *Claar* with *Ambrosini v. Labarraque*, 101 F.3d 129 (D.C. Cir. 1996) (the possibility of some uneliminated causes presents a question of weight, so long as the most obvious causes have been considered and reasonably ruled out by the expert). (4) Whether the expert "is being as careful as he would be in his regular professional work outside his paid litigation consulting." *Sheehan v. Daily Racing Form, Inc.*, 104 F.3d 940, 942 (7th Cir. 1997). This is quite similar to the "intellectual rigor" consideration from *Kumho Tire Co. v. Carmichael*, 119 S.Ct. 1167, 1176 (1999). (5) Whether the field of expertise claimed by the expert is known to reach reliable results for the type of opinion the expert would give. See *Kumho Tire Co. v. Carmichael*, 119 S.Ct. 1167, 1175 (1999).

142   Advisory Committee on Evidence Rules, "Proposed Amendment: Rule 702," citing *United States v. 14.38 Acres of Land Situated in Leflore County, Mississippi*, 80 F.3d 1074, 1078 (5th Cir. 1996).

143   509 U.S. at 595

144   *In re Paoli R.R. Yard PCB Litigation*, 35 F.3d 717, 744 (3d Cir. 1994)

plaintiff. As a result critics of the tort law have frequently used this litigation as an exemplar that there are substantial problems with the tort law.

Direct monetary costs to Bendectin defendants might have been "in the range of $100 million" with plaintiffs' firms spending "tens of millions."[145] Moreover, the tort system tends to impose a tax of 50–70 percent on every dollar transferred from defendants to plaintiffs. However, in the Bendectin litigation, this tax might have approached 100 percent, because little money changed hands despite two thousand cases and twenty years of litigation.[146]

Indirect costs included the withdrawal of Bendectin from the market because of litigation pressures and the alleged deterrence of research and innovation in the pharmaceutical industry, which has substantial capacity to improve public health and welfare.

Finally, more strident critics have argued that "there is no statistically significant association between Bendectin and birth defects,"[147] and that "Bendectin is safe for both the mother and the unborn child . . . "[148] In the extreme, some claimed that the number of birth defects actually *increased* since Bendectin was removed from the market, because violent nausea might cause injuries to developing embryos.[149]

Correctives

In his extensive study, *Bendectin and Birth Defects*, Michael Green argues that the allegations about the tort law are far from established. "Many commentators disagreed with several aspects of the [initial] crisis account, its causes, and its consequences."[150] There was a substantial increase in tort cases filed from 1974–1985, with asbestos, a quite potent toxicant, making up 31 percent of the cases, but significantly, "in absolute terms, the incidence of claiming is well below the incidence of injurious events that might justify a claim."[151] Other scholars agree; the best studies available about the tort law indicate that only a small percentage of persons wrongfully injured by a doctor or a company's products ever approach a lawyer seeking redress for their injuries. For example, when there are known tortiously actionable injuries, only about 2–3 percent

---

[145] Green, *Bendectin*, 335.
[146] Green, *Bendectin*, 335.
[147] Peter Huber, *Galileo's Revenge: Junk Science in the Courtroom* (New York: Basic Books, 1991), 111–129.
[148] Howard Denemark, "Improving Litigation Against Drug Manufacturers for Failure to Warn Against Possible Side Effects: Keeping Dubious Lawsuits from Driving Good Drugs Off the Market," *Case Western Reserve Law Review* 40 (1987): 427–438.
[149] Green, *Bendectin*, 337.
[150] Green, *Bendectin*, 19.
[151] Green, *Bendectin*, 20.

become lawsuits, a fairly common finding.[152] In federal law, only a small part of the total tort filings, the tort law area was hardly the fastest growing area of litigation, with general *nontort* filings growing faster.[153]

More specifically on the Bendectin litigation, Merrell Dow withdrew Bendectin from the market because of the litigation. This has "no doubt deprived some pregnant women of relief from the nausea and vomiting of pregnancy, . . . [but] the loss of Bendectin is not nearly as tragic as some of the critics' semi-hysterical claims have made it out to be."[154] One study found that Bendectin "relieved morning sickness in only 10% more of the women than took a placebo . . . [and for nausea alone it provided] benefit to 23 percent more of those receiving Bendectin than those who were given a placebo." For vomiting there was only a 7 percent difference.[155] (These are "relative benefit" ratios of 1:1.1, 1:1.23, and 1:1.07. Compare them with defense and some court claims that human epidemiological studies must exhibit "relative risks" greater than 2.0 before an expert can rely on them for expert testimony.)

Moreover, the absence of Bendectin from the market was not necessarily a bad thing as this "avoided the significant overuse of the drug that occurred in the 1970s . . . " Green notes that physicians and women should be cautious in exposing a developing embryo to many such substances, since this is one of the most biologically vulnerable periods in a human life as an embryo grows from one cell to billions in a short period of time.[156]

On the scientific claims, Green concludes that some of the most strident critics have gone much too far in asserting the safety of Bendectin or absence of scientific studies showing adverse effects. For example, one critic claimed that ". . . overwhelming scientific evidence [shows] that Bendectin is safe for both the mother and the unborn child . . ."[157] Green counters, "The range of risk [of shortened limbs from exposures to Bendectin] that is consistent with the scientific evidence is *small, but it still exists*."[158] Nonetheless, that risk is too small to permit a plaintiff to satisfy the proof conditions in a toxic tort case.

Is the tort system a social drag on the economy? "[W]e simply do not know. . . . Moreover, there is good reason to be skeptical that Bendectin signals

---

[152] Michael J. Saks, "Do We Really Know Anything about the Behavior of the Tort Litigation System — and Why Not?" *Pennsylvania Law Review* 140 (1992): 1184–1185. (Saks cites numerous studies showing how few legitimately injured persons actually file suits and fewer still proceed to trial.)

[153] Federal government suits for recovery of overpayments to individuals or firms, social security cases, and contract litigation all increased faster than tort cases, yet these areas were not "in crisis." (Saks, "Do We Really Know Anything," 1200–1201.)

[154] Green, *Bendectin*, 336.

[155] Green, *Bendectin*, 336.

[156] Green, *Bendectin*, 337 (quoting a standard textbook on the effects of drugs on the fetus).

[157] Green, *Bendectin*, 330 (quoting Howard Denemark, "Improving Litigation Against Drug Manufacturers," 413, 427–428).

[158] Green, *Bendectin*, 330 (emphasis added).

much of anything about the net social impact of tort law on the pharmaceutical industry."[159] A Rand study "observes that liability effects on innovation 'cannot be observed or quantified.'"[160] At most tort liability might shift some research funding from research on "modest drugs" to research on those that would represent "a major break-through and the promise of huge profits."[161]

Consequently, "[r]ather than being emblematic, the Bendectin litigation may be idiosyncratic [or even aberrational] in assessing the role of the tort system's impact on pharmaceutical technology and innovation."[162] Although in the end Green would add the Bendectin litigation to the negative side of the mass toxic tort ledger, he is cautious in "overemphasizing its impact."[163] Bendectin's negative impact must be balanced against the litigation concerning the Dalkon Shield IUD, asbestos, MER/29, thalidomide, alachlor, atrazine, formaldehyde, and perchloroethylene, all justified tort claims.[164] The tobacco litigation, which had not developed extensively at the time he completed his book, should be added to the positive side of the ledger as well.

CONCLUSION

The review of the *Daubert* trilogy of cases that modified the law on the admissibility of expert testimony and its scientific foundation sought to show where in the legal process this occurs. However, much more is required to analyze the impact of these changes on the legal system, the scientific community, and ordinary citizens whose lives are affected by the tort law. To evaluate these changes, we need a deeper understanding of some of the legal implications as well as a better understanding of the science that will be needed in such cases. These are subjects for the chapters that follow.

[159] Green, *Bendectin*, 339.
[160] Green, *Bendectin*, 339.
[161] Green, *Bendectin*, 340.
[162] Green, *Bendectin*, 341.
[163] Green, *Bendectin*, 341.
[164] Berger, "Eliminating General Causation," 2135.

3

Institutional Concerns about the Supreme Court's Trilogy

In *Daubert,* the Supreme Court correctly saw that lower courts had reviewed the admissibility of expert testimony and its foundation on the basis of a principle – the *Frye* "general acceptance" test – that had been superseded by the more liberal admissibility guidance of the Federal Rules of Evidence. At the same time, when it sought to articulate guidance for this activity, it heightened the gatekeeping duties of judges. However, in doing this, it entered intellectual territory that is not readily accessible to judges with their typical training.

The Supreme Court did not mention and seemingly disregarded its own decision of a decade earlier in *Barefoot v. Estelle.* This decision had held that cross-examination and jury assessment of witnesses' credibility and reliability were sufficient to protect a criminal defendant in a death penalty case against dubious and unreliable expert testimony that was widely criticized by the expert's own profession.[1] By the time *Daubert* was decided in 1993, instead of merely rejecting *Frye,* as Chief Justice Rehnquist argued in dissent, and going beyond the plain language of the Federal Rules of Evidence, it created a "reliability" screen for expert testimony.[2] This contrasted with *Barefoot v. Estelle* and with much of the previous application of the *Frye* test. In many jurisdictions, the *Frye* test only applied to generic tests, studies, technological devices, and scientific procedures that provided the foundation of scientific testimony, not to scientific opinions or the inferences of scientists.

In this chapter, I sketch some issues the court created by entering the intellectual terrain of epistemology, philosophy of science, and the nature of causal inferences. None of these issues is easy, but the Court took them up anyway. The easy part of the *Daubert* opinion was the rejection of the *Frye* test. A much more

---

[1] *Barefoot v. Estelle,* 463 U.S. 880, at 899 (1983). See also Michael H. Gottesman, "From Barefoot to Daubert to Joiner: Triple Play or Double Error," *Arizona Law Review* 40 (1998): 753, for further discussion of this.

[2] Faigman *et al., Modern Scientific Evidence,* 12 (suggesting that the meaning of the Federal Rules of Evidence was far from "plain," and that *Daubert* substantially changed past practice).

difficult issue for the courts and for the rest of us is understanding the import of the decisions and how they should guide the admissibility of expert testimony and its scientific foundation. Subsequently, the Federal Rules of Evidence were amended to reflect the Supreme Court's opinions and to guide federal judges; this is also introduced.

OBVIOUS LESSONS

First, the Court gave federal trial judges a heightened "gatekeeping" duty to review expert testimony and its scientific basis. This gatekeeping duty has loomed much larger than the amount of space the Court devoted to discussing and characterizing it. Only two places in the majority opinion *Daubert* did the Court use the word "gatekeeping."[3] The Court has clearly been understood as authorizing trial courts to serve as *nontrivial* "gatekeepers" of expert testimony.

The screening responsibility conveyed by the gatekeeping requirement has become quite substantive. Experts are not merely reviewed, as they were previously in federal courts and as they continue to be in some state jurisdictions, (a) to see that they are properly qualified by knowledge, skill, experience, training, or education to testify about technical issues they are asked to address; and (b) to ensure that their scientific opinions are based upon generic techniques, tests, studies, and scientific procedures that are viewed as reliable by the scientific community. Subsequent to the *Daubert* decision if an expert *opinion* is not judged to be sufficiently reliable, judges may exclude it.

The Court's language suggests that judges must ensure that expert testimony purporting to be scientific must indeed be based upon scientific reasoning and methodology.[4] The aim of this requirement seems to be to ensure that legal decisions will comport more closely with what is known scientifically or what can be reasonably inferred from the science that is relevant to the legal issues. However, at least some commentators have suggested that the courts were really struggling with a much more basic issue – how to preclude charlatans or perhaps even "liars" from testifying.[5] This was a perceived concern about torts in the late 1970's and early 1980's – perhaps some experts could be found to testify on nearly any subject and say nearly anything that their employers needed to be said if they were paid for testifying. Indeed, it is likely that some experts on both sides of tort cases testified as their employers wanted. And there are a

---

[3] *Daubert v. Merrell Dow Pharmaceuticals, Inc.*, 509 U.S. 579, at 589, 597.

[4] "Faced with a proffer of expert scientific testimony, then, the trial judge must determine at the outset . . . whether the expert is proposing to testify to (1) scientific knowledge that (2) will assist the trier of fact to understand or determine a fact in issue. This entails a preliminary assessment of whether the *reasoning or methodology underlying the testimony is scientifically valid and of whether that reasoning or methodology properly can be applied to the facts in issue.*" *Daubert*, 509 U.S. at 592–593 (emphasis added).

[5] Gottesman, "From *Barefoot* to *Daubert* to *Joiner*," 753.

variety of incentives and more subtle relationship processes that might select for experts to testify as their employers wish.[6] Courts also might have been concerned about experts who expressed "unsupported speculation," where they had insufficient knowledge about which they are testifying or perhaps had mere "subjective beliefs" that were not as fully grounded in scientific studies as might be reasonably be required. In order to address these issues the Court sought to ensure that experts base their testimony on what is known or what can be reasonably inferred from them.

The principle from *Daubert* is that expert testimony that is not "reliable," that is, that is probably not grounded "in the reasoning or methodology" of science should be excluded.[7] According to *Daubert*, when courts determine the admissibility of evidence, they should ask whether the evidence was more likely than not based upon scientific reasoning and methods.[8] If the answer is no, the evidence should be excluded. If the answer is yes – that the evidence probably resulted from scientific reasoning – then it should be admitted. The courts are vague about "scientific reasoning." I consider it in several chapters that follow.

Although courts have considerable latitude in screening evidence, if the questions are framed properly, the answers to them appear to be more determinate than some appellate opinions suggest. The reason for this is that scientists routinely utilize certain kinds of evidence to come to their conclusions concerning toxicity: epidemiological evidence, if it is available, as well as animal, short-term toxicity, structure-activity, and mechanistic studies. If a particular scientist relies on such scientifically relevant evidence and evaluates it as do other respectable scientists, but assigns somewhat different weights to the studies, the scientist more likely than not has utilized scientific reasoning and methods in making inferences from the data, even if her *conclusions* do not necessarily accord with other experts' conclusions. Thus, it may be more difficult than courts have suggested to show that an expert's reasoning is *probably not reflective of respectable scientific reasoning* on a particular toxicological issue. This is especially the case when respectable scientists have a range of views on an issue, as they often do. Scientific experts frequently disagree, even when evaluating the same evidence and engaging in quite good science.[9] I return to these issues in Chapters 4, 5, and 6.

[6]   Gross, "Expert Evidence," 1113–1232.
[7]   *Daubert*, 509 U.S. at 588.
[8]   *Daubert*, 509 U.S. at 589–590.
[9]   Not all judicial rulings on scientific evidence raise issues of toxicology. Some merely deal with correctly assessing circumstantial evidence involving exposures to toxic substances. These are not addressed here, but for examples see *Moore v. Ashland Chemical, Inc.,* 151 F.3d 269 (5th Cir. 1998) (considering the adequacy of circumstantial and scientific evidence that exposure to a spilled solvent caused respiratory tract disorders); *Wright v. Willamette Indus., Inc.,* 91 F.3d 1105 (8th Cir. 1996) (concerning circumstantial and scientific evidence that exposure to formaldehyde-impregnated wood dust caused respiratory disorders); and *Zuchowicz v. United States,* 140 F.3d 381, 389–391 (2nd Cir. 1998).

The amended Rule 702 appears to be an improvement on the original *Daubert* trilogy. The modified Rule 702 permits expert testimony provided *"(1) the testimony is based upon sufficient facts or data, (2) the testimony is the product of reliable principles and methods, and (3) the witness has applied the principles and methods reliably to the facts of the case."*[10] Judges accordingly have three tasks. They must assess whether experts have relied on the kinds of studies scientists typically would utilize and whether such studies (taken together?) constitute "sufficient" evidence for expert testimony. (For courts to evaluate the scientific "sufficiency" of such evidence may be difficult [Chapter 4].) They must assess whether the testimony (one might say the "inferences") from the data are based on reliable principles and methods. (This, too, is not easy.) And they must judge whether the testimony is properly applied to the facts of the case. Rule 702 appears to be an improvement on the Supreme Court decisions because it distinguishes different tasks for courts; this may assist their analysis. However, it also may indicate a further shift in substantive legal policy, about which some have already expressed concerns.[11]

According to *Daubert* (and echoed in Rule 702 comments) trial court review is to be guided by four nondefinitive factors, if they are appropriate for the review in question. The *Kuhmo Tire* case emphasizes the flexibility in their use. Judges must rule on the admissibility of litigants' evidence based on the considerations that are pertinent to the facts of the case in question.[12] Moreover, to *what* are the various *Daubert* factors to be applied? There seems to be some confusion on this point. Do they apply to the underlying tests, studies, or technologies for generating information, as is often suggested, or do they apply to the *inferences* experts make from the studies? Two of the original four factors seem more naturally to apply to the underlying studies – testability (falsifiability) and error rate – and some commentators recommend this.[13] Sometimes these two factors are applied to scientists' inferences, but they seem much less at home there, much more difficult to utilize and scientists themselves seem

---

[10] Advisory Committee on Evidence Rules, "Proposed Amendment: Rule 702" (December 2000) (emphases in original and indicate new material).

[11] Margaret Berger expresses concern about testimony being based on "sufficient facts or data," since this may well indicate a significant shift in legal policy and give federal courts a more substantive role than they should have in reviewing the mere admissibility of expert testimony for cases originating in state courts. (Berger, "Upsetting the Balance Between Adverse Interests," 323. The concern is that federal courts could intrude on state rights to jury trial by means of an admissibility hearing.)

[12] "The conclusion, in our view, is that we can neither rule out, nor rule in, for all cases and for all time the applicability of the factors mentioned in *Daubert*, nor can we now do so for subsets of cases categorized by category of expert or by kind of evidence. Too much depends upon the particular circumstances of the particular case at issue.... Engineering testimony rests upon scientific foundation, the reliability of which will be at issue in some cases.... In other cases, the relevant reliability concerns may focus upon personal knowledge or experience" (*Kumho Tire v. Carmichael*, 526 U.S. 137, 150).

[13] Faigman *et al.*, *Modern Scientific Evidence*, 28–37.

unlikely to use them for this purpose. The other two – general acceptance and peer review – appear to apply to "more fundamental activit[ies] of scientific community."[14] Of the factors identified by subsequent courts and noted by the Advisory Committee on Evidence Rules[15] two seem to go to assessing the credibility of the expert (whether experts propose to testify about matters growing naturally out of their own research, and whether an expert is being as careful in legal testimony as he or she would in professional work outside the courtroom). One concerns the field itself (whether it is known to be reliable). Two concern scientific inferences from studies (whether there is "unjustifiable extrapolation from an accepted premise to an unfounded conclusion" and whether an expert has adequately accounted for obvious alternative explanations).

The *Daubert* and *Joiner* rulings reveal a tension between different Court concerns. One "emphasizes that the Federal Rules are *designedly permissive* with respect to expert testimony."[16] The other draws attention to the "gatekeeper" role of the trial court. The attention to the gatekeeper role emphasizes that they "have a heavy responsibility to exclude unreliable evidence; that they are to take this gatekeeper responsibility more seriously than perhaps they did in the past; and that the exclusionary [provisions of the] Federal Rule[s] should be used more aggressively with respect to expert testimony, because such testimony can have an undue impact on the jury."[17] The *Kumho Tire* decision may ameliorate the strong gatekeeping role that some courts appear to have utilized, but it is not entirely clear. For example, Associate Justice Breyer, who wrote the opinion, clearly envisions that some cases involving experts will require little review, while other will require a more extensive assessment.

> The trial court must have the same kind of latitude in deciding *how* to test an expert's reliability, and to decide whether or when special briefing or other proceedings are needed to investigate reliability, as it enjoys when it decides *whether or not* that expert's relevant testimony is reliable. . . . Otherwise, the trial judge would lack the discretionary authority needed both to avoid unnecessary "reliability" proceedings in ordinary cases where the reliability of an expert's methods is properly taken for granted, and to require appropriate proceedings in the less usual or more complex cases where cause for questioning the expert's reliability arises. Indeed, the Rules seek to avoid "unjustifiable expense and delay" as part of their search for "truth" and the "jus[t] determin[ation]" of proceedings.[18]

---

14 Faigman *et al., Modern Scientific Evidence,* 38.
15 Advisory Committee on Evidence Rules: Proposed Amendment: Rule 702.
16 Daniel J. Capra, "The Daubert Puzzle," *Georgia Law Review* 32 (1998): 699, 704, referring to *Daubert* at 588–589 (emphasis added).
17 Capra, "The Daubert Puzzle," 704.
18 *Kumho Tire v. Carmichael,* 526 U.S. at 152–153.

As already noted, the Court states that experts' testimony may be excluded when it falls "outside the range where experts might reasonably differ, and where the jury must decide among the conflicting views of different experts, even though the evidence is 'shaky.'"[19]

The language from *Kumho Tire* is to be commended, but it is not clear that it has penetrated the federal court system, because it appears that tensions between the "substantive gatekeeping" and the liberal admissibility remain. The presence of tensions between different court goals invite lower courts to make admissibility decisions in different directions: toward more or less permissive admissibility decisions, and it has resulted in some contrary decisions between courts and between circuits. For example, recall the Parlodel cases from Chapter 1 as well as other disagreements.[20]

There is a more pessimistic view as well. By formulating their standard of appellate review as they did in *Joiner* and *Kumho Tire,* the Court has sent the message that trial courts will be upheld on admissibility decisions unless their decisions are "manifestly erroneous." An implicit message might be that they do not want appellate courts to be bothered to review admissibility decisions, unless there is some quite mistaken decision. Thus, there will be less oversight of district courts by appellate courts than there would have been had *Joiner* been decided differently.

The other side of this issue is that trial courts have greater responsibilities *on their own* to ensure that their decisions are reasonable and fair, as appellate courts have limited authority to correct any lower court mistakes. Ultimately, if trial courts have too much difficulty in addressing the admissibility of scientific testimony, appellate courts may have to intervene to a greater extent simply to ensure basic fairness between litigants.

Social science evidence about federal law is beginning to suggest that trial courts are excluding more experts and the decisions are strongly asymmetrically against plaintiffs. For example, as already noted, since the *Daubert* decision, of the cases ending in summary judgments before trial, the rate has more than doubled with 90 percent of the terminated cases going against plaintiffs.[21]

---

[19] *Kumho Tire v. Carmichael,* 526 U.S. at 153, referring to *Daubert,* 509 U.S. at 596, 113 S.Ct. 2786.

[20] Compare recent cases from the Third Circuit Court of Appeals (e.g., *Paoli R.R. Yard PCB Litigation,* 35 F.3d 717 (1994), *Holbrook v. Lykes,* 80 F.3d 777 (1996), *Kannankiril v. Terminix,* 128 F.3d 802 (1997), and *Heller v. Shaw Industries,* 167 F.3d 146 (1999)) with those from the Fifth Circuit Court of Appeals (e.g., *Allen v. Pennsylvania Engineering Corp.,* 102 F.3d 194 (1996), *Moore v. Ashland Chem.,* Case No. 95–20492 (1998), *Black v. Food Lion,* Case No. 97–11404 (1999), *Tanner v. Westbrook,* 174 F.3d 542 (5th Cir. 1999)). See also Jerome P. Kassirer and Joe S. Cecil, "Inconsistency in Evidentiary Standards for Medical Testimony: Disorder in the Courts," *Journal of the American Medical Association,* 288, 11 (13 Sept. 2002): 1382–1387.

[21] Dixon and Gill, *Changes in the Standards for Admitting Expert Evidence in Federal Civil Cases.*

Moreover, some scholars have found evidence that *appellate* courts more often rule against plaintiffs than the district courts where cases originate and the judges are closer to the evidence.[22] As I argue later, some courts appear to be making substantial scientific errors in excluding experts, their evidence or their reasoning. These are troubling cases, given that the aim of *Daubert* was to ensure that legal decisions comport much better with the science on which they are based. Of course, when there are court errors that mistakenly exlude evidence, this also affects justice between parties.

Other issues posed by the *Daubert* trilogy are left open or appear to be more troubling than those just reviewed. These include the epistemic issues, judge versus jury responsibilities for deciding cases, the Court's suggestion of an "intellectual rigor test" from *Kumho Tire* for expert testimony, its rejection of Joiner's "weight-of-the-evidence argument, and the "methodology/conclusion distinction, which was originally quite sharp in *Daubert*, but subsequently modified in *Joiner*. Finally, there are two deeper issues about access and procedural bias in toxic tort suits, and truth and justice in torts.

MORE TROUBLING ISSUES

Epistemic Presuppositions

The *Daubert* decision presupposes some epistemic and philosophy of science views that at a minimum are confusing. Moreover, they suggest a search for a method that has ceased to be a concern of most philosophers of science and appears not to exist as a precise universal procedure.[23]

In an apparent effort to ground admissibility decisions in the methodologies of reputable philosophy of science the Court endorsed both Karl Popper's "falsifiability" views and Carl Hempel's confirmation theory, two inconsistent philosophies of science.[24] Popper is concerned largely with the view that scientific claims should be "falsifiable" – "no scientific claim or theory can ever be shown to be true or even probable."[25] Hempel's work emphasizes the *confirmation* of scientific views, a view according to which scientific theories that are

[22] Clermont and Eisenberg, "Anti-Plaintiff Bias in the Federal Appellate Courts," 128 (new research "reveals an unlevel appellate playing field: defendants succeed significantly more often than plaintiffs on appeal from civil trials – especially from jury trials (128)).

[23] Thomas S. Kuhn, "The History of Science," in *The Essential Tensions: Selected Studies in Scientific Tradition and Change* (Chicago: University of Chicago Press, 1977), 105–126. Susan Haack (personal communication, June 2003) additionally suggests that philosophers of science have ceased to be concerned with a "scientific method." There may be a vague inferential process – indeed I consider the nondeductive inference structure typical of empirical inferences, not just scientific inferences – but it hardly offers a precise method to assist admissibility decisions (although it does suggest useful reminders).

[24] Haack, "An Epistemologist in the Bramble-Bush," 231–232.

[25] Haack, "An Epistemologist in the Bramble-Bush," 232.

better supported by the evidence or *confirmed* should be adopted (but he also allows for them to be disconfirmed).[26] Thus, by referring to one philosopher who denies that scientific theories can be true or probable and another who believes they can be confirmed, it is difficult to know what the court intended. Inconsistencies do not provide good guides to decisions.

Beyond this scholarly problem, however, at least three distinct issues are conflated in *Daubert*. The Court fails to distinguish the science–nonscience *demarcation problem* – the issue of distinguishing scientific claims from nonscientific claims – from the extent to which specific scientific claims are *warranted* – the issue of how well warranted or supported scientific claims are – from the issue of "the reliability of specific scientific techniques or tests."[27] Thus, the court tends to conflate issues of demarcating science from nonscience, the degree of epistemic support for particular scientific claims, and how reliable "specific scientific techniques or tests" can be.[28] These are simply different issues with different answers as Susan Haack has pointed out. I do not address these issues except indirectly, but merely note that they create confusion in the original decision and suggest difficulties in knowing more precisely what the Court's concerns are.[29] Finally, there is a fourth issue the court did not note, but is of concern, namely, a scientist's inferences from studies to conclusions about adverse health effects.

In addition, on the reliability issue, as Haack, a philosopher of science puts it, the Court sought to find a *method* "that distinguishes the scientific and reliable from the nonscientific and unreliable."[30] But she argues, "There is no such method. There is only making informed conjectures and checking how well they stand up to evidence, which is common to every kind of empirical inquiry..."[31] She notes that there are difficulties with judges determining

---

26 Haack, "An Epistemologist in the Bramble-Bush," 232.
27 Haack, "An Epistemologist in the Bramble-Bush," 232.
28 Haack, "An Epistemologist in the Bramble-Bush," 232.
29 Some, such as Joe Hollingsworth and Erick Lasker have argued that every expert's testimony must be based on specific "objectively based" scientific studies directly on the point at legal issue, and they suggest it is strongly preferred (or judges should require) that such studies be on humans. Such suggestions are much too narrow, given how scientists themselves consider problems, as I will argue in later chapters, especially Chapter 7. (Joe G. Hollingsworth and Eric G. Lasker, "The Case Against Differential Diagnosis: *Daubert*, Medical Causation Testimony, and the Scientific Method," *Journal of Health Law* 37, 1 (Winter 2004): 85–112.)
30 Haack, "An Epistemologist in the Bramble-Bush," 232.
31 Haack, "An Epistemologist in the Bramble-Bush," 232. See also Susan Haack, "Trial and Error: The Supreme Court's Philosophy of Science," *American Journal of Public Health, Supplement 1* 95 (2005): S66–S74; Sheila Jasonoff, "Law's Knowledge: Science for Justice in Legal Settings, *American Journal of Public Health, Supplement 1* 95 (2005): S49–S58, esp. S53–S54 ("The Myth of the Scientific Method"); and Kenneth J. Rothman and Sander Greenland, "Causation and Causal Inference in Epidemiology," *American Journal of Public Health, Supplement 1* 95 (2005): S144–S150, esp. S150. ("Just as causal criteria cannot be used to establish the validity of an inference, there are no criteria that can be used to establish the validity of data or evidence.").

whether a claim is well warranted or not because this "requires substantive scientific knowledge."[32] I concur and develop reasons for this in Chapters 5, 6, and 7. Nonexperts risk being at sea in attempting to evaluate the *substantive quality of scientific research and inferences from* it when they lack the appropriate scientific background to do so. For example, in order to determine whether particular pieces of evidence such as studies of baby mice injected with PCBs (as in *Joiner*) are scientifically relevant evidence that PCBs promote cancer in human, judges need to have "substantive scientific knowledge" about the pertinent studies and what they reasonably show.[33] For courts fairly to review (as they needed to in *Allen v. Pennsylvania Engineering*) whether ETO induced brain cancer in rats, plus suggestive human studies, and knowledge that ETO is a potent multispecies mutagen are scientifically relevant evidence for the case in question, they must have an understanding of the science on these issues. Traditionally, judges have not been well prepared to do this, as Chief Justice Rehnquist worried in his *Daubert* dissent, but the Court assigned them the responsibility anyway. In later chapters, we will return to the reasons judges give in carrying out such tasks, in order to provide a window into how well some of them are carrying them their duties.

Judge-Jury Responsibilities and the Right to a Jury Trial

Beyond epistemic and philosophy of science concerns, the Court in its trilogy edged into problematic constitutional territory. In the background of these issues about the admissibility of evidence are generic concerns about whether judges' evidentiary rulings would unconstitutionally interfere with plaintiffs' or defendants' rights to have their claims heard by a "jury of peers" as required by the Seventh Amendment right to a jury trial.[34] This issue has two points to it: a constitutional issue, the right to a jury trial, and an issue about the distribution of legal power to decide the outcome of legal cases – judges or juries – and how much each should have and how that authority should be distributed.

If judges are too intrusive in reviewing expert testimony, they could easily infringe on the authority to decide on the weight and persuasiveness of evidence, which constitutionally should be left to juries. Some courts and commentators express the view that the Constitution gives juries the task to "weigh the evidence," to determine the credibility of the expert whose testimony to believe, and to assess the correctness of the evidence.[35]

---

[32] Haack, "An Epistemologist in the Bramble-Bush," 233, 235.
[33] Haack, "An Epistemologist in the Bramble-Bush," 235.
[34] Breyer, "Introduction," 4, and Metzger, "The Demise of *Daubert* in State Courts."
[35] For example, it is for the jury to weigh evidence and assess its credibility. A court may not substitute for a jury and conduct the fact-finding (unless the court is also the fact finder). It

Michael Gottesman additionally argues that, given how the Court reviewed evidence in the *Joiner* case,

> what is really going on beneath the surface is a transfer of the jury's 'truth-determining' functions to the trial judge under the guise of an evidentiary ruling. What is more, the transfer is stacked against plaintiffs; if they persuade the trial judge, they earn the right to a jury's consideration. To win, they must win twice. If the trial judge is not persuaded, however, the case is over. The defendant need only win once.[36]

His concern about plaintiffs having to win twice was also voiced by the Court of Appeals for the Third Circuit.[37] An obvious concern about scientific issues in court is whether juries can adequately address such issues compared with judges. However, social science research suggests that this is not a substantial problem.[38] And it remains an open question at what point a judge's evidentiary ruling might unconstitutionally intrude on the right to a jury trial. Nonetheless, judges, taking an enhanced and too intrusive role in deciding evidentiary issues with many of them resulting in dismissals may have additional adverse effects. They may deprive the public of important discussions of what happened between the parties and behavior of institutions within the community, decrease incentives for defendants to appropriately test their products, and increase the burdens on plaintiffs (Chapter 8).

---

may not predetermine facts for a jury. (Metzger, "The Demise of *Daubert* in State Courts.") Some courts have begun expressing concern about these issues: *Howerton v. Arai Helmet, Ltd.* (2004) 348 N.C. 440, 697 S.E.2d 674, 692 (Under the authority of *Daubert* courts "may unnecessarily encroach upon the constitutionally-mandated function of the jury to decide issues of fact and to assess the weight of the evidence."); *Brasher v. Sandoz Pharmaceuticals Corp.* (N.D. Ala. 2001) 160 F. Supp. 2d 1291, 1295 (applying *Daubert*, but noting that "[f]or the trial court to overreach in the gatekeeping function and determine whether the opinion evidence is correct or worthy of credence is to usurp the jury's right to decide the facts of the case"); *Logerquist v. McVey*, 196 Ariz. 470, 488, 1 P.3d 113, 131 (2000) ("The *Daubert/Joiner/Kumho* trilogy of cases . . . puts the judge in the position of passing on the weight or credibility of the expert's testimony, something we believe crosses the line between the legal task of ruling on the foundation and relevance of evidence and the jury's function of whom to believe and why, whose testimony to accept, and on what basis."); *Bunting v. Jamieson*, 984 P.2d 467, 472 (Wyo. 1999) (adopting *Daubert*, but nonetheless expressing concern that "application of the Daubert approach to exclude evidence has been criticized as a misappropriation of the jury's responsibilities. . . . '[I]t is imperative that the jury retain its fact-finding function.'").

36 Gottesman, "From *Barefoot* to *Daubert* to *Joiner*," 40 *Ariz. L. Rev.* 753 at 776.
37 *In re: TMI Litigation*, 193 F.3d 613, 665.
38 Neil Vidmar, "Expert Evidence, the Adversary System, and the Jury," *American Journal of Public Health*, Supplement 1 95 (2005): S137–143, esp. 142. ("Claims about jury incompetence, irresponsibility, and bias in responding to expert evidence is not consistent with a review of the many studies that have examined these issues from various methodological perspectives.")

The Intellectual Rigor Test

Another issue that could become more immediately troubling, depending on how the courts interpret and utilize it, is the "intellectual rigor" test used by the *Kumho* Court to which a few courts and commentators have drawn attention. The Justices note that

> The objective of [the *Daubert* gatekeeping] requirement is to ensure the reliability and relevancy of expert testimony. It is to make certain that an expert, whether basing testimony upon professional studies or personal experience, employs in the courtroom the same level of *intellectual rigor* that characterizes the practice of an expert in the relevant field.[39]

The term comes from a decision by the Seventh Circuit Court of Appeals. The relevant legal cases that led to this language were *Rosen v. Ciba-Geigy Corp.* and *Braun v. Lorillard Inc.* In *Rosen v. Ciba-Geigy Corp.* the issue was whether a heavy smoker with a history of serious heart disease could have an expert admitted who would testify that plaintiff's wearing a nicotine patch while continuing to smoke precipitated plaintiff's heart attack.[40] The District Court excluded the expert, a distinguished cardiologist, for his opinion that plaintiff's wearing the nicotine patch could and did precipitate the heart attack. The Seventh Circuit Court of Appeals affirmed the lower court's exclusion, stating that the object of *Daubert* was "to make sure that *when scientists testify in court they adhere to the same standards of intellectual rigor that are demanded in their professional work.*"[41] Chief Judge Posner explained that the cardiologist's opinion deserved

> careful attention, even though he has not himself done research on the effects of nicotine. But the courtroom is not the place for scientific guesswork, even of the inspired sort. Law lags science; it does not lead it. There may be evidence to back up [the cardiologist's] claim, but none was presented to the district court.[42]

This passage suggests that at a minimum the expert would need to offer some reason or evidence for holding the view that wearing the nicotine patch precipitated or contributed to the heart attack. Apparently, none was forthcoming.

In *Braun v. Lorillard Inc.*[43] plaintiff Braun, who suffered from mesothelioma, a signature asbestos-caused injury, sued the manufacturer of his brand of cigarettes, claiming that crocodolite asbestos fibers in the cigarettes' filters had caused his illness. Plaintiff's attorney tried to introduce expert testimony that crocodolite asbestos fibers, the kind most likely to cause mesothelioma, were found in the deceased plaintiff's lung tissues. The expert in question was

[39] *Kumho Tire v. Carmichael*, 119 S.Ct. at 1176 (emphasis added).
[40] *Rosen v. Ciba-Geigy Corp.*, 78 F.3d 316 (7th Cir.), *cert. denied*, 519 U.S. 819 (1996).
[41] 78 F.3d 316, at 318 (7th Cir.), *cert. denied*, 117 S.Ct. 73 (1996).
[42] 78 F.3d 316, at 319.
[43] 84 F.3d 230 (7th Cir.), *cert. denied*, 117 S.Ct. 480 (1996).

an engineer who normally tested for asbestos in building materials but had never applied his methodology before this case to test for asbestos in human or animal tissues. Other plaintiff's experts who utilized a methodology to test for asbestos in human or animal tissue had failed to find the presence of crocodolite fibers in plaintiff's lung tissues. The Seventh Circuit noted the following difficulties with this expert.

> The scientific witness who decides to depart from the canonical methods [of his or her field] must have grounds for doing so that are consistent with the methods and usages of his scientific community. The district judge did remark at one point that *Daubert* requires that the expert's method be one "customarily relied upon by the relevant scientific community" which is incorrect [because it echoes the "general acceptance" test]. But she did not rest her decision to exclude his testimony on that ground. Her ground was that [plaintiff's expert] had testified' that he really didn't have any knowledge of the methodology that should be employed, and he still doesn't have any information regarding the methodology that should be employed with respect to lung tissue. It seems to me that this witness knows absolutely nothing about analyzing lung tissue and asbestos fibers.[44]

This passage suggests that the expert must have some evidence or scientifically good reason to believe that a method for detecting asbestos fibers in building materials is also reliable for detecting asbestos fibers in human tissue.

Margaret Berger glosses the intellectual rigor test as follows.

> Experts must show that the conclusions were reached by methods that are consistent with how their colleagues in the relevant field or discipline would proceed to establish a proposition were they presented with the same facts and issues.[45]

Professor Berger's understanding of this test is plausible, but only a beginning, because the "intellectual rigor" test admits of a more benign or more troubling interpretation.

---

[44]   84 F.3d 230, at 234. The court went on.
>   If, therefore an expert proposes to depart from the generally accepted methodology of his field and embark upon a sea of scientific uncertainty, the court may appropriately insist that he ground his departure in demonstrable and scrupulous adherence to the scientist's creed of meticulous and objective inquiry. To forsake the accepted methods without even inquiring why they are the accepted methods in the case, why specialists in testing human tissues for asbestos fibers have never used the familiar high temperature baking method and without even knowing what the accepted methods are, strikes us, as it struck Judge Manning, as irresponsible. (84 F.3d 230, at 235)

[45]   Margaret A. Berger, "The Supreme Court's Trilogy on the Admissibility of Expert Testimony," *Reference Manual on Scientific Evidence*, 2d ed. (Washington, DC: Federal Judicial Center, 2000), 25–26.

The courts' discussions to this point do not appear to set a stringent requirement on "intellectual rigor," because the Braun's expert appeared not to have *any* appropriate idea of the needed methodology and Judge Posner argued that he needed proper grounding in how to test for crocodolite in biological materials. In *Rosen v. Ciga-Geigy* Posner also does not appear to impose a stringent standard because he appears to require that the expert have good reasons for his opinion, but the expert has neither conducted the appropriate research nor does he appear to cite studies by others.

Whether the "intellectual rigor" idea is a desirable one or not will depend on how it is understood and utilized by the courts. It is open to abuse or sensitive use. There is the possibility of a troubling interpretation, if too much emphasis is placed on "rigor." That is, if courts insist that scientific reasoning must comport with the most *rigorous* reasoning in the fields of the typical toxicological sciences, this would be a mistake in the tort law. For example, if courts insist that an expert before testifying on causation in toxic tort cases must have confirmation by multiple kinds of tests and multiple kinds of evidence of the sort illustrated in scientific textbooks, this would be a mistake because scientists tend to be more flexible in reasoning about the toxic effects of substances than some idealized textbook views would suggest. Or if courts insist that experts' conclusions must rest on consensus scientific judgments or judgments that will become part of the permanent fabric of science, this would be much too demanding. If courts emphasize too strongly the "rigor" in the test, they will impose a much more stringent demand on scientific testimony than experts themselves use in their own research.

By contrast, courts could adopt a variety of heuristics compatible with the "intellectual rigor" that scientists utilize in their own diagnoses of disease, judgments of disease causation and the like. If courts permit experts to testify on the basis of the weight of the evidence available to them as, for example, toxicologists or consensus scientific committees do when asked to make judgments about the likely toxicity of substances or likely causes of disease, or as physicians do in diagnosing diseases before recommending treatment, this would not be such an undesirable understanding of the intellectual rigor of the field.[46]

There is another way of making this point. If *Daubert* and other courts are concerned to prevent *charlatans* from testifying, this is one thing. This is a problem some have suggested that might be better addressed by juries who have ordinary expertise in judging honesty and credibility.[47] But if their aim is to ensure that experts are so reliable that they make almost no scientific *mistakes*, this could result in a much different and vastly more stringent screen for experts. Such reviews, however, would conflate the issue of *reliability* – whether

---

[46] Kassirer and Cecil, "Inconsistency in Evidentiary Standards for Medical Testimony," 1382–1387.
[47] Gottesman, "From *Barefoot* to *Daubert* to *Joiner*," 759–760.

an expert's testimony is more likely than not reliable – with the issue of its *correctness* – is the expert's testimony more likely than not correct – in a contested area. Courts' insistence on a high standard of correctness will distort the law, especially when issues are highly contested and not fully settled. This would greatly increase the effective burdens of proof plaintiffs must satisfy in order to bring their case to trial. Moreover, it also would intrude on the jury's right to decide factual issues. Some courts have recognized this potential problem and have cautioned against it.[48]

If courts in reviewing expert testimony emphasize the similarities between inferences experts draw in the courtroom and in their out-of-court scientific profession in making practical decisions of importance about whether substances cause or contribute to disease with all the *variety* and *sensitivity* this involves, this would be a much more defensible interpretation.[49] Language in *Kumho Tire* suggests just such a view,[50] and provides the seeds of a plausible approach to admissibility (Chapter 7).

Review of Weight-of-the-Evidence Methodology

After the *Joiner* Court articulated its "abuse of discretion" standard, it then applied that standard of review to the evidence on which Joiner's expert relied and argued that "a proper application of the correct standard of review indicated that the District Court did not abuse its discretion."[51] The trial court had critiqued each individual piece of evidence, finding it "unreliable" to support the ultimate causation claim. It then held that plaintiff's expert could not satisfy the recently articulated admissibility standards of *Daubert*.[52] After ruling on procedural issues the Supreme Court decided to do something it need not have done. It could have remanded to the Eleventh Circuit Court of Appeals the decision about whether the district court had "abused its discretion" on the admissibility of evidence. Instead, it chose to adjudicate whether the district court had "abused its discretion" in making the admissibility decision. However, to do this the Court had to review plaintiffs' substantive scientific arguments and rule on whether the district court had abused its discretion. In doing so, it largely echoed district court's argument in critiquing the studies and ruled that the lower court had not abused its discretion.

---

[48]   *Paoli R.R. Yard PCB Litigation*, 35 F.3d 717, at 750 (1994).
[49]   In re Ephedra Products Liability Litigation, 393 F. Supp. 2d 181, at 197 (2005).
[50]   *Kumho Tire v. Carmichael*, 526 U.S. 153 (citing *Daubert*, 509 U.S. at 596, 113 S.Ct. 2786). (The Court noted that if testimony "fell outside the range where experts might reasonably differ, and where the jury must decide among the conflicting views of different experts, even though the evidence is 'shaky'," it could be judged "unreliable" and thus inadmissible.)
[51]   *General Elec. Co. v. Joiner*, 522 U.S. at 141–143.
[52]   *Joiner v. General Electric Company*, 864 F.Supp. 1310, 1322–1326 (1994).

The Court argued that the baby mice studies were "so dissimilar to the facts presented in this litigation that it was not an abuse of discretion for the District Court to have rejected experts' reliance on them."[53] The court argued that the baby mice received "massive" doses of PCBs (whereas Mr. Joiner, an *adult*, did not),[54] that they received a more pure form of PCBs and the kinds of cancers were different between the mice and Mr. Joiner.

To a layperson reading the full account of the Court's review of the evidence, these reasons probably sound persuasive, but in fact are potentially quite misleading on scientific grounds. Plaintiffs' arguments considered out of the context of scientific expertise and by themselves are so far from a normal person's experience that they appear implausible on their face. Does this implausibility result from a gap between an expert's understanding and a layperson's understanding of the issue or are the arguments not persuasive? I will return to them in Chapter 7 after providing some scientific background. It appears that neither the district court nor the Supreme Court understood the significance of these studies. Perhaps plaintiffs' attorneys did not explain them well; perhaps the issues were not briefed well on appeal (although that was not the appellate issue). However, because judges are now reviewing the scientific substance of expert testimony, they run the risk of failing to understand the scientific relevance and probative value of scientific evidence and reasoning, particularly when unusual patterns of evidence are assembled to draw conclusions.

The Supreme Court, after believing it had disposed of the animal studies on which plaintiffs' experts had relied, then addressed individually four epidemiological studies on which plaintiffs had relied.[55] Without discussing the Court's characterization of these studies, the particularly troubling aspect of the opinion is that it held that "the studies upon which the experts relied were not sufficient, whether individually or in combination to support their conclusions that Joiner's exposure to PCBs contributed to his cancer, the District Court did not abuse its discretion in excluding their testimony."[56]

By conducting this review and reaching the conclusions it did the Court endorsed a critical review of *each study* taken by itself, finding reasons for each study not supporting plaintiff's ultimate conclusion. In addition, although the Supreme Court used the language of considering the studies "in combination," it did not assess them as an integrated whole and in combination. (It also did not address them in combination with the infant mice studies.) It recited the trial court's reasons for thinking that each study considered *by itself* was inadequate to support plaintiffs' ultimate conclusion or so "dissimilar" to plaintiffs' exposure circumstances as to render the study irrelevant.

53   *General Elec. Co. v. Joiner*, 522 U.S. at 144–145.
54   *General Elec. Co. v. Joiner*, 522 U.S. at 144.
55   *General Elec. Co. v. Joiner*, 522 U.S. at 145.
56   *General Elec. Co. v. Joiner*, 522 U.S. at 146.

Thus, the Supreme Court's *Joiner* opinion appears to invite and to give its imprimatur to a lower court to reject a litigant's experts' testimony as "unreliable" if *each piece* of evidence fails to support his ultimate conclusion as to causation, instead of evaluating the reliability of the evidence *as a whole* for the conclusion. There are several drawbacks to this strategy of review, only a few of which I address (but I return to the issue in later chapters). The most serious problem is that the court appeared to reject plaintiff's use of the "weight-of-the-evidence" argument that has such widespread acceptance in the scientific community and scientific literature. The Eleventh Circuit pointed out that

> Opinions of any kind are derived from individual pieces of evidence, each of which by itself might not be conclusive, but when viewed in their entirety are the building blocks of a perfectly reasonable conclusion, are reliable enough to be submitted to a jury along with the tests and criticisms cross-examination and contrary evidence would supply.[57]

Justice Stevens dissented in *Joiner* on this issue, noting that

> [Joiner's experts] did not suggest that any one study provided adequate support for the conclusions, but instead relied on all the studies taken together (along with their interviews of Joiner and their review of his medical records). The district Court, however, examined the studies one by one and concluded that none was sufficient to show a link between PCBs and lung cancer.[58]

Scientists, whether engaged in risk assessment (as Stevens notes) or scientific detective work about causation, utilize this form of argument.[59] Moreover, such a method of evidence evaluation is quite widespread as the discussion in the next few paragraphs suggests and as I elaborate in Chapters 4 and 7.

These points rest on deeper issues about the differences between valid and invalid deductive arguments as well as strong versus weak nondeductive inferences. I develop most of these points in the following chapter, but introduce a distinction in the next few paragraphs to point the way.

Arguments in support of conclusions are of two kinds: deductive and nondeductive, sometimes called "inductive." Deductive arguments are typical of mathematics and formal logic. The defining property of such arguments is that the conclusion is "guaranteed" logically or semantically by the premises: if the premises are true, the conclusion must be true.[60] In other words, in a deductively valid argument if one finds the conclusion to be false, at least one of the premises must be false as well. Or, if one accepts the truth of the premises, but

---

[57] *Joiner v. General Electric Co.*, 78 F.2d 524, at 532.

[58] *General Elec. Co. v. Joiner*, 522 U.S at 152 (Stevens's dissent).

[59] Moreover, it is plausible that courts themselves utilize a weight-of-the-evidence approach in their own proceedings, as it is unlikely in most cases that any single piece of evidence is sufficient to support a factual conclusion leading to a criminal conviction or a civil judgment of responsibility.

[60] Larry Wright, *Practical Reasoning* (New York: Harcourt Brace Jovanovich, 1989), 38–46.

rejects the truth of the conclusion in a *valid* argument, one contradicts oneself. For example, if one accepts that A > B and B > C, but denies that A > C, on the face of the argument one contradicts oneself. Logical tightness is an especially important feature of deductive arguments that gives them great inferential power, as the success of mathematics and formal logic shows. However, it also limits their scope of application. The limitation is that it is difficult to find sufficiently categorical claims for premises that are plausibly true to provide the kind of semantically tight support needed for sound deductive arguments.[61] Although the conclusions would follow logically from the premises in a valid argument, the premises would not be sufficiently categorically true to ensure *true* conclusions.[62]

By contrast, nondeductive arguments are simply those whose conclusions are *not guaranteed* by their premises. Philosophers have called such arguments "inferences to the best explanation," "diagnostic arguments," "diagnostic induction," "inductive arguments," and "differential diagnosis."[63] I largely use the phrase "inference to the best explanation." Even if the premises are true, the nondeductive link between premises and conclusions will have varying degrees of strength, unlike a deductive argument (which is either valid or invalid). Thus, in a nondeductive argument the premises will provide strong, weak, or moderate support for the conclusion or one might say that the argument will be strong or weak or in between, but not valid or invalid.[64]

Such arguments are the core of scientific (as well as most legal) inferences and they have several important features (discussed in Chapter 4). The truth of the conclusion is not guaranteed by the truth of the premises. In addition, scientists making such arguments would consider *all the evidence* that is relevant to the conclusion. That is, they typically would consider all the evidence that tends to

---

[61] The premises of deductive arguments must be sufficiently categorical to "eliminate rival substantive conclusions semantically" (Wright, *Practical Reasoning*, 81). But when premises are put in appropriate categorical form, they begin to look implausible. For example, in arguing deductively that the robbery of a mansion was an "inside" job, one would have to write premises to rule out different kinds of break-in, e.g., no one could rob the mansion unless he fooled the guard or picked the lock, and no one could be both an expert locksmith and a convincing actor (Wright, *Practical Reasoning*, 81).

[62] Consider a simple argument. "Either the butler, the maid, or the wife killed the husband of the house. It was not the butler or the wife. Therefore, it was the maid." While the form of the argument is valid, the dubious premise is the first one; does the person making the argument know enough to ensure that these are the only three people who could have killed the husband? Were there no other possible suspects? What is the basis for ensuring that the critical premise is true?

[63] Wright, *Practical Reasoning*; Gilbert Harman, "The Inference to the Best Explanation," *Philosophical Review*, 74 (1994): 89–90 (noting that the term "corresponds approximately to what others have called 'abduction,' 'the method of hypothesis,' 'hypothetic inference,' 'the method of elimination,' 'eliminative induction,' and 'theoretical inference'"); Brian Skyrms, *Choice and Chance: An Introduction to Inductive Logic* (Belmont, CA: Dickenson Publishing Company, Inc., 1966).

[64] Wright, *Practical Reasoning*, 48–54.

make a conclusion more true or less true. Finally, in assessing such arguments, an expert must consider different plausible explanations of the evidence (or conclusions to the argument) in order to assess which explanation best accounts for the evidence (or alternatively, which conclusion is best supported by the premises of the argument).

The second point is most important for understanding the courts' reviews of plaintiffs' evidence in *Joiner*, as I note in Chapter 4. The district court judge in *Joiner might* have found that the evidence *taken as a whole* was not sufficiently *reliable* to support the conclusion that Joiner's exposure to fluids and smoke containing PCBs caused or contributed to his lung cancer.[65] That is not what she said nor how she appeared to analyze the evidence (and, it appears, not what the Supreme Court endorsed), however. She addressed each piece of evidence individually and then dismissed the case because there was too great an "analytic gap" between each piece of evidence taken individually and the conclusion that PCBs had caused Joiner's lung cancer. Such a "corpuscular" review procedure[66] is clearly at odds with the scientific community and would undermine every scientific inference. Moreover, as we will see in Chapter 7, current scientific evidence suggests that plaintiffs had a much more plausible case resting on the infant mice studies plus suggestive epidemiological studies than the courts gave them credit for.

The Distinction Between Methodology and Conclusions

The *Daubert* Court carefully drew a sharp distinction between the scientific *methodology and reasoning* underlying scientific testimony and the *conclusions* drawn using the data at hand and the relevant methodology.[67] A trial court should only examine the reliability of the underlying methodology used in determining the admissibility of scientific evidence; it should not engage in an evaluation of the correctness of the conclusions reached by an expert, the admission of whose testimony is at issue.[68] The concern was that judges could assess the methodology, but only juries should review the conclusions for correctness. The latter is a task that is part of weighing and evaluating the evidence. But methodologies and the conclusions reached can be difficult to separate. Moreover, some subsequent decisions have noted that if a judge disagrees with an expert's conclusions, she is likely to take issue with the methodology as well.

[65] *General Elec. Co. v. Joiner*, 522 U.S at 152.
[66] This term comes from Thomas O. McGarity, "*Daubert* and the Proper Role for the Courts in Health, Safety, and Environmental Regulation," *American Journal of Public Health*, Supplement 1 95 (2005): S95.
[67] See *Daubert*, 509 U.S at 592–595.
[68] See *Daubert*, 509 U.S. at 592–595.

An early case illustrates an aspect of this issue.[69] In *Wade-Greaux v. Whitehall Laboratories, Inc.*,[70] a district court excluded the plaintiffs' scientific evidence regarding the alleged teratogenic effect of an over-the-counter asthma medication. This court appeared to blur the methodology/conclusion distinction in its opinion by incorrectly *examining the conclusions* offered rather than reviewing the underlying methodology or focusing on a certain subset of studies that might suffice to satisfy admissibility requirements. It disagreed with plaintiffs' experts that cited numerous epidemiological studies in support of the conclusion that the agent does in fact cause birth defects.[71]

A worry is that when courts reject scientific testimony on the grounds that the conclusions generated by the methodologies run counter to the conclusions of most other experts, it is rendering a decision based on the *weight* to accord that expert's testimony and her *credibility* on the science, two issues that constitutionally should be left to the jury. Consideration of the strength of all the proffered evidence offered by one side compared with the evidence and arguments offered by the other side is proper in the context of deciding *motions for judgment as a matter of law* or *judgments notwithstanding the verdict*, where a court explicitly considers the weight of the conclusions and the evidence on each side. However, consideration of the strength of the evidence should be improper in the context of ruling on admissibility.

The discussion in *In re Paoli Railroad Yard PCB Litigation* is instructive. That court noted that the "reliability" requirement on an expert's methodology is "lower than the merits standard of correctness."[72] Going on, the *Paoli* Court emphasized that a flaw in the expert's reasoning process *does not involve a question of admissibility*, unless the flaw is large enough to render the expert's reliance on an underlying study unreasonable.[73] Thus, where the underlying methodology meets the *Daubert* admissibility criteria, the court should not

---

69   The methodology/conclusion distinction is even more problematic, since in places the Court refers to "reasoning or methodology." See *Daubert*, 509 U.S. at 593.

70   *Wade-Greaux v. Whitehall Laboratories, Inc.*, 874 F. Supp. 1441 (D.V.I. 1994).

71   See *Wade-Greaux v. Whitehall Laboratories, Inc.*, 874 F. Supp. 1441, at 1477, 1483.

72   See *In re Paoli R.R. Yard PCB Litigation*, 35 F.3d 717, 744 (3d Cir. 1994), *cert. denied*, 115 S.Ct. 1253 (1995). The court noted

> [Plaintiffs] do not have to demonstrate to the judge by a preponderance of the evidence that the assessments of their experts are correct, they only have to demonstrate by a preponderance of evidence that their opinions are reliable.... A judge will often think that an expert has good grounds to hold the opinion that he or she does even though the judge thinks that the opinion is incorrect.... The grounds for the expert's opinion merely have to be good, they do not have to be perfect. The judge might think that there are good grounds for an expert's conclusion even if the judge thinks that there are better grounds for some alternative conclusions, and even if the judge thinks that a scientist's methodology has some flaws such that if they had been corrected, the scientist would have reached a different result.

73   *In re Paoli R.R. Yard PCB Litigation*, 35 F.3d at 743 n.9 (3d Cir. 1994). Later, the *Paoli* court noted however:

> [A]fter *Daubert*, we no longer think that the distinction between a methodology and its application is viable.... [A]ny misapplication of a methodology that is significant

allow errors or gaps in the expert's reasoning from the underlying methodology or, more generally, conclusions drawn from the underlying methodology (however tenuous those conclusions may be) to render the expert's testimony *inadmissible*. "The judge should only exclude the evidence if the flaw is large enough that the expert lacks 'good grounds' for his or her conclusions."[74]

The Supreme Court spoke to this issue in *Joiner*, contradicting its clear conclusion in *Daubert*, seemingly under the guise of providing a further interpretation of *Daubert*. In *Joiner* it noted, "conclusions and methodology are not entirely distinct from one another."[75] Perhaps the Court was responding to some concerns about the possibility of mutual dependence between a "methodology" used and a "conclusion" reached that had been raised subsequent to the *Daubert* decision.[76] Although there is some good sense to this point, it is not as easy as it seems.

Certainly, it is difficult to separate conclusions from methodology in the *deductive* arguments of mathematics or formal logic because of the logically tight relationship between them. It might or might not also be true of some laboratory procedures as the Third Circuit notes (I do not assess this).[77] However, it is not true to the same extent of nondeductive inferences from scientific evidence to conclusions, simply because of the nature of those inferences. Even though the premises of a nondeductive argument do not guarantee its conclusion, it may still be an inductively strong argument. The particular example discussed in *Joiner* – the weight-of-the-evidence methodology – stands as a shining instance of a procedure for assessing evidence that could easily lead different experts to different conclusions, without violating the procedure or violating the logic of the inference.[78]

We will return to the idea of inference to the best explanation and some of its implications for admissibility reviews, but enough has been discussed at this point to pose the issue and to note there can be difficulties when courts

> enough to render it unreliable is likely to also be significant enough to skew the methodology. (*Id* at 745)

Further on, it adds

> The methodology/conclusion distinction remains of some import, however, to the extent that there will be cases in which a party argues that an expert's testimony is unreliable because the conclusions of an expert's study are different from those of other experts. In such cases, there is *no* basis for holding the expert's testimony inadmissible.

In re Paoli R.R. Yard PCB Litigation, 35 F.3d at 746 n.15 (citation omitted) (emphasis added); see also *Cavallo v. Star Enter.*, 892 F. Supp. 756, 769 (E.D. Va. 1995) (excluding plaintiff's scientific evidence even though the methodology used by the expert was acceptable because the conclusions he reached were not a reasonable application of that methodology).

74   *In re Paoli R.R. Yard PCB Litigation*, 35 F.3d 717, at 746.
75   118 S.Ct. 512, 519 (1997).
76   Faigman *et al.*, *Modern Scientific Evidence*, 31.
77   *In re Paoli R.R. Yard PCB Litigation*, 35 F.3d 717, at 745.
78   I do not address the relationships between methodologies and conclusions in scientific studies.

criticize non-deductive arguments for having a "gap" between premises and conclusions. This is an endemic feature of nondeductive arguments since there is not a logically tight relationship between the premises and the conclusions. Consequently, if an expert witness is utilizing an inference to the best explanation (as all surely are), there is likely to be some "gap" between his premises and his conclusions – all nondeductive arguments have such gaps – but it does not necessarily undermine them. However, if the "gap" is too great, this can become a problem, but the issues are subtle (Chapter 4).

"Fit"

In *Daubert* the Court held that expert testimony must be "reliable" and "fit" the facts of the legal case ("be applied to the facts of the case").[79] However, there appears to have been some difficulties with "fit." The idea of fit has been used in a couple of different ways: (1) to judge whether a scientist's opinions relate to some specific issues in dispute" (a more traditional question of relevance); and (2) to assess "whether the research basis for the expert's opinion generalizes to the legal issues in dispute."[80] As an example of the first point an expert testified that 180-degree coffee caused greater burns than 150-degree coffee, but the appellate court (not challenging the issue) wanted the expert to speak to whether cooler coffee was "even possible" and whether defendant "was unreasonable for failing to make such a modification."[81] The court excluded the testimony as not fitting the case. Apparently the expert did not address the needed point.

On (2), a court addressed whether animal research extrapolated to show human harm in the legal case in question. A divided court ruled that it did.[82] The authors of *Modern Scientific Evidence* correctly note that such extrapolations should be based on "scientific principles of extrapolation," but suggest it is open to judges to make a judgment on such issues as part of their gatekeeping duties.[83]

Point (2) is more worrisome, if courts are too quick to rule against the scientific relevance of animal studies. Although the Supreme Court has given courts the authority to review scientific testimony substantively, this is an extremely difficult task because it requires substantive scientific knowledge. Once non-deductive arguments are understood, and experts are testifying based on all the evidence they regard as *scientifically relevant* to making their inferences (the first issue of fit), courts will need to exercise great care in contravening scientists on such issues. Moreover, it is not clear that they can properly assess

---

[79] *Daubert v. Merrell Dow Pharmaceuticals, Inc.*, 509 U.S. 579, at 592.
[80] Faigman *et al.*, *Modern Scientific Evidence*, Pocket Part, 5–6.
[81] *Garlinger v. Hardee's Food Systems, Inc.*, 16 Fed. App. 232 2001 929767 (4th Cir. 2001), at *4.
[82] *Metabolife International v. Wornick*, 264 F.3d 832, at 859 (9th Cir. 2001).
[83] Faigman *et al.*, *Modern Scientific Evidence*, Pocket Part, 6.

scientific data in this way (Chapter 4). Is it even proper scientific procedure to assess by itself whether a study can assist a scientist in drawing conclusions in absence of other data (apart from quite extreme cases)? I will return to this in later chapters.

Access and Process Bias in Toxic Tort Suits

How courts administer admissibility decisions following the *Daubert* trilogy and the modified by FRE Rule 702 can have a substantial impact on citizens obtaining access to the tort law. In order for citizens to have the possibility of justice for injuries they have suffered as a result of others' conduct, they must have realistic *access* to the law and the *process* must not be too tilted against them. In a trivial sense, of course, anyone can file a suit and have this minimal access. The more important concern is whether a person will know that she has been injured by another (toxic substances make this more difficult to know) and if she has been, whether there is a sufficiently plausible case to motivate an attorney to take it and pursue it. Both *features of toxic substances* and recent rulings on the admissibility of evidence *increase* citizens' difficulties in obtaining access to the law and both increase the tilt in process against them.

In order to understand the effect of recent legal changes on the admissibility of scientific testimony and their consequences for the tort law, we need to place the procedural changes in the broader context of the tort law as an institution. In 1990 Clayton Gillette and James Krier reviewed the regulation of "public risks" by means of the regulatory and tort law.[84] Consider only their view of torts. Public risks, they argued, pose several problems for plaintiffs trying to bring suits for redress of harm. Toxic substances pose risks that are a subclass of public risks. Consider them as examples.[85]

The recent rulings concerning judicial review of expert testimony and scientific evidence are not restricted to cases concerning toxic substances and not even to the tort law. Nonetheless, toxic tort cases pose special problems because of the particular kind of risks toxicants pose, the difficulty of detecting the harms they might cause, and the subtle science needed to substantiate the harms. When these risks result in harm, it is more difficult for plaintiffs to have *access* to the courts, raising a barrier to their even beginning a legal action for injuries they may have suffered.

---

[84] Gillette and Krier, "Risk, Courts and Agencies," 1077–1109.
[85] In some ways, focusing on toxic torts makes the task of addressing the use of scientific evidence in tort litigation more difficult, because toxic substances have properties that stress and strain many of the institutions that must regulate them. The stresses are especially great on the tort law because of the particular properties of many toxic substances and the difficulties of establishing causation. However, two of the three cases modifiying the admissibility of expert testimony – *Daubert* and *Joiner* – adjudicated just such an issue. And the tort law must accommodate litigation concerning toxicants.

First, many toxic substances pose risks that tend to have comparatively long latency periods before they materialize into harm.[86] That is, there is typically a significant time-delay between exposure to a substance and manifestation of disease that can be clinically detected. This may be because the diseases progress via a biological mechanism that produces a disease slowly, such as cancer, or because their effects are multigenerational. If disease effects are subtle and difficult to detect, the end result can be similar.

Second, risks from toxic substances tend to have a low probability of materializing; often they will have catastrophic consequences for individual victims, such as cancer or reproductive effects, or for the larger society (in the case of a nuclear meltdown).[87] In short, harms from toxicants tend to be low probability, high consequence risks (at least for individuals) that materialize.

Third, harms from some toxicants are diffusely "spread over many victims, so the costs to any one victim might be small even though the aggregate cost to the total victim population is very large this gives each individual victim little incentive to initiate action on her own because the personal cost-reward trade-off is not clear."[88] Gillette and Krier's examples include harm from chemical additives, recombinant DNA, mass-produced vaccines, nuclear power plants, leakage and contamination in the disposal of nuclear wastes, the production of synthetic chemicals, which may be toxic, carcinogenic, mutagenic, or teratogenic.[89] If citizens' calculation of the benefits and rewards of winning a suit discounted by the probabilities of success are not clear, they may decide not to pursue legal remedies. Similarly, lawyers considering such cases also have to make a strategic decision about whether the likely payoff of a case is sufficiently high to justify investment in the research and preparation to bring a case compared with the chances of losing the case, the chances of not receiving a settlement prior to trial, or even the chances of an award from a jury decision.

These "structural features"[90] of *public* risks pose *access* barriers to plaintiffs successfully bringing a suit in the first place. To put these into context, consider

---

[86] Cranor, *Regulating*, 3, 30–31; Gillette and Krier, "Risk, Courts and Agencies," 1046–1047.

[87] Gillette and Krier, "Risk, Courts and Agencies," 1039.

[88] Gillette and Krier, "Risk, Courts and Agencies," 1039. As they put it,

> [t]he characteristic diffuseness of public risks . . . can mean small costs per victim notwithstanding large losses in the aggregate. From the individual litigant's perspective, a relatively small injury usually will not warrant the substantial costs associated with proving a case and recovering a judgment. The situation is aggravated by process concerns, legal doctrines that complicate the plaintiff's job . . . for example, the requirement of identifying a particular defendant who more probably than not caused the plaintiff's injury.

> Gillette and Krier may overemphasize free rider problems, but their analysis points to quite serious issues for access to the legal system.

[89] Gillette and Krier, "Risk, Courts and Agencies," 1029; Talbot Page, "A Generic View of Toxic Chemicals and Similar Risks," *Ecology Law Quarterly* 7 (1978): 207.

[90] Gillette and Krier, "Risk, Courts and Agencies," 1047.

first some properties of *private* risks, such as auto and property accidents, that do not pose such problems. These have several features that make them easier to litigate in torts. Private risks tend to result in "injuries [that] are typically discrete, immediate, and readily cognizable, [thus] the obstacles to recovery (identifying the responsible defendants, establishing their liability, showing causation, providing the dimensions of loss) may be relatively low."[91] Moreover, because lawsuits are costly with their prosecution requiring "investment of time and money, and [with] success . . . hardly assured," only those among the injured whose ultimate monetary judgments discounted by the probability of success exceed the costs of litigation "will likely seek access to the adjudication process."[92] However, because of the properties of private risks between parties, the "expected recoveries for victims of private risk are often sufficient to create incentives to sue, though even here collective goods effects can damp the rate of litigation."[93]

Public risks that result in harm pose more difficult issues. Diffusely and widely distributed injuries reduce the chances that injured parties will even identify the source of harm. They also decrease the odds that they will identify a commonalty of interests between themselves and others injured by a particular exposure. Such risks complicate the identification of a defendant, as well. This is surely a problem with widely dispersed risks caused by a common exposure or drug. It can even be a problem for occupationally caused harms where people work at the same facility. For example, employees at a plant manufacturing 1, 2-dibromo-3-chloropropane (DBCP) discovered the adverse reproductive effects (low sperm counts) caused by this substance as a result of casual discussions at company softball games about their inability to have children.[94] For environmental exposures that might affect a diffuse and widely scattered population, these problems only exacerbate the identification problem.[95] There are likely injuries caused by products whose victims have not identified the cause of harm because the causal path is so difficult to trace and a person might not even know she had been exposed. For example, a person might not know she had been exposed to perchlorate, trichloroethylene, endocrine disrupters, and the like through drinking water at least until there was more public knowledge of such exposures.

---

[91]   Gillette and Krier, "Risk, Courts and Agencies," 1046.
[92]   Gillette and Krier, "Risk, Courts and Agencies," 1046.
[93]   Gillette and Krier, "Risk, Courts and Agencies," 1046.
[94]   Personal communication, Robert Spear, School of Public Health, University of California, Berkeley.
[95]   Tomas Alex Tizon, "Cases Against Nuclear Plant Finally Heard: After 15 years of delays, 2300 plaintiffs who say radioactive releases at the Hanford site made them seriously ill wait for a jury's decision," *Los Angeles Times*, 16 May 2005.

Before the *Daubert* decision Gillette and Krier argued that "public risk litigation is structurally biased against victim *access*. Victims who might wish to seek redress in the courts confront significant obstacles that diminish the incentive to sue."[96] Although there are collective strategies that even widely scattered plaintiffs might pursue – utilizing class action suits and entrepreneurial lawyers to pursue them – Gillette and Krier "argue that these do not have much application to the litigation access difficulties [they discuss]."[97] They concluded,

> public risk litigation [which is required to address toxic substances] is probably marked by *too few claims* and *too little vigorous prosecution*, with the likely consequence that too much public risk escapes the deterrent effects of liability. Those who think otherwise must believe that public risk claimants find a easy path into court and effective representation once there. (emphasis added)[98]

Gillette's and Krier's analysis of the balance of access and procedural biases for the tort law is important for admissibility decisions. They note first that "[t]he producers of public risks will be inclined to overindulge [in creating risks],

---

[96] Gillette and Krier, "Risk, Courts and Agencies," 1049 (emphasis added).

[97] Gillette and Krier, "Risk, Courts and Agencies," 1049 note 62, 1051–1053. These possibilities have been decreased in 2005 with recently passed legislation restricting most class action suits to the federal courts.

[98] Gillette and Krier, "Risk, Courts and Agencies," 1054. Their thesis, however, is largely premised on a wider social phenomenon of whether our legal institutions permit the optimum amount of risk in U.S. society, where they define the optimum risk as the sum of the total costs of the risks permitted and the costs of preventing the risks in question. In philosophic terms, their overriding concern is a utilitarian or quasi-utilitarian concern that there be the right amount of social resources devoted to preventing risks and the right amount of total risks allowed. Although this is an important consideration and clearly does bear on the question of whether the tort law permits too many or too few risks, their emphasis tends not to present a fuller picture of the extent to which the tort law as it is constituted provides individuals with reasonable protections from harm, including the combined effect of plaintiffs' accessibility to the tort law and any procedural biases they may face once in a courtroom.

An implicit concern of this book is with the total effect of any access biases and procedural biases on *individuals* who seek redress for injuries from which they may suffer as a result of exposure to toxic substances. The underlying normative view (but not explicitly argued for) is different from theirs. I am concerned with *fair treatment of individuals* throughout the legal process, not so much with whether the law permits the optimal amount of risk in society. Although their arguments support and reinforce the view argued for here, it is conceivable that their premises might not support sufficient access if, for example, they thought that legal rules supported the "right amount" of risk production. I do not ignore deterrence arguments – indeed, they are important in an overall assessment of an institution – I just do not give them pride of place or make them overriding. There is a fairly direct relationship between the extent to which plaintiffs are successful in receiving redress for grievances in the tort law and the efficacy of tort law deterrence effects. The more successful meritorious plaintiffs are in receiving redress, the better the deterrent effect of the tort law; the less successful they are, the worse the deterrent effect of torts.

absent signals that align their self-interest with the larger social interest."[99] One of their conclusions is that biases against citizen access to the tort law

> *viewed in isolation*, may make the expected value of the signal generated by court judgments too low. When claims go unfilled, the social costs they represent are not brought to bear on producer decision-making. Because the signal emanating from the courts is thus weakened, there is likely to be too much public risk.[100]

They were responding to critics who claimed that the tort law process made it too easy for plaintiffs to have cases decided in their favor. These critics claimed that

> Victim claims are treated too tenderly. Too many costs are internalized. Public risk producers are saddled with burdens that other risk producers avoid, and exit the market even though their activities are the less hazardous. There is likely to be too little public risk.[101]

However, Gillette and Krier argued that the process bias in favor of plaintiffs balances the access bias against plaintiffs. Thus, although too few cases make it to court to produce an optimal amount of public risk because of access bias, once a plaintiff has succeeded in court, the liability imposed on risk producers creates some deterrent effect that *all* risk producers must acknowledge and take into account.[102] Since all must take the possibility of liability into account, this results in some deterrence against the overproduction of public risks.

How might the *Daubert* decision have affected these institutional issues to which Gillette and Krier call attention? If the tort law in conjunction with the *Frye* rule, which was largely used in federal courts at the time they wrote, resulted in more expert testimony being admitted, it might have made plaintiffs' access easier and might not have erected high procedural barriers. If the *Daubert* decision had left the access and process biases unchanged, their analysis would

---

[99]   Gillette and Krier, "Risk, Courts and Agencies," 1055. (There are some market mechanisms that may help reduce the overproduction of risk [compared with an optimum amount], for example, prices that reflect some of the costs of producing risks. Of course, the government through its administrative agencies can generate deterrence price signals in the form of "compliance costs of rules and regulations." And, the tort system can generate price signals through the deterrence mechanism of liability judgments, insofar as it is effective.)

[100] Gillette and Krier, "Risk, Courts and Agencies," 1056.

[101] Gillette and Krier, "Risk, Courts and Agencies," 1056.

[102] Gillette and Krier, "Risk, Courts and Agencies," 1057. ("[P]rocess bias increases the expected liability that must be anticipated by *all* public risk producers in the market, so long as public risk claims enter the liability system on an essentially random basis. On this view, the social costs resulting from inflated liability in any particular case are simply the premium paid for the service of augmenting expected values that are probably otherwise too low. The enhanced recoveries amplify a signal that is weak at its origin. The premium exacted in the process may be unavoidable, and in any event worthwhile.")

remain the same. If the *Daubert* trilogy *increased* access and procedural barriers, it would exacerbate the problems plaintiffs' face.

The legal landscape has changed substantially in the aftermath of *Daubert, Joiner,* and *Kumho*. The consequences of these changes will depend upon how judges utilize scientific evidence in toxic tort suits subject to these decisions. If judges follow comparatively liberal rules in admitting scientific evidence within the *Daubert* principles, the changes may be comparatively modest, but arguably still more burdensome than when Gillette and Krier wrote in 1990. However, it remains worrisome simply because of the signals sent by greater scrutiny of experts since they wrote. Even the perception of change in the direction of more stringent review and as well as preparation needed for the possibility, in all likelihood would change the overall balance of access and process biases for plaintiffs in toxic tort suits.

However, if judges follow more restrictive rules in admitting evidence, they will likely bias the legal process much more against plaintiffs than it was in 1990. On Gillette and Krier's analysis this would result in a less than optimum number of cases reaching court because of existing access bias and an even smaller number being decided for plaintiffs once they had been litigated because of legal procedures concerning the admission of scientific evidence (which is so crucial to a plaintiff's case) in pretrial hearings.

There is no necessity to plaintiffs being worse off than Gillette and Krier's analysis suggests; it depends very much upon how judges treat scientific evidence that is available in toxic tort suits. What is important is to see that procedural decisions, as arcane and as seemingly far removed as they appear to be from discussions of justice, can have a profound impact on the lives of individuals and whether they are treated justly or not by the tort law. At a minimum how easy or difficult it is for plaintiffs to have their cases adjudicated at trial can easily affect the possibility of justice between parties and deterrence signals sent by the law.

Pursuit of Truth and Justice in Torts

The Gillette and Krier analysis, together with the increased gatekeeping duties placed on federal judges to review scientific testimony and its foundation, pose an issue to which Justice Breyer called attention in his concurring opinion in *Joiner*. He noted

> [M]odern life, including good health as well as economic well being, depends upon the use of artificial or manufactured substances, such as chemicals. And it may, therefore, prove particularly important to see that judges fulfill their Daubert gatekeeping function, so that they help assure that the powerful engine of tort liability, which can generate strong financial incentives to reduce, or to eliminate, production, *points towards the right substances and does not destroy the wrong ones*. It is . . . essential in this science-related

area that the courts administer the Federal Rules of Evidence in order to achieve the "end[s]" that the Rules themselves set forth, not only so that proceedings may be "justly determined," but also so "that the truth may be ascertained."[103]

It matters how judges screen scientific experts as courts pursue "the truth" about scientific matters. One of Justice Breyer's concerns is to ensure that the powerful engine of the tort law is directed toward the "right substances," the ones that in fact cause harm, but "does not destroy the wrong ones." The emphases of his comments appear to be a brief for the social good that has come and can come from the products of our technological society. He stresses that the tort law not falsely condemn nonharmful substances, calling attention to what might be lost if beneficial products are mistakenly identified as causing adverse health effects when they are (relatively?) harmless. Although he expresses the tort law's concern for justice, his greater emphasis seems to be that judges should avoid decisions that admit evidence that could be scientifically mistaken. This does several things that can be problematic.

His view tends to reinforce the scientific concern with false positives, a topic I consider in the next two chapters. Moreover, does he give sufficient attention to another mistake: legal false negatives – that is, legally failing to identify a harmful substance or failing to admit evidence that would show a substance harmful? Does he undervalue avoidance of mistakes that disadvantage plaintiffs? Does he tend to downplay the importance of the possibility of justice for plaintiffs, despite his language and the importance in torts to provide plaintiffs with just compensation for injuries suffered?

These concerns raise a more difficult and subtle point about truth and procedures for arriving at it. Many of us might be tempted to urge that factual truth about the toxicity of substances should precede or be a prerequisite to determination of just compensation for plaintiffs. Why should we not insist on the scientific truth about toxicity in torts? What degree of certainty should courts demand for the scientific evidence admitted to assist legal decisions?

Although the questions are easily put, indeed they seem almost rhetorical, their presuppositions are not so straightforward. We may be tempted to think that truth about the toxicity of substances is easily knowable and relatively quick to obtain. However, these claims are mistaken, it seems to me, about many toxic substances. Moreover, judges in their admissibility rulings according to the Courts should not be determining the truth of the underlying toxicity claims. This would intrude on the right to a jury trial. A court's task is only to review expert testimony for its reliability and relevance.

To get at the truth about toxicants for legal purposes, one must understand, first, the procedures of the needed fields of science, and, second, legal procedures

---

[103] *General Elec. Co. v. Joiner*, 522 U.S at 149 (emphasis added).

and how these interact. Neither guarantees the truth, *at least in the short run.* And, as we will see, scientific procedures ordinarily do not reveal the truth about toxicants quickly. Before we know the answers to such questions in the long run, while in the middle of scientific and legal debates, we must rely on scientific and legal procedures to guide us. What, one might ask, are the *tendencies* or *biases* of the different procedures during the period when the answers are not clear? Are the tendencies of scientific procedures biased toward one outcome or another? If so, what are they? How will these manifest themselves in different institutional settings? These questions of process bias are of concern both in science and in the science/law interaction in toxic tort cases. How will these manifest themselves when science is used in the law?

We cannot answer these questions at this time. Instead, they will be postponed until Chapters 4, 5, and 6 provide sufficient background to fully appreciate and articulate the issues. However, in order not to be manipulated by litigants, judges must understand the process biases of science and the law and appreciate a much wider range of mistakes against which they must guard. It is easy to argue for pursuing truth through application of the Federal Rules of Evidence and interpretations of *Daubert,* but it matters importantly how this is done and what mistakes judges tolerate or try to prevent by reviewing expert testimony.

Moreover, there are some practical procedural points. As I consider in Chapters 6 and 7, how trial courts administer admissibility rules might either increase or ease the procedural barriers to recovery that plaintiffs face. Appellate Courts might endorse rules for the admissibility of scientific evidence that are too restrictive or support admissibility principles that ease or at least do not increase platintiffs' barriers. Which direction trial and appellate courts might go will substantially affect plaintiffs' access to the legal system, the pursuit of truth in the law, and the possibility of justice between parties.

CONCLUSION

How courts review scientific testimony and its foundation is quite important in day-to-day decisions by trial court judges who are on the front lines of federal and state court litigation. In addition, their individual decisions affect not only parties at the bar, but the larger institution. The principles they use to guide their decisions are crucial, hence the importance of some of the more general concerns addressed above. In the chapters that follow, I introduce major kinds of scientific evidence and inferences from them for judgments about toxicity. Then I consider some lower court and appellate court cases that have used the Supreme Court's guidance on the admissibility of scientific testimony and whether these correspond appropriately to how scientists themselves evaluate scientific evidence. In the remainder of the book the question is "Whither the law in using scientific evidence in pursuit of justice?"

4

Studies of Toxicity and Scientific Reasoning

The law provides the institutional rules within which science will be utilized. Science often provides important content needed to assist in the resolution of legal disputes. However, scientific evidence is arcane, complex, and subtle. In order to better understand the law-science interaction, then, one should understand some of basic toxicity studies that are needed in the law as well as scientific reasoning from them to conclusions about human harm. This chapter reviews these subjects.

Early in this chapter, I provide some basic information about some of the main kinds of studies on which experts rely to make inferences about the potential of toxicants to cause adverse effects in persons. This summary seeks to acquaint readers, who might not be fully familiar with the science, with some of the types of studies and their features. I also review more extensively other kinds of evidence with which courts have had greater difficulties and that are less well understood. However, they are or potentially can be quite important in tort cases.

Later in this chapter I discuss less visible and less well-understood issues: scientific (nondeductive) inferences and some of their implications for scientific testimony. Surprisingly, a number of courts in their written opinions appear not to have understood different scientific studies, some of the reasonable inferences that can be made from them, and some of their limitations.

However, a deeper and broader understanding of the science and its context for the tort law is needed as well. There are implicit, explicit, and subtle barriers to providing the scientific evidence needed in toxic tort suits that may not be understood by courts or the wider public. Consequently, Chapter 5 explores some of these subtler but important pragmatic barriers to providing the needed science.

FEATURES OF BIOCHEMICAL RISKS THAT HINDER
IDENTIFICATION AND ASSESSMENT OF HARMS

Chemical substances have some special features that in general make the identification and assessment of their causal properties difficult. In the tort law, these features pose particular problems, stressing and straining the institution in various ways. Although many substances could serve as examples, consider one: polychlorinated biphenyls (PCBs) and some of the risks they pose. PCBs were the main substances at issue in *Joiner*, but that is not the reason for presenting them here. This is a class of substances that are clearly toxic, but whose properties have not been quickly or easily understood.

PCBs are thermally stable, are resistant to oxidation, acids, bases, and a number of other chemical substances, have excellent dielectric properties and make good commercial products. Until 1972 they were used as transformer cooling liquids, hydraulic fluids, lubricants, plasticizers, surface coatings, sealants, pesticide extenders, and copy paper. However, because of the risks they pose and harms they cause, since 1974 all U.S. uses have been confined to closed systems such as transformers and vacuum pumps.[1]

By now PCBs are well-recognized human, mammalian, and ecosystem toxicants (including reproductive toxicants and probable human carcinogens). It was not always so. It took scientists considerable time to identify and document their toxic properties. Moreover, even though their toxicity is partially understood, the means by which they are transported through the environment has just recently become better appreciated. Because of their stability and lipophilic properties they were known to bioaccumulate and move through the food chain from small organisms to increasingly larger organisms and eventually to mammals such as polar bears and whales, and finally to humans who consume fish and large mammals. Although this remains an important part of the route of transmission, scientific understanding of the processes has deepened and revealed a more worrisome one. In 1991 Travis and Hester reported that PCBs, dioxins, and pesticides, persistent organic pollutants all, tend to

> volatilize to the atmosphere and are transported globally. During transport, organics attach to particles in the atmosphere and are eventually transferred back to the Earth through processes of wet and dry deposition. After deposition from the atmosphere, lipophilic compounds bioaccumulate in vegetation, beef, milk and fish; [and then] the food chain becomes the primary path of human exposure for most global pollutants.[2]

---

[1]   U.S. Department of Health and Human Services, National Toxicology Program, *Ninth Annual Report on Carcinogens*. Rev. 20 Oct. 2000. Available at: http://ehis.niehs.nih.gov/roc/ninth/known.pdf.

[2]   Curtis C. Travis and S. T. Hester, "Global Chemical Pollution," *Environmental Science and Technology* 25 (1991): 814–819.

In particular, such substances are volatilized in warmer climates or at warmer times of the year in moderate or colder climates, transported to the colder areas of the earth (especially the north and south poles) and then deposited when it becomes too cold to support their volatilization. Moreover, ecosystems appear to have little capacity to degrade such substances because of their stability.[3] In addition, several researchers have reported, and the U.S. EPA has endorsed the view, that "bioaccumulated" PCBs are transformed into more persistent and more toxic variants than commercial PCBs as they move through the food chain.[4]

This is a broader picture about their features than is needed for a typical tort suit, but it suggests how little scientists collectively have understood about PCBs and how long it has taken them to comprehend what they now know. Indeed scientists are still learning about them. Recent discoveries revealed a new process of transmission and that bioaccumulation increased their toxicity. As a consequence of these processes researchers have found that humans and other large mammals in the arctic have near toxic body burdens of PCBs even though they are far removed from the original sources of pollution or spills.[5]

PCBs are only one example of molecular substances that can have toxic and other harmful effects. Other examples, such as benzene, arsenic, and so on, would have made many of the same points.

There are several generic features of biochemical risks that pose scientific difficulties and create problems that can be exacerbated by the practices of scientific inquiry. Carcinogens, reproductive toxicants, and neurotoxicants are invisible and undetectable intruders. Some of them can have long latency periods (a long period between the initiation of disease and its clinical identification). When they harm humans they typically leave no signature effects (the adverse effects are identical in most cases to diseases resulting from other causes). Too often they operate by means of unknown, complex, subtle molecular mechanisms that harm humans (and often the environment) in ways that can remain hidden for years. Scientists tend to lack information for the most part about the mechanisms by which substances are transmitted (as in the case of PCBs) and by which they harm us, which makes their causal path difficult to trace. Exposure to toxicants can cause catastrophic consequences for the affected individuals, but this typically occurs with low probability.

3   Joe Thornton, *Pandora's Poison: Chlorine, Health and a New Environmental Strategy* (Cambridge, MA: MIT Press, 2001).
4   U.S. EPA, "PCBs: Cancer Dose-Response Assessment and Application to Environmental Mixtures," APA/600/P-96/001F (September 1996); M. J. Brunner, T. M. Sullivan, A. W. Singer, M. J. Ryan, J. D. Toft II, R. S. Menton, S. W. Graves, A. C. Peters, "An Assessment of the Chronic Toxicity and Oncogenicity of Arochlor-1242, Aroclor-1254 and Aroclor-1260 administered in diet to rats" (Columbus, OH: Batelle Study No. SC920192, Chronic Toxicity and Oncogenicity Report, 1996).
5   Travis and Hester, "Global Chemical Pollution," 814–819.

What are some of the scientific consequences of the subtle biochemical interactions involved? At the most general level they include the following.

For one thing, the harms they cause, the mechanisms by which they harm (if they will ever be understood), and the methods of transmission must be inferred from more visible evidence. Thus, injuries from toxic substances are quite unlike typical harms that the tort law has traditionally addressed, such as automobile accidents, trespasses, property damage, and so on. That is, the causal mechanisms by which harms result are too often not understood. Frequently, scientific understanding may take decades, occasionally centuries,[6] unlike grosser forms of harm typical of more ordinary torts. Understanding the properties of such substances and assessing any risks they pose requires subtle scientific expertise that is usually on the frontiers of existing scientific knowledge.

For another thing, one should understand some differences between biochemical risks and those of more ordinary physical objects such as cars, airplanes, or guns about which we also make causal judgments. When a car traveling at moderate to high speed hits someone, we are rarely in doubt about what caused the person's injuries. Or, if our car stops working in the middle of a busy street, we no doubt quickly search for a causal explanation, one we hope we can diagnose quickly and repair so we do not hold up traffic. Has it run out of gas? Is the battery dead or has the alternator quit? Do we have a clogged fuel line? Without going into a detailed example, we know enough to know that we, or a local mechanic, will be able to find the problem, diagnose it, repair it, and we can go on our way.

Such problems are more or less accessible to us. For the most part, sophisticated scientific tests are not required to diagnose the problems, and they are comparatively tractable to assess and fix (although car troubles can also befuddle us). Things are not so easy concerning molecular disease causation.

STUDIES THAT ASSIST CAUSAL UNDERSTANDING

What kinds of studies do scientists utilize to understand the contributions substances make to human harms? Once studies have been conducted that provide some of the needed data, how do scientists infer that exposures can harm humans? Typical data consist of statistical and other studies in humans, experimental studies in animals, studies about chemical structure and biological activity, and mechanistic and molecular information, when it is available. All can assist causal understanding. And, each kind of evidence can make a greater or lesser contribution to understanding causation, depending on what other evidence might be available about a potential toxicant.

---

[6] Paul Thagard, *How Scientists Explain Disease* (Princeton: Princeton University Press, 1999), 120.

Human Studies

Studies of toxic effects in people are the most direct evidence of human harm simply because humans are the objects of study. Such studies fall into three categories: randomized clinical trials, epidemiological studies, and human case reports. In this section I describe *randomized clinical trials* and *epidemiological studies*, but postpone discussion of case reports until a later section.

An ideal in scientific experiments would be "the creation of duplicates sets of circumstances in which only one factor that is relevant to the outcome varies, making it possible to observe the effect of variation in that fact. Achievement of this object requires an ability to control all the relevant conditions that would affect the outcome under study."[7] For biological experiments, however, the hope of having duplicative circumstances, which vary by only one factor "is unrealistic." There is too much biologic variation.[8] The best that can be hoped for is to keep the "extent of variation of extraneous factors that affect the outcome . . . small in relation to the variation of the factor under study."[9]

Randomized Clinical Trials

For inferring the toxic effects of a molecular substance in humans sufficiently large randomized clinical trials might be considered to be the gold standard. Clinical trials are as close to human experimental studies as researchers might get. In these the investigator assigns "the exposure to the [study] subject . . . [with the intention of achieving] the scientific objective of the study."[10] Typically, researchers would randomly assign the subjects to "exposed" and "control" groups to ensure similarity between them. Exposures would be carefully monitored as well. In addition, the best studies would be "double-blind," that is, those administering the treatment or exposure would be "blinded" from knowing whether they were administering the exposed and control groups a treatment or a placebo. (Testing the effects of prescription drugs would be typical in this regard.) Double-blind studies make it more difficult for scientists to inadvertently influence the outcome.

Researchers would then evaluate any differences in adverse effects between the two groups and subject them to various statistical tests to see if the study showed an increased association for either a beneficial or adverse effect. Moreover, the best studies would be sufficiently large to minimize various statistical mistakes that could result from smaller studies (but ordinarily clinical trials are conducted on comparatively small numbers of persons).

However, clinical trials would not be conducted on potential toxicants for obvious moral reasons: participants would be deliberately exposed to

[7] Kenneth Rothman, *Modern Epidemiology* (Boston: Little, Brown and Company, 1986), 51.
[8] Rothman, *Modern Epidemiology*, 51.
[9] Rothman, *Modern Epidemiology*, 51.
[10] Rothman, *Modern Epidemiology*, 52.

something considered possibly harmful. Clinical trials tend to be utilized for prescription drugs and other potentially beneficial interventions precisely because the products are believed to be beneficial (researchers would compare the drug treatment with a placebo), but testing potential toxicants on humans would typically would be out of ethical bounds. A clinical trial of a potentially beneficial product might reveal adverse effects, but the study would have been aimed primarily at ascertaining any beneficial effects; data about adverse effects would be a by-product of the research.

Epidemiological Studies

Consequently, most human studies utilized to learn about potential toxicants are *non-experimental.* They are typically conducted in circumstances in which people are "willingly or unwillingly expose[d] . . . to . . . potentially harmful factors."[11] Exposures might be those from cigarette smoking, hormone substitution therapy during menopause, the taking of birth control pills, a variety of exposures in the workplace, for example, asbestos, benzene, ethylene oxide, vinyl chloride, and so on. Often exposures are quite adventitious, so exposure data is likely poorly recorded.

In nonexperimental studies investigators must conduct research so as "to simulate the results of an experiment, had one been possible. . . . [Since] the investigator cannot control the circumstances of exposure . . . he or she must rely heavily on the primary source of discretion that remains, the selection of subjects" to mimic as close as possible an experiment.[12]

Nonexperimental epidemiological studies are of three types: follow-up or cohort studies, case-control studies, and ecological (sometimes called "correlational") studies. Cohort and case-control studies focus on observations of the effects of exposures on individual persons, whereas in ecological studies "the unit of observation is a group of people rather than an individual . . ."[13]

Follow-up or *cohort* studies are those "in which two or more groups or people that are *free of disease* and that differ according to extent of exposure to a potential cause of disease are compared with respect to incidence of the disease in each of the groups. . . . The essential element of a follow-up study is that [disease] incidence rates are calculable for each group."[14] That is, researchers compare those *exposed* to a potential disease-causing substance or process with a control group in order to determine whether exposure causes adverse effects, what any disease rates might be, and what range of effects might be associated with exposure.

---

[11] Rothman, *Modern Epidemiology,* 55.
[12] Rothman, *Modern Epidemiology,* 56.
[13] Rothman, *Modern Epidemiology,* 74.
[14] Rothman, *Modern Epidemiology,* 57 (emphasis added).

In *case-control* studies researchers consider a group of individuals "that has *contracted a disease*, [compare] the characteristics of that group and its environment with a properly representative control group [an appropriate "sample" of individuals who are not exposed] and [try] to isolate factors that might have caused the disease."[15] In this case, scientists seek to infer what differences between the two different groups might have caused or contributed to the diseases.

Follow-up studies provide the basis to evaluate a "range of effects related to a single [type of] exposure." For example, what range of diseases does cigarette smoking cause? What diseases do exposures to benzene cause? By contrast, a case-control study can look for different possible causal antecedents of the particular disease being studied. When individuals have lung cancer, what are likely causes of it – smoking, smog, asbestos, radiation, or other things? Thus, a case-control study can investigate a wider range of potential causes or contributors of disease, whereas a cohort study might reveal a variety of effects from one kind of exposure.

For the law, these differences may be important in particular cases. If the legal issue is whether a particular toxic exposure produced a variety of adverse effects, a cohort study may be superior, whereas a case-control study is limited to only the disease from which the diseased persons suffer. If there is an issue about whether a toxic substance or something else caused a disease, a well-done case-control study might be more useful than a cohort study in sorting out different explanations of a particular disease. And it would not be surprising to find litigants on different sides of an issue emphasizing one kind of study or the other depending on their interests.

Cohort studies are limited in their ability to evaluate the effects of rare diseases because large samples are required (making them difficult and expensive to conduct), whereas case-control studies can much better study the causes of rare diseases.[16] The greater size needed for cohort studies tends to make them much more expensive.[17]

Cohort studies can have difficulties of tracking study subjects over the study period. The longer the study the more difficult this is likely to be. In case-control studies researchers must try to ensure that there is comparability between cases (those with disease) and controls (those without).

Case-control studies may suffer from "recall bias in classifying exposure" because those with the disease may misremember any exposure conditions that

---

15 Cranor, *Regulating*, 29 (emphasis added).
16 Rothman, *Modern Epidemiology*, 68.
17 Cranor, *Regulating*, 36 (note 107) (citing J. J. Schlesselman, "Sample Size Requirements in Cohort and Case-Control Studies of Disease," *American Journal of Epidemiology* 99 (1974): 381, 382–383).

might have been present prior to disease, or recall exposures as higher or lower than they really were. However, this is not a problem with cohort studies.[18]

In both kinds of studies researchers must be explicit about exposure assumptions.[19] A study must allow sufficient time for the *induction* period of disease and its *latency* period in order to detect a disease reliably. For a disease to manifest itself, a sufficient period of time must have elapsed for all of the causal antecedents of the disease process to have been completed (the *induction period of the disease*). For some causal antecedents this may be a short time; for others it may be considerably longer. For example, there appears to be a long induction period between exposure to diethylstilbestrol (DES) *in utero* and cancer of the vagina in young women that occurs between the ages of fifteen and thirty.[20] However, if hormones at puberty also contribute to these cancers after the DES exposure, there would be a much shorter induction period between hormonal exposures and the disease. Once all the causal antecedents needed to produce the disease have materialized, there can still be a *latency period* between the completion of these jointly sufficient conditions and the clinical manifestation of the disease.

Exposure to a potential disease-causing substance does not count as sufficient exposure until enough time has elapsed to ensure that the exposure, plus other biological conditions, has triggered the disease process (the *induction period* of the disease).[21] Moreover, in following up the individuals who have been exposed, ample time must be allowed for the latency period to have been completed. Thus, it is especially important for epidemiological studies to make some assumptions about the "timing between exposure and disease" and to allow a sufficient follow-up period to be able reliably to detect a disease when it is present.[22]

Courts will face issues concerning induction and latency periods in reviewing epidemiological studies. They can easily be confronted with studies in which there was an insufficient follow-up period to reliably detect diseases that were the object of the study; a disease effect might easily be missed. For example, two scientists critiqued a study by Otto Wong, who found no adverse effect between exposure to styrene and disease. They argued that Wong's study had too short a follow-up period – seven years – even though the author had a large sample population to study.[23] Thus, they argued, this defect "should caution against a premature negative evaluation of cancer risk in the reinforced plastics industry."

[18] Rothman, *Modern Epidemiology*, 68–80.
[19] Rothman, *Modern Epidemiology*, 72 (arguing that "no epidemiologic study can be conducted or epidemiologic data analyzed to evaluate cause and effect without making some assumptions, explicit or implicit, about the timing between exposure and disease").
[20] Rothman, *Modern Epidemiology*, 14.
[21] Rothman, *Modern Epidemiology*, 58.
[22] Rothman, *Modern Epidemiology*, 58, 72.
[23] Manilas Kogevinas and Paolo Boffetta, *British Journal of Industrial Medicine* 48 (1991): 575–576 (1991) (letter to editor criticizing a study by O. Wong, "A Cohort Mortality Study and

The particular study had substantial chances of mistakenly reporting "no effect" between exposure and disease simply because the follow-up was too short.

A third kind of epidemiological study is an "ecological" or "correlational" study.[24] The unit of study in this case is whole groups of people – in schools, factories, areas of cities, counties, or even whole nations.[25] Researchers would measure the *incidence* of disease or *mortality* that might have been caused by exposure. However, *individual exposure* would not be measured as might be the case with drugs or with some particularly well-done studies in occupational settings with excellent records. Rather, ecological studies would utilize some overall index that *averages* exposure across the entire study group in question. The use of summary measures of exposure and the disease endpoint in question makes it difficult to rule out alternative explanations of the adverse effects. The end result is that researchers regard ecological studies of "questionable validity"[26] and make causal relationships "less easy to infer . . . than from cohort and case-control studies."[27]

In reviewing epidemiological studies researchers assess both the quality of the study and the extent to which the study might support an inference of a causal relationship when an association is found between exposure and disease. For quality control, scientists consider the possible roles of bias, confounding and chance in the interpretation. *Bias* or *systematic error* would result from the "operation of factors in study design or execution that lead erroneously to a stronger or weaker association than in fact exists between disease and an agent, mixture or exposure circumstance."[28] For example, the persons studied might have been chosen in a way that produces a systematic error. Volunteers in a colon cancer study may have a lower disease rate because they are more health conscious and have a diet less likely to produce colon cancer.

Confounding would result from a factor that made the "relationship with disease . . . to appear stronger or to appear weaker than it truly is as a result of an association between the apparent causal factor and another factor that is associated with either an increase or decrease in the incidence of the disease."[29] Consider a silly example. A study that found a greater association between ashtrays in households and lung cancer might mistakenly suggest that the presence of ashtrays caused the cancer, when in fact it was smoking that caused cancer and that led to the presence of ashtrays.

a Case Control Study of Workers Potentially Exposed to Styrene in Reinforced Plastics and Composite Industry," *British Journal of Industrial Medicine* 47 (1990): 753–62).

[24] Rothman, *Modern Epidemiology*, 74; International Agency for Research on Cancer [IARC], *Monographs on the Evaluation of Carcinogenic Risks to Humans*, Preamble. Rev. Aug. 18 2004. Available: http://www-cie.iarc.fr/monoeval/preamble.html.

[25] Rothman, *Modern Epidemiology*, 74; IARC, *Monograph Series*, Preamble.

[26] Rothman, *Modern Epidemiology*, 74.

[27] IARC, *Monograph Series*, Preamble, section 8.

[28] IARC, *Monograph Series*, Preamble, section 8.

[29] IARC, *Monograph Series*, Preamble, section 8.

The role that statistical chance (random errors) can play in effecting the interpretation of statistical studies is in some ways overrated and in other ways underrated. Scientists and (recently) the law have given a good deal of attention to the *statistical significance* of studies. In order to review this I need to present a bit of the theory of hypothesis acceptance and rejection (even though this practice is being deemphasized in recent theoretical literature).

Consider the following account presented elsewhere.

> In trying to determine whether a substance such as benzene is a human carcinogen, a scientist considers two hypotheses. The first (the null hypothesis, H_o) predicates that exposure to benzene is not associated with greater incidence of a certain disease (e.g., leukemia or aplastic anemia) than that found in a nonexposed population. The second (the alternative hypothesis H_1) indicates that exposure to benzene is associated with a greater incidence of such diseases.
>
> Since epidemiology considers *samples* of both exposed and unexposed populations, by chance alone a researcher risks inferential errors from studying a sample instead of the whole population in question. A scientist runs the risk of false positives [the study shows that the null hypothesis should be rejected (and the alternative hypothesis accepted) when in fact the null hypothesis is true] or false negatives [the study shows that the null hypothesis should be accepted when in fact the null hypothesis is false (and the alternative hypothesis is true)]. A false positive is designated a *type I error,* and a false negative is called a *type II error*.... Statistical theory provides estimates of the probability of committing such [sampling] errors by chance alone. The probability of a type I error is normally designated α and the probability of a type II error is designated β. Conventionally, α is set at .05 so that there is only a one in 20 chance of rejecting the null hypothesis when it is true. The practice of setting $\alpha = .05$ I call the "95% rule," for researchers want to be 95% certain that when knowledge is gained [a study shows new results] and the null hypothesis is rejected, it is correctly rejected.
>
> Conventional practice also sets β between .05 and .20 when α is .05, although conventions are less rigid on this than for values of α. When β is .20, one takes 1 chance in 5 of accepting the null hypothesis as true when it is false, for example, the chance of saying benzene is not associated with leukemia when in fact it is. When $\beta = .20$, the *power* $(1 - \beta)$ of one's statistical test is .80, which means scientists have an 80% chance of rejecting the null hypothesis as false when it is false. The low value for α probably reflects a philosophy about scientific progress and may constitute part of its justification. It is an instantiation of a cautious scientific attitude.... When the chances of false positives are kept low, a positive result [departure from the null] can be added to scientific knowledge with considerable confidence that is not the result of random chance. Were one to tolerate higher risks of false positives, take greater chances of [studies showing] new information being false by chance alone, the edifice would be much less secure. A secure edifice of science, however, is not the only important social value at stake.

One can think of α, β (the chances of type I and type II errors, respectively) and $1-\beta$ as measures of the "risk of error" or "standards of proof." What *chance of error* is a researcher willing to take? When employees in an industry or the general public may be contracting cancer (unbeknownst to all) even though a study (with high epistemic probability) shows they are not, is a risk to their good health worth a 20% gamble?

. . .

In order to see some tradeoffs [that must be made in interpreting epidemiological studies] we need two other variables: N, the total number of people studied in the exposed and unexposed samples, and, δ the relative risk one would like to be able to detect. Relative risk is the ratio of the incidence rate of disease for those exposed to a disease-causing substance to incidence rate among those not exposed:

$$\text{Relative risk} = \frac{\text{incidence rate among exposed}}{\text{incidence rate among nonexposed}}$$

For instance, if the incidence rate of lung cancer in the nonexposed population is 7/100,000, and the incidence rate among heavy smokers is 166/100,000, the relative risk is 23.7. The value of concern, depends upon many factors, including the seriousness of the disease, its incidence in the general population, and how great a risk, if any, the exposed group justifiably should be expected to run. (Relative risk can be misleading, if the disease rate in the general population is quite low, for example, 1/10,000,000. Thus, one needs to take into account this and other factors in evaluating the overall seriousness of the risk.) With α and β fixed, the relative risk one can detect is inversely related to sample size: the smaller the risk to be detected, the larger the sample must be.

The variables α, β, δ and N are mathematically interrelated. If any of the three are known, the fourth can be determined. Typically, α is specified at the outset, although it need not be. Because the variables are interdependent, however, crucial tradeoffs may be forced by the logic of the statistical relations . . . [30]

For example, when researchers are forced to utilize small samples, they cannot have studies with small chances of false positives, small chances of false negatives, and reliably detect small relative risks – at least one of them must be sacrificed.[31] This result is simply a function of the mathematics of small sample sizes. (Larger studies can reduce the effects of random statistical errors, but they are more expensive.)

There is a more important policy point however. When an epidemiological (or any statistical) study does not have large enough samples to ensure both

---

[30] Cranor, *Regulating*, 32–34.
[31] Cranor, *Regulating*, 34–39.

low chances of false negatives and low chances of false positives and detect relatively small relative risks, how one interprets a study is important both for science and the law. If researchers insist on having small chances of false positives, then the chances of a "no effect" study being falsely negative increase. Similarly, if one wants to ensure that the chances of false negatives are quite low, the chances that a positive study is falsely positive increase. In short, with smaller samples than might be ideal, the chances of false positives and false negatives are inversely (but not directly) related. This is an important source of tension between science and the law, to which we return in Chapter 6.

From Statistical Association to Causal Conclusion

Even after researchers have found an "association" between an exposure and the presence of disease, they need to evaluate whether the association is causal or not. That is, they must *make an inference* about whether the association is causal or whether it is the result of some accidental feature, a bias in the study, or a confounding factor. How might researchers ferret out misleading associations from those revealing causal associations?

In 1965 Sir Austin Bradford Hill, a distinguished British epidemiologist, called attention to various factors that would assist in making causal inferences. Subsequently, scientists have used his considerations with greater or lesser stringency (sometimes despite his cautions).[32] His factors must be utilized carefully, as Hill himself, as well as Rothman, Greenland and Weed all independently argue. The important underlying aim is to make an *inference* about whether there is a causal relationship or not between the exposure and the disease. Hill's factors can serve as *reminders about* features of studies as well as the literature to review in making such inferences, but are *not automatic indicators* of causation or substitutes for reviewing the studies and drawing inferences from them. Indeed, a careful reading of Hill himself shows that he did not embrace these "considerations" as necessary for judging a causal relationship between exposure and disease.

Hill proposed nine "aspects" – *not "criteria"* – of a statistical association between two variables to consider in assessing whether the most likely interpretation of the relation between them is one of causal connection.[33] They follow below with Hill's own cautionary notes about each consideration.

> (1) Strength. First upon my list I would put the strength of the association [or relative risk between the exposed and unexposed population with the greater the difference between the two groups suggesting that a causal

---

[32] Austin Bradford Hill, "The Environment and Disease: Association or Causation?" *Proceedings of the Royal Society of Medicine* 58 (1965): 295–300, reprinted in *Evolution of Epidemiologic Ideas: Annotated Readings on Concepts and Methods*, ed. Sander Greenland (Newton Lower Falls, MA: Epidemiology Resources, Inc., 1987), 15–20.

[33] Hill, "The Environment and Disease," 15–16.

relationship is more likely]. . . . [However], [i]n thus putting emphasis upon the strength of an association we must, nevertheless, look at the obverse of the coin. We must not be too ready to dismiss a cause-and-effect hypothesis merely on the grounds that the observed association appears to be slight. There are many occasions in medicine when this is in truth so. Relatively few persons harbouring the meningococcus fall sick of meningococcal meningitis. Relatively few persons occupationally exposed to rat's urine contract Weil's disease.[34]

For another example, the relative risk of lung cancer for those exposed to secondhand cigarette is quite low. For example, lung cancer tends to be about 1.2 times higher in those exposed to secondhand smoke than in those who are not so exposed. Even though this is a low relative risk, scientists are convinced that there is a causal relationship between the exposure and disease.

(2) *Consistency:* . . . Has it been repeatedly observed by different persons, in different circumstances and times. [The more often independent researchers have found an association between exposure and disease, the more this increases the chances of a causal relationship.]. . . . Once again looking at the obverse of the coin there will be occasions when repetition is absent or impossible and yet we should not hesitate to draw conclusions.[35]

(3) *Specificity:* If . . . the association is limited to specific workers and to particular sites and types of disease and there is no association between the work and other modes of dying, then clearly that is a strong argument in favour of causation.

We must not, however, over-emphasize the importance of the characteristic. [Exposures can cause multiple adverse effects and diseases may have more than one cause]. . . . One-to-one relationships are not frequent. . . . In short, if specificity exists we may be able to draw conclusions without hesitation; if it is not apparent, we are not thereby necessarily left sitting irresolutely on the fence.[36]

(4) *Temporality:* My fourth characteristic is the temporal relationship of the association – which is the cart and which the horse?[37]

This is the one Hill factor that must exist before a causal relationship can exist between exposure and disease, because a cause must precede its effect.

(5) *Biological gradient:* Fifthly, if the association is one which can reveal a biological gradient, or dose-response curve, then we should look most carefully for such evidence. For instance, the fact that the death rate from cancer of the lung rises linearly with the number of cigarettes smoked daily,

---

[34] Hill, "The Environment and Disease," 15–16.
[35] Hill, "The Environment and Disease," 16–17.
[36] Hill, "The Environment and Disease," 17.
[37] Hill, "The Environment and Disease," 17.

adds a very great deal to the simpler evidence that cigarette smokers have a higher death rate than non-smokers. The comparison would be weakened, though not necessarily destroyed, if it depended upon, say, a much heavier death rate in light smokers and lower rate in heavier smokers. We should then need to envisage some much more complex relationship to satisfy the cause-and-effect hypothesis. . . .[38]

(6) *Plausibility*: It will be helpful if the causation we suspect is biologically plausible. But this is a feature I am convinced we cannot demand. *What is biologically plausible depends upon the biological knowledge of the day. . . . In short, the association we observe may be one new to science or medicine and we must not dismiss it too light-heartedly as just too odd . . .*[39]

(7) *Coherence*: On the other hand the cause-and-effect interpretation of our data should not seriously conflict with the generally known facts of the natural history and biology of the disease – in the expression of the Advisory Committee to the Surgeon-General it should have coherence . . . while such laboratory evidence can enormously strengthen the hypothesis and indeed, may determine the actual causative agent, the lack of such evidence cannot nullify the epidemiological observations in man. Arsenic can undoubtedly cause cancer of the skin in man, but it has never been possible to demonstrate such an effect on any other animal.[40]

(8) *Experiment*: Occasionally it is possible to appeal to experimental, or semi-experimental, evidence.[41]

He seems to have contemplated that removing an exposure from a population would reduce the disease rate. This consideration has also been taken by others to mean that experimental studies of some other kind add support to a causal inference. For example, early evidence that vinyl chloride was a potent human carcinogen was provided by a small number of case reports, but scientists were greatly assisted in their inferences by experimental animal studies conducted in Italy by Cesare Maltoni.[42]

(9) *Analogy*: In some circumstances it would be fair to judge by analogy. With the effects of thalidomide and rubella before us we would surely be ready to accept slighter but similar evidence with another drug or another viral disease in pregnancy . . .[43]

---

[38] Hill, "The Environment and Disease," 18.
[39] Hill, "The Environment and Disease," 18 (emphasis added).
[40] At the time Hill wrote, this was the status of the research. Subsequent studies have provided some evidence for the tumorigenicity of arsenic in animals. IARC, *Monograph Series*, Supplement 7 (1987), 100–106. Rev. 11 Feb. 1998. Available at: http://www-cie.iarc.fr/htdocs/monographs/suppl7/benzidinedyes.html.
[41] Hill, "The Environment and Disease," 18–19.
[42] Markowitz and Rosner, *Deceit and Denial*, 183.
[43] Hill, "The Environment and Disease," 18–19.

This suggestion appears to be that analogies might open up new areas of research or make observed phenomena more plausible than in the absence of the analogy.

Hill's discussion concluding this section of his address is particularly striking:

> Here then are nine different viewpoints from all of which we should study association before we cry causation. *What I do not believe – and this has been suggested – is that we can usefully lay down some hard-and-fast rules of evidence that must be obeyed before we accept cause and effect. None of my nine viewpoints can bring indisputable evidence for or against the cause-and-effect hypothesis and none can be required as a* sine qua non. What they can do, with greater or less strength, is to help us to make up our minds on the fundamental question – is there any other way of explaining the set of facts before us, is there any other answer equally, or more, likely than cause and effect?[44] (emphasis added)

Some courts and some commentators have not followed the science or Hill's own advice on this point (I return to this point in Chapter 6). Thus, Greenland notes

> It is unfortunate that in the ensuing decades, this list or similar ones have been presented in textbooks as "criteria" for inferring causality of associations, often in such a manner as to imply that all the conditions are necessary. A careful reading of Hill shows that he did not intend to offer a list of necessary conditions; on the contrary, . . . he warned against laying down "hard and fast rules of evidence that *must* be obeyed before we accept cause and effect." . . . Hill's only real mistake was to say that *none* of his nine aspects could be considered necessary if the association were indeed causal; in fact, temporality (no. 4) is obviously necessary, as cause must precede effect.[45]

Finally, Hill's factors tend to be asymmetric: if they can be satisfied, they tend to strengthen a causal inference. If they are not satisfied, they do not tend to undermine it (except for temporality). I will return to inferences of causation from statistical associations after introducing scientific reasoning later.

Animal Studies

Whereas studies in humans can provide direct evidence of adverse effects in humans, they have limitations. Often there is not yet "sufficient human

---

[44] Hill, "The Environment and Disease," 19.
[45] Greenland, *The Evolution of Epidemiological Ideas*, p. 14. More recently, a distinguished group of cancer researchers expressed concern that several of Hill's factors "have not stood the test of time and cannot be considered essential: specificity, analogy, plausibility and coherence." Michele Carbone, George Klein, Jack Gruber, and May Wong, "Modern Criteria to Establish Human Cancer Etiology," *Cancer Research* 64 (2004): 5518–5524, esp. 5519.

experience with the agent to determine its full toxicological potential."[46] "Exposure estimates are often crude and retrospective..."[47] They are also limited "in...the ability to identify and adjust for confounding exposures or genetic susceptibility..."[48] Frequently, they "are not sufficiently sensitive to identify a carcinogenic hazard except when the risk is high or involves an unusual form of cancer."[49] Moreover, because of the latency period of cancers in particular, if scientists rely upon human studies, years of preventable human exposures and likely cases of cancer would occur before epidemiological studies could be adequately conducted.[50] In many instances they simply have not been conducted for a risk of interest. Humans may be subjected to numerous exposures that can cause harm, thus contaminating studies.[51] Finally, they are expensive to conduct.

For these reasons, scientists utilize other evidence to infer the causal properties of substances. In particular, researchers regard animal studies as especially important for inferring that substances cause adverse effects in humans. Animal studies are *controlled experiments*, usually with rodents, such as rats or mice, but may also involve other species, such as hamsters, monkeys, or dogs. In this respect they resemble human clinical trials, only the experiments are conducted on animals.

In studies for purposes of identifying carcinogens ordinarily scientists would randomly assign animals to exposed and control groups. Typically, they would expose three groups of experimental animals to different doses of the suspect substance in question, for example, benzene, ethylene oxide (ETO), polychlorinated biphenyls (PCBs), or vinyl chloride, to compare the tumor rates in the experimental groups with the tumor rate in a control group of similar animals. If according to statistical tests the tumor rate is significantly greater in the exposed than in the control groups, scientists then extrapolate from the response rates in the experimental animals to those in humans. Usually, this involves extrapolating from higher-dose effects in animals to lower-dose effects in animals and then from low-dose effects in animals to low-dose effects in humans in order to estimate the toxicity effects in humans.[52]

---

[46] Huff and Rall, "Relevance to Humans," 433.
[47] Faustman and Omenn, "Risk Assessment," 86.
[48] Carbone et al., "Modern Criteria," 5519.
[49] Vincent James Cogliano, Robert A. Baan, Kurt Straif, Yann Grosse, Marie Beatrice Secretan, Fatiha El Ghissassi, and Paul Kleihues, "The Science and Practice of Carcinogen Identification and Evaluation," *Environmental Health Perspectives* 112 (2004): 1269–1274, esp. 1270.
[50] Cogliano et al., "Science and Practice," 1270.
[51] Huff and Rall, "Relevance to Humans," 433.
[52] There are a variety of considerations scientific bodies utilize to assess the quality of animal studies, but I do not consider these because the scientific bodies themselves, as well as other groups, have considered these issues. Guidelines from the International Agency for Research on Cancer can be found at IARC, Preamble to the Monographs, Section 9: Studies

Animal studies have "a complementary set of strengths and limitations" compared with epidemiological studies.[53] They are genuine experiments and exposure is clearly defined. However, "the question of relevance [to human carcinogenesis] must be addressed."[54]

There are, of course, readily apparent differences between laboratory animals and humans. Humans are larger, have longer life spans, suffer concomitant diseases, may be quite differentially exposed, may "process (i.e., metabolize, store, excrete) the agent in question in a different manner and . . . are much more genetically heterogeneous . . ."[55] These differences often receive greater attention than the similarities. Moreover, because of these dissimilarities it is relatively easy to persuade laypeople to misunderstand animal studies. Thus, judges may have difficulty sorting out cogent versus irrelevant criticisms. Nonetheless, there are solid scientific reasons that experimental animal studies can assist inferences about human harm. One might even think of these as defeasible biological principles that provide support for inferences from animals to humans.

First, leading scientists have noted that "experimental evidence to date certainly suggests that there are more physiologic, biochemical, and metabolic similarities between laboratory animals and humans than there are differences."[56] For example, the close relationship between mice and humans at the gene and protein levels has now been confirmed by recent studies of the human and mouse genomes.[57]

Second, "biological processes of molecular, cellular, tissue, and organ functions that control life are strikingly similar from one mammalian species to another. Such processes as sodium and potassium transport and ion regulation, energy metabolism, and DNA replication vary little in the aggregate as one moves along the phylogenetic ladder."[58]

Third, based on current information, there is great similarity in the carcinogenic processes between animals and humans.[59] This is the reason that animals

of Cancer in Experimental Animals, *Monographs*. Rev. 5 Jan. 1999. Available at: http://www-cie.iarc.fr/monoeval/studiesanimals.html.

[53] Carbone et al., "Modern Criteria," 5519.

[54] Carbone et al., "Modern Criteria," 5519.

[55] Huff and Rall, "Relevance to Humans," 433.

[56] Rall et al., "Alternatives to Using Human Experience in Assessing Health Risks," *Annual Review of Public Health* 8 (1987): 356.

[57] Mark S. Boguski, "Comparative Genomics: The Mouse that Roared," *Nature* 420 (2002): 515–516; The Mouse Genome Sequencing Consortium, Alec MacAndrew, "Comparison of Mouse and Human Coding Genes," *Nature* 420 (5 December 2002): 520–562.

[58] Huff and Rall, "Relevance to Humans," 434. (Significant scientific understanding of neural transmission, renal function, and cell replication and development of cancer have come from non-human species, often species far removed phylogenetically from humans.)

[59] Some researchers believe the relationships are even closer. For example, see Huff, "Chemicals and Cancer," 201, 204 (stating that the array and multiplicity of carcinogenic processes are virtually common among mammals, for instance between laboratory rodents and humans).

are used as *models* for biological responses in humans. This is the point of animal studies – good animal models demonstrate either beneficial or harmful effects in humans so the substance or condition causing the effects can be studied and manipulated in controlled experiments. By conducting such studies researchers can better understand the effects of a substance. Animal studies are utilized extensively in pre-market drug testing as well as in testing for toxic substances.[60]

Fourth, a leading scientist has argued that the more "we know about the similarities of structure and function of higher organisms at the molecular level, the more we are convinced that mechanisms of chemical toxicity are, to a large extent, identical in animals and man."[61] The U.S. EPA and the Federal Judicial Center's Manual on Scientific Evidence echo these points.[62]

Fifth, there are some differences in carcinogenic responses from one species to another and from animals to humans.[63] However, researchers have identified particular response patterns in animals that greatly increase the likelihood that a carcinogenic response in one mammalian species will produce a carcinogenic response in another mammalian species.[64] Cross-species predictions are substantially higher for mutagens (agents that cause mutations) than non-mutagens, for substances that are toxic at low doses,[65] for substances that show a dose-response relationship or reduced latency period, and for substances that induce uncommon tumor types or tumors at multiple sites and tumors

---

[60] See, generally, U.S. Department of Health and Human Services, Taskforce on Health Risk Assessment, "Determining Risks to Health: Federal Policy and Practice" (Dover, Mass: Auburn House Publishing Company, 1986), but especially 10–13, for information on testing in the Food and Drug Administration. For more general discussions see, U.S. Congress, Office of Technology Assessment, *Identifying and Regulating Carcinogens* (Washington, DC: U.S. Government Printing Office, 1986) and National Research Council, *Risk Assessment in the Federal Government* (Washington, DC: U.S. Government Printing Office, 1983).

[61] Huff, "Chemicals and Cancer," 204.

[62] U.S. Environmental Protection Agency, "Proposed Guidelines for Carcinogen Risk Assessment," *Federal Register* 61 (1996): 17,977 ("[T]here is evidence that growth control mechanisms at the level of the cell are homologous among mammals, but there is no evidence that these mechanisms are site concordant [i.e., must be in the same tissue in rodents and humans]."); Bernard D. Goldstein and Mary Sue Henifin, "Reference Guide on Toxicology," in *Reference Manual on Scientific Evidence*, 2nd ed., ed. Federal Judicial Center (New York: LEXIS, 2000), 419.

[63] For example, rats and mice differ at least 25 percent of the time. See George M. Gray, Ping Li, Ilya Shlykhter, and Richard Wilson, "An Empirical Examination of Factors Influencing Prediction of Carcinogenic Hazard Across Species," *Regulatory Toxicology & Pharmacology* 22 (1995): 283, 284, 287 (arguing in general that a positive carcinogenic response in mice is associated with a positive carcinogenic response in rats 76 percent of the time, and the converse association from rats to mice is 71 percent [chance would produce positive response rates of 48 percent from mice to rats and 43 percent from rats to mice]).

[64] See Gray et al., "An Empirical Examination." The elevated concordance across species for the above comparisons ranges from 84 percent to 98 percent, depending on the comparison considered, all well above the average positive predictive value of carcinogenic responses between rodents and much above chance concordance (284, 287).

[65] See L. Gold et al., "Interspecies Extrapolation in Carcinogenesis: Prediction between Rats and Mice," *Environmental Health Perspectives* 81 (1989): 211, 211–219.

in both sexes of one test species.[66] "[I]f a chemical causes multiple tumors in one species it is virtually certain to increase the tumor rate in the other species as well."[67] Cross-species carcinogenic responses constitute evidence scientists utilize to help conclude that substances with these properties in animals are more likely to be carcinogenic in humans. Some factors can modify these inferences. If exposures for animals and humans are radically different, it may not be proper to extrapolate to humans. If there are well-established and highly certain mechanisms of action in animals that do not extend to humans (a quite rare occurrence), this may modify the conclusions.[68]

Thus, the International Agency for Research on Cancer notes, "[A]nimal studies generally provide the best means of assessing particular risks to humans" and notes that "toxicokinetics and mechanisms" can be utilized to address the relevance of animals studies to human cancer.[69]

Sixth, a group of well-known researchers concludes,

[f]rom data available so far, therefore, it appears that chemicals that are carcinogenic in laboratory animals are likely to be carcinogenic in human populations and that, if appropriate studies can be performed, there is qualitative predictability. Also, there is evidence that there can be a quantitative relationship between the amount of a chemical that is carcinogenic in laboratory animals and that which is carcinogenic in human populations.[70]

Distinguished scientific committees have concurred, including the National Academy of Sciences.[71] Utilizing the language of rebuttable presumptions, the Academy notes that

in the absence of countervailing evidence for the specific agent in question, it appears reasonable to assume that the life-time cancer incidence induced

---

[66] See Gray et al., "An Empirical Examination," 288.

[67] See Gray et al., "An Empirical Examination," 288.

[68] See Gray et al., "An Empirical Examination," 290.

[69] Cogliano et al., "Science and Practice," 1270.

[70] Huff and Rall, "Relevance to Humans," 437.

[71] See Huff, "Chemicals and Cancer," 205 (quoting the National Academy of Sciences, "Pest Control: An Assessment of Present and Alternative Technologies," in *Contemporary Pest Control Practices and Prospects: The Report of the Executive Committee* (1975), 66, 66–83); see also Victor A. Fung et al., "The Carcinogenesis Bioassay in Perspective: Application in Identifying Human Cancer Hazards," *Environmental Health Perspectives* 103 (1995): 680, 682 (arguing that chemicals shown to unequivocally induce cancer in laboratory animals, especially in multiple species, must be considered capable of causing cancer in humans). Moreover, a group of researchers from the National Institute of Environmental Health Sciences, the University of North Carolina, the International Agency for Research on Cancer, the Linkoping University in Sweden, the National Cancer Institute, and the National Institute of Occupational Safety and Health have concluded that experimental results, in particular long-term carcinogenicity tests, have proven to be valid predictors of human risk. See Lorenzo Tomatis, James Huff, Irva Hertz-Picciotto, Dale P. Sandler, John Bucher, Paolo Boffetta, Olav Axelson, Aaron Blair, Jack Taylor, Leslie Stayner, and J. Carl Barrett, "Avoided and Avoidable Risks of Cancer," *Carcinogenesis* 18 (1997): 95–105, esp. 97.

by chronic exposure in man can be approximated by the life-time incidence induced by similar exposure in laboratory animals at the same total dose per body weight.[72]

A 2005 Institute of Medicine and National Research Council report gives them a strong endorsement, echoing numerous earlier reports. Animal studies are

powerful because controlled studies can be conducted to predict effects that might not be detected from customary use by humans until they result in overt harmful effects. Animal studies are especially useful in detecting effects of chronic exposures and effects on reproductive and developmental processes because epidemiological methods of studying humans are especially problematic in these areas . . .[73]

In general, adverse effects observed in well-designed and well-conducted animal studies should be treated as if they would occur in at least some members of the human population, assuming humans receive a sufficiently high dose.[74] Yet they will need to be evaluated to determine the extent of their relevance to humans. Bioassays involving the use of high doses and the evaluation of large numbers of tissues, as well as the testing of strains of laboratory animals prone to high incidences of spontaneous tumors, can sometimes produce results that may not be reproducible or likely to occur in humans under normal exposure conditions.[75] However, even such studies may be directly pertinent to workers, especially susceptible individuals, or those subject to accidental exposures. In addition, although some scientists believe that some chemical agents induce tumors in animals through mechanisms that do not operate in humans,[76] this is far from settled.[77]

---

[72] Huff and Rall, "Relevance to Humans," 437 (quoting the National Academy of Sciences, "Pest Control"). Subsequent to this paper, Curtis Travis recommended that the appropriate interspecies scaling factor be the dose per body weight to the three-quarter power, a value somewhat different from the Academy's scaling factor. There now appears to be a substantial consensus on Travis's point. See Curtis C. Travis, "Interspecies Extrapolation of Toxic Data," in *Health Risk Assessment: Dermal and Inhalation Exposure and Absorption of Toxicants*, ed. R.G.M. Wang, James B. Knaak, and Howard I. Maibach (Boca Raton, FL: CRC Press, 1993). IARC concurs with the National Academy of Sciences: "[I]t is biologically plausible . . . to regard agents and mixtures for which there is sufficient evidence of carcinogenicity in experimental animals as if they presented a carcinogenic risk to humans." IARC, *Monograph Series*, Preamble, Section 9.

[73] Institute of Medicine and National Research Council, Committee on the Framework for Evaluating the Safety of Dietary Supplements, *Dietary Supplements: A Framework for Evaluating Safety* (Washington, DC: National Academy Press, 2005), 157.

[74] Institute of Medicine and National Research Council, *Dietary Supplements*, 157.

[75] Animals are exposed to high doses to overcome problems of small sample sizes typically used in animal bioassays. See National Research Council, *Risk Assessment*, 24–27; see also OTA, *Identifying and Regulating Carcinogens*, 39, 46.

[76] See IARC, *Monograph Series*, Preamble; U.S. Department of Health and Human Services, *Ninth Annual Report on Carcinogens*; Jerry M. Rice, "Editorial: On the Application of Data on Mode of Action to Carcinogenesis, *Toxicological Sciences* 49 (1999): 175–177.

[77] J. Huff, "Alpha-2u-Globulin Nephropathy, Posed Mechanisms, and White Ravens," *Environmental Health Perspectives* 104 (December 1996): 1264–1267; R. L. Melnick, M. C. Kohn,

Finally, animal studies take at least five years to conduct and interpret, many person-hours of effort, and are also expensive. Thus, they too are not quick and easy tests for determining toxic effects. Ideally, scientists need to find quicker, short-term tests to identify toxicants.[78]

Other Data Relevant to Toxicity Assessments

Other kinds of evidence can assist scientists in inferring a causal relationship between exposure to a substance and a disease: chemical structure-biological activity relationships, genetic and chromosomal damage data, and some other short-term tests.

A standard toxicology textbook notes the importance of chemical structure-biological activity relationships, that is, the relation between a substance's chemical structure and its biological effects on mammalian or other systems.

> An agent's structure, solubility, stability, pH sensitivity, electrophilicity, volatility and chemical reactivity can be important information for hazard identification,[79]

that is, identifying hazards caused by substances. Moreover, "[h]istorically, certain key molecular structures have provided regulators with some of the most readily available information on the basis of which to assess hazard potential."[80] These include information about some carcinogens, structural alerts for "aromatic amine groups," and certain dyes as potential carcinogens. Some provide important information about developmental toxicants.[81] Industry relies on structure-activity relationships to help identify toxicants in their product development and testing.[82]

The Institute of Medicine and National Research Council note the scientific importance of structure-activity information for identifying adverse effects (from dietary supplements and other toxicants).

> The physical-chemical properties and biological effects of a substance are derived from its chemical structure. If the chemical structure of a dietary supplement is known, but additional insight into the biological activity is needed, then it is scientifically appropriate to consider the information about the biological activity of structurally related substances. It is assumed that the biological effects of chemicals, including toxic effects, are implicit in their molecular structures (referred to as toxicophores when they are

---

J. Huff, "Weight of Evidence Versus Weight of Speculation to Evaluate the Alpha2u-globulin Hypothesis," *Environmental Health Perspectives* 105 (September 1997): 904–906.

[78] Huff and Rall, "Relevance to Humans," 440.

[79] Faustman and Omenn, "Risk Assessment," 86.

[80] Faustman and Omenn, "Risk Assessment," 86.

[81] Faustman and Omenn, "Risk Assessment," 86.

[82] Richard Dennison, "U.S. HPV Challenge and Beyond," Presentation to Ward, Kershaw, and Center for Progressive Regulation Environmental Law Symposium: The Data Gaps Dilemma: Why Toxic Ignorance Threatens Public Health, 6 May 2005.

associated with toxic effects). This concept is most clearly illustrated with the example of ephedra, which is considered by some scientists to have similar physiological actions, although less potent, to the chemically related substance amphetamine, as well as the recently banned pharmaceutical agent phenylpropanolamine.[83]

For other examples, scientists recognize that certain classes of structure-activity relationships are important in identifying developmental toxicants or in identifying chemical groups that are known to interact with mammalian DNA or proteins. Such relationships provide *strong*, but not quite infallible, reasons for thinking that substances with chemical similarities have similar biological activity.[84]

Courts, as we consider in Chapter 6, can be quite impatient with molecular or chemical structure data. One reason, apart perhaps from their simply not understanding the significance of chemical data, is that similar chemical structures are not mathematically certain guides to similar toxicity effects. However, this data, properly understood, can contribute substantial evidence of causation for certain classes of substances and should be part of scientifically reasonable patterns of evidence of causation.

If the courts seek to make the law better comport with the pertinent science, they must recognize the *scientific relevance* and sometimes *quite strong evidentiary weight* of structure-activity relationships. They should not automatically exclude such evidence, but also recognize their limitations. Judges will need to adopt a much more sensitive approach to this data and other short-term tests, because such evidence is part of reasonable scientific assessments of toxicity.

Beyond mere structure-activity relationships, there is other molecular evidence that can be quite valuable. Even a cursory review of a toxicology textbook reveals that when scientists understand a good deal about the mechanisms of toxicity, much of this data is at the molecular level. For example, some substances bind to molecules in the body through electron transfer, so-called covalent binding, which turns out to be very important. It is irreversible, and if the substance is bound to DNA, so that it interferes with the replication or other

---

[83] Institute of Medicine and National Research Council, *Dietary Supplements*, 205–206 (citing Food and Drug Administration, "Final Rule Declaring Dietary Supplements Containing Ephedrine Alkaloids Adulterated Because They Present an Unreasonable Risk," *Federal Register* 69 (2005): 6787–6854; I. Furuya and S. Watanabe, "Discriminative Stimulus Properties of Ehedra Herb (*Ephedra sinica*) in rats, *Yakubutsu Seishin Kodo* 13 (1993): 33–38; C. R. Lake, and R. S. Quirk, "CNS Stimulants and the Look-Alike Drugs," *Psychiatry Cin. North American* 7 (1984): 689–701).

[84] Faustman and Omenn, 83–104; J. Ashby, R.W. Tennant, "Chemical Structure, Salmonella Mutagenicity and Extent of Carcinogenicity as Indicators of Genotoxic Carcinogenesis among 222 Chemicals Tested in Rodents by the U.S. NCI/NTP," *Mutation Research* 204 (1988): 17–115; David A. Eastmond, Chair, Department of Environmental Toxicology, University of California, Riverside, personal communication, 2002.

DNA functioning, this may well trigger cancer or other serious conditions.[85] Still other compounds may activate or inactivate various molecular pathways that lead to adverse effects.[86] If toxicologists know that a substance has a chemical structure that binds to an oncogene – one that tends to cause cancer – or binds to a tumor suppressor gene so as to interfere with their function, this is very important information for making toxicity judgments. Aflatoxins, for example, are known to induce mutations of both tumor suppressor genes and oncogenes, leading to cancer.[87] As a second example, federal and state agencies have classified a large number of dioxins and related compounds as carcinogens based not on human or whole animal studies, but on their propensity to bind to the aryl-hydrocarbon (Ah) receptor. This is a biological feature that humans and other mammals have in common.[88] If other compounds exhibit *sufficiently similar* properties in mammalian systems, this information would contribute significantly to a toxicity judgment. Other chemical reactions can "alter the primary structure of molecules" in the body, thus rendering them dysfunctional or toxic.[89]

The preceding point generalizes to a larger point. Molecular level data plus information about how toxicants are transformed within mammalian bodies and other mechanistic information assist scientists' inferences about adverse effects in humans. Combined with animal data this information can be especially helpful.[90] Thus, with animal evidence alone or animal evidence plus the right kinds of complementary evidence, scientists can infer that a substance is a human carcinogen without needing human evidence.[91] As molecular studies are refined, their use is likely to increase. Recently a distinguished group of cancer researchers has even called for increased research "to identify potential carcinogens *primarily from mechanistic information,* even in the absence of epidemiological or experimental animal studies in which the tumors are observed."[92]

---

[85] Zoltan Gregus and Curtis D. Klaassen, "Mechanisms of Toxicity," in *Casarett and Doull's Toxicology,* 6th ed., 28–76.

[86] Carbone et al., "Modern Criteria," 5519.

[87] Gregus and Klaassen, "Mechanisms of Toxicity," 28–76.

[88] Faustman and Omenn, "Risk Assessment," 86; Lauren Zeise, Director, Office of Health Hazard Assessment, California EPA, personal communication, July 2004; David A. Eastmond, Chair, Environmental Toxicology, University of California, Riverside, personal communication, July 2004.

[89] Gregus and Klaassen, "Mechanisms of Toxicity," 47.

[90] Cogliano et al., "Science and Practice," 1270 and Carbone et al., "Modern Criteria," 5519–5520.

[91] A distinguished group of cancer researchers has noted, "when there is sufficient evidence of carcinogenicity in animals and when there is molecular pathology proof that in human cells the agent interferes with key molecular pathways that lead to tumor formation," this information can be used to identify carcinogens and co-carcinogens." Carbone et al., "Modern Criteria," 5519.

[92] Carbone et al., "Modern Criteria," 5519 (emphasis added).

Scientists also utilize various short-term or in-vitro (test-tube) tests, rang-ing from test-tube experiments to skin-painting tests on mice.[93] These might be used to assist in identifying carcinogens or reproductive toxicants. Such studies, for example, can be especially important for identifying geneotoxic carcinogens, that is, substances that cause DNA damage, but are less successful for identifying non-genotoxic carcinogens. The skin-painting tests appear to be quite good at identifying substances that *promote* cancer once cells have been mutated to trigger the initial stages of cancer.[94]

Short-term tests for identifying chromosomal abnormalities hold promise for identifying the carcinogenic potential of substances, but they are somewhat more complicated and expensive than other short-term tests. Nonetheless, if such data are available, they can be quite valuable in assessing carcinogenicity.[95]

A scientific body such as the International Agency for Research on Can-cer utilizes a variety of data from short-term tests, data about gene mutation and chromosomal damage, cell transformation, and even short-terms tests in simpler biologic systems, such as "prokaryotes, lower eukaryotes, insects and cultured mammalian cells."[96]

This brief review of some short-term tests and other kinds of data about car-cinogenicity or other toxic potential of substances is not meant to be complete. Such data are scientifically relevant and can be quite important. Consensus scientific bodies routinely utilize such information. The studies can and do contribute substantially to judgments of toxicity. Some courts have overre-acted and directed too much skepticism toward expert testimony based on scientific studies that do not include human data. Such studies should not face the high skepticism they often do, given their scientific relevance and impor-tant contribution to causation assessments. As we consider in later chapters, how much any particular piece of scientific data can contribute to a toxicity judgment about a substance depends on how good that data is, what other data are available, how well the different kinds of data fit together to provide information on toxicity, and what background knowledge there is about the different kinds of data.

The above are some of the main kinds of "standard" evidence that are sci-entifically relevant and used to identify substances as carcinogenic to humans. The Institute of Medicine and National Research Council have identified sim-ilar kinds of evidence for assessing the toxicity of dietary supplements.[97] Thus,

---

93   Faustman and Omenn, "Risk Assessment," 87–88.
94   Faustman and Omenn, "Risk Assessment," 87–88.
95   Henry C. Pitot III and Yvonne P. Dragan, "Chemical Carcinogenesis," in *Casarett and Doull's Toxicology*, 6th ed., 290–291.
96   IARC, *Monograph Series*, Preamble, Section 8. See also Cogliano et al., "Science and Practice," 1271, and Carbone et al., "Modern Criteria," 5519.
97   Institute of Medicine and National Research Council, *Dietary Supplements*, 126–291.

there is nothing particularly special about assessing the toxicity of carcinogens (except perhaps that it is more difficult) – similar categories of evidence must be utilized whether scientists are assessing the adverse effects of potential carcinogens, reproductive toxicants, neurological toxicants, or dietary supplements.

SCIENTIFIC REASONING

Beyond basic scientific studies there is a concern that courts may not understand fully critical features of scientific reasoning. Such reasoning is the means by which scientists make inferences from studies to conclusions about the toxic properties of substances. These inferences are central to the scientific enterprise, but some courts seem not to have understood their features. In fact, some judges have had a tendency to adopt comparatively simple indicators of reliable scientific reasoning, indicia that must be jettisoned or modified in favor of a more subtle understanding of scientific reasoning.[98]

Before turning full attention to scientific reasoning, I consider one other kind of human evidence that may "get little respect" from some scientists and "gets almost no respect," as the late Rodney Dangerfield might say, from the courts: case studies. This kind of evidence should be reviewed in the context of scientific reasoning because what makes case studies good evidence about causation is the *analysis* to which they are subjected and how *scientists reason about them*. Good case studies rest on a principle of diagnostic or nondeductive reasoning that is essential to all causal judgments. Understanding this reasoning about case studies thus serves two purposes: it shows how case studies can be good evidence for causation and it sheds light on a much more fundamental form of reasoning that judges must recognize in reviewing scientific expert testimony.

Case Studies

Case studies or case reports typically "arise from a suspicion, based on clinical experience, that the concurrence of two events – that is, a particular exposure and occurrence of a cancer – has happened rather more frequently than would be expected by chance."[99] Unfortunately, case reports, typically reports of single observations, do not comprehensively identify all cases of the same disease in any population or the population at risk and do not estimate the number

---

[98]   I return to these issues in Chapters 6 and 7.
[99]   IARC, *Monograph Series*, Preamble, Section 8.

of cases of disease when there is no exposure.[100] Consequently, case reports cannot be utilized to establish the prevalence of an adverse condition in the exposed population or even to establish a relative risk between exposed and unexposed populations. Thus, case studies do not provide some information that statistically based research can. However, when they are combined with other animal or other kinds of evidence they can provide quite useful information. On occasion, very good case studies can establish causation by themselves. Thus, despite these limitations, sometimes case reports can contribute to or even be quite good evidence of causation on their own.

Case reports for vaccines and drugs are often part of what health professionals call "passive reporting schemes that rely on the vigilance of health care providers to detect events that are felt to be due to the administration of a drug product..."[101] They also are utilized to provide early warnings of adverse reactions to occupational exposures. Such systems rely on the collection of case reports by some centralized agency, such as the Centers for Disease Control or the Food and Drug Administration in the United States, the Vaccine-Associated Adverse Events Surveillance Program in the Division of Immunization, Bureau of Infectious Diseases in Canada, or the Occupational Safety and Health Administration in the United States. These are then utilized to provide early warnings of adverse health effects and to alert agencies to possible broader problems when a wider population is exposed. Moreover, their importance increases when the law does not require premarket testing of products and that basic data is missing.

Case series provide "a description of a number of patients who exhibit the same exposure, disease or [unusual drug events].... A single case report may indicate an individual reaction and/or an extremely rare phenomenon. A case series provides evidence that a finding, even though still rare, is repeated."[102]

Case studies can be good, scientifically relevant evidence of causation or not, depending upon the quality of the study. Merely *descriptive* case reports – reports that do not rule out alternative causes of disease, do not assess features of a patient that might have led to an adverse reaction, do not address the biological plausibility of the adverse reaction, or are not at all subtle about the temporal relations involved – are quite poor evidence or may constitute no evidence at all. They can fail to provide evidence of causation because they are simply instances of physicians or nurses noticing adverse effects in a patient following exposure to a drug, vaccine, environmental contaminant, or poison, and reporting these facts to a governmental agency. Health care workers are

[100] IARC, *Monograph Series*, Preamble, Section 8.
[101] J. P. Collet et al., "Monitoring Signals for Vaccine Safety: The Assessment of Individual Adverse Event Reports by an Expert Advisory Committee," *Bulletin of the World Health Organization* 78, 2 (2000): 178–185.
[102] Abraham G. Hartzema, Miquel Porta, and Hugh H Tilson, eds., *Pharmacoepidemiology: An Introduction*, 3rd ed. (Cincinnati, OH: Harvey Whitney Books Co., 1998), 77.

strongly encouraged to issue such reports in order to facilitate monitoring – to provide a basis for early warnings if significant patterns of adverse effects emerge.[103]

Case studies function best to reveal adverse causal reactions to vaccines, drugs, poisons, some anesthetics, and even dietary supplements. Their evidentiary value tends to increase when there is a fairly short interval between exposure and reaction and where adverse reactions are reasonably easily identified.[104] In some instances, case studies have been used to identify carcinogens and, perhaps, some other toxicants.

What constitutes a good case report? The argument that follows proceeds by several steps: I review five examples in which case studies provide good evidence of causation, and then review science methodologists' support for the use of case studies. Finally, I show how the inferences from case studies are founded on a much more fundamental and generally accepted form of reasoning that is foundational for both case studies and scientific reasoning more generally.

The Scientific Data

The examples that follow are instances in which scientists on the basis of case reports have judged that the exposure in question probably or certainly caused or contributed to the adverse reaction. Three of these are taken from adverse reactions to drugs or vaccines, the fourth is an example of an adverse reaction to a known carcinogen that functioned as a poison, and the fifth shows how occupational physicians inferred that vinyl chloride was identified as a potent carcinogen by case studies as causing cancer in some industrial employees.

Example 1: The first example shows how physicians diagnose the cause of an adverse reaction from an anesthesia on the basis of a single case study, but regard it as quite good evidence.

A forty-four-year-old physician began his training in anesthesiology July 1961, and was exposed to low concentrations of halothane almost daily thereafter. On June 26, 1962, "increasing malaise, fatigability, anorexia, nausea and occasional vomiting began. One week later, the urine darkened, but the stools remained normal in color. There was no accompanying pruritus [severe itching], abdominal pain, chills, fever or rash. Mild jaundice appeared on July 6, the

---

[103] The FDA, for example, removed Parlodel (bromocriptine), a postpartum lactation suppression drug from the market simply on the basis of a series of case reports indicating a relationship between use of Parlodel and patients suffering strokes or heart attacks. The FDA took this course of action without addressing whether exposure to Parlodel *caused* either strokes or heart attacks. It had sufficient legal authority to act short of establishing a causal relation between a patient taking Parlodel and experiencing a heart attack or stroke. U.S. Department of Health and Human Services, Food and Drug Administration, "Sandoz Pharmaceuticals Corp.; Bromocriptine Mesylate (Parlodel) for the Prevention of Physiological Lactation; Opportunity for a Hearing on a Proposal to Withdraw Approval of the Indication," 59 Federal Register 43347 (23 August 1994): 43347.

[104] Institute of Medicine and National Research Council, *Dietary Supplements*, 131–132.

tenth day of the illness, but the patient continued to work until July 16 when he consulted a physician for the first time, and was advised to enter the hospital."[105]

Physicians ruled out infectious mononucleosis and chest abnormalities. The laboratory and clinical tests "were considered typical of acute viral hepatitis so that the patient was kept at bed rest for approximately three weeks."[106] He convalesced at home for three weeks and about two months after the onset of the first illness he returned to work. "Within 5 hours of resuming his duties as an anesthetist, he had a shaking chill followed by a rise in temperature to 101 F and the appearance of headache, myalgia, anorexia and nausea. The fever subsided within 24 hours, but the other symptoms persisted." This illness was "attributed to an intercurrent viral infection, and he was allowed to continue working." Liver function studies revealed abnormalities that "were interpreted as evidence of a relapse of the hepatitis.[107]

To shorten a six-year scientific detective story, he suffered four more relapses of his hepatitis-like condition over a five-year period, all after substantial exposure to halothane. On a few other occasions he was exposed to halothane, but because he was taking prednisone, a steroid, he appeared not to suffer symptoms. Finally,

> [b]ecause of the possible relation of the relapsing hepatitis to repeated exposure to halothane, and the evidence of progressive damage to the liver, the patient was advised to discontinue the use of halothane in his practice. [However, before doing that] he wanted more substantial evidence that his liver disease was attributable to halothane exposure.... [and sought a halothane challenge, that is, exposure to halothane, under controlled conditions].[108]

He took the halothane challenge at a hospital and suffered an episode of "acute hepatitis within 24 hours" that resembled previous episodes after his exposure to halothane. Once he abandoned exposure to halothane in his work as an anesthesiologist, he did not suffer a relapse. The authors of the study conclude, "It is highly probable that halothane was responsible for the recurrent attacks of hepatitis in this case."[109]

---

[105]   Gerald Klatskin and Daniel V. Kimberg, "Recurrent Hepatitis Attributable to Halothane Sensitization in an Anesthetist," *The New England Journal of Medicine* 280 (1969): 515.
[106]   Klaskin and Kimberg, "Recurrent Hepatitis," 515.
[107]   Klaskin and Kimberg, "Recurrent Hepatitis," 516.
[108]   Klaskin and Kimberg, "Recurrent Hepatitis," 519.
[109]   Klaskin and Kimberg, "Recurrent Hepatitis," 515. Inferences such as this in which the exposure was present, followed by the adverse reaction, contrasted with circumstances in which the exposure was absent with no adverse reaction, each repeated several times followed by a deliberate challenge under controlled conditions (which was preceded by no exposure and no adverse conditions) is very close to John Stuart Mill's Method of Difference. That Method is to "have every circumstance in common save one, that one occurring only in the [circumstance in which the phenomenon under investigation occurs]; the circumstance in which alone the two instances differ is the effect, or the cause, or an indispensable part of the cause, of the phenomenon." J. S. Mill, *A System of Logic: Ratiocinative and Inductive* (London: Longman, Green and Co., LTD, 1941), 256.

In the above example every time the halothane was present, the hepatitis occurred; when the halothane was withdrawn, the hepatitis subsided and soon disappeared only to occur again when halothane was reintroduced. Moreover, this occurred over several years in a number of different circumstances, including the essentially experimental condition of deliberate exposure to halothane in order to test whether exposure to it would reintroduce the adverse liver conditions. In medical terminology this amounts to a classic example of challenge-dechallenge and then rechallenge in the experimental exposure.

Example 2: A forty-two-year-old man developed Guillain-Barré Syndrome (GBS), an acute inflammatory demyelinating polyneuritis following tetanus shots. This disease "is characterized by the rapid onset of flaccid motor weakness with depression of tendon reflexes and elevation of protein levels in CSF without pleocytosis. The annual incidence of GBS appears to be approximately 1 per 100,000 for adults" and approximately the same for children.[110] This individual "developed GBS on three separate occasions (over a 13-year period) following receipt of tetanus toxoid [vaccine]. The relation between tetanus toxoid and GBS is convincing at least for that one individual, even though this man [subsequent to his last episode of GBS caused by tetanus toxoid] experienced multiple recurrences of demyelinating polyneuropathy, most following acute viral illness. . . . [Two other cases] are recorded in enough detail to be accepted as GBS."[111]

This example reveals several points about inferences leading to causal judgments. First, on every occasion in which the individual received a tetanus vaccine he contracted GBS. The latency periods for three episodes "were 21, 14, and 10 days, respectively," time periods well within biological plausibility.[112] In each case he had a "self-limited episode of clear-cut, well-documented polyneuropathy of the GBS variety . . .", and "made a full functional recovery" following each episode. Following one of the episodes, the disease was confirmed by biopsy, showing lesions in the peripheral nervous system. Moreover, no other plausible explanations seemed available for his contraction of GBS; for example, there appeared to be no immunological basis for his reaction.[113]

However, the patient did contract GBS on several occasions independent of receiving the tetanus virus, thus suggesting that he also had some predisposition to GBS either as a result of his reaction to tetanus toxoid or independent of it. Nonetheless, this did not deter independent evaluators from asserting that "because [this] case by Pollard and Selby (1978) demonstrates that tetanus toxoid *did* cause GBS, in the [IOM] committee's judgment tetanus toxoid *can*

---

[110]   Institute of Medicine, *Adverse Events Associated with Childhood Vaccines: Evidence Bearing on Causality*, ed. Abraham G. Hartzema, Miquel Porta, and Hugh H. Tilson (Washington, DC: National Academy Press, 1994), 86.
[111]   Institute of Medicine, *Childhood Vaccines*, 89.
[112]   Institute of Medicine, *Childhood Vaccines*, 87.
[113]   Institute of Medicine, *Childhood Vaccines*, 88.

cause GBS."[114] This conclusion is significant in several ways for legal cases, to be discussed later, as it shows that a single case study can provide a plausible basis for general causation in the law.

Second, the authors note that the few case reports that exist cannot establish "whether the frequency of cases is higher than the expected background rate of GBS."[115] From a scientific point of view the main function of disease rates following exposure appears to be a public health concern. If it is rare for tetanus toxoid to cause GBS above background, then there is little or no public health concern as a result of tetanus inoculations. An occasional adverse reaction is a small social price to pay for having protection against tetanus. By contrast, if tetanus toxoid–caused GBS were substantially above background, public health authorities would have to be concerned about whether or not to provide tetanus shots, or perhaps tetanus shots from a particular vaccine batch. In addition, one might think that rare GBS reactions to tetanus vaccines might suggest that the GBS reaction was a *coincidence,* since it is at least conceivable that on an occasion when a person received an inoculation he also inexplicably suffered GBS independent of inoculation. Such an explanation seems implausible in the present example according to the experts' assessment, however, because of the consistency of the person's reaction to each of three tetanus shots he received.

Third, in some respects this case, like some others, is a comparatively easy one in which to judge causation, since there is a fairly direct and consistent relationship between exposure to tetanus vaccine and contraction of GBS. Defacto this case is equivalent to challenge-rechallenge with the patient acting as the control, because the repeated vaccinations were always followed by adverse reactions.

Fourth, the authors describing this case study go to some lengths to rule out other possible explanations of the patient's GBS, an important aspect of a *good* case study.

Example 3: This third example shows how physicians could diagnose the cause of an adverse drug reaction on the basis of a case study with the primary emphasis on the timing of the onset of adverse reaction. The authors in effect argue that *a particular temporal period* between exposure and onset of reaction can be highly important evidence in distinguishing between an adverse reaction caused by drug exposure and an adverse reaction caused by an underlying disease.

> [First of pair]: A patient with clinically stable lupus erythematosus develops renal dysfunction (an increase in serum creatinine from 1 to 2 mg%) 1 day after starting aspirin therapy. The renal dysfunction could conceivably be due to the underlying disease, but if so it would have approximately the same chance of appearing at any stage of this life-long disease. Hence, in this

---

[114]   Institute of Medicine, *Childhood Vaccines,* 89 (emphasis in original).
[115]   Institute of Medicine, *Childhood Vaccines,* 89.

case the concordance of the timing with the hypothesis of aspirin causation, compared to the diffuseness of the timing distribution for the alternative etiology, gives fairly conclusive evidence for drug causation, and so methods should not bound the potential effect of timing information from above.

[Second of pair]: As above, except that the increase in the serum creatinine is detected 1 hr after the first aspirin tablet is taken. In this case, the latency period is too short (even with the renal shutdown it would take at least 12 hr for the serum creatinine to rise by 1 mg%) and so information about timing conclusively refutes drug causation, showing that the effect of timing information on probability of [drug]-causation should not be bounded from below, even when the patient received [the drug] before [the effect] occurred.[116]

The authors go on to make two important observations about this pair of examples. A generic point is that there should be "no a priori constraints on the effects of factors [that might contribute to causation]."[117] That is, sometimes particular kinds of information can virtually establish the causal relationship, even though from some abstract point of view and before considering an individual case, one might think that it would be a mistake for such information to be decisive. Second, they observe that "under certain conditions timing information can virtually prove or rule out drug causation."[118]

This is a case in which the authors believe that a single case could establish the causal relationship between aspirin therapy and renal dysfunction, combining the timing of dose with background information on what an increase of creatinine levels means for kidney function and the plausibility of aspirin causation. The *time interval* together with *background knowledge* provides much of the biological plausibility of the causal relationship.

The particular temporal proximity of exposure and adverse effect can by itself establish, in conjunction with appropriate background knowledge, a causal relationship. Moreover, it is not just that the cause precedes the effect, but the *particular time interval in question* that can be quite important in helping to show causation. In the first of the pair, timing would virtually establish causation (given background knowledge) and in the second decisively rule out causation.

Example 4: Several members of the family of a woman who had rejected the romantic advances of a man suddenly became ill following ingestion of lemonade. The first victim, Chad Shelton, was an eleven-month-old child. Diagnosis of his symptoms ranged from gastroenteritis, otitis media (inflammation of

---

[116]   Tom A. Hutchinson and David A. Lane, "Standardized Methods of Causality Assessment of Suspected Adverse Drug Reactions," *Journal of Clinical Epidemiology* 42 (1989): 12.

[117]   Hutchinson and Lane, "Standardized Methods of Causality Assessment," 11.

[118]   Hutchinson and Lane, "Standardized Methods of Causality Assessment," 12. (They go on to note that "[s]imilarly, in some situations, other categories of case information (dechallenge, rechallenge etc.) can have a determining effect on the assessment.")

the middle ear), and tonsillitis to Reyes syndrome (a disease characterized "by vomiting, central-nervous system damage and liver damage"). After continuing to deteriorate, baby Chad died the day following his admission to the emergency room. The pathologist who performed the autopsy concluded that, given the poor condition of the liver, "this pattern is more consistent with a toxic ingestion of an unknown agent rather than Reye's syndrome or other infectious etiologies."[119] Chad Shelton had died from liver failure.

A second patient, Duane Johnson, uncle of Chad Shelton, was admitted to a different hospital and after exhibiting symptoms of chills, diarrhea, vomiting, and severe nose-bleeds, became comatose, and was judged to have "gone into . . . a neurological situation from which he cannot be retrieved."[120] Johnson died two days later. Johnson's three-year-old daughter was sick with stomach pains and vomiting, his sister-in-law Sally Shelton, Chad's mother, had been sick. It turned out some members of this extended family were quite sick, some died, but some were quite well.

In both deaths, the liver was the only organ affected. Most toxic substances that affect the liver also affect other organs, but that was not the case here. The substance also had to be soluble in water since it was believed (but not proven) to have been in the lemonade that some, but not other, members of this extended family had ingested. The substance was more or less tasteless. This permitted toxicologists to narrow the group of substances that might cause such problems to some "readily modifiable hydrocarbons called alkylating agents."[121] (There were no traces of the substance in the bodies, only certain kinds of damage had occurred.) The list of alkylating agents could be further narrowed to eight. A toxicologist ruled out several for being too weak, one because it causes damage to red blood cells, which was not seen in this case. Another was eliminated because it was not consistent with the kind of liver damage seen and causes damage in only large amounts. This left one substance, dimethylnitrosamine that fit all the facts of the case. Moreover, the liver lesions identified under the microscope were identical with textbook examples from *animal studies*. Finally, there was one test that could be performed that would reveal a particular kind of liver damage. A blind study on several tissue samples performed by a UC Irvine researcher, Ronald Shank, identified the substance as dimethylnitrosamine.

This was a case of murder caused by dimethynitrosamine placed in the family's lemonade by the jilted boyfriend of an older daughter in the Shelton family. He only intended to give the family cancer over a much longer period of time, but the dimethylnitrosamine concentrations in the lemonade were sufficiently high that it was toxic to those who drank much of it.

---

[119] Beron Roueché, "The Lemonade Mystery," *The Saturday Evening Post* (May/June 1982), 59.
[120] Roueché, "The Lemonade Mystery," 59.
[121] Roueché, "The Lemonade Mystery," 120.

There were no human epidemiological studies; there was no background rate of disease for this liver condition. On the basis of the facts of this case and some laboratory studies based on animal testing, they were able to identify the substance and ultimately to trace it to the murderer, a former employee in a cancer institute.[122]

It is clear in this case that the scientific and forensic investigators ruled out various causes partly based upon symptoms, partly on the context of the poisoning, partly on some laboratory tests, and partly on tissue damage similar to that in animals exposed to dimethylnitrosamine. It was a highly unusual event, but causation was inferred nevertheless – on the basis of the information particular to the case. In effect they had to infer causes from circumstantial evidence without having other direct human studies. This example has become a toxicological case study classic.

In addition to the points in the preceding two paragraphs, what can we infer? A good case study rules out alternative explanations of the events. Here the ruling out rested on circumstances surrounding the poisoning, sorting through symptoms, some non-human laboratory results that identified the particular kind of liver damage, some background knowledge based on the kinds of substances that could cause the kind of liver damage seen here, and finally some very specialized lab tests to pinpoint chemical changes in the liver attributed to dimethylnitrosamine.

The authorities were *certain* about causation without having some kinds of evidence that tort courts have insisted upon – they had no human epidemiological studies and no background rates of liver damage – and with only a few human case studies and some animal studies on the effect of the substance on the liver to lend any additional support. The causal judgment *in this murder case* was made without reliance on such evidence. This, I submit, was a quite convincing *causal judgment* based on a case study and made without reliance on many other kinds of statistically based evidence that some courts have demanded and scientists would find desirable.

Example 5: In 1974 Creech and Johnson, two occupational physicians, and their collaborators reported three cases "of angiosarcoma of the liver among workers at a polyvinyl chloride (PVC) production plant in Louisville."[123] A follow-up search revealed eight additional cases. On the basis of the three cases and other considerations present (which I discuss next), these scientists came to the conclusion that there was a causal relationship between exposure to vinyl chloride (VC) monomers and contraction of angiosarcoma of the liver (ASL). They expressed this in different ways. One expression was, "The reason an

---

[122]   Cranor and Eastmond, "Scientific Ignorance," 39.

[123]   Henry Falk, John L. Creech, Jr., Clark W. Heath, Jr., Maurice N. Johnson, and Marcus M. Key, "Hepatic Disease Among Workers at a Vinyl Chloride Polymerization Plant," *Journal of the American Medical Association* 230 (7 Oct. 1974): 59.

etiologic association between VC work and tumor could be inferred so readily on the basis initially of only 3 cases is that ASL is extraordinarily rare."[124] Later in the same publication they conclude, "In light of recent animal experiments and of clinical observations reported in European VC workers, it seems likely that exposure to VCM in the course of VC polymerization work *is responsible* for malignant and nonmalignant liver disease in these cases."[125]

I quote the actual language of the scientists, because, despite the phrase "etiologic *association*" and slight hedging in the second expression ("it seems likely"), the italicized phrases in both sentences above contain language explicitly implicating a causal relationship between exposure to VC and ASL. Moreover, subsequent researchers generally attribute the identification of VC as the cause of ASL to Creech et al.'s observations of a small number of case studies.[126] In short, working scientists attributed angiosarcoma of the liver to vinyl chloride exposure on the basis of a few cases without the use of statistical studies.

The scientists based their causal inferences on several considerations. First, they note the rarity of disease and the unusual number of ASL cases in one PVC plant in Kentucky. They estimated a relative risk of about 400:1 by comparing the rate of ASL in VC plants with the disease rate in the general population. Before these cases appeared in PVC plants, there were only about twenty-five cases of ASL *per year* in the United States, whereas they found up to eight cases in a comparatively short time in VC plants. Second, they additionally note that both animal studies and some case observations elsewhere also add support to the judgment. Finally, they had some knowledge of other kinds of exposures that would cause similar liver disease – excessive alcohol usage, arsenic compounds, or thorium dioxide – but were able to rule these out as alternative

---

[124] Clark W. Heath, Jr., Henry Falk, and John L. Creech, Jr., "Characteristics of Cases of Angiosarcoma of the Liver Among Vinyl Chloride Workers in the United States," *Annals of the New York Academy of Sciences* (1975): 231 (emphasis added).

[125] Heath, Falk, and Creech, "Characteristics of Cases of Angiosarcoma," 235 (emphasis added).

[126] David B. Clayson, *Toxicological Carcinogenesis* (New York: Lewis Publishers, 2001), 11–12 ("Even in 1974, Creech and his colleagues reported that those working with 'vinyl chloride', the raw material from which the commercially important plastic polyvinylchloride (PVC) is made, were at risk from an exceedingly rare form of liver cancer, liver angiosarcoma. They found four cases of angiosarcoma of the liver in a factory population of less than 5000 workers engaged in the manufacture of the monomer and the plastic. In the total population of the U.S. (about 250,000,000) only about 25 of these tumors were reported to develop on an annual basis; therefore, Creech's observation, by itself, was almost an adequate indictment of the chemical."); John Craighead, *Pathology of Environmental and Occupational Disease* (St. Louis, MO: Mosby, 1995), 60 (Clinical observations that workers chronically exposed to vinyl chloride had an unusually high incidence of hepatic angiosarcoma, a rare form of cancer in the United States, provided the initial evidence that it was carcinogenic. Subsequent studies have verified the increased incidence of hepatic angiosarcoma following chronic occupational exposures, particularly in those workers exposed to the highest concentrations of vinyl chloride.").

explanations for ASL in the stricken individuals relatively easily. Moreover, they were able to find patterns and duration of exposure that were comparatively consistent among those affected. They were even able to construct a crude dose-response relationship between exposure and latency of disease before manifestation.[127]

It is unusual for carcinogens to be identified mainly on the basis of case studies for several reasons. For one thing, cancers tend to be fairly common diseases. As a consequence it will be more difficult to identify common cancers on the basis of a small number of cases. However, when the disease is quite rare, as is ASL, it becomes comparatively easier. For another, cancers are multifactorial diseases with typically long latency periods. Consequently, because over a long period of time a person will be subjected to a number of bodily insults that might complete the induction of disease and contribute to the contraction of cancer, it can be difficult to identify one factor as a significant causal contributor to the disease. Moreover, often cancers caused by workplace or environmental exposures are not elevated much above background rates of disease; this, too, makes identification of the etiology of the disease difficult, since even the best scientific tools are comparatively insensitive. It would be much more difficult for case studies to be helpful in such cases. However, when the disease is rare, highly elevated above background with few other exposures likely to cause the particular disease in question, and other causes easily ruled out, the evidentiary value of case studies rises and may be quite compelling for identifying the cause of disease as they were in this instance.

Scientific Reasoning in Good Case Studies

The above constitute clear instances in which experts in the field concluded on the basis of a singular or small number of events, typically short of a sufficient number for an epidemiological study, that the exposures in question *caused* or *probably caused* the adverse effects. In the argot of philosophy, these examples constitute comparatively fixed points for theorizing about causal judgments.

The persuasiveness of the examples is strengthened by the considerations utilized by the U.S. Institute of Medicine in assessing whether vaccines in fact caused or probably caused an adverse reaction in a person. As they pose it, this is the "Did it?" Question – *did* the substance in question cause the adverse reaction? The IOM specifically considers evidence from case reports and other studies that bear on the likelihood of a causal relation between exposure to a vaccine and an adverse reaction. They utilize the following considerations in identifying causal relations from case studies or case series. These considerations are *defeasible criteria* that must be taken into account in assessing the quality and plausibility of case reports for vaccines, but the criteria can

---

[127]   Heath, Falk, and Creech, "Characteristics of Cases of Angiosarcoma," 234.

be generalized to other kinds of adverse reactions.[128] Their considerations are posed as questions to be addressed by physicians who provide the case reports.

1) *Previous general experience with the vaccine*: How long has it been on the market? How often have vaccine recipients experienced similar events? How often does the event occur in the absence of vaccine exposure? Does a similar event occur more frequently in animals exposed to vaccine than in appropriate controls?

2) *Alternative etiologic candidates*: Can a preexisting or new illness explain the sudden appearance of the adverse event? Does the adverse event tend to occur spontaneously . . . ? Were drugs, other therapies, or diagnostic tests and procedures that can cause the adverse event administered?

3) *Susceptibility of vaccine recipient*: Has he or she received the vaccine in the past? If so, how has he or she reacted? Does his or her genetic background or previous medical history affect the risk of developing the adverse event as a consequence of vaccination?

4) *Timing of events*: Is the timing of onset of the adverse event as expected if the vaccine is the cause? How does that timing differ from the timing that would occur given the alternative etiologic candidate(s)? How does the timing, given vaccine causation, depend on the suspected mechanism (e.g., immunoglobulin E versus T-cell-mediated)?

5) *Characteristics of the adverse event*: Are there any available laboratory tests that either support or undermine the hypothesis of vaccine causation?

6) *Dechallenge*: Did the adverse event diminish as would be expected if the vaccine caused the event? . . .[129] [This feature rarely contributes useful information.[130]]

7) *Rechallenge*: Was the vaccine readministered? If so, did the adverse event recur?[131] [They note that this will often have "a major impact on the causality assessment."[132]]

Moreover, the IOM committee concluded that

[I]n the absence of epidemiologic studies favoring acceptance of a causal relation, individual case reports and case series were relied upon, provided that the nature and timing of the adverse event following vaccine administration

---

[128] "Defeasible criteria" are features of a reasoning process that a scientist might follow, and if the features are present, he/she will likely arrive at a correct causal conclusion. However, these criteria are *defeasible*, that is, they do not guarantee, or are not sufficient for, a correct outcome. A scientist might make a mistake, ignore some important background information, and so on, even though he/she was formally following all the steps that one should in coming to a conclusion about causation. I owe this point to my colleague Peter Graham.

[129] Institute of Medicine, *Childhood Vaccines*, 23–24.

[130] Institute of Medicine, *Childhood Vaccines*, 26.

[131] Institute of Medicine, *Childhood Vaccines*, 26.

[132] Institute of Medicine, *Childhood Vaccines*, 26.

and the absence of likely alternative etiologic candidates were such that a *reasonable certainty of causality* could be inferred . . . from one or more case reports. The presence or absence of demonstrated biologic plausibility was also considered in weighing the overall balance of evidence for and against a causal relation."[133]

Finally, the committee concludes that the evidence

favors acceptance of a causal relation [when] the balance of evidence from one or more case reports or epidemiologic studies provides evidence for a causal relation that *outweighs* the evidence against such a relation. Demonstrated biological plausibility was considered supportive of a decision to accept a causal relation but was insufficient on its own to shift the balance of evidence from other sources . . .

[The evidence] *establishes a causal relationship* "when epidemiological studies and/or case reports provide *unequivocal evidence* for a causal relation, and biological plausibility has been demonstrated."[134]

The considerations advanced by the IOM are not unusual; other national or international bodies (such as the World Health Organization[135]) and thoughtful methodologists in the biomedical sciences have endorsed them.[136] Quite recently a second IOM report has emphasized the importance of case reports as evidence of adverse effects from dietary supplements.[137] Moreover, the importance of case reports increases when products have not been subjected to

---

[133]   Institute of Medicine, *Childhood Vaccines*, 31 (emphasis added).

[134]   Institute of Medicine, *Childhood Vaccines*, 32–33 (emphasis added).

[135]   After explaining the number of considerations it uses to guide causal assessment, the WHO gives the following summary guidelines. A causal relation is defined as "very likely/certain," when there is a "[c]linical event with a plausible time relationship to vaccine administration . . . [that] cannot be explained by concurrent disease or other drugs or chemicals." A causal relation is "probable" when there is a "clinical event with a reasonable time relationship to vaccine administration, and is unlikely to be attributed to concurrent disease or other drugs or chemicals." J.-P. Collet, N. Macdonald, N. Cashman, R. Pless, and the Advisory Committed on Causality Assessment, "Monitoring Signals for Vaccine Safety: the Assessment of Individual Adverse Event Reports by an Expert Advisory Committee," *Bulletin of the World Health Organization* 78 (2000): 181.

[136]   Hutchinson and Lane argue that a causality assessment must utilize "any fact, theory or opinion that can affect an evaluator's belief that drug D caused an adverse event E {especially including" all the background information such as theories from the basic sciences, data from laboratory experiments and clinical experience, as well as epidemiological data about the relative incidence of events of type E when D is and is not administered [to patients similar to the patient in question]},

[compare] how much more (or less) compatible the findings are with drug vs. non-drug causation [what they call "etiologic balancing," [or one might call "ruling out alternative explanations"], and [place] no "*a priori* constraints" on the effects of various factors or pieces of information on a scientist's "degree of belief."

Hutchinson and Lane, "Standardized Methods of Causality Assessment," 10–11. See also a related quite thoughtful article, Michael S. Kramer and David A. Lane, "Causal Propositions in Clinical Research and Practice," *Journal of Clinical Epidemiology* 45 (1992): 639–649.

[137]   Institute of Medicine and National Research Council, *Dietary Supplements*, 130.

premarket testing since important information that could have been generated in such testing is absent.[138]

Different considerations were relied on in examples (1)–(5) above to assist in revealing causality – sometimes one was more important, sometimes another. The particular timing illustrated in example (3) can be important. The repeated GBS reactions following tetanus shots in example (2) and the repeated contraction of hepatitis following halothane exposure in example (a) constitute a kind of accidental rechallenge. Many of these features correspond to recommendations in a recent IOM report. For example, they suggest that "a temporal relationship between medical product and adverse event, positive dechallenge, and rechallenge can make individual reports conclusive as to product-event association."[139]

Principles of Reasoning Underlying Causal *Inference*

The IOM's, WHO's, and methodologists' considerations, should be sufficiently persuasive for accepting causal judgments based on singular or a small number of events, because such reasoning is widely accepted and utilized in the scientific and medical community.[140] However, we can strengthen the argument here and add to the persuasiveness of the analysis of case reports by anchoring both to a deeper form of inference that is operative in these cases – *inference to the best explanation* (introduced in Chapter 3). That is, the considerations scientific methodologists utilize to infer causation in case reports are simply those implicit in inference to the best explanation, diagnostic inference, or nondeductive inference. This form of reasoning is widely utilized: by consensus scientific bodies, including the IOM and WHO, by methodologists, by physicians in differentially diagnosing diseases from symptoms, and by physicians diagnosing the causes of disease (some call this "diagnostic etiology" – the search for causes of disease), and by fire, airplane, and shuttle accident investigators. It is widely (universally) endorsed across many fields and accounts for the particular characteristics of causal inferences to which methodologists and others call attention in good case studies. In short, it is also the foundation of virtually all scientific inferences.

Recall that inferences to conclusions are of two kinds: deductive and nondeductive. The defining feature of valid deductive inferences, typical of mathematics and formal logic, is that the conclusion is "guaranteed" logically or semantically by the premises: if the premises are true and the argument is *valid*,

---

[138] Institute of Medicine and National Research Council, *Dietary Supplements*, 131–134.

[139] Institute of Medicine and National Research Council, *Dietary Supplements*, 132 (citing R. Temple, "Meta-analysis and Epidemiologic Studies in Drug Development and Postmarketing Surveillance," *Journal of the American Medical Association* 281 (1979): 841–844).

[140] Moreover, in another venue the National Transportation Safety Board usually has only case studies, single accidents, by which to evaluate the cause of airplane accidents.

the conclusion must be true.[141] There is, thus, a "logically tight" relationship between premises and conclusions.

By contrast, nondeductive inferences are simply those whose conclusions are supported but *not guaranteed* by their premises. Even if the premises are true, the nondeductive link between premises and conclusions will have varying degrees of strength, unlike a deductive argument. In nondeductive arguments if the premises are true, they may offer much to little (or no) support for the conclusion in question.[142] Moreover, the given premises will provide support for different possible conclusions (or as the literature puts it, support different *explanations*). The task, then, in evaluating such inferences is to determine which conclusion is the most plausible (or best supported) given the premises or which explanation best accounts for the evidence.

How does one *infer* the best explanation of an event? Gilbert Harman sketched the generic inferential process, but some elaboration is needed.

> In making this inference one infers, from the fact that a certain hypothesis would explain the evidence to the truth of that hypothesis. In general, there will be several hypotheses, which might explain the evidence, so one must be able to reject all such alternative hypotheses before one is warranted in making the inference. Thus, one infers, from the premise that a given hypothesis would provide a "better" explanation for the evidence than would any other hypothesis, to the conclusion that the given hypothesis is true.[143]

Providing a philosophic account of causal explanation is quite difficult on its own terms. There are different philosophic views about the correct approach to causal inferences – some suggest the idea of making inferences to the best explanation,[144] some are Bayesians,[145] and so on. There is no need to choose between them; my modest aim is to provide some understanding of how to assess scientific inferences in the law and some of the major steps, common to the different approaches, in coming to conclusions about the causal effects of exposures to substances. I seek to provide a sufficiently accurate overview of nondeductive scientific reasoning to provide a characterization of such inferences, and then

---

[141] Larry Wright, *Practical Reasoning* (San Diego: Harcourt Brace Jovanovich, 1989), 38–46.

[142] Wright, *Practical Reasoning*, 48–54.

[143] Harman, "The Inference to the Best Explanation," 89.

[144] Harman, "The Inference to the Best Explanation," 89–90, and Wright, *Critical Thinking: An Introduction to Analytical Reading and Reasoning* (New York: Oxford University Press, 2001), 206–217. Thagard adopts much of this view, indicating that scientists "can infer that the factor causes the disease if this hypothesis is part of the best explanation of the full range of evidence." . . . [and that the factor that is identified as causing] "the disease must be a better explanation of the correlation between the factor and the disease than the assertion that some other cause is responsible for both the factor and the disease" (Thagard, *How Scientists Explain Disease*, 129).

[145] Brian Skyrms, *Choice and Chance: An Introduction to Inductive Logic* (Belmont, CA: Dickenson Publishing Company, Inc., 1966).

in later chapters use this to contrast with how courts have reviewed experts' reasoning in coming to causal conclusions about toxicity.

A typical first step in reasoning about the causes of disease is an observation of something to be explained. We could think of this as a correlation or association between some exposure or condition and a disease. Once such correlations have been observed, they invite explanation, if they are sufficiently interesting, or perhaps alarming.[146] In the case of ulcers, researchers noticed the greater frequency of the bacteria *Helicobacter pylori* in patients who had peptic ulcers than in those who did not. Once a correlation has been noticed, two important questions are "Does the observed correlation have a causal explanation?" and "What is it?" A related question in the law is, "If there is a causal explanation for an observed association, is it one for which a responsible party should be held accountable?"

Second, in trying to understand casual relationships a researcher needs to consider a sufficiently complete list of plausible explanations to account for the evidence. This is one of the "most basic, . . . least understood" and difficult steps in non-deductive inferences.[147] Philosophers who endorse making inferences to the best explanation would emphasize finding a list of reasonable or plausible explanations to try to account for the phenomena, and would argue that this is based on scientists' experience, expertise, background knowledge, and other evidence of the effects. More Bayesian-oriented philosophers would, as Skyrms puts it, try to ascertain

> what factors are likely to be relevant to the conditioned property in which we are interested [the thing to be explained]; there must be some way of setting up a list of *reasonable length* of possible conditioning properties which probably contains the necessary or sufficient conditions being sought. The only way to do this is to apply inductive logic to previously acquired body of evidence.[148]

(Conditioning properties on Skyrms's view are those that produce a causal effect.[149]) Recall, for example, that in identifying vinyl chloride monomer as the cause of angiosarcoma of the liver scientists had a very short list of possible causes of this rare disease – excessive alcohol usage, arsenic compounds, thorium dioxide and, of course, a possible new cause, exposure to vinyl chloride monomer in the workplace.[150] Their list of possible explanations was

---

[146] As Wright notes, the mere fact that there are correlations between two things often provides something to be explained (Wright, *Practical Reasoning*, 154).

[147] Skyrms, *Choice and Chance*, 107.

[148] Skyrms, *Choice and Chance*, 107. Skyrms's account of "conditioning properties" may in fact be somewhat wider than "possible explanations" endorsed by the other view, but this is not germane to our discussion (I owe this point to Larry Wright).

[149] Skyrms, *Choice and Chance*, 81–87.

[150] Clayson, *Toxicological Carcinogenesis*, 11–12.

fortuitously short, as often the list of possible causes of an adverse condition might be much longer.

Third, scientists would then rank the list of rival explanations according to their plausibility based on the evidence available at the time. Such evidence would include both evidence collected at the time of the investigation and background knowledge about the subject being studied. "Plausibility rankings" refers to "the list of rival explanations [to explain what is going on] in the order of their plausibility."[151] Thus, "[w]hen we judge the [explanatory] rivals [of nondeductive arguments] to be more or less plausible, we are estimating how well or badly they explain what happened, or what is going on, given what we know about it."[152] Such plausibility and associated strength judgments have many degrees of gradation or many degrees of strength.[153]

Fourth, a scientist would use the initial plausibility rankings to try to discern what *other evidence* might be available that would distinguish between the explanations – to separate more plausible from less plausible explanations – and seek it out. That is, she would identify research, typically in the form of tests, studies or background information that could assist the search, help discriminate between different explanations and then look up the data or conduct the studies when that was appropriate and feasible. Of course, this may be easier said than done. Sometimes experiments cannot be conducted, studies available may not directly address needed issues and disease processes can be quite complex.[154]

Fifth, methodologists, regardless of their views about issues in philosophy of science, agree that *all relevant* information bearing on possible explanations must be considered in drawing a conclusion about which explanation or conditioning property is most likely.[155] "Relevant information" is information that has any impact on the probability of a scientist's conclusions, the plausibility

---

[151] Wright, *Practical Reasoning*, 101.
[152] Wright, *Practical Reasoning*, 107.
[153] Wright, *Practical Reasoning*, 47. Individuals can develop skills in ranking the different conclusions from the premises based on their *plausibility*. Such skills are quite important for scientists and the explanations they consider within their fields. Courts need to recognize the importance of the implicit skill in recognizing and utilizing scientific inferences to the best explanation.
[154] Thagard, *How Scientists Explain Disease*, 131.
[155] See, for example, Thagard, *How Scientists Explain Disease*, 129; Skyrms, *Choice and Chance*, 107; Hutchinson and Lane, "Standardized Methods of Causality Assessment," 10; and Jerome P. Kassirer and Joe S. Cecil, "Inconsistency in Evidentiary Standards for Medical Testimony: Disorder in the Courts," *Journal of the American Medical Association* 288, 11 (13 September 2002): 1382–1387, esp. 1386, for writers from different methodological perspectives who agree on this point. Hutchinson and Lane put this point especially strongly, "A causality assessment method must respect Fisher's fundamental rule of uncertain inference – *never throw information away*. That is, any fact, theory or opinion that can affect an evaluator's belief that [a particular exposure] caused an adverse event E must be incorporable by the method into the 'state of information' on which the assessment is based" ("Standardized Methods of Causality Assessment," 10).

of explanations or conditioning properties.[156] Relevance judgments may not always be without controversy, but the standard for what constitutes "relevant" information is quite minimal, since typically *any* information that can effect a scientist's belief, ranking of possible explanations, probability of conditioning properties or conclusions should be included. (Importantly, legal conceptions of "relevant" evidence appear to be identical to relevant evidence in scientific reasoning.[157])

What is or should be less controversial for legal purposes is that what constitutes *scientifically relevant information or data* for drawing a scientific conclusion is a matter of *scientific judgment*. That is, scientists are the arbiters of what constitutes relevant evidence. This is not to say that the judgment that goes into this assessment is totally subjective or that it can be idiosyncratic. It also recognizes that *scientists* may differ about relevance judgments. However, in many instances there will be widespread agreement between scientists about what constitutes scientifically relevant data. Moreover, even in cases in which conclusions may be controversial, what constitutes relevant data may be less controversial than the conclusions drawn from the data. In some highly contested instances there may be scientific disagreement about relevance, but it would be a *scientific disagreement*. However, even if scientists agree that evidence is relevant to the judgment, they may still disagree about the weight to attach to it.

The scientific relevance of particular kinds of studies has become an issue in the law because some judges appear to have excluded individual pieces of evidence as insufficiently *scientifically* relevant to an expert's inferences in question, when they were clearly relevant. There might have been disagreements about how much *weight* or *ultimate value* a particular piece of evidence can contribute to an inference, but that is a different, more complicated, and much more controversial issue.[158] This is something that courts have found difficult. Consider what a physician and legal scholar note on this point:

> [C]ourts tend to assess separately the reliability of each component rather than assessing the reliability of the *"totality of the evidence"* including all *relevant clinical factors. In doing so, courts fail to take into account the complex inferential process that lies at the heart of clinical medical reasoning.*[159]

156 See for example, Wright, *Practical Reasoning*, 104, and Wright, *Critical Thinking*, 206–217.
157 *McCormick on Evidence*, 541–542, and *The Federal Rules of Evidence*, section 401 ("evidence having any tendency to make the existence of any fact that is of consequence to the determination of the action more probable or less probable than it would be without the evidence").
158 Two such examples are the neonatal mice studies suggesting that PCBs are cancer promoters utilized in *General Elec. Co. v. Joiner* and the rat studies in *Allen v. Pennsylvania Engineering* suggesting that ethylene oxide can cause cancer.
159 Kassirer and Cecil, "Inconsistency in Evidentiary Standards," 1386 (emphasis added).

They might have added that this inferential process for which they argue applies to *all scientific reasoning.*

Sixth, the search for causal understanding then focuses on how much more probable an effect is with a cause or conditioning property than without that cause or conditioning property.[160] For example, was it more plausible that employees in the polyvinyl chloride plants contracted their liver cancer from exposure to thorium oxide or alcohol consumption or from exposure to vinyl chloride monomer? Was it more plausible that the anesthesiologist in case study (1) contracted his hepatitis just by accident, from exposure to halothane, or from some other exposure or condition? The Institute of Medicine concluded that it was highly certain that he contracted it from exposure to halothane. Whether the results of an epidemiological study "reveal a causal relation requires one to consider alternative explanations of the observed association, such as chance, bias in the design of the study and confounding alternative causes" (well-known alternative explanations that need to be ruled out) as well as more substantive explanations.[161]

In pursuit of a best explanation, one would seek evidence that would *modify the plausibility "gap"* between the highest ranked explanation and the next highest ranked one. That is, during one's investigation the initially top-ranked explanation may gain in strength and plausibility, or it may lose strength, and, thus, the gap between it and other possible explanations would narrow, which shows that its strength and plausibility compared with rival explanations is weakening (or the others have risen in plausibility). On Wright's view, a scientist does not so much *reject* all other explanations (as Harman argued), but one finds evidence or relies on background knowledge that permits one to judge that one explanation is more or less plausible than others. If additional evidence or background knowledge is quite persuasive, then one might even *reject* all other hypotheses in favor of one supported by the bulk of the evidence and background knowledge.[162] Of course, if two hypotheses are approximately equally plausible, there might be no "best" explanation, but two equally plausible rival explanations. In other cases, the plausibility of a hypothesis might be so great compared with the others that it clearly stands out as highly probable.[163]

---

160 Thagard, *How Scientists Explain Disease*, 102.
161 Thagard, *How Scientists Explain Disease*, 104.
162 Harman, "The Inference to the Best Explanation," 89–90, appears to be thinking of clear cases in which one explanation is so superior to all others that one can properly be said to *reject* them. One explanation can be better than another without rejecting the second.
163 Wright, *Critical Thinking*, 206–217. The better the quality and quantity of evidence for the highest ranked explanation compared with the quality and quantity of evidence for the next ranked explanation, the greater the plausibility gap between the two. When the evidence becomes quite compelling, one might properly "reject" the alternative explanations as so

Although there are different theoretical accounts of the above reasoning process just reviewed and its proper form, the overall strategy in the search for explanations is broadly similar. And, it is widely endorsed by epidemiologists,[164] toxicologists, methodologists inferring causes from well-analyzed case studies,[165] governmental scientists assessing risks, investigators seeking to explain airplane or space shuttle accidents, and many other technical experts.

Paul Thagard points to an additional desirable feature of medical or biological causal inference, namely, finding an appropriate *mechanism* or "mode of action" (to use a term from toxicology). Finding such mechanisms, he argues, can assist in explaining diseases, identifying causes and suggesting treatments.[166] However, he also notes that even though "[r]easoning about mechanisms can contribute to causal inference,... it is *not necessary* for such inference."[167] Especially "in less well-understood domains, correlations and the consideration of alternative causes can get causal knowledge started in the absence of much comprehension of mechanisms."[168]

This cautionary note about disease mechanisms is important because, although mechanisms of action can importantly assist the diagnosis of disease, and they likely will become increasingly important in the future,[169] the literature suggests that at present they tend to be rare. Sometimes for scientists to identify the mechanisms of disease can take decades if not far longer, as it did with the mechanisms of scurvy.[170] For example, understanding the mechanisms by which aspirin reduces pain and inflammation may not add to the *certainty* that it has this effect, but it likely would deepen scientific *understanding* of that substance and its properties.[171] The point is

lacking in plausibility that they are no longer in the running. This has obviously occurred for explanations about the force of gravity, the explanation of scurvy, and many other well-established results in science. Haack claims that Watson and Crick's explanation for the double-helix structure of DNA, despite the seeming weakness of individual pieces of evidence, was "the only entry that fits." (Haack, "An Epistemologist in the Bramble-bush," 217–237.)

164 Hill, "The Environment and Disease," 15–24. See also, Douglas Weed, "Underdetermination and Incommensurability in Contemporary Epidemiology," *Kennedy Institute of Ethics Journal* 7 (1997): 107–114.

165 See, for example, Hutchinson and Lane, "Standardized Methods of Causality Assessment," 12.

166 Thagard, *How Scientists Explain Disease*, 107.

167 Thagard, *How Scientists Explain Disease*, 109 (emphasis added); see also 112, 120, 124, 132.

168 Thagard, *How Scientists Explain Disease*, 109.

169 Carbone et al., "Modern Criteria," 5519.

170 Thagard, *How Scientists Explain Disease*, 120 (taking from about 1498 to the twentieth century to understand the mechanism of scurvy).

171 In addition, Larry Wright (personal communication) suggests that mechanistic understanding may be much more useful when we are not sure about the causal properties of a substance than when we are quite certain. For example, we are certain about the relationship between

that scientists in many cases can understand that there is an effect without fully understanding the mechanism by which it is produced.

Finally, for some scientific research there is a *social side* to the search for causation; this is especially true in medicine. Although consensus eventually develops in many other fields of science, it appears more haphazard than in medicine where conferences are explicitly organized to serve the *shared* goal of finding effective treatments as a result of understanding causes. Such conferences contribute to the "reliability, fecundity [conveying results to a large number of practitioners] and practical benefit of medical beliefs."[172]

Some commentators on *Daubert*, seeming to echo Thagard's point, have come close to suggesting that judges should rely upon consensus scientific committees for whether an expert's view is "scientifically valid."[173] This would be a mistake in the law. It would erect an extremely high barrier if plaintiffs had to satisfy it for admissibility, especially in hotly contested areas on the frontiers of science in which tort litigation arises. There would be no shared goals as there are in medicine; committed opponents would likely resist consensus. And, it would likely take a long time for consensus to develop. Meanwhile plaintiffs would likely go uncompensated and suffer with diseases or die. Moreover, if there were a consensus on a particular scientific issue at law, there likely would be little or no need for a trial on the scientific issues.

One can illustrate the above points about nondeductive reasoning with a mundane case of explaining what happened to Joe Smith in the Atlantic Ocean. If we know that Joe left the east coast of the United States in a rowboat to cross the Atlantic Ocean on a course for Europe, that a week later a storm intersected his course, and that a few days later his boat was found, empty, near that point of intersection, these premises may suggest several different conclusions (or alternatively several different explanations). He might have fallen out of his boat and swum hundreds of miles to shore. He might still be treading water. He might have drowned. He might have been a spy and rendezvoused with a Soviet submarine. A passing ship could have rescued him. He might have been taken on board an alien spaceship and is now living on another planet. Martians might have beamed him into outer space.[174]

In trying to explain Joe's fate one can rank the possible explanations of his disappearance by their plausibility. However, one may not have much confidence in any one explanation (conclusion), except for ruling out the most

---

drinking alcohol and poor mental judgment by an agent, but likely not the mechanism by which this occurs.

172 Thagard, *How Scientists Explain Disease*, 198. (For the importance of social processes in shaping causal knowledge in medicine, see generally Thagard, *How Scientists Explain Disease*, 167–198.)

173 Kenneth R. Foster and Peter W. Huber, *Judging Science: Scientific Knowledge and the Federal Court* (Cambridge, MA, and London: MIT Press, 1997), 241–245.

174 Example from Wright, *Critical Thinking*, 102–103.

outrageous ones, unless there is further evidence to support a particular conclusion. The available evidence might support several different conclusions
about equally well or badly.

In the dimethylnitrosamine poisoning case (example (4)), the explanation
that dimethylnitrosamine was the cause of liver damage and death, not only rose
to the top of the plausibility rankings, but in the end it was so far above all the
others that it was presumably established *beyond a reasonable doubt*, providing
much of the factual foundation for a criminal prosecution. In example (2),
the patient's GBS following injection of tetanus shots was so consistent and so
related to receipt of each of three tetanus shots that the explanation that tetanus
toxoid–caused GBS was much more probable than any alternative explanation.

The strength of scientific inferences depends on both the truth of the evidentiary claims in the premises and the *cumulative support* the premises offer for
the conclusions in question. Yet another name for these arguments is "*weight-
of-the-evidence*" arguments. This is a term from both scientific and regulatory
contexts.[175] In regulatory science, for example, researchers might be concerned
whether a substance is a human carcinogen. In such circumstances scientists
consider which rival conclusions the *weight of the available evidence better supports*: Is the substance a human carcinogen, is it is a probable human carcinogen,
is the evidence so equivocal that one cannot decide, or is it not a human carcinogen at all? The implicit question to be addressed is whether the weight of
the available scientific evidence better supports the claim that a substance is
likely to cause cancer or to support some other claim.[176] In short, scientists
must integrate the relevant evidence to infer conclusions.

Integrating Evidence

In order to come to conclusions about a substance's toxicity, good scientific
practice dictates that scientists consider human evidence, if it is available, evidence from experimental animals, structure-activity evidence, mechanistic evidence, and so on to come to a conclusion about what the overall weight of the
evidence shows about a substance. Often the metaphor of fitting the pieces of
a puzzle together is used to describe this process.[177]

At the International Agency for Research on Cancer (IARC), for example, the scientific committees explicitly go through a stepwise process. The

---

[175] For example, IARC researchers note that for the conclusions of a consensus scientific committee "the final overall evaluation [of evidence that a substance is carcinogenic to humans]
is a matter of scientific judgment, reflecting the *weight of the evidence* derived from studies in humans, studies in experimental animals and mechanistic and other relevant data."
Cogliano et al., "Science and Practice," 1272 (emphasis added).

[176] For a discussion of the weight of the evidence procedure in regulation, see the U.S. Environmental Protection Agency, "Proposed Guidelines for Carcinogen Risk Assessment," *Federal
Register* 61, 79 (April 23, 1996), section 2.6, 17960–18011.

[177] Haack, "Trial and Error," S70, and Margaret A. Berger, "What Has a Decade of *Daubert*
Wrought?" *American Journal of Public Health, Supplement 1* 95 (2005): S59–S65, esp. S61.

scientists consider any evidence that a substance causes cancer in humans and any evidence that it causes cancer in animal studies. These lines of evidence are then combined to provide a default evaluation of the substance's likelihood of causing cancer in humans. The committee then considers mechanistic and other kinds of evidence to "determine whether the default evaluation should be modified."[178] The current director of that program gives this gloss on final judgment.

> The final overall evaluation is a matter of *scientific judgment*, reflecting the weight of the evidence derived from studies in humans, studies in experimental animals, and mechanistic and other relevant data.[179] (emphasis added)

In a group meeting such as this, although consensus of all members of the committee is sought, sometimes the overall evaluation must be decided by majority vote.[180] A distinguished group of cancer researchers recommends similar integrative approaches to evidence, but, because they are not recommending approaches for an institution, their recommendations are more informal.[181]

The Institute of Medicine and National Research Council articulate similar guidelines for integrating evidence to assess the adverse effects of dietary supplements. They point out that individual pieces of evidence can be "weak" or "strong." Also, evidence is of "different types," including animal, human case reports, structure-activity, mechanistic, and the like. After describing different lines of evidence (like those considered in this chapter), they then provide several examples to illustrate the integration of different lines of scientifically relevant evidence to assist scientists or committees in coming to an overall evaluation of risks or harms from dietary supplements. They note that

> summing or synthesizing data addressing different linkages [between kinds of data] forms a more complete causal evidence model and can provide the biological plausibility needed to establish the association between a dietary supplement and an adverse event. . . . [Even though] a single category of data supporting a causal evidence model is incomplete or weak, precluding firm conclusions, [b]y linking data from more than one category, such as human and animal data, causal models create a more complete picture of the data and provide a more complete understanding of the relationship between biological effects and potentially adverse health outcomes.[182]

Such recommendations for integrating evidence are not unusual; quite the contrary, they are routine. For another more theoretical example, consider a

---

178 Cogliano et al., "Science and Practice," 1272.
179 Cogliano et al., "Science and Practice," 1272.
180 Cogliano et al., "Science and Practice," 1272.
181 Carbone et al., "Modern Criteria," 5519.
182 Institute of Medicine and National Research Council, *Dietary Supplements*, 262. (I describe two of their models in Chapter 7.)

basic discovery in science resulting from an inference that integrates disparate pieces of evidence.

> Chargaff's discovery that there are approximate regularities in the relative proportions of adenine and thymine, guanine and cytosine in DNA is hardly, by itself, strong evidence that DNA is a double-helical, backbone-out macro-molecule with like-with-unlike base pairs; Franklin's X-ray photographs of the B form of DNA are hardly, by themselves, strong evidence that DNA is a double-helical, backbone-out macro-molecule with like-with-unlike base pairs. That the tetranucleotide hypothesis is false is hardly, by itself, strong evidence that DNA is a double-helical, backbone-out macromolecule with like-with-unlike base pairs, and so on. But put all these pieces of evidence together, and the double-helical, backbone-out, like-with-unlike base pairs, structure of DNA is very well warranted (in fact, the only entry that fits).[183]

This esoteric but fundamental discovery of the structure of DNA is likely much more difficult than inferring whether an exposure to a substance has made a causal contribution to disease. Yet, it points to the necessity for scientists, whether in the courtroom or laboratory, to piece together in a *scientifically plausible* way *relevant evidence* to understand substantive claims.

Scientists, whether as individuals or as members of scientific committees, must integrate different lines of relevant evidence to come to conclusions about the toxicity of substances. Different lines or kinds of evidence may play a greater or lesser role in supporting a toxicity judgment, *depending upon what other evidence may be available in a particular case.* A distinguished group of cancer researchers has argued that

> There should be no [hierarchy of state-of-the-art approaches for making tox-icity decisions]. Epidemiology, animal, tissue culture and molecular pathol-ogy should be seen as integrating evidences in the determination of human carcinogenicity.[184]

Moreover, the mere fact that one piece of evidence does not strongly support a conclusion does not imply that all the evidence taken together fails to support it (or to provide some support for the conclusion, even if it is not the strongest argument). Or, to put this point more positively, a particular piece of evidence might be flawed, but the total weight of the evidence may still more probably

---

[183]   Susan Haack, "An Epistemologist in the Bramble-Bush: At the Supreme Court with Mr. Joiner," *Journal of Health Politics, Policy and Law* 26 (2001): 217–237.

[184]   Carbone et al., "Modern Criteria," 5522. See also the Institute of Medicine and National Research Council, *Dietary Supplements*, 254. ("It is also not appropriate to develop a hier-archical approach to considering the different types of data – human data, animal data, *in vitro* data or information about related substances – for various reasons. In part, such an approach is not feasible because of limitations in the quality of the data and what different types of studies can reveal, but these limitations can be overcome with other types of data.")

than not support the conclusion in question. The National Research Council and Institute of Medicine put the point as follows:

> Available evidence from each category of data, by itself may be insufficient to indicate concern [from dietary supplements], but when a pattern of mechanistically related adverse effects is observed across two or more categories in a consistent manner, this can establish biological plausibility and warrant heightened concern for potential harmful effects in humans.[185]

(The language is about "concern" not "causation" because of the committee's particular issues and the legal framework within which their recommendations are considered.) For example, molecular evidence by itself often may not be greatly supportive of causation (but in some cases it can be). However, it might be especially helpful for toxicological judgments in combination with animal studies, but not human studies. To illustrate: scientists used molecular pathological evidence to determine that viral infections could cause human cervical cancer five to seven years earlier than epidemiological studies established the relationship.[186] In other circumstances, if there are very good human studies available (this tends to be rare), molecular data might add substantially to understanding, but not contribute a great deal of certainty to the causal conclusion.

In toxic tort cases, there are usually at least two, and possibly more conclusions that litigants may claim are supported by the totality of the evidence. Plaintiffs typically claim that exposure to defendants' substance, such as asbestos or radiation, caused or contributed to plaintiffs' injuries, for example, lung cancer, whereas defendants will claim that *something else*, such as smoking, genetic predisposition, unknown antecedents, and so on caused plaintiff's injuries. Thus, the large issue for a jury is the comparison of two or more explanations: is the explanation that defendant's action contributed to plaintiff's harm more probable than the explanation that defendant's action did not contribute to plaintiff's harm?

In Chapter 3, I noted that the *Joiner* Court struggled with plaintiffs' weight of the evidence reasoning. It should now be clear that the proper procedure for reviewing nondeductive arguments, as Justice Stevens argued in his Joiner dissent, is to evaluate whether all the scientific evidence, taken together, supports the expert's inference in question, and whether the support is sufficiently strong and contains the right kind of scientific evidence to comply with the *Daubert* mandate that the expert's testimony is more likely than not "reliable." If a judge is permitted to evaluate whether each piece of evidence supports the conclusion and to reject the evidence if it does not, and do this for each piece of evidence without considering the evidence as a whole, then few or

---

[185]   Institute of Medicine and National Research Council, *Dietary Supplements*, 255–256.
[186]   Carbone et al., "Modern Criteria," 5519.

no scientific arguments to conclusions about general causation or about harm to a particular plaintiff are going to survive scrutiny. It is a simple mistake of scientific reasoning to assess nondeductive arguments in this way.

Thus, the proper procedure for reviewing nondeductive arguments is for a court to determine whether an expert in assembling and integrating *all* the scientifically relevant evidence, taken together, is engaged in reasoning that is scientifically reliable.[187] And is the support that the expert utilizes sufficiently strong and does it contain the right kind of scientific evidence to constitute a reasonable and defensible scientific inference? A proper comparison in such instances would be whether the particular pattern of evidence exhibited in arguments was generally reliable or had been reliable in the past. For instance, the district court judge in *Joiner* (and the Supreme Court as well) *might* have found that the evidence *taken as a whole* was not sufficiently *reliable* to support the conclusion that Joiner's exposure to fluids containing PCBs caused or contributed to his lung cancer. That was not her view (and the Supreme Court appeared to support her), however. She addressed each piece of evidence individually and then dismissed the case because there was too great an "analytic gap" between each piece of evidence taken individually and the conclusion that PCBs had caused Joiner's lung cancer. Such a review procedure is clearly at odds with recommendations by experts on reasoning and by the scientific community.

Also in Chapter 3 I noted that courts had had some struggles with evidence "fitting" a legal case. In light of the preceding discussion one should note that while courts could be tempted, as the *Joiner* court was, to exclude evidence such as the baby mice studies as not "fitting" the case, this can easily be a mistake. Making such judgments of *scientific relevance* (the first issue of fit) requires substantive scientific expertise. Ordinarily, scientists should be accorded great deference in such judgments. Only in the most extreme circumstances should judges preclude scientists from making scientific inferences on the basis of studies they regard as scientifically relevant. A large measure of scientists' expertise consists in judging relevant from irrelevant evidence. Moreover, it is not clear that courts can properly judge the "fit" of one piece of evidence in absence of the other evidence a scientist utilizes to come to a conclusion about human harm. That is, it is not a single study but the integrated studies combined with background knowledge that support a conclusion about human harm. Courts should be extremely cautious in second-guessing scientists on whether studies on which they rely can be used to assess human harm (I consider the *Joiner* case on this issues in Chapter 7).

Causal Inferences in Epidemiology

Consider the above points about scientific inferences applied to epidemiological studies. I approached Hill's considerations as reminders that epidemiologists

---

[187] *General Elec. Co. v. Joiner*, 522 U.S at 152.

should consider in judging whether an association between exposure and disease shows a causal relationship or not. Properly understood they are, I believe, better seen as part of a larger inference to the best explanation.

Some judges, urged on by some litigants and some scientists, appear to believe that epidemiological studies are the *best* kind of evidence (and a few seem to suggest that they may be the *only* kind of evidence) for inferring that an exposure contributes to a disease or other adverse effect. Perhaps the judges who hold this view do so because they believe that epidemiological studies carry the conclusions "on their face" as it were. This would be a mistake; even epidemiological studies require nondeductive *inferences* in order to determine what they show about any causal relations between exposures and disease. Moreover, recall that a distinguished group of scientists has argued that there is "no hierarchy of evidence."[188]

Like all scientific evidence, epidemiological evidence *underdetermines* the explanation that can account for the evidence.[189] This is another way of saying that the evidence is logically insufficient to *guarantee* a particular conclusion as the premises of a valid mathematical argument might logically ensure a conclusion. Thus, researchers must make *inferences* from the data combined with background biological understanding and good judgment to draw conclusions about what they show.

The inferential strategy is "to distinguish among several alternative hypotheses, all of which are underdetermined by the evidence."[190] Douglas Weed argues this point using Hill's factors. His argument is that even if researchers use the same study and agree that Hill's factors are useful guides to assist causal inferences, the conclusion is underdetermined and the different factors need interpretation for application; for example, what does "consistency" or "biological plausibility" mean, and how should they be applied to the evidence?

Moreover, as neither the data nor the form of inference guarantee a single conclusion, such inference drawing can result in "many opportunities within the practice of causal inference for scientists to hold different opinions about which scientific values are important to the assessment of evidence."[191] One researcher might, for example, place greater emphasis on *lack of consistency* between one study and others. Another might have a different understanding of *biological plausibility* than professional peers, even though both agree that biological plausibility is an important consideration. Some of these differences *in scientific judgment* might lead to different conclusions about causation. Researchers could reasonably disagree on their interpretations of criteria that

---

[188] Carbone et al., "Modern Criteria," 5522. See also the Institute of Medicine and National Research Council, *Dietary Supplements*, 254.

[189] Willard Van Orman Quine, *Word and Object* (Cambridge, MA: MIT Press, 1960), 78.

[190] Weed, "Underdetermination," 107–114.

[191] Weed, "Underdetermination," 108.

assist in assessing whether a study shows a causal relationship, for example, strength of association, coherence, or confounding. Thus, even when competent, well-intentioned, conscientious scientists utilize *identical data* and agree on *identical generic criteria* for interpreting it, they might reasonably and *without mistake* interpret the data and criteria somewhat differently, utilize somewhat different "rules of inference" for applying the criteria, and, as a result, reach different conclusions.[192]

Weed's paper illustrates several major points. First, human data do not guarantee a single conclusion. Second, the data must be interpreted – the conclusions are not carried on the face of the study. Third, even if an epidemiologist believes that Hill's considerations can assist understanding of whether or not an association is evidence of causation, these are not sufficient by themselves to guarantee a particular conclusion. A scientist must still attempt to determine whether the data, guided by Hill's considerations and the inference rules based on them, provide *a good explanation* for a causal relationship or not. Fourth, in order to address the third point, one makes an inference to the best explanation to see what conclusions the data together with one's background knowledge and knowledge of the disease processes best supports. Finally, a fifth point emerges from the first four: scientific judgment on the part of the researcher is essential to making these inferences – there is no automatic or algorithmic procedure.

The Importance of Scientific Judgment

Implicit in scientific inference is the role of professional judgment. Inferences about causation typically rest on scientific judgment at several points. An expert reviews data that appear to bear on causal judgments, selects scientifically relevant data, weighs the importance of different kinds of data vis-à-vis one another (e.g., animal studies vs. human studies vs. short-term studies vs. structure-activity relationships vs. any case studies), utilizes the studies that in her judgment are stronger, and brings her background understanding of biology and toxicology, as well as her understanding of the phenomena, to the causal issues. She then evaluates different possible explanations in light of all the evidence and the phenomena (i.e., a disease) she wants to explain. That is, an expert integrates the scientifically relevant evidence in order to assess what it shows. Finally, expert judgment enters into an assessment of the strength of the best explanation vis-à-vis alternative explanations. As both medical and legal commentators put the point:

> In the final analysis, assessment of evidence and causal inferences depend on accumulating *all* potentially relevant evidence and making a subjective judgment about the strength of the evidence.[193]

---

[192]   Weed, "Underdetermination," 107–114.
[193]   Kassirer and Cecil, "Inconsistency in Evidentiary Standards," 1384. See also Jerome P. Kassirer, "Diagnostic Reasoning," *Annals of Internal Medicine* 110 (1989): 893–900, and Jerome

A similar point guides consensus scientific committees: "The final overall evaluation [by IARC] is a matter of scientific judgment, reflecting the weight of the evidence derived from studies in humans, studies in experimental animals and the mechanistic and other relevant data."[194] A very recent Institute of Medicine and National Research Council Report echoes this point.[195]

In short, experts' inferences about causation are permeated by considerations of professional judgment. Moreover, this fact and the nature of nondeductive arguments open up the possibility that different experts may evaluate the same evidence differently depending upon their assessment of the quality of studies, their background beliefs about the weight different kinds of evidence should have, and so on.

Courts understandably are likely to be concerned about the possibility of subjectivity in scientific inferences. Scientific judgment might seem to permit greater latitude than courts would prefer, given the reputation of science as "objective." However, they may expect too much and may underestimate the role of expert judgment in inferring causal conclusions. They might think scientific inferences are more objective than in fact they are or believe that since studies are "objective," inferences from them are similarly "objective."

The short answer to this is that after a group of scientists have studied some phenomenon for a sufficient period of time and discovered the right kinds of evidence about it, for example, the effects of benzene on human bone marrow or the effects of ozone on human lungs, they may come to some "objective" or at least quite firm conclusions about it. This is a property of groups or group judgments. However, an *individual scientist* must review the available data, previous studies, background information, her own understanding of the issues and current papers on the topic and then make an inference to the best explanation to come to a scientific conclusion. The role of judgment is essential for an individual scientist or consensus scientific committees. Group consensus and objective views over the long run arise out of the collision of professional arguments and judgments.

Consider another way to illuminate this point. Laypeople may have something of an idealized view of science and scientific judgments from textbooks. When there is a settled scientific view, for example, about the laws of mechanics or the toxicology of benzene, numerous studies will have been done and the relevant scientific community has come to a consensus, it may appear that there

---

P. Kassirer and R. I. Kopelman, *Learning Clinical Reasoning* (Baltimore, MD: Williams and Wilkins, 1991).

[194] Cogliano et al., "Science and Practice," 1272.

[195] Institute of Medicine and National Research Council, *Dietary Supplements*, 254. ("In the absence of scientific studies specifically designed to assess the safety of dietary supplement ingredients, it is not possible to apply a specific algorithmic or formulaic approach to determining safety, and *expert judgment in the interpretation of data* is likely to be important, as it is for other substances" emphasis added.)

is no or little room for scientific judgment. *Textbook science*, however, is a far cry from the state of science that is developing or even when there is a partial consensus. It is further yet from the circumstance of an expert who has to integrate studies, piece together evidence, rely on her background knowledge of what has been established in order to address whether a substance more likely than not causes adverse health effects. This is the position scientists in toxic tort cases find themselves and that judges must review. In such circumstances experts must exercise considerable judgment about evidence, its relevance, its weight, pertinent background knowledge, and the exposure circumstances of the plaintiff. When this occurs, it is likely that there will be disagreements; it is the judge's task to ensure that experts fall within a range of reasonable, respectable disagreement within the relevant field. Morever, there will probably be a range of reasonable scientific disagreements within an area until issues are fully settled.

Courts have been concerned about scientific inferences from data. Indeed the Supreme Court noted in *Joiner* that it is not enough that opinion evidence is "connected to existing data only by the *ipse dixit* of the expert."[196] I concur in this point and do not urge otherwise. A mere scientist's say so should not constitute sufficient reason to accept her reasoning from data to conclusion. However, courts need to fully recognize the myriad roles that scientific judgment play in experts' reviewing data and coming to conclusions on the basis of them. Moreover, they should not reject scientific testimony simply because it is clear that an expert has had to utilize considerable judgment in coming to conclusions. Neither should courts reject testimony because others come to different conclusions.

Even though professional judgments are central to a working scientist's conclusions, there are constraints on expert reasoning. Their views must be consistent with the body of evidence; experts are not free to come to any conclusions they want about evidence – some might be outrageous or speculative. Reasoning can be better or worse and is subject to intersubjective constraints and correction by equally well-trained peers. Scientists also need to be able to explain the data that are in need of explanation, to consider major alternative explanations of the evidence and to rule out with a sufficient degree of confidence major alternative explanations of the phenomena in question. However, the possibility of disagreements between experts cannot be avoided, simply because of the "fact of reasonable scientific disagreement," the final issue in this chapter.

Scientific Disagreement

Theoretical progress in science (and other fields) tends to occur and become consolidated when there is considerable certainty about conclusions and a

---

[196] *General Electric Company v. Joiner*, 522 U.S. at 146. "*Ipse dixit*" means "he himself said it," and is "something asserted but not proved." *Black's Law Dictionary*, 8th ed., 847.

resulting consensus has developed among researchers. However, judges and other laypeople should not forget that there can be considerable reasonable disagreement concerning scientific conclusions before some ultimate consensus on an issue is reached. Scientific disagreement is *real* and *legitimate* and also *important* to the enterprise. Yet, I want to develop the point a bit further for the law.

Disagreement is essential to the functioning of science and its development. However, in the short-run and even for a period of time scientific disagreement may delay the relevant community in coming to a consensus about what the totality of relevant studies shows. Because disagreements can so easily arise between scientists about either fundamental theoretical issues or more practical issues such as the toxicity of a substance, the disagreements can become barriers to quick resolution of disputes and to a common understanding of the issues.

David Goodstein, Vice Provost and a distinguished professor of physics at California Institute of Technology, calls attention to and embraces scientific disagreement:

> [S]cience is, above all, an adversary process. It is an arena in which ideas do battle, with observations and data the tools of combat . . . it is crucial that every idea receive the most vigorous possible advocacy, just in case it might be right. Thus, the Popperian ideal of holding one's hypothesis in a skeptical and tentative way is not merely inconsistent with reality, it would be harmful to science if it were pursued.[197]

Such disagreements are manifested at the most fundamental levels in science, about practical issues concerning the toxicity of substances and at the frontiers of the field as they are likely to be in toxic tort suits.

Scientific Disagreement about Fundamental Issues

Thomas Kuhn, the noted historian of science, speaks to disagreements concerning the choices at fundamental levels of explanation between scientific *theories*. In "Objectivity, Value Judgment and Theory Choice," Kuhn argues that scientists, trying to choose between theories to explain phenomena, resort to a number of "rules" or as he prefers to call them "values" to help guide their choice of the best theory to explain phenomena.[198] He lists five leading considerations pertinent to theory choice. First and foremost, a theory should be accurate "within its domain, that is consequences deducible from a theory should be in demonstrated agreement with the results of existing experiments and observation."[199] Second, it should be not only internally consistent, but consistent with "other currently accepted theories applicable to related aspects

197   David Goodstein, "How Science Works," in *Reference Manual on Scientific Evidence*, 74 (see also 78).
198   Thomas Kuhn, *The Essential Tension* (Chicago: University of Chicago Press, 1977), 320–339.
199   Kuhn, *The Essential Tension*, 321.

of nature."[200] Third, its scope should be broader rather than narrower, that is, its "consequences should extend far beyond the particular observations, law, or subtheories it was initially designed to explain."[201] Fourth, it should be "simple" in "bringing order to phenomena that in its absence would be individually isolated and as a set, confused."[202] And, finally, it should be fruitful of new scientific research.[203]

Such considerations, important in choosing between theories, are "imprecise" and may conflict with one another in particular cases.[204] More importantly for our purposes, Kuhn argues that scientists may attach different degrees of importance, significance, or weight to these considerations. As a result, they will disagree about whether one theory is acceptable or not compared with another theory. One scientist might find theory X more accurate than another, but with a lesser scope than Y. Others might find theory Y somewhat less accurate within a domain compared with X, but more consistent with theories and data in neighboring areas of science and judge Y the better theory. Thus, although all involved in the debate about the theories in question might agree on the list of considerations that bear on theory choice, they may still disagree about whether one theory or another is acceptable because of different weights each attaches to the considerations on which they all agree.[205] And, they all could have reasonable views within the field that are entitled to a respectful hearing.

Kuhn's essay on theory choice can help us to understand scientific disagreements more generally. Scientists coming to agreement is difficult because so many different considerations and values are in play for any one scientist, which considerations may be weighed differently by or have different significance for different researchers. He concludes:

> What I have been suggesting here is that theory choice, too, can be explained only in part by a theory which attributes the *same properties* to all the scientists who must do the choosing. Essential aspects of the process generally known as verification will be understood only by recourse to the features with respect to which *men may differ* while still remaining scientists.[206]

[200] Kuhn, *The Essential Tension*, 322.
[201] Kuhn, *The Essential Tension*, 322.
[202] Kuhn, *The Essential Tension*, 322.
[203] Kuhn, *The Essential Tension*, 322.
[204] Kuhn, *The Essential Tension*, 322.
[205] Thus, he notes that two scientists

  fully committed to the same list of criteria for choice may nevertheless reach different conclusions. Perhaps they interpret simplicity differently or have different convictions about the range of fields within which the consistency criterion must be met. Or perhaps they agree about these matters but differ about the relative weights to be accorded to these or to other criteria when several are deployed together. (Kuhn, *The Essential Tension*, 324. A similar point is made at 331.)

[206] Kuhn, *The Essential Tension*, 334.

Whereas some may see scientific disagreements as imperfections resulting from imperfect reasoners, Kuhn sees this as part of "the *essential nature* of science."[207] Individual judgment, which leads to debate and disagreement, but also ultimately to scientific advance, is critically important to the scientific enterprise.[208]

Scientific Disagreement about More Practical Issues

Kuhn's account is important for our inquiry, not because scientists involved in litigation are usually choosing between global theories to explain toxicological phenomena. Rather, the kinds of considerations pertinent to choosing between *theories* provide analogs to considerations that bear on more *practical* judgments about the toxicity of particular substances that scientists might have to render. Moreover, the structure of the choice is similar in critical respects to Kuhn's: There are different lines of evidence that typically must be integrated to come to a judgment about a substance's toxicity. Different scientists might weigh the different lines of evidence differently or they might legitimately utilize different kinds of considerations to assist their decisions. Or, as Weed argues, they might agree on the relevant studies and on considerations for interpreting them, but still disagree on ultimate conclusions. Some of these commitments may be traceable to an individual's own scientific background – epidemiologists may favor epidemiology, toxicologists may give greater weight to animal studies because they understand and work with them, and so on. Thus, scientists may well disagree about the importance or significance of each kind of evidence or other consideration, and as a consequence, there may be quite legitimate disagreements within a community of respectable, conscientious scientists about the toxicity of particular substances or whole classes of substances.

More complex scientific judgments where experts must integrate human, animal, and short-term studies pose greater challenges. For MOCA,[209] for an anti-cancer drug 1-(2-chloroethyl)-3-cyclohexyl-1-nitrosourea (CCNU),[210]

---

207   Kuhn, *The Essential Tension*, 330 (emphasis added).
208   Kuhn, *The Essential Tension*, 330.
209   MOCA is 4,4'-methylenebis(2-chloroaniline). IARC's overall evaluation is as follows: "MOCA is probably carcinogenic to humans" and "[t]here is *inadequate evidence* in humans for the carcinogenicity of 4,4'-methylenebis(2-chloroaniline) (MOCA)." See IARC, "Occupational Exposures of Hairdressers and Barbers and Personal Use of Hair Colourants; Some Hair Dyes, Cosmetic Colourants, Industrial Dyestuffs and Aromatic Amines," *Monograph Series, Supplement 57* (1993): 271. Available at: http://www-cie.iarc.fr/htdocs/indexes/vol57index.html. ("There is sufficient evidence in experimental animals for the carcinogenicity of 4,4'-methylenebis(2-chloroaniline) (MOCA).") There is a somewhat fuller presentation of this evidence in Chapter 7.
210   See IARC, *Monograph Series, Supplement 7*, 150. ("No epidemiological study of CCNU as a single agent was available to the Working Group . . . ; there is sufficient evidence in animals, and CCNU is a directly-acting, bifunctional alkylating agent. On the weight of all the evidence, CCNU is probably carcinogenic to humans.")

and for benzidine-related dyes,[211] there is inadequate evidence[212] of carcinogenicity in humans and sufficient evidence of carcinogenicity in animals. The International Agency for Research on Cancer and the National Toxicology Program classify all of these as probable human carcinogens.[213] Here, traditional human epidemiological evidence did not directly contribute much to the judgment that the substance is a likely human carcinogen. For example, the inference that MOCA is a human carcinogen is based upon integrated evidence from animal studies, chemical structure–biological activity similarity between related substances, and additional supportive evidence.

Yet some scientists, more strongly committed to wanting human evidence, might argue that MOCA is not a human carcinogen because there is as yet no *human* epidemiological evidence even though there is cellular, molecular, and quite good animal evidence. For some scientists, the absence of epidemiological studies would defeat the claim that MOCA more likely than not is capable of causing human cancer. For many others, including these consensus scientific bodies, however, the accumulated animal, cellular, molecular, structure-activity evidence would be sufficient for a conclusion that MOCA more likely than not is a human carcinogen. The small number of different kinds of evidence that bear on scientific judgments about the toxicology of substances − structure-activity relationships, animal studies, in vitro studies, mechanistic studies, human epidemiological studies, and human case reports − should not obscure the fact that scientists reviewing this data may draw somewhat different respectable conclusions from it. Just as scientists who make judgments about theory choice on the basis of a small number of criteria once disagreed even about issues we now know are settled, so can they disagree in their judgments about the toxicity of substances even though a comparatively small number of considerations bear on the issue. However, when scientists legitimately disagree, judges should not take sides, but permit both to present their arguments to court. (There will be more on this in Chapters 6 and 7.)

---

[211] See IARC, "Benzidine-Based Dyes," *Monograph Series, Supplement 7*. There is inadequate evidence for carcinogenicity to humans, but sufficient evidence for carcinogenicity to animals. However, "[b]enzidine-based dyes are structurally related to benzidine, exposure to which is causally associated with cancer in humans, and commercial material may contain small amounts of benzidine." The overall evaluation is that benzidine-related dyes are probably carcinogenic to humans.

[212] "The available studies [of carcinogenicity] are of insufficient quality, consistency or statistical power to permit a conclusion regarding the presence or absence of a causal association between exposure and cancer, or no data on cancer in humans are available." IARC, Preamble, Evaluation, *Monograph Series*.

[213] See IARC, "Overall Evaluation of Carcinogenicity to Humans," *Monograph Series*, available at: http://www-cie.iarc.fr/monoeval/crthgr02a.html; U.S. Congress, *Ninth Annual Report on Carcinogens*.

Disagreement at the Frontiers of Scientific Knowledge

The issue of disagreements is especially important in toxic tort cases when the scientific discussion in all likelihood will be "at the frontiers of scientific knowledge." For a particularly dramatic example of such disagreements consider Christina Ruden's study of twenty-nine different assessments of the carcinogenicity of trichloroethylene (TCE) conducted by consensus scientific committees. She reviewed the assessments, not by individuals, but by national or international scientific committees concerning the carcinogenicity of TCE – some committees were governmental, some private, and some nongovernmental. Six committees judged TCE negative in animals, negative in epidemiological studies, and negative for humans overall. Ten judged the substances positive in animals, but negative in epidemiological studies and negative for humans overall. The remaining thirteen judged TCE positive in animals, either negative (9) or positive (4) in humans, but posing a "non-negligible human cancer risk" overall. To a considerable extent group judgments that there was not a significant human risk tended to be earlier when TCE had been less well studied. Groups that reviewed TCE evidence later tended to find that there was a nonnegligible risk. Ruden's conclusion and final assessment is quite revealing.

About one fourth of the most cited primary carcinogenicity data (bioassays and epidemiological studies) referred to in the TCE database have been interpreted differently by different risk assessors. The main reasons for differences in the interpretations of bioassay results were different assessments of statistics and different assessments of the toxicological relevance of the results obtained.

Regarding the assessment of statistics, there were differences in the choice of statistical methods and in how statistically non-significant effects were assessed and communicated. There were furthermore examples of when a change in the interpretation of one individual primary data correlated to a change in the overall conclusions.

Regarding the assessment of toxicological relevance of the data evaluated, one example of when a risk assessor (IARC) assessed the relevance of primary data results differently than other risk assessors and differently than the authors of the original paper was presented. In this example the IARC changed their relevance assessment of the results obtained in a particular bioassay from 1987 to 1995. I.e. the IARC considered the mouse lymphomas reported in Henschler et al. (1980) to be relevant to human health risk assessment when the IARC meta-analysis of new epidemiological data indicated that TCE exposure caused an increased risk of lymphomas in humans. Hence, the interpretation of this individual primary data was changed in the light of new data. This change also correlated to a change in the overall conclusions.

Seven [groups of] risk assessors all face the same available epidemiological data. Three of them conclude that epidemiology is positive. However, these three risk assessors base their conclusions on different studies, reporting carcinogenic effects in different organs. One of them (IARC) motivates the conclusion with a meta-analysis of individually negative findings. Another motivates the conclusions by evaluating the quality of a study differently than all the other TCE risk assessors. The third makes a cautious interpretation and extrapolation of uncertain data. The other four risk assessors conclude that the TCE epidemiology is negative. Their motivations are (1) that the majority of the epidemiological data are negative, and (2) that the positive data are insufficient due to lack of consistent findings, limited statistical significance, or questionable quality. None of these four risk assessors has utilized the meta-analysis performed by the IARC, and none considers the Henschler et al. study to be conclusive.

This study provides examples of when and why risk assessors interpret toxicological data in different ways. *The scope of possible interpretations of individual primary data for risk assessment purposes only becomes apparent to the reader if he or she either has carefully studied the original primary data, or compares different possible interpretations of one and the same primary data (as made by different risk assessors). The differences in the interpretations of particular primary data, as presented by the TCE examples, may be small and seemingly insignificant. They are for instance all well within the scope of the scientifically acceptable interpretations. Yet, such seemingly subtle differences have the potential to affect the overall risk assessment conclusions.*[214]

These are not individual scientists assessing the carcinogenicity of TCE, but consensus scientific bodies. Moreover, some of the same bodies, such as the International Agency for Research on Cancer, revisited the toxicity of TCE as the evidence changed. Consequently, if, for example, one considers the latest studies (from 1995) there is somewhat more agreement that overall TCE poses carcinogenic risks to humans: two groups judge that it is not, whereas five judge that it poses a nonnegligible risk to humans.[215]

The Ruden study is quite helpful in understanding scientific disagreement on the frontiers of scientific knowledge, since consensus scientific bodies were assessing the likelihood that TCE could cause harm as the science was developing. In toxic tort cases this is particularly pertinent for "first" or "early" plaintiffs who have been exposed to a suspect toxicant. Because they might be among the first persons affected by a toxicant, there may be a limited scientific record to assist their case. Thus, there may be disagreements concerning the science. However, recall Ruden's point that the different committee judgments over a twenty-four-year period were "all well within the scope of the scientifically acceptable interpretations." This illustrates the point of the next section – the "fact of reasonable scientific disagreement." Moreover, recall her point that it is difficult to assess the quality of studies without going into their details,

[214] Christina Ruden, "Interpretations of Primary Carcinogenicity Data in 29 Trichloroethylene Risk Assessments," *Toxicology* 169 (2001): 209–225, esp. 223 (emphasis added).
[215] Ruden, "Interpretations of Primary Carcinogenicity Data," 212.

which often exhibit "seemingly subtle differences." Rothman and Greenland have reinforced this point: An assessment of a scientific study

> is not one that can be done easily by someone who lacks the skills and training of a scientist familiar with the subject and the scientific methods that were employed. Neither can it be applied readily by judges in court, nor by scientists who either lack the requisite knowledge or who do not take the time to penetrate the work.[216]

In addition to the above, plaintiffs may also face time limits within which they must file a complaint alleging injury (statutes of limitation). In such instances they risk being squeezed between legally mandated filing limitations and a limited scientific record (and certainly incomplete compared with an ideal set of studies).[217] When this occurs, this, too, will increase disagreements. If plaintiffs' injuries have been caused by products that have been little studied and few scientists are available to address the cause of their injuries, this increases their proof problems. There will likely be considerable skepticism on the part of other scientists that such exposures cause harm, simply because the substances will have been poorly or minimally studied.

The Fact of Reasonable Scientific Disagreement

Disagreements between respectable scientists will arise for a number of reasons: the nature of nondeductive inferences, the underdetermination of an explanation by the evidence, the complexity of evidentiary patterns experts may need to consider, and the need to cogently integrate different lines of evidence to come to conclusions. However, it is not simply *that* there will be disagreements, but these disagreements are perfectly *reasonable*, given the complex inferences that must be made. *Reasonable and legitimate disagreement* should be expected. (I borrow the idea of *reasonable disagreement* from Rawls.[218])

We have seen how easy it is for scientists to disagree concerning fundamental theories, epidemiological studies, and more practical judgments concerning the toxicology of particular substances. Moreover, there are often disagreements on scientific advisory panels about how well the evidence supports a toxicity

---

216 Rothman and Greenland, "Causation and Causal Inference in Epidemiology," S150.

217 This point was illustrated, but in reverse, in the Bendectin litigation. Some early litigation was successful based on a limited scientific record suggesting Bendectin caused birth defects. Now, however, based on a much more mature scientific record most commentators seem convinced that Bendectin does not sufficiently increase human birth defects to a level that warrants compensation. The success of the defense in later litigation sometimes might increase as it did in the Bendectin cases, but it could also be less successful, if more evidence were found in support of adverse effects. However, the longer the time lag between injury and the development of scientific evidence needed for admissibility, the more plaintiffs risk having their cases precluded because of statutes of limitation. The general point is that if the scientific record changes, the legal results may also change; this may or may not assist plaintiffs depending on the evidence and statutes of limitations.

218 John Rawls, *Political Liberalism* (Cambridge, MA: Harvard University Press, 1993), 54–58.

conclusion about a substance. Such panels usually must *vote* in order to come to conclusions.[219] It is even easier for legitimate disagreements to arise when complex inferences must be drawn based on the varieties of evidence and various considerations that scientists typically must assemble in coming to conclusions. When evidence is conflicting and complex, it is more difficult to assess and evaluate. The relevant concepts are often vague and subject to difficult cases, which results in indeterminacy that may add to reasonable disagreements. And, an expert's judgment will not unreasonably be affected by his or her total scientific and personal experience up to the time of judgment. Finally, because of how individual scientists assess different kinds of evidence, the weight they give to it, and the background knowledge they bring to it, there is an (almost) *irreducible scientific judgment* that enters into assessing scientific evidence and inferring that a substance causes a disease. The idea of an irreducible scientific judgment is a central feature of an individual scientist's view of a phenomenon under study. When such conditions obtain for scientific experts, it is quite *reasonable* for respectable experts to disagree with one another.

In the final section of this chapter I apply some of the above results to an issue the Supreme Court has addressed and that other courts have referenced.

THE METHODOLOGY-CONCLUSION DISTINCTION

The *Daubert* decision drew a sharp distinction between the scientific *methodology and reasoning* underlying scientific testimony and the *conclusions* drawn using the data at hand and the relevant methodology.[220] In determining the admissibility of scientific evidence a trial court should only examine the reliability of the underlying methodology or reasoning used; it should not engage in an evaluation of the correctness of the conclusions reached by an expert, the admission of whose testimony is at issue.[221] This is a task that should be left to the jury weighing and evaluating the evidence.

Unfortunately, the Court also spoke to this issue in *Joiner*, contradicting its earlier conclusion in *Daubert*, noting,

> conclusions and methodology are not entirely distinct from one another. Trained experts commonly extrapolate from existing data. But nothing in either *Daubert* or the Federal Rules of Evidence requires a district court to

---

[219] National Institute of Environmental Health Sciences of the National Institutes of Health, *Assessment of Health Effects from Exposure to Power-line Frequency Electric and Magnetic Field* (Research Triangle Park, NC: The Institute, 1998); Raymond R. Neutra, Vincent DelPizzo, and Geraldine M. Lee, *An Evaluation of the Possible Risks from Electric and Magnetic Fields (EMFs) from Power Lines, Internal Wiring, Electrical Occupations, and Appliances* (Oakland: California Department of Health Services, 2002); Haack, "An Epistemologist in the Bramble-Bush," 217–237.

[220] See *Daubert v. Merrill Dow Pharmaceuticals*, 509 U.S. 579, at 592–595.

[221] See *Daubert v. Merrill Dow Pharmaceuticals*, 509 U.S. 579, at 592–595.

admit opinion evidence that is connected to existing data only by the *ipse dixit* of the expert. A court may conclude that there is simply too great an analytical gap between the data and the opinion proffered.[222]

In understanding these passages, we should recognize that there is substantial ambiguity about the idea of methodology that needs attention before addressing the issue. The term "methodology" might be applied to the scientific procedures used in designing and conducting a study. It also might apply to how one interprets the study. Or it might also apply to how a scientist makes inferences from several studies to overall conclusions about the toxicity of a product.[223] I consider only the last point, since it seems clear that this is what the Court had in mind in *Joiner*.

The Court was addressing plaintiff's experts' use of the weight-of-the-evidence methodology for conclusions about whether PCBs can cause lung cancer. Plaintiff's experts, piecing together several different kinds of data, had argued that a combination of infant mice studies, several human epidemiological studies, plaintiff's smoking history, and other evidence supported an inference that exposure to PCBs more likely than not could contribute to or promote his lung cancer.

The discussion concerning scientific reasoning can clarify some issues around the Court's claims about scientific argumentation. To fix ideas, recall the kinds of evidence that IARC used to conclude that MOCA (and some other substances) are known human carcinogens.[224] It was based on little human data, but the scientists had some good studies in animals, some chemical structure similarities, and some mutagencitiy data. From these *studies*, background knowledge about the chemicals, the kind of mutagen involved and mammalian biology, they had to *infer* whether or not exposure likely caused cancer in humans. They concluded that it does. Such an argument is not as logically tight as an argument of mathematics, but it is scientifically quite sound.

Conclusions of nondeductive arguments are logically distinct from the premises that support them and disagreement is possible. Consequently, *every* nondeductive argument will have *some gap* between premises and conclusion. We might say the gaps are *irremovable*; they will always be present. The strongest nondeductive arguments will have a logically possible "gap" as long as it is logically possible to think of an alternative conclusion for the premises. For example, it is *logically possible* that Newton's laws of gravity might only be a local phenomenon on the surface of the earth and near planetary system but inapplicable elsewhere in the universe. Thus, even very strong arguments

---

222   *Joiner v. General Electric Co.*, 118 S.Ct. 512, 519 (1997).
223   Recall from the methodologists and scientists themselves that there is no distinctive scientific method. Haack, "An Epistemologist in the Bramble-Bush," 232; Haack, "Trial and Error," S70; Rothman and Greenland, "Causation and Causal Inference in Epidemiology," S150.
224   For a more detailed presentation of the evidence on these points see Chapter 7.

will have some gap as long as another conclusion has some possibility. It's also *possible* that MOCA does not cause human cancer, but it's improbable. For some especially weak or bad arguments, there could be such a large "gap" that the conclusion is hopelessly implausible, for example, that the space shuttle Columbia's disintegration was caused by beams from Martian spaceships.

Courts should not be surprised, then, to discover a "gap" in every scientific argument; that is in their nature. But if there is always some gap, how should judges review scientific arguments? Can they review expert testimony without comparing plaintiff's conclusions with defendant's conclusions, as the original *Daubert* decision cautioned against?

First, not every nondeductive argument admits of *legitimate* critique simply because there is the possibility of a gap. Some will be quite good and strong, others weak or even implausible. (However, it is important to recognize that because there are irremovable gaps in such arguments, this provides opponents with openings to critique the arguments. They might challenge the inference or provide another explanation to account for the evidence.) Second, courts will need to consider an expert's conclusion in reviewing her testimony, but only *relationally*. That is, a judge would need to consider the *relation* between the expert's premises (or data) and conclusion, in order to evaluate the overall plausibility of her inferences. Thus, a judge would have to attempt to make some minimal assessment of the strength of her nondeductive argument to see whether it is sufficiently minimally plausible to be more likely than not "reliable" as *Daubert* requires. Or to put this point in the language of *Kumho Tire*, a judge must review the relation between a scientist's premises and her conclusion to ensure that she is not testifying "outside the range where reasonable experts would disagree" in making such inferences. (This is not an easy task (recall Ruden's point about the need to examine individual studies), but it is the job the Court assigned to trial judges.)

Thus, judges will need to consider, not an expert's conclusion in isolation or in comparison with the conclusion of experts on the other side of the case. Instead their focus should be on an expert's conclusion in relation to the premises of her own argument in order to make some sense of the plausibility of her argument to ensure that it crosses the "reliability" threshold for admissibility. There can be, of course, arguments in which the data on which experts rely so poorly support the inferences drawn that one might say they have no support at all. When this occurs it is probably better to say not that there is "too great a gap between data and the conclusions drawn from them," but, rather, that the conclusion is simply too "speculative" given the premises.[225]

---

[225] Michael J. Saks, "The Aftermath of Daubert: An Evolving Jurisprudence of Expert Evidence," *Jurimetrics Journal,* 40 (2000): 229 at 236.

The law of civil procedure suggests that courts should avoid judging the plausibility of one expert's scientific conclusion versus another's conclusion or even judging one expert's argument vis-à-vis another's in order to choose between them. These are comparisons that legally should be left to the jury (Chapter 2). A court might judge whether litigants have offered evidence to support each element of their cause of action. That is, does expert testimony and its foundation plus other information sufficiently support causal claims to create a triable issue on causation? If a court were to reject scientific testimony on the grounds that a conclusion generated by the methodologies (nondeductive inference) is counter to the conclusions of most other experts, it would appear to invade the constitutionally protected authority of a jury because it would seem to be rendering a decision based on the *weight* to accord that expert's testimony and her *credibility* on the science, two issues that constitutionally should be left to the jury. Consideration of the strength of all the proffered evidence offered by one side compared with the evidence and arguments offered by the other side is proper in the context of deciding motions for summary judgments or judgments notwithstanding the verdict, where a court is explicitly authorized to weigh the conclusions on one side versus the conclusions on the other. As we saw in Chapter 2, such comparative assessments should only result in a dismissal of a case when a reasonable jury could not find for one side or the other or when the evidence on one side so overwhelms the other side that there is not reason for a jury trial.

CONCLUSION

Having some appreciation of the basic data – human, animal, mechanistic, structure-activity, and other studies – is only the first step in understanding scientific evidence and testimony in toxic tort cases. Epidemiological studies are one kind of evidence that has received considerable discussion in the courts. As we will see in the chapters that follow, some of that discussion is correct, but some of it is mistaken. Other kinds of evidence are less well understood and have posed problems for courts: animal, molecular, and human case studies. I have tried to develop some better understanding of these. Courts will need to address this evidence better.

Deeper and more difficult issues concern the inferences that scientists must make about what integrated data show about the toxicity of substances. Nondeductive inferences are neither simple nor easy for non-experts to assess substantively. Courts must recognize that these arguments will have gaps between premises and conclusions, but the mere presence of gaps is not a sufficient reason for excluding the testimony. Moreover, in coming to conclusions about theories, epidemiological studies, case reports or the properties of particular substances, a scientist's *professional judgment* is an essential component. Because it is, reasonable experts might well disagree about what the evidence shows. Courts must make a place for this.

For all that has been said in this chapter, the reader might have the impression that scientific studies are comparatively accessible and relatively easy to obtain. This is far from true – there are a variety of pragmatic barriers to obtaining good evidence about the causal properties of substances that further complicate the use of science in the tort law. This is the subject of Chapter 5.

5

Excellent Evidence Makes Bad Law

Pragmatic Barriers to the Discovery of Harm and Fair Admissibility Decisions

The theoretical tools available to assist scientists in discovering the adverse effects of toxicants in humans are one thing. Their actual use with what is not known about substances, practical difficulties in using them, the time it takes to conduct studies, the rareness of background diseases at issue, and the adventitious exposure circumstances of torts are quite another. These and other limitations need to be appreciated in order to better understand how the utilization of science in the tort law affects the institution.

The courts in the *Daubert* litigation might not have had a realistic understanding of the kinds and quality of evidence that could be available in toxic tort litigation. The evidence in the original *Daubert* decision was particularly good and the Bendectin litigation in general had an unusual amount of high quality, readily available direct human evidence about the product.[1] Indeed, it may be one of the "best studied substances" ever.[2]

Such excellent evidence, however, can result in bad law. How could this be, since the common aphorism is that "bad evidence can make bad law"?[3] Moreover, in cases subsequent to *Daubert* courts might mistakenly believe that nearly ideal evidence is always available or easily obtainable. If they do, they are likely to demand it in other cases. Suppose litigants lack similarly good evidence in other cases. Will courts think that the lawyers who file the case or the scientists who are prepared to testify in it have not done their homework? Are they trying to fool the courts? Are they basing their litigation on "junk science"? Are they trying to keep costs down? Are they not acknowledging

---

[1]   Green, *Bendectin*, 31 2–17; Green, "Expert Witnesses," 679–8; Cranor and Eastmond, "Scientific Ignorance," 5–48. There were excellent, fairly large epidemiological studies with good exposure data and good medical records to identify any health effects of concern.

[2]   Gina Kolata, "Controversial Drug Makes a Comeback," *New York Times*, 26 Sept. 2000, F1 (quoting Dr. Anthony Scialli, Professor of Obstetrics and Gynecology at Georgetown University School of Medicine).

[3]   See Alex Berenson, "For Merck, Vioxx Paper Trail Won't Go Away," *New York Times*, August 21, 2005, for a news report on the affect of "bad evidence," namely, a paper trail indicating cover-ups and bad behavior on the part of Merck.

unfavorable evidence? I don't know. However, it becomes easy for courts to mistakenly generalize from a few cases with excellent evidence to most others where the evidence is far from the best and is not easily produced.[4] Such an assumption can lead to errors.

This chapter tries to present a more realistic, and, I hope, more accurate picture of some barriers to the discovery of harm that can easily affect the kind and amount of evidence that litigants might have available and that affect the fairness of courts' admissibility decisions. There are substantial impediments to the production of the best scientific evidence needed for tort law litigation. The practical difficulties are so great in most cases that unless courts recognize them and apply the law sensitively, the tort law risks sacrificing justice to mistaken conceptions of available evidence or to some conventions of science that can pose problems for the tort law. If the realities of providing scientific evidence and documenting toxicological claims are not recognized, fewer plaintiffs injured by exposure to toxicants will have the possibility of corrective justice.

What are some of these hindrances and the problems they pose? Many laypeople are likely to believe that some governmental agency, such as the U.S. EPA or the Food and Drug Administration, have required the testing of products before they enter commerce. Thus, they might suppose considerable testing of products is required before they enter commerce and that a good deal is known about them. Moreover, the public may also believe that the toxicity of such substances is reasonably well understood. Both views are mistaken for large numbers of substances. Consequently, evidence that many might assume to be available or easily obtainable for litigation simply may not be there. Moreover, if courts also have a mistaken idea about available evidence, this risks distorting their thinking about the kinds, quality, and amount of evidence that should be presented in court cases. They may be tempted to set unwise standards for the scientific basis of expert testimony as a consequence.

Many substances have properties that make them difficult to study or that lessen the chances of detecting any toxic properties they possess, or both. Substances that cause harm in low concentrations or cause diseases that have long latency periods, that are quite rare or even quite common, or that lack signature effects possess these features to some extent. Such properties aggravate scientists' difficulties in determining which substances cause harm. Judges reviewing evidence about such substances might face much more difficult tasks because any evidence is likely to be pieced together from many sources. They can review such evidence well or poorly.

Scientific epistemology and conventions internal to science can also present problems: a concern to strongly prevent false positive mistakes, a tendency

---

[4] See Lucinda M. Finley, "Guarding the Gate to the Courthouse: How Trial Judges Are Using Their Evidentiary Screening Role to Remake Tort Causation Rules," *DePaul Law Review* 49 (1999): 117; and Green, "Expert Witnesses," 120.

to demand more and better evidence to support a scientific view, and even an inattention to distributive issues in the presentation of evidence. These in turn can distort the law. Judges cannot change these matters. However, as the administrators of the law, they have institutional responsibilities to ensure that such conventions do not inadvertently and mistakenly affect the fairness of admissibility decisions.

The very language scientists utilize to describe their findings is easily misunderstood by laypeople, including judges. If judges misapprehend scientific language in reviewing the basis of expert testimony, this can easily and mistakenly preclude litigants their day in court.

As we saw in Chapter 4, scientists can and do legitimately disagree with one another. Judges (and others) might believe that there is a greater consensus in "objective" science than they tend to see in court. Thus, they might come to expect it. (A more plausible view is that legitimate scientific disagreements are much wider and more common than judges and other laypeople recognize.) Or, judges might be drawn into the fray and choose sides between experts rather than acknowledge that there could be such legitimate disagreements. To remedy this, courts must recognize the range of legitimate disagreements and the myriad patterns of evidence that can bear on toxicity judgments.

Finally, in the law several of the above barriers invite considerable manipulation by the parties to a dispute that are in the position to play defense. These are often expressed as "There are no human studies...," "There are no statistically significant studies showing a relative risk of 2 or greater...," "There is not enough knowledge...," "We cannot be certain that...," "There are no definitive studies showing...," "More evidence is needed...," "Animals are not humans and provide no evidence for human toxicity..."[5] These are phrases that suggest arguments, which can in turn mislead courts to construct misguided templates for reviewing scientific testimony and its foundation. Such arguments in short rest on a kind of "insidious science" produced by litigants. Courts can learn to review such arguments thoughtfully or not.

As I argue later, the conjunction of the above barriers, the post-market structure of the tort law, and stringent gatekeeping following *Daubert* create counterproductive incentives that invites defendants to emphasize such arguments and to refrain from developing information about their products (Chapter 8). Because such arguments are so attractive, judges must learn how to separate the valuable wheat from the irrelevant chaff of such challenges.

These issues can affect judicial decisions. And judicial decisions can impact them. I return to both points in the conclusion.

---

[5] Many of the strategies suggested by these phrases are instances of "manufacturing uncertainty." See David Michaels and Celeste Monforton, "Manufacturing Uncertainty: Contested Science and the Protection of the Public's Health and Environment," *American Journal of Public Health*, Supplement 1 95 (2005): S39–S48.

SCIENTIFIC IGNORANCE ABOUT THE CHEMICAL UNIVERSE

First, as surprising as it may seem, there is somewhat spotty, but quite persuasive evidence that scientists know relatively little about the toxicity of chemical substances.

It is estimated that there are about 20,500,000 unique organic and inorganic chemicals.[6] There are about 70,000 chemical substances registered for use in U.S. commerce. If one adds to these their derivatives, there are about 100,000 substances registered for use in commerce. The vast majority of these have not been well assessed for their health effects.[7]

Moreover, another fifteen hundred to two thousand substances are added to the existing stock each year with no legally required toxicity testing.[8] Under the Toxic Substances Control Act (TSCA) firms are required to inform the U.S. EPA of whatever they know about substances they propose to manufacture, but unless the EPA requires testing of specific substances after they have been submitted, no testing is legally required.[9] Manufacturers *may* submit test data, but only about one-half do so, and in 1987 only about 17 percent of the notifications had "any test information about the likelihood of the substance's causing cancer, birth defects or mutations – three biological effects that were singled out for special concern in TSCA"[10] when it was enacted.

This point about minimally tested substances that enter commerce each year should not be overemphasized or underemphasized. Although many substances are proposed for manufacturing and are authorized by the U.S. EPA, probably large numbers of these are never pursued. Moreover, there is probably no need for a full toxicity assessment of most of these substances.[11] However,

---

[6] James Huff and Ronald Melnick, "Chemical Carcinogenesis Bioassays: Critical for the Sensible Application of the Precautionary Principle for Protecting Public Health," Presentation to Collegium Ramazzini, 23–24 October 2002.

[7] National Research Council, *Toxicity Testing*, 84 (estimating about seventy thousand substances registered for use in commerce); James Huff and David Hoel, "Perspective and Overview of the Concepts and Value of Hazard Identification as the Initial Phase of Risk Assessment for Cancer and Human Health," *Scandinavian Journal of Work Environment and Health* 18 (1992): 85 (estimating 50,000–100,000 chemicals in the marketplace); U.S. Congress, Office of Technology Assessment, *Screening and Testing Chemicals in Commerce* (Washington, DC: U.S. Government Printing Office, 1995) (estimating seventy thousand chemicals in commerce). If derivatives and metabolites are included, some experts suggest that the more appropriate number is one hundred thousand (Lauren Zeise, Chief, Reproductive and Cancer Hazard Assessment Section, California EPA, personal communication, Dec. 1999; Huff and Melnick, "Chemical Carcinogenesis Bioassays").

[8] Dennison, "U.S. HPV Challenge and Beyond." Two thousand new substances each year represents an increase over reports of 15 years ago: OTA, *Identifying and Regulating Carcinogens*, 127.

[9] OTA, *Identifying and Regulating Carcinogens*, 127.

[10] OTA, *Identifying and Regulating Carcinogens*, quoting OTA, *The Information Content of Premanufacture Notices* (Washington, DC: U.S. Government Printing Office, 1983), 222.

[11] Nicholas Ashford, personal communication, Collegium Ramazinni, October 29–30, 2004.

it may be difficult in advance to know which require closer scrutiny and which do not, although EPA procedures are designed to try to identify these. Wide anecdotal evidence, however, suggests that the public believes that products to which they are exposed *are* legally required to be tested before they enter the market; this is clearly mistaken.

Some premarket laws require testing of substances or products before they enter commerce: laws concerning pesticides, drugs, new food additives, and some medical devices.[12] Although there is little testing of substances other than those explicitly subject to premarket screening laws, firms have some reasons to conduct short-term tests and use structure-activity information to prevent obvious toxicants from entering commerce. This results in some congruence between a firm's private interest in being safe rather than sorry later and the public interest in health protections. Nonetheless, the U.S. Congress' Office of Technology Assessment found that some substances approved for manufacturing under pre-market notification laws (that do not require testing) have "demonstrated toxicity."[13]

Of the approximately 100,000 substances in commerce, perhaps one-third present little or no exposure and another 23 percent are polymers, which pose minimal threats because of their large size.[13] Thus, such estimates suggest that somewhat more than 50 percent present little or no threat to the wider public or even to employees in the workplace.

Nonetheless, there are substantial reasons for concern when one looks closer. In 1984 the U.S. National Academy of Sciences found that there were

- 12,860 substances produced in volumes exceeding one million pounds per year for 78 percent of which there is *no* toxicity information available; 11 percent had minimal toxicity information,
- 13,911 chemicals produced in volumes of less than 1 million pounds (76 percent with no toxicity data, 12 percent had minimal toxicity information),
- 8,627 food additives; 46 percent had no toxicity data, 34 percent had some toxicity information (but it was below the minimal level), 1 percent had minimal toxicity information,
- 1,815 drugs, 25 percent of which had no toxicity data, 36 percent had some toxicity data (but below the minimal level), 3 percent had minimal toxicity information,
- 3,410 cosmetics, 56 percent of which had no toxicity data, 18 percent had some toxicity data (but below the minimal level), 10 percent had minimal toxicity information, and

---

12 Richard Merrill, "FDA Regulatory Requirements as Tort Standards," *Journal of Law and Policy* 12 (2004): 549–558.
13 Huff and Hoel, "Perspective and Overview," 85.

- 3,350 pesticides of which 36 percent had no toxicity data, 26 percent with some toxicity data (but below the minimal level), 2 percent had minimal toxicity information.[14]

From this, one can see that out of about 13,792 substances subject to more extensive premarket testing, 7,537 or 41 percent had no toxicity data. This was an improvement over general chemicals, but not impressive. Moreover, even when there was some data, for most substances it was only "minimal" toxicity data.[15] On average for substances subject to premarket testing, about 30 percent had such minimal data.[16] For the large majority of substances (not subject to pre-market testing), the percentages lacking all toxicity data were much greater.

In the early 1990s there was insufficient change in the data to justify updating the National Academy Report.[17]

Of a group of three thousand substances produced in the highest volume, there remained substantial knowledge-gaps for about 75 percent of them as recently as 1998, when the U.S. EPA entered into a voluntary agreement with the producers to close the knowledge gaps.[18] These were likely the most worrisome of substances, but even in 1995 the U.S. Congress Office of Technology Assessment found that there are another one thousand to twelve thousand, for which extensive toxicological information would be quite important but that was not available.[19]

Not only is little known about this universe of substances, but it will be quite difficult to close the knowledge gaps. According to the National Academy of Sciences, obtaining the relevant knowledge about most substances will not be easy because an endemic problem of identifying and assessing their toxicity properties is the "sparseness and uncertainty of the scientific knowledge of the health hazards addressed, and this problem has no ready solution."[20] Even when there is an understanding of some features of toxicants, there may be woeful ignorance about many other toxic properties.[21] In addition, even if some substances are, for example, known carcinogens, there may be lesser understanding of the organs in which they cause cancer, because they may not have been fully evaluated. (This more specific information, often needed in tort cases, would have to be inferred.)

---

[14] NRC, *Toxicity Testing*, 118–119.
[15] NRC, *Toxicity Testing*, 83. ("Minimal toxicity information was defined as specific combinations of five basic types of tests prescribed by the Committee on Toxicity Data Elements: acute, subchronic, chronic, reproductive/developmental, and mutagenicity.")
[16] NRC, *Toxicity Testing*, 84.
[17] John C. Bailor and Eula Bingham, personal communication, Collegium Ramazzini, 2002.
[18] "EPA, EDF, CMA Agree on Testing Program," 193.
[19] OTA, *Screening and Testing Chemicals in Commerce*.
[20] NRC, *Risk Assessment in the Federal Government*, 6.
[21] NRC, *Risk Assessment in the Federal Government*, 6.

These facts suggest that there is a huge backlog of substances, especially those produced in the highest volume, about which scientists are largely ignorant (through no fault of their own). And, of course, producing data for them would do nothing to keep up with current production of new substances, if some of them merit more extensive testing. (It should be added that to date the new substances do not appear to have been the most significant problems (rather, existing substances have posed greater toxicity problems), but the institutions do not have control of potentially toxic substances.) Thus, the large number of substances about which so little is known represents an overwhelming task for the scientific community that is likely to go unattended until particular toxicity issues rise to some high level of public or scientific concern.[22]

There will also likely be no reason to try to characterize the toxicity of all these substances, as many will present no exposure, others may no longer be used, and so on. Nonetheless, it appears there are thousands of substances that pose substantial exposure problems whose properties are poorly understood or not understood at all. The public, consequently, in effect becomes guinea pigs for determining whether there are any adverse effects from these substances.

The lack of scientific knowledge about the universe of substances has also impacted federal agencies charged with protecting the public health. They are aware of the toxic properties of some substances, but have been slow to conduct tests and follow-up health assessments needed to identify toxicants for regulatory purposes. In addition, even when agencies have toxicity studies of substances, they have been slow to take regulatory action. For example, the Office of Technology Assessment found in 1987 that of the known carcinogens within the regulatory jurisdictions of federal agencies, the agencies had addressed only one-half to one-third of the substances for which they were responsible.[23] For substances for which animal studies had been completed (the typical foundation of toxicity data and regulations), regulatory agencies had conducted risk assessments on only about 15%.[24] One of the most widely used governmental databases contains substantial gaps.[25] In short, basic toxicity

---

[22] Whether there are any systematic attempts to characterize a broader range of substances is not known to the author. Theoretical toxicologists may have incentives to study a small number of already characterized substances in greater depth and detail, because this will result in a better understanding of toxicity mechanisms than will the same effort characterizing a wider universe of substances.

[23] OTA, *Identifying and Regulating Carcunogens*, 9–22 See also *American Federation of Labor and Congress of Indus. Organizations v. Occupational Safety and Health Admin., U.S. Dept. of Labor*, 965 F.2d 962 (11th Cir. 1992). (The court recognized the need for OSHA to regulate a large number of substances quickly simply in order to make major strides in protecting worker health and safety, but invalidated its attempt to do so (987).)

[24] OTA, *Identifying and Regulating Carcinogens*, 20, 194.

[25] Katherine Baer and Matt Shudtz, Center for Pregressive Regulation, "Data Gaps White Paper," presented at the Ward, Kershaw Environmental Law Symposium, The University of Maryland School of Law, 6 May 2005.

data is not available concerning most substances. And even when it is available, regulatory assessment is lagging well behind basic toxicity studies.

Moreover, each year the National Toxicology Program authorizes only a small number of animal tests on substances it suspects might cause cancer.[26] Thus, postmarket testing, assessment and follow-up of suspect substances lags far behind the production of new substances. If federal or state agencies have not assessed the toxicity of substances, it is unlikely that others have.

Institutionally it is important to recognize that if the regulatory agencies have not reviewed substances for their toxicity, this is an additional reason to ensure that the tort law is not rendered so legally toothless that it cannot serve as a backup institution to regulatory failures to determine the toxicity of substances. To put the point more positively, a well-functioning tort law is needed to repair the damage done to humans and the environment by regulatory shortcomings in testing and in regulations (as well as accidents). How well the tort law works is in part a function of how stringently or sensitively judges review expert testimony.

However, in the context of the tort law, waiting until toxicity issues arise poses two problems: (1) humans exposed to substances in commerce that have not been sufficiently tested in effect become exposure and research subjects, whether or not anyone intended this outcome; and (2) there are evidentiary problems. Because scientists typically will have developed little or no evidence about the toxicity of most substances, persons injured by exposure to unstudied substances will not be able to recover damages for injuries suffered until sufficient data are compiled to provide evidence of the harm.[27] In that context, science delayed risks being justice denied.

These institutional facts suggest that the identification and assessment of chemical substances is out of control of our public institutions. The legal system as it currently functions is not up to the task with which it is charged. The rate of production of substances far exceeds the ability of institutions to ensure that the public is not put at substantial risk or harmed as a result of the activities of a free enterprise system.

---

[26] Ronald Melnick, personal communication, Collegium Ramazzini, 25 October 2002.

[27] A broader public health issue is that, by exposing employees and the general public to so many substances, it will be increasingly difficult to obtain a truly untainted, "unexposed" database of individuals against which to compare those who are more obviously exposed. By such population exposures our institutions have ensured that the controls for a good scientific study of the effects of substances on humans in effect have been contaminated, thus preventing the best kinds of studies on them. Thus, except for unusually virulent substances such as vinyl chloride or diethylstilbestrol (DES), both of which exhibited quite high relative risks, or substances that leave their signatures, such as asbestos, which leaves physical traces behind in the body, it may be difficult to detect disease effects above background. This will be especially true for substances that cause common diseases or other adverse effects that are not highly elevated above background. Scientific difficulties in detecting diseases will only exacerbate the problems plaintiffs face in trying to establish that particular exposures have likely caused or contributed to their diseases.

Resource Limitations

Closing even the most important scientific gaps is costly in terms of time, resources, and scientists available. For substances that are the object of study, it takes time as well as substantial monetary and human resources to do the needed toxicity research on particular substances in order to remove the lack of information and to increase scientific understanding of their properties.[28]

As we considered in Chapter 4, the most obvious and morally best route to understanding the toxicity of substances would be to conduct animal and other nonhuman tests and make inferences from them to effects in humans. However, simply accumulating the needed scientific evidence can be quite slow. At a minimum, utilizing various kinds of non-human evidence and conducting expedited studies generally takes six years or more to have a basic battery of test results with which to assess the basic toxicity of a substance.[29] This might be expedited to some extent, but conducting appropriate studies is not quick. Moreover, the costs of long-term animal studies alone are estimated to range from $2 million to $5 million.[30]

Providing human evidence can be even more vexed and expensive. It is morally unacceptable to deliberately expose humans to a potentially toxic substance and then conduct epidemiological studies to try to determine whether there are any adverse effects. Even exploiting adventitious circumstances for research purposes in which people have been exposed to toxicants in effect uses humans as guinea pigs, when existing institutions are inadequate to provide appropriate preventive protections.[31] Moreover, when courts *require* human evidence, this only further delays evaluation and legal remedies.

In addition, there must be sufficient numbers of scientists to provide the needed data. There are a limited number of toxicologists and epidemiologists who could address their attention to particular problems. If there are not ample resources devoted to studying a problem, this will slow understanding. If there are few scientists interested in a problem, this will delay scientific research. If substances and their exposures do not present problems of interest to fundamental research interest, scientists are unlikely to study them. If there is little or no funding for studying potential toxicants, they are unlikely to be addressed.

Even if it made sense to test individually each substance that was registered for commerce in the United States, *which it does not*, in 1992 Huff and Rall

---

28   Huff and Rall, "Relevance to Humans," 439.
29   R. C. James, "General Principles of Toxicology," in *Industrial Toxicology: Safety and Health Applications in the Workplace*, ed. Phillip L. Williams and James L. Burson (New York: Lifetime Learning Publications, 1985), 7–26.
30   Jerold Last, Director, University of California Toxic Substances Research and Teaching Program, personal communication, 18 April 2004.
31   Of course, it is better to try to learn what we can from such adventitious exposures in order to preclude more serious problems in the future, but it is indeed unfortunate that failures of our institutions force us into such choices.

estimated that there were sufficient world resources to begin only about two hundred new chemical carcinogenic studies each year.[32] Using those data and assuming *arguendo* (with the 1995 OTA study) that there were several thousand existing substances that pose serious risks, it would require at least many years to begin the studies and longer yet to complete and interpret them. None of this takes into account the many untested substances that are introduced each year.

Corporate Failure to Determine the Safety of Their Products

These problems might arise from the regular, seriously flawed, but nonculpable, operations of a laissez-faire economic system and the resource limitations of scientific and legal institutions. This alone should raise questions about whether our legal structure is adequate to review the myriad substances produced by companies, to ensure adequate understanding of any toxic properties, to provide compensation to wrongly injured victims and to prevent others from being harmed.

However, there is some evidence suggesting that lack of scientific knowledge about the chemical universe is not simply a matter of institutions being out of control. Some ignorance may be culpable, for it appears to arise in part from the deliberate actions of those who manufacture and use potentially toxic substances. Professor Berger summarizes this by noting that often

> the corporation in question did not test its product adequately initially, failed to impart information when potential problems emerged, and did not undertake further research in response to adverse information. It appears that the corporations took virtually no steps to determine or minimize the possibility of harm until their hands were forced, *usually by litigation*. Only after extensive and expensive discovery have documents and witnesses come to light that showed the corporations' awareness of potential problems. (emphasis added)[33]

---

[32] Huff and Rall, "Relevance to Humans," 439.

[33] Berger, "Eliminating General Causation," 2135. She cites in particular studies of Agent Orange, asbestos, Bendectin, breast implants, the Dalkon Shield, thalidomide, tobacco, MER/29 (a cholesterol-reducing drug that caused cataracts), alachlor, atrazine, formaldehyde, and perchloroethylene.

For a discussion in the toxicological literature of some of these and other issues, see also Barry Castleman, "Regulations Affecting Use of Carcinogens," in *Cancer Causing Chemicals*, ed. N. Irving Sax (New York: Van Nostrand Reinhold, 1981), 78; David E. Lilienfeld, "The Silence: The Asbestos Industry and Early Occupational Cancer Research – A Case Study," *American Journal of Public Health* 81 (1991): 791, 791–798; David Michaels, "Waiting For The Body Count: Corporate Decision Making and Bladder Cancer in the U.S. Dye Industry," *Medical Anthropology Quarterly* 2 (1988): 21 5–27; see also Donald R. Mattison and John E. Craighead, "Reproductive System," in *Pathology of Environmental and Occupational Disease*, ed. John E. Craighead (St. Louis: Mosby, 1995), 55 9–72.

In some instances, even responsible firms may also fall prey to ambiguity and difficulty in interpreting data and scientific studies.

Similar conclusions are suggested in not infrequent newspaper reports (resembling the recent concern over Bridgestone/Firestone tire failures) that merit further investigation.[34]

Such conduct is not restricted to the private sector, as governmental agencies may not always be forthcoming. This has been particularly in evidence concerning workplace exposure to radiation and atomic weapons fallout.[35] In addition, for another example, it is only comparatively recently in Southern California and elsewhere that communities have been informed by governmental contractors and the Department of Defense that groundwater has been contaminated by perchlorate, a component of rocket fuel. Rocket fuel deteriorates fairly rapidly. Companies that manufactured and used such substances as potassium and aluminum perchlorate (as well as governmental agencies) frequently dumped deteriorating fuel components directly into the ground or into groundwater injection wells. After thirty years, the perchlorate salts that are readily soluble in water and percolate rapidly through the groundwater have migrated to contaminate sources of drinking water for fairly large communities.[36] Perchlorate interferes with the uptake of iodide by the thyroid gland, which in turn may pose risks of reproductive, hormonal, neurodevelopmental, developmental, carcinogenic, and immune system diseases.[37] (The concentrations at which these effects occur represent another issue.)

Moreover, corporate failures to test substances for toxicity or corporate hiding or falsifying test results appear not to belong to ancient history or even U.S. history of several decades ago. For example, in the 1990s, court documents indicate that there had been some sixty-three reported cases of seizures in women taking Parlodel,[38] a lactation suppression drug. However, given the

---

[34] Ricardo Alonso-Zaldivar and Davan Mahara, "Tests Show Firestone 'Had to Know,' Probers Say; Safety: Congress Cites New Evidence Against Tire Maker as Sentiment Swings in Favor of Criminal Penalties in Such Cases," *Los Angeles Times,* 12 September 2000, C1; Richard A. Oppel, Jr., "Environmental Tests 'Falsified', U.S. Says," *New York Times,* 22 September 2000, A14; Melody Petersen, "Settlement Is Approved in Diet Drug Case," *New York Times,* 29 August 2000, C2; David Willman, "The Rise and Fall of the Killer Drug Rezulin; People Were Dying as Specialists Waged War Against Their FDA Superiors," *Los Angeles Times,* 4 June 2000, A1; David Willman, "Risk Was Known as FDA Ok'd Fatal Drug," *Los Angeles Times,* 11 March 2001, A1.

[35] See for example, Gayle Greene, *The Woman Who Knew Too Much: Alice Stewart and the Secrets of Radiation* (Ann Arbor: University of Michigan Press, 1999) (describing governmental attempts in the U.S. and Great Britain to preclude researchers from data and to vigorously fight their findings concerning exposures to nuclear radiation); and Matthew L. Wald, "U.S. Acknowledges Radiation Killed Weapons Workers," *The New York Times,* 29 January 2000, A1.

[36] *In re: Redlands Tort Litigation* (2001).

[37] U.S. Environtmental Protection Agency, "Perchlorate," available at: http://www.epa.gov/swerffrr/documents/perchlorate.htm.

[38] U.S. Food and Drug Administration, "Notice of an Opportunity for a Hearing on a Proposal to Withdraw Approval of the Indication [of Bromocriptine Neslate (Parlodel) for the Prevention of Physiological Lactation]," *Federal Register* 59 (1994): 43347, 43351.

information available to Sandoz Pharmaceutical, the manufacturer of Parlodel, the number of seizures might have been much higher. For another example, in June 2002, the *Los Angeles Times* reported that "internal documents show that Warner-Lambert Co. executives who promoted the diabetes pill Rezulin masked early indications of the drug's danger to the liver from federal regulators and later delayed sharing information about its lethal toxicity with family doctors."[39] Although this diabetes drug received "fast-track" approval from the Food and Drug Administration in 1997, it was withdrawn from the market in 2000 after ninety-four liver failures, including sixty-six deaths, were attributed to the drug by the FDA. Physicians and others suspect that more than 556 deaths may be attributed to the drug, according to the *Times* investigation.[40] Pfizer, the parent company of Warner-Lambert following a merger, is facing "2000 law suits filed on behalf of approximately 5,100 Rezulin users or their survivors" and is under investigation for criminal behavior in concealing information about the safety of the drug.[41] Recently internal documents of the Americal Petroleum Institute (unveiled in litigation) strongly suggest that API knows what its studies will find before they are ever conducted.[42] Finally, as this book went to final publication the editors of the *New England Journal of Medicine* went on record expressing concern about Merck scientists who deleted positive results from studies that sought to identify harms from exposure to the pain drug Vioxx.[43]

Sometimes, laboratories used by industries have been subject to criminal liability for their testing failures. Some firms or industries have aimed to subvert the results of independent scientific studies or deliberately manipulated data and studies for their own benefit.[44] At other times, firms have delayed sending information of adverse test results to appropriate government agencies and fought withdrawal of harmful products from market.[45] Such actions further

---

[39] David Willman, "Hidden Risks, Lethal Truth," *Los Angeles Times*, 30 June 2002, 1.
[40] Willman, "Hidden Risks," 1.
[41] Willman, "Hidden Risks," 1.
[42] American Petroleum Institute, Shaghai Study: Internal Documents (unveiled in litigation), 54–57; D. Capiello, "Oil Industry Funding Study to Contradict Cancer Claims," *Houston Chronicle*, April 29, 2005, AD; A1.
[43] C. D. Curfman, S. Morrissey, J. M. Drazen, "Expression of Concern: Bombardier, et al., Comparison of Upper Gastrointestinal Toxicity of Rofecoxib and Naproxen in Patients with Rheumatoid Arthritis," *New England Journal of Medicine* 343 (2005): 2813–2814.
[44] Elisa K. Ong and Stanton A. Glantz, "Tobacco Industry Efforts Subverting International Agency for Research on Cancer's Second-hand Smoke Study," *The Lancet* 355 (8 April 2000): 1253 (notes that an independent research group such as IARC spent $1.5–$3 million to study second hand smoke, while one tobacco company planned to spend up to $6 million to undermine the credibility of IARC's work (1254, 1256).); Samuel S. Epstein, "Corporate Crime: Why We Cannot Trust Industry-Derived Safety Studies," *International Journal of Health Services* 20 (1990): 433; Richard A. Oppel, Jr., "Environmental Tests 'Falsified,' U.S. Says," *New York Times* (September 2000), A14.
[45] As Michael Green reports occurred with Bendectin (*Bendectin and Birth Defects*, 129–130) and as one can see from the Food and Drug Administration withdrawal notice concerning

delay, or eliminate altogether, the possibility of just resolution of meritorious claims and undermine any deterrent effect of torts.

In addition, as we will see later, even if firms do not deliberately conceal or delay turning over evidence, it is comparatively easy to conduct or design studies that are unlikely to detect harms or risks of concern, although standardized test protocols are designed to minimize this. There are temptations or pressures to refrain from testing altogether, given the incentives created by the tort law and its procedures for reviewing scientific evidence and expert testimony (I will return to this in Chapters 7 and 8).

There is, thus, considerable absence of scientific knowledge about the universe of chemical substances, some of which will harm individuals exposed to them. And, the costs in terms of time, person-power, and money will only delay closure of the data gaps suggesting that assessment will only fall further behind the existing backlog of substances as well as behind the creation of new substances.

In large part the failure of firms to test substances and any further failure to report adverse effects are engendered by incentives created by the legal system. Companies introducing substances subject to post market-laws, for example, are not legally required to test them, and in most cases will only have a legal duty to turn over any data they have on the substances subject to the TSCA rules (different laws apply to drugs, food additives, and pesticides). Once products are in commerce, if firms' tests reveal adverse health effects they *may* be required to report these results to a regulatory authority under some laws, but they also may not be. In addition, the test results are certainly subject to discovery if there is eventually a tort suit. So, once products are in commerce, why test them? It only invites legal trouble.

These conditions can have a profound effect on the tort law. Sometimes defendant's failure to test results in inadequate scientific studies of substances, poor understanding of their toxicity properties, and failure to identify toxicants before they cause harm. Yet, in the tort law, it is the plaintiff, a possible victim, who has the legal duty to bring such evidence forward and make a sufficient case to change the legal status quo. Thus, given current institutional structures there appears to be little incentive for firms to conduct the relevant scientific studies that would permit victims to make a case that particular substances contributed to their harm.

In sum, there are several reasons for lack of scientific information and understanding about substances:

- General institutional failure to demand health and environmental studies, contemporaneous with the introduction of new substances.

Parlodel (U.S. Food and Drug Administration, "Notice of an Opportunity for a Hearing," 43347, 43351). A similar problem was recently revealed by the *New England Journal of Medicine* (Curfman et al., "Expression of Concern," 2813–2814).

- Insufficient public resources to investigate potentially toxic substances.
- Some industry culpability.
- Legal structures that discourage testing and that reduce or remove incentives to report known adverse effects.

Beyond these points there are features of chemical substances that compound the problems.

FEATURES OF TOXIC SUBSTANCES THAT FRUSTRATE THE DISCOVERY OF TOXICITY

Low Concentrations Can Be Toxic

Molecules are submicroscopically small objects, unlike bullets, knives, or cars that are often the carriers of harm and the object of legal attention. Yet they can harm us just the same, only in almost vanishingly small amounts. For example, in 1978 the Occupational Safety and Health Administration (OSHA) became concerned about workplace exposures to benzene and issued a regulation lowering the permissible exposure from ten parts per million to one part per million (ppm), a level that was not necessarily safe, but the lowest level they could reliably detect in the workplace.[46] At 10 ppm, the agency was concerned that employees exposed to benzene would contract leukemia or aplastic anemia, typically both life-ending diseases.[47] More recently, research has shown that benzene exposure at .1 part per million (100 times lower than ten parts per million) reduces the white cell count in humans, compromising their immune systems.[48]

To put these concentrations of benzene in perspective, the ratio of 1 ppm is equivalent to the ratio of 1 inch to 16 miles (length), 1 cent to $10,000 (money), or 1 minute to 2 years (time). Thus, extremely tiny concentrations of such substances can cause great and permanent harm to a person. Other substances appear to cause harm down to parts per billion, one thousand times lower concentrations.[49]

---

[46] Even this level might not be sufficiently protective. See Peter F. Infante, "Benzene and Leukemia: The 0.1 ppm ACGIH Proposed Threshold Limit Value for Benzene," *Applied Occupational Envrionmental Hygene* 7 (1992): 253–262.

[47] Subsequent analysis showed that 35% of leukemogenic diseases appeared to be caused by exposures below 6 ppm and that increased chromosomal breakage occurred at exposures at 1 ppm, so OSHA was hardly being too cautious in setting its exposure levels (Infante, "Benzene and Leukemia")

[48] Qing Lan et al., "Hematoxtoxicity in Workers Exposed to Low Levels of Benzene," *Science* 306 (2004): 177 4–1776.

[49] For example, the U.S. EPA and the California EPA are considering evidence which suggests that exposure to perchlorate, a product of rocket fuel manufacturing that has contaminated groundwater, should be set at between one to six parts *per billion* for purposes of protecting the public health.

Detection methods to accurately measure such low concentrations may or may not be available, as such small amounts can require very sensitive analytical testing. And, even if advanced equipment could detect such low concentrations in laboratory settings there may or may not be pragmatic and cost-effective *monitoring* devices that can be used in workplaces or the general environment to easily measure exposures.

However, the important point for exposures that lead to tort suits is that even if there are excellent monitoring devices for particular substances, *actual measurement* of them in circumstances from which tort suits often result does not occur. Exposures may be quite adventitious. Thus, it may be that exposures are rarely measured, or in some cases not measurable. If courts demand, as several have,[50] fairly specific and precise exposure levels before cases can advance to trial, this will ensure that many otherwise meritorious cases will not receive a jury trial.

Discovering the properties and reliably evaluating the risks and harms caused by such low concentrations of such substances can be quite difficult. Quite subtle exposure and molecular detective work is required. The research needed to tease out the effects of toxic substances is not different from other more mundane contexts, just more difficult.

Scientific investigations to identify and assess the toxicity of the substances involved take time, because the tasks are sufficiently subtle and labor intensive. The lower the concentrations and the more subtle the effects, the more difficult such tasks are. Umberto Eco, in his medieval detective story *The Name of the Rose*, reminds us of the difficulties of discerning the nature of the world around us in the comparatively ordinary and mundane world of a human murder mystery. However, his reminder captures some of the problems researchers face in trying to detect the effects of toxic substances in the much more esoteric world of scientific investigation:

> But, we see now through a glass darkly, and the truth, before it is revealed to all, face to face, we see in fragments (alas how illegible) in the error of the world, so we must spell out its faithful signals even when they seem obscure to us . . .[51]

The vanishingly small concentrations of tiny substances that can threaten us, and the difficulties detecting them should not conceal that there are real human

---

50   *Wright v. Willamette Indus., Inc.*, 91 F.3d 1105, at 1107 (8th Cir. 1996); *Moore v. Ashland Chemical Inc.*, 151 F.3d 269 (5th Cir., (Tex.) 1998).

51   Umberto Eco, *The Name of the Rose* (New York: Harcourt, Brace Jovanovich, Inc. 1983), 3. Later the protagonist, the medieval detective, Brother William, speaking to his apprentice, Adso, says "My good Adso . . . during our journey I have been teaching you to recognize the evidence through which the world speaks to us like a great book" (18). The suggestion, insofar as it is correct, fits well with the discussion developed below, since the evidence for toxicity effects on human beings is subject to a great deal of interpretation, and often sharply differing interpretations, before one can reach conclusions about a substance's toxic effects.

consequences from exposures to toxic substances. Such exposures can harm us just as much as the grosser forms of violence, theft, and deception, traditional legal concerns. Indeed, toxic molecules might cause more suffering than much larger and more mundane sources of harm. Carcinogens, for example, can kill us just as surely as, and often more agonizingly than, a gunshot or knife wound. Walter Allen contracted brain cancer and died from it; Karen Magistrini contracted leukemia. Robert Joiner contracted and died from lung cancer. Exposure to toxic substances might have caused or contributed to all of these diseases. However, those exposed might be unaware of an invasion of their bodies, unaware when it occurred, and, because such substances can have long latency periods, even unaware of the source of harm.

Reproductive toxins may not kill us. But they might maim our children, for example, causing them to be born with stub arms or legs.[52] Or worse, they might make it impossible for families to have children because of low sperm counts.[53] In a kind of double whammy, they might give women cervical cancer and possibly give their offspring health problems as well, all because the women's mothers took the drug diethylstilbestrol (DES).[54]

Neurotoxins, such as lead, might lower a child's Intelligence Quotient or those of a whole generation. Thus, the effects caused by such substances might be as serious or more serious than the effects of the grosser forms of violence, theft, and deception in our lives, but much more difficult to detect.

The issues just reviewed only exacerbate some problems with the tort law. Simply understanding the toxicity effects of substances will be difficult enough. Even more problematic is the discovery, assessment, and evaluation of the lowest concentrations of substances that pose harms to biologically quite diverse human populations. Individuals with an "eggshell skull" biology – those who may be more susceptible to lower concentrations than the average person or the vast majority of people – may be vulnerable at quite low exposures. Yet, there is a need for addressing such problems in torts, because according to the "eggshell skull" doctrine in the tort law, even especially vulnerable people are entitled to legal protections.[55] This issue has far-reaching implications for the

---

[52] This resulted to children whose mothers took the drug thalidomide during pregnancy. For a general discussion, see J. Manson, "Teratogens," in *Casarett and Doull's Toxicology*, 5th ed., ed. C. Klaassen, M. Amdur, and J. Doull (New York: McGraw-Hill, 1996).

[53] 1,2-dibromo-3-chloropropane (DBCP) causes such harms. For a general discussion, see R. Dixon, "Toxic Responses of the Reproductive System," in *Casarett and Doull's Toxicology*, 3rd ed., ed. C. Klaasen, M. Amdur, and J. Doull (New York: Macmillan), 432–477.

[54] Diethylstilbestrol (DES) has been found to cause cervical cancer in the daughters of women who took DES during pregnancy (*Sindell v. Abbott Laboratories*, 26 Cal.3d. 588, 607 P. 2D 924 (1980)). Some have suggested that DES might even cause third generation effects, but this effect is not well established.

[55] Carl F. Cranor, "Eggshell Skulls and Loss of Hair from Fright: Some Moral and Legal Principles that Protect Susceptible Subpopulations," *Environmental Toxicology and Pharmacology* 4 (1997): 239–245.

tort law and especially important consequences for courts considering claims about the pertinent exposure levels to which people are exposed.

Long Latency Periods

Some substances have long latency periods. Recall the latency of a disease is the time between the completion of the disease induction period and the clinical manifestation of disease.[56] The latency period for cancers typically varies from a few months to more than forty years.[57] For reproductive toxicants, neurotoxicants or others the latency period may not be as pronounced as it is for cancers, but for many of these it can take considerable time for adverse effects to be identified.[58] Some adverse reproductive effects, such as shortened limbs, which triggered the *Daubert* litigation, are manifested at birth, whereas others, including multigenerational effects, may take much longer to appear. When the adverse effects are difficult to detect, for example, reduction in intelligence due to exposure to lead, compared with reduction in limb length, there will be additional problems.

Long latency periods add to the complexity of a disease process and make the identification of causal connections between exposures and contraction of diseases more difficult. During the time lag between exposure and clinical manifestation of disease, it is at least possible that there are a variety of intervening factors that could make some contribution to the disease and, thus, confound the explanation of its causes. If substances had nearly instantaneous effects as some poisons or vaccines do, they would be considerably easier to identify and assess.

Rare Diseases

Both rare and common diseases additionally burden the identification and assessment of disease causation by means of either epidemiological or animal studies. A rare disease does not occur in very many people exposed to a disease-causing substance. Consequently, statistical studies, which are traditionally used to detect disease effects in populations, require *large enough numbers*

---

[56] Rothman, *Modern Epidemiology*, 15.
[57] Malcolm A. Smith et al., "Therapy-Related Acute Myeloid Leukemia Following Treatment with Epipodophyllotoxins: Estimating the Risks," *Medical & Podiatric Oncology* 23 (1994): 86–87 (latency period as short as 10 months, with a median of 30 months, from chemotherapy treatments); U.S. Department of Health and Human Services, *Toxicological Profile for Asbestos* 6, 28 (1995) (latency period from exposure to asbestos is ten to forty years).
[58] For example, there might be a twenty- to forty-year latency period for multi-generational reproductive toxicants such as diethylstilbestrol (DES). For a neurotoxin such as lead, although the adverse effect might be manifested early, the effects of decreased IQ (intelligence quotient) might be so subtle that they would be difficult to detect except on the basis of very large longitudinal population studies, another factor that would delay identification of effect, but one that would not be due to latency.

of exposed and control groups, as well as sufficiently large responses in the exposed group for scientists to reliably detect them. If a cause of disease is rare, it requires *larger studies* to detect it than if it is more common. It is much easier to identify the cause of a disease that has a background rate of 1/1000 than it is to identify the cause of leukemia, which only occurs naturally in about 1/100,000 people in the general population.[59]

In addition, when diseases are rare, a difference in one or two affected people in an exposed or control group can make a substantial difference in deciding whether exposure to the substance results in a statistically significant disease rate.[60] At that point, the small numbers of people adversely affected can become controversial simply because anyone can see that a difference of a person or two classified as having the disease in an exposed group would make a substantial difference in interpreting the risks from a substance. Thus, in the law there will be tremendous pressures on judges to preclude epidemiological studies involving rare diseases, as the numbers of diseased individuals is likely to be quite small. For example, many vaccine-caused illnesses are comparatively rare. Judge Golkiewicz notes that "the rarity of certain reactions makes it logistically impossible to create a reliable study *because of the need for an inordinately large population*."[61] Even if they could be studied it would be difficult and costly to do so.

It is possible for animal studies to detect comparatively rare adverse effects from exposures to toxic substances, but they can face statistical difficulties similar to those that confront epidemiological studies. Moreover, as we saw in the previous chapter, two significant extrapolations are required to estimate effecting humans, which can invite critiques. Such criticisms are often exaggerated, but the use of animal studies opens up such possibilities.

Occasionally, if a disease effect is *extremely* rare, this can facilitate its detection. Thus, vinyl chloride–caused angiosarcoma of the liver that researchers were able to identify as a result of a small number of case studies (described in Chapter 4) was just such a disease. It was so rare that there were only about 25 cases per year in a U.S. population of about 250,000,000 (one case per ten million people). Consequently, the rareness of this disease actually helped identify

---

[59] Cranor, *Regulating Toxic Substances*, 35–39.

[60] David A. Savitz and Kurtis W. Andrews, "Risk of Myelogenous Leukaemia and Multiple Myeloma in Workers Exposed to Benzene," *Occupational and Environmental Medicine*, 33 (1996): 357–358. (The movement of a single case of disease from one category to another in an epidemiological study of comparatively rare diseases could substantially affect the result of the study.)

[61] *Stevens v. Secretary of the Department of Health and Human Services*, 2001 OL 387418 (Fed. CI). (Discussing the reasons that epidemiological and mechanistic evidence are so rare for vaccine-induced injuries. ["First, relevant research regarding causation is often extremely limited. A number of factors restrict the medical community's efforts to conduct such studies including the *costliness* of the research and the *rarity of the illnesses studied*" (14, emphasis added)]. In a footnote he adds, "Ethical concerns, such as giving a placebo to a child, may also prevent statistical research" [14].)

its cause, because there were comparatively more cases in a vinyl chloride plant with a modest number of exposed people than in the general population, resulting in an approximate relative risk of 400:1. When exposures are much more diffuse and diseases are rare, it will take a particularly large epidemiological study to detect the etiological association because the disease effect will only infrequently reveal itself.

Common Diseases

When a disease end point is common, this will hinder detection of a *new cause* of that particular disease. If a disease is widespread in the general population, it will be difficult to detect a new cause of the disease, simply because it will be difficult to notice a few *new* cases among the many already present. It likely will be difficult to distinguish a new cause of a common disease from *random variation* in the existing disease rate. This effect will be aggravated when the new cause of the disease is not a frequent one, since the vast number of cases will be attributable to variation in the disease rates and not to the new exposure. Even if common diseases are induced at a "much higher frequencies," they can still be difficult to detect.[62]

If a disease is common and the result of a fairly long latency period, this doubly complicates causal contributors to disease. *Long latency* allows time for a number of different disease factors to make a contribution, while causing a *common* disease endpoint is likely to slow and complicate identifying particular factors contributing to disease, for example, genetics, smoking, lifestyle, and so on.

Lack of Signature Effects

Substances that leave unique or highly unusual effects are comparatively easier to identify, but such substances are rare. Asbestos-caused diseases are one group that are easier to identify. In clear cases asbestos, "a silicate mineral in fiber form," leaves traces of silica behind in the organ affected. Because the body cannot fully absorb silicon, this can provide a unique trace of the cause of disease.[63] Heavy metals appear to cause readily identifiable adverse effects.[64] Substances that cause extremely rare diseases but with very high relative risks, such as diethylstilbestrol or vinyl chloride also provide very good evidence for

[62] Huff and Rall, "Relevance to Humans," 437.

[63] Hanspeter Witsche and Jerrold Last, "Toxic Regulation of the Respiratory System," in *Casarett and Doull's Toxicology* (6th ed.), ed. C. D. Klaassen (New York: McGraw-Hill, 2001), 515–534, 526.

[64] Mark R. Cullen, Linda Rosenstock, and Stuart M. Brooks, "Clinical Approach and Establishing a Diagnosis of an Enviromental Medical Disorder," in *Environmental Medicine*, ed. Stuart M. Brooks (St. Louis: Mosby, 1995), 221.

identifying a substances. Similar difficulties detecting rare effects are seen with vaccine-induced adverse reactions.[65] Judge Golkewicz notes that such evidence is usually "unavailable."[66]

Weak vs. Strong Causal Effects of a Substance

Substances are often said to have "strong" or "weak" effects. A "weak" effect "confers only a small increment in disease risk [over a population], whereas a strong cause will increase disease risk substantially [over a larger number in a population]."[67] To illustrate this point, consider an example from an animal experiment. The B7C3F1 experimental male mice have a liver tumor incidence of about 31 percent (with a range of 7 to 55 percent), while females of the species have a spontaneous liver incidence rate of about 6 percent (with a range of 2–8 percent). The parental strains of these mice exhibit either a higher incidence of spontaneous liver tumors (C3H/He mice: 60–80 percent) or a lower incidence of spontaneous liver tumors (C57BL/6J mice: 0–4 percent). When Phenobarbital, a commonly prescribed antiepileptic drug, is administered to those mouse strains that are tumor-susceptible – C3H/He and B6C3F1 mice – the mice have a 100 percent liver tumor incidence rate. However, an identical dosage administered to mice that are not susceptible to liver tumors (the C57BL/6J mice) does not result in the induction of additional liver tumors.[68]

The generic point is that the same dosage has a *strong effect* in one group of mice (i.e., produces tumors in 100 percent of the mice), whereas it fails to produce a similar effect in a different group of mice. Although the dosage is the same, the presence of *something else* in the mice makes the phenobaritol have a greater or lesser effect in the populations of different strains of mice.

Similar effects are seen in humans. For example, humans that are "fast acetylators" are less likely than "slow acetylators" to "develop bladder cancer from cigarette smoking and from occupational exposure to bycyclic aromatic amines."[69] Acetylation is biologic process by means of which a chemical substance is transformed in the body that may assist in its elimination and excretion. This can be a comparatively quicker or slower process in individuals. In addition, acetylation can facilitate the detoxification of some substances and

---

[65] *Stevens v. Secretary of HHS*, 14.

[66] *Stevens v. Secretary of HHS*, 14. ("The presence of such 'vaccine footprints' leaves little doubt in the mind of the experts and the factfinder that the vaccination is the likely cause of the injury. Unfortunately, most petitioners cannot benefit from the introduction of such evidence because it is unavailable. On this point, the competing experts agree.")

[67] Kenneth J. Rothman, "Causes," in *Evolution of Epidemiologic Ideas: Annotated Readings on Concepts and Methods*, ed. Sander Greenland (Chestnut Hill, MA: Epidemiology Resources Inc, 1987), 39–45, 43.

[68] Fox and Goldsworthy, *Chemical Industry Institute of Toxicology News* 13, 7 (1993): 1–6.

[69] Andrew Parkinson, "Biotransformation of Xenobiotics," in *Casarett and Doull's Toxicology*, 6th ed., ed. Curtis D. Klaassen (New York: McGraw-Hill, 2001), 210.

activation of others, making them more toxic.[70] Moreover, the particular features of acelylation appear to vary with population groups – populations of Middle Eastern descent appear to be slow acetylators, whereas those of Asian descent tend to be faster acetylators.[71]

Whether the causal effect of a substance is "strong" or "weak," then is not merely the result of the toxicity of the substance in question, but also the distributions of the *other components that are jointly needed to produce the causal effects.*[72] For exposure to bicyclic amines, if other components that are needed to facilitate the production of liver cancer are widely distributed in the population, the bicyclic amines will be a "strong" risk factor for liver cancer. If the other components are not widely distributed, bicyclic amines will be "weak" risk factors. Thus, a substance's having a weak or strong effect is not a *universal property of the substance* (or exposure), but is in effect a *relational property* that exists between the substance and *other factors* needed to produce the disease effect.[73]

Scientists must utilize considerable care in what they infer from a study that shows a substance has either a weak or a strong effect. A study showing that a substance has overall an average "weak" effect might disguise *subpopulations* in which the effect would be stronger simply because the subpopulation had a biology that facilitated the production of disease and made them more susceptible. Analogously, a study that overall showed exposure to a substance had an average "strong" effect might well disguise that it produced weaker effects in subpopulations lacking the necessary components to complete the disease process.

Consequently, the issue of whether a substance has a strong or weak effect in contributing to a disease is just another instance in which a scientific study needs considerable care in its interpretation. The results, as it were, are not necessarily carried on the face of the study.

These issues can pose problems in toxic tort cases. Judges who review testimony about such studies need to be sensitive to these issues. Even if a study shows that a particular substance arguably has a "weak" effect in producing disease, it may be that if some subpopulations could be identified that had a greater presence of risk factors that facilitated the production of disease, for example, "fast acetylators" exposed to bycyclic aromatic amines will be more

---

[70] Parkinson, "Biotransformation," 208–211. For exposure to cigarette smoke and bicyclic aromatic amines the same dosage can have different effects in different persons depending on what other features of their biology are present, namely their rate of acetylation.

[71] Parkinson, "Biotransformation," 209.

[72] Rothman, "Causes," 24–23.

[73] Another way to put this point is to say that an inference of the causal effects of a particular substance is dependent upon the presuppositions of the context, in particular presuppositions about how the substance interacts with other conditions or biological processes that affect the causal properties of the substance. I owe this generalization of the point about weak and strong causal effects to my colleague, Larry Wright.

susceptible. Whether or not such "other" factors have been identified, whether populations can be easily identified that have such properties and whether this information can be utilized in a particular instance, especially in the context of a toxic tort case, is a more difficult issue. Because average responses in a study may disguise important differences, courts should inquire about these issues by asking whether there are features of the population studied that might result in over- or underestimates of the risks involved.

Lack of Mechanistic Understanding

As we saw in Chapter 4, identifying and understanding the biological mechanism or "mode of action" (to use a term from toxicology) by which a substance causes disease can be quite important. It can help explain diseases, identify causes, and suggest treatments.[74] Those seeking to understand causation strongly seek to find the mechanisms of action, as it helps to "connect cause and effect" beyond mere correlations.[75] And in the future mechanisms of actions in all likelihood will be more important.[76] Moreover, the mechanisms of a number of disease processes are known, including scurvy, smoke causing lung cancer, and bacteria-causing stomach ulcers, to name a few.[77] Thus, one might suppose that the biological mechanisms for many diseases are understood. This hope is not realized for many substances.

Even when substances have been studied extensively, there can remain substantial gaps in understanding. Simply put, the biological world and toxicological reactions within it are complicated, which makes substantial understanding of a toxicant's effects difficult and rarely complete. Consider, for example, what a standard toxicology textbook has to say about the widely used and well-studied over-the-counter drug, aspirin.

> Many compounds exhibit a multiplicity of biological effects. Some of these, in the case of drugs, are beneficial, others may be inconsequential to the well-being of the organism, and others are harmful and may even be lethal. . . . It is probable that, if we look hard enough, all chemicals will be found to have multiple effects and it is unlikely that the mechanisms are the same for all effects. Thus, the term *mode of action* when referring to a biological property of a chemical compound is meaningless unless qualified by the biological action that is of interest.
>
> Consider, for example, the widely used nonprescription drug aspirin. Its well known therapeutic effects are on the central nervous system (CNS),

---

[74] Paul Thagard, *How Scientists Explain Disease* (Princeton: Princeton University Press, 1999), 107.

[75] Thagard, *How Scientists Explain Disease*, 109.

[76] Michelle Carbone, George Klein, Jack Gruber, and May Wong, "Modern Criteria to Establish Human Cancer Etiology," *Cancer Research* 64 (1 August 2004): 5518–5524.

[77] Carbone et al., "Modern Criteria," 5518–5524.

causing analgesia and antipyresis, and as a local anti-inflammatory agent and inhibitor of platelet aggregation. Aspirin at therapeutic doses also uncouples oxidative phosphorylation, causing an increase in the production of CO_2, which stimulates the medullary center. An increased alveolar ventilation balances the increased CO_2 production. At higher doses of aspirin there is direct stimulation of the respiratory center leading to decreased plasma CO_2, which is compensated by renal excretion of bicarbonate. This phase of toxicity seen with intensive aspirin therapy rarely proceeds further. However, at high doses of aspirin, CNS effects are seen in the form of tinnitus and hearing loss and central respiratory paralysis. Since production of CO_2 continues, plasma pCO_2 increases but is poorly buffered because of the already lowered plasma bicarbonate. In addition, there is accumulation of organic acids due to aspirin induced derangement of carbohydrate metabolism. Finally, very high doses of aspirin lead to central respiratory paralysis and circulatory collapse due to vasomotor depression. These are just a few of the biological effects of aspirin. *We know the mechanism of action of some of these effects, but little about the mechanism of others.*

Some chemicals affect the function of a tissue or the structure of a particular kind of cell in a way so specific that even *without any clue to its chemical basis* the observed change can be spoken of as a mode of action. However, each observation of this sort constitutes a challenge to discover the underlying physical or chemical mechanism that must exist.

Each explanation offers the promise not only of understanding the action of a particular chemical but also of acquiring a better knowledge of the function of the normal body. Based on this point of view, [there are] a number of examples of highly specific, but *in many instances unexplained*, changes induced by chemicals.[78] (emphases added)

The example of aspirin suggests that despite the success of science to date in increasing our knowledge of the world, there are substantial and even critical limitations to scientists' understanding of many features of both beneficial and potentially toxic substances, even those that have been well studied for more than one hundred years. The biological world and toxic reactions in it are quite complex. Courts must be quite careful to prevent this complexity from mistakenly preventing a plaintiff's day in court when they have good but not perfect evidence for a substance's toxicity.

As if to underscore this point a Special Magistrate in the National Vaccine Injury Compensation Program discussed this issue concerning mechanistic evidence for vaccine-caused injuries. Judge Golkiewicz notes that

other desirable direct evidence [than epidemiological studies] is dispositive clinical or pathological markers evidencing a direct causal relationship. The

---

[78] Kenneth S. Santone and Garth Powis, "Mechanism of and Tests for Injuries," in *Handbook of Pesticide Toxicology*, ed. W. J. Hayes, Jr., and E. R. Laws, Jr. (New York: Harcourt Brace Jovanovich, 1991), 169.

presence of such "vaccine footprints" leaves little doubt in the mind of the experts and the factfinder that the vaccination is the likely cause of the injury. Unfortunately, most petitioners cannot benefit from the introduction of such evidence *because it is unavailable.* On this point, the competing experts agree. (emphasis added)[79]

Novel Scientific Detective Problems

Once a substance is the object of study, it may pose a comparatively novel scientific detective problem. The complex biochemical world appears to permit few generalizations at least at this point in the development of the relevant fields. This especially appears to be the case concerning the underlying mechanisms of disease.[80] To the extent that previously unknown modes of action pose new scientific problems, this will further burden the identification of adverse effects and their causes. Even though sometime in the future there may be generalizations on which scientists will be able to rely on in order to assess the risks from substances, this appears to be limited at present. For example, within the category of carcinogenic processes there are many different diseases and somewhat different processes leading to cancer responses.[81] And these are different yet from reproductive or neurotoxic effects. Consequently, researchers, while learning from the stock of existing knowledge, are frequently faced with new challenges in identifying the toxicity of substances each time they consider a different substance.[82]

Thus, although the subtle, complex mechanisms of toxicity suggest it will be difficult to understand the major modes of action and nearly impossible to describe the detailed causal path from exposure to disease, some commentators suggest and some courts appear to insist on such detailed information for tort law purposes.[83] This would be a mistaken demand that exacerbates the difficulties litigants would face in court.

Substances That Are of Little Research Interest

There will likely be substantial knowledge gaps for some kinds of substances, such as fuels or the dust from coal tars.[84] Some fuels may have their chemical

---

79   *Stevens v. Secretary HHS,* 14. The court might be referring either to a toxicity mechanism or to a "signature effect" from which causation could be inferred, but the judge is correct whichever one he is referring to.

80   Gregus and Klaassen, "Mechanisms of Toxicity," 28–76.

81   David A. Eastmond, personal communication, July 2004.

82   As we will see in Chapter 8, although often each new adverse effect often will create a new scientific puzzle to solve, there can be characteristic *types* of evidence that researchers utilize to try to identify and understand the disease mechanisms. Judges must understand these.

83   See, for example, *Black v. Food Lion, Inc.,* 171 F.3d 308, at 309 (5th Cir. 1998).

84   *Donaldson v. Central Illinois Public Service,* 199 Ill.2d 63 (2002).

composition modified sufficiently frequently that there is something of a moving target to study. Dust from coal tars may not have presented a sufficiently interesting scientific problem for study. The generic issue is that some substances will hold so little fundamental intellectual or scientific interest for researchers or funding agencies that they will be poorly studied. Yet, as some recent cases indicate, they may come to the attention of the tort law because they are involved in accidental exposures.[85] If there is not funding for research on substances, they are unlikely to be studied.

In sum, the preceding concerns – little mechanistic information, low concentrations that are toxic, long latency periods, rare diseases or extremely common diseases, as well as poorly studied substances – reduce the likelihood of obtaining human evidence and exacerbate the slow identification of any toxicity properties.[86] They also force scientists to piece together different kinds of available evidence for toxicity inferences. For example, it is not surprising that lawyers and experts had limited and varied toxicological data to use to assess the cause of Walter Allen's brain cancer. Brain cancer is quite rare and slow to develop. Thus it would be difficult to determine by means of insensitive epidemiological studies whether or not ETO made a causal contribution to his disease. Mr. Allen appeared to have had infrequent, but occasionally high exposures that probably diminished over the years. While many of the toxicity properties of ETO are well understood, there was no definitive *human* evidence that it caused or contributed to brain cancer in humans, even though there was quite plausible animal evidence. Thus, his experts had to rely largely upon animal studies and molecular data to see what they would show.

If exposure has been widespread, it may be more difficult to have "clean" unexposed groups, simply because even many in the unexposed group will have had some exposure. This contamination of seemingly "unexposed" groups will burden the detection of the disease in question.[87] As our world and our bodies are increasingly contaminated (already been observed), these problems only increase. Moreover, it can be quite difficult to obtain historical exposure data, since "times of introduction and removal of materials overlap," and often there is poor or no recordkeeping.[88] Thus, studies based on historical data are at risk of either over- or of underestimating exposure simply because the data are so poor.

---

[85] *Cavallo v. Star Enter.*, 892 F.Supp. 756 (E.D.Va. 1995); *Moore v. Ashland Chemical Inc.*, 151 F.3d 269 (5th Cir. 1998).

[86] See D. Schottenfeld and J. F. Haas, "Carcinogens in the Workplace," *CA* 29 (1979): 144, 156–159. For example, a National Institute of Occupational Health epidemiological study was noted to have an 80 percent chance of detecting a nine-fold relative risk of bladder cancer in a cohort of workers exposed to 4,4'-methylenebis (2-chloroaniline) (MOCA) in 1985, but by 1995 the same study would have an 80 percent chance of detecting a fourfold relative risk. See Elizabeth Ward et al., "4,4'-Methylenebis (2-Chloroaniline): An Unregulated Carcinogen," *American Journal of Industrial Medicine* 12 (1987), 537, 542.

[87] Huff and Rall, "Relevance to Humans," 433.

[88] Huff and Rall, "Relevance to Humans," 433.

SCIENTIFIC EPISTEMOLOGY BURDENS THE DISCOVERY OF TOXIC EFFECTS

These concerns are heightened by some pragmatic limits on scientific studies and by some broader, but perhaps under-appreciated features of science, its epistemology, and how it is interpreted and implemented by at least some in the scientific community. All of these can have adverse effects on providing the scientific basis needed for tort law purposes.

Once scientific studies have been performed to provide the basic data needed to help identify and assess the potency of substances, the interested scientific community will have to interpret the results and come to conclusions concerning any toxicity effects. This is typically not a quick process, especially if there are scientific disagreements about what the tests show, as there inevitably will be. (It would take much longer still, except in highly unusual cases, for a *consensus* to develop.)

There are a number of general considerations that suggest that it can be a slow, often difficult task to assemble much of the basic scientific information, interpret it, and come to conclusions about what the evidence shows. In addition, there are some more specific scientific practices or *conventions for interpreting studies* that will complicate and further delay the identification and assessment of risks and harms from substances. Judges must understand the same processes, since they are now important consumers of scientific information. Failure to understand and sensitively review scientific studies in the law will affect the justice of their decisions.

General Considerations

A background feature of scientific inquiry is that research is open-ended. Conclusions, even comparatively settled ones, are open to revision upon the presentation of new data, theories, or discoveries. As a result, scientists can be reluctant to come to conclusions or reluctant to assert their views with great assurance for a variety of reasons (more on this at the end of the chapter). Sometimes this reluctance reflects the degree of confidence with which they hold their views, but often it has more to do with the complexity of the biological world and conventions of scientific discussion, politeness, and persuasion (discussed later in the penultimate section on hedging).

In a legal setting, the possibility of new data or theories about to be produced may serve as a barrier to drawing scientific conclusions based on all the available evidence. This occurred with U.S. regulatory agencies concerning the toxicity of dioxin; new studies were often "just around the scientific corner."[89]

---

[89] Lauren Zeise, Chief, Reproductive and Cancer Hazard Assessment, California Environmental Protection Agency, personal communication, March 2003.

Accumulating data, forging minimal consensus, and taking regulatory action has similarly been slow with respect to arsenic.[90] To the extent that conclusions are expressed too tentatively, this may mislead judges and bar tort cases. It also can inadvertently, but mistakenly, distort some of the aims of the tort law.

Interpretive Issues

There are several epistemic practices typical of the most demanding scientific procedures that can compound the problems posed by molecular toxicants. These, combined with the open-endedness of science, can increase the chances of unfair admissibility decisions.

In general, scientists are typically quite demanding in preventing factual false positives. For assessing the toxicity of substances this would mean that their procedures are designed to minimize study results that show that a substance has a toxic property when in fact it does not. Tests might show that a substance is harmful or that it is not. The studied substance might *in fact* be harmful or not. There are, thus, four possibilities. Tests might show correctly that a substance is harmful or show correctly that a substance is not harmful. Or the tests might mistakenly show that a substance is harmful when it is not (a *false positive*) or show that a substance is not harmful when in fact it is (a *false negative*). Without having a god's-eye view of the correct outcome, scientists must interpret the tests to try to determine the actual properties of substances in the world.

Scientists appear to have a lesser concern to prevent false negatives than to prevent false positives. It is difficult to find systematic statements about the stringency of scientific inferential views in preventing false positives, as they are rarely articulated. However, the following considerations provide some evidence for this claim.

First, scientists are vigilant toward random statistical errors producing false positive results, demanding that support for their conclusions must be *statistically significant*.[91] A common cause of a false positive is that the *sample* in an experimental group being studied is not sufficiently representative of the population of interest and as a matter of statistical chance contains a higher than representative number of adverse effects compared with the population as a whole. The risk is that a study might suggest that there is an elevated rate of disease, when in fact there is not one. This difference results from random variation in the samples being considered. Thus, there are a variety of tests and procedures to determine whether the difference between adverse effects

---

[90] National Research Council, *Arsenic in Drinking Water* (Washington, DC: National Academy Press, 1999).

[91] That is, there must be less than 5 percent (or sometimes less than 1 percent) odds by chance alone (as a result of sampling or experimental error) of a factual false positive.

in an experimental group and a control group are due to random (statistical) chance or to real differences in responses. Judges may be told that scientists seek to ensure that they have no more than a 1 percent to a 5 percent chance of a false positive.[92] Some scientists may hold rigidly to such standards but the assertion can be misleading. The particular percentage that a scientist uses for statistical significance need not be so low, as we considered in Chapter 4. Moreover, working scientists indicate a much greater flexibility on this point than is often found in court decisions. That is, there is a lesser concern with a particular level for statistical significance, for example, .05, but more concern with what the study reveals using various statistical tools.

Suppose there is an epidemiological study showing there is an elevated liver cancer rate from exposure to vinyl chloride. An obvious question is, what explains it? Is it a real effect, for example, from the vinyl chloride exposure, or is it an artifact of the study, that is, merely a statistical accident suggesting there are more liver cancers in the exposed than in the nonexposed group, or is it something else? A scientist demanding low statistical significance, in effect insists that it is highly important to rule out statistical anomalies that might mistakenly show a study is positive when there would be no real effect in the world. Of course, it is important to distinguish between real effects and artifacts of the studies. However, this effort must be conducted sensitively and well because there are a variety of pitfalls from utilizing overly simple interpretive rules.

A second kind of evidence for epistemic conservatism is a demand for multiple kinds of evidence. Consider what Arthur Furst, a well-known toxicologist, would require to show *scientifically* that something is a human carcinogen. He argues that one needs multiple epidemiological studies, multiple animal studies subjected to strict experimental conditions (to have an animal model for the toxic effect), and multiple short-term studies and other detailed features of the substance.[93] In effect, he would want to see evidence of toxicity from a variety of tests. This would ensure quite a full characterization of a substance and better understanding of its adverse effects. In the absence of such complete information, he would be cautious and reluctant to judge that a substance is a human carcinogen *for scientific purposes.*[94]

There are a variety of problems with this view even within a scientific field. It is time-consuming – it might well take one or more decades to accumulate the recommended data about substances such as carcinogens. It is quite expensive. (Thus, the object of study would need to be considered of great enough importance to be worth such an investment of time and resources.) And, the scientific community has such substantial information for very few substances.[95]

---

92 Rothman, *Modern Epidemiology*, 115–118.

93 Arthur Furst, "Yes, But Is It a Human Carcinogen?" *Journal of the American College of Toxicology* 9 (1990): 1–18.

94 Personal communication when both Professor Furst and the author made presentations to the University of California Toxic Substances Research and Teaching Program, April 1995.

For example, Professor Furst's requirements might necessitate requiring even more kinds of evidence than was available in the Bendectin cases.

Furst's view represents a standing temptation that has just enough legitimacy to make it difficult for scientists or public officials to resist. A failure to pursue certain kinds of evidence makes a scientist or an official appear impervious to new evidence or uninterested in a *good* scientific foundation for legal purposes. Indeed such arguments are in effect utilized to try to persuade officials to demand further scientific investigations. Who can be against being more certain about or having a better scientific foundation for testimony or a conclusion?

Answering this apparent rhetorical question, however, is not so obvious. Giving in to the temptation may delay or prevent public health protections or prevent corrective justice to a wrongfully injured plaintiff. Regulatory officials in administrative agencies must use good judgment in assessing and evaluating how much evidence is needed for addressing particular substances for regulation. They must carefully consider whether more and better evidence, and how much, if any, is needed for their purposes.

Judges, the administrators of the tort law, will be similarly urged to demand more and better data or face claims that there are insufficient data to support an expert's testimony. They will likely face demands for epidemiological or mechanistic evidence, neither of which is necessary to make causation inferences about substances (Chapters 6 and 7). In fact some courts appear to have endorsed such views (Chapter 6). If courts embrace such requests as minimum standards of scientific support for the admissibility of expert testimony, this is contrary to current scientific practice. It also will greatly burden litigants, especially injured parties, and could easily deny them a trial. Other courts have seen the pitfalls of such requests and have resisted them.[96] There are several combinations of

---

[95] Out of 736 agents that the World Health Organization had evaluated for carcinogenicity as of 1998, 74 substances were known human carcinogens (these *might* satisfy Furst's criteria), 56 were "probably" human carcinogens (which would not satisfy his criteria), and 225 were classified as "possibly" human carcinogens. See IARC, *Monographs*, vols. 1–71 (1972–1998), summarized at the International Agency for Research on Cancer Web site http://www-cie.iarc.fr/monoeval/grlist.html (updated 5 March 1998). (Not surprisingly, firms whose products are threatened by regulation often demand multiple kinds of evidence and insist on the need for human evidence.)

[96] Judge Putnam of the Northern District of Alabama chided his district court brethren for insisting on too much *scientific certainty* for admissibility decisions concerning the toxicity of Parlodel, a breast milk lactation suppression drug (*Brasher v. Sandoz Pharmaceuticals Corp*, 160 F. Supp. 2d 1291, at 1296 (2001)). Moreover, he felt the need

to explain [why he reached] a conclusion about the admissibility of this scientific testimony different from that reached in [other] cases.... The court believes that in those cases the *Daubert* standard [for admitting expert testimony] was applied incorrectly, creating much too high a standard of admissibility. [The earlier] cases seem to equate *Daubert's* reliability standard with *scientific certainty*, which is far from what the Supreme Court intended in *Daubert*. Science, like many other human endeavors, draws conclusions from circumstantial evidence when other, better forms of evidence are not available. As already noted above, one cannot practically conduct an epidemiological study of the association of Parlodel with postpartum AMI.

respectable scientific evidence that implicate substances as toxic to humans well short of the demanding standards Furst proposes. And, not all respectable scientists are so extreme in their reluctance to draw inferences.[97]

Another scientist, perhaps enamored with the passé philosophy of science of Karl Popper,[98] has articulated analogous views about the importance of ruling out alternative hypotheses that might explain an adverse effect before drawing a conclusion. Scientists, he claims, seek to establish causal connections between exposure and disease with "proof... usually accepted in science" or proof "beyond a reasonable doubt" because alternative explanations will slay "a beautiful [but mistaken] hypothesis."[99] Trying to falsify an existing hypothesis by proposing an alternative explanation is a feature of Popper's philosophy of science. Moreover, the "beyond a reasonable doubt" language is revealing since it is one of the most demanding in the law. This standard of proof is used in the criminal law to protect a person's vital interests and to serve as a bulwark against mistakenly convicting an innocent person. Adopting it in toxicology would require that if there were any reasonable doubts about the toxicity properties of a substance, one should not conclude that a substance has them. This is much too demanding for the tort law's admissibility standards and for its ultimate standard of proof. In the criminal law, as commentators have put it, there are "preeminent values at stake," such as loss of life, liberty, and good standing in the community.[100] Although defendants in tort suits stand to lose money as a result of a legal decision, these are not the same *preeminent values* that criminal defendants face and the law does not provide them the same degree of protection provided by high degrees of certainty. Judges should not impose such high protection for tort defendants inadvertently by what they require for admissibility decisions in torts.

James Huff and David Rall, two leading environmental health experts, have suggested a third consideration arguing that toxicologists in particular may be

---

Moreover, one cannot ethically experiment on human beings, exposing them to the near certainty of some number of deaths, simply to satisfy some evidentiary standard. *Hollander* and *Brumbaugh* failed to recognize that *Daubert* does not require, or even allow, the trial court to determine the scientific "correctness" or certainty of the evidence, but only that the facts from which the opinion is *inferred* are themselves scientifically reliable. (emphasis added)

97   I consider these points in Chapter 7.
98   David Goodstein, "What is Science?" *Reference Manual on Scientific Evidence* (Washington, DC: Federal Judicial Center, 2000), 71 (noting, along with many others, that the testability of a scientific claim is not adequate to demarcate scientific from nonscientific claims or methods). Karl Popper's views have long been rejected by philosophers of science as a criterion demarcating science from non-science. See Gary Edmond and David Mercer, "What Judges Should Know About Falsificationism," *Expert Evidence* 5 (1997): 29.
99   H. J. Eysenck, "Were We Really Wrong?" *American Journal of Public Health,* 133 (1991): 42 9–32, but compare Sander Greenland, "Invited Commentary: Science versus Public Health Actions: Those who Were Wrong Are Still Wrong," *American Journal of Public Health* 133 (1991): 43 5–36.
100   *McCormick on Evidence,* 3rd ed., 962.

reluctant to conclude that substances are harmful to humans. Scientists who normally propose and test hypotheses on animals and other nonhuman systems may be reluctant to predict effects on humans from exposures to substances. However, because of legitimate moral constraints on testing humans, scientists are for the most part denied the opportunity to test predictions of effects on humans. Thus, the

> laboratory scientist, accustomed to being able to close the circle from hypothesis, to test, to acceptance or rejection, to new hypothesis generation, is uncomfortable when lawyers, economists, journalists, and politicians take the hypothesis and use it in a system in which the circle cannot be closed and in which the answer often cannot be known *with certainty*.[101]

To the extent that scientists are implicitly uncomfortable with less than *certain* conclusions as Huff and Rall suggest, they may be reluctant to urge that, based on animal studies, there are adverse human effects with that degree of certainty. The open-endedness of science and the complexity of biology also will caution scientists against urging conclusions concerning toxicity to humans with the high degree of certainty to which Huff and Rall refer. Nonetheless, they go on to add that this research circle has been "closed" in a number of instances and that when one considers the body of animal and human evidence that has been compiled over a thirty-five-year period by consensus scientific bodies and governmental research institutions, "it appears likely that the natural or synthetic compounds that are carcinogenic in animal models will likewise be carcinogenic in humans."[102]

Fourth, in assessing the risks from toxic substances, scientists typically presume that substances have no properties in particular until these have been established by appropriate studies. That is, if we were to hand a scientist an unknown substance and ask her whether it was toxic or not, she would remain *agnostic* until she had done appropriate tests on it. Agnosticism, as we know from discussions about religion, is the view that on the evidence available, one cannot know whether or not the thing in question has an alleged property. Agnostics *suspend* judgment about the object of inquiry until there is further evidence.

If scientists were to ask a more difficult questions, such as, "At what exposure levels might it be toxic to humans?" it would take a much longer time for our scientist to come to respectable conclusions. Answering questions about the *mechanism of action* would take even longer, if it were ever understood.

Scientific agnosticism, however, can easily be transformed by individual scientists into something much more insidious for both science and the law. Courts will need to be alert to such testimony. Recent examples from litigation

---

[101] Huff and Rall, "Relevance to Humans," 434 (emphasis added).
[102] Huff and Rall, "Relevance to Humans," 440.

illustrate this point. A scientist, instead of being agnostic about the properties of a substance, might *assume* that they have *no toxicity properties* until proven otherwise. Sander Greenland, one of the leading epidemiologists in the country, has called this approach the "tyranny of the null hypothesis." One scientist has been quoted as saying, "If the human data do not compel me to reject the null hypothesis, then I must conclude that exposure to the chemical does not pose a risk of the disease."[103] Moreover, "if you do not observe an increase in the incidence of the disease in the exposed population, then you cannot reject the null hypothesis *and therefore must accept it.* . . . In other words, if you do not have sufficient evidence that exposure to a chemical poses a risk of the disease, then you conclude that the exposure does not pose a risk."[104] As Greenland notes, this means that "In the absence of sufficient evidence, adhering to the null hypothesis, Dr. [X] states that we will always find that a chemical does not pose a risk to humans. . . . [this constitutes] the *fallacy of assuming what is to be proved.* It is a very common logical fallacy and is built into the methods that form the basis of Dr. [X's] testimony, namely, statistical methods that test only the null hypothesis and no other possibility" (emphasis added).[105]

Greenland goes on to explain the problem with such an approach.

> The claim that an epidemiologist must start with the assumption that a chemical does not pose a risk of disease to humans is false, both logically and in common-sense terms, as many scientific and every day examples demonstrate. To believe otherwise can lead to premature and untrustworthy judgments, with consequent serious damage to public health. By such reasoning, the Food and Drug Administration should approve for market every new and untested product, for with no testing there will be no evidence that the product poses a risk; with no evidence, you will be unable to reject the null hypothesis, and by Dr. [X's] reasoning you must then conclude that the product does not pose a risk. Needless to say, impartial scientists, regulators, and lay persons alike reject such reasoning. By the same token, it should come as no surprise that industry seeks out experts who still promote such fallacies.[106]

The approach Greenland critiques is in essence a very skeptical view combined with an unproven, nonneutral *assumption* that exposure to a substance does not cause or contribute to disease. Moreover, this view appears to license the inference that no evidence of an adverse effect is evidence that there is no adverse effect. But this is an obvious fallacy. Such a view, thus, nicely reinforces a defendant's position in the law – to assume that a substance does not cause adverse effects until this is *definitively established* by quite good evidence. Thus,

103 "Written Direct Testimony of Sander Greenland, Dr. P. H., in Opposition to Baxter Healthcare Corporation's Petition for Declaratory Judgment," 30 April 1999, 22 (quoting Dr. Patricia Buffler, School of Public Health, University of California, Berkeley).
104 "Written Direct Testimony of Sander Greenland," 22.
105 "Written Direct Testimony of Sander Greenland," 22.
106 "Written Direct Testimony of Sander Greenland," 22–23.

this methodology *predisposes scientists not to find toxicity* (because it assumes there is no toxicity) and *begs the question against findings of toxicity*, at least until there is "sufficient evidence" that exposure to a substance causes or contributes to disease.

If a scientist also demands either multiple sources of evidence or high degrees of certainty before concluding that a substance is toxic, this ensures that few substances will be found to be toxic or that it will take a considerable period of time and great expense to come to such a conclusion.

In summary, combining a demand for a high degree of certainty with a demand for multiple kinds of evidence before scientists may infer a toxicity judgment together with the assumption that a substance has no toxicity properties until scientific tests *compel* one (with considerable certainty) to make toxicity judgments, will ensure that few, if any, substances will be judged to have toxic properties. Such views create intellectual traps of which judges must be aware when reviewing admissibility decisions.

Fourth, the scientific burdens of proof and the standards of proof with which they must be satisfied that are suggested by some scientists are usually reinforced by considerable skepticism and inferential caution. Such views are often motivated by basic scientific training to develop intellectual virtues, skills, and techniques that tend to prevent false positives, resist casually proposing views that overturn the hard-earned epistemic status quo, add carefully to the knowledge status quo, and improve their understanding of the mechanisms by which phenomena work. (It does not appear that the same effort and training is devoted to preventing false negatives.)

There are several reasons for these epistemic tendencies. Scientists develop inferential caution to avoid mistakenly changing the knowledge theoretical status quo that has been carefully established over time. Healthy skepticism discourages scientists from overenthusiastic advocacy of their own ideas and discourages them from wasting their own research efforts. It assists the profession in self-regulation by discouraging large segments of a field from chasing research chimeras and wasting collective efforts.

However, skeptical attitudes, inferential caution, and epistemic virtues can have quite unintended and unexpected effects depending on the context in which they are used and how extreme are the attitudes in resisting claims to new knowledge and insights.

In the law, agnosticism about the toxicity of substances preserves the current legal status quo ante, whatever it may be. If harmful substances are in commerce, they remain there until a case is made for removing them. If people are exposed to toxicants, they remain exposed. If they are exposed to substances that are believed to be toxic but are not, they will be unharmed. If substances are not permitted into commerce until there has been substantial testing of their safety under a pre-market regulatory statute, they remain out of commerce until the testing is complete.

The points in the preceding two paragraphs raise the issue discussed in the next few paragraphs.

Inattention to the Distribution of Mistakes in Scientific Research

Scientists for the most part appear not to attend to the distribution of mistakes that can result from their epistemic procedures (except to prevent mistakenly adding to the theoretical scientific status quo).[107] This is quite proper and appropriate for scientific research for its own sake. However, it can have unintended consequences for other institutions.

By not attending to distributive effects I mean several things. Minimally, scientific conventions and practices are not to be designed to serve other social institutions; they *serve the internal needs of science.* Consequently, conventions and practices that arose to internally serve the needs of science may or may not be well-suited for providing scientific information for other institutions. The powerful tendency to prevent false positives serves the epistemic norms of science.[108]

More important, in most research science there is little or no attention to the distribution of mistakes between false positives and false negatives, with prevention of false positives given priority.[109] This can have a substantial impact on other institutions if administrators of those institutions (including federal judges), are not aware of these features. Yet when scientific procedures are utilized in other institutions, the distribution of mistakes can be quite important (Chapter 6).

---

[107] That is, it is not part of basic scientific research to address how scientific mistakes might affect other institutions, and there appears to be a much lesser concern with how false negatives might affect the institution of science. This is very different from the law, for example, which ordinarily has a self-conscious concern with the distribution of mistakes (Chapter 6).

[108] This is a tendency not equally stringent across all fields (e.g., compare public health fields with subatomic physics), but as a generalization it is not misleading.

[109] One area of scientific research for which this is less true is public health research and medical practice – two scientific areas concerned with protecting the public from disease. For example, the U.S. National Research Council indicates that

> Whether in law or science, the inference of causation must be understood as a process that involves judgment and interpretation. Because the basic mechanisms of most modern chronic diseases are not well understood, analysts are forced to interpret observational data to find clues about etiology. Despite the immense public interest in the effect of hazardous wastes on public health, rather few empirical data are available. Nevertheless, public health policy requires that decisions be made despite the incomplete evidence, with the aim of protecting public health in the future.
>
> Where this committee *emphasizes the need to protect the public health* in the face of knowledge gaps and scientific uncertainty, the conclusion of a *scientific research report is much more likely to emphasize the uncertainty, knowledge gaps, and need for further research* with little or no comment about protecting public health. (National Research Council, 1991, 44) (emphasis added)

Recently, the environmental justice movement in the United States has high-lighted concerns about the distribution of mistakes in a third sense: distribution of risks across populations, because some might be especially susceptible or highly exposed. Scientists and risk assessors, who at least until recently typically conducted their studies based on the toxicity effects on 70-kilogram, healthy males, tended not to take account of the effects of substances on children, infants, the sick, the infirm, and those already exposed to substances. For example, a major study concerning the effects of perchlorate in drinking water on humans was a two-week study of a small number of adult men and women. No children, infants, elderly people, pregnant women, bottle-fed babies, or diseased individuals were in the study. As a result, it was inadequate to address the effects of perchlorate on the general population.[110] (Fortunately, some of these issues are now receiving greater attention both in science and the law.[111]) Consequently, studies must be reviewed to determine who was the study population and what implications this might have for parties at the bar.

The previous point is especially germane for the tort law. Many studies are done to determine whether an exposure to a substance causes or contributes to disease in healthy, *adult* males. Epidemiological studies are often based on *workplace exposures*. However, those who work are *usually healthier* than the general population (the "healthy worker" effect). This has two consequences: (1) when no adverse effect has been found in adult males or in workers, the study probably has few implications for biologically vulnerable individuals (if they could be determined); and (2) if some adverse effect has been found in males or in workers, it is likely that the adverse effect will be worse in the general population at the same or lower exposures. In a more varied general population, comprised of individuals with greater vulnerabilities and susceptibilities, there will be adverse effects shown in more individuals.

The administrators of other social institutions must be especially sensitive to the distributive effects of scientific procedures and methodologies *on their institutions* in order to ensure that practices internal to science for its own purposes or studies done for quite different purposes do not distort conclusions they need for their institutions when evidence is transferred to a new context. That is, they must be alert to possible shortcomings of the scientific studies and how these might affect the social institutions for which they have responsibility. Judges, administrators of the legal system, must be especially vigilant to ensure that seemingly neutral scientific impartiality does not inadvertently predispose the tort law toward one side or the other in the law.

---

[110]   *Perchlorate in Drinking Water: A Science and Policy Review*, University of California, Irvine (June 2004).

[111]   Michael Gerrard, ed., *The Law of Environmental Justice: Theories and Procedures to Address Disproportionate Risks* (Chicago: Section of Environment, Energy, and Resources, The American Bar Association, 1999).

HEDGING IN SCIENTIFIC COMMUNICATION

Scientists' reports of research can have substantial but often hidden impacts on the evidentiary value of research for the law. In particular, communication of scientific results can *inadvertently* diminish the evidentiary value of reports needed for legal purposes. Scientists have a tendency to *hedge* their claims in scientific papers; this can have unintended consequences in other contexts.

Hedging is a convention of communication with several features that has been well studied by applied linguists and rhetoricians. Hedging "express[es] tentativeness and possibility in communication,"[112] and may reflect "a lack of complete commitment to the truth value of... a proposition, or a desire not to express that commitment categorically" or a variety of other conventions.[113] This is an endemic rhetorical practice of scientists that can substantially affect communication between scientists and the larger public, including judges who may be reviewing scientific papers that contain hedging language. More important, if judges do not understand hedging, it is likely to mislead them.

For example, there are a variety of linguistic expressions by means of which scientists hedge the claims they make or assert in research papers: "it seems that," "it might be speculated that," "it could be suggested that," "it could be explained by," "if correct, this prediction might explain why," and "although a causal relationship between the latter processes remains to be verified, the correlation may not reflect mere coincidence."[114] Scientific papers often conclude with the claim that research only "suggests" a toxicity effect or that the research "may" support a conclusion that a substance is toxic.

Content-Oriented Hedging

Some hedging clearly focuses on the content of a scientific proposition being articulated in a research article. One writer has proposed that there may be two kinds of content-oriented hedges: *attribute* and *reliability* hedges.[115]

Attribute hedges seek to qualify the relations between actual experimental results and what might have been expected. An attribute hedge "indicates that results vary from an assumed ideal of how nature behaves and allows a better match with familiar descriptive terms."[116] Thus, writers utilize "attribute hedges to seek precision in the expression, and ... encode variability ..." For example, a writer might say that "This appearance of kinase activity correlates

---

112   Ken Hyland, *Hedging in Scientific Research Articles* (Amsterdam: John Benjamins Publishing Company, 1997), 1.
113   Hyland, *Hedging*, 3–5.
114   Hyland, *Hedging*, 3–5.
115   Hyland, *Hedging*, 163.
116   Hyland, *Hedging*, 164.

quite well . . . "[117] (Or, for those who recall the kinetic theory gases, this theory explains Boyle's law as long as one does not demand too much precision, since the kinetic theory of gases is an idealization.) Such a statement indicates that the result, although *reasonably accurate* or close to what might have been expected, was not *wholly accurate* or *exactly what might have been expected* or *what might be found under more ideal condtions.*

Related to this are *"reliability-oriented"* hedges. These "acknowledge the writer's uncertain knowledge and indicate the confidence he or she is willing to invest in the validity of a claim: they say, 'I do not speak from secure knowledge.'" As one of Kenneth Hyland's scientific informants puts this, "You're dealing with living organisms and, at whatever level you study, its very hard to say definitively 'this is how things are'. Actual truths are not easily dug out.'"[118] Instead of saying definitely that *is* how things are, a scientist might say, "This is how they *seem* or *appear* to be."

Common to content hedges is that they try to "provide a specification of the state of knowledge rather than hedge the writer's commitment to the claim. . . . Both forms . . . seek to increase the exactness with which a proposition is expressed, either by indicating how far entities approach an ideal endpoint on a cognitive scale, or by stating more precisely the writer's assessment of the certainty of a statement."[119] Such hedging language is likely to be expressed by phrases such as "we suspect," "it appears possible," or the claim is "probably" correct.

The kinds of hedging language just sketched are what one might expect from scientists who tend to be cautious about the accuracy and scope of their claims. The major function of these hedging features "is to provide a *specification of the state of knowledge* rather than hedge the writer's commitment to the claim. Both [kinds of hedging] are principally concerned with the interpretation of the world . . . and seek to increase the *exactness* with which a proposition is expressed . . ."[120] (emphasis added). If a result does not quite come out as expected the author hedges to show she is being accurate. Especially in the biological sciences, if the world does not work according to tidy rules so that she can say how things *are*, she hedges and says this is how they *seem*.

Writer-Oriented Hedging

However, there are other uses of hedging language that have important functions in scientific writing and communication that have much less to do with accuracy or degrees of certainty with which scientists might believe something

[117] Hyland, *Hedging*, 168.
[118] Hyland, *Hedging*, 168.
[119] Hyland, *Hedging*, 169.
[120] Hyland, *Hedging*, 169.

about features of the world. It is these that have considerable potential to mislead those who are unfamiliar with such cautious, hedging language. Borrowing from others we might say that hedging can be "writer-oriented" or "reader-oriented" as well as serving the aims of politeness.

Since research articles and reports "publicly link *scientists* with their *knowledge claims*, [the articles] therefore represent careful decisions concerning the degree of commitment the writer wishes to invest in them."[121] Use of various hedging devices in these contexts tends to "*diminish* the author's presence in the text" in order "to *shield* the writer from the possible consequences" of later being proven wrong in her results and *limiting damage to her reputation* that might occur from categorical commitments.[122] Phrases such as "these data indicate" or "taxonomic evidence suggests," or "the model implies," *hedge the writer's commitment to the ultimate claim*, resting it instead on "the data," the "evidence," or "the model." Thus, if there is something wrong with the result it is the *data*, the *evidence*, or the *model*, *not the author* who was mistaken. Such phrases suggest that the writer is avoiding full commitment to the truth of what is claimed in order to *shield* him or her from reputational damage should the claims not ultimately be accepted or ultimately be shown to be mistaken. One scientist reported the rationale for this:

> Scientists are fallible and so are their methods. Most of the time you could be right but there is often a chance that it might be something different and you'd better make sure you let people know that before they let you know.[123]

In addition, such assertions let the authors establish claims to the findings (that is, discovering it first), but the hedging keeps them at a sufficient distance so that their reputations are not irrevocably damaged if the claims turn out to be problematic in some way.

Although such strategies could be interpreted as lack of confidence in the content of the claim, Hyland's informants "unanimously interpreted these forms [of hedging] as *protective strategies.*[124] Thus, they "diminish personal responsibility for a variety of reasons . . . [and afford] . . . protection from the full effects of the eventual overthrow of the claim by colleagues."[125]

Reader-Oriented Hedging

There are also "reader-oriented" hedges. Hedged statements implicitly addressing the readers of scientific articles "mark claims as provisional . . . invite readers

---

121 Hyland, *Hedging*, 170 (emphasis added).
122 Hyland, *Hedging*, 170 (emphasis added).
123 Hyland, *Hedging*, 170 (quoting unnamed informant).
124 Hyland, *Hedging*, 175 (emphasis added).
125 Hyland, *Hedging*, 176.

to orientate themselves to the discourse and engage in a dialogue. . . . [That is, they] invite the audience to respond in some way, they solicit collusions by addressing the reader as someone possessing good sense and an ability to participate in the discourse with an open mind."[126] Others have suggested that an important aspect of hedging for this purpose involves politeness. These two aspects of hedging are related.

The idea is that if one submits one's ideas politely and humbly to the research community without overtly challenging extant views and without causing others to lose face by how one's ideas are presented, this facilitates one's own ideas being considered and, perhaps, ultimately being accepted by other researchers. By contrast, the suggestion is that if one submits a paper with strong, unhedged conclusions, saying how they will obviously overturn decades of accepted research, this will offend the research community, invite resistance to the ideas and create something of a barrier to the consideration and acceptance of the ideas.

Such reader-oriented aspects of hedging appear to have nothing to do with the content of the thesis defended but are largely utilized because of social conventions within the research community. The aim appears to be to submit ideas to others in sufficiently humble ways to have them considered, debated, and taken seriously, as well as helping to persuade others of one's views without offending or insulting them by the means of the presentation. This aspect of hedging has to do with courtesy and deference toward others, including those whose views one might seek to overturn, as a means of trying to get one's ideas considered and ultimately accepted by them.

An author's only "suggesting" a conclusion and inviting others to consider it, also indicates a kind of politeness and invites them to become part of the enterprise, to consider the viability of the proposed idea, thus, perhaps to help persuade them of the truth of the claim. To the extent that conventions of politeness and persuasiveness influence scientific reports, they may misleadingly understate the conclusions.

Thus, scientific conclusions or statements are hedged for numerous reasons other than the firmness of a researcher's conviction about his or her results. There clearly are reasons for hedging that have little or nothing to do with weak support for one's conclusions. This was notably illustrated in Watson and Crick's justly famous paper on the structure of DNA. While telling "anyone who would listen that they had discovered the secret of life," their published conclusion was "We wish to suggest a structure for . . . DNA . . . [which] has novel features which are of considerable biological interest."[127] Their beliefs in their

---

126 Hyland, *Hedging*, 178.
127 Hyland, *Hedging*, 65. (While telling "anyone who would listen that they had discovered the secret of life," their published conclusion was "We wish to suggest a structure for . . . DNA . . . [which] has novel features which are of considerable biological interest.")

conclusions and their beliefs in the revolutionary import of their discoveries were much stronger than their research papers expressed.

Similar points can be made about toxicity judgments. Even though a scientific paper does not claim certainty for a conclusion that a toxic substance causes human harm – "there may be an association between exposure and tumors" – the author may well have believed that harm was probable (or even fairly certain).

The results of or assertions in scientific papers may be hedged in part because of the scope of *accuracy* of the results and *limits of the authors' confidence* in the conclusions, in part because the authors are seeking to *shield themselves* from future criticism or overturning of their results and in part because they are making *humble and polite* submissions of research reports for consideration by the scientific community in order to facilitate consideration of their ideas and, ultimately, their acceptance.

As a result of hedging, and this is quite important, the degree of certainty with which scientists *believe* conclusions *is not necessarily accurately expressed in the language of their published papers* that are implicitly addressing a variety of other conventions in the scientific community. There could, thus, be a substantial disconnection between a scientist's published papers on a subject and that scientist's beliefs about it. The various hedges of published papers amount to terms of art – or *arcane features of less visible conventions with which the wider public and judges are not likely to be familiar.* Hedging language becomes a term of art or has technical meanings and nuances that diverge from ordinary uses. Thus, a scientist might have or verbally express greater confidence in her research than is indicated in her published papers and would not be trying to mislead others. Moreover, hedging is such an ingrained psychological tendency for individual and social features of the scientific profession that even comparatively strong conclusions may be hedged out of habit, politeness, or an attempt to persuade others.

Laypersons, including judges and most of the rest of us, are likely to understand hedged comments as a lack of epistemic confidence in research conclusions. In some instances this may be the case. However, in many other cases this would be a mistake because other conventions are at work.

This last point is strongly buttressed by some observations about scientists and scientific practice by one of the authors in the Federal Judicial Center's *Reference Manual on Scientific Evidence.* David Goldstein notes that scientific debates are strongly adversarial, with "every idea receiv[ing] the most vigorous possible advocacy, just in case it might be right."[128] If these observations are correct about the practices of science or even of many scientists within a field, they suggest a significant incompatibility between how scientific results are presented in professional papers and how strongly scientists believe in them

[128] Goodstein, "How Science Works," 74 (see also 78).

(or at least major aspects of their research). Consequently, the tentative, hedging language of professional papers would be a poor guide to how strongly the original author, or even others who held similar views, believed in the results of research.

Thus, courts risk mistakes when they use or permit published results to be used to impeach a scientist's stated belief in research conclusions, since the contexts might be quite different. Courts should be open to accepting stronger statements from testifying experts in recognition of the hedging practices in the literature or they must learn to translate scientific articles in order to read them as expressing stronger conclusions than existing language suggests.

Finally, even if a scientist offers published results in tentative, hedged language, *other scientists, reviewing the same data*, might come to *stronger* conclusions. This, too, would not necessarily be a mistake. Individually written and humbly submitted research products – appropriately sensitive to the standing and face of others in the community – are more likely to win approval and ultimately adoption and endorsement by the community. Moreover, as others review accumulated studies and *become persuaded* of the claims (the aim of the original articles), *even though no new evidence has emerged to support them*, scientists' confidence in the results increases. This is part of consensus formation in the scientific community.[129] Thus, one function of hedging is to assist in persuading others of the correctness of he study. Others reading and incorporating the hedged results of several authors might come to have and articulate more certain views of the issue than any of the individual study reports. In legal contexts, judges should exercise great care in permitting individual scientific reports to impeach a more comprehensive, carefully formed scientific view.

COMMUNICATION BETWEEN SCIENCE AND THE LAW

Hedging will substantially affect communication between science and the law. Scientists are not likely to write papers with strong, unhedged conclusions, saying how they are certain that they have discovered a causal relationship and that their discovery will overturn decades of accepted research. Even though a scientific paper does not claim certainty for a conclusion that a toxic substance causes human harm, the author may well have believed that harm was probable (or even fairly certain). Some distinguished scientists have informed me that when they say there is an *association* between an exposure and harm, this is what they mean by a causal relation between the exposure and the harm.[130]

---

[129] Personal communication, David A. Eastmond.
[130] Ellen Silbergeld of Johns Hopkins University is the most recent scientist to express this point. She means by this that if one has appropriate replicated studies showing the association, there is not some addition "causal" relation one will find. (Personal communication, Collegium

Moreover, as noted above, when others review accumulated studies (including papers expressed in quite tentative language) and become persuaded of the claims (the aim of the original articles), even though no new evidence has emerged to support them, scientists' confidence in the results increases. This is part of consensus formation in the scientific community.[131]

Laypersons, including judges and most of the rest of us, are not likely to understand hedged comments. Or we might understand them as a lack of epistemic confidence in research conclusions. As we have seen this only accounts for a portion of hedging and in some cases may not be a significant reason because other conventions are at work (recall Watson and Crick).

Carefully hedged scientific papers, then, could pose at least two problems in the law. Judges might well take the hedged terms in their ordinary senses without recognizing the linguistic conventions and scientific practices that are behind them, and without recognizing that such language is a term of art, be persuaded by the cautionary terms, and perhaps reject plaintiffs' experts as a result. In addition, defendants could exploit this cautious language to try to persuade judges that plaintiffs have not made a case for causation simply because of the hedged language in journal articles.

Thus, courts risk mistakes if they accept without scrutiny or qualification published results to impeach a scientist's stated belief in research conclusions based on a range of studies and background information, since the contexts are likely quite different. Courts should be prepared to accept stronger statements from testifying experts, who have reviewed and integrated a variety of studies, in recognition of the hedging practices in the literature and in recognition of the weight of accumulated evidence for their conclusions.

In short, courts should not necessarily accept at face value individual scientific reports and permit them to impeach more comprehensive, carefully formed and integrated scientific views based on wider evidence, without undertaking a more careful and sensitive review of the reports and the experts opinion based on all the evidence he or she has considered. One court reports an instance of trying to understand cautious language. A judge in the Vaccine Injury Compensation Program sought to determine what the phrase the "evidence is consistent with a causal relationship" meant (used by the Institute of Medicine). After comparing two different reports and further inquiries

Ramazzini, October 2004.) One also sees similar assertions in the early vinyl chloride papers, although the authors there used language more strongly implicating causal connections: one expression was "*an etiologic association* between VC work and tumor" and the other was that VC work exposure "was responsible for malignant and nonmalignant liver disease." (Clark W. Heath, Jr., Henry Falk, and John L. Creech, Jr., "Characteristics of Cases of Angiosarcoma of the Liver Among Vinyl Chloride Workers in the United States," *Annals of the New York Academy of Sciences* (1975): 231 (emphasis added).)

[131] David A. Eastmond, personal communication.

he concluded that "is consistent with" means "favors acceptance of" a causal relationship. He then went on to interpret that to mean that this language would satisfy the more likely than not standard of the law.[132] On the face of the language "is consistent with" does not mean "more likely than not." Scientific conventions in that case hid important information.

Similar differences in language between scientific and ordinary contexts also need to be recognized. Scientists might say that substances *may be* human carcinogens instead of saying that they *are*. Or they might say that substances have the *potential* to be human carcinogens, not that they *are* human carcinogens. Or they may say that there is an *association* between exposure and disease and mean by that exposure makes a causal contribution to disease.[133] In short, they hedge.

If lawyers exploit for tactical legal purposes scientists' cautious language, this will have an asymmetric effect in the tort law. Hedged language *may not be a good guide to the scientific reality in question.* Language can change subtly from one context to another and judges must be sensitive to the misuse of adversarial strategies, which seek to discredit respectable scientists in court contexts.

I had a similar experience on a science advisory panel. The issue being considered was whether aspirin had adverse reproductive effects, especially on developing fetuses during the third trimester. There was evidence both for and against this claim, but strong theoretical reasons and some evidence for believing that this could be a problem. During a break in presentations I asked the occupational physician who sat next to me what he thought of the issue. After reviewing the pro and con evidence, and thinking for a minute, he then said, "Well, if my wife were pregnant, I sure would not let her take aspirin during the third trimester of pregnancy." He did not know *for sure* that aspirin would cause intracranial bleeding in a developing fetus *in utero*, but he thought the scientific community knew enough to put warning labels on aspirin bottles to inform women that there was a reasonable chance that this could occur. And, he would protect his own child from this possible low-level risk. Similarly, in other practical contexts, including the tort law, scientists could be fully prepared to judge that a substance was more likely than not a carcinogen, but might not be quite willing to assert in so many words in professional journals because of existing publication and professional communication conventions. The reluctance would not be the result of disingenuousness, but of different contexts from professional publishing to more practical life judgments. Publication contexts raise the stakes, author's caution, and critics' skepticism. However, these should not be determinative for all other contexts in which scientific judgments are called for.

---

132   *Snyder v. Secretary of Health and Human Services*, 2002 WL 31965742 (Fed.Cl. 2002).
133   Personal communication, Ellen Silbergeld, Johns Hopkins University.

CONCLUSION

There are a variety of pragmatic considerations that frustrate, slow, or burden the detection of substances that are likely to harm persons. How might these issues impact courts' admissibility decisions or conversely?

- There is substantial ignorance about the universe of substances. Any knowledge gaps will be slow to close because of a shortage of monetary and scientific resources. The production of chemical products appears to be out of control of the legal institutions that should ensure protection of the public health. Researchers will continue to identify and discover toxic substances largely *after* people have been injured or died as a result of exposures. Judges cannot change this, but they can shape admissibility rules to address the problem in context. (1) Admissibility reviews that demand ideal evidence or that are quite stringent will exacerbate this problem. (2) Because of the paucity of data, judges should be prepared to recognize the limited kinds of evidence that can be integrated to conclude that a substance contributes to human harm. This would allow expert testimony even without ideal or excellent evidence.
- Tiny substances in low concentrations can cause harm. When the resulting diseases are rare, but not exceedingly rare, or, conversely, quite common, or when they have long latency periods or they result from substances that do not leave signature effects, this makes identifying any toxic properties difficult. Other substances create novel scientific detective puzzles or are of so little theoretical interest that they pose problems that exacerbate their identification and timely use in tort suits. Limitations of the data-generating tools of science will aggravate problems in quickly identifying disease-causing substances, or preclude their identification all together by some studies. Judges cannot change these facts about science and the world, either. However, what courts require as support for expert testimony can affect legal outcomes. They can easily expect or demand too much in light of what is available or can be readily generated. Their analyses of evidence at the bar can be too crude to properly credit the science. Courts will need to learn enough about science to recognize that human studies will frequently be unavailable (as well as why) and to learn how to recognize how other kinds of toxicological evidence can support testimony.
- The conventions and practices internal to theoretical research science can exacerbate problems with admissibility decisions. Great attention to the prevention of false positives (which can increase false negatives), reinforced by considerable skepticism toward assertions challenging the status quo, inattention to the distribution of scientific mistakes, and even scientific disagreement itself will all slow the identification of toxicants

and their full range of adverse effects. This, too, creates a task for courts in order for them to ensure fair admissibility reviews. Subtle and sensitive court reviews of evidence will be needed to ensure simple fairness between litigants.

- Inevitably, there will be scientific disagreements about studies and what they show. Indeed disagreement, as Ruden shows, may be much wider and potentially more extensive than most of us believe. Yet scientific disagreements may be a particularly difficult issue for the law. Courts might consider disagreement as an occasion to take sides, believing that one side or the other was scientifically mistaken, when that would not necessarily be knowable in the current state of the science. (Moreover, this would intrude on the jury's role.) Courts must allow for an appropriately wide range of legitimate scientific disagreement.

- Finally, hedged scientific assertions are such constitutive features of scientific communication that it may be a barrier to conveying accurate results of scientific studies to other audiences and a barrier to more formal testimony in other institutional contexts. Judges should not be misled by scientifically hedged language and permit it to be exploited for legal purposes.

Scientific ignorance, overly cautious inference drawing for the institutional context, skepticism, hedging in scientific articles, and slow knowledge accumulation taken together present difficulties for toxic tort law. If scientific information about a substance had been produced contemporaneously with its commercialization, some of the pragmatic issues discussed above would not be of concern. If *accurate evidence* about adverse effects in humans could be found or produced instantaneously, there would be less need to piece together like the elements of a puzzle different streams of human and nonhuman evidence to try to determine the toxicity of a substance. If there were studies that would permit scientists to determine accurately adverse effects for the wide range of individuals who might be susceptible to a substance, this would greatly facilitate regulatory and tort law tasks where scientific evidence is needed. If diseases could be identified at an early stage, left their signatures, or did not have long latency periods, there might be a lesser need for various kinds of evidence and inferences to make toxicity judgments. If scientists were as concerned to avoid missing the toxicity of a substance as they are about mistakenly convicting it of toxicity, there would be fewer concerns about the effect of scientific conventions on the law. Unfortunately, this is not the social and scientific world in which we live.

In our complex biological world with little knowledge about commercial products and with insensitive tools for determining adverse effects, in most cases scientists face substantial hurdles. They must integrate sketchy and incomplete human evidence with animal, structure-activity, genetic, mechanistic (if it's available) and other less direct but scientifically relevant evidence in order to infer the contributions of substances to human disease. This is a more complex task and involves inferences, but inferences that can invite skepticism by those uninformed of the scientific procedures and inferences, even when it is not well warranted. Courts need to recognize the legitimacy of such evidentiary patterns (Chapter 7).

Excellent Evidence Makes Bad Law

I have spent considerable time reviewing these issues, because some courts may have misunderstood or learned the wrong lessons from the Bendectin (and possibly the Agent Orange[134]) litigation that provided the legal occasion for the reform of scientific scientific. In the interest of leavening the evidentiary reform of *Daubert*, scholars have called on courts to shape the law appropriately to avoid distorting its fundamental aims.[135] If the arguments of this chapter are correct, the problems may be much worse than even these scholars have suggested. In effect, the excellent evidence available in the Bendectin cases makes for particularly bad law, because human evidence was readily available, exposure information was quite good, the studies were comparatively quick to conduct, and large groups of exposed individuals were available, thus reducing the chances of no effect studies being falsely negative. But this makes the Bendectin cases poor precedents for a world in which excellent evidence is rarely available.

Injuries Can Long Precede the Scientific Understanding of Their Causes

In more typical cases likely to reach the tort law, injuries from a substance might easily precede scientific understanding and documentation of that fact, and they might precede it by years, if not decades. The point is not merely that tort law compensation is retrospective (which it is), but a much deeper one that in some cases it can take years to have clues that substances cause harm, even longer to document the cause of damage, and longer yet to develop some degree of confidence about the issue. (Whether scientists will ever have a full understanding of the range of toxicity effects from a substance is an even more open issue.)

Recall (from Chapter 1) the example of benzene, a well-known human carcinogen. As early as the 1890s, it was known to cause various blood diseases and, by the 1920s, it was reported to cause leukemia.[136] It would be another sixty

---

[134] *In re Agent Orange Prod. Liab. Litig.*, 611 F. Supp. 1223 (E.D.N.Y. 1985).

[135] See Green, *Bendectin*, 312–317; Green, "Expert Witnesses," 679–681; and Finley, "Guarding the Gate to the Courthouse," 120.

[136] R. Snyder, "The Benzene Problem in Historical Perspective," *Fundamental and Applied Toxicology* 4 (1984): 692–699; H.G.S. van Raalte and P. Grasso, "Hematological, Myelotoxic, Clastogenic, Carcinogenic, and Leukemogenic Effects of Benzene," *Regulatory Toxicology and Pharmacology* 2 (1982): 153–176; *Casarett and Doull's Toxicology*, 4th ed., ed. Mary O. Amdur, John Doull, Curtis D. Klaassen (New York: Pergamon Press, 1991), 686.

years before there was extensive scientific documentation of and substantial agreement on benzene's leukemogenic properties and that it was "carcinogenic to man."[137] The scientific community likely could have discerned the disease patterns from benzene exposure much earlier, but regrettably it did not.[138] People obviously contracted leukemia and other bone marrow diseases from benzene long before the mid–nineteen eighties. However, during this period, there likely was little or no compensation for anyone who contracted leukemia from benzene exposure.[139] Benzene is not an isolated case; similar problems have attended the regulation of the adverse health effects of asbestos,[140] arsenic,[141] lead,[142] benzidine dyes,[143] dioxin,[144] and other substances.

Although there is little systematic evidence on this point, benzene may be more representative than a substance such as Bendectin, for which there was a relatively quick scientific evaluation.[145] Thus, slow knowledge accumulation exacerbated by considerable ignorance about most substances and other pragmatic difficulties pose serious problems for discovering and documenting adverse health effects in humans. In torts, science delayed can easily be justice denied.

Judges cannot change the science or the pace of discovery. However, they can have a more realistic view of the availability of evidence, change what they expect of it and modify how they treat the evidence before them. Overly restrictive admissibility reviews will exacerbate these problems, affect fairness between litigants, and reduce the possibility of justice for deserving victims. By

---

[137] International Agency for Research on Cancer, "Benzene," *Monograph Series, Supplement 7*. Rev. 6 Feb. 1998. Available at: http//www-cie.iarc.fr/htdocs/monographs/suppl7/benzene.html (emphasis added).

[138] European Environmental Agency, *Late Lessons from Early Warnings: The Precautionary Principle 1896–2000, Environmental Issue Report no. 22* (Luxembourg: Office for Official Publication of the European Communities, 2001), 38–51, esp. 39.

[139] Recall that physicians altered their discharge diagnoses from leukemia to aplastic anemia so widows could receive some compensation for their husbands' deaths. ("Hearings for Benzene Standard, Occupational Safety and Health Administration," *Federal Register* 50, 239 (10 December 1985): 50518–50519.)

[140] Brodeur, *Outrageous Misconduct* (see, for example, his presentation that company physicians certainly knew in the early 1930s of the deadly effects of asbestos exposure), 113, 327, 348.

[141] NRC, *Arsenic in Drinking Water* (reporting that the drinking water standard for arsenic had not been updated since 1942) (also reported at http://www.nap.edu/books/0309076293/html/).

[142] Markowitz and Rosner, *Deceit and Denial*, 303 (companies knew of adverse health effects from lead as early as 1920).

[143] Michaels, "Corporate Decision Making and Bladder Cancer," 215, 218–221.

[144] Kyle Steenland, Pier Bertazzi, Andrea Baccarelli, and Manolis Kogevinas, "Dioxin Revisited: Developments Since the 1997 IARC Classification of Dioxin as a Human Carcinogen," *Environmental Health Perspectives* 112, 13 (2004): 1265–1268.

[145] W. J. Nicholson, "IARC Evaluations in the Light of Limitations of Human Epidemiologic Data," *Annals of the New York Academy of Sciences* 534 (1988): 44–54 (showing for about eighteen substances, exposure conditions or processes that are carcinogenic (and that have quite high relative risks), there has been evidence of their human carcinogenicity for many decades, but action on them occurred only recently).

contrast, courts could recognize the myriad kinds of evidence that are available and that can be integrated to provide evidence that a product causes human harm. Moreover, if the above pragmatic barriers are common, as they appear to be, courts should permit testimony as early as possible in the history of knowledge of the toxicity of a substance. This will facilitate compensation for wrongfully injured parties and strengthen deterrence messages to firms who manufacture and market products that can harm fellow citizens.[146]

Thus, courts have alternatives in how they conduct admissibility reviews. How have they chosen and what reasons have they given for some of their decisions? This is the topic of Chapter 6.

[146] Green, *Bendectin*, 192, 208.

6

Science and Law in Conflict

When scientific evidence is centrally needed to assist legal decisions, the Supreme Court, *inter alia*, aimed at increasing the chances that legal decisions would more closely follow or at least not be at great odds with the relevant science. This is not as easy a task as it might have seemed. For one thing, generic tensions between the law and science hamper easy pursuit of this goal. In addition, given the complexity, subtlety, and near inscrutability of some scientific evidence, judges understandably, but regrettably often struggle with scientific studies and reasoning. These difficulties increase the more complex and subtle the evidence becomes.[1] Moreover, judges may have disagreements with one another about how scientific evidence should be reviewed, given its complexity.[2] Finally, the chances that admissibility decisions will result in mistaken judgments are even greater given some of the pragmatic problems reviewed in the previous chapter. That is, even when judges review quite good evidence, there are numerous opportunities for errors. When there are myriad pragmatic barriers to obtaining good evidence about the toxicity of substances and less than optimal evidence is available, the potential for stresses and strains increases. Failures to attend successfully to these issues pose threats to the legitimacy of the law as an institution.

The current chapter focuses on some of these issues; the next chapter suggests a partial corrective to them. This chapter first reviews some tensions between science and the law that can affect how well they can function together. Different standards of proof central to each, different time frames within which each operates, different concerns about the distribution of mistakes, and different approaches to uncertainty, simplicity, and complexity create a context

---

[1] Wright, *Practical Reasoning*, 231–233.

[2] This is a problem Judge Golkiewicz notes in *Stevens v. the Secretary of Health and Human Services*, 2001 WL 387418 (Fed. Cl.). He was concerned that federal magistrates' decisions in vaccine injury cases were utilizing different conceptions of scientific evidence in deciding cases and proposed a common framework.

in which judges can err. Such tensions on top of the pragmatic barriers already considered increase courts' burdens.

Next, I review some district and appellate court cases in which the admissibility of scientific evidence has been at issue and assess the *reasons* courts have given for their decisions in light of how scientists typically address similar evidence. The examples suggest that some courts have had difficulty in reviewing and understanding scientific studies and reasoning, or have adopted quite different standards for assessing scientific evidence than scientists themselves would. These problems are of concern, because it appears that at least some courts are struggling with the task of admitting and excluding evidence. To the extent they do, this undermines the aim of making the law more consistent with the science pertinent to the cases and affects the just resolution of legal issues. Recognizing the shortcomings of simple and restrictive guides can serve as a corrective to past errors and point the way to improving how the tasks could be approached better and more sensitively (Chapter 7).

Before the *Daubert* decision, a number of commentators were concerned that some courts might have permitted into trial scientific testimony that in Justice Breyer's words (quoting the physicist Wolfgang Pauli) might not have been "good enough to be wrong."[3] Published district and appellate court opinions now suggest that some judges in reviewing scientific evidence are issuing decisions on scientific testimony and its foundation contrary to how most scientists themselves would assess the same evidence. Some courts excluded experts who had utilized the kinds of evidence on which scientists would routinely rely for making causal inferences about human harm, whereas others have required that testimony must be based on evidence that scientists might find quite valuable, but not necessary for causal inferences. They appear to have had difficulties with the scientific relevance of some evidence and even have had difficulties appreciating how complex pieces of evidence can fit together to provide a scientific explanation that is more likely than not reliable.

It is important to note, however, that although judges might have arrived at these judgments on their own, litigants on the other side of the case may have contributed to their views. Litigants often urge that courts should demand higher certainty, human studies or other stringent requirements. In some respects we should not be surprised by such arguments. We saw how tempting this could be from a scientific point of view (Chapter 5). Moreover, some have adopted it as a more conscious strategy. "Doubt is our product," has long been used by the tobacco industry to avoid responsibility for the adverse effects of tobacco exposure.[4] Other industries have followed suit, including the lead,

---

[3]   Breyer, "Introduction," *Reference Manual on Scientific Evidence*, 1–10.

[4]   Brown & Williamson – Smoking and Health Proposal, Doc. No. 332506, at http://tobaccodocuments.org/bw/332506.html. See also David Michaels, "Doubt Is Their

vinyl chloride,[5] and asbestos industries,[6] *inter alia.* Thus, some defense lawyers and experts appear to have engaged in "junk science" of precisely the kind the Supreme Court aimed to exclude. This newer junk science is more insidious because it often has a patina of acceptability to it that can be difficult to pierce to its misleading core.

When courts rule on evidence and reasoning in ways that are at odds with the scientific community, these rulings are often propagated throughout the legal system and then perpetuated via a written record in the form of precedents or merely from "following the Joneses" of sister courts. This multiplies mistakes of science and decreases the possibility of justice throughout the legal system.

GENERIC TENSIONS BETWEEN SCIENCE AND THE LAW

Tension in Goals

A common *aim* of science is epistemic: Scientists first seek to describe and, then to explain and understand accurately the phenomena they study. Their accumulating data and describing phenomena are the easier parts of research. Making inferences from the descriptions and data to explain and understand the phenomena are more difficult.

An overriding virtue of science might be seen as pursuit of truth about the world or the small portions of it under study, with an emphasis on pursuit of this truth for its own sake – not typically a means to something else.[7] This last point needs qualification, of course, as much contemporary discussion of science emphasizes the value of scientific discoveries for developing beneficial technologies and other products that will improve human life. On the one hand, scientists might study quarks, which at the moment appear to have little pertinence for human institutions, or, on the other hand, they might try to understand the causes of AIDS or how a drug controls cancer, both of which can have substantial consequences for humans. An appealing virtue underlying scientific inquiry, however, is pursuit of truth about a subject for its own sake.[8]

This sketched reminder about scientific research is most apt for what we might consider theoretical science where pursuit of the truth for its own sake to answer empirical questions seems most at home. The picture is more complicated for scientific fields that have more varied goals such as toxicology.

Some toxicologists aim to recognize, identify, and quantify the hazards from toxic substances to humans and the environment, some to create new drugs or

---

Product," *Scientific American* 96 (June 2005): 96–101. 4 *Daubert v. Merrell Dow Pharmaceuticals, Inc.*, 509 U.S. 579 (1993).
[5] Markowitz and Rosner, *Deceit and Denial.*
[6] Brodeur, *Outrageous Misconduct.*
[7] Kitcher, *The Advancement of Science*, 3.
[8] Kitcher, *The Advancement of Science*, 3–4.

pesticides, whereas some engage in more basic research in order to understand the mechanism(s) of acute and chronic illnesses caused by toxicants.[9] This last is the theoretical focus of the field. Toxicology is representative of many fields that courts need to assist them in addressing the adverse effects of human exposures to substances – they have both theoretical and more pragmatic or applied aspects. Failure to distinguish between these different parts of a field may lead to some confusions. One that can be of importance in the law is to conflate procedures and implicit standards of proof used for theoretical advances in a field with the epistemic procedures and standards that would be more germane for pragmatic areas of the same field. The procedures and standards may not be identical. For example, Michael Gallo writes that toxicology "is both a science and an art" . . . with the science being the observation and data gathering that is typical of the discipline and the art being utilization of that same data to "predict outcomes of exposure in human and animal populations."[10] His very use of different terms for these activities suggests some substantive differences between the areas they designate. He adds that toxicological *theories* have "a higher level of certainty than do [*predictions*]" of toxic effects from a group of animals to humans or to another group of other animals, thus suggesting that the different facets of the field are subject to somewhat different standards.[11]

Typically, scientific research embodies systematic procedures for developing explanatory answers to empirical questions that scientists have posed and are trying to answer. Indeed, part of what gives science its honorary connotation in at least some contexts is the fact that the systematic procedures for answering questions are paradigmatic of some of the best ways of addressing and answering empirical questions.[12] As David Goodstein of the California Institute of Technology puts it, "The things that science has taught us about how the world works are the most secure elements in all of human knowledge" . . . although he distinguishes between "science at the frontiers of knowledge (where not all is understood) and "textbook science that is known with great confidence."[13]

The *time scale* of scientific research differs from that of the law, as one might suppose for an intellectual area in which pursuit of truth for its own sake is a leading virtue. A scientist pursuing research questions for their own sake cannot anticipate when discoveries will be made, satisfying explanations reached and

---

[9] Michael A. Gallo, "History and Scope of Toxicology," in *Casarett and Doull's Toxicology*, 6th ed., ed. Curtis D. Klaassen (New York: McGraw-Hill, 2001), 3.

[10] Gallo, "History and Scope of Toxicology," 3.

[11] Gallo, "History and Scope of Toxicology," 3.

[12] As indicated (Chapter 3), the use of systematic procedures for finding answers to empirical issues does not necessarily mean that there is a univocal "scientific method" or that such systematic procedures are the same from field to field, or subdiscipline to subdiscipline.

[13] Goodstein, "How Science Works," 79.

understanding achieved. In addition, when experiments can take considerable time to conduct, the problem is especially difficult, or progress must depend on the efforts of many researchers, this will add to the time before scientific understanding is achieved.

Moreover, the end products of scientific research are relatively open-ended, because of complexity, scientists' inability to predict the outcome of experiments and when understanding will be reached, and researchers using nondeductive inferences to explain the phenomena. Even comparatively settled conclusions are open to revision on the presentation of new data, theories, or discoveries that might overturn existing explanations in favor of better ones. The open-endedness of science and the practices that accompany it can affect the communication between science and the law, as we have seen. Scientists, thus, may hedge even well-supported claims in which they strongly believe. Judges need to recognize this practice because it can mislead courts and disadvantage meritorious litigants who have respectable evidence but who must carry the burden of proof to establish a claim.

In scientific endeavors, there is a collaborative aspect that has several features. Typically, research results are cumulative – one scientist or research group builds on the progress of others; personal collaborations across space and more impersonal collaboration across time contribute to the development of fields. In developing a theory or insight into how the world works, scientists typically assimilate the results of others, augment that with their own contributions and then develop or refine a new view. In addition, progress in science typically results in developing a consensus about the subject of study. The new results are much better secured when an appropriate subfield of scientists have been persuaded of the view.

Finally, as we discussed earlier, scientists for the most part do not attend to the distributive consequences of their results or mistakes that can result from research outcomes.[14] They give less attention to false negatives than to false positives. Much toxicity research, conducted in workplaces, does not attend to adverse effects for more varied subpopulations.

By contrast with science, torts is a body of law that seeks to provide the means by which individuals who have been harmed by the actions of others may receive compensation for the injuries they have suffered. As a means to this end it provides a forum to adjudicate disputes between parties where one is claiming that the other wrongly harmed her.

---

[14] That is, it is not part of basic scientific research to address how scientific mistakes might affect other institutions, and there appears to be little concern within science with how false positives and false negatives might affect the institution of science (apart from avoiding false positives). This is very different from the law, which has a self-conscious concern with such matters.

Justice is the leading virtue of the law. Adjudication must be done in such a way that the parties are treated fairly in the process and that, when a decision is rendered, justice has been done between the parties. Other normative goals also shape and guide legal dispute resolution, such as, *inter alia*, efficiency, administrative cost, wealth distribution, and morality. The law is, thus, "normative to the core."[15] This is something unlikely to be said of science, even though there are normative elements manifested in scientific inquiries and the institution at large.[16]

It is more difficult to point to readily identifiable systematic procedures that are characteristic of legal institutions in the same way that some systematic empirical investigations are characteristic of science. Of course, in litigation the adversarial presentation of facts, theories and interpretations of the law are central to getting at the legal truth of the issues and resolving disputes between parties. Adversarial procedures can attain the truth about an issue, but they can also mislead or create a much messier picture.

Although the time frame of science is open-ended, the law imposes several generic time constraints on the resolution of disputes. It seeks to ensure that disputes are addressed within a reasonable period of time and then resolved in a timely and conclusive manner. Thus, a plaintiff's allegations of harm must be brought within specified periods of time fixed by statutes of limitations or they will not be considered.[17] Once allegations are timely filed, the legal system imposes on itself some time constraints within which the issues must be taken up in court proceedings. After the legal issues have been litigated, typically they are considered settled once and for all by *res judicata* – "an issue that has been definitively settled by judicial decision."[18] *Res judicata* rules recognize the fact that "the purpose of a lawsuit is not only to [allow enough time] to do substantial justice but to bring an end to controversy."[19] The latter provides legal judgments that have stability and certainty so that "the parties and others may rely on them in ordering their practical affairs . . . but also so that the moral force of court judgments will not be undermined."[20] Although contemporary law seeks to provide sufficient time for legal issues to develop,

---

[15] Peter H. Schuck, "Multi-Culturalism Redux: Science, Law, and Politics," *Yale Law and Policy Review* 11 (1993): 1, 24.

[16] Sheila Jasanoff, *Science at the Bar: Law, Science and Technology in America* (Cambridge, MA: A Twentieth Century Fund Book, Harvard University Press, 1995), 7–11.

[17] A statue of limitations is a "statute establishing a time limit for suing in a civil case, based on the date when the claim accrued (as when the injury occurred or was discovered). The purpose of such a statute is to require diligent prosecuting of known claims, thereby providing finality and predictability in legal affairs and ensuring that claims will be resolved while evidence is reasonable, available, and fresh." *Black's Law Dictionary*, 8th ed., Bryan A. Garner (St Paul, MN: West Publishing, Thomson Business, 2004), 1450–1451.

[18] *Black's Law Dictionary*, 1336–1337.

[19] James and Hazard, *Civil*, 532.

[20] James and Hazard, *Civil Procedure*, 532.

it may not permit enough for the requisite scientific research to be completed to ensure full documentation of any adverse effects from suspected toxicants. Meanwhile, *res judicata* rules typically foreclose revisiting issues even if new evidence becomes available at a later time.[21]

The finality of law, Peter Schuck argues, creates another legal "bias" that can in turn generate tensions with science.

> Because much law must be predicted, understood, and applied by many ordinary people with limited resources, simplicity is often a compelling legal virtue. Law cannot afford to be as nuanced as the realities it seeks to shape; it necessarily draws lines and creates categories that force many legal decisions into a binary mold; one is either in or out of the category, and it matters a great deal which.[22]

By contrast scientists, trying to understand the natural world of biology or toxicological relationships, must take their subject as they find it, with all its subtlety, complexity, and uncertainty about effects. Even when scientists seek to model the biological world, their resulting products often have considerable complexity. Vern Walker has more extensively argued a similar point in a forthcoming paper. He notes not only the differences between the two areas of endeavor but also how legal pressures for more simple and understandable legal guides tend to push scientists in their testimony away from the needed complexity of their discipline.[23] As we will see later, there are a number of temptations for judges to adopt comparatively simple rules to guide the review of evidence. However, if they aim to remain faithful to the science, they will have to approach this subject much more subtly and sensitively. More subtle approaches toward the science will serve both accuracy and fairness between litigants (Chapter 7). Courts will need to be sensitive to the simplicity-complexity tension between these two institutions in order to do justice to both, but also will need to review the scientific foundations of expert testimony in a way that does credit to the complexity of the science.

Finally, although the distributive effects of scientific research usually receive little attention, the distributive effects of legal rules and decisions are of preeminent importance. Distributive considerations are central to many issues in the law, but consider only two: that there be justice between parties and that admissibility procedures treat litigants evenhandedly (discussed in the next section).

[21] In some circumstances courts have crafted rules to permit toxic tort issues to be reopened if a disease actually develops (after permitting recovering under causes of action short of actual harm); see *Hagerty v. L&L Marine Services, Inc,* 788 F 2d 315 (1986).

[22] Schuck, "Multi-Culturalism Redux," 28 (citing an earlier work: see Peter Schuck, "Legal Complexity: Some Causes, Consequences, and Cures," *Duke L.J.* 42(1992): 1, 27–31.

[23] Vern R. Walker, "Transforming Science into Law: Transparency and Default Reasoning in International Trade Disputes," *Rescuing Science from Politics,* ed. Wendy Wagner and Rena Steinzor (New York: Cambridge University Press, 2006).

Tensions between Scientific and Legal Epistemic Practices

In the tort law, evidentiary procedures with which adversaries must comply might be considered part of the requirements that collectively aim at not exceeding a tolerable balance of mistakes – of legal false positives/false negatives – between parties and at achieving other nonepistemic institutional goals, such as serving justice, providing fair procedures to litigants, and the like. Although tort law does not endorse casual rejection of the status quo, the *standards of proof* embedded in its burdens of persuasion do not appear as demanding as scientific standards of proof, and there is a different concern with mistakes that might result.[24]

For example, there is a *normative* evenhandedness between litigants that is central to the tort law as revealed by the ultimate standard of proof to which plaintiffs must persuade a jury, the *preponderance of evidence standard*. This is a long-standing norm from the traditions of civil law and the Supreme Court has endorsed it.[25] Unlike the criminal law, which embodies procedural rules that tend to prevent the wrongful conviction of innocent persons, the tort law more equally balances the concerns of avoiding mistakenly holding defendants accountable and mistakenly denying plaintiffs recovery. There is substantial legal history supporting this view. In *Speiser v. Randall*, Justice Brennan noted:

> There is always in litigation a margin of error, representing error in factfinding, which both parties must take into account. Where one party has at stake an interest of transcending value – as a criminal defendant his liberty – this margin of error is reduced as to him by the process of placing on the other party the burden of ... persuading the factfinder at the conclusion of the trial of his guilt beyond a reasonable doubt.[26]

Justice Harlan developed this theme in a concurring opinion in *In re Winship*:

> The standard of proof influences the relative frequency of these two types of erroneous outcomes. If, for example, the standard of proof for a criminal trial were a preponderance of the evidence rather than proof beyond a reasonable doubt, there would be a smaller risk of factual errors that result in freeing guilty persons, but a far greater risk of factual errors that result in convicting the innocent. Because the standard of proof affects the comparative frequency of these two types of erroneous outcomes, the choice of the standard to be applied in a particular kind of litigation should, in a rational world, reflect an assessment of the comparative social disutility of each.[27]

---

[24] See *In re Winship*, 397 U.S. 358, 371–372 (1970); *Speiser v. Randall*, 357 U.S. 513, 525–526 (1958); see also Green, "Expert Witnesses," 643–699, at 697.
[25] *Speiser v. Randall*, 357 U.S. 513, 525–526 (1958).
[26] 357 U.S. 513, at 525–526. (1958).
[27] *In re Winship*, 397 U.S. 358, at 371 (1970).

Note that the two types of erroneous outcomes possible are a factual outcome that favors the plaintiff when the facts warrant an outcome for the defendant or an "erroneous factual determination" for the defendant when a correct understanding justifies a judgment for the plaintiff. Justice Harlan then discussed the preponderance of the evidence standard:

> In a civil suit between two private parties for money damages, for example, we view it as no more serious in general for there to be an erroneous verdict in the defendant's favor than for there to be an erroneous verdict in the plaintiff's favor. A preponderance of the evidence standard therefore seems peculiarly appropriate for, as explained most sensibly, it simply requires the trier of fact to "believe that the existence of a fact is more probable than its nonexistence . . ."[28]

Moreover, recently the Supreme Court in *Santosky v. Kramer*, adopted the standard set forth in *Addington* that "in any given proceeding, the . . . standard of proof . . . reflects not only the weight of the private and the public interests affected, but also a societal judgment about how the risk of error should be distributed between the litigants."[29] It then added that the preponderance of the evidence requires litigants to "share the risk of error in roughly equal fashion."[30]

The same standard of proof is utilized in the vaccine "off table" injury cases and is articulated as follows:

> Petitioners must only demonstrate more probably than not (50% and a feather) that the vaccine can and did cause the injury alleged.[31]

Thus, the tort law, based on the "more likely than not" standard of proof, is "indifferent as between a plaintiff's erroneous recovery [a legal false positive] and a defendant's erroneous non-liability [a legal false negative]," reflecting important non-epistemic values, such as the risk of injustice between parties.[32] The distribution of the risk of mistakes just reviewed rests on an interpretation of the ultimate standard of proof in the tort law that must be established to a jury's satisfaction.

It is barely possible that admissibility decisions might be seen as embracing a different standard for risks of mistakes, but that would be odd. Instead, a reasonable presumption in the law appears to be that judges should be at least

---

[28]   397 U.S. 358 at 371–372.
[29]   *Santosky v. Kramer*, 455 U.S. 745, 755 (1982).
[30]   *Addington v. Texas*, 441 U.S. 418, 423 (1979).
[31]   *Stevens v. the Secretary of Health and Human Services*, 2001 at 32.
[32]   *Santosky v. Kramer*, 455 U.S. at 755 (1982) (adopting the standard set forth in *Addington v. Texas*, 441 U.S. at 423 (1979); Green, "Expert Witnesses," 687. Legal and factual false positives (or false negatives) are not identical, of course. However, when there are a few pieces of evidence that are critical to a litigant's case, a factual error will more likely translate into a legal mistake.

as evenhanded in admitting and excluding experts as the civil law is in its ultimate adjudication of civil litigation. The argument for this point would be that although both the tort law and the criminal law have different standards of proof to which a jury must be persuaded, judges in both cases are presumed to be equally evenhanded in admitting and excluding evidence in the two areas of law. That is, the legal risk of mistakes in admissibility does not follow the risk of mistakes as represented by the ultimate standard of proof and the only reasonable presumption is that judges must be equally evenhanded toward each side.[33] Thus, it seems that the litigants should share the "risk of error" in admissibility "in roughly equal fashion."[34] Judges, hewing to this standard, must exercise care in treating scientific evidence evenhandedly in admissibility decisions because of the mistake norms of the law.

Science has different commitments that can pose tensions and even undesirable consequences for the law. The goals of understanding phenomena and adding carefully to the knowledge status quo have led the scientific community to adopt selective evidentiary procedures in order to ensure that new (typically theoretical) knowledge is securely added to the field. As I argued in Chapters 4 and 5, in general, scientists are typically quite demanding in preventing factual false positives, that is, their procedures are designed to minimize study results that show that a substance has a toxic property when in fact it does not. At the same time, scientists seem to have a lesser concern to prevent false negatives. Although this is appropriate for theoretical scientific research, it risks problems in other institutional contexts, such as, in public health institutions or in either the regulatory or the tort law that have different mistake norms.

Scientific epistemology is blind to the law's evenhanded norms; it is not indifferent between preventing these two different kinds of factual mistakes. Thus, courts need to be sensitive to these differences when they make admissibility rulings – erring in ways that *neither favor plaintiffs nor defendants* as they review expert testimony and its foundation. Judges will need to exercise special care when reviewing expert testimony resting on scientific studies that, because of the epistemic norms implicit in science, do not protect as well against factual false negatives as against factual false positives. Such errors can have substantial effects on the legal interests of the litigants. If they fail to recognize such issues they risk being unfair to litigants.

To further illustrate this, the special magistrates in vaccine-injury cases are sensitive to this issue insofar as it pertains to the preponderance of the evidence burden of proof, as Judge Golkiewicz puts it in his *Stevens'* opinion:

---

[33] Another possibility is that the review of evidence might follow the stringency of the standards of proof. This would increase the screening of the government's evidence in criminal cases because of the high burden of proof it faces, but the screening of evidence in civil litigation would continue to be evenhanded because its ultimate standard of proof is as well.

[34] *Santosky v. Kramer*, 455 U.S. at 755.

Of course, the court's reliance on the [Institute of Medicine's scientific] committees' reports in no way suggests that a petitioner must demonstrate causality under the same strict scientific principles employed by the panel members. Petitioners [analogous to plaintiffs in tort suits] must only demonstrate more probably than not (50% and a feather) that the vaccine can and did cause the injury alleged; petitioners need not prove their case to a scientific certainty.[35]

However, there is a further point to which we will return later. In ruling on the admissibility of expert testimony that rests on a few individual studies, courts must exercise care so that the scientific concern to prevent falsely positive results does not greatly increase the possibility of falsely negative results of studies to the detriment of plaintiffs. As we saw in Chapter 4, this can be a particularly vexing issue when statistical studies are too small to equally reduce random mistakes. This example is particularly dramatic and mathematically certain, but it only serves to highlight a much more general problem that judges can face in admissibility rulings. They also must exercise caution not to fall prey to insisting on high standards of proof from science and demand those for the law; this, too, would distort legal norms.

Critical Stresses

Which of the tensions just reviewed might pose the greatest problems for the law-science interaction? One obvious difference between the two institutions is in the time frames of scientific inquiry and the legal resolution of disputes, respectively. There are several time-sensitive issues that can make a difference.

1) Typically, scientific curiosity must have been pricked to lead scientists to pursue a problem. Scientific inquiry tends to be driven by curiosity and question answering, whereas the law imposes various time-constraints on bringing legal cases within statutes of limitation. A scientist must have a research problem in which she is interested and have the funding and other resources to pursue it before the research will be done.[36]

Any research needed in legal settings may or may not be available within the limitations imposed by the law. If research has not been conducted by the time injuries have been noticed and the toxicity of substances suspected, it may be difficult to provide results to assist the legal issues. This occurred in the toxic tort suit described in *A Civil Action*: shortly after the case was settled, the U.S. EPA issued a report indicating that trichloroethylene did reach the water wells of Woburn, Massachusetts, which plaintiffs' had alleged caused leukemia

---

[35] *Stevens v. the Secretary of Health and Human Services*, at 32.

[36] Of course, scientists might well conduct research on more practical problems not primarily driven by curiosity, provided sufficient funding were available.

in several children. The author, Jonathan Harr, notes, "On the face of it, the verdict appeared to stand for an example of how the adversary process and the rules and rituals of the courtroom can obscure reality."[37]

2) Research itself takes time. Even if investigating the toxicity of a new substance is on a scientist's research agenda, research may not be quick to conduct. A reasonable battery of animal testing to provide a variety of data points about the toxicity of a substance can take up to six years to complete. Epidemiological research also can take time, depending on the availability of data.

3) Biological systems impose their own constraints. For example, epidemiologists must study exposed individuals for a sufficient duration to ensure that both the induction and latency periods have elapsed so that the studies are not falsely negative because researchers have violated these fundamentals. This is particularly a problem for diseases such as cancer that have long latency periods.[38] In general nature does not always reveal her secrets quickly. Courts must be sensitive to such issues to ensure fairness between litigants.

4) Once a legal case has been adjudicated, it cannot be reopened even though scientists might have uncovered compelling new evidence that could change the outcome. The generic issue recently received the attention of the U.S. Supreme Court in *Dow Chemical Company, Monsanto Company, et al., v. Stephenson and Isaacson*.[39] Although earlier a district court had overseen a settlement between Vietnam veterans who alleged they had contracted a variety of diseases from exposure to Agent Orange, new scientific evidence has now strongly suggested that a broader class of individuals had contracted disease than were part of the earlier settlement. Will the veterans who are alleging new kinds of diseases be permitted to pursue their legal claims?

A second difference between science and the law is that there are funding constraints on scientific inquiry that influence the development of a research agenda. Even if a scientist suspects that a substance adversely affects humans, because research is expensive, she must have sufficient funding to carry out the studies. She must find a funding source and needed personnel. This is not always easy. Some problems are not of interest to national funding agencies. Some problems might be of interest to the firm that created and distributed the substance, but, as we have seen, testing can often only invite legal problems, so this source of funding may be closed. Victims likely do not have resources for

---

[37] Jonathan Haar, *A Civil Action* (New York: Random House, 1995), 456.

[38] Similar concerns apply to animal studies, although because animals have shorter lifetimes and faster metabolisms research can be done more quickly on them than on humans.

[39] *Stephenson v. Dow Chemical Co.* 273 F.3d 249 C.A.2 (N.Y.), 2001.

the funding and plaintiffs' attorneys' funding will be criticized as suspect (the same critique should apply to defendants).

A third and most significant feature that distinguishes between the institutions is their respective standards of proof. We have discussed these differences earlier and suggested why judges should exercise great care not to substitute one for the other.

A fourth difference is in their approach to the complexity of the subjects before them. Scientists recognize the need to be sensitive to the subtlety and complexity of their subject (hence some of their hedging), whereas courts need to make the law more or less accessible to the citizenry and tend to simplify.

A fifth and related difference concerns approaches to uncertainty. Uncertainty is endemic to science; indeed, part of the integrity of scientific claims is that researchers exercise considerable care in saying what they do and do not know about the subject under consideration (or they assign probability judgments to claims). Moreover, they usually do not need to make action-guiding decisions based on their uncertain knowledge (other than how to pursue research further). They acknowledge and are quite comfortable with varying degrees of certainty and uncertainty about their subject. By contrast, although the law recognizes and has decision rules for addressing uncertainty (e.g., legal presumptions as well as burdens and standards of proof), if there is too much uncertainty for a particular decision rule, the party with the burden of proof on the issue loses (recall Chapter 2). In a trial context, courts do not have the luxury of avoiding a decision in the face of uncertainty. Moreover, it is usually forced into a binary choice – for one party or the other – despite uncertainty. (The mere presence of uncertainty in the law may make it easier to decide against the party with the burden of proof. And, it leads to deliberate strategies to emphasize or exaggerate the uncertainties facing that party.[40])

A sixth critical distinction is in the distributive concerns between the two institutions: (1) differences in standards of proof can also produce substantive tensions between law and science on distributive issues because the two institutions have different approaches to the distribution of mistakes. Thus, judges must ensure that scientific inattention to false negatives does not distort the legally mandated equal concern with the risk of errors between plaintiffs and defendants in admissibility decisions or in the ultimate outcome of a trial; and (2) human toxicity studies may have been conducted independently of legal concerns, thus ignoring issues of biological variability that can arise between different subpopulations of exposed persons: infants, children, the elderly, women, pregnant women, and diseased individuals. In Chapter 7, I consider specific examples of this issue.

---

[40] See Michaels and Monforton, "Manufacturing Uncertainty," S39–S48, for a discussion of the use of this strategy going back to the 1950s.

JUDICIAL RESPONSES TO THE SCIENCE-LAW INTERACTION

The tensions just described create a context in which courts can understandably, regrettably err. At the same time they can be exacerbated or ameliorated by judicial reviews. On the one hand, for example, courts' failure to recognize the less than textbook evidence that is often available in legal venues can lead them to impose admissibility that requirements that are simply too stringent for the practical decision making of the law. This might well put at risk the possibility of justice between parties. In addition, a tendency for simple and restrictive rules may deny parties some of the more complex evidence they might need in support of their cases. This would undermine one of the main goals of the *Daubert* trilogy – having legal decisions better supported by the pertinent scientific evidence.

On the other hand, how judges review evidence can aggravate or reduce tensions between the two institutions. If courts adopt some of the more extreme views toward the *prevention* of false positives from the scientific community or require numerous kinds of evidence (more than needed) for expert testimony, they can exacerbate tensions. By failing to observe the "mistake norms" of the law and adopting some of the more extreme mistake norms of science, courts can upset the legally mandated balance of mistakes between plaintiffs and defendants. This would end plaintiffs' cases for legally and scientifically mistaken reasons. This could invite criticism from the scientific community as courts impose conceptions of scientific evidence and reasoning in opposition to scientific norms. By contrast, when courts are too lenient toward experts and scientific evidence, this opens the possibility that courts will permit scientific evidence and testimony that would not be within the boundaries of acceptable scientific disagreement, invites criticisms from the scientific community from a different direction, and creates opportunities for final court decisions to be at odds with existing scientific evidence. Thus, there are risks of mistakes on both sides of admissibility decisions.

However, there can be an asymmetry from the scientific community's responses to admissibility errors. On one side, at the time of the Bendectin decision some courts had admitted expert testimony at odds with the prevailing science about the substance in question; this in turn might have invited and probably did invite a wider critical response from the scientific community.[41] Legal decisions at odds with the *known* scientific evidence (if it is indeed *known*) creates a target that is easy to publicize. On the other side, when judges exclude evidence that should be admitted, this is comparatively invisible – resulting from an admissibility hearing, not a public trial – and probably receives little or no attention. These decisions do not become such an inviting target simply

---

[41] Donald Kennedy, Editorial: "Science, Law and the IBM Case," *Science*, 305, 16 (July 2004): 309.

because they are below the public radar screen. Pressures from the scientific community that might serve as correctives to judicial admissibility mistakes tend to be asymmetrical: more strongly arrayed against decisions that mistakenly admit flawed scientific evidence, but likely much less or nonexistent against decisions that mistakenly exclude good evidence and reasoning. This may have begun to change with some papers by legal scholars and scientists in special issues of journals or books that are about to appear concerning the disregarding of reasonable scientific evidence.[42]

I do not argue that the generic tensions between science and law have created the problems about to be considered, but they set the stage for mistakes and invite them. Judges, like the rest of us, can become trapped by our own context or by idealized views of a tool we need to use, in this case science. The earlier section sought to highlight some differences between science and the law, so that those who must work with both can better see how to use them more compatibly.

The remainder of the chapter conducts a philosophic analysis of some reasons courts have given for excluding evidence in existing cases.[43] The cases considered merit review for several reasons. First, they provide some windows into the effects of the doctrinal changes instituted by the Supreme Court.[44] Second, they provide some, but not fully comprehensive, information about whether the Court's reform is making law and science more or less compatible. Fragmentary evidence to date indicates that although it may be that courts are excluding some scientific experts whose reasoning and methodology exceed the boundaries of respectable scientific disagreement in their testimony, other courts are overreaching and excluding experts whose testimony appears to be within the boundaries of respectable scientific disagreement – they are

---

[42] Cranor and Eastmond, "Scientific Ignorance," 5–48; Finley, "Guarding the Gate to the Courthouse Door, 49 (1999): 335; Michael D. Green, "The Road Less Well Traveled (and Seen): Contemporary Lawmaking in Products Liability," *DePaul Law Review* 49 (1999): 377; Michael H. Graham, "Gatekeeping Test of Daubert, Kumho and Proposed Amended Rule 702 of the Federal Rules of Evidence," *University of Miami Law Review* 54 (2000): 317; Berger, "Eliminating General Causation"; a special issue of *American Journal of Public Health, Supplement 1: Scientific Evidence and Public Policy* 95 (2005), ed. David Michaels; Wendy Wagner and Rena Steinzor, eds., *Rescuing Science from Politics* (New York and London: Cambridge University Press, 2006).

[43] The analysis is philosophical in the sense that I consider various reasons judges have given for admitting, or more commonly, excluding evidence. To what extent are these reasons consistent with those scientists would utilize? The scientific comparison is based on reasons that consensus scientific committees would provide for their conclusions.

[44] It is, of course, difficult to have a comprehensive view of this issue because evidence of mistaken judicial admissibility decisions is asymmetrical – when evidence is excluded which precludes a plaintiff's case from going forward to trial, the judge must write an opinion and it is subject to appeal (but whether or not an appellate court in fact reviews it is another matter). When evidence is admitted there is usually little or no record of the judicial reasoning, unless that decision is appealed.

excluding experts for reasons that are at odds with good scientific practice and whose testimony should be heard by juries, Third, how would such decisions affect the balance of interests between litigants in toxic tort cases?[45]

THE RISK OF SIMPLIFIED ADMISSIBILITY RULES

The *Daubert* opinion stressed the need for a flexible set of criteria to determine the admissibility of scientific evidence. Nevertheless, that decision left open the possibility for the use of overly simple admissibility rules because judges have great latitude in reviewing scientific evidence without appellate review. Many of the cases presented below suggest that courts often utilize relatively simple rules as guides for reviewing expert testimony and its foundation. Because of the evidentiary complexity in science, there is a risk that it may overwhelm judges who, as a result of their education, may not be prepared for the subtle and difficult task of evaluating and weighing the various kinds of evidence and scientific reasoning for the context in question. Simple rules may be endemic to and valuable in the law as Schuck and Walker suggest. And they are tempting in order to ease the task of court administration. However, to remain faithful to the letter and spirit of *Daubert*, judges should avoid using such guides. Their reviews should be as subtle and sensitive as the evidence demands. This will ensure that their reviews remain faithful to the science and better ensure fairness to litigants.

SPECIFIC CONCERNS FROM COURT DECISIONS

Some courts have demanded that experts base their testimony on particular kinds of evidence, even though scientists would not insist upon such evidence in order to make a toxicity judgment about a substance.[46] Other courts exclude testimony based on evidence that scientists routinely rely upon to draw inferences. When either occurs, it will frustrate the laudable aim of the law utilizing the pertinent science. Moreover, it is a reasonable conjecture that there is no minimum kind or amount of evidence for a judgment that substance S causes or contributes to an injury to humans and there is no required or

---

[45] Most of the cases I review are those in which evidence has been excluded (plaintiffs' evidence), thus the discussion has this bias, but it is one resulting from visible court cases. Admitted evidence is more difficult to obtain and have any legal opinion of it.

[46] This point must be phrased carefully; it is not that the kinds of evidence on which courts have insisted are poor kinds of evidence. Indeed, often it is quite the contrary, they may mistakenly insist on *ideal* evidence. The problem is that in a number of rulings the evidence courts have *required* may be evidence that scientists would ideally prefer, but it not necessary for inferences about the toxicity of substances.

privileged explanation that S causes or contributes to a disease. There are various explanatory paths to such conclusions and different kinds and patterns of evidence that can be assembled to come to such judgments, several of which I will present in Chapter 7.[47] If courts exclude evidence or expert testimony needed to show that a particular explanation is plausible, they may make an explanatory mistake – litigants utilizing such an inference are not permitted to utilize certain arguments to argue for an explanation of the harm.

If courts err, their mistakes can also have an abiding *legal* impact because they appear as a written opinion. Appellate decisions serve as *precedents* for the court in question and for lower courts in the same jurisdiction. Appellate or district court opinions can function as *supportive reasons*, but not as precedents, if the court is at the same level in a judicial hierarchy, but in a different circuit or jurisdiction (thus, the reason cannot act as an explicit precedent). "Following the Joneses" of other jurisdictions, however, can perpetuate mistaken evidentiary understandings through the legal system.[48]

Demands for Particular Kinds of Evidence

Ideal Evidence Is the Enemy of the Good

Shortly after *Daubert* was decided, a few courts insisted that experts testifying must base their testimony on what might be considered *ideal* toxicity evidence. *Wade-Greaux v. Whitehall Labs* illustrates this issue.[49] The plaintiffs argued that a mother's use of Primatene Tablets and Primatene Mist, over-the-counter asthma medications sold by the defendant "caused TiaNicole Wade-Greaux to be born with true malformation of her upper limbs and other skeletal defects."[50] The trial court held that plaintiffs, in order to have their scientific evidence admitted, had to show that their claims about causation were supported by "repeated, consistent epidemiological studies; . . . an animal model that duplicates the defects resulting in the human from the exposure; . . . a dose/response relationship between the exposure and the effect on the experimental fetus; and . . . the mechanism of teratogenicity of the agent should be understood and make biologic sense."[51] As we discuss later, most of the court's necessary conditions are scientifically problematic. A court's requiring that *all* of these conditions be satisfied for admissibility presents even greater difficulties.

---

[47] Cranor and Eastmond, "Scientific Ignorance," 34–45.

[48] For example, in *Casey v. Ohio Medical Products, Inc.,* 877 F. Supp. 1380 (N.D. Cal 1995), the district court judge did not permit plaintiff to rely upon case studies and this court's reasons have been perpetrated and perpetuated throughout the legal system (but not a matter of legal precedent), very likely resulting in mistakes.

[49] *Wade-Greaux v. Whitehall Lab., Inc.,* 874 F. Supp. 1441, at 1450 (D.V.I.), *aff'd,* 46 F.3d 1120 (3d Cir. 1994)

[50] *Wade-Greaux v. Whitehall Lab., Inc.,* 874 F. Supp. at 1448.

[51] *Wade-Greaux v. Whitehall Lab., Inc.,* 874 F. Supp. at 1450.

Although this decision is not a leading one,[52] and by now is probably seen as an outlier (but the trial court was upheld on appeal), it illustrates the some mistakes courts need to avoid. Moreover, it might have been correct to exclude the experts. Rather, the error consists in the *reasons* the court gave and the seemingly extreme standards the court articulated in order for litigants to have their experts admitted.

First, the court appears to have engaged in an assessment of the plaintiffs' experts' ultimate conclusions instead of their methodology, contrary to the *Daubert* teaching. *Daubert* suggests that the appropriate inquiry for admissibility concerns the reliability of an advocate's evidence and reasoning, not its probative value compared with the defendant's.[53] This should be considered in the context of a directed verdict.

Second and more seriously, the court seems to take a literal textbook approach to admitting scientific evidence. That is, because standard toxicology references suggest that there must be epidemiological, animal, and other evidence in support of the claim of causation,[54] courts should require *all of this evidence* before plaintiff's experts can testify in a trial.[55] Such multiple sources of evidence may be *the best* and ensure the most certain route to a correct scientific judgment.

---

[52] Summary judgment was granted because the plaintiff's evidence fell far short of the court's articulated criteria, and the decision was upheld without comment on appeal. See *Wade-Greaux v. Whitehall Lab., Inc.*, 874 F. Supp. at 1476–1486, and *Wade-Greaux v. Whitehall Lab., Inc.*, 46 F.3d 1120 (3d Cir. 1994) (unpublished table decision). Nonetheless, the announced criteria seem particularly problematic.

[53] See *Daubert*, 509 U.S. at 595. ("The focus, of course, must be solely on principles and methodology, not on the conclusions that they generate.")

[54] The court listed various factors for determining whether an agent is a human teratogen, noting that those factors (which included epidemiological evidence, animal models, and a demonstrated dose-response relationship) were generally accepted by the community of teratologists, taught in medical schools throughout the country, and included in highly esteemed treatises on teratology. See *Wade-Greaux v. Whitehall Lab., Inc.*, 874 F. Supp. at 1450–51.

[55] In its findings of fact on epidemiology, the court stated:

Absent consistent, repeated human epidemiological studies showing a statistically significant increased risk of particular birth defects associated with exposure to a specific agent, the community of teratologists does not conclude that the agent is a human teratogen.

... [P]ositive epidemiologic findings are, standing alone, insufficient to permit a conclusion that a particular agent is teratogenic because the scientific community also requires confirmatory evidence from experimental animal studies.

Wade-Greaux, 874 F. Supp. at 1453 (citations omitted). Toxicologist Arthur Furst appears to adopt a similar view (see Arthur Furst, "Yes, But Is It a Human Carcinogen?" *Journal of the American College of Toxicology* 9 (1990): 12), but it is more appropriate for the context within which he works. He was addressing a society of toxicologists and asking what criteria a scientist should require to be satisfied before *being certain* on substantive scientific grounds that a substance is a carcinogen. Courts assessing the admissibility of scientific evidence are operating in a much different context with different evidentiary rules and different guidance from the *Daubert* decision.

This approach, however, poses several difficulties. It is overly restrictive for what constitutes an appropriate explanation of plaintiff's causal claims. The court appears to require that certain categories of evidence must be present, even though not all of this evidence would be required for a scientist or consensus scientific body to come to a reasonable scientific conclusion that substances are toxic to humans.

Moreover, such demanding evidentiary standards should not be needed to survive an admissibility review. A court adjudicating a tort claim need not be persuaded to a scientific certainty that a substance is a teratogen. Such certainty would substitute the most demanding scientific standards of proof for tort law admissibility. Thus, the *Wade-Greaux* court appears to have required a more constraining evidentiary explanation than is necessary, and demanded the best or *most certain* evidence when *reasonable* evidence is the most that should be needed to survive the reliability requirement for admissibility.

Daubert only requires that for testimony to be admissible it must be more likely than not reliable and fit the facts of the case.[56] The more specific amended Rule 702 requires that testimony must be "based on sufficient facts of data," the testimony must be the "products of reliable principles and methods" and "reliably applied to the facts of the case."[57] Courts should assess a litigants' evidence as a whole for reliability, but it need not possess the highest degree of certainty, be the best evidence or even be more likely than not *correct.*[58] The evidence utilized by and conclusions of consensus scientific committees serve as counterexamples to the *Wade-Greaux* court's demands (Chapter 7).[59] Moreover, often scientists do not have such evidentiary luxury (except perhaps in pure research for its own sake). In many circumstances, they can come to *correct* conclusions with evidence well short of this ideal.

Such requirements are additionally odd if we recall that a decision on admissibility is a *preliminary* review of whether an expert's opinion rests on a sufficiently reliable basis to support the factual basis of plaintiffs' cause of action and assist a jury. In *Wade-Greaux* the ideal became the enemy of the good and possibly of the admissible; courts need to guard against this.

---

56   See *Daubert v. Merrell Dow Pharm., Inc.*, 509 U.S 579, 589 (1993).

57   Federal Rules of Evidence, Rule 702 (amended 2002).

58   *Daubert v. Merrell Dow Pharm., Inc.*, 509 U.S at 590. ("Of course, it would be unreasonable to conclude that the subject of scientific testimony must be "known" to a certainty; arguably, there are no certainties in science.") See also the more recent *Advisory Committee on Evidence Rules proposed Amendment: Rule 702*, Committee Note: "As the court stated in *In re Paoli R.R. Yard PCB Litigation*, 35 F.3d 717, 744 (3d Cir. 1994), proponents "do not have to demonstrate to the judge by a preponderance of the evidence that the assessments of their experts are correct, they only have to demonstrate by a preponderance of evidence that their opinions are reliable. . . . The evidentiary requirement of reliability is lower than the merit's standard of correctness."

59   Cranor and Eastmond, "Scientific Ignorance," 34–39.

Demands for Human Epidemiological Evidence

Other courts have approached the *Wade-Greaux* mistake, but the error is subtler. These courts have demanded that expert testimony must be supported by *human epidemiological studies*. This was particularly the case with decisions made prior to and immediately following *Daubert*,[60] but some courts continue to demand human data as a necessary foundation for expert testimony.[61]

For example, in the leading Agent Orange opinion,[62] Judge Weinstein stated that "[a] number of sound epidemiological studies have been conducted on the health effects of exposure to Agent Orange. *These are the only useful studies having any bearing on causation*" (emphasis added).[63] Similarly, in *Lynch v. Merrell-National Laboratories, Division of Richardson-Merrell, Inc.*,[64] the First Circuit Court of Appeals noted that nonepidemiological studies used "singly or in combination, do not have the capability of proving causation in human beings in the absence of any confirmatory epidemiological data."[65] Other courts hearing Bendectin cases came to similar conclusions.[66] Courts hearing toxic tort cases involving other substances have concurred as well.[67] Moreover, the influence of an epidemiological threshold continues to the present with courts often citing the *Brock* Bendectin case.[68] Even when epidemiological studies are not explicitly a necessary condition, the context may suggest "that epidemiological evidence is a necessary prerequisite for a plaintiff to prevail."[69]

However, it is simply a mistake to think that epidemiological studies are necessary for scientists to form reasonable views about toxic effects in humans.

---

[60] Cranor et al., "Judicial Boundary-Drawing," 31–32, 49–55.

[61] Cranor and Eastmond, "Scientific Ignorance," 29–30 and notes therein.

[62] *In re Agent Orange Prod. Liab. Litig.*, 611 F. Supp. 1223, at 1231 (E.D.N.Y. 1985).

[63] Although this statement is ambiguous as to whether it is a claim about the particular case or a more general criterion for admissibility, a number of courts appear to have taken his remarks as announcing a general criterion.

[64] *Lynch v. Merrell-National Lab., Div. of Richardson-Merrell, Inc.*, 830 F.2d 1190 (1st Cir. 1987).

[65] *Lynch v. Merrell-National Lab., Div. of Richardson-Merrell, Inc.*, at 1194.

[66] See *Brock v. Merrell Dow Pharm., Inc.*, 874 F.2d 307, 312 (5th Cir. 1989) (the court concluded that a Bendectin plaintiff must proffer a statistically significant study before satisfying her burden of proof on causation), *cert. denied*, 494 U.S. 1046 (1990); *Richardson v. Richardson-Merrell, Inc.*, 857 F.2d 823, 825, 831 n.59 (D.C. Cir. 1988), *cert. denied*, 493 U.S. 882 (1989) (noting that "epidemiological studies are of crucial significance").

[67] See *Renaud v. Martin Marietta Corp.*, 749 F. Supp. 1545 (D. Colo. 1990); *Carroll v. Litton Sys., Inc.*, No. B-C-88–253, 1990 WL 312969, at *47 (W.D.N.C. Oct. 29, 1990); *Thomas v. Hoffman-La-Roche, Inc.*, 731 F. Supp. 224 (N.D. Miss. 1989), *aff'd on other grounds*, 949 F.2d 806 (5th Cir. 1992); *Chambers v. Exxon Corp.*, 81 F. Supp. 2d 661 (M.D. La. 2000).

[68] See *Chambers v. Exxon*, 81 F. Supp. 2d 661, at 664. ("Epidemiological studies are necessary to determine the cause and effect relationship between an agent, in this case exposure to benzene, and a disease, CML [chronic myelogenous leukemia] (citing *Brock v. Merrell Dow Pharmaceuticals, Inc.*, 874 F.2d 307, 311 (5th Cir. 1989), modified by 874 F.2d 307, 311 (5th Cir. 1989).)

[69] Green, "Expert Evidence," 665 n.101.

Because of limited evidence, consensus scientific bodies in fact frequently utilize various kinds of nonepidemiological evidence in combination to conclude that a substance is a known or probable carcinogen to humans. Some courts have resisted the impulse to enshrine epidemiological studies as necessary before an expert can testify to causation and there appears to be a more recent and salutary trend away from an epidemiological threshold.[70]

The attraction of courts to epidemiological studies is understandable, as we saw in Chapter 4. Epidemiological studies are the most direct evidence of human harm. *Well-designed* and *well-done* epidemiological studies (much is built into these ideas), with *sufficiently large samples* that are *sufficiently sensitive* to detect the adverse effects in question and with a *sufficient duration* can greatly assist in identifying toxic effects of product. Unfortunately, such ideal studies appear to be the exception rather than the rule.[71] Other kinds of human data, such as clinical trials (even rarer), if there are any, well-substantiated human case studies, and molecular and toxicity data from humans, also can be important evidence of a substance's human toxicity. And there are other kinds of scientifically relevant evidence that support judgments of a substance's human toxicity.

There are both scientific and legal reasons against requiring epidemiological studies as the foundation for expert testimony in a toxic tort case. There are various scientific problems, limitations, shortcomings, and weaknesses that affect their usefulness, especially in toxic tort suits. For many substances, epidemiological data simply are not available.[72] Recall from Chapter 4 that there is often too little human experience with a toxicant to fully establish its toxicity, exposures tend to crude, and epidemiological studies are notoriously insensitive.[73] For example, there is good epidemiological evidence for only about half or less of the known or likely human carcinogens assessed by national or international scientific bodies.[74] How widespread a problem this is for other toxicants is difficult to know. Special Magistrates in the Vaccine

---

[70]   See, e.g., *Marder v. G.D. Searle & Co.*, 630 F. Supp. 1087 (D. Md. 1986); *Zuchowicz v. United States*, 140 F.3d 381, 389–390 (2d Cir. 1998); *Ambrosini v. Labarraque*, 101 F.3d 129, 138–139 (D.C. Cir. 1996); *Benedi v. McNeil-P.P.C.*, Inc., 66 F.3d 1378 (4th Cir. 1995); *McCullock v. H. B. Fuller Co.*, 61 F.3d 1038 (2d Cir.1995); *Hopkins v. Dow Corning Corp.*, 33 F.3d 1116 (9th Cir. 1994); *Glaser v. Thompson Med. Co.*, 32 F.3d 969 (6th Cir. 1994); *Mendes-Silva v. United States*, 980 F.2d 1482 (D.C. Cir. 1993); *Kennedy v. Collagen Corp.*, 974 F.2d 1342 (9th Cir. 1992); *Wells v. Ortho Pharm. Corp.*, 788 F.2d 741, 745 (11th Cir. 1986); *Globetti v. Sandoz Pharms., Corp.*, 111 F. Supp. 2d 1174 (N.D.Ala. 2000); *Graham v. Playtex Prod., Inc.*, 993 F. Supp. 127, 132 (N.D.N.Y. 1998); *Lakie v. Smithkline Beecham*, 965 F. Supp. 49, 56 (D.D.C. 1997).

[71]   Cranor and Eastmond, "Scientific Ignorance," 35–39.

[72]   Rall, et. al., "Alternatives to Using Human Experience," 355–385.

[73]   Huff and Rall, "Relevance to Humans," 433; Elaine Faustman and Gilbert S. Omenn, "Risk Assessment," in *Casarett and Doull's Toxicology: The Basic Science of Poisons*, 6th ed., ed. Curtis D. Klaassen (New York: McGraw-Hill, 2001), 86; Carbone, et al., "Modern Criteria," 5518–5524, esp. 5519; Cogliano, et al., "Science and Practice," 1269–1274, esp. 1270.

[74]   Rall et al., "Alternatives to Using Human Experience."

Injury Compensation Program have judicially noticed this point.[75] Because it is morally wrong to deliberately expose people to a toxicant for study purposes, any studies must be conducted when accidental exposures occur. However, this makes it difficult to have accurate exposure information and accurate results.

Even when epidemiological studies can be conducted, they tend to be expensive. And, if studies are too small or of too short duration, they may fail to detect adverse effects even if the substance in fact causes or contributes to them (Chapter 4).

Surprisingly also, human studies that are conducted too long after exposure can also result in underestimations of risks. For example, studies conducted on retired workers who were exposed to benzene during their working years show a lower relative risk than would be expected in such circumstances.[76] Finally, it is a reasonable conjecture that for many exposures typical of toxic tort suits, conducting an appropriate epidemiological study is simply not an option, for example, too few may be exposed, exposure data is not likely to be present, the diseases may be rare, or the studies will be quite expensive.[77]

In addition, because epidemiological studies are not *controlled* experiments, their reputation in the scientific community may not be nearly as strong as the standing they appear to have with federal judges, especially those who have said that human epidemiological evidence is the only or the best kind of evidence in toxic tort suits. An epidemiologist at the National Cancer Institute describes their relative strength as follows:

> There is a perception in the scientific community that epidemiological evidence, observational in nature and prone to confounding and bias, is weaker evidence than animal model studies and other types of laboratory-based toxicological studies. The perception is decades old.
>
> This perception is likely to be mitigated by the recent development and successes of molecular epidemiology and multidisciplinary programs in disease prevention that develop and use evidence from many different scientific disciplines.[78]

[75] *Stevens v. Secretary of the Department of Health and Human Services*, at 14. ("Unfortunately, . . . epidemiology and [toxicological] footprints are rarely available – such is the nature of science. This lack of direct evidence leaves petitioners no other recourse than to corroborate their causation claim with circumstantial evidence.")

[76] Rinsky, et al., "Benzene Exposure and Hematopoietic Mortality," 474–480; S. R. Silver, R. A. Rinsky, S. P. Cooper, R. W. Hornung, and D. Lai, "Effect of Follow-Up Time on Risk Estimates: Longitudinal Examination of the Relative Risks of Leukemia and Multiple Myeloma in a Rubber Hydrochloride Cohort," *American Journal of Industrial Medicine* 42 (2002): 481–489.

[77] Cranor and Eastmond, "Scientific Ignorance," 5–48.

[78] Douglas L. Weed, M.D., Ph.D., Dean, Education and Training, Chief, Office of Preventive Oncology; Director, Cancer Prevention Fellowship Program, Division of Cancer Prevention, National Cancer Institute, personal communication, January 2003.

Epidemiological studies are, however, just one kind of evidence; there are others (Chapter 4). Moreover, an insistence on epidemiological evidence obviously privileges "holistic" human body evidence over other quite good evidence on which scientists rely.[79]

There are legal problems with requiring epidemiological evidence. To insist that plaintiffs, for example, alleging that exposure to a substance such as ethylene oxide caused brain cancer, must have epidemiological studies on which to base testimony by scientific experts is to require a study that is extremely difficult to do. Causes of rare diseases, of which brain cancer is one, can be quite difficult to detect without a large, expensive study that is sufficiently sensitive to detect the effect. In most cases, there are not persons appropriately exposed to serve as the basis of a study.

Special Restrictions on Epidemiological Studies

Some courts and commentators have gone further and have required that the epidemiological studies must satisfy additional conditions before they can provide a foundation for expert testimony in toxic tort cases. Some have insisted that such studies be "statistically significant."[80] Others have insisted that the studies find a relative risk of at least two between the exposed and control populations.[81] Still others have suggested that all or most of Hill's factors must be satisfied by epidemiological studies before they should be admitted.[82] Such considerations help interpret studies. However, if they become necessary conditions on scientific evidence that forms the foundation of expert testimony, this poses problems.

Statistical Significance Requirements: Both before and after the *Daubert* decision, several courts and numerous commentators have insisted that epidemiological studies must be "statistically significant," a not unreasonable, but possibly misleading, requirement.[83] This requirement means that studies must

---

[79] Jasanoff, *Science at the Bar*, 125.

[80] See, e.g., *Brock v. Merrell Dow Pharm., Inc.*, 874 F.2d 307, 312 (5th Cir. 1989), *cert. denied*, 494 U.S. 1046 (1990).

[81] See, e.g., *Daubert v. Merrell Dow Pharm.*, 43 F.3d 1311, 1321 (9th Cir.), *cert. denied*, 116 S.Ct. 189 (1995).

[82] See, e.g., David E. Bernstein, "The Admissibility of Scientific Evidence After *Daubert v. Merrell Dow Pharmaceuticals Inc.*," *Cardozo Law Review* 15 (1994): 2139, 2167–2170 (discussing the imposition of nine "aspects" of a statistical association between two variables, which were first proposed by Sir Austin Bradford Hill in 1965).

[83] See, e.g., *Brock*, 874 F.2d at 312; and "Development in the Law – Confronting the New Challenges of Scientific Evidence," *Harvard Law Review* 108 (1995): 1532, 1542. *Brock* is frequently cited for this proposition, even comparatively recently: *Chambers v. Exxon*, 81 F. Supp. 2d 661, at 665 (2000), also referring to *In re Breast Implant Litigation*, 11 F. Supp. 2d 1217, 1228 (2000).

have less than some low probability, for example, typically less than .05, that a statistical association between exposure to a substance and a disease is not the result of random chance.[84] Some judicial rulings suggest that if studies do not satisfy this condition, expert testimony based on them should be rejected as evidence in toxic tort cases.[85] Thus, statistical significance is treated as something like a *bright-line rule* that epidemiological studies must satisfy before they can be part of the foundation for expert testimony. However, many scientists, although recognizing its importance, do not necessarily regard statistical significance as decisive in judging whether epidemiological evidence can contribute to causal judgments of harm.[86]

A variety of considerations show demands for low statistical are problematic. First, although some courts suggest that studies should be statistically significant at the .05 level, scientists take a much more nuanced approach toward the exact level of statistical significance they utilize. Colleagues with whom I have collaborated would tolerate a wider range of statistical significance for interpreting studies, for example, higher than .05, but would understand properly what they do and do not show about the data. After all, statistical significance rules out only one possible explanation of a positive study result – chance distributions in the sample population under study. And there seems no necessity to adopt a low, for example, .05, value for litigation. If there is a .10 chance of a false positive, is this too much higher than a .05 chance? Yet courts will be pressured to utilize the lower number.

Second, statistical signficance compared with confidence intervals was an issue between *amici* in the *Daubert* case,[87] but recent discussions suggest that the cutting edge of the field seems to be moving away from tests of significance for two reasons. Tests of significance are a kind of *decision rule,* useful for certain purposes but not others. Moreover, tests of significance reveal less about the underlying data than other presentations of the evidence.[88]

---

[84] See David Ozonoff and Leslie I. Boden, "Truth and Consequences: Health Agency Responses to Environmental Health Problems," *Science Technology & Human Values* 12 (1987): 70, 73–74.

[85] See Ozonoff and Boden, 74; and Tom Christoffel and Stephen P. Teret, "Epidemiology and the Law: Courts and Confidence Intervals," *American Journal of Public Health* 81 (1991): 1661, 1665.

[86] See *Amicus Brief of Professor Kenneth Rothman, et al. In Support of Petitioners* at 3–7, *Daubert v. Merrell Dow Pharm., Inc.,* 509 U.S. 579 (1993).

[87] *Amicus Brief of Professor Kenneth Rothman,* 3–7; but compare *Amicus Brief of Professor Alvan R. Feinstein in Support of Respondent* at 4–8, *Daubert v. Merrell Dow Pharm., Inc.,* 509 U.S. 579 (1993).

[88] For discussion of this point, see Joseph L. Fleiss, "Significance Tests Have a Role in Epidemiologic Research: Reactions to A.M. Walker," *American Journal of Public Health* 76 (1986): 559, 559–560; Steven N. Goodman and Richard Royall, "Evidence and Scientific Research," *American Journal of Public Health* 78 (1988): 1568, 1568–1574; Green, "Expert Witness," 685; Charles Poole, "Beyond the Confidence Interval," *American Journal of Public Health*

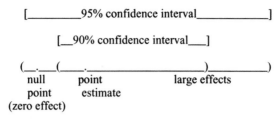

Figure 6.1. Recreated from figure 9-1 in Rothman, *Modern Epidemiology*, p. 120.

Even if tests of significance were treated as decision rules for scientific research purposes, it is not obvious that the same decision rule should be utilized for admissibility decisions in the law, because the aim is to see if a litigant has an integrated body of evidence that could reliably support the legal conclusion.

Moreover, it should be in the interest of tort law to have evidence presented in the most informative manner possible, which again argues against strict and uniform tests of significance. However, if the aim is to present evidence in the most informative way, Kenneth Rothman *inter alia* has argued that scientists should use *confidence intervals*. Confidence intervals display information about the *magnitude* and *the inherent variability* of an effect that is more accurate and informative than a decision cutoff. Thus, for example, even if one end of a confidence interval includes a "no effect" point (suggesting that the study shows "no effect" (a point for which defendants might argue)), if the other end of the confidence interval is asymmetrically beyond the point estimate of the study, it is compatible with the study showing a marked effect.[89] This is illustrated in Figure 6.1.

In this figure, whereas a 95 percent confidence interval according to some experts and lawyers would be interpreted as showing that "there is 'no effect' from exposure," Rothman argues that the asymmetry in the uncertainty distribution around the point estimate suggests an effect. Moreover, the smaller *90 percent confidence interval* (analogous to a 10 percent statistical significance rule) is consistent with an adverse effect, because it does not include the "no effect" point (but there is a 10 percent chance that a positive study might be a statistical anomaly). This second point reinforces the point made above that courts should not routinely reject higher statistical significance cutoffs, for example, .10 or confidence intervals of 90 percent because these, too, can

195, 77 (1987): 195–199; W. Douglas Thompson, "Statistical Criteria in the Interpretation of Epidemiologic Data," *American Journal of Public Health* 77 (1987): 191, 191–194; and Alexander M. Walker, "Reporting the Results of Epidemiologic Studies," *American Journal of Public Health* 76 (1986): 556, 556–558.

89 Rothman, *Modern Epidemiology*, 120–121.

be informative and there is nothing sacrosanct about a 95 percent confidence interval.[90]

The important evidentiary point is, "What does the evidence show about the phenomena?" Thus, Rothman argues for not using some automatic procedure to decide the issue, but more informationally rich means of exhibiting the data. Judges should be similarly willing to tolerate more relaxed confidence intervals or rules concerning statistical significance (if they insist on that) because scientists do. (This will make their review tasks more difficult, but the Supreme Court has given them the job.)

Third, if scientific results are excluded merely because they are not statistically significant, decision makers risk excluding important evidence and the decision might result in "far greater inaccuracy."[91] Greater inaccuracy can result because demanding tests of significance asymmetrically prevent false positives, but permit more false negatives (Chapter 4). And, "[p]reemptorily rejecting all studies that are not statistically significant would be a cursory and foolish judgment, particularly if there are multiple studies tending to show a consistent effect."[92] Thus, court decisions might be more accurate on factual grounds if a wider range of epidemiological data were admitted.[93]

In addition, Rothman points out, when tests of significance dominate the interpretation of epidemiological data, they also can be quite misleading in another way. For example,

> [i]n a review of 71 clinical trials that reported no 'significant' difference (P > 0.05) between the compared treatments, Freiman et al. [1978] found that in the great majority of such trials the data either indicated or at least were consistent with a moderate or even reasonably strong effect of the new treatment. In all of these trials, the original investigators interpreted their data as indicative of no effect because the P-value was not 'statistically significant.' The misinterpretations arose because the investigators relied solely on 'significance' testing for their statistical analysis rather than on a more descriptive and informative analysis. On failing to reject the null hypothesis, the investigators in these 71 trials inappropriately 'accepted' the null hypothesis as correct, resulting in a probable type II error [false negative] for many of these so-called 'negative' studies.[94]

---

[90] Rothman, *Modern Epidemiology*, 119–120.

[91] Green, "Expert Witnesses," notes one reviewer who identified seventy-one epidemiologic studies that failed to satisfy statistical significance, but concluded that the "studies were consistent with a moderate or strong effect of the treatment under investigation" (685) (citing Jennie A. Freiman et al., "The Importance of Beta, the Type II Error and Sample Size in the Design and Interpretation of the Randomized Control Trial: Survey of 71 'Negative' Trials," *New England Journal of Medicine* 299 (1978): 690).

[92] See Green, "Expert Witnesses," 686.

[93] See Green, "Expert Witnesses," 686; see also Cranor et al., "Judicial Boundary-Drawing," 71–81.

[94] Rothman, *Modern Epidemiology*, 117–118 (emphasis added).

There are also policy reasons to be concerned about stringent statistical significance rules. Recall the inverse relationship between preventing false positives and preventing false negatives (Chapter 4).[95] Thus, one cannot, without using very large sample sizes, have very low false positives, very low false negatives, and a study that will detect comparatively small relative risks, for example, of around two or three. For studies with small samples trying to detect the causes of comparatively rare diseases, researchers will be unable to detect some outcomes of scientific interest and perhaps of social import.

Moreover, determining which factual error one should risk in legal decisions is a policy matter.[96] If courts adopt a legal concern strongly to protect against false positive mistakes they are committed to the view that in the law it is more important to protect against false positives than to protect against false negatives. Mathematically, this favors defendants and makes it more difficult for plaintiffs to provide probative evidence.

In addition, when judges demand low statistical significance, they are also implicitly insisting that one explanation for a positive test result must be ruled out with a very high degree of confidence (95 percent), namely, that the positive result was a statistical anomaly. Thus, an interpretive tool of scientific inquiry, and a seemingly neutral one, can have quite unintended asymmetric effects in another institutional context and adversely affect the social outcomes of those institutions.[97]

Moreover, such a screening rule seems at odds with the evenhandedness with which torts treats plaintiffs and defendants as revealed by its ultimate burden of proof and reasonable admissibility procedures.[98] The law in embracing scientific mistake norms as expressed in rigid statistical significance rules undermines its own mistake norms. Such rules will systematically disadvantage the party seeking to establish a fact with statistical evidence, typically the plaintiffs. This consequence is even more worrisome if, as some suggest, juries and judges accept statistical evidence much less critically than other kinds of evidence. Statistical evidence is then given greater credibility, and likely imposing particular hardships on plaintiffs.[99] None of this is to suggest that judges should

---

[95] Green, "Expert Witnesses," 681, 687; Cranor et al., "Judicial Boundary Drawing," 30–39.

[96] The issue is somewhat more complex than this even. One must make tradeoffs between preventing false positives, preventing false negatives and being able to detect comparatively low relative risks. With samples that are smaller than an "ideal size" to ensure all three, something must give. See Chapter 4 and Cranor, *Regulating Toxic Substances*, 36–40. See also Green, "Expert Witnesses," 691–692 (providing an example showing that the chances of a false negative can easily be nearly 10 times the chances of a false positive) and Cranor, *Regulating Toxic Substances*, 71–78.

[97] As we have seen, there are other mistakes that can be artifacts of studies, such as biases in the design of studies and confounders, but because these are somewhat less likely to result in asymmetric errors that can adversely affect the law, I do not review them.

[98] See Green, "Expert Witnesses," 691–692; Cranor, *Regulating Toxic Substances*, 71–78.

[99] See Green, "Expert Witnesses," 693.

accept all epidemiological studies. Rather, they must become better consumers of scientific evidence so that their admissibility decisions concerning scientific evidence and reasoning do not distort the law.

We would do well to heed both a scientist and a legal scholar on the issue of statistical evidence. Sir Austin Bradford Hill, whom we met earlier, posed some fundamental questions scientists should ask themselves regarding causation: "[I]s there any other way of explaining the set of facts before us, is there any other answer equally, or more likely than cause and effect?" He then proceeded to sum up the views of many working scientists concerning statistical significance:

> No formal tests of significance can answer those questions. Such tests can, and should, remind us of the effects that the play of chance can create, and they will instruct us in the likely magnitude of those effects. Beyond that they contribute nothing to the "proof" of our hypothesis.[100]

Michael Green, an academic lawyer concerned about the inordinate influence of the Bendectin and Agent Orange cases, concludes a discussion of statistical significance as follows:

> [T]he art of teasing out causal inferences in the absence of a mature epi-demiologic record is far too complicated for courts seriously to review the methodologies and analyses involved. Making the ultimate causal inference requires an assessment not only of the quality of the epidemiology but the biological plausibility, based on what is understood about the mechanisms of toxicity. Indeed, one of the lessons of the Bendectin cases is that the courts are not truly engaging in greater scrutiny of experts' opinions; rather, they are adopting a few relatively simple screening devices.... Especially as the available universe of evidence gets thinner, inadmissibility decisions have significant risks.[101]

I concur. Rigid and low statistical significance rules perhaps simplify the job of screening epidemiological studies. They also risk ignoring salient scientific evidence, encourage less accurate and less nuanced decision making, systemat-ically disadvantage plaintiffs, and, thus, risk upsetting the balance of interests between plaintiffs and defendants.

Relative Risk Rules: Still other courts have required that epidemiological studies must find a relative risk of at least two. Carruth and Goldstein found thirty-one cases in which relative risks greater than two (RR > 2) were discussed. In twenty-nine cases, courts addressed whether RR > 2 is a threshold for proof of causation, with twelve saying that RR > 2 "was required to support a reasonable inference of causation"; whereas fourteen indicated that it was

---

[100] Hill, "The Environment and Disease," 15, 19
[101] Green, "Expert Witnesses," 693–694.

not.[102] In addition, twenty-one of the opinions discussed whether RR > 2 is a threshold for the admissibility of an expert opinion on causation, with ten saying that "RR > 2 is required" and eleven that it is not. Thus, nearly half of the opinions that discuss this issue require it for ultimate proof of causation and about one-third make it a threshold for the admissibility of expert testimony. For the discussion here, I focus on the use of RR > 2 in support of expert testimony for admissibility.

Before discussing this suggested admissibility constraint, what is attractive about it? A judicial rule that makes having a RR > 2 necessary for expert testimony seems to hope for a certain ideal. It seems to require an evidentiary foundation for testimony that is objective, directly pertinent to human harm, is free or at least freer from subjective scientific judgment by the experts than studies that provide more complex and less direct evidence of human harm, and finally, is one that seemingly carries the legal burden of proof on its face in the statistics of the study.

It is seemingly objective because it is a scientific study, not simply an expert's opinion. It is directly pertinent to assessing human harm in a way that animal or some other kinds of evidence are not because any revealed adverse effects are on humans. It appears to limit the latitude of experts in their judgment about the probability of causation because scientific judgment superficially appears not to enter into reporting and using the results of such studies. Finally, it seems to provide a scientific answer to either the standard of proof that must be met for general or specific causation. It appears that the statistics alone indicates that a randomly chosen diseased person in the exposed group "more probably than not" had his or her disease caused by the substance, thus plausibly satisfying the ultimate tort law standard of proof on specific causation. Similar considerations might be invoked in an argument for general causation.

Many pre- and post-*Daubert* courts and a number of commentators have endorsed the idea that an epidemiological study must reveal a relative risk of at least two in order for testimony based on such evidence to be admissible.[103] Prominent among these is the Ninth Circuit Court of Appeals. It utilized such

---

[102] Russellyn S. Carruth and Bernard D. Goldstein, "Relative Risk Greater than Two in Proof of Causation in Toxic Tort Litigation," *Jurimetrics Journal* 41 (2001): 195, 200–201.

[103] See, e.g., *Daubert v. Merrell Dow Pharm., Inc.*, 43 F.3d 1311, 1320–21 (9th Cir. 1995), *on remand from* 509 U.S. 579 (1993); see also *In re Joint E. & S. Dist. Asbestos Litig.*, 758 F. Supp. 199, 203 (S.D.N.Y. 1991), *aff'd*, 52 F.3d 1124 (2d Cir. 1995), and the Supreme Court of Texas in *Merrell Dow Pharmaceuticals, Inc. v. Havner*, 953 S.W.2d 706 (1997). Carruth and Goldstein reported that twelve of twenty-nine cases discussing a relative risk greater than two argued that RR > 2 "was required to support a reasonable inference of causation," whereas opinions in fourteen cases indicated that RR > 2 was not required for proof of causation (Carruth and Goldstein, "Relative Risk Greater than Two," 200–201). Commentators who argued early on for requiring a relative risk even greater than two are Bert Black and David E. Lilienfeld, "Epidemiologic Proof in Toxic Tort Litigation," *Fordham Law Review* 52 (1984): 732, 769. More recently, Joe G. Hollingsworth and Eric Lasker argued for the same

a consideration to decide the *Daubert* case on remand without returning it to the trial court of origin.

> California tort law requires plaintiffs to show not merely that Bendectin increased the likelihood of injury, but that it more likely than not caused their injuries. . . . In terms of statistical proof, this means that plaintiffs must establish not just that their mothers' ingestion of Bendectin increased somewhat the likelihood of birth defects, but that it more than doubled it – only then can it be said that Bendectin is more likely than not the source of their injury. Because the background rate of limb reduction defects is one per thousand births, plaintiffs must show that among children of mothers who took Bendectin the incidence of such defects was more than two per thousand.[104]

The Texas Supreme Court concurred in *Merrell Dow Pharmaceuticals, Inc. v. Havner:*

> The use of scientifically reliable epidemiological studies and the requirement of more than a doubling of the risk strikes a balance between the needs of our legal system and the limits of science.[105]

There are several problems with courts requiring relative risks greater than two for admissibility rulings. Some of the issues arise because of what one might consider pragmatic issues in a study, whereas others reflect fundamental methodological problems in epidemiology. Finally, they also pose legal problems.

Consider the pragmatic issues. First, as epidemiological studies are ordinarily conducted to identify public health problems from environmental or workplace exposure, once a causal relationship is suspected between exposure and disease, if preventive actions can be taken for those who continue to be exposed, they ordinarily will be. An epidemiological study is essentially a "snapshot in time,"[106] but it is as early a snapshot as might be helpful for public health purposes. Consequently, for diseases with any significant latency period, there will likely be additional diseases that were not detected by an early study and thus, the early study will suffer from incomplete accrual of diseases.[107] This is likely to underestimate the severity of the disease causation. If courts insist on relative risks of at least two in published studies as a foundation for expert testimony, they will exclude some evidence of disease effects in humans. Moreover, if it is in a study that did not allow for complete accrual of disease, they exclude possible evidence of a higher rate of disease.

point: "The Case against Differential Diagnosis: *Daubert,* Medical Causation Testimony and the Scientific Method," in *Journal of Health Law,* 37 (Winter 2004): 85–112.

104 *Daubert v. Merrell Dow Pharm., Inc.,* 43 F.3d at 1320.
105 *Merrell Dow Pharmaceuticals, Inc. v. Havner,* 953 S.W.2d 706, at 718 (1997).
106 Carruth and Goldstein, "Relative Risk Greater than Two," 207.
107 Carruth and Goldstein, "Relative Risk Greater than Two," 207.

Second, in many cases epidemiological studies are done in occupational settings. Those who are employed tend to be healthier than the general population, producing a "healthy worker effect." Thus, "comparing exposed workers to the general population tends to understate relative risk" because the general population has a greater variability and wider range of susceptibility to diseases than healthy workers.[108] Courts must be sensitive to such effects and realize they have limited applications to children, the diseased, the elderly and so on.

Third, when a population at risk has been studied, if there is an elevated disease rate, there typically would be efforts to reduce exposures and, thus, disease. If a follow-up study is then conducted on populations for which remedial measures have been taken, disease rates will be lower, and lower relative risks will be likely. Thus, follow-up studies can easily underestimate the potential substances have for causing adverse effects. Courts should inquire about the context of the studies.

Fourth, a study typically reports an average relative risk from exposure to a toxic substance, which may disguise higher or low relative risks, on the one hand, resulting from higher or lower exposures respectively, or, on the other hand, disguise more or less sensitive individuals. For example, higher exposures might result in relative risks of four, whereas lower exposures might reveal relative risks of only 1.7. The weighted average of the different relative risks might yield an overall average relative risk less than 2. As scientists become increasingly aware of sensitive subpopulations, for example, resulting from genetic or other susceptibilities,[109] they may discover that average relative risks inadequately reveal real risks to sensitive subgroups. (The causal basis for this was considered in Chapter 5 under "weak and strong" causal contributions.)

The tort law clearly protects sensitive subgroups, those with "eggshell skulls,"[110] but overly stringent admissibility rules risk frustrating this aim. Thus, admissibility rules that preclude studies with overall relative risks less than two might prevent the admissibility of studies which included relative risks greater than two for individuals exposed to higher levels of a toxic substance or relative risks greater than two for particularly vulnerable groups. The automatic exclusion of testimony based on such evidence unfairly disadvantages both biologically sensitive plaintiffs and those subject to greater exposures than the study average. Unless courts (or legislatures) make policy decisions to exclude such subpopulations from tort compensation, epidemiological studies

[108]   Carruth and Goldstein, "Relative Risk Greater than Two," 208 (noting that a 1.5 relative risk in an exposed worker population might well reflect a doubling of disease rate compared with the appropriate unexposed population).

[109]   See, e.g., Frederica Perera, "Molecular Epidemiology: Insights into Cancer Susceptibility, Risk Assessment, and Prevention," *Journal of the National Cancer Institute* 88 (1996): 496, 496–509 (discussing the interaction of environmental factors and genetic and acquired susceptibilities to cancer).

[110]   See W. Page Keeton et al., *Prosser and Keeton on Torts*, 291–292.

with relative risks less than two can provide scientifically relevant evidence and should not automatically be excluded from trial (or experts excluded for using it as part of their testimony).

The proceeding point is supported by a striking example from radiation epidemiology that suggests it is a serious mistake to exclude expert testimony based on epidemiological studies with relative risks less than two. Ionizing radiation has long been a known carcinogen. It causes cancer in many human organ systems. One study shows that atomic bomb survivors from Hiroshima and Nagasaki contracted leukemia and multiple myeloma, as well as cancer of the esophagus, stomach, colon, other segments of the digestive system, urinary tract, lung, lymph nodes, and a number of other sites.[111]

Contrary to widespread belief,[112] the radiation exposures for many in these study populations were relatively low. What is striking about these findings is that epidemiological studies show with (interestingly) 90 percent confidence that all malignant neoplasms taken together except leukemia have a relative risk of less than two. Individual cancers that have a relative risk less than two include stomach, other parts of the digestive system, lung, and some other sites. Only leukemia, multiple myeloma, urinary tract, and colon cancer have relative risks greater than two from radiation exposure.

Such findings would be problematic for courts that have ruled inadmissible testimony based on epidemiological studies with relative risks less that two. Because ionizing radiation is one of the best-known carcinogens and one that scientists are certain causes cancer, courts, faced with plaintiffs who have been exposed to radiation, must either rule inadmissible testimony based on epidemiological studies for all neoplasms for which there is not a relative risk of greater than or equal to two, or must admit the evidence and then engage in the sensitive and complex task of assessing and weighing testimony based on evidence that exposure to ionizing radiation caused the cancer in question. Clearly, given the substantial evidence and degree of certainty about this carcinogen, the latter course seems much more defensible on both scientific and legal grounds. Several courts have judicially recognized the carcinogenic potential of radiation.[113] Moreover, courts should apply this lesson to studies of other toxicants.

There is also a subtler theoretical point about relative risks of the two. Sander Greenland and Jamie Robbins in a series of papers have argued that it is difficult

---

[111] See H. Kato, "Cancer Mortality," in *Cancer in Atomic Bomb Survivors*, ed. I. Shigematsu and A. Kagan (Japan Scientific Societies Press, 1986), quoted in Arthur K. Sullivan, "Classification, Pathogenesis, and Etiology of Neoplastic Diseases of the Hematopoietic System," in *Wintrobe's Clinical Hematology*, ed. G. R. Lee et al., 9th ed. (Philadelphia: Lea and Febiger, 1993), 1725, 1750.

[112] See Julius C. McElveen and Chris Amantea, "Risk Symposium: Legislating Risk Assessment," *University of Cincinnati Law Review* 63 (1995): 1553, 1556.

[113] *In re Hanford Nuclear Reservation Litigation* 292 F.3d 1124, at 1137 (C.A.9 (Wash. 2002), citing *In re TMI Litigation*, 193 F.3d at 643 (3d Cir. 1999).

to determine how much disease to attribute to an exposure. Thus, it is difficult to utilize epidemiological studies as a very good guide to the increase in disease causation.[114] For example, exposure to a toxicant might cause new cases of disease, that is, diseases in individuals who would not have contracted the disease at all, or it might accelerate the onset of disease in individuals who would have contracted the disease in any case, but not as early. Thus, exposure may not only be an on-off switch for the disease in question, that is, turning it on; it may also function as an accelerator of disease that would have occurred in any case, only at a later time in a person's life. Both contributions to disease should be attributed to the exposure. However, epidemiological studies ordinarily would only record the new cases of disease. This theoretical point constitutes an additional reason to be skeptical about treating relative risks of two as any kind of important cutoff for legal purposes. (How much practical import their point has is less clear since pragmatically it will be quite difficult to estimate the acceleration of disease in those who would have contracted it in the natural course of events.) Robbins and Greenland, thus, argue that utilizing epidemiological studies as evidence for attributing disease to exposure risks under-reporting disease rates and some other approach should be taken.[115]

Moreover, studies showing a relative risk of two or greater simply may not be available, as the *Stevens'* judge notes for epidemiological data in vaccine injury cases.[116] Judge Golkiewicz argues that the best evidence in vaccine cases are epidemiological studies or vaccine "footprint" evidence ("dispositive clinical or pathological markers").[117]

> Unfortunately, few petitioners are afforded this evidentiary luxury since epidemiology and footprints are rarely available – such is the nature of science. This lack of direct evidence leaves petitioners no other recourse than to corroborate their causation claim with circumstantial evidence.[118]

---

[114] See, for example, Sander Greenland and James M. Robins, "Conceptual Problems in the Definition and Interpretation of Attributable Fractions," *American Journal of Epidemiology* 128 (1988): 1185, 1185–1196; James M. Robins and Sander Greenland, "Estimability and Estimation of Excess and Etiologic Fractions," *Stat. Med.* 8 (1989): 845, 847–854; James Robins and Sander Greenland, "The Probability of Causation Under a Stochastic Model for Individual Risk," *Biometrics* 45 (1989): 1125, 1129–1136; Sander Greenland, "Relation of Probability of Causation to Relative Risk and Doubling Dose: A Methodologic Error That Has Become a Social Problem," *American Journal of Public Health* 89 (1999): 1166, 1166–1169; and Sander Greenland and James M. Robins, "Epidemiology, Justice, and the Probability of Causation," *Jurimetrics Journal* 40 (2000): 321. Two of the more accessible (and less technical scientific) articles are the last two in the series.

[115] Carruth and Goldstein, "Relative Risk Greater than Two," 206 (also citing Greenland and Robbins's work).

[116] *Stevens v. Secretary of the Department of Health and Human Services,* at 14.

[117] *Stevens v. Secretary of the Department of Health and Human Services,* at 14.

[118] *Stevens v. Secretary of the Department of Health and Human Services,* at 14.

Finally, there is a much more serious ethical and policy issue. A demand for human epidemiological studies with relative risks greater than two commits the tort law to the view that other people must have suffered serious diseases or death from a similar exposure before a plaintiff at the bar even has a chance at a jury trial in an attempt to receive just compensation for injuries suffered. In short, a necessary condition of admissibility of expert testimony is death or serious diseases suffered by others in order for an expert to have an epidemiological study on which to rely. Moreover, although the tort law is not on the front line of protecting the public's health, deterrence of harmful conduct or products is a substantial part of the justification of torts.

For these reasons, one should be skeptical on both scientific and legal grounds of legally requiring a relative risk of two for the admissibility or the sufficiency of epidemiological evidence. The American Law Institute in modifying the Restatement of Torts on tort law causation has now also come out against requiring RR > 2.[119]

Sample Size and Duration of Studies: Sample size and duration of epidemiological studies are topics, which, although not explicitly utilized by judges (or recommended by commentators) as restrictions on expert testimony based on epidemiological studies, nonetheless merit a brief caution because both can be shortcomings of a study that can adversely affect their legal value. Recall that epidemiological studies that are of *too short a duration* may fail to reveal an existing relative risk because the induction and latency periods of the disease is longer than the study. Similar problems attend studies that are based on too small a sample. Both could produce mistaken "no effect" results (Chapter 4). Such outcomes would be particularly likely for studies that sought to identify cancers, which tend to have much longer induction and latency periods than many diseases.[120] A longer study would likely be more sensitive to lower risks.[121]

Finally, there is a further point related to duration of exposure. Studies that are conducted *too long after exposure has ceased* can also underestimate risks; the "observed relative risk may not be the maximum risk experienced by the cohort."[122] Benzene researchers have found that the relative risks from benzene

---

[119] American Law Institute, *Restatement of the Law: Torts: Liability for Physical Harm* (Proposed Final Draft) (2005), 14.

[120] See D. Schottenfeld and J. F. Haas, "Carcinogens in the Workplace," *CA – Cancer J. for Clinicians* 29 (1979): 144, 156–159.

[121] A National Institute of Occupational Health epidemiological study was noted to have an 80 percent chance of detecting a ninefold relative risk of bladder cancer in a cohort of workers exposed to 4,4'-methylenebis (2-chloroaniline) (MBOCA) in 1985, but by 1995 the same study would have an 80 percent chance of detecting a fourfold relative risk. See Elizabeth Ward et al., "4,4'-Methylenebis(2-Chloroaniline): An Unregulated Carcinogen," *American Journal of Industrial Medicine* 12 (1987): 537, 542.

[122] Silver et al., "Effect of Follow-up Time on Risk Estimates," 488. See also Rinsky et al., "Benzene Exposure and Hematopoietic Mortality," 474–480.

exposure decrease the greater the time that has elapsed between the last exposure and the time of study. The data suggest that leukemia may have a relatively short latency period or that the most susceptible individuals "succumbed to the disease early, leaving a less susceptible population at risk for the majority of the follow-up period."[123] These findings show how critical the timing of a study can be. If studies conducted quite long after last exposure are utilized as the basis for estimating the risk of disease from contemporaneous exposure, this would substantially underestimate risks. Consequently, epidemiological studies simply cannot be taken at face value for what they show without an inquiry into their duration, context of study, or sample size.

Extrapolation from Women to Men and Middle-Aged to Old and Young Persons: Recently, a federal court case in Washington state produced a new allegation from defendants about why even an exhaustively peer-reviewed, well-conducted, statistically significant epidemiological study showing a relative risk greater than two for women between the ages of eighteen and forty-nine should *not* provide evidence for adverse effects of the same substance for either children, those older than the study group, or some groups of men.[124] This study showed that women using phenylpropoanaline (PPA)-containing appetite suppressants had a *16.85 times greater risk* of suffering a hemorrhagic stroke when compared with those not using it, and a *3.13 relative risk* of hemorrhagic stroke for *any* use of PPA (also in cough or cold products). There were an insufficient number of men using these products to provide any data on increased risks. Defendants challenged plaintiffs' evidence on a number of grounds, only a few of which I mention.

Defendants objected that extrapolating from the eighteen- to forty-nine-year-old age group was not *good science.*[125] They argued that because those older than forty-nine tend to have more strokes than those under forty-nine, extrapolation to older individuals should not be permitted. Quoting a defense scientist, however, Judge Barbara Rothstein rejected this argument, noting, "There are no drugs I'm aware of that get safer the older you get."[126]

Defendants also called attention to differences between the women studied and extrapolations to men and children. However, Judge Rothstein found "wide support" in the scientific and medical literature for extrapolations to children, anticipating that toxic effects will be "as great, if not greater in children."[127] And,

---

[123] Silver et al., "Effect of Follow-up Time on Risk Estimates," 487. For protective purposes, they also show how important it is to reduce exposures once a risk has been identified.

[124] *In re: Phenylpropanolamine (PPA) Products Liability Litigation,* 289 F. Supp. 2d 1230 (2003).

[125] *In re: Phenylpropanolamine (PPA) Products Liability Litigation,* 289 F. Supp. 2d at 1244.

[126] *In re: Phenylpropanolamine (PPA) Products Liability Litigation,* 289 F. Supp. 2d at 1244.

[127] *In re: Phenylpropanolamine (PPA) Products Liability Litigation,* 289 F. Supp. 2d at 1245.

defendants "failed to introduce any evidence that plaintiffs' experts' reasoning was not scientifically valid."[128]

The issues just discussed about extrapolations are not problems with judicial rulings. Quite the contrary. We see defendants trying to introduce some skepticism about plaintiffs' excellent scientific studies and a knowledgeable judge properly rejecting it. This judicial opinion shows plausible sources for possible judicial mistakes concerning scientific evidence, namely, one party to the litigation suggests some skepticism about the science, which a less astute judge might not have noticed (although defense arguments in this case were implausible).

Using "Hill's Factors" for Excluding Evidence: Subsequent to *Daubert* courts have reviewed experts' "methodologies." One such methodology is an expert's use of Hill's considerations as a guide to inferring causation from association. However, some courts have merely noted that these are some considerations that experts use to guide their inferences,[129] whereas other courts have made more rigid uses of it.[130] Some commentators, like courts, have merely noted the helpfulness of Hill's considerations.[131] Others have urged the courts in more rigid directions. [132] They appear to suggest that failure to satisfy some or many

---

128   *In re: Phenylpropanolamine (PPA) Products Liability Litigation*, 289 F. Supp. 2d at 1246.

129   See, for example, *Amorgiano v. National Railroad Passenger Corporation*, 137 F. Supp. 2d 147 (E.D. N.Y. 2001) ("Epidemiologists generally look to several additional criteria to determine whether a statistical association is indeed cause. These criteria are sometimes referred to as the Bradford Hill criteria . . ."); and *Magistrini v. One Hour Martinizing Dry Cleaning*, 180 F. Supp. 2d 584 (2004). (These factors, first set forth by Sir Austin Bradford Hill, also have been referred to as "viewpoints," emphasizing that one or more of the factors may be absent even where a causal relationship exists and that no factor is a sine qua non of causation (593).)

130   *Merrell Pharaceuticals v. Havner* 953 S.W. 2d 706, 724 (It must be reiterated that even if a statistically significant association is found, that association does not equate to causation. Although there may appear to be an increased risk associated with an activity or condition, this does not mean the relationship is causal. There are many other factors to consider in evaluating the reliability of a scientific study including, but certainly not limited to, the sample size of the study, the power of the study, confounding variables, and whether there was selection bias (724).); *In re Breast Implant Litigation*, 318 F. Supp. 2d 879 (Colorado D.C. 1998) (The Bradford-Hill criteria are then used "to establish scientific cause and effect . . . such criteria as the *temporal sequence of events*, the *strength of the association*, the *consistency* of the observed association, the *dose-response* relationship, and the *biologic plausibility* of the observed association.") *In re Joint E. & S. Dist. Asbestos Litig.*, 827 F. Supp. 1014 (S.D.N.Y. 1993).

131   See Linda A. Bailey et al., "Reference Guide on Epidemiology," in *Reference Manual on Scientific Evidence*, 2d ed. (Washington, DC: Federal Judicial Center, 2000), 45, at 121, 161. All of Koch's Postulates are included in Hill's considerations except "consideration of alternative explanations," which is always considered for epidemiological studies, usually under the consideration of "confounders" (at 160–163). Hill's considerations include two additional features not explicitly included in Koch's Postulates: the possibility of appealing to experimental evidence and argument by analogy. See Hill, "The Environment and Disease," 18–19.

132   An early work, which appears to insist on using Hill's criteria, is Bert Black and David Lilienfeld, "Epidemiologic Proof in Toxic Tort Litigation," *Fordham Law Review*, 52 (1984):

of Hill's factors should defeat or cast great doubt on an epidemiological study as relevant evidence for a causal relationship between exposure and disease.

Such court requirements or commentators' recommendations misunderstand Hill's considerations. They turn his guides to interpretation or implicit questions to ask about a study into "criteria" for accepting or rejecting studies. This is contrary to his own view (recall his counterexamples to each factor) and to standard epidemiological practice in interpreting such studies. He was quite clear on this point in the concluding remarks of his paper:

> What I do not believe – and this has been suggested – is that we can usefully lay down some hard-and-fast rules of evidence that *must* be obeyed before we accept cause and effect. None of my nine viewpoints can bring indisputable evidence for or against the cause-and-effect hypothesis and none can be required as a *sine qua non.*[133]

Contemporary epidemiologists agree with him, except for temporality.[134]

The federal district court for the Southern District of New York, in *In re Joint Eastern & Southern District Asbestos Litigation,*[135] contravened both Hill's and Greenland's cautionary points concerning Hill's factors. It evaluated evidence post-*Daubert* using Hill's considerations to argue that if the plaintiff's epidemiological studies do not satisfy any of Hill's considerations, then plaintiff's experts' testimony based on epidemiological evidence is not sufficient to survive a judgment as a matter of law following a jury verdict for the plaintiff.[136] Apart from the temporality factor the court's assertion is problematic. It

---

132–785, at 764 (arguing that all of Koch's hypothesis should be satisfied). See also Bernstein, "The Admissibility of Scientific Evidence," 2166, 2168. Bernstein's remarks are ambiguous between the claim that *all* of Hill's criteria must be met for a study to be admissible (a view that is clearly at odds with good scientific practice) and the claim that if *none* (which would include the temporal criteria) of the criteria are met a study is not admissible. The second contention would be correct while the first I would sharply disagree with, as did Hill himself. See Hill, "The Environment and Disease," 19. Furthermore, Bernstein argues that if "proffered epidemiological evidence meets some but not all of the criteria a judge would do well to consult with a court-appointed epidemiological expert to assist her in judging the reliability of the evidence." Bernstein, 2168–2169. Based on Hill and contemporary epidemiologists' views, judges should be hesitant to rule epidemiological studies inadmissible on such grounds since the absence of any single criteria (with the exception of temporality) is consistent with causation.

[133] Hill, "The Environment and Disease," 19.

[134] Recall Greenland, *Evolution of Epidemiologic Ideas*, 14, from Chapter 4 (at 105).

[135] *In re Joint E. & S. Dist. Asbestos Litig.*, 827 F. Supp. 1014 (S.D.N.Y. 1993).

[136] See *In re Joint E. & S. Dist. Asbestos Litig.*, 827 F. Supp. at 1038. The court stated:

> While none of the Sufficiency Criteria is decisive by itself in determining the sufficiency of a plaintiff's epidemiological evidence in the context of a Rule 50(b) motion, sufficient epidemiological evidence will necessarily satisfy several of these criteria. More significantly, when epidemiological evidence fails to satisfy any of the Sufficiency Criteria, it cannot be relied on to support a jury verdict in the face of a motion for judgment as a matter of law.

turned Hill's *considerations* into *criteria* for judging the admissibility of expert testimony based on epidemiological evidence.

Subsequent epidemiological articles and the Federal Judicial Center's *Reference Manual* also reject the court's reasoning.[137] Rothman notes that although *strength* retains "some meaning as a description of the public health importance of a factor . . . [it] is devoid of meaning in the biologic description of disease etiology" because whether an association is "weak" or "strong" depends on the "prevalence of complementary component causes in the same sufficient cause. . . . [T]his prevalence is often a matter of custom, circumstance or chance, and is not a scientifically generalizable characteristic."[138] Other epidemiologists echo Hill concerning the plausibility and coherence factors. Susser notes, "Coherence is an ultimate and yet not a necessary criterion for causality. . . . But coherence supports existing inference and theory."[139] He continues: "[i]ncoherence may also have a more general explanation, in which instance it will generate a new theory. As Lilienfeld has said: 'the finding of a biologically implausible association may be the first lead to this extension of knowledge.'"[140]

Some of their sharpest criticisms are saved for those who would emphasize "specificity." Some have noted that although there may be:

> a tendency toward clustering of specific clinical features and other manifestations among patients afflicted with a particular cause of disease . . . and [it is possible to] find diseases in which there is very high association of a particular cause with a particular effect[,] . . . the majority of causal agents that are chosen as criteria for constructing disease entities are associated with a great diversity of clinical, pathological, and biochemical patterns.[141]

Others are more critical.

> [A]rguments that demand specificity are fallacious, if not absurd. There can be no logical reason why any identifiable factor, and especially an unrefined one, should not have multiple effects. . . . By now it is evident that the associations of health disorders with smoking depend on a variety of mechanisms,

---

[137] *In re Joint Eastern*, 827 F. Supp. at 1038. Epidemiologists and the *Reference Manual* have rejected that view.

[138] See Rothman, *Modern Epidemiology*, 43. This subtle point concerning a common model of causation was discussed in Chapter 4.

[139] Mervyn Susser, "Judgment and Causal Inferences Criteria in Epidemiologic Studies," *Am. J. of Epidemiology*, 105 (1977): 1, 9, reprinted in *Evolution of Epidemiologic Ideas: Annotated Readings on Concepts and Methods*, 69, 77.

[140] Susser, "Judgment and Causal Inferences," 77.

[141] Brian MacMahon and Thomas F. Pugh, "Causes and Entities of Disease," in *Methods of Preventive Medicine*, ed. D. W. Clark and B. MacMahon 1967, 11, 16 reprinted in Greenland, *Evolution of Epidemiologic Ideas*, 26, 31.

some causal and some not. Specificity enhances the plausibility of causal inference, but lack of specificity does not negate it.[142]

In sum, in the cases just reviewed the courts have made more stringent use of Hill's considerations than he and other leading epidemiologists would. Hill's considerations constitute questions scientists should ask about epidemiological studies to assist in their judgments about the strength of the evidence, but they must serve an explanatory function within a nondeductive inference to the best explanation (discussed in Chapter 4).

The Unfortunate Consequences of "No Effect" Studies

Although this point is more difficult to document, it appears that judges may take "no effect" epidemiological studies at face value and conclude that because a study fails to show an effect between exposure and disease, this demonstrates that the exposure does not cause the disease.[143] Frequently, courts are presented with epidemiological studies that show no relation between exposure and disease. Because plaintiffs must establish the basis of causation, if there is no epidemiological evidence for a causal relationship between exposure and disease, they must establish causation in some other way, provided it can be done. For example, they may have to use animal studies, case reports, structure-activity relationships, other molecular studies, and the like. If courts are reluctant to allow such evidence for causation, this precludes plaintiffs from going forward.

However, courts sometimes appear to go further and suggest that because epidemiological studies do not show evidence of an effect, there is not one. That is, they appear to assume that no effect studies compared with other kinds of evidence show there is no adverse effect. Such a view would commit multiple mistakes. That is, courts may believe that negative epidemiological studies *trump* all other kinds of evidence. In only a few cases do courts note that a "no effect" study might fail to show there is evidence of no effect; usually they are silent on this issue.

First, a defendants' evidence compared with plaintiffs' evidence should be irrelevant for an admissibility decision in which a court considers only the evidence on one side of the case. Second, comparing evidence between parties is applicable only for assessing whether plaintiffs' evidence is legally sufficient to create a material issue of fact for a jury to consider. Third, and most seriously, courts that make such an assessment risk a serious error on the science.

---

[142] See Susser, "Judgment and Causal Inferences," 81.

[143] See *Chambers v. Exxon Corp.*, 81 F. Supp. 2d 661, at 665–666 (M.D. La. 2000) (holding that expert testimony that benzene exposure causes chronic myelogenous leukemia ("CML") was inadmissible for lack of scientific reliability, in the absence of an epidemiological study that *conclusively* established a *statistically significant* risk of contracting CML from exposure to benzene (emphasis added)).

There are two possibilities for no effect studies. A study might only show *no evidence of an effect* or it might show the much more difficult point that there is *evidence of no effect* (this second possibility is not likely except in very special circumstances as I discuss below). On the first, one might say that there is not any human evidence of an adverse effect. On the second, there is more affirmative evidence of *no* effect.

These two judgments are clearly different as an analogy suggests. Suppose that I am looking over a large plain at some distance. If someone asks me if there are people down on the plain, not having seen any I might say "There is no evidence that there are." However, this does not mean that humans are not present. I might not have had very good evidence that no one was on the plain. I might have poor eyesight. I might have used a telescope that had insufficient magnification to reveal people at such a distance. I might not have investigated the issue in any other way. I could better claim that there was evidence that no one was on the plain if I had verified that my telescope had sufficient magnification to reveal people if they were there, and used it carefully in examining the terrain, but still was unable to see anyone. However, even a high-resolution telescope might still be insufficient if I looked at the wrong time, for example, during the daytime and people only moved about on the plain at night. If I wanted to be highly certain that there was no one on the plain, then I might need to undertake a number of other investigations, such as leaving my vantage point and going to investigate much closer.

Thus, judges need to recognize the difference between "there is no evidence of an effect" and "there is evidence of no effect." Even if they did this, however, neither result should legally contravene admissibility, as that is concerned only with plaintiffs' evidence. Even if defendants believe they have no evidence of an effect, plaintiffs might well have evidence of an effect based on other kinds of data. For example, cancer researchers recently observed that epidemiological evidence that exposure to human papilloma virus caused cervical cancer lagged other kinds of evidence by five to seven years.[144] The question then becomes, do plaintiffs' experts have a reasonable enough foundation for their testimony to be admitted?

For judging the legal sufficiency of plaintiffs' evidence on a directed verdict the "no effect" studies defendants have proffered is pertinent, but even here they are quite limited. If plaintiffs have offered *some evidence of an effect* based on other kinds of studies, simply because defendants have *no evidence* of an effect in particular epidemiological studies does not show there is evidence of no effect; it should not trump plaintiffs' evidence. Defendants' evidence could trump plaintiffs' other evidence of an effect, only if defendants' evidence could sufficiently establish that *there was evidence of no effect* from human studies

---

[144] Carbone et al., 5518–5519.

and it so overwhelmed plaintiffs' evidence that no reasonable jury could find for plaintiffs. However, this is an extremely difficult showing to make.

Scientists are extremely careful to avoid inferring from the fact that there is "no evidence of effect" that there is "evidence of no effect," because of its invalidity and because of the enormous consequences that attach to such an inference. Thus, a consensus scientific body, such as the International Agency for Research on Cancer, requires that some highly specific and detailed conditions should be met before making such an inference. Even then they apply only to the disease end point of interest and not to unrelated diseases (the conditions are indicated in the footnote).[145] Judges should become quite skeptical of no effect studies. They only show that there is evidence of no effect when the highly specific conditions IARC discusses are satisfied.[146]

Demanding Mechanistic Evidence

The Fifth Circuit Court of Appeals in *Black v. Food Lion, Inc.*, decided subsequent to *Kumho Tire*, reversed a trial judge for admitting medical testimony that

---

[145]   For example, the International Agency for Research on Cancer addresses the issue in the following way:

> When several epidemiological studies show little or no indication of an association between an exposure and cancer, the judgement may be made that, in the aggregate, they show evidence of lack of carcinogenicity. Such a judgement requires first of all that the studies giving rise to it meet, to a sufficient degree, the standards of design and analysis described above. Specifically, the possibility that bias, confounding or misclassification of exposure or outcome could explain the observed results should be considered and excluded with reasonable certainty. In addition, all studies that are judged to be methodologically sound should be consistent with a relative risk of unity for any observed level of exposure and, when considered together, should provide a pooled estimate of relative risk, which is at or near unity and has a narrow confidence interval, due to sufficient population size. Moreover, no individual study nor the pooled results of all the studies should show any consistent tendency for relative risk of cancer to increase with increasing level of exposure. It is important to note that evidence of lack of carcinogenicity obtained in this way from several epidemiological studies can apply only to the type(s) of cancer studied and to dose levels and intervals between first exposure and observation of disease that are the same as or less than those observed in all the studies. Experience with human cancer indicates that, in some cases, the period from first exposure to the development of clinical cancer is seldom less than 20 years; latent periods substantially shorter than 30 years cannot provide evidence for lack of carcinogenicity. (International Agency for Research on Cancer, *Monographs on the Evaluation of Carcinogenic Risks to Humans*, Preamble, section 8, Studies of Cancer in Humans. Rev. Aug. 18 2004. Available at: http://193.51.164.11/ monoeval/StudiesHumans.html.)

[146]   See *Ambrosini v. Labarraque*, 101 F.3d 129, at 136 (1996), for a case in which the court recognizes the need to consider statistical power in order to assess the plausibility of a negative epidemiological study. (The court pointed out that plaintiffs' expert "explained that an epidemiologist evaluates studies based on their 'statistical power.' Statistical power, he continued, represents the ability of a study, based on its sample size, to detect a causal relationship. Conventionally, in order to be considered meaningful, negative studies, that is, those which allege the absence of a causal relationship, must have at least an 80 to 90 percent chance of detecting a causal link if such a link exists; otherwise, the studies cannot be considered conclusive.")

plaintiff's fall in defendant's grocery store had caused her to develop fibromyalgia. This is a syndrome characterized by "generalized pain, poor sleep, an inability to concentrate, and chronic fatigue."[147] The physician had followed approved methods for identifying fibromyalgia. However, the appellate court found that because there is no known etiology for fibromyalgia (which the expert conceded), it held that it was scientifically illogical for expert to conclude that the disease must have been caused by the fall merely because she had eliminated other possible causes. The court argued that the district should have determined "whether [the diagnosing physician] tied the fall at Food Lion by some specific train of medical evidence to Black's development of fibromyalgia," then continued into more troubling territory:

> The underlying predicates of any cause-and-effect medical testimony are that *medical science understands the physiological process* by which a particular disease syndrome develops and knows what factors cause the process to occur. Based on such predicate knowledge, it may then be possible to fasten legal liability for a person's disease or injury.
>
> In this case, neither Dr. Reyna nor medical science knows the exact process that results in fibromyalgia or the factors that trigger the process. Absent these critical scientific predicates, for which there is no proof in the record, no scientifically reliable conclusion on causation can be drawn. Dr. Reyna's use of a general methodology cannot vindicate a conclusion for which there is no underlying medical support.[148] (emphasis added)

Such a requirement seems much too optimistic for many diseases and, thus, too demanding as a requirement for the admissibility of expert testimony.[149] We have seen the importance of mechanistic information.[150] Moreover, the court in *Black v. Food Lion* might well have made the correct admissibility decision in the particular case (I take no position on that). However, its *reasons* are mistaken, its rationale is too general and its view that mechanistic evidence is needed suggests a misunderstanding of various ways the scientific community can identify causal relationships.

Although the court's general point is correct – understanding the mechanisms of disease can greatly assist causal inference, and scientists would like such data – it is a scientific mistake to make it a necessary condition of good causal inferences and a legal error as well. Scientists can and do make causal inferences without such evidence, and, unfortunately, frequently it is often not available. Recall the point from Chapter 5 about the widely used and well-studied over-the-counter drug, aspirin. Its therapeutic and adverse effects have

---

147 *Black v. Food Lion, Inc.*, 171 F.3d 308, at 309 (5th Cir. 1998).
148 *Black v. Food Lion, Inc.*, 171 F.3d at 314.
149 For another decision that expresses such a view see *McClain v. Metabolife International, Inc.*, 2005 WL477861 (11th Cir. (Ala)), at 14–15.
150 Thagard, *How Scientists Explain Disease*, and discussion in Chapter 4.

been well documented. However, as recently as 1991 the mechanisms by which aspirin produces them were not understood.[151]

Benzene constitutes another example. Consensus scientific committees have documented for more that two decades that benzene causes leukemia and aplastic anemia at very low exposure levels, for example, between one part per million and ten parts per million, perhaps as low as .1 ppm. Yet research scientists as of this date do not understand the physiological processes and mechanisms by which benzene causes these diseases.[152]

Moreover, mechanistic evidence is asymmetrical – when it is present it can greatly strengthen a causal inference, but when it is absent it does not necessarily undermine the inference.[153] Thus, it is not a scientifically necessary condition of causal inference.

The legal error is twofold. First, by requiring mechanistic evidence, courts demand something that often does not exist and something that is more than science may be able to deliver in the short run (and sometimes even in the very long run, e.g., recall scurvy). In addition, if experts must understand the "physiological predicate by which a particular disease syndrome develops" this will ensure that very few experts will be permitted to testify when such understanding is absent, thus, excluding nearly all litigants from court.

This is another instance in which a court has conflated particularly help-ful evidence with necessary evidence for causal inference. When judges insist on ideal or very good evidence, they risk overlooking other good and quite reasonable evidence that could serve admissibility purposes. Again, the ideal becomes the enemy of the good.

Second, the courts' words suggest that understanding the physiological process by which a disease develops is something that is known in every case or known easily or known in many cases in which scientists ascribe a disease to a particular cause. Although physicians and toxicologists have substantial under-standing of diseases and their grosser causes, it appears to be comparatively rare that they understand the detailed step-by-step physiological processes and biological mechanisms by which the disease develops. It is only in the most well-studied diseases, even those that have been studied for decades, that such basic physiologic and mechanistic understanding is present.

In addition, often such understanding is irrelevant. For public health pur-poses, once the causation pattern between exposure and disease is well estab-lished, many researchers may have little incentive to investigate further the physiological route by which that exposure results in that particular disease.

---

[151] Santone and Powis, "Mechanism of and Tests for Injuries," 169.
[152] David A. Eastmond, Director, Environmental Toxicology, University of California, Riverside, personal communication.
[153] *Electric and Magnetic Fields Risk Evaluation Guidelines* (California Department of Health Services, 1999).

They have established to the satisfaction of their scientific community that a particular exposure contributes to a particular disease. Moreover, they now would know enough to take steps to prevent the exposures from occurring, which would prevent the disease in question. Continuing to study the physiological processes by which diseases occur is in the interests of researchers only if it appears to hold out the promise of making a wider contribution to the field or to understanding basic biology or toxicology. If the mechanism of biological action were always required before protective or compensatory legal actions were taken, few substances would have been addressed by regulatory or tort law.

The Mistaken Exclusion of Evidence

The Denigration of Animal Evidence

Some courts have excluded animal evidence as pertinent for experts making causal judgments about the effects of toxicants on humans or excluded it unless it was accompanied by epidemiological evidence. Yet this is a kind of data on which toxicologists and other scientists routinely rely for making toxicity assessments. Although animal studies do not provide mathematically certain means by which to infer the causal effects of a toxicant on humans, they are scientifically good and relevant evidence for identifying substances as human toxicants.[154]

Judge Weinstein's decision in *In re Agent Orange Product Liability Litigation*,[155] has influenced a number of courts to exclude animal studies *per se* from evidence in toxic tort suits.[156] He argued that, "[T]he studies on animal exposure to Agent Orange, even Plaintiffs' expert concedes are not persuasive in this lawsuit.... There is no evidence that plaintiffs were exposed to the far higher concentrations involved in [the animal studies] ..."[157] Moreover, he argued that because the animal studies involved *different biological species*, they were not helpful to the case.[158] He said the studies "are of so little probative force and are so potentially misleading as to be inadmissible.... They cannot be an acceptable predicate for an opinion under Rule 703."[159] Although Judge Weinstein placed an emphasis on "this lawsuit," his opinion has been widely interpreted as excluding reliance on animal studies, unless they are accompanied by epidemiological evidence.[160] Even when there has been no absolute legal barrier to the use of animal studies, they have faced undue skepticism

---

[154] See Chapter 4.
[155] *In re Agent Orange Prod. Liab. Litig.*, 611 F. Supp. 1223 (E.D.N.Y. 1985).
[156] See, e.g., *In re Paoli R.R. Yard PCB Litig.*, 706 F. Supp. 358, 366–368 (E.D. Pa. 1988), *rev'd*, 916 F.2d 829 (3d Cir. 1990), *cert. denied*, 499 U.S. 961 (1991).
[157] *In re Agent Orange*, 611 F. Supp. at 1241.
[158] *In re Agent Orange*, 611 F. Supp. at 1241.
[159] *In re Agent Orange*, 611 F. Supp. at 1241.
[160] See, e.g., *In re Paoli R.R. Yard PCB Litig.*, 706 F. Supp. at 367–368.

from courts. In a Bendectin case the Fifth Circuit Court of Appeals in *Brock* regarded animal studies of "questionable applicability to humans," especially in the absence of some reference to epidemiological studies. Moreover, the court used as support for its legal rationale a highly controversial regulatory case from 1983 in which it objected to animal studies that show a risk of cancer from urea formaldehyde foam insulation.[161] Courts' difficulties with animal studies, thus, have considerable history; perhaps it is time for them to better understand the science.

Apart from what may be errors in an understanding of toxicology, a generic exclusion of animal studies is mistaken on two counts. First, it appears contrary to the *Daubert* Court's emphasis on the consideration of scientific evidence that is relevant to expert testimony concerning causation. Clearly, scientists consider them quite relevant evidence in making toxicity judgments. Second, if one believes that it is appropriate for courts to consider the science that is available for assessing the toxicity of substances and their effects on human beings, then such evidence should ordinarily be permitted to be part of the foundation of expert testimony. Recall that such evidence is much more likely to be available than human studies, for instance.

For toxicologists, the fact that there is information from "other" biological species is both *scientifically relevant* and *probative evidence*. Moreover, contrary to Judge Weinstein, such studies have considerable probative force even if they might not always be as direct evidence of human harm as thorough, well-designed epidemiological studies with sufficiently large samples conducted for a sufficiently long duration to detect any toxic effects.

Animal evidence can and does have considerable explanatory power for toxicologists (Chapter 4). It also can, importantly, supplement or cast doubt on human data. For example, animal data might rule out a positive epidemiological study as having little biological plausibility. For a more specific example, it has been quite difficult to duplicate in animal studies the adverse effects seen in humans from exposure to electromagnetic fields. For some scientists, this casts doubt on some fairly consistent human epidemiological studies.[162] By

---

[161] *Gulf South Insulation v. Consumer Product Safety Commission*, 701 F.2d 1137 (1983) (noting that "had 20 fewer rats or 20 more developed carcinomas, the risk predicted by [the risk assessment mode] would be altered drastically"). The U.S. Congress Office of Technology Assessment noted, "This is very close to saying that if the victim of the gunshot wound had not died, the defendant wouldn't be guilty of murder." (OTA, *Identifying and Regulating Carcinogens*, 208).

[162] This discussion occurred when the author served on California's Electric and Magnetic Fields Science Advisory Panel from 1999 to 2002. The National Institute of Environmental Health Sciences Working Group "concluded that there is inadequate evidence in experimental animals for the carcinogenicity of exposure to [Extremely Low Frequency Electric and Magnetic Fields] . . ." (National Institute of Environmental Health Sciences, U.S. National Institutes of Health, U.S. Department of Heath and Human Services, Public Health Service, *Assessment of Health Effects from Exposure to Power-line Frequency Electric and Magnetic Fields*, ed. Christopher J. Portier and Mary S. Wolfe [Research Triangle Park, NC: NIH Publication No. 98–3981, 1998], 397.)

contrast, there are a number of substances identified as possible or probable human carcinogens on the basis of animal or mechanistic studies by the National Toxicology Program (NTP) and IARC, even though there are no (or only inadequate) epidemiological studies (discussed in Chapter 7).[163]

Fortunately, however, Weinstein's *In re Agent Orange* opinion and other courts that follow it may be quite limited. There were special considerations present in that litigation at that time, which partially explain his views.[164] (Did the court and others ignore the possibility that no effect studies were falsely negative because they were of too short a duration, the samples were too small, or there was inadequate data?) Conflicting epidemiological studies were considered to be either inapposite or flawed.[165] Subsequent studies have provided evidence of adverse effects.[166]

Other courts have recognized the limitations of Weinstein's views.[167] They have ruled that, as a matter of scientific practice, animal studies are the kind of evidence on which scientists rely for evidence of causation from toxic substances. Of particular note is a decision from the Third Circuit Court of Appeals, which discussed the mixed state of case law on admissibility of animal studies and noted that "[m]any cases have held that the studies are admissible."[168] The court added:

> While other cases have held that animal studies are inadmissible, these cases are for the most part distinguishable because most involved the exclusion of animal studies in the face of *extensive* epidemiological data that failed to support causation, because none involved studies on animals particularly

---

[163] See Rall et al., "Alternatives to Using Human Experience," 356.

[164] At the time, governmental epidemiological studies did not show adverse long-term health effects from exposure to Agent Orange. ("These epidemiological studies alone demonstrate that on the basis of present knowledge, there is no question of fact: Agent Orange cannot now be shown to have caused plaintiffs' numerous illnesses." *In re Agent Orange Prod. Liab. Litig.,* 611 F. Supp. 1223, 1241.)

[165] See *In re Agent Orange Prod. Liab. Litig.,* 611 F. Supp. at 1241.

[166] For a summary of some of this work, see Committee to Review the Health Effects in Vietnam Veterans of Exposure to Herbicides, Institute of Medicine, *Veterans and Agent Orange* (1996), 14 (Some subsequent studies that show that people exposed to the herbicides used in Agent Orange in occupational or environmental exposure had increased risks of various cancers and other diseases and that at least Vietnam veterans with very slight exposure to Agent Orange "could have risks approaching those in occupational and environmental settings."); and Brief *Amici Curiae* of the Lymphoma Foundation of America, Carl F. Cranor, Devra Davis, Peter L. Defur, Brian G. Durie, Alan H. Lockwood, David Ozonoff, Arnold J. Schecter, and David Wallinga in support of Respondents, in *Dow Chemical Company, Monsanto Company v. Stephenson, and Isaacson* (Supreme Court of the United States, 2002).

[167] See, e.g., *In re Paoli R.R. Yard PCB Litig.,* 35 F.3d 717, 780 (3d Cir. 1994), *cert. denied,* 115 S.Ct. 1253 (1995); *Hines v. Consolidated Rail Corp.,* 926 F.2d 262, 271 (3d Cir. 1991); *Villari v. Terminix Int'l, Inc.,* 692 F. Supp. 568, 572 (E.D. Pa. 1988).

[168] The *Paoli* court's own citation provides helpful support. See, e.g., *In re Bendectin Prod. Liab. Litig.,* 732 F. Supp. 744, 749 (E.D. Mich. 1990) (experts in the field think it is reasonable to rely on nonepidemiological studies to link Bendectin to birth defects); *Hagen v. Richardson-Merrell,* 697 F. Supp. 334, 337 (N.D. Ill. 1988) (defendants did not adequately demonstrate

similar to humans in the way they react to the chemical in question, and because none involved studies the federal government had relied on as a basis for concluding the chemical was a probable health hazard [as was true in this case].[169]

The *Paoli* opinion is on much firmer scientific ground than some of the opinions noted earlier.[170]

However, even the Third Circuit's view of the pertinent evidence may not be fully accurate. That is, given what toxicologists know and how they view the evidence that is pertinent to making causal judgments, courts should be open to a wider range of toxicological evidence than even the Third Circuit suggests. Animal studies should not be *excluded* even in the face of no effect epidemiological evidence to the contrary (as indicated earlier). Such evidence might or might not be ultimately legally sufficient, given evidence on the other side of the case, but that is a separate matter. Moreover, animal evidence typically is scientifically pertinent to judgments of whether toxic substances cause human harm. As Judge Golkiewicz in *Stevens* points out, animal evidence can provide "biological plausibility" of an effect or perhaps suggest doubt about a human study because it cannot be replicated in an animal model.[171] Moreover,

that expert opinion based partly on animal studies should be excluded); *and Saakbo Rubanick v. Witco Chem. Corp.*, 242 N.J. Super. 36, 576 A.2d 4, 7, 15 (1990) (under New Jersey law reversing trial court's exclusion of expert testimony, which was partly based on animal studies that PCBs caused cancer). In *Villari v. Terminix Int. Inc.*, 692 F. Supp. 568, 570 (E.D. Pa. 1988), Judge Pollak explained that:

> [W]hile it may be true that defendant can offer tests and experiments that do not support the findings of plaintiff's expert, the defendant cannot deny that animal studies are routinely relied upon by the scientific community in assessing the carcinogenic effects of chemicals on humans. Even defendant's own expert acknowledges that animal experiment studies are built on "prudent presumptions," although he concludes that they should not be admitted.

[169] *In re Paoli R.R. Yard PCB Litig.*, 35 F.3d (citing *In re Agent Orange*, 611 F. Supp. at 1241 (excluding animal studies of Agent Orange based partly on the court's earlier conclusion that there was significant epidemiological data, that the Center for Disease Control had concluded that the animal studies did not demonstrate adverse human health effects, and that the animal studies gave pregnant females high doses at critical times); *Viterbo v. Down Chemical Co.*, 826 F.2d 420 (5th Cir. 1987) (excluding the evidence where there was only a single animal study and it showed a link to a disease completely different than plaintiff's diseases); *Richardson v. Richardson-Merrell, Inc.*, 857 F.2d 823, 830 (D.C. Cir. 1988) (excluding animal studies of Bendectin because of the overwhelming body of contrary epidemiological evidence and the admission of the expert that animal studies merely raise a suspicion of causation in humans); *Lynch v. Merrell-Nat. Lab.*, 830 F.2d 1190, 1194 (1st Cir. 1987) (excluding animal studies of Bendectin where they stood in the face of significant contrary epidemiological data); *Turpin v. Merrell Dow Pharm., Inc.*, 959 F.2d 1349, 1360 (6th Cir. 1992) (excluding the testimony where the record failed to make clear how the animal studies were sufficient to show that Bendectin causes birth defect more probably than not).

[170] See Chengelis and Gad, "Introduction," *Animal Models*, 1–2.

[171] *Stevens v. the Secretary of Health and Human Services*, 23, 24 (citing the Institute of Medicine at note 68).

animal evidence appears to be available for a wider range of substances than human evidence.

An interesting counterexample to a claim about the irrelevance of animal evidence is provided by the scientific detective story considered in Chapter 4 concerning dimethylnitorsamine poisoning. Recall that this was a scientific and legal case in which animal evidence and a small number of human case reports combined with other circumstances, revealed the cause of two deaths and led to the criminal conviction of the person who was responsible for poisoning them with dimethylnitrosamine. Data about mechanism, carcinogenic doses, and lethal doses came from animal or *in vitro* studies, not human epidemiological studies.[172] If some of the rules concerning the nonadmissibility of animal evidence in tort cases had been applied to exclude the evidence in that criminal case, a criminal would have gone free. More important, the scientists used all of the toxicological evidence they had available to them.

What is needed to establish causation in a tort case is an explanation based on scientifically relevant studies that is more probably than not true connecting the defendant's actions to the plaintiff's injuries. However, providing an appropriate explanation does not automatically require the use of only human epidemiological evidence. For admissibility only a respectable scientific explanation that is supported by sufficient data, which is reliably applied to the facts of the case are needed. Thus, judicial and commentator insistence that the explanations must have certain necessary components is mistaken. Moreover, there are instances in which animal evidence conjoined with short-term test and structure-activity relationships might well be sufficient to show more probably than not that a substance is a human carcinogen.[173] We return to some of these issues in Chapter 7.

Discriminating among Animal Studies

More recently, in *Allen v. Pennsylvania Engineering*, both a district court and the Fifth Circuit Court of Appeals rejected plaintiff's evidence and held that the fact that ethylene oxide caused brain tumors in *rats* could not be evidence for the claim that ETO could cause brain tumors in humans. The reason: ETO did not correspondingly cause brain tumors in phylogenetically similar mice.[174] There is generic plausibility to such an argument. However, the court did not

---

172 See Renate D. Kimbrough, "Case Studies," in *Industrial Toxicology: Safety and Health Applications in the Workplace*, ed. P. L. Williams and J. L. Burson (New York: Lifetime Learning Publications, 1985), 414, 417–420. Kimbrough notes that the evidence showing the toxicity of dimethylnitrosamine was based on studies in rats and then an amount lethal to adult humans was calculated from the results of those studies. See Kimbrough, "Case Studies," 417–420.

173 See, e.g., Kimbrough, "Case Studies," 417–420 (describing cases where case studies on cancer in animals were useful in determining cause of death in humans).

174 See *Allen v. Pennsylvania Eng'g Corp.*, 102 F.3d 194, 197 (5th Cir. 1996).

probe further and, thus, left a problematic decision. There tends to be general concordance of toxicity effects between two phylogenetically close species such as rats and mice, but there is no necessity to it. Substances may well be more toxic in one species than another, and still be toxic to humans.[175] The underlying principle is that different species may show different toxic effects to a greater or lesser degree. Rats may be more or less susceptible to a given toxicant than mice.[176] For example, both the human carcinogens Direct Black 38 and Direct Blue 6, two benzidine based dyes, are carcinogenic in rats but not in mice under the same experimental conditions and routes of exposure.[177] MPTP – 1-methyl-4-phenyl-1,2,3,6-tetrahydropyridine – a chemical causing a Parkinson's disease–like condition in humans, induces a similar neurotoxic effect in mice, but not in rats.[178] Melphalan, a human carcinogen, is positive in rhesus monkeys and shows no effects in the phylogenetically similar cynomologous monkeys.[179] If substances are carcinogenic in two species, the probability that they are carcinogenic in humans is greatly increased; but a substance might be quite potent and harmful to humans even though it did not result in carcinogenicity in at least two rodent species. Frequently, substances have not been tested, or not adequately tested, in other species. Toxicologists try to design studies to have the best chance of detecting toxic results that are pertinent to humans.[180]

---

[175] See S. C. Gad, "Model Selection and Scaling," in *Animal Models in Toxicology*, ed. C. P. Chengelis and S. C. Gad (New York: Marcel Dekker, 1992), 841, 849, and Tables 5, 6.

[176] See Gad, "Model Selection and Scaling," 841, 849, and Tables 5, 6.

[177] *U.S. Department of Health and Human Services, National Toxicology Program, Ninth Annual Report on Carcinogens.* Rev. 20 Oct. 2000. Available at: http://ehis.niehs.nih.gov/roc/ninth/known.pdf.

[178] See Richard E. Heikkila et al., "Dopaminergic Neurotoxicity of 1-Methyl-4-Phenyl-1,2,5,6-Tetrahydropyridine in Mice," 224 *Science* 1451, 1451–53 (1984); and Rajesh N. Kalaria et al., "Correlation of 1-Methyl-4-Phenyl-1,2,3,6-Tetrahydropyridine Neurotoxicity with Blood-Brain Barrier Monoamine Oxidase Activity," *Proceedings Acad. Sci. U.S. Am.* 84 (1987): 3521–3525.

[179] See *Summary of Carcinogenic Potency Database by Chemical: Nonhuman Primates and Dogs.* Available at: ftp://potency.berkeley.edu/pub/tables/ chemicalsummary.other.text (visited February 2, 2001).

[180] The literature on these issues is substantial. See Gad, "Model Selection and Scaling," 813–840.

This entire book is directed at the premises that (1) animals can serve as accurate predictive models of toxicity in humans (or other species); (2) the selection of an appropriate species to use is key to accurate prediction in man; and (3) understanding the strengths and weaknesses of any particular model is essential to understanding the relevance of specific target organ toxicities to what would be expected in humans.

A fundamental hypothesis of toxicology is that adverse effects caused by chemical entities in animals are generally the same as those induced by those entities in humans. Many scholars point to individual exceptions to this, and conclude that the general principle is false. Yet, as our understanding of molecular biology advances and we learn more about the similarities of structure and function of higher organisms at the molecular level, the more it becomes clear that the mechanisms

Even though the ETO toxicity results in rats were not duplicated in mice, could they be good evidence? The court should have inquired whether (or plaintiffs should have argued that) there was something important about the rats as a model for humans. Did they have more plausibility than might have been apparent? I return to this in Chapter 7.

Target-Site Arguments

Judges also will need to adjudicate a general criticism of animal evidence that because the target sites of cancer in animals are different from the target sites in humans, this cannot be evidence for carcinogenicity in humans.[181] This is another view that is tempting, but not generally correct.[182] For example, benzidine is a *known human bladder carcinogen*, but is not a bladder carcinogen in animal species (except for dogs), although it induces tumors in hamsters (liver tumors), rats (liver, ear duct, mammary, and intestinal tumors), and mice (liver tumors).[183] Moreover, there appears to be no scientific agreement that there must be tissue concordance between animals and humans.[184] Concordance in tumor sites, although considerably strengthening the evidence, is not essential.

of chemical toxicity are largely identical in humans and animals. (Gad, "Model Selection and Scaling," 813)

Other experts and the EPA concur. See Romualdo Benigni and Alessandro Giuliani, "Tumor Profiles and Carcinogenic Potency in Rodents and Humans: Value for Cancer Risk Assessment," *Journal of Environmental Science and Health. Part C, Environmental Carcinogenesis and Ecotoxicology Reviews* 45 (1999): 63 (reporting that key information concerning the probity of animal evidence for human cancer lies in carcinogenic potency, not in the specificity in the response of a species); Environmental Protection Agency, "Proposed Guidelines for Carcinogen Risk Assessment," *Federal Register* 61 (1996): 17,960, 17,967, 17,977; see also Michael P. Waalkes et al., "The Scientific Fallacy of Route Specificity of Carcinogenesis with Particular Reference to Cadmium," *Regulatory Toxicology and Pharmacology* 20 (1994): 119:

[T]he mechanisms of control of cell growth and differentiation are remarkably homologous among species and highly conserved in evolution.... Thus far, there is evidence that growth control mechanisms at the level of the cell are homologous among mammals, but there is no evidence that these mechanisms are site concordant. Moreover, agents observed to produce tumors in both humans and animals have produced tumors either at the same (e.g., vinyl chloride) or different sites (e.g., benzene) (NRC, 1994).

[181] See, e.g., Bernstein, "The Admissibility of Scientific Evidence," 2167; *Allen v. Pennsylvania Eng'g Corp.*, 102 F.3d 194, 197 (5th Cir. 1996) (holding that animal studies are too unreliable). For a general discussion of this issue, see James Huff, "Applicability to Humans of Rodent-Specific Sites of Chemical Carcinogenicity: Tumors of the Forestomach and of the Harderian, Preputial, and Zymbal Glands Induced by Benzene," *Journal of Occupational Medicine and Toxicology* 1 (1992): 109–141.

[182] See James Huff, "Long-Term Chemical Carcinogenesis Bioassays Predict Human Cancer Hazard: Issues, Controversies and Uncertainties," *Annals of the New York Academy of Sciences* 56, 62 (1999): 895; and U.S. EPA, *Proposed Guidelines for Carcinogen Risk Assessment*, at 17,977.

[183] See *Toxicological Risk Assessment, Vol. I: Biological and Statistical Criteria*, ed. D. B. Clayson, D. Krewski, and I. Munro (Boca Raton, FL: CRC Press, 1985), 105–122.

[184] See Huff, "Long-Term Chemical Carcinogenesis Bioassays," 62; U.S. EPA, *Proposed Guidelines for Carcinogen Risk Assessment*, 17,977.

As indicated earlier and in Chapter 4, the results of well-conducted animal tests can provide reliable evidence for the toxicity and carcinogenicity of chemical and physical agents. As already noted, these results need to be evaluated sensitively for reproducibility and relevance to humans.

In reviewing animal studies, some courts and commentators have suggested enshrining into law more stringent criteria for judging the validity of scientific inferences and explanations than are required in the science itself. Courts are not being faithful to the science. Moreover, the adoption of rigid rules places more stringent legal restrictions on litigants than scientists themselves adopt. These constraints will legally skew admissibility decisions, a point to which we return in the conclusion of this chapter.

Chemical Structure–Biological Activity Evidence

Many courts have routinely excluded expert testimony based in part on chemical structure–biological activity relationships as pertinent to assessments of causal effects of toxicants on humans, arguing that *at best* they form the basis of a hypothesis, not evidence, of causation. Indeed, structure-activity relationships have a number of well-known difficulties. One legal scholar whose comments have now been repeated by courts noted that a small difference in chemical structure can make a major difference in biological activity.[185] There is truth to this point, but that is not the end of the story, as some courts seem to regard it.

As already discussed (Chapter 4), properly understood chemical structure–biological activity evidence can contribute substantially to causation in certain contexts and in any case could be part of any scientifically integrated evidence of causation. In general, it is not the strongest scientific inference to argue from similarity in chemical structure to similarity in biological activity, as even some specific similarities in chemical structure with minor dissimilarities elsewhere can result in fairly significant differences in biological effects. Recall, however, the Institute of Medicine's and National Research Council's view of the importance of structure-activity relationships from Chapter 4.[186]

However, for chemical families with certain properties, there also are scientifically quite strong inferences. For example, molecules with chemical groups

---

[185] Sanders, *Bendectin on Trial.* ("Molecules with minor structural differences can produce very different biological effects" [46].)

[186] Institute of Medicine and National Research Council, Committee on the Framework for Evaluating the Safety of Dietary Supplements, *Dietary Supplements: A Framework for Evaluating Safety* (Washington, DC: National Academy Press, 2005), 205–206 (citing Food and Drug Administration, "Final Rule Declaring Dietary Supplements Containing Ephedrine Alkaloids Adulterated Because They Present an Unreasonable Risk," *Federal Register* 69 (2005): 6787–6854; I. Furuya and S. Watanabe, "Discriminative Stimulus Properties of Ephedra Herb (*Ephedra sinica*) in rats, *Yakubutsu Seishin Kodo*, 13 (1993): 33–38; and C. R. Lake and R. S. Quirk, "CNS Stimulants and the Look-Alike Drugs," *Psychiatry Cin. North American*, 7 (1984): 689–701 ("the biological effects of chemicals, including toxic effects, are implicit in their molecular structures")).

that are known to interact with mammalian DNA or proteins provide *strong*, but not infallible, reasons for thinking that substances with chemical similarities have similar biological activity.[187] For another example, scientists regard substances that bind to the Ah receptor (aryl-hydrocarbon receptor) as being sufficiently similar that they can assign a toxicity equivalence factor to judge the toxicity of different substances.[188] Clearly, structure-activity relationships can assist scientists in assessing the toxicity of a substance to humans; the data needs to be evaluated sensitively. If substances are members of classes that have strong chemical and biological relationships as some of the examples just suggested, they have even greater evidentiary value.[189]

How much structure-activity relationships can contribute to a given toxicity judgment depends on the particular structure-activity data, on the other evidence available and on how it all "fits together." Courts in assessing expert testimony should permit experts to utilize all the kinds of evidence on which scientists themselves rely in making their judgments of causation, including appropriate structure-activity evidence.

Moreover, there can be wider kinds of evidence at the molecular level that can be powerful evidence. For example, ethylene oxide is a small, direct-acting molecule (it does not need metabolic transformation) that can reach nearly any tissue and cause mutations. Most substances may not have this property, but courts need to allow for such possibilities.

The Exclusion of Case Studies as Evidence

In Chapter 4, I discussed some of the circumstances in which case studies could be good evidence for causation or at least contribute to judgments of causation. However, case studies have tended to fare quite badly in toxic tort suits. As a co-author and I will report elsewhere,[190] judges in fifteen of seventy-seven tort cases admitted case reports as a substantial basis of expert testimony for the purpose of proving causation.[191] Eight of these cases involved adverse drug/nutritional supplement reactions (three Parlodel cases, two cases involving psychiatric medications, two cases involving diet pills, and a phenylpropoanaline (PPA)

---

187   J. Ashby and R. W. Tennant, "Chemical Structure, Salmonella Mutagenicity and Extent of Carcinogenicity as Indicators of Genotoxic Carcinogensesis among 222 Chemicals Tested in Rodents by the U.S. NCI/NTP," *Mutation Research* 204 (1988): 17–115; David A. Eastmond, Chair, Department of Environmental Toxicology, University of California, Riverside, personal communication.

188   Elaine Faustman and Gilbert S. Omenn, "Risk Assessment," in *Casarett and Doull's Toxicology: The Basic Science of Poisons*, 6th ed., ed. Curtis D. Klaassen (New York: McGraw-Hill, 2001), 86; European Environmental Agency, *Late Lessons from Early Warnings: The Precautionary Principle 1896–2000*, 67–68.

189   Faustman and Omenn, "Risk Assessment."

190   Carl F. Cranor and David Strauss, "Case Studies in Science and the Law" (submitted).

191   One of these cases is *Cella v. United States*, 998 F2d 419 (C.A. 7 (Ind.) 1993), an appellate case that appears to have been decided under the *Frye* test.

case). In three cases, typing on a keyboard or lifting a heavy object was alleged to have caused muscular/skeletal injuries. Another nineteen of the seventy-seven cases remain on the list because they contain relevant comments regarding the uses of case reports. However, they do not make explicit rulings regarding the admissibility of case reports as evidence for medical causality assessments.[192] The forty-three remaining cases all found expert testimony based in part on case reports to be inadmissible. In two of these cases, the judges explicitly stated that expert testimony based on some case reports *can satisfy Daubert* criteria; but the particular case reports presented to the court were not reliable. Among the remaining forty-one cases rejecting case reports, many judges rejected case reports categorically, but several were ambiguous as to whether case reports can ever be admissible.[193]

We also examined forty legal cases from litigation under National Vaccine Injury Compensation Program, a body of law that has somewhat different procedural rules. There are somewhat less formal procedures for introducing evidence. In addition, although the judges are not explicitly required to use *Daubert* procedures and standards, many of them indicate they are following it. Finally, the judges use the preponderance of the evidence standard of proof.

Vaccine injury cases also are somewhat different from normal tort cases in that the judge serves both as the adjudicator of the law and is the fact-finder; there is no jury to protect from mistaken evidence or expert testimony. Nonetheless, judges must still decide whether or not to resolve the factual issues based in part or, more rarely, almost totally on case reports.

Judges in vaccine injury cases are much more receptive to the use of case reports supporting causal judgments than are most of the judges in traditional torts. Although case reports were not accepted as causation evidence in every hearing, they were accepted quite frequently. What is most interesting is that *none* of the seven judges who decided the forty cases categorically rejects the scientific relevance of case reports. This highlights a notable inconsistency between the judges in vaccine injury cases and many federal tort judges in the ways that case reports are perceived for supporting causal judgments. And since both sets of judges are reviewing case reports for their probative value as evidence for medical causation, the inconsistency appears to be based on a basic disagreement between judges as to the reliability or scientific relevance of case reports. The judges in the vaccine injury cases are much more nearly correct on the scientific issues than are the majority of the Article III federal judges, who tend to reject case reports. The reason for this appears to be that

---

192 For example, several of these cases discuss the use of case reports for establishing enough evidence to constitute a "duty to warn."

193 The primary decision that judges are required to make in *Daubert* hearings is whether the testimony (based on certain evidence) offered to the court is admissible. Because some judges found the particular case reports presented to the court to be unreliable, they did not bother to evaluate whether case reports are categorically bad evidence.

they are much more familiar with case reports and how they can inform or be decisive for causation judgments.

Like structure-activity relationships, case studies are not mathematically certain guides to causal relationships. Some case studies are good evidence; others are not. Thus, not every positive case study provides evidence of causation. However, not every positive epidemiological study or every positive animal study provides evidence of causation as well. If tort judges are to carry out their gatekeeping duties well, they must learn to evaluate and sift the evidence at the bar in order to admit expert testimony based on biological evidence that is scientifically relevant evidence of causation. In Chapter 4, I reviewed clear examples of good case studies, well accepted in the scientific community, and discussed considerations that consensus scientific bodies use to judge which case studies are good ones.

Good case studies are less rare than the recitation of a few examples might suggest. The World Health Organization has found that about 17 percent of case studies they considered are the basis of certain or probable casual relationships between vaccine exposure and adverse reactions. Seventeen percent is a comparatively small percentage, but it is not negligible. Moreover, because courts are required to review carefully *all the evidence* litigants present that might assist the jury in coming to its decision, they need to consider whether the case studies at the bar are scientifically relevant evidence of causal relationships or not. Finally, even if one case report (or several) is (are) not sufficient by itself (themselves) to support a causal judgment, they can importantly contribute to other evidence that is available.[194]

Sometimes a case report by itself can support a causation judgment. For example, the Special Magistrates from the Vaccine Injury Compensation Program utilize such evidence and sometimes found single case studies quite compelling. Consider the opinion in *Stevens v. the Secretary of Health and Human Services.*[195] Judge Golkiewicz points out that the special masters "have debated the utility of case reports" for causation inferences. Moreover, even some who initially opposed them

> concluded that a single persuasive case report and a petitioner whose symptoms matched the case report's facts adequately supported petitioner's actual causation claim for a tetanus toxoid cased GBS. . . . Later, . . . [the same special master] opined that a single case report may support the possibility that a vaccine can cause a certain injury, "[i]f sound medical and scientific

---

[194] See for example both a scientific judgment by IARC, "Chloroethyl Nitrosoureas," *Monograph Series, Supplement 7* (1987): 150. Rev. 6 Feb. 1998. Available at: http://www-cie.iarc.fr/htdocs/monographs/suppl7/chloroethylnitrosoureas.html (noting a few case reports of cancer in patients exposed to this anticancer drug), and a tort case in which case studies provided supporing evidence (*In re: Phenylpropanolamine (PPA) Products Liability Litigation*, at 1242, 1244, 1246)).

[195] *Stevens v. the Secretary of Health and Human Services*, at 13–15 .

principles have been applied in that one case and the matter has been published for peer review."[196]

The tetanus toxoid case referred to was example (2) from the case studies discussed in Chapter 4.

Never Throw Evidence Away

In order to evaluate possible explanations of a phenomenon, a scientist must consider *all the scientifically relevant evidence.* In the law, however, some courts have been excluding as irrelevant individual pieces of evidence that certainly appear to be relevant to scientific judgments. Particular courts appear to decide *a priori* that whole categories of evidence, for example, structure-activity relationships, case studies, or animal studies, scientifically *cannot* contribute to (or cannot support by themselves) a scientific inference of causation and proceed to eliminate them as well as the expert who relied on them. However, as discussed in Chapter 4, a scientist's inference to a conclusion must be evaluated based on all the relevant evidence.

A number of consensus scientific committees have argued that scientists should, "Never throw evidence away."[197] For example, a large group of scientists and physicians involved in assessing adverse events from immunization proposed a method for assessing vaccine-caused adverse events that is "based on the best available information, [such that] [m]aximum use is made of *all available information and nothing is arbitrarily discarded*" (emphasis added).[198] Some scientific methodologists make the same point in even stronger terms:

> A causality assessment method must respect Fisher's fundamental rule of uncertain inference – *never throw information away.* That is, any fact, theory or opinion that can affect an evaluator's belief that [a particular exposure] caused an adverse event E must be incorporable by the method into the "state of information" on which the assessment is based.[199]

In the law, if a particular kind of evidence is scientifically relevant to scientists' causality judgments, it should be available as part of a body of integrated evidence that a court then considers when reviewing scientific testimony for

---

[196] *Stevens v. the Secretary of Health and Human Services,* at 15 (quoting *O'Leary v. Secretary of HHS,* No. 90–1729V, 1997 WL 254217, at 3).

[197] Scientists and physicians involved in assessing adverse events from immunization propose a method for assessing vaccine-caused adverse events that is "based on the best available information, [such that] [m]aximum use is made of *all available information* and nothing is arbitrarily discarded." Gerald M. Fenichel, David A. Lane, John R. Livengood, Samuel J. Horwitz, John H. Menkes, and James F. Schwarrtz, "Adverse Events Following Immunization: Assessing Probability of Causation," *Pediatric Neurology* 5 (1989): 287–290, esp. 290.

[198] Fenichel et al., "Adverse Events Following Immunization," 290.

[199] Hutchinson and Lane, "Standardized Methods of Causality Assessment," 10 (emphasis added).

admission. The court procedure for judging overall admissibility might be the following: Presumptively, courts should not rule as irrelevant any *individual* scientific fact, theory, or opinion that plausibly can affect a scientist's belief that a particular exposure caused an adverse event. Courts should consider all the relevant evidence on which a scientist bases her inferences, then review whether it is integrated or "fits together in the right way"[200] to support reliable expert testimony. Or, in the words of Rule 702, does the expert testimony rest on sufficient data (all data taken together), is it the product of reliable principles and is it reliably applied to the facts of the case? Specifically Rule 702 should be interpreted so that courts consider all an expert's scientifically relevant evidence to determine whether that body of integrated evidence sufficiently supports expert testimony.

Such evidence might ultimately be *inadmissible* if the body of a litigant's evidence, *taken as an integrated whole* did not support "scientifically reliable" expert testimony or if it did not fit the facts of a case. Yet to date some courts appear to have violated the aphorism − "never throw evidence away" − excluding individual pieces of evidence that are scientifically relevant to a scientist's judgment about causation.

Requiring Detailed Exposure Information

In assessing expert testimony courts need to determine whether plaintiffs can "demonstrate 'the levels of exposure that are hazardous to human beings generally as well as the plaintiff's actual level of exposure.'"[201]

In *Wright v. Willamette Industries*, the court reasoned that "a plaintiff in a toxic tort case must prove the levels of exposure that are hazardous to human beings generally as well as the plaintiff's actual level of exposure to the defendant's toxic substance before he or she may recover." Arguing that courts and juries in toxic tort cases must "make more particularized inquiries into matters of cause and effect . . . ,"[202] it goes on to argue that

> At a minimum, we think that there must be evidence from which the factfinder can conclude that the plaintiff was exposed to levels of that agent that are known to cause the kind of harm that the plaintiff claims to have suffered. . . . We do not require a mathematically precise table equating levels of exposure with levels of harm, but there must be evidence from which a reasonable person could conclude that a defendant's emission has probably

---

[200] See Haack, "An Epistemologist in the Bramble-Bush" for some discussion of the puzzle metaphor.

[201] *Westberry v. Gislaved Gummi AB*, 178 F.3d 257, at 263 (quoting *Mitchell v. Gencorp Inc.*, 165 F.3d 778, 781 (10th Cir. 1999) (quoting *Wright v. Willamette Indus., Inc.*, 91 F.3d 1105, 1106 (8th Cir. 1996)); see *Allen v. Pennsylvania Eng'g Corp.*, 102 F.3d at 199.

[202] *Wright v. Willamette Indus., Inc.*, 91 F.3d 1105, at 1107 (8th Cir. 1996).

caused a particular plaintiff the kind of harm of which he or she complains before there can be a recovery.

Despite this seemingly reasonable language, the court adds that

> In this case, while the Wrights proved that they were exposed to defendant's emissions and that wood fibers from defendant's plant were in their house, their sputum, and their urine, they failed to produce evidence that they were exposed to a hazardous level of formaldehyde from the fibers emanating from Willamette's plant. Their experts' information on this subject was simply insufficient.[203]

Although exposure is a needed factual predicate in an argument concerning injury from toxic substances, it is often a particularly difficult one to establish. Frequently, people are unaware that they are exposed. This occurred with radiation near the Hanford nuclear site in Washington state.[204] Exposures can be quite accidental as they were in *Moore v. Ashland Chemical Co.* (chemicals spilled in the back of a truck, which the driver had to clean up in a very closed space),[205] or otherwise difficult to document or measure. Victims do not carry monitors with them to document the extent of their exposures. Exposure information is difficult enough to provide for risk assessments by regulatory agencies (because of poor exposure records even in workplaces), and often there is a considerable demand for high degrees of quantification in that context. However, given the adventitious and often accidental exposures typical of toxic tort cases, it is an even more difficult factual issue to quantify with any degree of precision. Yet defendants may press strongly on this point because it is in their interest to do so. Courts should not expect or demand considerable precision or quantification of exposures.

The Federal Judicial Center's advice on this issue, endorsed by some courts, seems correct:

> Only rarely are humans exposed to chemicals in a manner that permits a quantitative determination of adverse outcomes.... Human exposure occurs most frequently in occupational settings where workers are exposed to industrial chemicals like lead or asbestos; however, even under these circumstances, it is usually difficult, if not impossible, to quantify the amount of exposure.[206]

203 *Wright v. Willamette Indus., Inc.*, 91 F.3d 1105, at 1107 (8th Cir. 1996)
204 Tomas Alex Tizon, "Cases Against Nuclear Plant Finally Heard: After 15 years of Delays, 2300 Plaintiffs who Say Radioactive Releases at the Hanford Site Made Them Seriously Ill Wait for a Jury's Decision," *Los Angeles Times*, 16 May 2005.
205 *Moore v. Ashland Chemical Inc.*, 151 F.3d 269 (5th Cir. (Tex.) (1998)).
206 Federal Judicial Center, *Reference Manual on Scientific Evidence* 187 (1994). *Westberry v. Gislaved Gummi AB*, 178 F.3d 257, at 264 (4th Cir. 1999), endorses this view.

Courts have adopted views ranging from the quite stringent to more flexible toward the amount of exposure that must be shown to satisfy the exposure requirement in typical toxic tort suits. The *Wright* court seemed especially stringent on this issue. Clearly, the Wrights had considerable exposure from formaldehyde impregnated wood dust and fibers – it was in their sputum and urine – but the court was sufficiently unsure about the formaldehyde exposure to admit the testimony. Given the fortuitous nature of such exposures, it appears that those courts that are more flexible on the issue provide a fairer forum to the parties involved. More flexible views appear to have been endorsed by the Fourth Circuit Court of Appeals in *Westberry v. Gislaved Gummi AB*,[207] as well as the Third Circuit Court of Appeals in *Heller v. Shaw Industries*.[208]

Thus, although excellent exposure information would be very helpful in toxic tort suits, it is usually quite poor and often difficult to obtain. Courts need to be quite sensitive in reviewing this part of plaintiff's case because a too-stringent and rigid approach will eliminate meritorious cases. The concern about exposure is heightened in light of (a) susceptible subpopulations and (b) the law concerning susceptible individuals. As we considered earlier, some individuals are more susceptible to toxic exposures than others. Thus, too demanding an approach toward explicit exposure data risks leaving susceptible individuals uncompensated for wrongfully inflicted injuries. Moreover, as a result of the eggshell skulls doctrine in torts, such persons are entitled to protection.[209]

Lumping vs. Splitting Toxicological Evidence

Defendants often argue that if there are two related human diseases, judges should consider them separately and assess how much evidence is available showing that a potentially toxic substance causes each disease. For example, benzene is well known for being associated with a number of blood and bone marrow related diseases, such as acute myelogenous (AML), myelomonocytic (AMMoL), monocytic (AMoL), and chronic mylegenous leukemias (CML), as well as several others.[210]

---

[207]   *Westberry v. Gislaved Gummi AB*, 178 F.3d at 264 (4th Cir. 1999). ("Consequently, while precise information concerning the exposure necessary to cause specific harm to humans and exact details pertaining to the plaintiff's exposure are beneficial, such evidence is not always available, or necessary, to demonstrate that a substance is toxic to humans given substantial exposure and need not invariably provide the basis for an expert's opinion on causation" (264).)

[208]   167 F.3d 146, at 157 (3d Cir. 1999) (noting "that even absent hard evidence of the level of exposure to the chemical in question, a medical expert could offer an opinion that the chemical caused plaintiff's illness").

[209]   Keeton et al., *Prosser and Keeton on Torts*, 291–292 (1984).

[210]   Peter F. Infante, "Benzene and Leukemia: Cell Types, Latency and Amount of Exposure Associated with Leukemia," in *Advances in Occupational Medicine and Rehabilitation*, vol. Q, no. 2 (May–August 1995): 108–109.

A common defense strategy is to separate these diseases into subtypes and ask how much particular evidence favors the claim that benzene exposure (and at what levels) causes each subtype of leukemia. Splitting the diseases into subcategories can separate some diseases that are more common from some that are much less common. Even if associations between exposure and disease have been documented for more common diseases, they may not have been as well documented or not documented at all for rare subtypes or relatives of the same generic diseases. Moreover, for reasons that seem not to be understood, some diseases are particularly rare in some countries or cultures – chronic myelomonocytic leukemia is much rarer in China than it is in other countries (or cultures).[211] With respect to leukemias Peter Infante, one of the major researchers on leukemia and for many years an official of the National Institute of Occupational Safety and Health, the research agency of the Occupational Safety and Health Administration, notes the problem with this approach:

> One of the difficulties in determining whether a specific type of leukemia is associated with an elevated relative risk from formal epidemiologic study of benzene exposed workers stems from the fact that leukemia is a relatively rare form of cancer and further subdivision into specific types results in very little statistical power to evaluate such relative risk.[212]

David Savitz and Kurtis Andrews, epidemiologists at the University of North Carolina at Chapel Hill, echo his view.[213]

Dr. Infante argues that when rare subtypes of diseases have not been identified because epidemiologic studies are too insensitive, he would rely upon other kinds of evidence, such as case reports, animal studies, if they were available, and more generic modes of action arguments, to assist in determining whether exposure to benzene was associated with rarer subtypes of leukemia.[214] This is in keeping with standard scientific approaches in understanding disease causation.

Nonetheless, such scientific arguments did not persuade a federal judge, who accepted defense arguments for splitting diseases into rarer subtypes. In *Chambers v. Exxon*, the judge argued that Exxon produced "a number of scientifically performed studies which demonstrate *no association* between exposure to

[211] B. Chen, W.-L. Zhao, J. Jin, Y.-Q. Xue, X. Cheng, X.-T. Chen, J. Cui1, Z.-M. Chen, Q. Cao, G. Yang, Y. Yao, H.-L. Xia, J.-H. Tong, J.-M. Li, J. Chen, S.-M. Xiong, Z.-X. Shen, S. Waxman, Z. Chen, and S.-J. Chen, "Clinical and Cytogenetic Features of 508 Chinese Patients with Myelodysplastic Syndrome and Comparison with Those in Western Countries," *Leukemia* 19 (2005): 767–775.

[212] Infante, "Benzene and Leukemia," 108–112.

[213] David A. Savitz and Kurtis W. Andrews, "Review of Epidemiological Evidence on Benzene and Lymphatic and Hematopoietic Cancers," *American Journal of Industrial Medicine* 31 (1997): 287–295.

[214] Infante, "Benzene and Leukemia," 108–112.

benzene and development of CML [chronic mylogenous leukemia]."[215] He ruled Infante's argument "unreliable" and plaintiff's case was at an end. We have already seen that "no effect" epidemiological studies do not necessarily imply that there is evidence of no effect and that they might well be falsely negative. That is a greater problem when courts permit rare diseases to be split into even more rare subtypes, which may or may not be scientifically plausible. (In addition, even if there are good scientific reasons to split diseases, courts should not then insist on epidemiological studies (which may be much too insensitive to detect such rare subtypes), but permit other kinds of evidence to support causation inferences.)

Further Confusions about Weight-of-the-Evidence Arguments

The failure of courts to understand inference to the best explanation, beginning with the *Joiner* district court and endorsed by the U.S. Supreme Court, has led to several confusions about scientific arguments that must be addressed to better align legal outcomes with the needed science in each case.

Confusing the Form of the Argument with the Standard of Proof

Recall that the term "weight of the evidence" is often utilized by regulatory agencies when they assess the toxicity of substances. Recall also that "weight of the evidence" is simply another term for nondeductive inferences. However, some courts, noting that regulatory agencies utilize this term and that they are interested mainly in assessing *risks*, not causal relations as required by torts, dismiss "weight-of-the-evidence" arguments in torts for two reasons: (1) because they are merely about *risks*, not retrospective causation; or (2) because the standard of proof may be lower. The view of the Fifth Circuit Court of Appeals in *Allen v. Pennsylvania Engineering*, is representative and sometimes repeated.

> We are also unpersuaded that the "weight of the evidence" methodology these experts use is scientifically acceptable for demonstrating a medical link between Allen's EtO exposure and brain cancer. Regulatory and advisory bodies such as IARC, OSHA and EPA utilize a "weight of the evidence" method to assess the carcinogenicity of various substances in human beings and suggest or make prophylactic rules governing human exposure. This methodology results from the preventive perspective that the agencies adopt in order to reduce public exposure to harmful substances. The agencies' threshold of proof is reasonably lower than that appropriate in tort law, which "traditionally make[s] more particularized inquiries into cause and

---

[215] *Chambers v. Exxon*, 81 F. Supp. 2d 661, at 665 (2000).

effect" and requires a plaintiff to prove "that it is more likely than not that another individual has caused him or her harm."[216]

There are at least two confusions in such reasoning. First, the term "weight-of-the-evidence argument" is merely another term for nondeductive inferences. Weighing and evaluating the extent to which evidence supports one explanation compared with another is pertinent to assessing both *risks* and *retrospective causation*; it is not restricted to assessing risks.[217] Taken literally the phrase "weight of the evidence" refers to which explanation has the *stronger balance of evidence* in support of it. Thus, one might think of it as referring both to a reasoning process, and to the kind and amount of evidence in support of one explanation compared with others. Courts appear to have confused the *form of inference* and the subject to which they apply – risks or retrospective causation. Such argument forms apply to both.

Federal or state regulatory agencies routinely rely on human, animal, and other kinds of studies to predict risks to humans. However, although some agency deliberations are predictive and preventive in nature, others search for retrospective causal effects, as in the tort law. The Food and Drug Administration (FDA) (e.g., for drugs and new food additives) and parts of the U.S. EPA (for pesticides) are required by law to evaluate substances before they enter the market (acting under so-called premarket approval statutes) and before there is any significant exposure.[218] Toxicological evaluation of substances in these circumstances is more predictive and explicitly preventive in nature.

However, other agencies engage in less predictive assessments. A number of regulatory bodies, such as the Occupational Safety and Health Administration and other parts of the EPA, act under postmarket statutes. In this capacity, they must act as scientific investigators and reconstruct a *causal explanation* of what led to disease or death with a further aim of reducing the adverse effect.[219] These scientific inquiries are much more like those needed in the tort law; thus, the conclusions and deliberations are quite pertinent to tort law inquiries.

---

[216] *Allen v. Pennsylvania Engineering*, 102 F.2d at 198, quoting *Wright v. Willamette Industries, Inc.*, 91 F.3d 1105, 1107 (8th Cir. 1996).

[217] Moreover, weighing and evaluating evidence of the relation between exposures and risks is not substantially different from weighing and evaluating evidence for evidence of a retrospective causal relation between exposure and harm. In fact, scientists regard both activities as like those of scientific detectives, as the evidence for *risks* from exposures is likely to be some kind of harm that the exposures have caused to people, animals, mammalian cells, organs, or DNA, or some combination of these – the same kind of evidence scientists would use for assessing causes of *harm* (personal communication, David A. Eastmond, Chair, Program in Environmental Toxicology).

[218] See Ping Kwong Chan and A. Wallace Hayes, "Principles and Methods for Acute Toxicity and Eye Irritancy," in *Principles and Methods of Toxicology*, 2nd ed., ed. A. Wallace Hayes (New York: Raven Press, 1989), 169, 206–212.

[219] Chan and Hayes, "Principles and Methods," 212.

Second, some courts seem to have confused the *level of proof* required to establish an explanation with the *form of the argument* (nondeductive arguments) utilized to explain an event (e.g., the Fifth Circuit). There are numerous problems with this view. The nondeductive *form of argument* does not determine the *standard of proof* used to judge the strength of an explanation for an event. Instead, the institution in question typically provides the standard of proof. Does the institution require that the best explanation be certain, beyond a reasonable doubt, highly probable, or only marginally probable compared with alternative explanations? Thus, a scientific inference to the best explanation might support the best inference by highly certain evidence, by highly probable evidence, by only 51 percent of the evidence, or only by some of the evidence. To illustrate: diagnostic arguments are used to discover the cause of disease for treatment purposes and to discover or explain some of the properties of black holes in physics. Different standards of proof might easily be used to judge their explanatory success in different scientific contexts. Consider another example. The criminal law might require a much greater weight of the evidence to show that a DNA sample from a crime scene matched the defendant's (because of its "beyond a reasonable doubt" standard of proof) than might be required for an analogous showing in the tort law to establish paternity (because of its "more likely than not" standard of proof). In either case, more evidence (the weight of the evidence) should favor the better explanation than alternative explanations.

Thus, it would be a mistake for courts to reject a *form of argument* – weight of the evidence – because a different standard of proof might (or might not [I have not conceded that point]) be utilized in regulatory settings. The form of argument is correct; the degree of certainty by which a conclusion is judged the most plausible of the explanatory alternatives is quite different. Moreover, agency personnel who write regulations do not see that the burden of proof used in support of them as a lesser standard than the tort law. In fact, at least some view agencies as seeking to ensure that regulations are supported by evidence beyond a reasonable doubt.[220]

Confusing the Likelihood of Causation with Statistical Evidence for It

A second major issue is that some courts also have confused the degree of certainty of causation with frequency of adverse effects indicated by a statistical study. This is evident in the demand for statistical studies showing a doubling of risks in exposed populations. A fundamental legal issue concerning causation (where general and specific causation are bifurcated) is what is the likelihood that a particular exposure *can cause* a disease, and what is the likelihood that

---

[220] Raymond R. Neutra, Chief, Environmental Epidemiology, California Department of Health Services, discussion at Electromagnetic Fields Science Advisory Panel (2000).

a particular exposure *in fact caused a particular plaintiff's disease*? In both instances, the issue is what is the likelihood of disease causation.

Statistical evidence *is not necessarily needed* to show probability of causation; it just happens to greatly facilitate the task. Chapter 4 presented five examples of disease causation based on singular (or a small number of) events. For each of them, scientists judged that exposure to the substance in question certainly or probably caused the adverse reaction, but there were no statistical studies showing causation.[221] Moreover, accident investigators assess the causes of airplane accidents or space shuttle disasters without statistical studies of all such accidents; there are simply too few.

The conclusion: to the extent that courts *demand* statistical evidence for probability of causation, they have it *backwards*. What must be shown is that it is more likely than not that exposure to defendant's substance can cause injuries like the plaintiff's and more likely than not did cause plaintiff's injury. Statistical evidence is merely *one way*, sometimes the only way, and often a particularly persuasive way to establish this claim (because it has a kind of objectivity to it whereas experts' probability judgments may concern courts). However, there may be other ways to show this using inference to the best explanation arguments, depending on the evidence that is available in a particular case. The examples of good case studies as well as accident investigations show this quite clearly. The procedure for establishing the likelihood of causation by means of a nondeductive argument is to show by means of the evidence available that it is more likely than not that defendants' substance caused plaintiffs' injuries (compared with other explanations to account for plaintiff's disease). Although this is a less *algorithmic* way to show such claims compared with statistical evidence, it is how scientists and the rest of us make such judgments all the time.

General and Specific Causation

There are also some issues that merit clarification concerning general versus specific causation. In federal toxic torts cases (something not necessarily true in all state jurisdictions[222]), courts tend to insist that a plaintiff must first show that it is more likely than not that a substance *can cause* the disease in question (general causation), and then show the substance *did cause* the particular plaintiff's injury (specific causation). Some courts (and some recent articles) insist on the particular order of showing – first, general causation and then specific causation. This makes sense in many cases, but there is no necessity to the order. Recall the case studies example concerning GBS (example 2, Chapter 4).

---

[221] This is clearly the case with examples (1), (2), (4), and (5) in Chapter 4.

[222] See, for example, *Donaldson v. Central Illinois, Public Service Company*, 199 Ill.2d 63 (2002). ("Illinois law does not define causation in terms of 'generic' or 'specific' causation. Rather, our case law clearly states that in negligence actions, the plaintiff must present evidence of proximate causation, which includes both 'cause in fact' and 'legal cause'" (90).)

In that instance, Institute of Medicine scientists explicitly concluded, "because [this] case by Pollard and Selby (1978) demonstrates that tetanus toxoid *did* cause GBS, in the committee's judgment tetanus toxoid *can* cause GBS."[223] That is, because specific causation had been shown by the evidence available, by *deductive reasoning* they concluded the possibility of general causation followed as a logical consequence. It is not clear how often such inferences will be possible. However, there is nothing wrong with the inference in question concerning GBS, and there is *no statistical evidence* in support of it. Consequently, courts and commentators must exercise care in laying down hard and fast rules about the order of demonstration between general and specific causation.

Consider this point with respect to what is called "differential diagnosis," yet another term for inference to the best explanation. Joe Sanders and Julie Machal-Faulks have argued that the majority of decided legal cases suggests that in differential diagnosis, a physician or scientist must "rule in" the possibility of a general causal relationship between an exposure and a disease before "ruling out" all other possible explanations.[224] A number of courts have held that it is not enough in differential diagnosis for an expert to rule out all other explanations and then find that the remaining one – that defendant's substance caused plaintiff's disease – can be ruled in and the only explanation left standing.

There is some good sense to this suggestion, but again *no necessity*. A particular explanation must be a plausible one – *ceteris paribus*, it must be biologically plausible, typically must be consistent with what is known (although we have seen that these two considerations can be overemphasized), and satisfy other *explanatory* considerations. However, as the tetanus toxoid and vinyl chloride case studies show, given background information, particular exposures, and ruling out of other explanations, *a previously unsuspected causal relationship can be revealed on the basis of a singular event or small number of events.* Moreover, because a particular exposure *did cause* an adverse reaction, it follows that the exposure *can cause* that reaction. In such cases, because there was such a powerful inference to the best explanation from the evidence available, *specific causation* implies *general causation*. In the tetanus vaccine–GBS example, a particular explanation was ruled in by *compelling singular circumstances* and *background information* without general causation having been independently established. *General causation was simultaneously shown by specific causation.* A similar inference occurred in the vinyl chloride case. When there is such evidence one rightly can say the scientists *discovered* general causation as a result

[223] Institute of Medicine, *Childhood Vaccines*, 89 (emphasis in original).
[224] Joe Sanders and Julie Machal-Faulks, "The Admissibility of Differential Diagnosis Testimony to Prove Causation in Toxic Tort Cases: The Interplay of Adjective and Substantive Law," *Law and Contemporary Problems* 64 (2001): 107.

of specific causation in the particular case(s) they were investigating. Such outcomes are probably unusual, but in the spirit of *Daubert* it seems courts should allow for this in their review of expert testimony and its foundation.

Statistical evidence can serve another purpose for medical and legal purposes by indicating the rate of disease in exposed populations compared with background rates. For public health purposes, if exposure to a vaccine or an anesthetic greatly increases disease rates above background, this is important information concerning whether or not to pursue a vaccination program or allow exposures to an anesthetic. If exposure only slightly increases disease rates above background, there may be no public health concern. For legal purposes, if courts have such statistical information, this can provide some evidence about the likelihood of causation. It is helpful but not a necessary condition (recall the discussion in Chapter 5).[225]

The last two points raise a more significant one for which I will not argue, but for which I will offer a conjecture. Certainly courts, and the scientific world more generally, have become captivated by the idea that various kinds of statistical support are needed for scientific conclusions. Statistical studies seem especially important for biological research given the high degree of variability within populations. Moreover, the emphasis on statistical studies is neither surprising nor remarkable, given the methodological and other progress that has been made with statistical reasoning in science in the twentieth century. In addition, certain kinds of statistical evidence – in particular double-blind clinical trials with large numbers in the control and the exposed groups – can be paradigmatic of excellent scientific studies. The mistake, and it is a mistake, is to confuse a common example of good scientific reasoning for what is required of *all* scientific and factual reasoning. Austin Bradford Hill is especially sharp on this point.[226] Harman and Wright both argue that induction by enumeration

---

[225] On a separate legal issue, if a defendant is subject to a negligence standard of liability, a plaintiff must show that defendant failed to exercise the kind of care a reasonable person in the circumstances would. Thus, in order to establish the defendant's liability, the plaintiff would need to show that the harm was foreseeable. The foreseeability requirement would need some substantiation that an *ex ante* risk was being imposed on those exposed to a product or substance. Thus, having a disease rate elevated above background would be one kind of evidence to show foreseeability, but this is a separate issue from showing causation.

[226] See his discussion at Hill, "Environment and Disease," 19:

> Between the two world wars there was a strong case for emphasizing to the clinician and other research workers the importance of not overlooking the effects of the play of chance upon their data. Perhaps too often generalities were based upon two men and a laboratory dog while the treatment of choice was deduced from a difference between two bedfuls of patients and might easily have no true meaning. It was therefore a useful corrective for statisticians to stress, and to teach need for, tests of significance merely to serve as guides to caution before drawing a conclusion, before inflating the particular to the general.
>
> I wonder whether the pendulum has not swung too far – not only with the attentive pupils but even with the statisticians themselves.

is a special case of inference to the best explanation. The statistical evidence shows why one conclusion is the best explanation.[227]

Causal inference is needed in science. Inference to the best explanation is the reasoning process by which scientists infer that a causal relation holds between exposure and disease. There are a variety of kinds and patterns of evidence that could be used in inferences to the best explanation to conclude that a causal relationship more likely than not existed. Statistical studies of one kind or another are merely *one* means (one pattern of evidence, if you will) of supporting causal inferences, not the only one and not a necessary form of inference that every causal inference must have.

It is a reasonable conjecture that at least some courts have mistaken *an important species* of causal inference for the *genus* or *necessary condition* of all causal inferences. Instead, they should recognize that the fundamental issue is the causal relationship between exposure and injury and that there are a variety of kinds and patterns of evidence that would license an inference to such conclusions. A variety of patterns of evidence – utilizing all the kinds of evidence available in a particular case – can support causal inferences.

DEFENSE CONTRIBUTIONS TO THE ABOVE ARGUMENTS

This book constitutes an essay about institutions and how administrators of the law shape and mold it by their decisions. It is not an essay that aims to assign blame. Quite the contrary, the tasks the Supreme Court gave federal judges are complex and difficult for judges with their generic and typically nonscientific education. It does not prepare them well for such tasks. If they err, it seems that such mistakes could occur because of too little acquaintance with the relevant fields. I do not assume that this is a deliberate strategy to protect one party at the bar; this would be an abandonment of their responsibilities as fair administrators of the law.

However, in the adversary system there are at least two sides to every dispute judges must adjudicate. If courts have erred in their rulings, their ideas about an appropriate test for scientific evidence have probably not, like Athena, been born fully mature from the head of a Zeus-like judge. It is likely that judges have been influenced in their rulings (largely against plaintiffs) by adversaries on the other side. Moreover, evidence is beginning to accumulate that industries, trade groups, and their lobbying firms have tried to construct a view of science that permits them to reduce or avoid responsibility for the adverse effects of their products. Often these arguments have been used in regulatory settings, but similar points are suggested in tort courts.

I do not make this point a major theme of the book, however, because that would change the nature of the project, take considerable documentation (but

---

[227] Harman, "Inference to the Best Explanation," and Wright, *Practical Reasoning*, 175–184.

some of that has been done), and be a distraction from the major institutional concern: wherever judges acquire their views about scientific evidence, they err in ways that profoundly affect the law.[228]

Nonetheless, there is evidence that defense attorneys and experts are constructing views of science that are contrary to those of consensus scientific committees and many (but perhaps not all) scientists. Much of this began with the tobacco industry. The tobacco industry was advised by Hill and Knowlton, a public relations firm, to emphasize three points about any relationship between smoking and lung cancer: "That cause-and-effect relationships have not been established in any way; that statistical data do not provide the answers; and that much more research is needed."[229] The primary means by which such a claim would be defended would be to invoke an account of causation so stringent that there could be few causal relationships in the world. Moreover, because of court documents made public through litigation, researchers now know that their generic strategy was to create doubt about scientific evidence that their products caused harm. "Doubt is our product" as one document puts it.[230]

Other industries appear to have followed the lead of the tobacco industry in preventing information reaching the scientific literature or mischaracterizing it. Such strategies have been mounted on behalf of asbestos,[231] vinyl chloride,[232] lead,[233] the general chemical industry (fighting the Delaney Clause),[234] and benzidine dyes.[235] It would be surprising that similar arguments were not used in toxic tort cases, as they have had some success in the larger area of public discourse.

In addition, there is a patina of plausibility to a claim that "more evidence is needed," because most scientific papers conclude with similar claims about the subject under consideration. Moreover, why would not judges (or regulators for that matter) not want to be more certain about scientific conclusions before incorporating them into the law? Such arguments rest on a certain ideal and are quite tempting, as we saw in Chapter 5. Yet they can be sufficiently misleading

---

[228] This concern is beginning to be addressed more broadly by special issues of journals or books: a special issue of *American Journal of Public Health, Supplement 1: Scientific Evidence and Public Policy* 95 (2005), ed. David Michaels; Wendy Wagner and Rena Steinzor, eds., *Rescuing Science from Politics* (New York and London: Cambridge University Press, 2006); and a special issue of the *International Journal of Occupational and Environmental Health: Corporate Corruption of Science* II(4) (2005), ed. David S. Egilman, Susanna Rankin Bohme, available at http://www.ijoel.com.

[229] Michaels and Monforton, "Manufacturing Uncertainty," S40, note 35.

[230] Michaels and Monforton, "Manufacturing Uncertainty," S40 (note 38).

[231] Brodeur, *Outrageous Misconduct,* and Barry Castleman, *Asbestos: Medical and Legal Aspects* (New York: Pantheon Books, 1985).

[232] Markowitz and Rosner, *Deceit and Denial,* 226–233, 300–301.

[233] Markowitz and Rosner, *Deceit and Denial,* 300–301.

[234] Michaels and Monforton, "Manufacturing Uncertainty," S41, note 46 (citing internal Hill and Knowlton memos).

[235] Michaels, "Corporate Decision Making and Bladder Cancer," 215, 218–221.

that they constitute their own version of junk science. Evidence is beginning to accumulate that similar strategies are being utilized in toxic tort cases.[236]

In closing, I consider two broader issues suggested by the courts that can be addressed given the resources of this and previous chapters.

THE INTELLECTUAL RIGOR TEST

The idea that courts should require of expert testimony the same "intellectual rigor" in court as in the field has become a frequently cited guide for judges to utilize in assessing expert testimony. However, whether the "intellectual rigor" idea is a desirable one or not depends on how it will be understood and utilized.

Surprisingly, there are at least two different concerns about it. On the one hand, the authors of *Modern Scientific Evidence* characterize it as "dangerous." Their concern is that because it is discipline specific, experts from fields that lack sufficient rigor might not be reviewed carefully enough by judges.[237] The intellectual rigor of the field might be insufficient. On the other hand, it tempts courts to emphasize the "rigor" too much and risks being overly stringent. This second concern seems more likely in toxic torts, because there seems to be little doubt about the quality of the pertinent scientific fields. If courts insist that an expert before testifying on causation in toxic tort cases must support his views by multiple kinds of tests and multiple kinds of evidence of the sort illustrated in textbooks or that were insisted upon by the *Wade-Greux* court, this would be at odds with much scientific practice and would erect nearly insuperable barriers for most plaintiffs. As we have seen, scientists tend to rely on a wide range of data in making inferences about the toxicity of substances, but without having the fullest panoply of evidence available in most cases. Scientists tend to be more flexible in reasoning about the toxic effects of substances than some idealized textbook or commentator views might suggest. Placing too much emphasis on "rigor," an interpretation that some courts might already have done, would not conform to scientific practice and it would have undesirable effects on the tort law.

By contrast, if courts permit experts to testify on the basis of the weight of the evidence available to them, as, for example, toxicologists do when asked to make judgments about the likely causes of disease or physicians do in diagnosing the causes of disease, this would be a much better application of the intellectual rigor test.[238] If courts emphasize the similarities between inferences experts

---

[236] Michaels and Monforton, "Manufacturing Uncertainty," S44.

[237] Faigman *et.al., Modern Scientific Evidence,* 48.

[238] Kassirer and Cecil, "Inconsistency in Evidentiary Standards for Medical Testimony," 1382–1387. Note also a very recent decision in which the court recognizes that to be admissible, an expert's "analogies, inferences and extrapolations connecting the science to the witness's conclusions must be of a kind that a reasonable scientist or physician would make in a

draw in the courtroom and in their out-of-court scientific profession with all the *variety* and *sensitivity* this involves, this would be a much more defensible interpretation.[239]

Finally, courts should preserve the legal distinction between a *preliminary review* of the evidence to assess its *reliability,* and *extremely rigorously arrived at scientific conclusions* on the same issues that might make their way into textbooks. Judges – even those assessing the intellectual rigor of scientific reasoning and methodology – must merely conduct a preliminary review of an expert's reasoning and methodology for it reliability and relevance to the facts of the case.

PURSUIT OF TRUTH AND JUSTICE IN TORTS

Recall that in his concurring opinion in *Joiner* Justice Breyer noted two goals that the Federal Rules of Evidence should serve and that should guide judges in reviewing the admissibility of scientific evidence and expert testimony: truth and justice – two of the great concerns of human institutions (Chapter 3, 88–89).[240] He explicitly seeks to ensure that the powerful engine of the tort law is directed toward the "right substances," the ones that in fact cause harm, but also does not "destroy the wrong ones." This is a concern that courts, after the results of a jury verdict, should yield a verdict, based on a correct (or reasonable?) scientific view about the toxicity of a substance and not mistakenly have eliminated beneficial, but (comparatively) harmless, products. He emphasizes the social good that has come and can come from the products of our technological society. He suggests that admissibility and trials be conducted so that substances that are part of beneficial products and that in fact do not cause adverse effects in humans do not become mistakenly judged legally as human toxicants. This would be a mistaken legal verdict for plaintiffs against defendants.

Whereas he also calls attention to the tort law's concern for justice and court procedures for finding truly harmful substances by means of its legal proceedings, his greater emphasis – that courts should avoid false positives – does several things that can be problematic. It reinforces the asymmetric scientific norm to prevent false positives. However, rather than needing support, this scientific norm about mistakes probably merits some countervailing attention in the law. To legally reinforce the scientific norms about mistakes further burdens plaintiffs.

Moreover, there is another possible legal mistake that appears to receive less attention: legal false negatives – that is, a mistaken legal outcome finding that

---

decision of importance arising in the exercise of his profession outside the context of litigation." (*In re Ephedra Products Liability Litigation*, 393 F. Supp. 2d 181, at 189.)

[239] This is a point we considered in Chapter 5.
[240] *Joiner v. General Electric Co.*, 118 S.Ct. at 520.

plaintiffs are not harmed by exposure to a substance when in fact they are. He is silent about this possible mistake. Does he undervalue admissibility procedures that would prevent errors that disadvantage plaintiffs? Does he inadvertently undervalue the importance of justice for plaintiffs, despite his articulated point about justice?

These topics raise a more difficult and subtle point about truth and procedures for arriving at it. Many of us might be tempted to believe that factual truth about the toxicity of substances should precede or be a prerequisite to determination of just compensation for plaintiffs. Why should we not insist on the *scientific truth* about toxicity in torts?

Although this question is easily posed, its answer is not so straightforward. For one thing, the *correctness* of an expert's conclusion is not the goal of an admissibility hearing, only the reliability of his or her testimony is. For another, we may be tempted to think that the truth about the toxicity of substances is easily knowable and relatively quick to obtain. Both claims about the science are not true for many kinds of toxic substances (Chapter 5).

To get at the truth about toxic substances for legal purposes, as a community we must utilize, first, the procedures of different areas of biology and toxicology, and, second, legal procedures. However, while we are in the middle of scientific and legal debates, we must rely on scientific and legal procedures to guide us.

What are the biases or tendencies of different procedures during the period before the science is fully settled and against the background of various practical hurdles to establishing scientific claims? How will these affect the law? What are the tendencies of scientific procedures? Is the process biased toward one outcome or another? These are, thus, questions of process tendencies both in science and in the science-law interaction in toxic tort cases. How will the process biases manifest themselves when science is used in the law?

Consider some of the evidentiary tendencies in scientific practices leading to consensus and truth concerning a toxic substance. First, if a scientist is given a substance and asked if it is toxic, she might respond that she does not know. Or perhaps, invoking the memory of Paracelsus who is responsible for the aphorism that "the dose makes the poison," she might note that at some concentrations it will be toxic and at some concentrations it will not be, but she would not know what those were without investigation. In short, she would be agnostic about such claims in the absence of evidence.[241]

Second, as I argued elsewhere and reviewed in Chapter 4, if a scientist attempts to study a substance's toxic effects with epidemiology, unless she has a

---

[241]   In addition, recall that some scientists begin with more controversial assumptions. If judges were to be convinced by defendants to adopt the presumption that substances caused no human health harms until overwhelming evidence established evidence to the contrary, this would raise quite high barriers to establishing appropriate toxicity claims.

very large sample population, conceptually she will be forced to choose toward which kind of mistake her study has a predisposition – a false positive or a false negative.[242] That is, if her study shows an elevated risk from exposure, is this a true elevated risk or an anomaly of the study? If her study yields a no effect result, is it truly no effect or falsely negative? And beyond that, can it provide any evidence at all that there is no harm from exposures? The smaller the samples used in the study, the greater these problems will be.

If our scientist tries to answer the question with animal studies there are additional problems. One is the extrapolation from high-dose results in animals (needed to have a study of any sensitivity) to low-dose effects in animals. Another is the extent to which positive animal studies provide evidence of likely human harm, although as I argued in Chapter 4 scientists understand such studies so as to provide reasonable estimates of these effects. Even though scientists routinely utilize animal studies, skeptics have intellectual space to challenge the inferences. Our scientist, again, might guard against false positives and might withhold judgment about human harm based on positive animal studies. However, *withholding judgment* – even if there is sufficient evidence for the legal conclusion – creates the possibility that there may be enough uncertainty to undermine the case.

Third, if human studies are positive, scientists may be tempted to search for positive animal studies to help confirm human evidence and to help provide a model for the disease process. For understanding the disease, even multiple human results may be insufficient. More study is needed. If animal studies are positive, but human studies are not, does this show there is no human effect or that the human studies were insensitive, poorly designed, too short, or just a statistical aberration? Human and animal studies may not agree – one or the other may be positive, the other negative. This could cloud the picture and further delay judgment about human effects.

Fourth, even if both human and animal results tend to agree, some scientists might still want to understand the *biological mechanisms* of action in order to eliminate mere statistical associations and in order to understand the disease process better. The ideal would be to understand the disease process "all the way down" from external exposure, to exposure at the target organ, to metabolic activation and distribution throughout the body, even to molecular effects resulting ultimately in disease or death at the cellular level. Moreover, with diseases such as cancer there may be multiple molecular changes before the disease is manifested clinically. However, a demand for mechanistic understanding is not likely to be met for most substances (Chapter 4 and above).

There also may be demands for multiple kinds of evidence in support of expert testimony. This, too, appears to be rarely met even for scientific purposes. It will be rarer yet in toxic tort law with its time frames. To permit such demands

---

[242] Cranor, *Regulating Toxic Substances*, 31–47.

to dominate the tort law would overturn reasonable standards of admissibility and proof.

Fifth, throughout the investigative process there may be lingering doubts about whether there are alternative hypotheses to explain the seeming toxic effects. Is the association between exposure and disease real or is something else occurring that accounts for the observed effects or is it an artifact of the studies themselves? What degree of certainty will our scientist seek to support her conclusions? If she seeks too much certainty her doubts will linger a long time. The legal question is the extent to which such demands for certainty are permitted to forestall the admissibility of testimony or the ultimate standard of proof in torts.

Without these kinds of confirmation supported by considerable certainty, the scientific picture *may* appear incomplete compared with one kind of theoretical ideal. This in turn can open space for doubt about toxic effects that can be exploited in legal proceedings. Lack of full understanding supported by a high degree of certainty – short of the ideal noted earlier – can invite doubt on one ground or another. The various kinds of doubt, plus demands for additional studies and demands for certainty all serve to *prevent false positive* mistakes (but increase the risks of false negatives). They also tend to reinforce legal inaction, or worse, end a tort case.

There are also some forces, mostly a result of human psychology, that might risk false positives. Because an individual scientist typically has a difficult, long-term project on which she is working, she tends to "become committed or attached to it; [she] strongly want[s] it to be correct and find[s] it increasingly difficult to envision the possibility that it might be false..."[243] If she believes that a substance is toxic to humans, her commitment to the project may lead her to overlook contrary evidence or to exaggerate the toxic effects. In addition, some have pointed to a "publication bias" which leads journal editors to publish positive scientific results more than negative ones (that some expected effect was not found by research is ordinarily not an exciting result). Both of these tendencies could lead to results that were falsely positive. (In the law, of course, there is the concern that experts will be motivated to modify their testimony to favor their employer, a concern that applies to both sides of litigation.) However, on balance, it seems that the process of winnowing and assessing evidence *in the scientific community* tends to guard more against false positives than against false negatives (Chapter 5).

Return now to admissibility and truth in toxic tort cases. It may be comparatively easy in retrospect to identify which scientific claims are true after a consensus has developed. However, in assessing the scientific basis of testimony for admissibility we should be more concerned about the *process* tendencies in

---

[243] James Woodward and David Goodstein, "Conduct, Misconduct and the Structure of Science," *American Scientist* 84 (1996): 479, 485.

science that are manifested during the search before consensus is achieved. If these arguments are correct – that scientific processes are biased to prevent false positives and reinforced by skepticism and demanding standards of proof – this suggests that in the early to middle stages of inquiry into the properties of toxic substances that, outside of those who are vested in establishing such results, there is likely to be skepticism toward the view that a substance causes injury making it more difficult to show that the substance causes injury. Thus, *in the short to intermediate term* during such investigations, courts are more likely to encounter skepticism and doubt about whether the substances are toxic than they are to encounter support and certitude that they are toxic.

Justice Breyer's admonition to trial judges – urging them to ensure that the tort law's outcome "*points towards the right substances and does not destroy the wrong ones*"[244] – simply reinforces a tendency already there in the scientific community. This point is especially clear when one considers how a judge might try to ensure that expert testimony based on positive scientific studies was correctly positive. A court, by insisting on quite stringent standards to prevent falsely positive results, could better increase the chances that when studies show an adverse effect they are correctly positive. That is, the best way to increase the probabilities that a positive scientific study is truly positive is to greatly reduce the chances that it is a falsely positive result – by having such demanding standards that it is highly unlikely to be falsely positive. (Recall, however, that admissibility decisions need not be correct, only reliable.)

The major downside is that courts might fail to analyze or undervalue studies that point to a substance's toxicity – for example, a no effect epidemiological study that is too small or too short to reveal a toxic effect or a failure to appreciate animal, molecular, or case studies that point to toxicity. In such instances, an effort to avoid false positives would lead to missing a more subtle assessment that points to human toxicity. Thus, if judges are encouraged by the highest court to adopt the approach that Justice Breyer tends to emphasize, this risks *doubly biasing* tort law procedures against the party seeking to establish the toxicity of a substance – both scientific processes and judicial rules on admissibility would be predisposed in the same direction. His admonition appears contrary to a *normative* evenhandedness in the law that tries to ensure neither factual nor legal mistakes favor plaintiffs or defendants.

There is a corrective to this difficulty. Judges in screening expert testimony and scientific evidence must be particularly vigilant to prevent the *process tendencies of science* from distorting the *process evenhandedness of the law*. If they are not, they may be at the mercy of lawyers reinforcing scientific skepticism for narrow purposes of their own. Thus, judges risk being manipulated by the party to litigation that benefits from skepticism and scientific uncertainty.

---

[244] *Joiner v. General Electric Co.*, 118 S.Ct. at 520.

In addition, the search for truth through scientific processes and seeing that justice is done between litigants can conflict; there is no certainty that they will converge. Moreover, they are likely to diverge in cases in which it is difficult to establish that a substance causes harm to humans, even if the substance in fact harmed the plaintiff. At least such circumstances invite those who have an interest in denying the causal relationship *to utilize the process tendencies of science* – demands for human studies, for mechanistic studies, and multiple confirmation of results, all supported by a high degree of certainty – to preclude a case from coming to a jury trial.[245] We might see this, for example, when substances cause common diseases or diseases that have long latency periods. This might have happened in an earlier period concerning exposure to benzene or arsenic, both of which have taken considerable time to establish just how toxic they can be at comparatively low levels.[246] When such conditions obtain, wrongly injured plaintiffs would be treated unfairly by the combination of scientific and legal process tendencies. Moreover, if plaintiffs cannot get past an admissibility hearing – because of process biases – they will not have their day in court and risk being treated unfairly. Meritorious individuals will be denied the possibility of justice and some of the important deterrence effects of torts will be lost.[247]

This issue about the pursuit of truth and justice in torts has another aspect to it. It is comparatively easy for judges to learn some simple rules for reviewing scientific inferences, but those reviewed in this chapter are mistaken or greatly misleading. More important, virtually all of them tend to prevent false positives, thus, asymmetrically benefiting one side in the litigation: the defense. However, in order to prevent manipulation by litigants, judges must recognize which screening rules are mistakes and come to understand a much wider range of mistakes against which they must guard. Fairness between litigants demands judicial evenhandedness in detecting both positive studies in support of expert

---

[245] For a representative view, consider Joe G. Hollingworth and Eric G. Lasker, "The Case Against Differential Diagnosis: *Daubert*, Medical Causation Testimony and the Scientific Method," *Journal of Health Law*, 37, 1 (Winter 2004): 85–112.

[246] Benzene appears to be toxic down to 1 ppm and possibly toxic to .1 ppm (see Infante, "Benzene and Leukemia," 253–262; and Qing Lan, Luoping Zhang, Guilan Li, Roel Vermeulen, Rona S. Weinberg, Mustafa Dosemeci, Stephen M. Rappaport, Min Shen, Blanche P. Alter, Yongji Wu, William Kopp, Suramya Waidyanatha, Charles Rabkin, Weihong Guo, Stephen Chanock, Richard B. Hayes, Martha Linet, Sungkyoon Kim, Songnian Yin, Nathanial Rothman, Martyn T. Smith, "Hematotoxicity in Workers Exposed to Low Levels of Benzene," *Science* 306 (2004): 1774-1776), whereas arsenic, which for years was believed to be comparatively safe at 50 parts per billion (ppb), is now judged to be toxic to levels perhaps as low as 10 ppb (or even less). See the U.S. Environmental Protection Agency, at http://www.epa.gov/safewater/arsenic.html, for discussion of the drinking water standard for arsenic.

[247] Some deterrence will remain, of course, simply because the threat of suit is available to those who believe they have been wronged. However, the deterrent effect is stronger, if meritorious cases succeed.

testimony that are falsely positive and negative studies at issue in expert testimony that are falsely negative (as well as those that simply fail to show evidence of no adverse effects). It is easy to argue for pursuing truth through application of the Federal Rules of Evidence and interpretations of *Daubert*, but it matters importantly how this is done and what mistakes judges tolerate or try to prevent by reviewing expert testimony.

CONCLUSION

If courts are to accurately review scientific testimony and its foundation, to fairly perform their admissibility responsibilities and to enhance the possibility of justice in torts, they must become knowledgeable, sensitive, thoughtful consumers of scientific studies and inferences. This will not make their tasks easier; in all likelihood, it will be more difficult to conduct reviews of evidence well. Judges will first need to avoid using overly simple and restrictive guides for reviewing evidence. The court decisions considered as examples in this chapter illustrate a tendency to look for comparatively simple heuristics and procedures to assist their work, something that is less true of scientists as they study the complex biological world. The evidentiary picture in science is more complicated than such simplified rules can reasonably accommodate. However, if the law is to be more compatible with science, courts will need to conduct admissibility reviews that better recognize the multifaceted, varied nature of scientific evidence and reasoning. Thus, they also need to be more sophisticated about subtle process tendencies of science that can undermine legal goals. To better serve science and law, they should avoid:

- Demanding ideal evidence.
- Insisting on epidemiological studies or placing misleading restrictions on them.
- Demanding mechanistic evidence.
- Routinely excluding animal studies and structure-activity evidence.
- Routinely excluding relevant case reports (they need to learn the indicia of *good* case reports).
- Excluding individual kinds of scientifically relevant evidence because by themselves they are insufficient for a causal conclusion.

More subtle and sensitive analyses will be needed in place of all of this.

Courts also will need to develop greater sensitivity to the process tendencies of science in order to review it more accurately and to be fair to litigants from both sides. *Inter alia* this includes the need to

- Recognize the difference between "no evidence of an effect" and "evidence of no effect."

- Recognize the variety of ways that studies can be misleadingly negative, because they are too small, too short, too specific for subspecies of disease, or conducted too long after exposure has ceased to identify real adverse effects.
- Understand the "healthy worker" effect.
- Exclude evidence on the basis of scientific irrelevance only with the greatest of care.
- Recognize other ways that the process tendencies of science can unfairly impact admissibility reviews.
- Review a scientist's evidence as an integrated whole.

The various mistaken reasons some courts have given for refusing to admit expert testimony pose one serious kind of problem – judges appear to be deciding issues about the *scientific* relevance of evidence contrary to good scientific practices. Such decisions are even worse, however, when they are considered against the background of pragmatic barriers to the identification of causal relations that exist. The result is an unfortunate synergism between mistaken court reasons for excluding evidence and pragmatic barriers to the discovery of causal relations. This synergism in effect greatly *heightens the barriers* for injured parties to successfully bring their cases before a jury and have a *public discussion* of the human and institutional relationships that led to exposure and possibly disease. I close this chapter with some highlights of the adverse consequences for the law.

The more demanding scientific requirements courts place on the evidence that forms the basis of expert testimony, the more this heightens plaintiffs' barriers to the law simply because so little is known about the universe of chemical substances. The less subtle judges are about science, the more likely it is that the process tendencies of science or uninformed skepticism will inadvertently trump the law's mandated evenhandedness in making admissibility decisions.

In addition, ignorance about the universe of substances burdens the extent to which it is possible in a particular case to obtain minimal evidence about whether exposure to a product has contributed to a plaintiff's disease. Thus, the more courts constrain with considerable specificity the kinds of evidence that must be used in support of testimony (instead of permitting scientists to utilize the wide range of evidence they would ordinarily rely on for causation judgments), the more this restricts scientists' tools of the trade and reduces plaintiffs' access to the legal system. Given the widespread ignorance about substances, a better presumption would be that there might be little or no human epidemiological evidence and no mechanistic information about the effects of any particular substance. When either is available, this is more a result of good fortune than a routine matter.

The higher the evidentiary standard that must be met before expert testimony is admitted, the burden of production is carried, or a scientific finding is justified to the satisfaction of a jury, the easier this makes an adversary's task because the opposing party may be "more inclined to rest on the non-credibility of the proponent's proofs, and less inclined to produce affirmative evidence."[248] Such standards will not minimize the weighted number of mistakes between plaintiffs and defendants,[249] and will reduce incentives for opponents to produce their own affirmative evidence frustrating two aims of the tort law.[250] The more legitimate scientific information courts have to arrive at a decision, the more accurate outcomes likely will be.

There is a further and important concern. By their rulings on the admissibility of expert testimony and its scientific foundations, courts are at least implicitly making policy for the tort law, but making it in ways that are hidden from the public and perhaps even from large numbers of the bar.[251] These are not merely policies concerning admissibility; courts are also constructing substantive law. For example, when a court precludes a case from going to trial unless there is statistically significant epidemiological evidence showing a RR > 2, such decisions in effect are predisposing legal outcomes, especially for those whose evidence may not match the *judicially* imposed standard. Admissibility rulings can have several broader policy implications:

- They can create a *legal view of science* that is at odds with many in the scientific community.
- They can establish a policy that precludes plaintiffs from recovery for harm suffered if they cannot provide specific kinds of evidence. Thus, a person's injuries are not legally *worthy of just rectification unless there is such evidence.* When this occurs, the law does not follow where science leads, but refuses to recognize a case for recovery, unless there is a special kind of evidence.
- There also can be different standards for admissibility in different courts. To the extent that there are, litigants are treated differentially depending on which circuit their case is heard. This invites "forum shopping" by litigants to find the most favorable venue for their trial.[252]

Short of major modifications in tort law liability and consistent with the requirements of *Daubert*, courts can take some steps to modestly, but, importantly, address the problems discussed earlier. To do this, however, they must

[248] Vern R. Walker, "Preponderance, Probability and Warranted Fact Finding," *Brooklyn Law Review* 62 (1996): 1075, 1115.
[249] Green, "Expert Witnesses," 643, 687.
[250] Walker, "Preponderance," 1115.
[251] Berger, "Upsetting the Balance Between Adverse Interests," noting a number of policy decisions that are implicitly made.
[252] Gottesman, "From *Barefoot* to *Daubert* to *Joiner*," 753–780; Margaret A. Berger, "The Supreme Court's Trilogy on the Admissibility of Expert Testimony," *Reference Manual on Scientific Evidence*, 2nd ed. (Washington, DC: Federal Judicial Center, 2000), 9–39, esp. 39.

correct some of the apparent mistakes noted in this chapter. Were they to do this, courts' admissibility decisions would not decide the cases, but they would permit testimony to be presented and critiqued before a jury.[253]

The gatekeeping rules and the public values at stake, however, increase courts' responsibilities to perform their tasks well to achieve the goals of torts within existing liability rules and available scientific evidence.[254] Failures in these tasks do not seem to be options; they are too threatening to the legitimacy of the law and the possibility of justice. To fulfill this responsibility and avoid some of these tendencies from materializing, courts need a better understanding of institutional tensions between science and the law and how better to review the scientific foundation of testimony.

---

[253] There is an important asymmetry between these two examples. By excluding cases from trial unless they have expert testimony that rests on very good human evidence, courts are in effect concluding that cases that fall short of this scientific standard as *without legal merit*. They *decide that class of cases*. By permitting experts to testify on the basis of less direct kinds of evidence, they are not necessarily deciding such cases; they are merely letting the proceedings continue further to be considered by juries and subject to later defense objections and motions and any appeals.

[254] In Chapter 8, I raise the question of whether current liability rules are adequate.

7

Enhancing the Possibility of Justice under *Daubert*

If some courts have been using unduly constrained, idealized, or overly simple heuristics for reviewing scientific testimony on causation, how might they conduct this task differently? How can they better address complex patterns of evidence? Can their admissibility decisions better serve the aims of both law and science?

Addressing these questions is the subject of the current chapter. I briefly consider the use of court-appointed experts, and then discuss an alternative, building on suggestions made by the Supreme Court in *Kumho Tire* and the Third Circuit Court of Appeals. After discussing this proposal, I consider some more nuanced patterns of evidence from consensus scientific committees to illustrate some complex patterns of evidence that courts might face, should be able to recognize and review favorably. I then present some decisions in which judges have recognized the subtlety of issues they faced or in which they addressed well the shortcomings of studies or reasoning against which they needed to guard. Toward the end of the chapter, I revisit some decisions discussed in Chapter 1 to suggest more specifically some of the problems they raise.

Courts have choices in how they implement *Daubert* and its progeny. They can unduly restrict scientific testimony, or fail to recognize more subtle scientific mistakes that can affect litigants. By contrast, they could review admissibility decisions on expert testimony to assess whether they fall within a "zone where reasonable scientists would disagree" (adopting a guiding heuristic from the Court in *Kumho Tire*).[1] Were they to do this, it is reasonable to expect several consequences to result.

Admissibility decisions should be better founded scientifically than at present and comport better with how scientists themselves assess evidence. Such outcomes would increase the acceptability of admissibility decisions within the scientific community and reassure respectable scientists who testify that their testimony will not be judicially condemned as inadequate.

---

[1] *Kumho Tire v. Carmichael*, 526 U.S. at 153.

When such decisions are within the range where scientists would reasonably disagree, this would likely improve the accuracy of tort decisions because it would reduce institutional biases that many of the simplified admissibility rules have produced. This is turn would lessen some of the admissibility barriers that have been erected as a result of the current implementation of *Daubert* and perhaps modestly increase plaintiffs' access to the law.

Decisions in accordance with these principles would reduce the risk of courts intruding on the right to a jury trial because judges would not exclude testimony when there are legitimate scientific disagreements. Finally, decisions in accordance with these principles might well increase just outcomes where both parties can have their experts admitted and can argue their cases before a jury of their peers. Whether the recommendations suggested here ultimately are enough is an issue we will consider in Chapter 8.

THE USE OF COURT-APPOINTED EXPERTS

One widely supported suggestion has been that judges should make greater use of court-appointed scientific experts to assist them in deciding the substantive issues of the admissibility of expert testimony. That is, courts should seek *substantive experts* to guide their substantive assessment of evidence. One can see the plausibility of this view by comparing it with an analogous concern in regulatory settings. When an agency proposes a regulation and provides interested parties with an opportunity for input, it would have information from a variety of sources. However, agency scientists are in a position to adjudicate in an informed way the scientific claims of opposing parties. Such an informed adjudicator is typically missing from tort law admissibility reviews. Thus, the strong suggestion by Justice Breyer and others to utilize court-appointed experts has a great deal of plausibility to it. Independent scientists could serve an important purpose in torts as agency experts do.

However, despite seeming good sense to the suggestion, there are several practical shortcomings that limit their use. Many agree that court-appointed experts are not particularly desirable in single plaintiff cases, as the costs can be comparatively high when relatively modest damages are at stake. Courts have quite limited resources to pay for their own experts, so typically litigants would have to contribute to paying for a court-appointed expert. However, if litigants, especially plaintiffs, were requested to provide additional funding, at the margins this would exclude some plaintiffs from court and exclude more than at present.

There also can be much worse outcomes. For example, in *Magistrini v. One Hour Martinizing Dry Cleaning* the plaintiffs and defendants both had scientists, but the judge, seeking external advice concerning each side's experts, gave both litigants the opportunity to have meta-experts speak to the reasoning and methodology of their primary experts. After that, still seeking further guidance, the judge appointed her own expert to assess the two sets of experts and meta-experts, but required that defendants and plaintiff share the cost of her advisor. Karen Magistrini, the plaintiff, suffering from leukemia with all that meant for treatment and medical bills, had to pay her share of those expenses out of her own pocket.[2] Moreover, this created a cost over and above already high costs Ms. Magistrini and her lawyers faced in bringing a case and trying to usher it through an admissibility review. This added financial insult and burdens to her physical injuries.[3] Moreover there have been single-plaintiff cases when judges have appointed their own experts, but in at least one notable case the judge appeared to disagree with some of his own experts' advice and failed to recognize legitimate scientific disputes that should go to trial.[4]

There appears to be much greater agreement that in mass toxic tort cases court-appointed experts can be quite helpful in deciding generic scientific issues that will affect many cases. If the expenses of experts do not become too high, this *may* be plausible, but even in such cases costs can be quite high. For example, an Alabama district court judge appointed an expert panel in consolidated silicone breast implant cases in the hope that this would assist in resolving some of the difficult scientific issues across many different district courts and several circuits. Unfortunately, its conclusions were perhaps less definitive than had been hoped for. The total cost was $989,983.74, with the federal judiciary paying $733,645 and the affected parties sharing equally the remaining $206,338.74.[5] Whether or not this was reasonable in the circumstances, others will have to judge.

Use of court-appointed experts could be quite helpful. This is particularly the case when judges lack expertise, the experts are sufficiently knowledgeable and sensitive to both the range of scientific evidence and the different contexts of the tort law admissibility decisions, and the costs are not disproportionate to the overall value of the case. If some of the judges discussed earlier had had such assistance, this might have prevented some of the judicial struggles discussed in Chapter 6.

However, this does not get at the heart of the issue. Even court-appointed experts must have some guidance and for the most part such principles have

2   *Magistrini v. One Hour Martinizing*, 180 F. Supp. 2d 584–613 (2002), and personal communication, Gerson Smoger, Smoger and Associates, Oakland, California.
3   Under Rule 54 of the Federal Rules of Civil Procedure judges have authority to shift costs from one party to the other, especially from the winning party to the losing party, but it appears that this did not occur in Magistrini (and Ms. Magistrini lost on admissibility, so it is unlikely the costs would be shifted).
4   *Soldo v. Sandoz Pharmaceuticals Corporation*, 2003 WL 355931 (W.D.Pa.).
5   Laural L. Hooper, Joe S. Cecil, and Thomas E. Willging, "Assessing Causation in Breast Implant Litigation: The Role of Science Panels," *Law and Contemporary Problems*, 64, 4, (2001): 139–189, 176.

been missing. What should they look for? How should they think about the issues? How are they to judge the testimony of the litigants' experts?

TOWARD A SOLUTION FOR REVIEWING EXPERT TESTIMONY

A Proposal

Admissibility guidelines formulated by the Third Circuit Court of Appeals in the *In re Paoli Railroad Yard PCB Litigation* supplemented by a useful heuristic in *Kuhmo Tire v. Carmichael* and subsequent cases provide a place to begin.[6] I focus particularly on the Third Circuit because its decisions seem to reflect considerable sensitivity and subtlety about scientific issues. I sketch the outlines of plausible principles for judges to follow in their assessment of evidence and to instruct their own experts should they decide to use them.

Of course, for an expert to be admissible his or her credentials would need to be reviewed for the pertinent qualifications, education, experience, standing in the professional community, or certifications needed to be eligible to testify. In addition, such considerations can all be *circumstantial evidence* about the quality and reliability of an expert's arguments. In scientific peer reviews, a scientist's standing is an important consideration for judging the quality of the research he or she does.[7] The *Paoli* court recognized its importance.

That court, following the Supreme Court's precedent, noted that proposed testimony "must be reliable," but noted that "the standard for determining reliability 'is not that high' . . ."[8] It then distinguished between an expert's reasoning "process or technique" and her "conclusions," adverting to the original distinction in *Daubert*, noting that judges must only review the reasoning, not the conclusion.[9]

In addition, the court noted that "The goal is [to assess the] reliability [of expert testimony], not [its] certainty. Once admissibility has been determined, then it is for the trier of fact to determine the credibility of the expert witness."[10]

Moreover, the Third Circuit argued, "'*the evidentiary requirement of reliability is lower than the merits standard of correctness.*'"[11] Thus, it recognized that testimony could be reliable, but possibly not correct. Courts must ensure that the reliability review does not become a correctness review, as this intrudes on the right to a jury trial.

In addressing the concern from *Joiner* that there could be too great a "gap" between the data and opinion offered, the Third Circuit noted that the judge

---

[6]   35 F.3d 717 (3d Cir. 1994), *cert. denied*, 513 U.S. 1110 (1995).
[7]   David A. Eastmond, personal communication, 2004.
[8]   *In re TMI Litigation*, 193 F.3d 613, 664 (3d Cir. 1999).
[9]   *In re TMI Litigation*, 193 F.3d at 664.
[10] *In re TMI Litigation*, 193 F.3d at 665 (citing *Paoli II* at 743–746).
[11] *In re TMI Litigation*, 193 F.3d at 665 (quoting *In re Paoli Railroad Yard PCB Litigation*, 35 F3d 717, at 744) (emphasis added).

must determine whether the litigants' experts' conclusions "could reliably flow from the facts known to the expert and the methodology used."[12] A reliability review aims to ensure that the testimony is not too likely "to lead the factfinder to an erroneous conclusion."[13] This suggestion appears similar to a point from Chapter 4 that a judge should review the relation between a scientist's premises and conclusion in a nondeductive argument to ensure that it is minimally plausible (or, as I will say later, that it falls within a "zone of reasonable scientific disagreement").

This court's view seemed to presage that of *Kumho Tire*, namely, that an expert's opinion should have enough reliability compared with other scientific reasoning that it is not outside the range of scientific inferences drawn by reasonable scientists familiar with the subject matter and appropriate studies on the issue (more on this below). Properly stated, this suggests that a *judge's* role is to review expert testimony to ensure that it is more likely than not *reliable* in order to be heard by a jury, whereas a *jury's* role is to review the testimony together with other evidence to see whether a litigant's case in the judgment of the jury is more likely than not *correct*.

Thus, its summary view was that "[t]he grounds for the expert's opinion merely have to be good, they do not have to be perfect."[14] Moreover, plaintiffs "*do not have to prove their case twice*."[15] By this, the court appears to mean that plaintiffs should not have to present their full scientific case for causation twice and have it meet the same standards for *correctness* that they would have to meet for a jury decision. Finally, it is the jury's responsibility to "determine the credibility of the expert witness."[16]

The Third Circuit's admissibility doctrine preserves several needed distinctions: between a preliminary admissibility review, and the correctness of an expert's testimony, and between the role of judge and jury, without setting the standards of admissibility unreasonably high and without requiring plaintiffs to prove their case twice.[17] Despite these useful distinctions, however, the court

---

[12]   *In re TMI Litigation*, 193 F.3d at 665 (quoting *Heller v. Shaw Industries, Inc.*, 167 F.3d 146, 153 (3d Cir. 1999)).

[13]   *In re TMI Litigation*, 193 F.3d at 666.

[14]   *In re TMI Litigation*, 193 F.3d at 665 And, "[t]he test of admissibility is not whether a particular opinion has the best foundation, or even whether the opinion is supported by the best methodology or unassailable research. Rather, the test is whether the 'particular opinion is based on valid reasoning and reliable methodology.' . . . The goal is reliability, not certainty. Once admissibility has been determined, then it is for the trier of fact to determine the credibility of the expert witness" (quoting *Kannankeril v. Terminix International Inc.*, 128 F.3d 802 (3d Cir. 1997)).

[15]   *In re TMI Litigation*, 193 F.3d at 665.

[16]   *In re TMI Litigation*, 193 F.3d at 665.

[17]   In *Paoli*, the Third Circuit twice reviewed district court decisions on the exclusion of expert testimony and evidence, overturning it each time, forcing the trial court finally to have a jury trial on the factual issues in the case. In a bifurcated trial in which causation issues were separated from liability, the jury decided nearly all issues against plaintiffs. When the jury trial and verdict were appealed to the Third Circuit, it upheld admissibility and other

has not specified what "reliable" reasoning is or how to judge it. This needs to be developed.

By having a general conception of what "reliable" reasoning could be, courts can ease their own or their appointed experts' tasks. Courts must recognize that scientific arguments are based on *nondeductive inferences* with all that implies. *Inter alia*, they should recognize that an expert's testimony must be based on *all* the *scientifically relevant evidence* she has assembled and integrated to draw conclusions about causation. In particular, judges should not review whether *individual* pieces of evidence considered by themselves support plaintiffs' causal conclusions. Instead, they should ask if the scientific data could contribute to the conclusion. In reviewing scientific evidence in support of expert testimony they should be extremely reluctant to substitute their own views of scientifically relevant evidence for those of scientists. After all, scientists have the substantive expertise to assess the scientific relevance of studies; judges typically do not. Reviewing individual pieces of evidence for whether they individually support a causal conclusion would undermine every well-established scientific inference. It is hardly consistent with how scientists assimilate and utilize the myriad evidence in making scientific inferences. It would seem that a judge who did this, *ceteris paribus*, would abuse his or her discretion, thus, could and perhaps should open the decision to being overturned on appeal, because it is so contrary to the fundamentals of scientific reasoning. In reviewing proposed testimony, courts then should consider whether litigants' inferences based on all the evidence are "reliable" forms of inference (developed in the next paragraphs).[18]

Judges will need to adjudicate the "fit" of evidence with care, for example, whether and to what extent animal studies might be pertinent to a judgment of human toxicity. An expert should be able to articulate the reasons for such extrapolations and how this assists causal inference. But recall that this is a kind of evidence on which scientists routinely rely for making judgments about the toxicity of substances. However, it is a kind of evidence that is easy to mischaracterize. In short, judges should use great caution in contradicting scientists on the *scientific relevance* of particular kinds of evidence for inferences they make.

Judges also should not be misled by *a priori* weighting of different kinds of evidence, something various interest groups have promoted. That is,

---

judicial decisions leading up to the jury verdict. The result? The appellate court appeared to insist that expert testimony and scientific evidence not be excluded for spurious reasons even though in the end a jury did not find for plaintiffs. That exemplifies a proper distinction between admissibility and ultimate legal correctness, leaving proper roles for both the judge (preliminary screening of the evidence) and the jury (the ultimate weighing and assessing of the correctness of plaintiff's versus defendant's evidence).

18 Of course, judges should not insist on what they regard as "correct" or "probably correct" expert testimony. Such a screening principle would resemble the *Wade-Greaux* decision, would be much too demanding for torts, would erect new and higher barriers for plaintiffs than at present, intrude on the jury's authority, and violate the Constitution, *inter alia*.

such groups claim, for example, that epidemiological studies are among the strongest, while animal studies or case studies are weaker kinds of evidence, with the suggestions that the strongest form of evidence should always trump weaker kinds of evidence or the possibility that so-called weaker kinds of evidence should not be relied upon at all. However, if several pieces of seemingly "weak" evidence fit together well, they can support strong findings of causation. Recall that some distinguished cancer researchers have argued that there should be no "hierarchy" of kinds of evidence at all. Moreover, not infrequently consensus scientific committees integrate less than the strongest evidence to infer with considerable certainty that a substance causes adverse effects to humans. There are numerous patterns of evidence in which evidence that is individually "weaker" considered by itself, when it is properly integrated can support strong conclusions about the human toxicity of a substance (discussed later).

The Supreme Court's *Kuhmo Tire* opinion provides an important heuristic to guide admissibility. On procedural issues that Court explains that a trial judge needs

> The discretionary authority . . . both to avoid unnecessary "reliability" proceedings in ordinary cases where the reliability of an expert's methods is properly taken for granted, and to require appropriate proceedings in the less usual or more complex cases where cause for questioning the expert's reliability arises. Indeed, the Rules seek to avoid "unjustifiable expense and delay" as part of their search for "truth" and the "jus[t] determin[ation]" of proceedings.[19]

It then goes on to say that an expert may not testify if the testimony is outside the

> range where experts might reasonably differ, and where the jury must decide among the conflicting views of different experts even though the evidence is "shaky."[20]

It follows from this claim that if an expert's testimony is *within the range of opinion where experts might reasonably differ on a scientific issue even though the evidence is shaky*, then they should be admitted to testify. Call such testimony within a *zone of reasonable scientific disagreement*. Of course such testimony should reliably apply to the facts of the case as *Daubert* and the Amended Rule 702 require.

Moreover, the *Kumho Tire* suggestion makes sense within the larger goals of the legal system. To see this, consider an analogy to an argument presented by Charles Nesson on the acceptability of jury verdicts. He argues that "directed verdicts," a legal device by means of which a judge decides a case without

---

[19]   *Kumho Tire v. Carmichael*, 526 U.S. at 152–153.
[20]   *Kumho Tire v. Carmichael*, 526 U.S. at 153.

permitting it to go to a jury, are a means of helping to ensure the social acceptability of the legal outcome.

> [Directed verdicts] prevent the legal system from generating *unacceptable* verdicts. The directed verdict permits the court to withhold from the jury those cases in which a finding of guilt or liability would be *patently untenable* in light of the case presented by the plaintiff. The trial judge allows a case to go to the jury only if the evidence suffices to support a verdict either way.[21]

A directed verdict is not equivalent to the admissibility decisions we have considered (and is subject to a more stringent appellate review), but we can use it as an analogy to show why expert testimony within a zone of reasonable disagreement would contribute to acceptable jury verdicts.

The *Daubert* decision generally seeks to ensure that the ultimate legal decision comports with or is compatible with the science reasonably available for a case. Thus, its aim seems to be to winnow expert testimony by means of admissibility reviews so that a jury decision based in part either on plaintiffs' or on defendants' scientists' accounts will not be "patently untenable" scientifically. Expert testimony, that is, will be *within the bounds of respectable scientific views* about the issue involved. Consequently, whether the jury decides for plaintiffs or for defendants it will not be beyond respectable scientific reasoning on that issue and will be (broadly) scientifically acceptable (or at least not unacceptable). This does not ensure that the overall verdict will be acceptable (because that will be dependent on all the evidence and the jury's view of it), but an important aspect of it will be. It does not even ensure that the science will be correct, but it should be within the boundaries scientists consider open to legitimate debate at the time.

The suggestion above does not directly address "reliability," but utilizes something of a sociological surrogate to get at it. Expert testimony that is within the zone of reasonable scientific disagreement is reliable; testimony outside it is not. On this view judges need only to be able to make *comparative judgments* –"How does this expert's reasoning compare with others on similar issues?" – not absolute substantive scientific judgments about the particular argument. In making this assessment they would need to have an idea of reasonable arguments in the field by other respectable practitioners. That is, they would need to make judgments about whether an expert's reasoning on a subject sufficiently resembles the reasoning of other respectable experts within a scientific community in order to permit the testimony or whether it is so far beyond the range where experts on the subject might reasonably differ that she should not be permitted to testify. (There are analogous suggestions in the same spirit, recognizing the importance of conducting a preliminary

---

[21] Charles Nesson, "The Evidence or the Event? On Judicial Proof and the Acceptability of Verdicts," *Harvard Law Review* 98 (1985): 1357, 1369–1370.

screening of the experts, without the judge conducting such a stringent review of the experts that he/she effectively decides cases by erecting high standard of proof barriers.[22]) They also need not, and indeed, should not make judgments about the correctness of the science.

The proposal also is consistent with the amended Rule 702 requirements. If scientific testimony is within a zone of reasonable disagreement, it should be supported by sufficient facts or data and the testimony should be the product of reliable principles and methods. And, as indicated, it must then be reliably applied to the facts at issue. The idea is that if the conditions of the proposal were satisfied, then the first two conditions of Rule 702 would also be satisfied. The proposal seeks to provide judges a heuristic to guide their deliberations so they have another way of assessing scientific testimony, but perhaps without feeling quite so much at sea with the task and feeling that they have to make substantive scientific judgments about it.

Of course, this does not dispose of the problem, as judges are not part of scientific communities and do not routinely encounter arguments with which to make the reasonable comparisons. The *Kumho Tire* principle would be of greater assistance to judges utilizing scientific experts because a well-chosen expert would be closer to the scientific field and better able to judge whether qualified scientific experts' testimony fell within a zone of reasonable scientific disagreement. Some have used it for this purpose.[23] As the nature of studies and scientific inferences suggest, it is difficult for judges as nonexperts to enter substantively into the culture and arcana of scientific evidence (recall Ruden's account of the difficulty in assessing scientific studies [Chapter 4]). It is unlikely judges will be able to substantively assess studies and nondeductive reasoning as the experts themselves would. Nonetheless, they have been given this task. Judges who must review scientific issues on their own must still assess the *substantive basis* of scientific reasoning compared with other experts in the field, a task for which they are not trained and in all likelihood lack the

---

22   Green, *Bendectin and Birth Defects*, 312–317. Green suggests that a "decision based on the preponderance of the *available evidence*, rather than imposing an evidentiary threshold, would be closest in keeping with the role of the civil justice system" (317). Thus, where mature epidemiological evidence does not exist "analysis of the sufficiency of plaintiff's evidence ... would begin by considering the universe of available evidence of toxicity" (316). This proposal may discomfit some because "plaintiffs with relatively thin and attenuated evidence" could bring a case to trial, "[b]ut the reality is that stronger and better evidence is unavailable (through no fault of anyone) and a decision based on the preponderance of the available evidence, rather than imposing an evidentiary threshold, would be closest in keeping with the role of the civil justice system" (317). For other suggestions, see Cranor and Eastmond, "Scientific Ignorance and Reliable Patterns of Evidence in Toxic Tort Causation," 47.

23   For example, the judge in *Soldo v. Sandoz Pharmaceuticals Corp.*, 244 Supp. 2d 434 was advised by the opinions of three extramural scientists. Court appointed experts also were used in the silicone breast implant litigation. (Hooper, Cecil, and Willging, "Assessing Causation in Breast Implant Litigation," 139–189.)

substantive background. What can they do to guide their assessment of studies and evidence sufficiently well to carry out their tasks? Here there are some minimal suggestions that may help advance the discussion.

Courts could compare the reasoning of experts under consideration with patterns of evidence and reasoning that scientists have utilized in other venues to come to conclusions about causation.[24] In fact, this is the way in which *good* – not mistake-free – legally articulated reviews of scientific evidence could be helpful to judicial brethren in deciding other cases. The Third Circuit opinions are good models in this regard; so are some court decisions in the vaccine injury cases, with the *Stevens* decision in particular being quite helpful.[25] (Courts have done this, but in reverse: They have followed other courts in repeating mistakes made in earlier decisions. They also could learn from good reasoning.)

More important, there are readily available sources of information from which courts could learn. There are reasonable patterns of evidence that have been utilized by consensus scientific committees to conclude that substances can cause human harm. Judges can learn of the *varieties of patterns of evidence* that have implicated substances as toxic.[26] That is, courts could learn from the kinds of studies that such committees have utilized and relied on to infer causation. What kinds of studies have scientists themselves taken seriously? How have they combined them to learn about causation? What reasons did they articulate for considering certain studies as being more important or less important in reaching decisions? Moreover, judges can even see some of the patterns of inference that consensus committees have utilized to arrive at judgments about toxicity causation. That is, they can also begin to have a sense of committees' reasoning – why they have found compelling structure-activity evidence, case reports, or less than fully adequate epidemiological studies. For example, it is especially important for courts to look for the kinds of evidence where there was not overwhelming human evidence, as good human evidence is likely to be rare in tort cases. Analogous patterns provide models for *which combinations of evidence have been judged scientifically plausible and which can serve as a guide to not implausible patterns in the future.*

The proposal for assessing expert reasoning and its scientific foundation has both a negative and a positive purpose. At a minimum it serves as a strong caution against some of the scientifically mistaken reasons courts have provided for excluding evidence. That is, if a judge knows that an appropriate combination of animal studies alone or animal studies plus evidence about "mode of action" have justified scientists on expert scientific bodies or within

---

[24] Judges sometimes have sometimes utilized this form of argument by analogy when they followed other courts in *mistakenly excluding* evidence.

[25] *Stevens v. the Secretary of Health and Human Services.*

[26] Developed later in this chapter.

governmental agencies in concluding that a substance is a known or probable human carcinogen or other toxicant, this should caution them to exercise care in excluding scientific testimony based on such foundations. It also provides them with a model for their decision.

Similarly, if judges recognize that scientists have utilized case studies plus animal studies, each taken individually not the strongest evidence by itself, to conclude that a vaccine causes adverse reactions in humans or vinyl chloride causes a rare form of liver cancer, this reminds them of the importance of such evidence and the strength that integrated evidence can have.[27] It also should preclude them from excluding analogous evidence for bad reasons. Whether such forms of reasoning based on such evidence are *correct* is another matter, but that, as the Third Circuit held, *is not the subject of an admissibility review*. (After all their task is not to prevent scientific mistakes, but to ensure that an expert's testimony falls within a zone of reasonable disagreement.)

There is also a more positive feature to my suggestion. If an expert utilizes an inference to the best explanation that has the same evidentiary components (e.g., animal studies plus case reports, or animal studies plus mode of action evidence) as other good scientific explanations have had, this provides a presumptive scientific reason for the plausibility of such arguments, unless there are good reasons to the contrary concerning the particular inference. That is, it could create an intellectual presumption of reliability.

Consequently, in order for a judge to assess the plausibility of an expert's testimony, he or she would consider *analogues* to other good arguments and utilize an informal inferential presumption. It spares judges making particular substantive scientific judgments, but provides guidance by analogy, unless there are good reasons against the form of reasoning. Of course, there will be a party ready to challenge both the argument on the other side and a judge's ruling. Moreover, even if the litigants' expert survives the admissibility review, at trial the opponent has the traditional devices pointed out by the *Daubert* Court and the Advisory Committee on Evidence Rules: "Vigorous cross-examination, presentation of contrary evidence, and careful instruction on the burden of proof . . . [to attack] . . . shaky but admissible evidence."[28] And, the judge retains the option of directing a verdict or issuing a judgment

---

[27] Although vinyl chloride was initially identified as causing cancer based on such evidence, it has been verified by more extensive epidemiological studies. (International Agency for Research on Cancer, "Vinyl Chloride," *Monographs on the Evaluation of Carcinogenic Risks to Humans, Supplement 7* (1987): 373. Rev. 10 Feb. 1998. Available at: http://www-cie.iarc.fr/htdocs/monographs/suppl7/vinylchloride.html ("A large number of epidemiological studies and case reports have substantiated the causal association between vinyl chloride and angiosarcoma of the liver. Several studies also confirm that exposure to vinyl chloride causes other forms of cancer, i.e., hepatocellular carcinoma, brain tumours, lung tumours and malignancies of the lymphatic and haematopoietic system.")

[28] *Daubert v. Merrell Dow Pharmaceutical, Inc.*, 509 U.S. at 595–596; Advisory Committee on Evidence Rules, "Proposed Amendment: Rule 702" (December 2000).

not withstanding the verdict, if the proffered evidence compares so unfavorably with an opponent's evidence that no reasonable jury could decide for the proponent.

Finally, there is a fariness rationale to the proposal. Based on what is known in a scientific field, if scientists reason about the known data in ways that are not outside the boundaries of reasonable scientific disagreement, it is a matter of fairness that courts admit such experts. This permits courts (a) to exclude scientific testimony that is outside the zone of reasonable disagreement as bad scientific reasoning, and (b) is fair to both sides in that jurors can hear reasonable intepretations of the evidence. When there is reasonable disagreement in a field about what studies show and what can be reasonably inferred from them, as a matter of fairness the experts should be heard.

Some Consequences of the Proposal

If courts were to review evidence in accordance with the above principles, what might change? It is plausible to suppose that admissibility decisions would be more scientifically accurate (at least not outside the boundaries of respectable scientific judgments on the issues) and comport better with how scientists themselves assess evidence.

Such decisions would increase the acceptability of admissibility decisions within the scientific community, because any admitted experts would be *within the range where reasonable experts could disagree*, to the extent judges were successful in assessing this. To the extent that judges review expert testimony more in line with actual scientific practice, this would foster greater acceptance of legal decisions in the scientific community. (This also might foster greater acceptability of court decisions within the larger community.)

Court admissibility decisions in accordance with the principles proposed would also reassure respectable scientists who testify within the zone of scientific reasonableness that their testimony will not be judicially condemned as inadequate. It would perhaps not drive scientific experts away from the law quite so quickly, as now occurs. As an additional benefit it might bring about greater scientific participation in the legal system (although this will likely be difficult given the controversial nature of the adversary system).

Admissibility decisions that permit more information within a zone of scientific reasonableness improves the chances of an accurate decision. This should also reduce the institutional bias exhibited by many of the restrictive admissibility rules reviewed in Chapter 6. Juries would then choose between reasonable scientific views. That is, if courts recognize a wider range of evidence as a reasonable basis of expert testimony, this would eliminate some of the past problems that have asymmetrically disadvantaged the party with the burden of proof. It would create a more even ground of competition on admissibility issues.

In addition, the suggested approach would lessen some of the admissibility barriers that have been erected as a result of the current implementation of *Daubert* and its progeny. It also would modestly increase plaintiff access to the law (because it will increase modestly plaintiffs' experts' admissibility) by slightly easing lawyer screening.[29] It would increase the possibility of justice for some plaintiffs.

Decisions in accordance with these principles would reduce or eliminate the risk of intruding on the right to a jury trial because judges should have less reason to intrude where there are legitimate scientific disagreements. There might still be mistakes because experts on one side or the other of a scientific debate could still be mistaken, or the analogical argument I suggest might not be unerringly accurate, but at the time of the trial the scientific issues would be legitimately contested. There do not appear to be significant downsides for defendants. They might have to defend more cases in court and might decide to settle more cases once plaintiffs' experts are admitted, but they are not without resources to address these issues and the quality of science would improve.[30]

Finally, decisions in accordance with these principles might well lead to more just outcomes where both parties to the bar can have their experts admitted and argue their cases before a jury of their peers. At least one side will not be asymmetrically excluded because of simplified admissibility guidance. If one side's experts testify outside the zone of respectable scientific disagreement, they should lose the admissibility review.

Implementation of the above suggestions would constrain scientific disagreements to those about which respectable scientists would disagree. It would bring greater congruence between the current but contested state of science and the outcome of legal cases with cases decided on the basis of the balance of available evidence. However, it has substantial disadvantages when viewed within a larger social and institutional context.

Given the woeful lack of scientific knowledge about the universe of chemical substances and the generic postmarket structural incentives created by a causation requirement in torts, even the most sensitive application of this proposal may not be adequate. Because the tort law considers causation claims after substances have been in the market, it leaves in place pernicious incentives for defendants whose products are subject only to postmarket regulation not to test their substances and not to report on the toxicity of their products.[31] The reason for this is that because plaintiffs have the burden of producing evidence in support of their causation claims, defendants need only to play defense and argue that the evidence is inadequate, or subject to so many uncertainties that

---

[29] There will remain substantial upfront costs for plaintiffs in particular because they have the burden of proof and because of judicial scrutiny of experts.

[30] *Daubert*, 595–596.

[31] Berger, "Eliminating General Causation," 2135.

it does not support a causation claim. In such circumstances, if defendants or others have not well tested their products for toxicity, they have no incentives to do so, because if test results show adverse effects, they can only cause them legal problems. When this context is added to the substantial ignorance of the products in the market, it creates substantial barriers to the tort law's functioning well, especially with respect to its deterrence function.

Because of these problems, there may be a need for different liability or admissibility rules to overcome these perverse structural incentives in order to provide compensation to plaintiffs and to create incentives for firms to better test and inform the public about potential harms from their products. This is a topic I sketch in Chapter 8.

In the remainder of this chapter, I amplify the suggestions made here for admissibility rules in order to give greater content to the procedure. I consider in more detail some features of good scientific arguments as revealed by expert scientific committees. This illustrates sound scientific arguments for toxicity conclusions, but not arguments based largely on human evidence. I hope this will usefully indicate the power of more complex patterns of evidence for causation conclusions. It seems these have largely been missing from much of the discussion of admissibility. And, because they are more difficult evidentiary patterns to assess, they provide examples of good patterns of integrated evidence and suggest models for how courts might better address more complex evidence when overwhelming amounts of human evidence are not available.

PATTERNS OF TOXICOLOGICAL EVIDENCE

There are various patterns of evidence that experts on consensus scientific committees have utilized to judge that a substance is a known or probable human carcinogen. These views are represented by international scientific bodies, such as the International Agency for Research on Cancer (IARC), national scientific bodies, such as the National Toxicology Program, and well-known scientists. Such views provide background and guidance for understanding scientific testimony for admissibility. I largely use carcinogens as the example because I have some familiarity with this area of science and there are well-recognized scientific bodies that articulate the scientific basis for assessing the toxicity of carcinogens. I also sketch two examples of scientific inferences concerning noncarcinogenic adverse effects to indicate the patterns of evidence are not unique to carcinogens.

However, the fact of consensus scientific views should not obscure that there will be some scientists who may depart from the consensus in one way or another – some may in good conscience judge that substances are carcinogens on the basis of less evidence than will be described as part of the consensus later, whereas others may in all good conscience demand more by way of evidence that substances are carcinogens than the consensus position represents. This does not mean that some are right and some are wrong; in the current state of knowledge that may be unknowable. Rather, courts need to be sensitive to legitimate scientific disagreements and permit experts to testify as long as their testimony is within the "zone of expert disagreement." This is critical for the fundamental fairness in torts concerning scientific testimony. In the pages that follow, I describe these consensus views in order to present some of the main patterns of evidence on which scientists base their views in judging whether a substance is more likely than not a human carcinogen, to present some good scientific arguments and to further illustrate show how some of the simple aphorisms for reviewing scientific evidence can be so misleading.

The International Agency for Research on Cancer

What I am calling consensus views are clearly expressed in documents from the International Agency for Research on Cancer (IARC). IARC is part of the World Health Organization. Most scientists consider it the definitive body for the identification of cancer-causing agents. The purpose of this program "is to prepare, with the help of international working groups of experts, and to publish in the form of monographs, critical reviews and evaluations of evidence on the carcinogenicity of a wide range of human exposures."[32] IARC carefully reviews studies from the peer-reviewed literature and decides which ones should be part of their deliberations. The *Monographs*, which record the evaluations of working groups created by IARC, then represent "scientific, qualitative judgements about the evidence for or against carcinogenicity provided by the available data."[33]

IARC categorizes the evidence for carcinogens into several classes based on consensus scientific judgments, "reflecting the strength of the evidence derived from studies in humans and in experimental animals and from other relevant data."[34] The evidence may support the judgment that an agent or mixture *is* "carcinogenic to humans [Group 1]," "probably carcinogenic to humans [Group 2A]," "possibly carcinogenic to humans [Group 2B]," "not classifiable as to its carcinogenicity to humans [Group 3]," or "probably not carcinogenic to humans [Group 4]."[35] Most important for our purposes are the evidentiary considerations that result in classification of substances as carcinogenic

32 IARC, Preamble, Section 2: Objective and Scope, *Monograph Series*. Rev. 5 Jan. 1999. Available at: http://www-cie.iarc.fr/monoeval/objectives.html.
33 IARC, Preamble, Section 2: Objective and Scope, *Monograph Series*. Rev. 5 Jan. 1999. Available at: http://www-cie.iarc.fr/monoeval/objectives.html.
34 IARC, Preamble, Section 12: Evaluation, *Monograph Series*. Rev. 5 Jan. 1999. Available at: http://www-cie.iarc.fr/monoeval/eval.html.
35 IARC, Preamble, Section 12: Evaluation, *Monograph Series*. Rev. 5 Jan. 1999. Available at: http://www-cie.iarc.fr/monoeval/eval.html.

to humans and probably carcinogenic to humans, as substances in these categories would easily satisfy the tort law standards of proof. The category "possibly carcinogenic" to humans is also worthy of consideration because IARC's standards for classification are so stringent that there might well be substances in this class that would satisfy the tort law's more likely than not standard of proof for toxicity. However, I do not discuss this class of substances. More important, however, a substance need not be in one of these categories in order for tort lawsuit to be successful. Under the new *Daubert* rules, a scientist should be able to advance a good argument for a product's toxicity and it should be admissible, provided the judge understands its reliability.

IARC classifies about sixty-six agents and groups of agents in Group I as carcinogenic in humans (this is a moving target, as the list changes frequently). There are another twenty-nine mixtures and exposure circumstances that are also classified as group I human carcinogens. In addition, there are about another sixty-six substances, agents, mixtures, and exposures that have been classified in group 2A as probably carcinogenic in humans.[36]

Substances are judged carcinogenic to humans, or as known human carcinogens, "when there is *sufficient evidence* of carcinogenicity in humans."[37] For most of the substances identified as known human carcinogens there is quite good human epidemiological data. However, IARC does not demand such evidence to classify something as a known human carcinogen. IARC classifies an agent as a human carcinogen "when evidence of carcinogenicity in humans is less than sufficient but there is *sufficient evidence* of carcinogenicity in experimental animals and strong evidence in exposed humans that the agent (mixture) acts through a relevant mechanism of carcinogenicity."[38]

This point should be emphasized. *Human* evidence is not necessary for IARC to judge that a substance is a human carcinogen. If there is good evidence that it is an animal carcinogen and strong supporting evidence that the agent acts via biological mechanisms that are likely to cause cancer in humans, it will classify such substances as human carcinogens. That is, other kinds of evidence may help support a judgment that a substance is a human carcinogen.

Consider the example of ethylene oxide (ETO), the same substance that was the object of litigation in *Allen v. Pennsylvania Engineering*. ETO, produced since the early 1900s, has been used as a chemical intermediate and in sterilizing medical instruments and supplies, as well as for the fumigation of spices. The

---

[36] IARC, "Overall Evaluations of Carcinogenicity to Humans, Group 1: Carcinogenic to Humans," *Monograph Series*. Rev. 7 July 2004. Available at: http://www-cie.iarc.fr/monoeval/crthgr01.html.

[37] "Sufficient evidence of carcinogenicity: The Working Group considers that a causal relationship has been established between exposure to the agent, mixture or exposure circumstance and human cancer. That is, a positive relationship has been observed between the exposure and cancer in studies in which chance, bias and confounding could be ruled out with reasonable confidence" (http://www-cie.iarc.fr/monoeval/eval.html [rev. 5 Jan. 1999]).

[38] IARC, Preamble, Section 12: Evaluation, *Monograph Series*. Rev. 5 Jan. 1999. Available at: http://www-cie.iarc.fr/monoeval/eval.html.

highest exposures to ETO typically occurred in sterilization (the exposure Mr. Allen faced) and fumigation.

At one time, IARC judged that ethylene oxide (ETO) was a *probable human carcinogen*, but in 1994 reclassified it as a known human carcinogen. It based the reclassification on the fact that there was *limited* evidence that ETO was carcinogenic in humans. This means that there was some evidence that ETO caused cancer in humans, but not all alternative explanations could be ruled out with *reasonable certainty*. IARC, however, had *sufficient evidence* that it was an animal carcinogen, and other information. The supporting evidence was that it

> induces a sensitive, persistent dose-related increase in the frequency of chromosomal aberrations . . . ; has been associated with malignancies in the lymphatic and haematopoietic system in both humans and experimental animals; induces dose-related increase in the frequency of hemoglobin adducts in exposed humans and dose-related increases in the number of adducts in both DNA and hemoglobin in exposed rodents; induces gene mutation and heritable translocations in germ cells of exposed rodents; and is a powerful mutagen and clastogen at all phylogenetic levels.[39]

In short, even though there was some epidemiological evidence that ETO is carcinogenic in humans, persuasive evidence for classifying it as a human carcinogen came from animal studies and a variety of short-term and mechanistic studies showing that it is a strong multisite mutagen (can cause DNA mutations in a variety of tissues and organs) and causes DNA damage to somatic and germ cells in humans and other mammals.

For substances that are *probably carcinogenic* to humans, IARC utilizes a wider range of evidence.

> This category is used when there is *limited evidence* of carcinogenicity in humans[40] and sufficient evidence of carcinogenicity in experimental animals. In some cases, an agent (mixture) may be classified in this category when there is *inadequate evidence* of carcinogenicity in humans and *sufficient evidence* of carcinogenicity in experimental animals and strong evidence that the carcinogenesis is mediated by a mechanism that also operates in humans.[41] Exceptionally, an agent, mixture or exposure circumstance

[39] IARC, *Monograph Series* 60 (1994): 73, 139.

[40] "Limited evidence of carcinogenicity: A positive association has been observed between exposure to the agent, mixture or exposure circumstance and cancer for which a causal interpretation is considered by the Working Group to be credible, but chance, bias or confounding could not be ruled out with reasonable confidence." IARC, Preamble, Section 12: Evaluation, *Monograph Series*. Rev. 5 Jan. 1999. Available at: http://www-cie.iarc.fr/monoeval/eval.html.

[41] "Inadequate evidence of carcinogenicity: The available studies are of insufficient quality, consistency or statistical power to permit a conclusion regarding the presence or absence of a causal association between exposure and cancer, or no data on cancer in humans are available." IARC, Preamble, Section 12: Evaluation, *Monograph Series*. Rev. 5 Jan. 1999. Available at: http://www-cie.iarc.fr/monoeval/eval.html.

may be classified in this category solely on the basis of *limited evidence* of carcinogenicity in humans.[42]

IARC's list of probable human carcinogens includes some comparatively familiar substances such as benzidine-related dyes, the pesticide captafol, a commonly used cleaning solvent trichloroethylene (one of the substances in the *Magistrini* case), the fire retardant tris(2,3-dibromopropyl) phosphate (once used to fireproof baby clothes), PCBs (the toxicant at issue in *Joiner*), and some naturally occurring exposures such as the herpes virus and ultraviolet radiation.[43] Many of these substances have been upgraded from possible to probable human carcinogens based on various kinds of nonhuman evidence, including animal evidence, molecular data, and evidence of mechanisms of action.

The National Toxicology Program

Similar, but not quite identical, categories of classification and similar principles of toxicology and biology are utilized by the U.S. Government's National Toxicology Program (NTP). According to NTP, a substance is classified as a known *human* carcinogen when "[t]here is sufficient evidence of carcinogenicity from studies in humans which indicates a causal relationship between exposure to the agent and human cancer."[44] It recognizes about fifty-four substances as known human carcinogens. NTP requires the use of human evidence to classify a substance as a human carcinogen, contrary to the view of IARC, although NTP may have a broader view of human evidence, perhaps, than IARC. We see this regarding benzidine-based dyes. Thus, we have two well-known and respectable scientific bodies that exhibit some scientific and normative disagreement about what they regard as a known human carcinogen.

NTP's second category is one in which a substance, mixture, or exposure is "reasonably anticipated to be a human carcinogen." There are about 185 substances in this class. This is analogous to IARC's "probable human carcinogen" category. For this classification, there are several alternative evidentiary patterns that might identify a substance as a probable carcinogen:

- limited evidence of carcinogenicity from studies in humans, which indicates that causal interpretation is credible, but that alternative explanations, such as chance, bias, or confounding factors, could not adequately be excluded, *or*

---

[42] IARC, Preamble, Section 12: Evaluation, *Monograph Series*. Rev. 5 Jan. 1999. Available at: http://www-cie.iarc.fr/monoeval/eval.html.

[43] IARC, *Monograph Series*. Rev. 5 Jan. 1999. Available at: http://www-cie.iarc.fr/monoeval/eval.html.

[44] National Toxicology Program, Introduction, *Eleventh Annual Report on Carcinogens*, 2. Available at: http://ntp.niehs.nih.gov/ntp/roc/toc11.html.

- there is sufficient evidence of carcinogenicity from studies in experimental animals which indicates there is an increased incidence of malignant and/or a combination of malignant and benign tumors: (1) in multiple species or at multiple tissue sites, or (2) by multiple routes of exposure, or (3) to an unusual degree with regard to incidence, site or type of tumor, or age at onset; *or*
- there is less than sufficient evidence of carcinogenicity in humans or laboratory animals; however, the agent, substance or mixture belongs to a well defined, *structurally related class of substances* whose members are listed in a previous Report on Carcinogens as either a known to be human carcinogen or reasonably anticipated to be human carcinogen, or there is convincing relevant information that the agent acts through mechanisms indicating it would likely cause cancer in humans.[45]

What is notable about these listing criteria for substances reasonably anticipated to be human carcinogens is that NTP will classify substances as likely human carcinogens on the basis of *good animal evidence* alone *or* on *similarity to a well defined "structurally related class" of substances known or likely to be carcinogens* or on convincing information about the *toxicological mechanism* indicating that it would likely *cause cancer in humans*. If courts are going to be reviewing substantive scientific data and inferences about the toxicity of substances, they need to obtain as much sophistication about the varied patterns of evidence as they can.

To summarize: two of the most important scientific bodies that evaluate the carcinogenic potential of substances, despite minor differences, are largely in agreement concerning pertinent criteria for classifying substances as known or likely human carcinogens. Although they judge that the best evidence for classifying something as a known human carcinogen is *good* human evidence, typically provided by good human epidemiological studies, importantly IARC does not consider it a *necessary condition*. Both IARC and NTP will conclude that a substance is a probable human carcinogen on the basis of animal evidence alone or on the basis of animal studies and various other kinds of supporting evidence.

These leading scientific bodies have a broader view of the pertinent *kinds* of scientific evidence and how it could fit together to provide an inference about the carcinogenicity of substances than do many federal judges who have been asked to rule on the admissibility of scientific evidence or expert testimony. Of course, this is not surprising. However, courts can learn from these consensus scientific bodies to guide their own reviews of scientific testimony. This would be especially important for understanding issues of general causation in toxic

---

[45] Criteria were first listed published on September 26, 1996, and are listed at the NTP Web site, http://ntp.niehs.nih.gov/ntpweb/index.cfm?objectid=03C9CE38-E5CD-EE56-D21B9.

tort cases. They can learn whether or not the substances likely cause cancer, some of the specific cancers they cause and, most important, the patterns of evidence committees have used to guide the conclusion.[46] The question of specific causation – whether a particular substance caused a particular plaintiff's injury – is different. Answering this question clearly requires much more specific information about the plaintiff, her context of injury and exposure information, in addition to the general causal properties of a substance.

Moreover, there is a wide range of data and theories that experts, whom the scientific organizations call on to judge the carcinogenicity of substances, utilize to make their inferences about toxicity, which is indicated by NTP:

> Conclusions regarding carcinogenicity in humans or experimental animals are based on scientific judgment, with consideration given to *all relevant information*. Relevant information includes, but is not limited to dose response, route of exposure, chemical structure, metabolism, pharmacokinetics, sensitive sub populations, genetic effects, or other data relating to mechanism of action or factors that may be unique to a given substance.[47]

Furthermore, these agencies recognize that mechanistic or toxicological information might either condemn or exonerate a substance as a likely human carcinogen. In many cases such data is used to support a judgment that a substance is a human carcinogen, but such data, as the NTP notes, may also indicate the agent acts through mechanisms that do not operate in humans and would therefore not reasonably be anticipated to cause cancer in humans.[48] Leading researchers tend to agree with these national and international bodies both in the general conclusions and in the principles underlying the conclusions as we consider at the end of this chapter.[49]

Toxicologically Reliable Patterns of Evidence

The general guidance just provided from IARC and NTP is further exemplified by particular scientific judgments these scientific bodies have made about the

---

[46] Courts must exercise care in concluding that exposures can only cause the cancers listed by such a committee, because a product's cancer-causing potential may be broader than has been indicated by the committee's deliberations. For example, because ethylene oxide is a multisite mutagen, it may cause a much wider range of cancers than those that have been identified in either human or animal studies.

[47] U.S. Department of Health and Human Services, National Toxicology Program, "Listing Criteria." Available at: http://ntp.niehs.nih.gov/ntpweb/index.cfm?objectid= 03C9CE38-E5CD-EE56-D21B94351DBC8FC3 (visited May 28, 1999) (emphasis added).

[48] U.S. Department of Health and Human Services, National Toxicology Program, "Listing Criteria." Available at: http://ntp.niehs.nih.gov/ntpweb/index.cfm?objectid= 03C9CE38-E5CD-EE56-D21B94351DBC8FC3 (visited May 28, 1999).

[49] Tomatis *et al.*, "Avoided and Avoidable Risks of Cancer," 97–105; Cogliano *et al.*,"Science and Practice," 1269–1274, esp. 1270.

likely human carcinogenicity of substances. I review several patterns of evidence for carcinogens from the literature. These are representative – not exhaustive – examples of the kinds and patterns of evidence that a substance probably or certainly causes cancer in humans.

There is, however, a cautionary note. In several respects, even these examples are *too robust* to serve as evidentiary models for courts to utilize to screen expert testimony and its foundations. Litigants' experts need only show that their testimony is "more likely than not *reliable,*" or as I have argued, "within a zone of reasonable scientific disagreement," not necessarily correct.[50] The patterns that follow, however, are models of evidentiary support for an *ultimate conclusion* that a substance is either a known human carcinogen or more likely than not a human carcinogen. Moreover, they represent peer-reviewed, *consensus judgments* (again, something not required for admissibility). The patterns are taken from quite cautious and respectable scientific bodies, and have a high degree of certainty of being *correct.* Thus, these patterns are much more than sufficient as models for a reliability judgment. They also do not represent necessary conditions because of the overwhelming evidence favoring them, the certainty with which they are assessed, their correctness, and the fact that they are consensus judgments.

Consider first some evidentiary patterns utilized by the International Agency for Research on Cancer to conclude that a substance certainly *is* a human carcinogen.[51] As indicated, most of these have good human epidemiological evidence to support that claim. (Analogously, when judges are reviewing good positive human epidemiological studies that all point in the same direction as evidence of causation in tort cases, their decisions are quite easy.) However, there are two substances and one form of radiation that are human carcinogens, but for which there is not sufficiently good human evidence for the judgment. In addition, the National Toxicology Program lists three benzidine-based dyes, Direct Black 38, Direct Blue 6, and Direct Brown 95, as known human carcinogens, but there is no epidemiological evidence to support these assessments (despite the language about human evidence).

Thus, between these two scientific bodies there are six substances classified as known human carcinogens, but for *none* of these is human epidemiological evidence sufficient to conclude that there is a causal relationship between exposure to the substance and human cancer.

50 For an extended discussion of "reliable," see Michael H. Graham, "The Expert Witness Predicament: Determining 'Reliable' under the Gatekeeping Test of Daubert, Kumho and Proposed Amended Rule 702 of the Federal Rules of Evidence," *Miami Law Review* 54 (2000): 317.

51 IARC, "Overall Evaluations of Carcinogenicity to Humans, Group 1: Carcinogenic to Humans," *Monographs.* Rev. 7 July 2004. Available at: http://cie.iarc.fr/htdocs/monoeval/crthgr01.html (visited September 9, 2000).

For two of these six substances – ethylene oxide (ETO)[52] and dioxin (2,3,7,8-tetrachlorodibenzo-para-dioxin)[53] – there is "limited" human evidence of carcinogenicity. Thus, "chance, bias or confounding could not be ruled out with reasonable confidence" in the relevant epidemiological studies.[54] For four – neutron radiation, Direct Black 38, Direct Blue 6, and Direct Brown 95 – there are no adequate epidemiological studies.

In all six cases, there was sufficient evidence of carcinogenicity in *animals* plus additional supporting evidence that led the scientific body to conclude that these substances were human carcinogens. ETO is an alkylating agent (which means that it places an alkyl chemical group on the DNA that interferes with its normal functioning) and induces genetic mutations and chromosomal breakage in a wide range of species.[55] Dioxin is a multisite carcinogen in experimental animals that acts through a receptor-mediated mechanism in cells that is believed to be common to animals and humans – the "aryl-hydrocarbon receptor" introduced in Chapter 4 under good structure-activity evidence.[56]

[52]   IARC, "Ethylene Oxide," *Monograph Series* 60 (1994): 73. Rev. 26 Aug. 1997. Available at: http://www-cie.iarc.fr/htdocs/monographs/vol60/m60--02.htm.

[53]   IARC, "Polychlorinated Dibenzo-*para*-Dioxins," *Monograph Series* 69 (1997): 33. Available at: http://www-cie.iarc.fr/htdocs/monographs/vol69/dioxin.html.

[54]   IARC, "Polychlorinated Dibenzo-*para*-Dioxins," *Monograph Series* 69 (1997): 33. Available at: http://www-cie.iarc.fr/htdocs/monographs/vol69/dioxin.html.

[55]   IARC, "Ethylene Oxide," *Monograph Series* 60 (1994): 73. Rev. 26 Aug. 1997. Available at: http://www-cie.iarc.fr/htdocs/monographs/vol60/m60--02.htm. ("There is limited evidence in humans for the carcinogenicity of ethylene oxide.

There is sufficient evidence in experimental animals for the carcinogenicity of ethylene oxide.

In making the overall evaluation, the Working Group took into consideration the following supporting evidence. Ethylene oxide is a directly acting alkylating agent that: (i) induces a sensitive, persistent dose-related increase in the frequency of chromosomal aberrations and sister chromatid exchange in peripheral lymphocytes and micronuclei in bone-marrow cells of exposed workers; (ii) has been associated with malignancies of the lymphatic and haematopoietic system in both humans and experimental animals; (iii) induces a dose-related increase in the frequency of haemoglobin adducts in exposed humans and dose-related increases in the numbers of adducts in both DNA and haemoglobin in exposed rodents; (iv) induces gene mutations and heritable translocations in germ cells of exposed rodents; and (v) is a powerful mutagen and clastogen at all phylogenetic levels.")

[56]   IARC, "Polychlorinated Dibenzo-*para*-Dioxins," *Monograph Series* 69 (1997): 33. Available at: http://www-cie.iarc.fr/htdocs/monographs/vol69/dioxin.html. ("There is limited evidence in humans for the carcinogenicity of 2,3,7,8-tetrachlorodibenzo-para-dioxin.... There is sufficient evidence in experimental animals for the carcinogenicity of 2,3,7,8-tetrachlorodibenzo-para-dioxin.

In making the overall evaluation, the Working Group took into consideration the following supporting evidence: (i) 2,3,7,8-TCDD is a multi-site carcinogen in experimental animals that has been shown by several lines of evidence to act through a mechanism involving the Ah receptor; (ii) this receptor is highly conserved in an evolutionary sense and functions the same way in humans as in experimental animals; (iii) tissue concentrations are similar both in heavily exposed human populations in which an increased overall cancer risk was observed and in rats exposed to carcinogenic dosage regimens in bioassays.")

Neutron radiation causes more severe tissue damage than x-rays and gamma rays, forms of radiation known to cause human cancer, thus by transitivity IARC concludes that neutron radiation also causes cancer.[57]

NTP's reasoning on benzidine-based dyes is the following.

> Dyes that are metabolized to benzidine are *known to be human carcinogens* based on the following evidence: (1) benzidine is *known to be a human carcinogen*, (2) metabolism of benzidine-based dyes results in the release of free benzidine in humans and in all experimental animal species studied, . . . and (3) benzidine exposure from exposure to benzidine-based dyes is equivalent to exposure to equimolar doses of benzidine . . .[58]

Thus, there is inadequate human evidence that these three dyes cause cancer, but it is by means of the above considerations that NTP lists them as known human carcinogens.

These constitute easy but illustrative cases. The evidence *taken as a whole* for each provides sufficient evidence for scientists to conclude certainly and unequivocally that each of the six is a human carcinogen. And it is important to emphasize that conclusions as to causation are *inferential* in nature. Scientists have inferred with high certainty that these substances are human carcinogens without having strong human epidemiological studies. Courts should not expect more. In toxic tort litigation they are not likely to see such robust and impressive evidence because of scientific ignorance about the universe of chemical substances. The conclusions concerning the six substances just mentioned are more obviously inferences because they involve integrating quite different kinds of evidence (a position a court typically finds itself in other areas). Finally, the various patterns of evidence are different from each other, but lead to the same conclusion – the substance *is* carcinogenic to humans.

Second, consider several substances that IARC classifies as *probable* human carcinogens. For four substances – 1,3-butadiene,[59] tetrachloroethylene,[60]

57   IARC, "Neutrons," *Monograph Series* 75 (2000): n.p. Rev. 19 Apr. 2000. Available at: http://www-cie.iarc.fr/htdocs/monographs/vol75/neutrons.html.

58   National Toxicology Program, "Benzidine and Dyes Metabolized to Benzidine," in *Eleventh Annual Report on Carcinogens* (Research Triangle Park, NC: U.S. Dept. of Health and Human Services, Public Health Service, National Toxicology Program, 2002). Available at: http://ntp.niehs.nih.gov/ntp/roc/eleventh/profiles/s020benz.pdf.

59   1,3-butadiene is used in high volume in the manufacture of a wide range of polymers, including styrene–butadiene rubber, polybutadiene, nitrile rubber, acrylonitrile–butadiene–styrene resins and styrene–butadiene latexes. It is also an intermediate in the production of various other chemicals. IARC, "1,3-Butadiene," *Monograph Series* 71 (1999): 109. Rev. 12 Apr. 1999. Available at: http://www-cie.iarc.fr/htdocs/monographs/vol71/002-butadiene.html.

60   IARC, "Tetrachloroethylene," *Monograph Series* 63 (1995): 159. Rev. 20 May 1997. Available at: http://www-cie.iarc.fr/htdocs/monographs/vol63/tetrachloroethylene.htm.

trichloroethylene,[61] and formaldehyde[62] − there is *limited evidence* of carcinogenicity in humans and *sufficient evidence* of carcinogenicity in animals. Again, there were some human epidemiological studies, but some alternative explanations for the results of the studies could not be ruled out with reasonable certainty. For these four substances, animal evidence and "other data relevant to the evaluation of carcinogenicity and its mechanisms" have provided reasons for the scientific body to judge that the substance probably is carcinogenic in humans. For each of these, human evidence contributed to the judgment but was not decisive.

For two other substances − MOCA,[63] and an anticancer drug − 1-(2-chloroethyl)-3-cyclohexyl-1-nitrosourea (CCNU),[64] there is *inadequate* evidence of carcinogenicity in humans and *sufficient evidence* of carcinogenicity in animals. IARC and the NTP classify these substances as *probable* human carcinogens. Here traditional human epidemiological evidence directly contributed little or nothing to the judgment that the substance is a likely human carcinogen. That inference is based on evidence from animals, human and animal studies of agents with similar properties, and additional supportive evidence.

The toxicology of 4,4'-methylenebis(2-chloroaniline) (MOCA) illustrates one of these patterns of evidence. MOCA produces a "significant excess of hepatoma" (liver tumors) in mice, lung tumors in rats, as well as "an excess of hepatomas and mammary carcinomas," whereas the target organ in dogs is the bladder.[65] In rats MOCA also produced tumors in the Zymbal (an ear) gland, an organ clearly present in rats, but possibly not in humans (there is controversy

---

[61] IARC, "Trichloroethylene," *Monograph Series* 63 (1995): 75. Rev. 20 May 1997. Available at: http://www-cie.iarc.fr/htdocs/monographs/vol63/trichloroethylene.htm.

[62] "Taken together, the epidemiological studies suggest a causal relationship between exposure to formaldehyde and nasopharyngeal cancer, although the conclusion is tempered by the small numbers of observed and expected cases in the cohort studies." "Because of the lack of consistency between the cohort and case-control studies, the epidemiological studies can do no more than suggest a causal role of occupational exposure to formaldehyde in squamous-cell carcinoma of the nasal cavities and paranasal sinuses." IARC, "Formaldehyde," *Monograph Series* 62 (1995): 217. Rev. 13 Aug. 1997. Available at: http://www-cie.iarc.fr/htdocs/monographs/vol62/formal.html.

[63] IARC's overall evaluation is as follows: MOCA is "probably carcinogenic to humans.... There is inadequate evidence in humans for the carcinogenicity of 4,4'-methylenebis(2-chloroaniline) (MOCA).

There is sufficient evidence in experimental animals for the carcinogenicity of 4,4'-methylenebis(2-chloroaniline) (MOCA)."

[64] IARC, "Chloroethyl Nitrosoureas," *Monograph Series, Supplement 7* (1987): 150. (No epidemiological study of CCNU as a single agent was available to the Working Group...; there is sufficient evidence in animals, and CCNU is "a directly-acting, bifunctional alkylating agent." On the weight of all the evidence, CCNU is "probably carcinogenic" to humans.)

[65] Elizabeth Ward, Alexander Blair Smith, and William Halperin, "4,4'-Methylenebis (2-Chloraniline): An Unregulated Carcinogen," *American Journal of Industrial Medicine* 12 (1987): 537, 538.

about this). These same authors report "[a]s yet, there is no direct evidence that MOCA is a carcinogen in humans. However, no *adequate* epidemiologic studies of workers exposed to this chemical have been conducted."[66] Although 178 workers in MOCA production plants with "random exposure" had been followed from 1971 to 1987, "no cases of bladder cancer had been observed . . ."[67] This is not surprising, the authors report, because "there was *limited statistical power* to detect an excess of cancer of the bladder . . ." [in a disease with an] "average latency . . . [of] 20 years or more."[68] Moreover, because the mean or median latency of occupational bladder carcinogens ranges from eighteen to forty-four years, in a prospective epidemiological study begun among workers exposed to MOCA from 1968 to 1979, it was unreasonable to have expected definitive results by 1987. In addition, at the time "the power of the study [was] 80% to detect a nine fold increase in bladder cancer incidence; by 1995, the power [would have been] 80% to detect a fourfold increase."[69] A ninefold relative risk is quite high, approaching that of cigarette smoke–induced lung cancer. Such a high relative risk would make the disease relatively easy to detect if MOCA were as potent a carcinogen as cigarette smoke and the study had had a study period appropriate to the latency period of the disease.

In spite of the evidence at the time this article was published MOCA was not *regulated* as a carcinogen.[70] Nonetheless, NIOSH, IARC, and the Committee on Amines of the National Research Council have reviewed the research. The U.S. National Institute of Occupational Safety and Health

> recommended that, based on oncogenic results in three animal test species, MOCA be treated as a potential human carcinogen. . . . The IARC concluded that MOCA is carcinogenic in the mouse and rat after oral administration and produces distant tumors in the rat after subcutaneous administration and noted that there were no conclusive epidemiologic studies on which an evaluation of MOCA's carcinogenic risk for humans could be based. The Committee on Amines of the National Research council concluded that "studies in test animals have demonstrated conclusively that MOCA is a carcinogen. This activity is to be expected from its structure, which is *similar to that of other aromatic amines* that cause tumors in humans as well as animals. Although the paucity of epidemiologic evidence does not

---

66 Ward, et al., "4,4'-Methylenebis (2-Chloraniline)," 539.
67 Ward, et al., "4,4'-Methylenebis (2-Chloraniline)," 539.
68 Ward, et al., "4,4'-Methylenebis (2-Chloraniline)," 539 (emphasis added).
69 Ward, et al., "4,4'-Methylenebis (2-Chloraniline)," 542. It is important to note what this sketch of the workplace epidemiology of MOCA presages for environmental epidemiology. Workplace exposures are ordinarily much higher than general environmental exposures and there is normally somewhat better exposure information, but the exposed population is generally healthier. How these would combine to produce disease effects is not clear (although recall the "healthy worker effect" from Chapter 5, which will result in a lowered relative risk for workers).
70 Ward et al., "4,4'-Methylenebis (2-Chloraniline)," 545.

permit an evaluation of the carcinogenic effects of MOCA, it is reasonable to assume that, given a sufficiently high exposure, it may also be carcinogenic in humans."[71]

Other countries have listed MOCA as a carcinogen: Australia, Germany, Sweden, and the United Kingdom. Finally, the authors of this study lamented that "[a]lthough experimental evidence has existed for more than a decade that MOCA is a carcinogen, worker exposure is not at this time specifically regulated by OSHA."[72]

This substance constitutes an interesting example for the tort law. Suppose someone alleged that MOCA had caused his bladder cancer. First, in some courts the expert testimony might not have been admitted because the evidence on which it rested consists only of animal studies, structure-activity similarities, and *resemblance to a class of substances* for which there is evidence that the substances cause cancer in humans, and bladder cancer in particular. There were no positive epidemiological studies when this article was published. Moreover, at least some courts would not let experts testify on the basis of this accumulated and integrated evidence that MOCA is more likely than not a *human* carcinogen. This would be a mistake. Other courts, it is important to note, probably would permit such expert testimony. Yet, second, the evidence that MOCA is a likely human carcinogen is quite strong. IARC regards it as a probable human carcinogen,[73] whereas NTP classifies it as "reasonably anticipated to be a [human] carcinogen."[74]

A plaintiff bringing a tort suit for recovery for appropriate damages for exposure to MOCA in a court should easily be able to have scientific experts admitted and to satisfy her burden of production on the issue of general causation on the basis of these scientific studies and expert testimony properly based on them. A showing of specific causation would depend on more specific factual information.

There may be experts who would insist on human studies before concluding that MOCA more likely than not is carcinogenic in humans,[75] but these would stand in contrast to IARC, NTP, and the authors of the scientific article on MOCA who clearly conclude that it a probable human carcinogen. Moreover, in the judgment of some toxicologists, most toxicologists would be comfortable

---

71 Ward et al., "4,4′-Methylenebis (2-Chloraniline)," 545 (emphasis added). The reader also should note the chemical structure-activity argument in this presentation.

72 Ward et al., "4,4′-Methylenebis (2-Chloraniline)," 547.

73 IARC's list of probable human carcinogens is listed at IARC Web site: http://www-cie.iarc.fr/htdocs/monoeval/crthgr02a.html (visited June 1, 1999).

74 NTP's list of substances reasonably anticipated to be a carcinogen is listed at NTP Web site: http://ntp.niehs.nih.gov/ntpweb/index.cfm?objectid=72016262-BDB7-CEBA-FA60E922B18C2540 (visited June 1, 1999).

75 Arthur Furst, "Yes, But Is It a Human Carcinogen?" *Journal of the American College of Toxicology* 9 (1990): 1–18.

concluding that MOCA should be regulated as a human carcinogen, despite the absence of human data in the form of traditional epidemiological studies.[76] Yet, even though there are scientific disagreements about MOCA, testimony should be permitted by both sides.

CCNU, an anticancer drug, is particularly interesting because it illustrates the importance of *chemical structure-biological activity similarities* to a well-defined class of substances in providing evidence for human carcinogenicity, even when there is inadequate human evidence.[77] Recall that many courts have not permitted structure-activity similarities to provide part of the basis of a scientific inference that a substance is a toxicant.

Consider the evidence that CCNU (1-(2-chloroethyl)-3-cyclohexyl-1-nitrosourea), an anticancer drug, is a probable human carcinogen. There are *no* human clinical trials or epidemiological studies showing that it is a carcinogen. In1981 IARC noted a few human *case reports* that patients administered CCNU (along with other cytotoxic agents) developed acute nonlymphocytic leukemia. However, the bulk of the evidence for its inference that CCNU likely caused cancer in humans was that CCNU produced lung tumors in rats and caused a slight increase in lymphomas in mice. Importantly, CCNU (and several related compounds) are directly acting alkylating agents *in animals*.[78] This means they place an alkyl chemical group on the DNA that induces genetic mutations and chromosomal breakage, which in turn is likely to lead to cancer in humans.[79]

The CCNU evidentiary pattern is interesting because virtually all the evidence that it is a carcinogen is from *animal studies*. There is a single study of "increased frequency of sister chromatid exchanges" in humans (a measurement of DNA repair and an indirect measurement of DNA damage).[80] Apart from the few case studies from 1981, there is no other direct evidence from human studies that it causes cancer in humans. There is a different kind of direct evidence that it causes cancer in humans, namely, that it causes DNA damage in mammalian (including human) cells.

---

[76] Cranor and Eastmond, "Scientific Ignorance," and personal communication, David A. Eastmond, July 2004.

[77] The case for benzidine-related dyes is assisted because of the structure-activity relationships between benzidine and benzidine-related dyes and because of a particularly toxic metabolite that is common to both groups of substances. (IARC, "Benzidine and Its Sulphate, Hydrochloride and Dihydrochloride," *Monograph Series* 29 (1982): 149. Rev. 9 Apr. 1998. Available at: http://www-cie.iarc.fr/htdocs/monographs/vol29/benzidine.html.) For another discussion of the importance of structure-activity relationships, see Goldstein and Henifin, "Reference Guide on Toxicology," 421 (note 51).

[78] IARC, "Chloroethyl Nitrosoureas," *Monograph Series, Supplement 7* (1987): 150. Rev. 6 Feb. 1998. Available at: http://www-cie.iarc.fr/htdocs/monographs/suppl7/chloroethylnitrosoureas.html.

[79] Gregus and Klaassen, "Mechanisms of Toxicity," 35–82.

[80] R. J. Preston and G. R. Hoffman, "Genetic Toxicology," in *Casarett and Doull's Toxicology*, 6th ed., 321–350.

Were a similar case in court, defendants might tell judges that there are *no statistically significant epidemiological studies* concerning adverse effects from exposure. This is clearly a red herring. None has been done, and they would be difficult to conduct. The sample sizes of those who have been administered CCNU are likely to be small and a much smaller number yet will likely develop tumors. If such studies could even be done, they would likely show no effect because of the small sample sizes and would run substantial risks of being falsely negative. There also will be many confounding factors, because those who have received CCNU have had cancer and likely will have received other potent drugs that can disrupt normal biological functioning. The CCNU evidence is persuasive because powerful *biological analogies* between animals and humans at the DNA, molecular, cellular, and tissue levels are sufficient to persuade scientists that CCNU is a probable human carcinogen, even though there is no specific human epidemiological or clinical trial evidence linking cancer to CCNU administration.

These examples illustrate the evidentiary strength of animal studies alone or combined with other evidence usually relying on accepted biological similarities at the DNA, molecular, cellular, or tissue levels. Scientists also rely on other kinds of evidence for inferring causation, depending on the information available. Occasionally they have relied on human case studies alone, in others on case studies combined with animal studies.

The general conclusions of IARC and NTP, as well as more specific examples I have described, are not isolated cases. They are representative of numerous others and merely serve to illustrate the larger points. As seen in a recent examination, IARC has found that out of about sixty-six substances or groups of substances (excluding mixtures and exposure conditions) that are *probable human carcinogens* more than forty of these substances have inadequate or limited evidence of carcinogenicity in humans.[81] Thus, about 60% of the substances lack good human data. The IARC scientific *inferences* are supported by controlled studies in animals and "other data relevant to the evaluation of carcinogenicity and its mechanisms."[82] Additional evidence may be that the substance has *substantial genetic effects* in relevant mammals, that it has *carcinogenic metabolites* common to humans and animals, that it belongs to a well-defined *structurally related class* of agents known to cause cancer, that it *binds to receptors* related to cancer in both humans and animals [Ah receptor], that it *binds to DNA* and is believed to contribute to *genetic mutations*, or that it causes *multiple tumors at multiple sites in one or more species of experimental*

[81] IARC, "Overall Evaluation of Carcinogenicity to Humans, Group 2A: Probably Carcinogenic to Humans," *Monograph Series.* Rev. 7 July 2004. Available at: http://www-cie.iarc.fr/monoeval/crthgr02a.html.
[82] IARC, "Overall Evaluation of Carcinogenicity to Humans, Group 2A: Probably Carcinogenic to Humans," *Monograph Series.* Rev. 7 July 2004. Available at: http://www-cie.iarc.fr/monoeval/crthgr02a.html.

animals. In order to infer that the substances are probable human carcinogens, the scientists ruled out alternative explanations, for example, that the animal studies were statistical accidents, that animal mode of action studies were not relevant to humans, that particular chemical structure-activity relationships were not relevant to humans, and so forth. They also accepted the animal evidence as powerful evidence of adverse effects in humans and that at the cellular and DNA levels similar adverse effects occur in animals and humans. Inferring how the evidence *taken as a whole* supports the conclusion and ruling out alternative explanations as being less likely are part of good scientific inferences.

For the NTP, the numbers are more dramatic. For substances that are reasonably anticipated to be a human carcinogen, the criteria specify that the best human evidence that will result in classification of a substance as a likely human carcinogen is "limited evidence of carcinogenicity in humans." Thus, of the 185 substances in this category, they are largely judged to be probable human carcinogens on the basis of animal and other data. NTP personnel confirm this.

In addition to this, the U.S. EPA classifies substances as probable human carcinogens based on animal studies, even if there is *inadequate* evidence that a substance is carcinogenic to humans. These are substances "likely to produce cancer in humans due to the production or anticipated production of tumors by modes of action that are relevant or assumed to be relevant to human carcinogenicity."[83] This, too, is reliable evidence for admissibility.

For a quite different kind of adverse end point (not cancer) but similar patterns of evidence, consider two kinds of adverse effects from dietary supplements reported by the Institute of Medicine. Saw palmetto is the active ingredient found in the American dwarf palm tree. *Inter alia*, it is used to treat the symptoms of benign hyperplasia of the prostate.[84] The Institute of Medicine (IOM) reports that it causes "inhibition of 5-α-reductase *in vitro* and in animal data."[85] The drug finasteride, to which it is chemically similar, has similar uses and "is also known to have this biological effect. Finasteride has been linked to developmental defects in male genitalia *in utero*."[86] The committee concludes,

> [T]his link between the biological activity (inhibition of 5-α-reductase) of the known teratogen finasteride and saw palmetto is sufficient to raise concern about the safety of saw palmetto use in women who could become pregnant because this inhibitory effect of finasteride on 5-α-reductase is considered causative in the teratogenic effect.[87]

83 U.S.Environmental Protection Agency, "Proposed Guidelines for Carcinogen Risk Assessment," 17,985.
84 Andrea E. Gordon and Allen F. Shaughnessy, "Saw Palmetto for Prostate Disorders," *American Family Physician* 67 (2003): 1281–1283.
85 Institute of Medicine and National Research Council, *Dietary Supplements*, 259.
86 Institute of Medicine and National Research Council, *Dietary Supplements*, 259.
87 Institute of Medicine and National Research Council, *Dietary Supplements*, 259.

Although there have been no documented birth defects caused by saw palmetto, the committee is quite concerned about potential risks to developing male fetuses. Because testosterone is needed for the development and maintenance of male sexual characteristics, the reduction of 5-α-reductase inhibits this process as well as the binding of another hormone to androgenic receptors.[88] Both kinds of inhibitions could affect this pathway *in vivo*. Moreover, such effects have been seen in animal studies in a dose-dependent manner. Even though the animal dose was 10 times higher than typical human doses, this was an insufficient gap to mitigate concerns for consumption by pregnant women. Thus, the Committee concludes, "consumption of saw palmetto poses a risk to unborn male fetuses."[89]

This inference about the risk of teratogenic effects was made on the basis of *in vitro* and animal studies, similar molecular pathways in animals and humans, and chemical similarities between saw palmetto and finasteride. There were no human epidemiological studies, but there was some decreased activity of 5-α-reductase in healthy young males who had consumed an extract of saw palmetto for 3 months.[90]

In another section of the IOM-NRC report, the Committee concludes that the scientific literature supports concerns about toxic effects of chaparral on the liver and kidney. The only human evidence is from nine human case reports "of definite hepatotoxicity temporally related to chaparral use as a single known agent," with five cases of "documented recovery after cessation of chaparral use," and one instance of rechallenge in which the patient "exhibited abnormal liver function." There also were animal studies showing kidney damage as well as liver damage by "structurally related chemicals."[91] The IOM in addition reported studies showing cell damage from the main active ingredient of chaparral, NDGA (nordihydroguaiaretic acid).[92]

The language of the IOM-NRC report is somewhat different from IARC's – it expresses "concern" about risks – but this seems more a matter of style and the context of that report than any substantive differences between it and IARC and NTP. The significant points from these examples are the varied patterns of evidence and more complex causal models the Committee uses to reach its conclusions. IOM-NRC utilizes the same kinds of nonhuman evidence to reach its conclusions about reproductive toxicity and liver/kidney damage, as do IARC and NTP to reach conclusions about the carcinogenicity of substances. The IOM-NRC committee uses models to show how several kinds of seemingly weak evidence can be integrated to conclude products are toxic or probably toxic to humans.[93]

---

[88] Institute of Medicine and National Research Council, *Dietary Supplements*, 457.
[89] Institute of Medicine and National Research Council, *Dietary Supplements*, 458.
[90] Institute of Medicine and National Research Council, *Dietary Supplements*, 458.
[91] Institute of Medicine and National Research Council, *Dietary Supplements*, 397–398.
[92] Institute of Medicine and National Research Council, *Dietary Supplements*, 386–387, 399.
[93] Institute of Medicine and National Research Council, *Dietary Supplements*, 253–268.

Finally, recall the unusual case study of dimethylnitrosamine poisoning considered in Chapter 4. In this instance a defendant was convicted in the criminal law of *murder* based largely on animal and molecular evidence. The conclusion that the substance dimethylnitrosamine, a carcinogen, was a human liver poison was based on acute toxicity studies in rats, inhalation studies in dogs and mice, three sets of case studies in humans (two people each), pathology evidence, some DNA studies, extensive circumstantial evidence, but *no* epidemiological studies. The only human evidence was the case studies and the dead and injured people in the murder case at the bar.[94]

LEARNING FROM RELIABLE PATTERNS OF EVIDENCE

What can we learn from these examples? First, there are a variety of explanatory or inference paths to a conclusion that a substance is more likely than not a human carcinogen. These toxicological conclusions can be supported by means of several different kinds of evidence.[95] Human evidence might be available and sufficient. If it is not, animal evidence alone or supported by other kinds of evidence might lead to the conclusion. Case studies with animal and other evidence also can suffice.

Second, direct epidemiological data is not necessary in judging whether a substance is a certain or likely human carcinogen, a reproductive toxicant, or a liver toxicant. There is considerable probative value to nonhuman evidence that is widely accepted in the scientific community. Animal, in vitro, and various forms of mechanistic evidence, including structure-activity similarities, can be particularly important, depending on its quality and other evidence available.

Third, the scientific judgments described earlier, based on combinations of studies and on good scientific reasoning from the data, are taken from those used by the International Agency for Research on Cancer, the National Toxicology Program, and the Institute of Medicine and National Research Council. They are similar to those used by the U.S. EPA and the California EPA, and are ones that toxicologists endorse.[96]

---

94 Renate D. Kimbrough, "Pathological Changes in Human Beings Acutely Poisoned by Dimethylnitrosamine," in *Nitrosamines and Human Cancer*, ed. Peter N. Magee (Cold Spring Harbor, NY: Cold Spring Harbor Laboratory, 1982), 25–34; Berton Roueché, "The Lemonade Mystery," *The Saturday Evening Post* 58 (May/June 1982); Ronald C. Shank and Deborah C. Herron, "Methylation of Human Liver DNA After Probable Dimethylnitrosamine Poisoning," in *Nitrosamines and Human Cancer*, 153–159.
95 Or one might say that several different nondeductive arguments utilizing different kinds of evidentiary support lead to the conclusion that a substance causes or contributes to human harm.
96 There may be some disagreement between these agencies on particular substances, reflecting legitimate scientific disagreement, but they agree in broad outline on these issues.

Fourth, because of their standing as sound *toxicological* inferences they are more than sufficiently *reliable* to satisfy an admissibility review (in fact they represent considerable overkill for admissibility), as they play such an obvious role in inferences endorsed by scientific bodies and experts in toxicology.

Fifth, however, the evidentiary pattern utilized for each substance also suggests that, *at the time these decisions were made, different kinds of evidence* were critical in identifying a substance as a carcinogen. Usually, animal evidence was particularly important. Sometimes, surprisingly, it was metabolic and structure-activity evidence (for benzidine-related dyes [for IARC] and CCNU). Sometimes it was largely molecular or mode of action evidence (CCNU, dioxin-like compounds, and saw palmetto), but not necessarily detailed step-by-step mechanistic pathway evidence that is usually quite difficult to provide. In many cases, it was the integrated evidence from animals, chemical structure, and other molecular considerations that led to a conclusion that the substance was a likely or known human carcinogen.

Sixth, *all the scientifically relevant evidence* in each case bears on a weight-of-the-evidence assessment of whether something is a likely human carcinogen (contrary to the Supreme Court and the district court views in *Joiner*[97]). For many of the carcinogens or reproductive toxicants the individual kinds of evidence were not necessarily strong, but the totality of integrated evidence was quite powerful. Thus, for courts to identify *one piece of relevant evidence* as inadequate by itself to implicate a substance as toxic or to evaluate each piece as inadequate for the ultimate conclusion and then to suggest that the evidence *as a whole* is inadequate, violates rules of good evidence evaluation.[98] It is contrary to weight-of-the-evidence procedures that are so important in the scientific evaluation of toxicants.[99]

Finally, patterns of evidence and lessons learned from them are, despite some of their complexity, *easy cases* because they resulted from consensus judgments of international or national scientific bodies or peer-reviewed judgments of the U.S. EPA. These scientific conclusions are not taken from marginal scientists, charlatans, or junk scientists. Yet the inference patterns are sufficiently varied to serve as a caution against judicially constrained admissibility reviews in toxic tort cases. Similar work should be done on neurotoxicants, reproductive toxicants, and others.

---

[97] See *General Electric Co. v. Joiner*, 522 U.S. 136, at 152–153. (Justice Stevens, concurring in part and dissenting in part, arguing that the majority's reliability ruling was not "faithful to the statement in *Daubert* that '[t]he focus, of course, must be solely on principles and methodology, not on the conclusions that they generate.'" He also argues that both the District Court and the Supreme Court evaluated each scientific study as inadequate for supporting the expert's ultimate conclusion but did not properly address Joiner's experts relying on a "weight-of-the-evidence" methodology.).

[98] Larry Wright, *Practical Reasoning* (New York: Harcourt Brace Jovanovich, 1987).

[99] U.S. Environmental Protection Agency, "Proposed Guidelines for Carcinogen Risk Assessment," 17981–17992.

PRINCIPLES OF TOXICOLOGY UNDERLYING THE
EVIDENTIARY PATTERNS

In addition to these patterns of evidence that scientific bodies have endorsed, recall some principles of carcinogen biology and toxicology noted in Chapter 4 that can assist judges in their review of expert testimony on general causation concerning carcinogens. These biological principles provide foundational support for the patterns of evidence and the scientific inferences just described. Just as in law in which more general principles provide reasons for drawing inferences about particular legal cases, these principles support inferences from particular biological experiments to conclusions about particular substances or patterns of evidence indicating a substance can cause human harm. Recall in particular some biological principles concerning inferences from animal studies, as they loom so large in the toxicology of carcinogens and have tended to fare badly in a number of legal cases.

First, despite apparent differences between laboratory animals and humans, "experimental evidence to date" suggests that there are greater similarities than there are differences between laboratory animals and humans at the physiologic, biochemical, metabolic, and genetic level."[100] Second, there are striking similarities from one mammalian species to another ("as one moves along the phylogenetic ladder") in the biological processes that control life.[101] Third, the more scientists "know about the similarities of structure and function of higher organisms *at the molecular level,* the more [they] are convinced that mechanisms of chemical toxicity are, to a large extent, identical in animals and man."[102] Fourth, despite differences in carcinogenic responses from one species to another, there are particular patterns of responses in animals that greatly increase the likelihood that a carcinogenic response in one mammalian species will produce a carcinogenic response in another mammalian species.

Fifth, a variety of formal and informal groups of scientists have concluded that for carcinogens "chemicals that are carcinogenic in laboratory animals are likely to be carcinogenic in human populations and that, if appropriate studies can be performed, there is qualitative predictability."[103] Indeed, the National Academy of Sciences notes that "in the absence of countervailing evidence for the specific agent in question, *it appears reasonable to assume that the life-time cancer incidence induced by chronic exposure in man can be approximated by the life-time incidence induced by similar exposure in laboratory animals at the*

---

[100] D. P. Rall et al., "Alternatives to Using Human Experience," 355, 356 (emphasis added). See also The Mouse Genome Sequencing Consortium, Robert Waterston et al., "Initial Sequencing and Comparative Analysis of the Mouse Genome," *Nature* 420 (5 Dec. 2002): 520–562.
[101] Huff and Rall, "Relevance to Humans," 434.
[102] Huff, "Chemicals and Cancer," 204.
[103] Huff and Rall, "Relevance to Humans," 437.

same total dose per body weight.[104] The IOM-NRC committee notes a similar principle concerning adverse effects other than cancer end points.[105]

The principles suggested support inferences, unless there is good substance-specific evidence to the contrary, and they help make inferences reliable concerning the toxicology of carcinogens. There are exceptions to these presumptions, but they are recognized as such. Analogues to these principles are likely to be applicable for other adverse effects as the IOM-NRC report shows, but I have largely focused on carcinogens.

In addition to these general principles and contrary to what some have suggested, Huff and Rall argue that there are some reasons to believe that humans are *as sensitive or more sensitive* than animals to exposures from various chemicals.[106] For several substances tested in animals, the animal exposures were

> the same or less than human exposures. In 20 chemotherapeutic agents the toxic doses were highly correlated if expressed on a dose per kilogram of body weight basis and almost identical if expressed as dose per body weight to the two-thirds power. This would suggest that humans may be up to ten times more sensitive than the typical small laboratory animal if the comparison is made on the basis of dose per kilogram of body weight.[107]

Furthermore, humans are genetically much more varied and would be expected to be more vulnerable to chemical insults than are animals bred for laboratory experiments.[108]

> Smaller animals tend to metabolize and excrete foreign organic chemicals more rapidly than do larger mammals; therefore, higher body burdens develop in humans over the years than develop in mice and rats in a 2-year experimental period. . . . Because chemically induced cancer is viewed

---

[104] Huff and Rall, "Relevance to Humans," 437 (quoting the National Research Council, Study on Problems of Pest Control, Executive Committee, *Contemporary Pest Control Practices and Prospects: The Report of the Executive Committee, Study on Problems of Pest Control, Environmental Studies Board, National Research Council* (Washington, DC: National Academy of Sciences, 1975), 66–83. IARC concurs with the National Academy. IARC, Preamble, Section 9: Studies of Cancer in Experimental Animals, *Monograph Series*. Rev. 5 Jan. 1999. Available at: http://www-cie.iarc.fr/monoeval/studiesanimals.html.

[105] Institute of Medicine and National Research Council, *Dietary Supplements*, 156. ("Even in the absence of information on adverse events in humans, evidence of harm from animal studies is often indicative of potential harm to humans. This indication assumes greatest importance when the route of exposure is oral, the formulation tested is identical or highly similar to that consumed by humans, and more than one species show the same or similar toxicity.")

[106] Huff and Rall, "Relevance to Humans," 439.

[107] Huff and Rall, "Relevance to Humans," 439. For a qualifier concerning the particular scaling factor, see Travis, "Interspecies Extrapolation."

[108] D. Hattis and K. Barlow, "Human Interindividual Variability in Cancer Risks. Technical and Management Challenges," *Health and Ecological Risk Assessment* 2 (1996): 194–220; Dale Hattis, "Variability in Susceptibility: How Big, How Often, For What Responses to What

as originating in one or a few cells, it is relevant that a human has hundreds of times more susceptible cells than does a mouse or a rat. . . . [T]he cells of small animals 'turn over' or replicate themselves at perhaps twice the rate of cells in larger mammals such as humans, and latent periods are longer in large animals. The human life span, however, is about 30 to 35 times that of the mouse or rat and this may make humans more susceptible.[109]

Beyond these generic considerations, infants, children, pregnant women, the elderly, the sick, and other vulnerable groups remind us of the variability within the general population.[110]

These observations raise several points. The human population with its greater genetic, metabolic, and other individual variability exhibits a wider range of responses to toxic exposures than mammalian species that have been uniformly bred for experimental purposes. Even if one overlooks specific, identifiable susceptible groups, some individuals will be more resistant and some will be more susceptible to toxic insults. For example, people with ataxia-telangiectasia (a DNA repair disorder) are highly susceptible to ionizing radiation exposure.[111] Persons with xeroderma pigmentosum (another DNA repair disorder) are highly susceptible to ultraviolet radiation.[112] Those who are slow (vs. rapid) acetylators (slow to metabolize certain compounds through acetylation [attaching an acetyl functional group to the molecule and altering its metabolic pathways]) are at higher risk for lupus from exposure to hydralazine or procainimide, whereas those who are rapid acetylators are believed to be at higher risk of carcinogenesis from heterocyclic amines.[113] Scientists know

Agents?" *Environmental Toxicology and Pharmacology* 4 (1997): 205–206; D. Hattis, P. Banati, and R. Goble, "Distributions of Individual Susceptibility Among Humans for Toxic Effects – For What Fraction of Which Kinds of Chemicals and Effects Does the Traditional 10-Fold Factor Provide How Much Protection?" *Annals of the New York Academy of Sciences* 895 (Dec. 1999): 286–316; S. Venitt, "Mechanisms of Carcinogenesis and Individual Susceptibility to 40 Cancers," *Clinical Chemistry* 40 (1994): 1421–1425.

[109] Huff and Rall, "Relevance to Humans," 439–440. Despite the value of animal studies for assessing risks and harms to humans, such research has limits because it is slow and costly like epidemiological studies.

[110] Institute of Medicine and National Research Council, *Dietary Supplements*, 48, 64.

[111] M. Swift, D. Morrell, R. B. Massey, and C. L. Chase, "Incidence of Cancer in 161 Families Affected by Ataxia-telangiectasia," *New England Journal of Medicine* 325 (1991): 1831–1836.

[112] A. C. Halpern and J. F. Altman, "Genetic Predisposition to Skin Cancer," *Current Opinion in Oncology* 11 (1999): 132–138.

[113] C. C. Deitz, W. Zheng, M. A. Leff, M. Gross, W. Q. Wen, M. A. Doll, G. H. Xiao, A. R. Folsom, and D. W. Hein, "N-Acetyltransferase-2 Genetic Polymorphism, Well-Done Meat Intake, and Breast Cancer Risk Among Postmenopausal Women," *Cancer Epidemiology Biomarkers and Prevention* 9 (2000): 905–910; J. Chen, M. J. Stampfer, H. L. Hough, M. Garcia-Closas, W. C. Willett, C. H. Hennekens, K. T. Kelsey, and D. J. Hunter, "A Prospective Study of N-Acetyltransferase Genotype, Red Meat Intake, and Risk of Colorectal Cancer," *Cancer Research* 58 (1998): 3307–3311; John Timbrell, *Principles of Biochemical Toxicology*, 3rd ed. (London: Taylor & Francis, 2000).

that there are biological variations that make some persons more and others less susceptible to toxicants. However, until there is greater study of these phenomena it may be difficult to know in particular cases which individuals have greater or lesser susceptibility to these or similar conditions. Moreover, as evidence of individual differences in biological susceptibility is understood, there may be tests to determine which individuals have such properties. However, until that time, the fact of widely differing susceptibility should caution judges against being too quick to reject *a priori* evidence of a toxic effect in a given individual.

The legal significance of variation in susceptibility is that courts in making admissibility decisions should allow for interindividual variability and for the possibility of greater sensitivity of some people to a toxic exposure. Indeed, the "eggshell skull" principle, part of tort law for more than one hundred years,[114] specifically recognizes that if a person's legitimate interests have been wrongly invaded by a tortfeasor, the defendant takes the victim as he finds him.[115] The principle appears to be that when there are wrongful invasions, everyone has equal standing to be protected from harm even though some have eggshell skulls, some are pregnant, and some have predispositions to disease or to "loss of hair from fright."[116] Thus, if some people are more sensitive to toxic exposures than other people or than animals, courts should allow for this. They should be sensitive to this consideration for admissibility decisions in toxic tort cases. This suggests that even if a plaintiff suffers a toxic effect identical in nature to those resulting from higher exposures, but his disease results from a lower

---

[114] *Prosser and Keeton on the Law of Torts*, 291–292.

[115] See *Maurer v. United States*, 668 F.2d 98, 99–100 (2nd Cir. 1981). ("It is a settled principle of tort law that when a defendant's wrongful act causes injury, he is fully liable for the resulting damage even though the injured plaintiff had a preexisting condition that made the consequences of the wrongful act more severe than they would have been for a normal victim. The defendant takes the plaintiff as he finds him.") *Prosser and Keeton on Torts*, 291–292. ("It is as if a magic circle were drawn about the person, and one who breaks it, even by so much as a cut on the finger, becomes liable for all resulting harm to the person although it may be death. The defendant is held liable when the defendant's negligence operates upon a concealed physical condition, such as pregnancy, or a latent disease, or susceptibility to disease [psychotic or neurotic predispositions, predisposition to amnesia, ruptured disc, delirium tremens], to produce consequences which the defendant could not reasonably anticipate. The defendant is held liable for unusual results of personal injuries which are regarded as unforeseeable, such as tuberculosis, paralysis, pneumonia, heart or kidney disease, blood poisoning, cancer or the loss of hair from fright. . . . One of the illustrations which runs through the English cases is that of the plaintiff with the 'eggshell skull,' who suffers death where a normal person would have had only a bump on the head . . . ")

It is important to note that there must be a "wrongful" invasion of interest before the eggshell skull principle can be invoked. Whether this will always be true as a result of exposure to a toxic substance is an issue that must be addressed.

[116] *Ominsky v. Chas. Weinhagen & Co.* (1911) 129 N.W. Rptr 845–846. Carl F. Cranor, "Eggshell Skulls and Loss of Hair from Fright: Some Moral and Legal Principles that Protect Susceptible Subpopulations," *Environmental Toxicology and Pharmacology* 4 (1998): 239–245.

exposure level, this could be considered a presumptive reason for inferring that the toxic substance contributed to plaintiff's disease.[117]

LEGAL DECISIONS EXEMPLIFYING SENSITIVE SCIENTIFIC REVIEWS

There are a number of legal cases that show sensitivity to the issues of scientific evidence presented earlier. These implicitly recognize that a variety of patterns of evidence would support a respectable scientific inference that a substance is a toxicant. It appears that some post-*Daubert* legal opinions are coming to this view, but there does not appear to be a legal consensus at this point.

In *In re Paoli Railroad Yard PCB Litigation*[118] the Third Circuit held that a district court abused its discretion in excluding animal studies as "irrelevant" and "unreliable" for conclusions that polychlorinated biphenyls are capable of causing cancer in humans. The defense had argued one scientific view (contrary to the scientific views documented in this book), namely, that "test animals are often very sensitive to chemicals due to breeding, overeating, and physiological, biological and metabolic pathways which are different than those of humans . . . [and that] studies of test animals identify many chemicals as carcinogenic in animals that are not carcinogenic in humans."[119] The Third Circuit, however, pointed out that there were other scientific views, thus recognizing, as I have put it, the *fact of reasonable scientific disagreement* on this issue. First, it noted that one of plaintiff's experts referred to some occupational studies consistent with the animal studies, that "scientists routinely use animal studies to assess the risks of chemicals to humans," that "animal studies are particularly valuable with respect to assessing the health effects of PCBs, because humans and monkeys have shown similar sensitivity to PCDFs and thus are likely to show similar sensitivity to PCBs."[120] Second, the Court noted that EPA relied on such studies, that it classified PCBs as "probable human carcinogens" on the basis of animal studies, and that EPA regarded PCBs as having the same carcinogenic potency as vinyl chloride (one of only fourteen substances proven to be carcinogenic by epidemiological studies, it argued). Third, the Court distinguished between case law in which there was overwhelming epidemiological evidence contrary to animal studies and legal cases in which there was little or

---

[117] For example, Carruth and Weinstein suggest if the plaintiff received a dose that is twice as much as the mean dose in an epidemiological study that reported a 50 percent increase in risk (putatively RR = 1.5), a toxicologist might conclude that the plaintiff's dose would lead to a doubling of risk. Carruth and Goldstein, "Relative Risk Greater Than Two," 195–209, esp. 209.

[118] 35 F.3d 717 (3d Cir. 1994).

[119] 35 F.3d at 779.

[120] 35 F.3d at 779.

no epidemiological evidence pertinent to the case.[121] Finally, the Court noted that animal studies "pass muster" when judged by *Daubert* criteria and are "one source by which plaintiffs can prove the harmful effects of PCBs.[122] The Third Circuit learned from the scientific and regulatory community in coming to its decision, although some aspects of its view were comparatively straight forward.

In *Ambrosini v. Labarraque*[123] the parents of a child who was born with birth defects brought action on behalf of the child against the manufacturer of a prescription drug Depo-Provera, alleging that birth defects in the child were caused by the drug. The District Court for the District of Columbia excluded plaintiff's experts and granted summary judgment to the defendants because plaintiffs could not substantiate their causation claims. Plaintiffs appealed to the District of Columbia Circuit Court of Appeals. On appeal, the D.C. Circuit overruled the District Court. The D.C. Circuit's discussion of standards for the admissibility of scientific evidence and the evidentiary value of different kinds of evidence is pertinent to the earlier discussion.

First, the court denied that *Daubert* establishes a "heightened" admissibility standard. It notes,

[T]he *Daubert* analysis does not establish a heightened threshold for the admission of expert evidence, but rather focuses on the court's "gatekeeper" role as a check on "subjective belief" and "unsupported speculation."[124]

Second, the court noted that "the threshold for admissibility has been lowered, both because of the liberal theory of admissibility adopted by the Federal Rules of Evidence and because *Frye's* "general acceptance" test is no longer dispositive of admissibility."[125] In particular, while the general acceptance of scientific theories or inferences may be sufficient for admission into a tort court, it is not required.[126]

Third, in a ruling clearly inconsistent with the Ninth Circuit on the *Daubert* remand (requiring statistically significant epidemiological studies with relative risks greater than two), the court held that just because an expert's testimony does not address "the relative risk between exposed and unexposed populations of cleft lip and palate, or any other of the birth defects from which [the child] suffers," this does not render his testimony inadmissible.[127] The question to ask of the expert is whether the testimony will "'assist the trier of fact to understand

[121] 35 F.3d at 780–781.
[122] 35 F.3d at 781.
[123] 101 F.3d 129 (D.C. Cir. 1996).
[124] *Ambrosini v. Labarraque*, 101 F.3d 129, at 134 (D.C. Cir. 1996) (citing *Daubert*, 509 U.S. at 590, 113 S.Ct. at 2795).
[125] *Ambrosini v. Labarraque*, 101 F.3d at 133.
[126] *Ambrosini v. Labarraque*, 101 F.3d at 133.
[127] *Ambrosini v. Labarraque*, 101 F.3d. at 135.

the evidence or to determine a fact in issue,' not whether the testimony satisfies the plaintiff's burden on the ultimate issue at trial."[128] Moreover, just because an expert's testimony alone might be insufficient to survive summary judgment (a ruling on this expert's testimony compared with evidence the defense presents) does not defeat its admissibility.[129] Thus, the court implicitly recognizes a distinction between the admissibility of evidence and the adequacy of that same evidence to survive a summary judgment.

Fourth, significantly, this court noted the importance of assessing the statistical power of negative studies to reliably detect toxic effects from exposures and noted that the no effect or negative studies cited by defendants in this case had too little statistical power to provide evidence of no effect.[130] These were "too small to be significant."[131]

Fifth, the court ruled on the admissibility of each expert's testimony based on the totality of evidence the expert utilized to come to an opinion. It did not, like the district and Supreme Court in *Joiner*, deconstruct each piece of evidence as inadequate to support the expert's conclusion.

Sixth, the court admitted the experts because it found they were utilizing a methodology well recognized in their field.[132]

Seventh, the court accepted plaintiffs' argument that some studies, by splitting types of birth defects into very specific subtypes and then testing for them, were negative simply because the studies had no statistical power to detect rare effects.[133]

None of this is to argue that the court necessarily made the correct admissibility decision or that the plaintiffs' experts were necessarily correct. Rather, the point is that the court understood many of the subtleties of scientific studies and inferences from them as well as sensitively assessing issues about them. It avoided many of the admissibility mistakes noted in Chapter 6, and appeared to use some of the same kinds of subtle considerations in assessing the evidence that the scientific community would.

There are other district and appellate court cases in which judges appear to have shown good judgment in assessing scientific evidence before the court. Many of these have been referenced throughout. Consider two others.

In *Blanchard v. Eli Lilly & Company*,[134] the court was faced with reviewing psychiatric testimony addressing whether the antidepressant Prozac could and did cause sufficient depression in a mother to move her to shoot and kill

---

128   *Ambrosini v. Labarraque*, 101 F.3d at 135 (quoting *Daubert*, 509 U.S. at 591, 113 S.Ct. at 2795 (quoting Federal Rules of Evidence 702)).
129   *Ambrosini v. Labarraque*, 101 F.3d at 136.
130   *Ambrosini v. Labarraque*, 101 F.3d at 136.
131   *Ambrosini v. Labarraque*, 101 F.3d at 136.
132   *Ambrosini v. Labarraque*, 101 F.3d at 135–136.
133   *Ambrosini v. Labarraque*, 101 F.3d at 139.
134   207 F. Supp. 2d 308 (D. Vt. 2002).

her minor children and then commit suicide. This was clearly a difficult case, given the scientific fields involved and the paucity of evidence. However, the court, after reviewing the evidence and some of its shortcomings, seemed to realize that there could be risks to employing a "checklist" of considerations or "cookbook" rules to decide whether to admit plaintiffs' experts.[135] Noting that "Strict adherence to traditional tests for reliability of 'hard science' would probably preclude Dr. Maltsberger's general causation testimony as well," the court then held, following the amended Rule 702, that its "task however [was] not to apply a rigid checklist to proposed opinion testimony, but to determine if it is based upon sufficient facts or data and is the product of reliable principles and methods, and if the principles and methods have been applied reliably to the facts of the case."[136] After taking a less "checklist" or "cookbook" approach, it still found the experts' testimony insufficiently well founded to be admitted for trial.

I do not comment on the ultimate admissibility ruling in this case, but use it only to point out that this judge appears to have taken extra steps to ensure that he was not captured by overly simple and restrictive rules concerning the admissibility of scientific evidence or perhaps rules that would unfairly disadvantage one side to the litigation. He appears to have engaged in the much more difficult task of sensitively reviewing the expert testimony based on the evidence before him and ultimately ruled that the expert should be excluded. Such an approach seems salutary.

A recent case, *In re Ephedra Products Liability Litigation,* exemplifies considerable sensitivity to the scientific issues discussed in this book.[137] In an opinion reviewing whether experts should be permitted to testify that exposure to ephedra caused or contributed to strokes, cardiac injury, or seizures in some people, Judge Rakoff wrote a scientifically well-informed opinion.

1) He recognized the importance of diagnostic or nondeductive inferences in science.

2) Simply because there are no statistically significant epidemiological studies showing an increased risk from ephedra, this does not bar plaintiffs' experts from testifying.[138]

3) On legal issues he notes that the Second Circuit Court of Appeals "affirmed admission of a physician's causation opinion even though he 'could not point to a single piece of medical literature that says glue fumes cause throat polyps.'"[139] Moreover, any legal opinion that would automatically exclude expert opinion testimony that is not based on statistically significant epidemiological studies would be "irreconcilable with" with [the Second Circuits'

[135]   207 F. Supp. 2d 308, at 317.
[136]   207 F. Supp. 2d 308, at 317.
[137]   *In re Ephedra Products Liability Litigation,* 393 F. Supp. 2d 181 (2005)
[138]   *In re Ephedra Products Liability Litigation,* 393 F. Supp. 2d 181, at 187.
[139]   *McCullock v. H. B. Fuller Co.,* 61 F.3d 1038, at 1043 (2d Cir. 1995)

opinions in] *Zuchowicz* and *McCullock* and with the admonition in *Amorgianos* that "[s]uch a bright-line requirement would be at odds with the liberal admissibility standards of the federal rules and the express teachings of *Daubert*" about the need for flexibility in the district court's gate-keeping role."[140]

4) Moreover he notes that Rule 702 permits experts to testify "even where the data falls short of proving the witness's conclusion."[141] To be admissible, an expert's "analogies, inferences and extrapolations connecting the science to the witness's conclusions must be of a kind that a reasonable scientist or physician would make in a decision of importance arising in the exercise of his profession outside the context of litigation."[142]

5) In addition, *Daubert* "was designed to exclude 'junk science.' It was never intended to keep from the jury the kind of evidence scientists regularly rely on in forming opinions of causality simply because such evidence is not definitive."[143] Admissibility rulings should be not "a more exacting standard of causality than more-probable-than-not simply because scientific issues are involved."[144]

6) He notes that because of the costs and time-consuming nature of epidemiological studies for ephedra-caused conditions, "the insurmountable practical obstacles would prevent injured parties from ever obtaining compensation even if such a study were theoretically possible."[145] And, a *retrospective* (v. a prospective) study would be "close to impossible."[146]

7) He then proceeds to recognize that scientific opinions could appropriately be based on peer-reviewed case studies, mechanistic information, adverse event reports (case studies), and the fact of particularly susceptible individuals.[147]

8) Finally, even though some "gaps" between the data plaintiffs utilize and definitive evidence of causality are real, "they are not so great as to require the opinion to be excluded from evidence."[148] The "inferences are of a kind that physicians and scientists reasonably make from good but inconclusive science when faced with practical decisions of importance."[149]

There are a couple of points that invite comment. Judge Rakoff held that "general causation has not been established by scientific standards of proof. Accordingly, [plaintiffs'] witnesses will not be permitted to testify with

---

140   *In re Ephedra Products Liability Litigation*, 393 F. Supp. 2d 181, at 186–187 (citing *Zuchowicz v. United States*, 140 F.3d 381, 386-87 (2d Cir. 1998), *McCullock v. H. B. Fuller Co.*, 61 F.Ed 1038 and *Amorgianos v. National Railroad Passenger Corp.*, 303 F.3d 256 (2d Cir. 2002)).

141   *In re Ephedra Products Liability Litigation*, 393 F. Supp. 2d 181, at 188.

142   *In re Ephedra Products Liability Litigation*, 393 F. Supp. 2d 181, at 189.

143   *In re Ephedra Products Liability Litigation*, 393 F. Supp. 2d 181, at 190.

144   *In re Ephedra Products Liability Litigation*, 393 F. Supp. 2d 181, at 190.

145   *In re Ephedra Products Liability Litigation*, 393 F. Supp. 2d 181, at 192.

146   *In re Ephedra Products Liability Litigation*, 393 F. Supp. 2d 181, at 193.

147   *In re Ephedra Products Liability Litigation*, 393 F. Supp. 2d 181, at 194.

148   *In re Ephedra Products Liability Litigation*, 393 F. Supp. 2d 181, at 195.

149   *In re Ephedra Products Liability Litigation*, 393 F. Supp. 2d 181, at 197.

any degree of medical or scientific 'certainty' that ephedra causes the listed injuries."[150] However, he added that plaintiffs' experts "have a reliable basis for forming a professional opinion that ephedra may be a contributing cause of cardiac injury and stoke in some people, such as those with a heart condition, high blood pressure, or a genetic sensitivity to ephedrine, if that opinion is appropriately qualified."[151]

The opinion suggests a distinction between data for causation that "[proves] a witness's conclusion" (suggesting that an appropriate epidemiological study might do this) and the evidence available in this case, which is likely fairly good for the conclusion that ephedra can cause adverse effects at least in more susceptible individuals.[152] The evidence he cites has many of the components quite good, nonepidemiological evidence can have and it is integrated to show that ephedra can contribute to the adverse events in question. Thus, there is a concern that his opinion inadvertently suggests too much importance can be attached to epidemiological studies. Second, in an otherwise excellent opinion, Judge Rakoff steps back from full recognition that the kind of evidence scientists have in this case and that he so well summarizes is in a large number of cases the best kind of evidence scientists likely will have in the practical decisions they must make. The distinctions, about which he is otherwise so punctilious, could invite difficulties in the future and may mislead other courts. One hopes they do not, for he appears to have reviewed the evidence in the case much as scientists would (and he notes that three of the experts already in their professional work had called attention to risks from ephedra exposure).

THE SOCIAL CONSEQUENCES OF ADMISSIBILITY DECISIONS REVISITED

In light of the suggestions made in this chapter, what can be said about the court opinions in the *Allen*, Parlodel, and *Joiner* cases introduced in the Chapter 1?

Allen v. Pennsylvania Engineering, Inc.

In *Allen* the 5th Circuit Court of Appeals, in upholding the trial courts cursory dismissal of plaintiffs' case, came close to imposing an epidemiological threshold for admissibility (no epidemiological study had found "a statistically significant link between ETO exposure and human brain cancer"[153]). It then ruled that plaintiffs' experts' reliance on rat studies (that provided a model showing ETO could case brain cancer) was "unreliable" because ETO did not

[150]   *In re Ephedra Products Liability Litigation*, 393 F. Supp. 2d 181, at 186–187.
[151]   *In re Ephedra Products Liability Litigation*, 393 F. Supp. 2d 181, at 187.
[152]   *In re Ephedra Products Liability Litigation*, 393 F. Supp. 2d 181, at 188.
[153]   207 F. Supp. 2d 308, at 317.

also cause tumors in the phylogenetically similar mice, and ruled that mutagenicity studies were only the "beginning not the end of scientific inquiry and proves nothing about causation without other scientific evidence."[154]

There are several problems with this opinion. First, the court appears to consider each type of study independently and rule it out as dispositive of causation. This suggests that the court did not understand nondeductive arguments and how all the evidence must be considered together in order to judge the plausibility of an expert's inference to a conclusion.

Second, the court appeared not to understand, or plaintiffs failed to explain well, the significance of the rat studies even in absence of similar results from mouse studies. It can be argued that in this case that rats could be a better model for predicting effects in humans simply because rats generally have a slower metabolism and breathing rate than mice, thus retaining ETO in the bodies more like humans.[155] They show that the small molecule of ethylene oxide can cross the blood-brain barrier, something that is typically difficult for chemicals to do. The blood-brain barrier is a physiological barrier that seems to have evolved to provide protections to the brain. If ETO can have this biological effect in rats with their metabolism more similar to humans than mice, it is plausible that it can do it in humans, which is what plaintiffs had argued.[156] Toxicologists would explain ethylene oxide's inability to cross the mouse blood-brain barrier as based on special features of mice that make them different from rats and humans. Rats' slower metabolism and respiratory rates result in them retaining ETO longer, giving that small molecule time for absorption into various bodily tissues, including the brain. The *Allen* court *assumed* that there was something special about rats that was not applicable to mice and to humans, when the opposite was true: the mice have special features that distinguish them from rats and make their responses less applicable to humans. The Court seemed to have misunderstood the significance of this evidence (or it was not well explained to them), excluded the expert testimony based on it, and denied plaintiff her day in court.[157]

Third, ETO is a multisite mutagen, a quite significant biological feature of a substance, which the court seemed not to understand or dismissed too easily.[158] Moreover, because it was a small molecule and required no transformation by human metabolism to produce toxic effects, it could reach nearly any target

---

[154] 207 F. Supp. 2d 308, at 198.

[155] David A. Eastmond, personal communication, June 2003.

[156] *Plaintiff's Expert Opinion Affidavit* by Karl T. Kelsey and Anthony D. LaMontagne, in *Allen v. Pennsylvania Eng'g Corp.*, 102 F.3d 194 (5th Cir. 1996).

[157] *Allen v. Pennsylvania Eng'g Corp.*, 102 F.3d 194, 197 (5th Cir. 1996).

[158] "Mutagenicieity testing, combined with an evaluation of chemical structure, has been found to identify a large proportion of trans-species, multiple-site carcinogens." R. Julian Preston and George R. Hoffmann, "Genetic Toxicology," in *Casarett and Doull's Toxicology*, 6th ed., ed. Curtis D. Klassen (New York: McGraw-Hill, 2001) 342.

site in the body; the rat studies showed it could cross the blood-brain barrier and reach the brain.

In addition, as part of an NSF research project at UC Riverside, David Eastmond and I sought scientific peer reviews of expert reports in a small number of legal cases. *Allen* was one. We sent the plaintiffs' and defendants' expert reports without names or affiliations attached to two extramural referees who were experts in the toxicology of ETO. Following the lead of some federal judges and the language from *Kumho Tire* we asked them whether the experts' opinions fell within a range where "reasonable experts would disagree."

One outside expert said of the Allens' plaintiffs' arguments:

> The evidence and interpretations offered by the plaintiff's experts are consistent with the information and reasoning used by expert panels that evaluate potential cancer risks from environmental and occupational agents. The evidence presented by these experts clearly establishes EtO as a carcinogen with a high likelihood of human risk. They appropriately cited literature showing that EtO is a direct-acting DNA alkylating agent, is mutagenic in multiple in vivo and in vitro studies including human cells, and consistently showed induction of chromosomal damage in peripheral lymphocytes of exposed workers (chromosomal aberrations, sister chromatid exchanges, and micronuclei). EtO also induces heritable translocations in rodents (not mentioned by the plaintiff's experts). The plaintiff's experts also cited studies showing tumor induction at multiple sites, including brain, in male and female rats exposed to EtO, and they cited studies demonstrating that EtO forms DNA adducts in the brain. The latter piece of information is important because it demonstrates that EtO can cross the blood brain barrier.[159]

A second expert on ETO with an industry affiliation reviewed the evidence as follows:

> Expert A provided the kinds of detailed data, information and background knowledgeable scientists would consider in assessing such a claim. Moreover, a step-wise rationale was presented to support Expert Witness A's contention that exposure to EtO more likely than not was associated with a brain tumor (high grade astrocytoma) in this individual. While I do not agree entirely on the finer points of interpretation of the literature on animal studies (hematopoetic tumors are more consistently related with EtO exposure than are brain tumors), nor with the general conclusion made from a review of the epidemiology studies (e.g., again, hematopoetic tumors are more consistent in these studies and past exposures were known to be very high [not necessarily low or unknown] as stated in Expert A's statement). These disagreements are within the boundaries of what might be expected among

---

[159] Peer review of plaintiffs' expert's report by anonymous reviewer, 12 Jan. 2004 (any emphases in the original).

different scientists knowledgeable on the topic and who review and interpret the same database.[160]

A third reviewer believed that experts could not infer much at all from the evidence about plaintiffs' injuries or defendants' counterarguments. He/she remained largely agnostic about what the evidence showed.

Plaintiffs, thus, according to two reviewers offered scientific arguments on general causation well within the range of respectable scientific arguments on this substance and on either straightforward *Daubert* grounds or on the more elaborate procedure suggested in this chapter, plaintiffs' experts should have been admitted.

Moreover, the first peer-reviewer found defense experts made several unsubstantiated assumptions that were contrary to good scientific methodology,[161] whereas the second thought that defense arguments were within a zone of respectability. Both peer reviewers were unsure about how to assess exposure, but one thought that were he a juror in the case, he would decide for plaintiff, whereas the other thought he would decide against plaintiff. Thus, as judged by knowledgeable experts, ultimately this might have been a close call because of exposure issues, but the admissibility decision was comparatively straightforward, but quite contrary to the trial and appellate judges' assessments.

In sum, the judge excluded plaintiffs by ruling individually on each of the kinds of evidence and failed to understand how the evidence taken as a whole could constitute a reasonable argument in support of plaintiff's claim. Whether the Allens would have won at a jury trial we do not know because they were

---

[160] Peer review of plaintiffs' expert's report by anonymous reviewer, 14 Apr. 2004 (bold in the orginal).

[161] "The defendant's experts made several unjustified assumptions and misstatements to support their contention that the plaintiff's brain tumor was not due to exposure to EtO. The limited epidemiological studies, which lack adequate exposure information, do not support any 'extremely firm conclusion' regarding the presence or lack of EtO brain cancer risk in humans. Differences in exposure patterns and possible differences in genetic susceptibility do not allow conclusions from available epidemiological data that deny the possibility that the plaintiff's brain cancer was due to exposure to EtO. Most epidemiologists would likely conclude that many key issues regarding brain cancer risk have not been adequately resolved. Defendant's expert Brown (Document D) assumes that if an epidemiological study did not mention brain cancer than no brain cancers were observed; this assumption is unreliable. While it may be true that epidemiology studies have not shown a doubling of brain cancer risk in workers, the determination of an individual's cancer risk must take into consideration the fact that EtO occurs in the general environment from several sources such that the unexposed reference populations used in the analyses of epidemiological data may actually have had some level of exposure to EtO, a healthy worker effect requires an upward adjustment to estimates of occupational cancer risk, different exposure patterns and genetic differences can affect the distribution of risks in exposed populations. Thus, an individual's likelihood of developing a brain cancer due to exposure to EtO cannot be denied simply because inadequate epidemiological studies have not detected a brain cancer risk greater than 2.0." Peer review of defendants' expert's report by anonymous reviewer, January 12, 2004 (any emphases in the original).

precluded from having that opportunity, but our peer reviewers suggest that the expert testimony should have been heard and that a jury verdict might have been a close call on scientific grounds. This appears to be precisely the kind of case that should be heard by a jury.

The Parlodel Cases

In the Parlodel cases, because the adverse effects that might have been caused by exposure to Parlodel – heart attacks, hemorrhagic strokes, and ischemic strokes – were sufficiently rare in women of childbearing age that they would be difficult for an epidemiological study to reliably detect (they could easily be falsely negative because of the rareness of the adverse effects), and there were no high-quality epidemiological studies. Consequently, plaintiffs' experts had to rely on other kinds of data and studies: case reports, including the French rechallenge study (for evidence that Parlodel can cause vasoconstriction and a heart attack),[162] some studies in animals, as well as chemical structure–biological activity evidence, and similarities with other compounds in the same chemical family.

As we saw in Chapter 1, these cases have been difficult for both courts and experts. There have been disagreements in different district courts about how nearly identical evidence should be treated. Also, in one district court case the judge sought the assistance of three extramural experts to assist in reviewing the scientific basis for expert testimony. The three experts disagreed with one another, two finding that plaintiffs' experts did not have a reasonable view about general causation and one finding that at least one of the experts did have a reasonable view.[163]

However, this difficulty has manifested itself in disagreements between federal judges on admissibility. For example, in one of the early cases that tended to set the tone for later opinions, the Eighth Circuit Court of Appeals in upholding a District Court's exclusions of plaintiffs' experts described a case report as

> [s]imply a doctor's account of a particular patient's reaction to a drug or other stimulus, accompanied by a description of the relevant surrounding circumstances. Case reports make little attempt to screen out alternative causes for a patient's condition, [and adding] case reports [is] not scientifically valid proof of causation.[164]

This court went on to recognize that rechallenge and dechallenge data "are substantially more valuable than run-of-the-mill case reports because a patient's reactions are measured against his own prior reactions" thus somewhat

---

[162] Considered in Chapter 1.

[163] However, given the discussion of this chapter, such disagreement among scientists concerning plaintiffs' experts' testimony shows that plaintiffs' experts were testifying with a "zone of scientifically reasonable opinions," thus satisfying the *Kumho Tire* test.

[164] *Glastetter v. Novartis Pharmaceuticals Corp.*, 252 F.3d 986, at 988 (8th Cir. 2001).

resembling a controlled experiment, but ultimately rejected them because the data were "statistically insignificant."[165] Thus, the *Glastetter* court seemed not to understand the causal pertinence of a rechallenge case report. However, as we have seen there are good and poor case reports; courts need to distinguish between them. In addition, rejecting rechallenge and dechallenge data as "statistically insignificant" suggests that the court may not have understood how individual case reports can be quite good evidence of causation (recall the case reports considered in Chapter 4).

In Chapter 1, I quoted Federal Magistrate Putnam, who disagreed sharply with his judicial brethren concerning the kind of evidence and the degree of certainty with which expert testimony should be supported for admissibility. He continued that line of argument in a companion case, *Brasher v. Sandoz Pharmaceuticals Corp.*[166]

> Although it is true that none of these bits of evidence establish conclusively that Parlodel can cause vasoconstriction and vasospasm, *taken together* they present a compelling picture, one which can support a reasonable scientific inference. *Daubert* does not require proof to a certainty, or even proof convincing to the trial judge. The trial judge is not required to find that the proffered opinion is scientifically correct, but only that it is trustworthy because it is tied to good scientific grounds. What *Daubert* does require is that the expert's opinion be based on sound methodologies of the type used by experts in the field in which the opinion is offered. There can be little question that scientists routinely use animal studies, case reports, and pharmacological comparisons of similar classes of drugs to infer conclusions, which are expressed in peer-reviewed journals and textbooks. Unquestionably, epidemiological studies provide the best proof of the general association of a particular substance with particular effects, but it is not the only scientific basis on which those effects can be predicted. In science, as in life, where there is smoke, fire can be inferred, subject to debate and further testing. The court is persuaded that the opinions offered here are reliably grounded on known scientific fact derived from recognized scientific methodologies. (emphasis added)

> Further, the fact that no epidemiological studies exist is due to the extreme difficulty, if not impossibility, of framing such a study. Because stroke is a relatively rare event in women of child-bearing years (although not unknown), it would require an extremely large pool of participants to reach statistically acceptable conclusions.[167]

Without judging the correctness of this decision, what is attractive about it is that Judge Putnam shows considerable understanding of the science. He recognizes that it is unreasonable to expect to find epidemiological evidence for the

[165]   *Glastetter v. Novartis Pharmaceuticals Corp.*, 252 F.3d 986, at 989 (8th Cir. 2001).
[166]   160 F. Supp. 2d 1291, at 1296 (2001).
[167]   160 F. Supp. 2d 1291, at 1296–1297.

kind of harm in question. He also appreciates the kinds of studies that are reasonably available and how they can plausibly "fit together" and be integrated to support a scientific inference. Finally, he makes the legal point that expert testimony need not be correct or fully convincing to a trial judge. This more nuanced judgment is refreshing given some that we have considered that endorse comparatively simple admissibility rules that do not do justice to the science.

General Electric v. Joiner

Recall that in *General Electric v. Joiner* the district court excluded plaintiffs' infant mice studies and found their epidemiological studies *individually* scientifically irrelevant to the issues or individually inadequate to support the ultimate causal conclusion. Without either type of study, plaintiffs could not make a causation case. Moreover, the U.S. Supreme Court not only upheld the exclusion as not being an abuse of discretion but also revisited these studies and in effect endorsed the district court's reasons for exclusion. I have already considered the problems that occur when courts individually reject each piece of scientific evidence in support of a causal conclusion in expert testimony.

The Court argued that the infant mice studies were "so dissimilar to the facts presented in this litigation that it was not an abuse of discretion for the District Court to have rejected experts' reliance on them."[168] It noted three points in support of its view: (1) The mice received "massive doses of PCBs injected directly into their peritoneums or stomachs," whereas Mr. Joiner was an *adult* human whose "alleged exposure to PCBs was far less than the exposure in the animal studies."[169] (2) The concentrations of the PCBs injected into mice were much greater than the concentration to which Joiner had been exposed. (3) The kinds of cancers were different: Joiner had "small cell carcinomas," whereas the mice had "alveologenic adenomas."[170] And, no study showed that *adult* mice developed cancer after being exposed to PCBs.

---

[168] *General Elec. Co. v. Joiner*, 522 U.S. at 144–145.

[169] *General Elec. Co. v. Joiner*, 522 U.S. at 144.

[170] The Court noted,

The studies involved infant mice that had developed cancer after being exposed to PCBs. The infant mice in the studies had massive doses of PCBs injected directly into their peritoneums or stomachs. Joiner was an adult human being whose alleged exposure to PCBs was far less than the exposure in the animal studies. The PCBs were injected into the mice in a highly concentrated form. The fluid with which Joiner had come into contact generally had a much smaller PCB concentration of between 0–500 parts per million. The cancer that these mice developed was alveologenic adenomas; Joiner had developed small-cell carcinomas. No study demonstrated that adult mice developed cancer after being exposed to PCBs. One of the experts admitted that no study had demonstrated that PCBs lead to cancer in any other species.

Respondent failed to reply to this criticism. Rather than explaining how and why the experts could have extrapolated their opinions from these seemingly far-removed animal

The baby mice studies are so far from a normal person's experience that they appear implausible on their face; how could someone believe such cockamamie arguments? This apparent implausibility, however, appears to result from a gap between an expert's understanding and a layperson's understanding of the studies in question. Judges will face considerable difficulties with more complex scientific arguments such as these simply because they do not bring scientific background knowledge, understanding of the literature, and years of training to the task.

The mouse experiments were appropriately conducted and designed to discover whether PCBs had the causal properties of increasing – in scientific argot, "promoting" – other cancer-causing cells that had already been initiated in a mammalian body. The biological idea is the following. Scientific models propose that the carcinogenic process is multistage. At least three stages have been proposed – initiation, promotion, and progression. Some agents tend to "alter the structure of DNA and/or chromosomes" in the cells; these are called "initiating agents."[171] However, for cells with DNA or chromosomal damage to become a cancer, they must be "promoted," that is the "clones of [induced or] spontaneously initiated cells" must expand and create many copies of the damaged cell.[172] Some substances to which mammals are exposed appear not to initiate the carcinogenic process and appear not to directly interact with DNA, but they do promote the process in this biologic sense. Finally, the cells "progress" into malignant or benign tumors.[173] Each of the steps in the processes can be and has been observed to be affected by exogenous agents, such as chemicals, with promotion seeming to require the continued exposure to a substance, either endogenous or exogenous, that facilitates this biological stage.

Scientists have long used generic initiation/promotion studies to help assess the carcinogenic potential of substances, including both skin paint studies and infant mouse studies.[174] Since the early 1960s, infant mouse experiments have

---

studies, respondent chose "to proceed as if the only issue [was] whether animal studies can ever be a proper foundation for an expert's opinion." Of course, whether animal studies can ever be a proper foundation for an expert's opinion was not the issue. The issue was whether these experts' opinions were "sufficiently supported by the animal studies on which they purported to rely. The studies were so dissimilar to the facts presented in this litigation that it was not an abuse of discretion for the District Court to have rejected the experts' reliance on them." (522 U.S. at 144)

[171] Pitot and Dragan, "Chemical Carcinogensesis," 267.
[172] Pitot and Dragan, "Chemical Carcinogensesis," 267, 278.
[173] Pitot and Dragan, "Chemical Carcinogensesis," 267.
[174] U.S. Department of Health and Human Services, Public Health Service, National Institutes of Health, National Toxicology Program, "Comparative Initiation/Promotion Skin Pain Studies of B6C3F1 Mice, Swiss (CD-1) Mice, and SENCAR Mice," *Technical Report Series*, No. 441; Lezlee G. Coghlan, I. Gimenez-Conti, Heather E. Kleiner, Susan M. Fischer, Joyce E. Runhaug, Claudio J. Conti, Thomas J. Slaga, and John DiGiovanni, "Development and Initial Characterization of Several New Inbred Strains of SENCAR Mice for Studies of Multistage Skin Carcinogenesis," *Carcinogenesis* 21, 4 (2000): 641–646.

been utilized extensively to provide evidence of the carcinogenicity of sub-stances.[175] Industry institutes accept such results.[176] Several scientists have won awards for research involving infant mice that showed the carcinogenic potential of substances.[177] The International Agency for Research on Cancer and the National Toxicology Program use such generic studies in their assess-ment of the carcinogenicity of substances[178] and both of them have utilized the PCB infant mice studies specifically in their assessments of the carcinogenic potential of PCBs.[179]

The particular PCB promotion data conducted at the National Cancer Insti-tute and referenced in *Joiner* resulted in a series of four scientific papers from the experiments. In one experiment the infant mice were divided into a control group and three experimental groups, one given PCBs only, one given an ini-tiator dimethynitrosamine (DMNS) only, and one given PCBs after receiving DMNS the initiator. The mice receiving both DMNS and PCBs had a substan-tially higher lung tumor rate.[180] Plaintiffs cited two of the four studies. The NCI

[175] Samuel M. Cohen, "Alternative Models for Carcinogenicity Testing: Weight of Evidence Eval-uations Across Models," *Toxicologic Pathology* 29 (suppl.) (2001): 183–190 ("The neona-tal mouse model has been used for more than 40 years."); R. Michael McClain, Douglas Keller, Dan Casciano, Peter Fu, James MacDonald, James Popp, and John Sagarts, "Neonatal Mouse Model: Review of Methods and Results," *Toxicologic Pathology* 29 (suppl.) (2001): 128–137.

[176] McClain et al., "Neonatal Mouse Model."

[177] Allan H. Conney, "Induction of Microsomal Enzymes by Foreign Chemicals and Carcino-genesis by Polycyclic Aromatic Hydrocarbons: G.H.A. Clowes Memorial Lecture," *Can-cer Research* 42 (1982): 3875–4917; Miriam C. Poirier, "In Memoriam: James A. Miller (1915–2000)," *Carcinogenesis* 22, 4 (2001): 681–683 (memorialized for beginning this line of research at McArdle Laboratory for Cancer Research).

[178] International Agency for Research on Cancer, "Consensus Report: The Use of Short- and Medium-term Tests for Carcinogens and Data on Genetic Effects in Carcinogenic Hazard Evaluation," *IARC Scientific Publications No. 146*, ed. D. B. McGregor, J. M. Rice, and S. Venitt (1999). Available at: http://www-cie.iarc.fr/htdocs/iarcpubs/pub146/pub146consensus.html; IARC, "Safrole, Isosafrole, and Dihydrosafrole," *Monograph Series* 10 (1976): 231. Rev. 22 March 1998. Available at: http://www-cie.iarc.fr/htdocs/monographs/vol10/safrole.html. ("Safrole also produced liver and lung tumours in male infant mice following subcutaneous injection." This indicates infant mice studies pro-vided some of the evidence that safrole was a carcinogen.) The National Toxicology Program also utilized such data for listing safrole. (National Toxicology Program, "Safrole, CAS No. 94–59–7," *Eleventh Report on Carcinogens* (first listed in 1981).)

[179] "Polychlorinated Biphenyls," *IARC Monograph Series, Supplement 7* (1987): 322 ("In one study, intragastric administration of PCBs to mice increased the incidence of lung tumours induced by intraperitoneal administration of N-nitrosodimethylamine." (refer-ences excluded)); "Polychlorinated Biphenyls," National Toxicology Program, *Tenth Report on Carcinogens*, Cas. No. 1336–36–3.

[180] Lucy M. Anderson, Jerrold M. Ward, Stephen D. Fox, Haleem J. Isaaq, and Charles W. Riggs, "Effects of a Single Dose of Polycholorinated Biphenyls to Infant Mice on N-Nitrosodimethylamine-Initiated Lung and Liver Tumors," *International Journal of Cancer* 38, 1 (1986): 109–116. ("Mice treated with the highest dose of PCBs after [Dimethylni-trosamine] (NDMA) presented approximately twice as many NDMA-initiated lung tumors

research was in line with several decades of similar work, and the experiments showed that the promotion effects of PCBs were well founded in more than one experiment.

In the laboratory mouse studies the cancers were alveologenic adenomas, initiated by dimethylnitrosamine, one carcinogenic chemical in cigarette smoke. Lucy Anderson et al., who conducted and reported the PCB infant mice studies, noted that the generic kind of study had been "shown to be a useful, reliable model for bioassay of tumor initiators (Shimkin and Stoner, 1975) and recently, *tumor promoters* (Witschi, 1985)" (emphasis added).[181]

Utilizing this data, plaintiffs argued that Joiner had had lung cancer initiated by exposure to cigarette smoke. Thus, if these kinds of experiments were well founded, they showed that PCBs promoted *whatever* cancer had already been initiated in the mice and, hence, if the analogy were biologically plausible (the reason for doing these experiments) PCBs would have promoted tumors that had been initiated in Joiner. However, if alveologenic adenomas had been initiated in infant mice as a result of exposure to dimethylnitrosamine (the initiating substance utilized in the NCI experiments), the PCBs would have promoted *that kind of lung cancer*. If "small cell" lung cancers (as defendants called them) in Joiner had been initiated by exposure to cigarette smoke, the PCB exposures would have promoted the small cell lung cancer, because *PCBs tended to promote the development of whatever cells had been initiated.*

In addition, the doses of PCBs may not have been as "massive" as the Court indicated. The doses administered by stomach tube or gavage (commonly used methods for administering test agents) were approximately 225 to 2250 micrograms per mouse.[182] Expressed in the more common milligram per kilogram body weight basis (mg/kg bw), these doses ranged from 50 to 500 mg/kg bw. It is not uncommon for a 500-mg/kg bw dose to be given on a continuing (frequently daily) basis to experimental animals in a long-term rodent cancer study.[183] The infant mice received only a single dose of this amount. In addition, it is common scientific practice to evaluate mammalian tumor responses to a carcinogen as a function of the *average dose* of a substance administered *over*

---

as those given only the carcinogen, at both 16 and 28 weeks. . . . These differences were of statistical significance. . . . In addition, after 28 weeks the values were suggestive of a dose-dependent increase in numbers of these tumors after 50 and 250 mg. PCBs/Kg" (111).)

[181] Anderson et al., "Effects of a Single Dose," 113. Moreover, these experiments were conducted at the Laboratory of Comparative Carcinogenesis, Division of Cancer Etiology, National Cancer Institute, Frederick, Maryland, one of the leading cancer research centers in the United States.

[182] A microgram is one millionth of a gram.

[183] David A. Eastmond, Environmental Toxicology Program, University of California, Riverside, personal communication.

a lifetime.[184] Using such an approach, a one-time dose of a substance averaged over a lifetime, even a one-time dose of a 100 percent PCB solution, may not be regarded as such a "massive dose."[185] And such lifetime average daily doses may or may not have been greater than the doses Mr. Joiner received as a result of much longer-term workplace exposures.

What is the significance of these features of the infant mice studies and the remarks above? The studies appear quite scientifically relevant and even important, contrary to the characterization by the two courts. In fact, the infant mice studies appear to have been quite compelling evidence of the promotion effects of PCBs. Plaintiffs' experts understood this point, but the written record does not indicate how well they articulated it in pretrial hearings or on appeal. (Their articulation of the issues might have been limited because they were presenting evidence so early in the new *Daubert* era.) In fact, all three reasons the Supreme Court gave for endorsing the exclusion of the studies appear to be off base: (1) comparing infant mice to an adult human being misses the point of the studies. The studies were designed to test the promotion effects of PCBs, not to test identical doses in mice and humans. (2) The doses were

---

[184] David A. Eastmond, Environmental Toxicology Program, University of California, Riverside, personal communication.

[185] See the accompanying tables created by David A. Eastmond, Environmental Toxicology Program, UC Riverside, taken from Anderson et al., "Effects of a Single Dose," 109–116.

Initiation Promotion Studies with PCBs and NDMA Animal doses

Single dose	Dose averaged over study period	
	LADD*	LADD
PCB	16 wks	28 wks
mg/kg	mg/kg	mg/kg
0	0	0
50	0.44	0.26
250	2.2	1.3
500	4.5	2.6
NDMA	16 wks	28 wks
mg/kg	mg/kg	mg/kg
0	0	0
5	0.045	0.026

Single dose	Dose averaged over study period			
	LADD	LADD	LADD	LADD
PCB	16 wks	28 wks	51.8 wks	64.5 wks
mg/kg	mg/kg	mg/kg	mg/kg	mg/kg
0	0	0	0	0
250	2.2	1.3	0.69	0.55
NDMA				
5	0.045	0.026	0.014	0.009

*Lifetime average daily dose

not necessarily "massive" given common practice and how scientists calculate the dose of a substance for purposes of assessing dosages associated with cancer. Moreover, although I do not argue this here, they may not have been massive compared with Joiner's exposure. That would need to be investigated. (3) The fact that the tumors in the mice were different from the tumors in Joiner appears to be tangential, given the study. PCBs tend to gravitate to the lungs and promote tumors that have been initiated in that tissue, whether alveologenic adenomas in mice or "small cell" lung tumors in humans.[186] The promotion of different kinds of tumors that had been initiated would be precisely what one would expect from a tumor *promoter*. Different tumors promoted were thus evidence in favor the plaintiffs' argument not evidence against it.

CONCLUSION

Courts have options in how they implement *Daubert* and its progeny. They can place overly restrictive, unscientific constraints on scientific inferences and their foundation. This decreases the kind and amount of scientific information available in a case. It reduces the chances of an accurate decision. It unfairly biases the legal process against the party with the burden of proof on the issue. And it likely denies them the possibility of justice. Or judges could more sensitively review scientific inferences and admit expert testimony that falls within a "zone where reasonable scientists would disagree." Several more complex patterns of evidence suggest legitimate evidentiary inferences scientists make and from which courts could learn.

Beyond the heuristics from *Kumho Tire* and suggestions made by the Third Circuit Court of Appeals, I reviewed some other decisions that exemplify more subtle assessments of expert testimony and its foundations more like those scientists would make. It can take considerable effort to learn the outlines of the science, conduct research about the pertinent or analogous substances, and thoughtfully review the reports and testimony. The courts discussed in the second group appear to have had some familiarity with the pertinent science.

Appellate courts could assist in these tasks. They could signal lower courts that they need not demand the most certain and best supported scientific evidence, if that would distort the aims of the tort law. More strongly, they could rule that failure to assess scientific evidence sensitively or to review reasoning as scientists would constitutes an abuse of discretion. Were they to do this, there would plausibly be several good consequences. Trial courts would likely produce greater scientific and tort law accuracy in their admissibility screening.

---

[186]   This distinction may or may not have significance, for it depends on the pathology studies in question, an issue that received no discussion in court and one which plaintiffs did not challenge (personal communication, Daniel Teitelbaum, Feb. 2002).

They would lessen some of the barriers erected by earlier decisions and reduce the risk of intruding on the right to a jury trial. They would ensure that wrongfully injured parties have a greater possibility of justice. Whether they will or not remains to be seen. Whether such modifications in the *Daubert* trilogy would be sufficient to serve the aims of the tort law and the larger society will be considered in the final chapter.

8

Is *Daubert* the Solution?

Courts need to become more sophisticated about the scientific issues in toxic torts along the lines suggested in Chapter 7 to better ensure that verdicts comport with the science needed in a case, that there are fair admissibility reviews, and that there is the possibility of justice for injured parties. However, even a sensitive review of scientific evidence within existing federal law may fall short in bringing the science of our technological society into the law to guide social decisions. It also may not be sufficient to ensure matters have been "set right" as corrective justice requires for citizens wrongfully harmed by others. Further analysis suggests that the *Daubert* trilogy has probably had a number of counterproductive, although perhaps unintended, consequences on this point. There are three structural issues that raise concerns: (1) Admissibility changes wrought by *Daubert*, whether conducted poorly or well, almost certainly decrease citizens' access to the legal system. In turn, this puts justice for injured parties at risk and reduces further tort law deterrence of harmful conduct or products. (2) In some respects, *Daubert* increases the acceptability of legal decisions that utilize scientific evidence. In others, it threatens their acceptability, creates counterproductive tendencies concerning the science, or has other untoward consequences. (3) Beyond these two more specific problems, *Daubert* admissibility screening, ignorance about the universe of substances, too little product testing and monitoring, and the causal requirement of torts together undermine protections of public health and the environment where toxic substances are concerned.

The first issue has to do with access and process biases in torts. The second with the difference between the acceptability of decisions based largely or solely on evidence versus legal decisions based on a full jury verdict. And the third, and broader, issue is the result of a legal-social system that pays too little attention to the uncertainties of the safety of products, and too much attention to removing uncertainties before regulating unsafe products or permitting plaintiffs' scientists to testify in court.

Daubert's changes in admissibility rules have decreased legal access and increased process hurdles plaintiffs must overcome. *Daubert* has almost certainly increased the scientific acceptability of jury verdicts, but it also likely had some counterproductive effects on this dimension. The modifications in admissibility are also too late in existing legal-social processes to ensure better scientific understanding of products and their health effects. These modifications reinforce unfortunate incentives for manufacturers and distributors of products to refrain from testing their products well and to refrain from monitoring them for adverse effects once they are in commerce. They also create institutional structures for defendants to use the resulting ignorance in defense of their products, and even to distort scientific studies and the literature of the field. All this tends to occur despite *Daubert*'s motivation to bring better science into the law. As a result, the legal system likely will be less successful in preventing harm from toxicants and wrongful conduct.

How might the law be altered to better address these issues? One possibility would be to have a major overhaul of our legal structure on the regulatory side to obtain better scientific information about products and better prevent injuries from toxicants. At present, there appears to be little political will for this alternative. Even worse, more and greater barriers are being raised to agencies pursuing more protective environmental and workplace health goals.[1] As a society, we seem too little concerned to ensure the safety of products before people are exposed and sometimes harmed. We also appear much more concerned about removing uncertainties concerning the toxicity of products before they are regulated or corrective justice is permitted. This hinders the reduction of risks to the citizenry. Political leaders continue to increase barriers to removing harmful products from market. In torts, some courts similarly seem to insist on removing considerable scientific uncertainty before a toxic tort trial is permitted. On their own courts could take some steps toward addressing these issues by modifying their reviews of expert testimony within a law that has a causation requirement or by modifying the liability rules themselves. What is to be said about these alternatives? These are the subjects of this chapter.

ACCESS AND PROCESS BIAS IN TOXIC TORT SUITS

In order for citizens to bring suits when they have been harmed by exposure to toxicants, they must have *access* to the law and the *process* must not be too tilted against them(Chapter 3). It is, of course, easy to file a suit. That is not the

---

[1]   Thomas O. McGarity, "Some Thoughts on 'Deossifying' the Rule-Making Process," *Duke Law Journal* 41(1992): 1335–1462. Thomas O. McGarity and Sidney A. Shapiro, *Workers at Risk: the Failed Promise of the Occupational Safety and Health Administration* (Westport, CT: Praeger, 1993).

issue; realistic access is. A plaintiff's case must have sufficient legal and factual merit for an attorney to commit to it. It also must have enough scientific merit for an expert to do the requisite preparation and to testify with integrity about causation.

Toxic tort suits raise both access and process concerns following the *Daubert* decision. The risks posed by toxic substances make it difficult for plaintiffs to have access to the courts, raising a barrier to their even beginning a legal action for injuries they may have suffered. Substances causing diseases with long latency periods are difficult to document.[2] Harms that are diffusely "spread over many victims" pose free rider problems.[3] Risks from toxic substances tend to have a low probability of materializing; yet they often will have catastrophic consequences for individual victims, such as cancer or reproductive effects, or for the larger society (in the case of a nuclear accident). These "structural features"[4] of public risks create access barriers for plaintiffs bringing a suit in the first place (Chapter 3). Moreover, diffusely and widely distributed injuries reduce the chances that injured parties will identify the source of harm and decrease the odds that they will identify a commonalty of interests between themselves and others injured by a particular exposure. We saw this problem concerning occupational exposures to DBCP. Such problems are enhanced for widespread environmental exposure from something like radiation. For example, the public living around the Hanford nuclear plant in the 1940s and 1950s was unaware of radiation in their presence, perhaps until the illnesses and deaths of neighbors led them to ask questions.

> Plutonium was extracted from uranium fuel rods in separation plants that measured 800 feet long and eight stories high. One step in the process involved dissolving the uranium rods in large vats of nitric acid. As the rods dissolved, gases that contained iodine-131 were released through the smokestacks.

> The emissions were mostly invisible.

> "You saw nothing!" said Harriet Fugitt, 66. Fugitt's father worked as an electrician at the Hanford plant, and the family lived near it for 12 years starting in the 1940s. Fugitt has suffered thyroid problems for decades.

> "There were no huge clouds," she said, recalling the smokestacks. "Sometimes there would be steam coming out. That's what they called it, anyway: steam."[5]

---

[2]   See the discussions in Chapters 4 and 5 on this point.

[3]   Gillette and Krier, "Risk, Courts and Agencies," 1039.

[4]   Gillette and Krier, "Risk, Courts and Agencies," 1047.

[5]   Tomas Alex Tizon, "Cases Against Nuclear Plant Finally Heard: After 15 Years of Delays, 2300 Plaintiffs who Say Radioactive Releases at the Hanford Site Made Them Seriously Ill Wait for a Jury's Decision," *Los Angeles Times*, May 16, 2005, A2.

As a consequence of such problems, Gillette and Krier argued in 1990,

> [P]ublic risk litigation [which is required to address toxic substances] is probably marked by too few claims and too little vigorous prosecution, with the likely consequence that too much public risk escapes the deterrent effects of liability. Those who think otherwise must believe that public risk claimants find a easy path into court and effective representation once there.[6]

And, because there is too little claiming in torts, "The producers of public risks will be inclined to overindulge, absent signals that align their self-interest with the larger social interest."[7] This absence of claiming, they argued, is not compensated for by market or regulatory mechanisms.

However, they also argued in 1990 that access bias against plaintiffs was balanced by "process bias" which favored plaintiffs. They saw no need, as tort law critics of that period had argued, to modify legal procedures for more stringent screening of scientific experts and their testimony. Yet this is precisely the authority the Supreme Court gave to trial judges in *Daubert*.

In light of the preceding discussion in this book, how does their view look fifteen years later? It should be clear that Gillette and Krier's view is now probably much too optimistic. The legal landscape changed substantially as a result of *Daubert, Joiner, Kumho Tire*, and amendments to Rule 702. Gillette and Krier advanced their thesis when courts arguably permitted most experts to testify and let the jury assess their testimony after cross-examination and presentation of contrary evidence. The *Frye* rule could in principle pose some barriers to the admission of novel *kinds* of studies, but most jurisdictions did not apply it to expert *testimony*. Subsequent to the *Daubert* trilogy with its substantive gatekeeping duty for expert testimony, evidence suggests admissibility reviews are less, and perhaps much less, permissive than in 1990. Moreover, as a result of *Joiner* it is difficult to appeal admissibility rulings, even those that are dispositive of a case.

The scientific difficulties appear greater than Gillette and Krier envisioned. The pragmatic barriers considered in Chapter 5 can frustrate the availability of good scientific evidence to support of expert testimony; this in turn exacerbates the access barriers for plaintiffs. There is substantial ignorance in general about potential toxicants. The fewer studies that have been done and the more difficult it is for scientists to conduct the needed studies, the less evidence will be available for adverse effects associated with exposure to a substance. For rare or very common disease end points, it will be difficult for scientific studies to detect them. Conventions of scientific practice can aggravate admissibility issues if courts are not sensitive to them. Court must recognize the fact of reasonable

---

[6]   Gillette and Krier, "Risk, Courts and Agencies," 1054.
[7]   Gillette and Krier," Risk, Courts and Agencies," 1055. See also, Saks, "Do We Really Know Anything about the Behavior of the Tort Litigation System – and Why Not?" 1184–1185.

scientific disagreement and not take sides when each group of experts is within the zone of reasonable disagreement.

In addition, how courts assess expert testimony and its scientific foundation is especially important, because of the pragmatic obstacles to detecting and substantiating the harms from toxic substances. Moreover, in admissibility hearings opponents can easily denigrate some of the elements of complex patterns of evidence that must be relied on in expert testimony. If such patterns in support of testimony are not permitted into evidence, this can determine the outcome of a trial. If courts follow more restrictive rules in admitting evidence, as some clearly have, this can easily bias the legal process much more against plaintiffs than it was in 1990. In Gillette and Krier's terms, this would greatly reduce the optimal number of cases reaching court because of increased access and process biases since 1990 that results from admissibility reviews.

If Gillette and Krier's original thesis was correct or reasonably close to it, even if the changes wrought by the *Daubert* trilogy were liberally construed by trial judges, they would still likely change the overall balance of access and process biases in toxic tort suits simply because of attorney's and plaintiffs' *perceptions* of the hurdles to be faced. Attorneys facing the new gatekeeping requirements and having to prepare cases would likely overcompensate in anticipation of evidentiary review, simply to avoid losing cases from inadequate preparation. Lawyers' caution would preclude them from taking some plaintiffs' cases, and thus deny plaintiffs access to legal assistance. Experts themselves also screen cases in which they are asked to testify. Can they in good conscience testify to the science? Is the preparation needed for testifying worth their time and any staff effort?

Courts can easily improve plaintiffs' access beyond what it is at present; it depends very much on how the many trial judges around the country treat scientific evidence and expert testimony that is available in toxic tort suits. To do this, courts should adopt admissibility screening procedures that are sensitive to the kind and range of scientific evidence that is available and can be submitted. They should permit reasonable, legitimate scientific points of view so as not to foreclose genuine scientific issues and disputes. Judges drawing boundaries around scientific evidence should not be seduced by univocal, overly simplified, or highly stringent standards of evidence in support of testimony. Such reviews could easily result in a cavalier rejection of perfectly sound, albeit sometimes not the best or most pristine, evidence and it would be inconsistent with scientific practices.[8]

---

[8]   See John J. Cohrssen and Vincent T. Covello, *Risk Analysis: A Guide to Principles and Methods for Analyzing Health and Environmental Risks* (Washington, DC: White House Council on Environmental Quality, 1989), 27–48 (describing factors scientists examine in identifying hazardous chemicals).

Unless courts conduct more sensitive admissibility reviews, respectable scientists testifying within a zone of reasonable disagreement might easily be excluded from court. Judges should adopt admissibility standards that serve the goals of torts and recognize the legitimacy of the range of evidentiary standards held by respectable practitioners of the pertinent disciplines, in order to ensure that jury decisions comport better with the pertinent science at the time of trial.

For example, a number of prominent epidemiologists believe the evidence between exposure to electromagnetic fields and the development of cancer is sufficient to warrant cost-effective protective actions and further studies into the adverse effects of this agent.[9] In contrast, other respected scientists, most notably biophysicists, claim the association between electromagnetic fields and cancer has "no persuasive scientific basis,"[10] largely because to date scientists have not found a plausible mechanism at the levels of exposure to EMFs to support a causal inference. There is legitimate scientific disagreement on these issues, often along disciplinary lines. Similar disagreements between well-respected scientists can be found for the health effects of other agents such as lead[11] and 1,3-butadiene.[12] Toxicologists can even disagree concerning the amount of evidence needed to justify claims of causation.[13] Such disagreements are not unusual or outside a zone of scientific reasonableness. Courts should allow for them, and not, as some appear to have done, choose sides in the face of reasonable disagreement.

Finally, placing too great a burden on the admissibility of scientific evidence hides important policy issues behind the science. These issues include the

---

[9] See Anders Ahlbom and Maria Feychting, "Studies of Electromagnetic Fields and Cancer: How Inconsistent?" *Environmental Science and Technology* 27 (1993): 1018–1020; B. Hileman, "Findings Point to Complexity of Health Effects of Electric, Magnetic Fields," *Chemical Engineering News* 72 (1994): 27, 33 (including related articles); and David A. Savitz, "Health Effects of Low-Frequency Electric and Magnetic Fields, Special Report Commentary," *Environmental Science and Technology* 27 (1993): 52, 54.

[10] Janet Raloff, "Physicists Offer Reassurances on EMF: Electromagnetic Fields and their Link to Cancer Might be Tenuous," *Science News*, 47 (1995): 308.

[11] See Joseph Palca, "Lead Researcher Confronts Accusers in Public Hearing," *Science* 256 (1992): 437, 437–438.

[12] *Compare* James A. Bond et al., "Epidemiological and Mechanistic Data Suggest that 1,3-Butadiene Will Not Be Carcinogenic to Humans at Exposures Likely to Be Encountered in the Environment or Workplace," *Carcinogenesis* 16 (1995): 165, 165–171, with Ronald L. Melnick and Michael C. Kohn, "Mechanistic Data Indicate that 1,3-Butadiene Is a Human Carcinogen," *Carcinogenesis* 16 (1995): 157, 157–163.

[13] For example, there is scientific disagreement on which substances constitute major human carcinogens. See Bruce N. Ames, "What Are The Major Carcinogens in the Etiology of Human Cancer? Environmental Pollution, Natural Carcinogens, and Causes of Human Cancer: Six Errors," in *Important Advances in Oncology*, ed. Vincent T. Devita, Jr., S. Hellman, and S. A. Rosenberg (Philadelphia: Lippincott, 1989), 237; Jean Marx, "Animal Carcinogen Testing Challenged," *Science* 250 (1990): 743; and Frederica P. Perera et al., "What Are the Major Carcinogens in the Etiology of Human Cancer? Industrial Carcinogens," in *Important Advances in Oncology*, 249.

following: Who should bear the risk of harm resulting from disease likely caused by exposure to toxic substances? When should wealth be shifted? Who should decide these decisions, a judge or jury? These policy issues should be addressed on their own merits, not decided through proxies such as debates about scientific evidence. Precluding juries from basing decisions on science that is too speculative is a legitimate and important concern. However, the effort to preclude so-called junk scientists from the courtroom has resulted in overly strong reviews or mistaken reasons for evaluating expert testimony. Moreover, this issue often overshadows and hides other important substantive debates that should be addressed openly.

HOW *DAUBERT* CAN UNDERMINE THE ACCEPTABILITY OF JUDICIAL DECISIONS AND CORRUPT SCIENCE

The Acceptability of Verdicts vs. a Focus on the Evidence

Charles Nesson, a well-known evidence scholar, argued for a distinction – the difference between the acceptability of verdicts that convey a liability judgment and verdicts that tend to focus on the evidence – that can assist this argument. In a well-known paper, Nesson introduced and argued for the following view.

> A verdict that a defendant is guilty or liable can carry two different meanings and project two different rules. The verdict can articulate a legal rule: "*You did the thing enjoined by the law*; therefore, you will pay the penalty." This message encourages each of us to conform our conduct to the behavioral norms embodied in the substantive law. Alternatively, the verdict can emphasize a proof rule: "We will convict and punish you only if your violation is proved by due process of law." This message invites people to act not according to what they know is lawful, but according to what they think can be proved against them. While the legal system requires judges to heed the proof rule, it encourages citizens to heed the legal rule and to conduct themselves accordingly. A primary objective of the judicial process, then, is to project to society the legal rules that underlie judicial verdicts.[14]

One way to make these points is to consider some of the "gaps" between comparatively raw scientific evidence and an ultimate legal conclusion about liability. Recall *Allen v. Pennsylvania Engineering, Inc.*[15] The Allens needed some scientific evidence showing that ETO *could cause* brain cancer and evidence that ETO *did cause* Mr. Allen's brain cancer. They also needed to show, given the causal claims, under the applicable law that Pennsylvania Engineering should be held *liable* for his brain cancer.

---

[14] Charles Nesson, "The Evidence or the Event? On Judicial Proof and the Acceptability of Verdicts," *Harvard Law Review* 98 (1985): 1357.
[15] 102 F.3d 194, 197 (5th Cir. 1996).

This argument has at least two major "gaps." There is an "evidence-causation" gap from basic scientific studies to the two causal judgments.[16] There is also a "causation-liability" gap from any causation established to a showing of liability. Both inferences are underdetermined. The evidence for each is likely to be compatible with different possible conclusions in a nondeductive inference to the best explanation. The issue for a court would be to determine which arguments are within a zone of reasonable scientific disagreement.

Recall the evidence from Chapter 7 that plaintiffs had in support of the claim that ETO could and did cause brain cancer in rats exposed to ETO compared with rats not so exposed (but not in mice). ETO is a small molecule that is a direct acting alkylating agent that can attach itself to DNA in a wide range of tissues in the body and disrupt DNA function.[17] There were also some suggestive epidemiological studies that ETO could cause brain cancers in persons occupationally exposed but a large meta-analysis of these small studies did not show an elevated risk. Did the studies show causation or not?

Defendants argued that because ETO did not cause brain cancers in mice, which are phylogenetically more similar to rats than rats are to humans, rat studies are *not evidence* that ETO can cause cancer in humans. Moreover, the defense greatly emphasized the significance of the meta-analysis of human studies and claimed that it showed that ETO did not cause cancer in humans. One defense expert opined, "For these reasons it is simply impossible to conclude that Mr. Allen's BT [brain tumor] was more likely than not caused by his occupational exposure to ETO."[18] The trial judge and the appellate court found that plaintiffs had insufficient reliable evidence for admissibility (mistakenly it appears (Chapter 7)).

Ultimately, if a case goes to trial, a jury must first assimilate the scientific evidence and expert testimony to make a causal judgment and then assimilate all of the causal and pertinent historical evidence of the events leading to the case and the applicable law to decide whether or not defendants were liable for the injuries. Nesson would argue that there is a difference between Pennsylvania Engineering being found *liable* for causing Mr. Allen's brain cancer, and the claim that the toxicological, epidemiological, and exposure evidence tended to favor the view that Pennsylvania Engineering's product caused Mr. Allen's brain cancer. A verdict or judgment of *liable* in civil litigation calls attention to the human and social events that transpired and to the legal rules that were violated. It also cautions people to avoid unlawful behavior and invites them to act according to what is lawful. An *evidentiary* claim by contrast calls attention to the evidence available and the extent to which a verdict might be proven,

---

[16] Some states do not require both general and specific causation, e.g., Illinois.

[17] These plaintiffs' and defendants' scientific arguments are taken from expert reports filed with the court and acquired by the author from plaintiffs' counsel.

[18] Report of Edward J. Calabrese, "Did Occupational Exposure to ETO Cause Mr. Walter Allen's Brain Tumor?" 13 Apr. 1993, 9.

in turn inviting citizens to act "according to what they think can be proved against them."[19] The scientific-evidence-only claim ultimately, first, leaves us in *doubt* about causation. Second, it leaves doubt about a liability claim. Third, it creates still further misgivings about whether justice has been done between the parties.

A citizen, by viewing a liability "verdict as a determination of what actually happened, [can] assimilate the applicable legal rule and absorb its behavioral message"; it also reminds a person of "what constitutes proper legal conduct in the circumstances."[20] If a citizen only regards a decision "as merely a statement about the evidence, he will assimilate only the proof rule, whose deterrent power [and behavioral message] is far less pronounced."[21]

Nesson appears to support his distinction by means of the following considerations. "The projection [and receipt] of the verdict as a statement about what happened is the key to conveying the legal rule and its behavior message. Projecting the verdict as such forges a link between the judicial account of the defendant's transgression and our own behavior."[22] The idea seems to be that those receiving the verdict about *the people involved* and *what happened* between them tend to identify with or perhaps recognize the significance of the *behavior* of those who were violating the law toward others. Receipt of this message and its recognition can have a significant impact on our and others' behavior to the extent the liability judgment is understood and internalized. We would tend to take the legal message embedded in the verdict seriously and, *ceteris paribus*, be disposed to modify our conduct accordingly. To the extent that a court decision conveys a message about the persons involved and their violation of the law, this creates the possibility that "[w]hen similar situations arise in the lives of those who have accepted the verdict as a determination about what happened, these citizens will govern their conduct in accordance with the behavioral rules that they have absorbed."[23]

By contrast, if a legal dispute is primarily about the *evidence* involved, this does not support, and, Nesson suggests, tends to undermine, a behavioral or deterrence message. Citizens typically would not recognize the significance of generic scientific evidence claims for their own behavior in the same way they would more readily identify with statements about the behavior of other citizens being held liable. And a focus on the evidence keeps the attention, first, on the extent to which evidence can or cannot establish causation, and, then, on the extent to which a legal violation can or cannot be established. Thus, instead

---

19   Nesson, "The Evidence or the Event?" 1357.
20   Nesson, "The Evidence or the Event?" 1361. Occasionally, a high-profile case, such as the criminal case involving O. J. Simpson, exhibits how an extreme focus on the evidence can distort the acceptability of a decision.
21   Nesson, "The Evidence or the Event?" 1361.
22   Nesson, "The Evidence or the Event?" 1367.
23   Nesson, "The Evidence or the Event?" 1367.

of conveying that the defendant negligently or wrongfully injured a plaintiff or created products that caused harm, it conveys and asks those receiving the evidence message to "assimilate the rule that one should not negligently injure others in a manner that allows them to prove it."[24] The evidentiary implications of a legal dispute to which Nesson calls attention appear to be greatly exacerbated by a focus only on scientific evidence that *Daubert* forces. An internal memo from Bayer Pharmaceutical concerning product testing suggests this point: "If the F.D.A. asks for bad news, we have to give, but if we don't have it, then we can't give it to them."[25] This suggests that Bayer lawyers act "according to what they think can be proved against them."[26] Their reading of the evidentiary message seems to be a self-interested, cost-benefit rule about the value of testing, not a rule aimed at protecting the public from wrongful behavior or harmful products. This statement seems oblivious to the importance of producing public scientific evidence about the effect of products on the citizenry.

Daubert and the Acceptability of Verdicts

The legal changes wrought by *Daubert* both can contribute to the acceptability of legal verdicts based on substantial scientific input and can undermine them. They can contribute to the acceptability of verdicts if screening is done well by ensuring that expert testimony rests on appropriate scientific foundation, and inferences from studies are within a zone of reasonable disagreement (Chapter 7). Verdicts whose science is within this zone will have greater acceptability from the scientific community than some earlier decisions might have (when some decisions might have been outside that zone). Thus, when judges do an accurate job of screening scientific evidence, making mistakes that favor neither plaintiffs nor defendants, this removes one way in which the acceptability of verdicts might be undermined.

However, *Daubert* modifications can also undermine the acceptability of verdicts. Poor implementation of *Daubert* will have this result. When courts err by requiring or excluding scientific evidence in support of expert testimony for reasons that are at odds with scientists' approaches to the same evidence or at odds with scientific reasoning, this makes the law vulnerable to legitimate scientific criticisms. When courts reject scientific inferences that are within a zone of reasonable disagreement, this too invites critiques from the scientific community. As such criticisms become known, this tends to subvert the legitimacy of the decisions and the legal system. When Courts mistakenly exclude

24 Nesson, "The Evidence or the Event?" 1367.
25 Alex Berenson, "Trial Lawyers Are Now Focusing on Lawsuits Against Drug Makers," *New York Times*, 18 May 2003, n.p.
26 Nesson, "The Evidence or the Event?" 1357.

plaintiffs' evidence and their legal actions end with a summary judgment, this denies plaintiffs a trial and the *possibility* of justice. To the extent that such results become known, this too affects the perceived *fairness* of the legal system.

Even if courts *properly implement* a reasonable version of *Daubert* as argued in Chapter 7, there are reasons, following Nesson, for being concerned about the heightened attention scientific evidence is receiving in admissibility decisions.

For one thing, it is arguable that plaintiffs have already been hurt by a focus on the evidence – analogous to Nesson's point about the difference between a focus on evidence and a focus on liability. A *pretrial* focus only on the evidence does not obviously require any consideration of past events, including discussions about defendant's improper treatment of plaintiff and the distribution of risks in the relationship. Instead, as in *Allen* the discussion is about the merits of rodent studies, small versus large epidemiological studies, structure-activity tests, other molecular data, and case studies. Such scientific arcana are difficult for most of us and we have little patience with them. The focus is not on what happened and the relations between people that led to litigation.[27] As important as the law as reasonable scientific evidence is, plaintiffs are handicapped because they can present only part of their account – the scientific evidence and expert testimony needed for causation. (They will have some account of past events in their complaints, but this is likely to be minimal.) It is difficult for them to offer a full account of defendant's behavior, whether it was negligent or not, and how the law was violated. Thus, *per force* plaintiffs' focus must be largely on what the scientific evidence and expert testimony would support about causation, that is, mainly on the evidence-causation gap.

Daubert hearings will bear resemblance to *scientific* debates or seminars about the quality of studies and the inferences from them. They will tend not to be a legal debate about defendant's treatment of plaintiff, and whether and to what extent legal rules have been violated. Some will think this is desirable since it forces a clarification of the quality of the science, free from "contamination" by stories about sympathetic plaintiffs, to see if there is a reasonable scientific basis for a plaintiff's complaint. It also promises court efficiencies (although these may be overrated).

Moreover, plaintiffs increasingly must invest substantial monetary and expert resources in preparation for an admissibility hearing simply in order to have a trial on what happened. By some estimates, the pretrial costs are now substantially higher than they were in an earlier period.[28] In general, the costs of testifying have increased for scientific experts following *Daubert*. This increases lawyers' costs and heightens their screening of plaintiffs and citizens' realistic

---

[27] There would not be such an emphasis under the earlier *Frye* rule that only required courts to inquire into the general acceptance of the kinds of studies on which experts relied, not their testimony.

[28] Personal communication from a major plaintiffs' expert.

access to the law. In an irony about which the law and larger community should be concerned, plaintiffs often must invest these resources because defendants or others did not test their products adequately in the first place. Some courts and some commentators are concerned that plaintiffs are at risk of having to prove most of their case twice: once at an admissibility hearing; again at trial, if their experts are admitted.[29]

The larger community also loses when cases end after admissibility reviews. First, there is likely to be little discussion of the relationships between people and the applicable law before a public trial. Second, there is no structured *public discussion* in a trial about what happened, the relationships between plaintiffs and defendants, the distributions of risks involved, and whether the law had been properly followed. Third, to the extent there is a legitimate dispute about proper legal behavior, there is no *public resolution* of this. Thus, the community is deprived of important kinds of information about its institutions and how they affect their neighbors.[30] At most, the community would learn that there was insufficient scientific evidence and expert testimony for the case to proceed. "Inadequate scientific evidence at present for the case to proceed," is a much different finding than "Defendant did not injure plaintiff." The former does much less to bring the legal proceedings to a satisfying social closure than the latter. It might well leave the community uneasy about the result, about how good a neighbor the company is and about how safe its products are.

In addition, the law has shifted focus. With *Daubert*, the Supreme Court itself has elevated the importance of the quality of scientific studies and expert opinions above other values in the system. Expert testimony and its basis must now be considered first chronologically, but they also have acquired an unusually high degree of importance for the legal system. The Court has seemed so concerned to secure these values that it permits judges to err on the side of mistakenly excluding evidence, which precludes adjudication of what happened between the parties, rather than permitting in the evidence and letting the trial and appellate process adjudicate what happened between parties. Adjudicating whether such relationships were legal and whether the treatment of plaintiffs was lawful is as important as (or more important than) whether every "i" is dotted and "t" crossed concerning scientific evidence. Thus, the concerns about scientific evidence and expert testimony appear to have taken precedence over *public* adjudication of past events and relations between people, norms of behavior exhibited therein, and the rules, norms, and ideals of the substantive law. Justice between parties has been deemphasized.

---

[29] *In re Paoli Railroad Yard PCB Litigation*, 35 F.3d 717 (3d Cir. 1994), and Gottesman, "From *Barefoot* to *Daubert* to *Joiner*," 753, 779.

[30] Owen M. Fiss, "Against Settlement," *Yale Law Journal* 93 (1984): 1073, decries the loss of public discussion of legal relationships that are blocked by settlements (although he largely appears to discuss settlements in public law, e.g., civil rights cases).

In short, the *Daubert* Court's decision and its implications appear to symbolize that it is more important *to the law to get the science right* by means of Daubert reviews *than to adjudicate more fully the justice of past events and lawful norms of behavior in a public forum.*[31]

There also appear to be worse effects on potential defendants and their behavior (the main focus of Nesson's concerns) with further adverse consequences for the community and plaintiffs. Structural issues can tempt defendants to exploit them. Defendants need only play "defense," an easy thing to do where science is concerned because of the burdens and standards of proof internal to science itself. Of course, this is defendants' position, but it has acquired added significance concerning scientific evidence. Implicit scientific burdens and standards of proof reinforce the defense position (as it does in the criminal law, but with a much different legal and social effect). Within science the burden of proof is typically on a scientist who would argue against the received scientific view, for example, that a substance is toxic when toxicity had not previously been established. Scientific standards of proof can be quite high, and typically are more demanding than the tort law's preponderance of the evidence standard (Chapter 6). Thus, if admissibility is not administered sensitively, the standard of proof to clear the admissibility barrier can be much higher than the plaintiff's ultimate standard of proof.[32] Moreover, because scientists typically demand removal of considerable uncertainty before they come to scientific conclusions, any uncertainty about a potential toxicant (which can be considerable) can tempt defendants to exploit it, unless judges are alert to these issues.[33] Any misunderstanding between the scientific community (including hedging) and the different context of the law can erect additional barriers. If scientists themselves fail to understand the different contexts, this too poses problems. And, of course, the party conducting the defense can exploit these differences; judges need to be alert to these issues as well. Even if admissibility reviews are conducted well, many of these issues remain.

These structural issues, plus the possibility of winning on evidentiary grounds alone before trial, heighten several temptations for defendants: to exploit uncertainty in the science, to exploit its high implicit standards of proof, or even to create a misleading idea of the science needed for toxicity assessments. In each case if they persuade a judge, *the case is over.* We have seen that defendants commonly insist that plaintiffs must have special or extensive evidence

[31] *Daubert* also may have encouraged an attitude toward risks very much favored by the technical community (vs. the public's conception of acceptable risk), which would further separate the public from its institutions. (Gillette and Krier," Risk, Courts and Agencies," 1077–1109.)

[32] The original *Daubert* decision suggested this should not be a significant issue.

[33] In Chapter 4, we saw that there can be considerable uncertainty in science for defendants to exploit. In Chapter 5, I suggested that emphasizing uncertainty in the science could easily become part of a deliberate strategy.

before scientific testimony is admissible, for example, epidemiological studies evidencing a relative risk greater than two or sometimes higher.[34] Moreover, even though defendants in their own product research typically rely on rodent studies, structure-activity relationships, molecular studies, mutagenicity studies, and even case studies to assess the toxicity of their products, they typically *dismiss, downplay,* or *denigrate* such evidence in admissibility hearings, simply because it is easy to raise various kinds of doubts about them that might appear persuasive to judges.[35] They appear to have had some success with such tactics.

Daubert also has created a legal environment for admissibility hearings that tempts defendants to act in ways that function to corrupt the scientific fields and their literature. There has always been the temptation for litigants on both sides to fund or use studies that favor their own view of the safety or harmfulness of products or even to cheat.[36] There have been systematic efforts to mislead the public and regulatory agencies about what scientific evidence shows.[37] Enhanced scrutiny of science has likely heightened this effect for several reasons: (a) Defendants have incentives to create a legally constructed picture of science that is at odds with scientists' understanding of the same evidence; (b) *Daubert* creates incentives for firms to distort scientific studies; and (c) it similarly creates incentives to distort the scientific literature.

(a) Because they are playing defense, some defendants utilize reasons contrary to those of most scientists to exclude studies or kinds of evidence, but reasons that have a patina of plausibility. Thus, they might denigrate certain kinds of studies as evidence that could invite naïve assent, for example, animal studies, case reports, or molecular data, even when this is contrary to scientific assessments of the same evidence. If judges acquiesce in such suggestions and individually exclude scientifically relevant evidence, this creates a misleading legal record of the science. Defendants also have reasons to try to persuade judges to erect barriers to studies that are difficult to satisfy; for example, they might argue for requiring human studies or argue that many of Hill's "factors" are necessary. All of this makes the defendants' task easier, and if they are successful, they do not have to go to trial or, as in many cases, to settle.

More insidiously, because *Daubert* encourages judges to use published results in peer-reviewed science journals as one consideration to assess the basis of expert testimony, this provides incentives for defendants to shape the scientific literature as well as the research. Studies can easily be designed to show negative outcomes: as we have seen they can be too small, too short, too specific for subspecies of disease, or conducted too long after exposure has ceased to

---

[34] Joe G. Hollingsworth and Eric G. Lasker, "The Case Against Differential Diagnosis: *Daubert,* Medical Causation Testimony, and the Scientific Method," *Journal of Health Law,* 37, 1 (2004): 85–112.

[35] Michaels and Monforton, "Manufacturing Uncertainty," S39–S48.

[36] Green, *Bendectin and Birth Defects,* 146.

[37] Markowitz and Rosner, *Deceit and Denial,* 195–233.

identify real adverse effects. For instance, a study like that by Wong, noted in Chapter 5, that is of too short a duration to allow for both the induction and latency periods for the disease to develop is misleadingly negative.[38] Evidence may be held from published reports or there may be no studies when risks are suspected, as occurred for the painkiller, Vioxx.[39] Research can be conducted too long after exposure has ceased to reliably identify adverse effects. Scientists *eventually* will probably detect and correct such misleading results as they did with the Wong study, but judges may not know of them, if the correctives have not been published, or someone in the legal process does not call them to judicial attention.[40] However, when misleading studies are deliberately published for legal purposes, this distorts the scientific literature. More recently, for example, drug companies have been criticized for only publishing studies that show their products are beneficial, while concealing studies that show no beneficial effects or that even show harmful effects.[41] This distorts the scientific record in another direction. The upshot is that the scientific literature is at some risk from misleading studies created for admissibility reviews as a consequent of the *Daubert* decision. The tobacco industry appears to have surpassed other industries in deliberately shaping and distorting the science used for regulation or tort suits.[42] Other industries have followed.

Defendants also have incentives to pay for studies critiquing others' scientific results and for studies that, legitimate or not, show that there are no adverse effects from products. One well-known example of this is the lead industry's attempt to discredit Herbert Needleman's studies showing that lead exposures lower the intelligence quotient (IQ) of children.[43] A recently publicized study to be conducted by the American Petroleum Institute suggests the organization

---

[38] Otto Wong, "A Cohort Mortality Study and a Case Control Study of Workers Potentially Exposed to Styrene in Reinforced Plastics and Composite Industry," *British Journal of Industrial Medicine* 47 (1990): 753–762.

[39] G. D. Curfman, S. Morrissey, J. M. Drazen, "Expression of Concern: Bombardier, et al., Comparison of Upper Gastrointestinal Toxicity of Rofecoxib and Naproxen in Patients with Rheumatoid Arthritis," *New England Journal of Medicine*, 343 (2005): 2813–2814. Located at www.NEJM.org. December 29, 2005. Alex Berenson, "First Vioxx Suit: Entryway into a Legal Labyrinth?" *New York Times*, 11 July 2005, n.p. ("Many Merck documents that have been produced by the company in the pretrial discovery process show that its top scientists were worried about heart risks from Vioxx, and considered and rejected conducting specific studies to examine those risks.")

[40] Manolis Kogevinas and Paolo Boffetta, *British Journal of Industrial Medicine* 48 (1991): 575–576 (letter to editor criticizing a study by Wong, "A Cohort Mortality Study," 753–762, for having too short a follow-up – seven years – even though the author had a large sample population to study).

[41] See, for example, Barry Meier, "Medical Editors Likely to Call for Registration of Drug Tests at Outset," *New York Times*, 8 Sept. 2004; and "Editorial: For Honest Reports of Drug Trials," *New York Times*, 11 Sept. 2004.

[42] Lissy C. Friedman, Richard A. Daynard, and Christopher N. Banthin, "How Tobacco-Friendly Science Escapes Scrutiny in the Courtroom," *American Journal of Public Health*, Supplement 1 95 (2005): S16–S19.

[43] Markowitz and Rosner, *Deceit and Denial*, 136–137.

knows what results the study will show before it is conducted.[44] In addition, a distinguished university scientist, who has testified for both plaintiffs and defendants, has informed me that highly paid professional critics follow his research in the scientific literature and publish articles misleadingly critical of it.[45] This, of course, is their First Amendment right and could be seen as part of the usual scientific give and take. It becomes more disturbing when critical scientists are highly paid simply for legal purposes to try to discredit scientific research carried out in the normal course of investigation and not aimed at litigation.

Defendants might have engaged in some of this conduct prior to the *Daubert* decision; indeed the attack on Needleman and the activities of the tobacco, lead, asbestos, dye, and vinyl chloride industries largely occurred before *Daubert* and were probably aimed more at regulatory rulemakings than tort law cases. Firms might well have paid for misleadingly negative studies before *Daubert* as well; it was clear in some early drug cases that firms sometimes falsified data or failed to report studies showing or suggesting harmful effects from their products, studies that would jeopardize approval or threaten removal.[46] However, the *Daubert* decision, with its emphasis on a separate scientific inquiry before a trial can even occur, has created a context that increases temptations to such conduct.[47]

Events reported in the developing Vioxx litigation illustrate a number of these points. Vioxx is a pain medication manufactured by Merck Pharmaceutical that studies have now shown to increase substantially the chances of heart attacks in patients who use it. In the first tort case to go to trial, the jury found that Merck hid the results of studies showing adverse effects and delayed informing the Food and Drug Administration about them for several months. If, contrary to the actual case, this legal proceeding had ended after an admissibility hearing because a judge would not permit the science to be heard by a jury, the public would have been deprived of important information and discussion about a major company and how its actions affect fellow citizens.[48]

To the extent that defendants are successful with some of the above strategies, this only reinforces their use in the future. One of Nesson's concerns is

[44] D. Capiello, "Oil Industry Funding Study to Contradict Cancer Claims, *Houston Chronicle*, April 29, 2005, AD; A1; American Petroleum Institute. Shaghai Study: Internal Documents (2003), 54–57.

[45] This distinguished toxicologist has requested anonymity, and I honor this.

[46] See some of the discussion from Chapter 2.

[47] Substantial regulatory oversight and intervention by scientific journals may reduce some of the more extreme practices by pharmaceutical companies. How likely this is to occur is a matter beyond the expertise of the author.

[48] Alex Berenson, "Jury Calls Merck Liable in Death of Man on Vioxx," *New York Times*, August 20, 2005; Bill Dawson and Alex Berenson, "Working Through a Decision Cut in Shades of Deep Gray," *New York Times*, August 20, 2005; Alex Berenson, "For Merck, Vioxx Paper Trail Won't Go Away," *New York Times*, August 21, 2005.

that a focus on the evidence can convey a message about "crude risk calculation ('estimate what you can do without getting caught')."[49] The *Daubert* admissibility requirements appear to exacerbate temptations not to conduct scientific studies and possibly increase the temptations to publish misleading results that bear on the science in toxic tort cases. My argument on this point is not that there is considerable evidence that such corruption has occurred (there is some evidence and such conditions are probably more widespread than the public is aware[50]), but the institutional rules of the game invite it.

When judges accept arguments that construct a misleading view of the science and repeat them in their admissibility opinions, this generates a more permanent legal environment that multiplies the mistakes, often throughout the legal system. To the extent that defendants have temptations to such behavior, courts have enhanced responsibilities – as protectors of the fairness of legal procedures and the justice of its outcome – to correct mistaken admissibility reviews and administer the law evenhandedly.

DAUBERT AND CAUSATION REQUIREMENTS

In order for plaintiffs to bring their cases they must have sufficient scientific evidence, provided by appropriate studies and expert testimony, that defendant's substance caused or contributed to their harm. However, there is the rub. Frequently such evidence is unavailable because it is beyond plaintiffs' control. Instead, in many cases there has simply been too little scientific evidence produced during the lifetime of a product from creation, to distribution, to postcommercialization use of the product for such evidence to be available.

Consider, for example, the case of polybrominated biphenyl ethers (PBDEs). PBDEs are added as flame retardants to foams, textiles, and high-impact plastics, and are typically found in electrical appliances, computers, TV sets, building materials, upholstery, the interiors of cars, and in drapery and rug textiles.[51] PBDEs are "selectively released over the products' lifetimes" and enter the environment and ultimately the bodies of animals and humans.[52] These are substances that interact with biological systems much like polychlorinated

---

[49] Nesson, "The Evidence or the Event?" 1362.

[50] Markowitz and Rosner, *Deceit and Denial*, 5, report such activities, and recent newpaper articles on the pharmaceutical industry also suggest this. As this book goes to print the *International Journal of Occupational and Environmental Health* published a special issue addressing these concerns. David S. Egilman and Susanna Rankin Bohme (Eds.), Corporate Corruption of Science [Special Issue]. *International Journal of Occupational and Environmental Health*, II(4) (2005), available at http://www.ijoel.com/.

[51] Kim Hooper and Thomas A. McDonald, "The PBDE's: an Emerging Environmental Challenge and Another Reason for Breast-Milk Monitoring Programs,"*Environmental Health Perspectives*, 108, 5 (2000): 387–388.

[52] Hooper and McDonald, "PBDE's," 387.

biphenyls (PCBs), the substances to which Robert Joiner was exposed. These chemicals (with chemical similarities to dioxins) tend to bind with a particular "hormone-receptor-like molecule called the aryl hydrocarcbon (Ah) receptor."[53] Some of them alter gene expression leading to cancers while others mimic the action of hormones. "[T]hey are stable (persistent), they are fat-seeking, and they have the potential to act as endocrine disruptors."[54] These properties cause them to concentrate as they move up the food chain; this in turn enhances their toxicity. Ultimately they "find their way into [mammalian] mother[s], where they pass tranplacentally to the developing fetus or through the breast milk to the nursing infant."[55]

PBDEs were introduced in the 1960s as flame-retardants, but their toxicology is not well understood.[56] There is only limited human data suggesting an association between some PBDEs and non-Hodgkin lymphoma (a type of cancer of the lymphatic system).[57] Only one congener (one chemical variant) has been studied in animals, producing cancer in mice and rats. And some studies indicate that some of the congeners will have "Ah receptor-mediated (e.g., dioxin like) effects . . ."[58] They are similar in genotoxic profile to PCBs in not being mutagenic in some short-term tests, but they disrupt thyroid hormone balance.[59] Numerous studies are needed to understand their toxicology: "ecologic, neurodevelopment, and thyroid function studies and 2-year rodent cancer bioassays . . ."[60]

The shocking thing about PBDEs is that they have been in the market since the 1960s, but they were below scientific radar screens until the mid-1990s or early 2000s.[61] Yet their concentrations in the breast milk of nursing mothers is doubling every year in Sweden and recent surveys of breast milk in U.S. women indicate levels that are the highest in the world.[62] Thus, here are widely utilized products whose toxicology is poorly understood even after they have been in the market for forty years. Whether or not the companies that created and distributed them knew of their adverse effects I do not know. It seems quite reasonable they should be required to understand the properties of their products. If firms creating them do not, who will? Should the broader public

---

[53] Hooper and McDonald, "PBDE's," 387.
[54] Hooper and McDonald, "PBDE's," 387.
[55] Hooper and McDonald, "PBDE's," 387.
[56] Hooper and McDonald, "PBDE's," 388.
[57] Non-Hodgkin's Lymphoma Information Centre at http://www.cancerbacup.org.uk/ Cancertype/Lymphomanon-Hodgkins/General/WhatareNHLs (visited on September 22, 2004).
[58] Hooper and McDonald, "PBDE's," 388.
[59] Hooper and McDonald, "PBDE's," 390.
[60] Hooper and McDonald, "PBDE's," 391.
[61] Hooper and McDonald, "PBDE's," 388; World Health Organization, "Brominated Diphenyl Ethers, IPCS Environmental Health Criteria", 163 (Geneva: World Health Organization, 1994).
[62] Hooper and McDonald, "PBDE's," 387; Marla Cone, "Cause for Alarm over Chemicals," Los Angeles Times, April 20, A1.

be required to experiment on nursing newborns in order to identify any toxic effects from PBDEs?

Now, PBDEs are not currently the subject of any tort suits; a Westlaw search yields no such results. Rather, they illustrate how little is often known about widely utilized products that have resulted in widespread exposures and actual contamination of the public. It is not implausible that there may be suits concerning PBDEs as there were for PCBs, but given the lack of evidence about their toxicity effects, they are not likely to be successful until scientists know more about their toxicity and some of the knowledge gaps are closed. However, because PBDEs have been scientifically invisible until recently, it likely will take considerable time for researchers to accumulate appropriate evidence about any toxic effects. Until there is more evidence about their effects, even if they are causing harm, nothing is likely to be done about them and citizens may be harmed by them. If any adverse effects are at all subtle, as they might well be, scientists will have great difficulty showing such results.

Although we live in a scientific and technological society and even though the Supreme Court in part acted in response to this scientific age by requiring better scientific support for legal decisions in toxic tort and other litigation, this is not enough to ensure that legal and social decisions, including social inaction,[63] are well informed by science. The Court only demanded greater scientific evidence in support of legal decisions *after* someone has been harmed and that person has sought legal action for redress of his injuries.[64] Thus, an injured parties' scientific experts may not have a sufficient scientific foundation for her testimony for a legal case to advance to a trial for a variety of reasons: (a) because of failures to test the product and monitor it for adverse effects at an earlier stage of its social life, (b) because human studies are too insensitive to detect adverse effects, (c) because in general it has been below or off the scientific radar screen as PBDEs were, and so on. The scientific community, the public, the legal system, and regulatory agencies that could address some of the risks before they materialize into harm frequently have too little scientific evidence earlier in the lives of products to provide better public health and environmental protections from their adverse effects.

Tort judges' demanding substantial amounts of scientific evidence so late in the social-legal process impose substantial barriers for plaintiffs and create perverse incentives for defendants. Because plaintiffs have the burden of proof on causation, they must come forward with enough credible scientific data and expert testimony to present their case to a jury. As I have argued, there are a variety of reasons to believe that plaintiffs' finding and producing the evidence needed for causation and passing through the judicial admissibility screen will

---

[63] An administration might refuse to take governmental actions on human contributions of carbon dioxide to global warming in the face of well-founded scientific evidence.

[64] Of course, the courts' alternatives to address problems are limited, but there were other possibilities.

be difficult for reasons beyond their control. Because defendants can preclude a case from going forward simply by playing defense and having courts accept the view that there is too little evidence or too much uncertainty about causal claims, it is in their interests not to produce evidence earlier in the lifetime of their products and not to monitor their products for adverse effects once they are in commerce. Defendants' legal incentives not to test, not to monitor, and not to produce scientific evidence about their products may well outweigh their self-interested reasons for testing to ensure that products do not pose adverse health effects that would in turn cause regulatory or tort law problems.[65] Such testing can only invite legal trouble or make the defense of products much more difficult. Thus, even if PBDEs harm people or the environment by their dioxin or PCB-like effects, there can be no redress until the science is developed. Until that time the companies that create, import, or distribute them can rest easy. Recall the internal memo from Bayer Pharmaceutical concerning product testing.[66] Testing and monitoring often only invite legal trouble.

We have seen the consequences of the current legal structure. There is substantial scientific and legal ignorance about the universe of chemicals. It is also difficult to produce scientific studies in a timely manner even if scientists have research interests in pursuing such issues. And even if these were not problems, there are a number of pragmatic barriers that stand in the way of producing the needed scientific evidence (Chapter 5).

In order to address these issues, the broader legal system (not just the tort law) may need to ensure that much more scientific evidence is provided about the products that enter commerce than is currently required. At present, for substances subject to postmarket regulatory laws there is simply too little science required up front before substances enter commerce and people are exposed.[67]

Next, there is too little scientific evidence produced along the way. There appears to be too little monitoring of the products – companies and governmental agencies know too little about what effects products have on human health and the environment once they are in commerce. There appears to be too few effective alerts when problems arise. And any alerts that might be used to prevent harm are too late for some people, if substances are toxic. The 1984 NRC report shows the consequences of such policies; there is little knowledge about most substances.[68]

---

[65] Berger, "Eliminating General Causation," 2135.

[66] Berenson, "Trial Lawyers Are Now Focusing on Lawsuits Against Drug Makers."

[67] As noted (Chapter 5), some products are subject to premarket testing – such as drugs and pesticides – but even when premarket testing is required substantial percentages of substances have not been well tested. National Research Council, *Toxicity Testing: Strategies to Determine Needs and Priorities* (Washington, DC: National Academy Press, 1984), 84. (See also, Richard Merrill, "FDA Regulatory Requirements as Tort Standards," 549–588, for a discussion of different legal requirements.)

[68] National Research Council, *Toxicity Testing*, 84.

Moreover, even if companies have monitored products out of self-interest, they rarely have *legal duties to report adverse effects* to a public agency that could publicize the problem or take legal steps to reduce exposures. There are, of course, some exceptions to this. For example, companies whose products affect employees in the workplace have a legal duty to report adverse effects to the Occupational Safety and Health Administration. Drug companies have a legal duty to report adverse effects of their products to the Food and Drug Administration, and physicians and other healthcare workers often do report adverse drug reactions to the FDA.[69]

However, even if there were duties to report such effects, nearly all agencies can only take legal actions by going through a fairly elaborate postmarket legal process called a "rule-making." This, of course, will be contested by affected parties and in most cases is subject to very burdensome procedural requirements that greatly delay the issuance of the rules. Governmental agencies usually have too few resources to protect well the public health, are overwhelmed by work, and are pressured by hostile Presidential administrations and Congresses. Beyond that, they are too often restrained by courts with judicial appointees hostile to regulation, even though they are charged with protecting public health and the environment.[70] For instance, it took the FDA several years to have Sandoz Pharmaceuticals place warnings on Parlodel and nearly five years to remove it from the market, once it had considerable evidence of Parlodel's capacity to cause strokes and heart attacks in the mothers of newborns who used it.[71]

WHERE MIGHT THE LAW GO FROM HERE?

If these are problems, what legal changes might address them? Solutions might go in at least two different directions. On the one hand, legislatures could demand much more scientific evidence before products enter commerce or legally require much more monitoring and reporting of adverse effects of products after they are in commerce, or, better, they could require both. This would necessitate considerable political will and a number of legislators to vote against the interest of many of their common supporters in a generally

---

[69] Merrill, "FDA Regulatory Requirements as Tort Standards," 555.
[70] McGarity, "Some Thoughts on 'Deossifying' the Rule-Making Process," 1335–1462; McGarity and Shapiro, *Workers at Risk*, 229–308.
[71] An FDA committee came to this conclusion in 1989 and asked Sandoz Pharmaceuticals voluntarily to withdraw Parlodel from the market. But Sandoz refused and in 1994 the FDA finally issued a regulatory rule to withdraw approval of Parlodel for this use. U.S. Department of Health and Human Services, Food and Drug Administration, "Sandoz Pharmaceuticals Corp.; Bromocriptine Mesylate (Parlodel) for the Prevention of Physiological Lactation; Opportunity for a Hearing on a Proposal to Withdraw Approval of the Indication," *Federal Register* 59 (23 Aug. 1994): 43347.

antiregulatory period in the United States. On the other hand, courts themselves could take some more modest steps to address some of these issues. Consider each in turn.

The first option, if it could be politically implemented, would produce scientific evidence that could better protect the public, the workforce, and the wider environment from the adverse effects of products. Legal requirements for "appropriate" premarket testing, for monitoring of adverse effects of products in commerce, and for legal authorization for relatively quick regulatory procedures to reduce exposures to products that caused adverse effects would all encourage the production of more scientific information about products and their consequences.[72] These in turn hold some promise for improving the information available to the public, the scientific community, and the regulatory community so better strategies can be devised to prevent some of the harms to humans and the environment that now occur and that become the objects of tort suits.

Although this is a seemingly quite desirable option, it faces great political hurdles, because it would substantially change the current legal structure and threaten many entrenched interests. Nonetheless, despite these major shortcomings, it should be held out as an ultimate goal. The Supreme Court's original motivation seemed to rest on an assumption that the legal system should more fully embrace the scientific age in which we live and utilize its information in support of social-legal decisions. That is, *Daubert's* underlying motivation aims at a greater convergence between what the scientific community knows, what can readily be developed, what can be reasonably inferred, and what the law requires for legal decisions. This same motivation should lead the body politic to develop laws and regulations that *encourage* rather than discourage the production of the biological and toxicological evidence. This would enable the society as a whole to have better scientific information about products in commerce, to better protect its citizens and its environment from substances that will harm them, and to have more data available for the tort law, when people in fact have been injured by the products.

If this is correct, then the law falls considerably short of encouraging the production of scientific data and information about the products and their consequences in society. *Daubert* addresses merely a small part of the problem and addresses it quite late in the social life of a product. By addressing only that piece it has created counterproductive incentives that discourage the production of scientific information about products and their consequences.

---

[72] Any premarket testing would need to be structured appropriate to the risks posed by the product in question. Thus, there might be more careful testing of some products and less testing of those that antecedently pose fewer risks to the extent this can be determined. (Carl F. Cranor, "Some Legal Implications of the Precautionary Principle: Improving Information Generation and Legal Protections," *European Journal of Oncology, Library Vol.* 2 (2003): 31–51.)

The tort law itself gives firms incentives not to test their products and not to monitor products and release that information to the public so it can protect itself against previously unknown and unanticipated consequences.[73] The *Daubert* trilogy of cases only enhances these perverse incentives. When *Daubert* is poorly implemented it further aggravates them. Even worse, it tempts firms to behave in ways that distort science (see earlier) – in presenting arguments that invite judges to adopt mistaken and simplified views of science, in failing to publish data, in harassing independent scientists, or in the funding of misleading studies that corrupt the scientific literature.

On the second option, there are a couple of alternatives that are different from broader regulatory reform. Courts themselves could implement some of these, and they hold modest promise of improving the use of scientific evidence over the *Daubert* status quo. One alternative is to return to different procedures for screening expert testimony and scientific evidence. Not all state court jurisdictions have followed the federal courts in imposing a *Daubert* screening procedure for expert testimony; indeed it may be that a majority of U.S. citizens are not subject to *Daubert* screening procedures in state courts.[74] Thus, there are models in state jurisdictions for resisting the *Daubert* approach and it is not obvious that they are measurably worse off than the federal court system, although comparative studies would need to be done on this issue. I will describe the approach adopted by the Illinois Supreme Court, which addresses two problems that exist in *Daubert* jurisdictions: the general causation requirement and stringent screening of expert testimony.

A second alternative is for courts to create a new cause of action that builds in some of the incentives to produce scientific data and information about products and their consequences following commercialization. At present, this is simply a proposal by Margaret Berger, a distinguished evidence scholar, although there are some models in state courts that approach this suggestion.

Consider each of these possibilities in turn.

A Return to *Frye*?

For an interesting example of a jurisdiction not utilizing *Daubert* admissibility rules but retaining the causation requirement in the tort law, consider a recent decision from the Illinois Supreme Court, *Donaldson v. Central Illinois Public Service*.[75] In this case cancer victims and their parents sought compensatory damages for diseases they alleged were caused by environmental exposure to coal tars and dust from coal tars during the cleanup of a former coal

---

73 Berger, "Eliminating General Causation," 2135.
74 Metzger, "The Demise of *Daubert* in State Courts" (noting that "some of the most populous states have rejected Daubert in favor of Frye or other standards, including California, Florida, Illinois, New York, New Jersey, Michigan, North Carolina, and Pennsylvania").
75 199 Ill.2d 63 (2002).

gasification plant. Several children living near the remediation site contracted neuroblastoma, a "peripheral nervous system cancer."[76] This rare cancer, typically occurring in only 9 of 1,000,000 children born was seen in four children in or near Taylorville, Illinois. "Statistically, a case of neuroblastoma occurs one time every 29 years in a community the size of Taylorville."[77] Perhaps because of the rareness of this disease, it had not been subjected to epidemiological studies and other extensive research. However, gases and other chemicals from coal tar were known to be potent carcinogens.[78]

Because Illinois is one jurisdiction that has not adopted *Daubert* screening of expert *testimony* – it continues to use the *Frye* test – defendants moved to have plaintiffs' experts reviewed under a version of the *Frye* test that mimicked *Daubert*, called the "*Frye*-plus-reliability standard of review." The trial court declined to accept this procedure, conducted an informal *Frye* hearing on the underlying studies and methodologies scientists used, and admitted plaintiffs' experts. After a jury awarded plaintiffs $3.2 million for the deaths of four children, defendants appealed the verdict. The jury verdict was affirmed by an intermediate appellate court. Defendants then appealed that decision to the Illinois Supreme Court.[79]

On appeal defendants, Central Illinois Public Service, argued that the trial judge denied them an appropriate *Frye* hearing to determine whether plaintiffs' experts *testimony* (not just their studies) was admissible and that the court "failed in its role as a 'gatekeeper' by permitting unfounded expert opinion testimony."[80] Thus, defendants were in effect arguing that the trial court should have conducted a *Daubert*–like hearing under *Frye* on plaintiffs' experts' *testimony* and excluded plaintiffs' experts because there were no epidemiological studies to support their testimony. Such arguments, urging the necessity of epidemiological studies, are not unusual, as we have seen.

The Illinois Supreme Court rejected the idea that a *Frye*-plus-reliability review of expert testimony was required in Illinois, even though some appellate courts had endorsed it.[81] Instead, *Frye* applies only to "novel" scientific principles, tests or techniques; it does not apply to expert *testimony*:

> On questions such as these, which stand at the frontier of current medical epidemiological inquiry, if experts are willing to testify that such a link exists, it is for the jury to decide whether to credit such testimony.[82]

---

[76] 199 Ill.2d 63, at 65.
[77] 199 Ill.2d 63, at 66.
[78] 199 Ill.2d 63, at 68.
[79] 199 Ill.2d 63, at 65.
[80] 199 Ill.2d 63, at 76.
[81] 199 Ill.2d 63, at 80.
[82] 199 Ill.2d 63, at 81 (citing *Ferebee v. Chevron Chemical, Inc.*, 736 F.2d at 1534).

Following this, the court proceeded to review plaintiffs' experts' testimony, which defendants argued was "not supported by specific scientific research establishing a cause and effect relationship between coal tar and neuroblastoma."[83] Moreover, the Court recognized that the cause and effect relationship between exposure to coal tar and neuroblastoma had "not been the subject of extensive study and research,"[84] because of rare effects (recall the discussion in Chapter 5). The court permitted plaintiffs' experts to testify, because it

> offers those with rare diseases the opportunity to seek a remedy for the wrong they have suffered. Thus in these limited instances, an expert may rely upon scientific literature discussing similar, yet not identical, cause and effect relationships. The fact that an expert must extrapolate, and is unable to produce *specific studies* that show the *exact cause and effect relationship* to support his conclusion, affects the weight of the testimony [for a jury to consider] rather than its admissibility.[85] (emphasis added)

On expert testimony, the Court first noted that "machines or procedures which analyze physical data" might mistakenly convey that the results were objective and infallible. It contrasted such studies or tests with expert testimony, especially experts "extrapolating" from existing studies, which the court argued carried the possibility of fallibility on its face for all, including a jury, to see.[86] Studies, machines, or tests need judicial screening; scientific testimony does not. In addition, as the *Frye* standard "does not demand unanimity, consensus, or even a majority to satisfy the general acceptance test, we find that extrapolation is sufficiently established to have gained general acceptance in these limited circumstances."[87] It concluded,

> in the interest of clarity, an expert's conclusion is subject to challenge by traditional efforts such as cross-examination. The general acceptance test should not replace the role of the advocate, who may expose shaky but admissible evidence by vigorous cross-examination or the presentation of contrary evidence.[88]

Thus, this court recognized that juries may need some protection against the possible spurious objectivity of scientific tests, but they will more naturally be

---

[83]   199 Ill.2d 63, at 82.
[84]   199 Ill.2d 63, at 87. (One expert explained that because few people are diagnosed with neuroblastoma, the disease is simply not the subject of extensive funding and study. Further, plaintiffs' experts testified that few studies exist regarding the specific cause and effect relationship at issue in this case because ethical considerations prevent exposing the human population to coal tar for research purposes (87).)
[85]   199 Ill.2d 63, at 85.
[86]   199 Ill.2d 63, at 87.
[87]   199 Ill.2d 63, at 88.
[88]   199 Ill.2d 63, at 88.

on their guard against the testimony of an expert, which can be tested under cross-examination. In short, the court saw little risk of the jury being overly awed by the testimony of an expert in the same way they might be awed by scientific studies or techniques.[89]

Going beyond these points the Court also addressed the general vs. specific causation issue, something that can be a barrier to presentation of early or new evidence of causation. Illinois law

> does not define causation in terms of "generic" or "specific" causation. Rather, our case law clearly states that in negligence actions, the plaintiff must present evidence of proximate causation, which includes both "cause in fact" and "legal cause."[90]

Illinois thus permits causation to be shown by means of circumstantial evidence and holds that plaintiffs' need not make a "showing of exposure, which must be quantified."[91]

This case presents a substantial contrast with the *Daubert* trilogy. It rejects judicial review of experts' testimony, rejects the necessity to show general causation at least in some kinds of cases, and does not impose high requirements for exposure information. The point about general versus specific causation is important, especially if courts are tempted to be highly demanding about general causation. If plaintiffs must first provide a *general scientific case* that exposure to coal tar gases and dust more likely than not cause neuroblastomas, this could be quite difficult (as it was with this rare effect). If, in addition, courts insist on a high degree of scientific certainty for general causation, this could be much more difficult to establish than causation in a single instance as *Donaldson* shows. Plaintiffs did not have the elaborate studies to show that in every case in which people were exposed to coal gasification residues some subset of them suffered an elevated risk of disease. The court correctly realized that more general scientific claims can be harder to demonstrate than causation in a single instance, especially when general scientific evidence may be quite limited as it was for the carcinogenicity for coal gasification by-products. (Recall the vinyl chloride case reports from Chapter 4.) In showing general causation, plaintiffs must show a general causation assessment for a very specific disease (modeled after a general risk assessment of the issue). The more courts demand in this regard, the harder it is for plaintiffs' cases to go forward. In this book we have seen some examples for which judges required quite elaborate scientific

---

[89] Recall that the U.S. Supreme Court noted the importance of cross-examination in 1983 to protect a criminal defendant from a possible death sentence (*Barefoot v. Estelle*, 463 U.S. 880 (1983)), but in 1993 still imposed a heightened duty to review expert testimony in *Daubert*. In *Daubert*, it suggested that the admissibility hurdle should not be that high and the cross-examination could be a corrective.

[90] 199 Ill.2d 63, at 90.

[91] 199 Ill.2d 63, at 91.

evidence in favor of general causation, for example, recall *Wade-Greaux v. Whitehall Labs* or some cases requiring human epidemiological studies.[92] The *Donaldson* court recognized the practical difficulties in such cases, but adopted a salutary pragmatic solution to them in order to ensure that those harmed by substances that cause rare diseases are not precluded from having a public trial for redress of grievances.

Courts that continue to use *Frye* will need to address some of the concerns traditionally raised about it (Chapter 2). However, these do not seem to be insuperable, especially concerning the scientific fields used in toxic tort cases.

Although various state courts remain committed to the older *Frye* test[93] and do not subject expert testimony to a *Frye* ruling, it may be difficult following the *Daubert* trilogy for federal courts (and state courts that adopted the *Daubert* rule) to return to *Frye*. This is especially the case for federal courts because the Federal Rules of Evidence were specifically created without reference to *Frye*. Moreover, *Frye* does nothing to encourage greater scientific testing of substances (one of the shortcomings of *Daubert*), except perhaps to have a somewhat more liberal court review of expert testimony. However, insofar as admissibility barriers are concerned, *Frye* appears open to a wider range of legitimate scientific evidence than some views of *Daubert* discussed previously.

Is There a Need for Tort Liability Reform?

Margaret Berger proposed an alternative to both *Daubert* and *Frye*. Her view seeks to address the woeful ignorance that plagues much scientific and agency knowledge of the universe of chemical substances. At present, it is both possible and likely that some toxic tort cases are dismissed simply because of ignorance about a particular substance and its general toxicity properties, leaving wrongfully injured plaintiffs without a possibility of justice, and undermining the deterrence function of the tort law. Beyond this, insofar as courts insist that plaintiffs must first establish the more difficult general causation case before specific causation, this increases barriers, especially when there is considerable scientific ignorance about products.

It is difficult to understand how extensive this problem might be – apart from general assessments about extensive scientific ignorance of substances and additional process barriers created by *Daubert* and its implementation. There is a concern, however, that tort law itself lacks adequate liability rules to motivate firms that create, distribute, and use potentially toxic substances to take steps to

---

[92] *Wade-Greaux v. Whitehall Lab., Inc.*, 874 F. Supp. 1441, at 1450.
[93] Ten states "have rejected the *Daubert* standard, at least for the time-being, preferring to remain with the *Frye* test or an alternative state formulation of general acceptance and relevancy. Seven "states follow their own state version of a relevance-reliability determination, usually based on the respective state code of evidence." Twenty-one "states have accepted the essential principles of *Daubert* . . ." Faigman, *et.al.*, *Modern Scientific Evidence*, 12–13.

properly test them before they enter commerce, test them when concerns arise about potential harms, monitor them for adverse effects, or report adverse effect data about them. Thus, at present it appears that there may be much less testing and review of the safety of substances than different or additional liability rules might produce. The present causation element required of tort liability creates a barrier to recovery in torts and creates an ostrich-head-in-the-sand effect, "incentives on the part of corporations not to know and not to disclose."[94] The public and workplace health is, thus, put at greater risk than it would be under alternative liability rules. Moreover, judicial review of the science needed to establish causation is a task with which judges may be quite uncomfortable. In light of these considerations, current law might be inadequate to cope with toxic substances. Tort liability rules may need to be modified in order for tort law better to address the extensive ignorance about the substances registered in commerce.

Professor Berger has made such a proposal:

> [L]iability in negligence [should] be imposed for failure to provide substantial information relating to risk and proof that the failure caused plaintiff's injury would not be required; defendants would be relieved of liability for injuries caused by exposure to their products, provided that they had met the required standard of care for developing and disseminating information relevant to risk.[95]

The idea would be to create "a new tort that conditions culpability on the failure to develop and disseminate significant data needed for risk assessment."[96] She illustrates this with respect to litigation concerning asbestos.

> [O]nce plaintiffs proved the manufacturers' negligence in failing to reveal substantial information highly relevant to assessing the potential risks of asbestos exposure, a prima facie case of liability would be made out for those able to substantiate exposure and ill health. Defendants should, however, be entitled to two special defenses: ... (1) to prove in general that certain adverse health reactions could not plausibly arise from exposure to defendant's product, or (2) to reduce damages by proof that a particular plaintiff's injury is attributable or partly attributable to another cause, such as smoking. Defendant should bear the burden of persuasion on these issues.[97]

It is correct, as at least one critic has argued, that as part of an affirmative defense defendants would have a burden of proof to show general causation to some extent on Berger's proposal.[98] Thus, Berger implicitly argues for the possibility of shifting the burden of proof on general causation. This is not a

---

94 Berger, "Eliminating General Causation," 2119.
95 Berger, "Eliminating General Causation," 2143.
96 Berger, "Eliminating General Causation," 2140.
97 Berger, "Eliminating General Causation," 2144–2145.
98 Alani Golaski, "General Causation at the Crossroads in Toxic Tort Cases, *Penn State Law Review* 108 (2003): 479–523, esp. 482–485.

bad idea. Often burdens of proof and presumptions are placed on parties in the best position to have or produce relevant evidence about contested issues of fact.[99] Manufacturers of products are surely in this position concerning the toxicity of their products. The value of her proposal is that it provides *tort law* incentives for firms to do better testing and monitoring of their products or compensate those exposed to them.

There are other possibilities. One strategy within existing rules might be to shift the burden of proof once "plaintiffs have made a specified threshold showing of causation."[100] Another might be somewhat analogous to duties to be informed about hazards and duties toward others in product liability cases.[101] At this juncture, the point is not to propose a specific alternative, but to sketch the types of legal modifications that should be explored in order

---

[99] James and Hazard, *Civil Procedure*, 251–253.

[100] Gottesman, "From *Barefoot* to *Daubert* to *Joiner*," 753, 779. This point was also suggested by Francis McGovern of the Duke University School of Law. Professor Gottesman suggests that

> if plaintiffs showed a specified number of epidemiological studies in which there were elevated incidences of cancer, coupled with evidence that the substance is causing cancer in animal studies and/or evidence that the chemical composition of the substance is similar to other substances known to be carcinogenic, a presumption of causation would arise . . . (779)

His scientific requirements appear to endorse an epidemiological threshold and thus are too strong. A better principle would suggest, in the spirit of this book, that if plaintiffs could present a pattern of evidence for a potential carcinogen similar to other patterns of evidence that had implicated substances as likely human carcinogens, then an intellectual presumption of causation would arise. The virtue of the alternative proposal is that it is neutral between different patterns of evidence, different explanatory paths to the same conclusion, and it does not require an epidemiological threshold.

[101] Gregory Keating of the University of Southern California Law School suggested this point. For a more specific articulation, see *Feldman v. Lederle Labs.*, 479 A.2d 374, 386 (N.J. 1984) (holding that drug companies will be negligent if they have failed to warn of a risk of which they knew "or should . . . have known . . . given the scientific, technological, and other information available when the product was distributed; . . . in other words, . . . actual or constructive knowledge of the danger . . ."). Constructive knowledge embraces knowledge that should have been known based on information that was reasonably available or obtainable and should have alerted a reasonably prudent person to act. Put another way, would a person of reasonable intelligence or of the superior expertise of the defendant charged with such knowledge conclude that defendant should have alerted the consuming public (386). "Further, a manufacturer is held to the standard of an expert in the field. A manufacturer should keep abreast of scientific advances . . ." (386). "Thus, for example, if a substantial number of doctors or consumers had complained to a drug manufacturer of an untoward effect of a drug, that would have constituted sufficient information requiring a warning" (387) (citing *Skill v. Martinez*, 91 F.R.D. 498, 514 (D.N.J. 1981), *aff'd on other grounds*, 677 F.2d 368 (3d Cir. 1982) (jury finding in products liability action for plaintiff upheld because "sufficient knowledge existed, in the form of articles of preliminary findings by two leading researchers in the field, of danger inherent in taking birth-control pill while smoking to warrant drug manufacturer's giving proper warning)); see *McKee v. Moore*, 648 P.2d 21, 24 (Okla. 1982) (finding that the duty to warn requires prescription drug manufacturer to maintain current information "gleaned from research, adverse reaction reports, scientific literature and other available methods").

to induce corporations to engage in far more scientific research when it matters – not to win lawsuits but to protect society against the risks posed by their products. The proper role for scientists with regard to toxic substances should be to provide needed information about possible latent defects, not to cast deciding votes on liability because causation has been made a surrogate for morally responsible corporate behavior.[102]

Courts need to recognize the role of the tort law in the context of the broader legal system, the inadequate testing and monitoring of products, and spotty record of reporting adverse effects. By doing this they might be more open to legal devices, new causes of action, such as the proposal by Margaret Berger, in order to provide better protections for the public and workforce health.

CONCLUSION

In preserving the central aims of the tort law, courts will need to do several things. They should recognize the wide variety of respectable, reliable patterns of evidence on which scientists themselves rely for inferring the toxicity of substances. The inference patterns presented in Chapter 7 serve as examples of some of the variety of inferences utilized in the scientific community. Courts need to be sensitive to a wider range of the shortcomings of scientific studies – especially those that would mistakenly preclude plaintiffs from trial. They should recognize the fact of reasonable scientific disagreements and permit experts to testify whose testimony falls within a zone of reasonable disagreement. Courts, recognizing a greater range of inferences, would then be able to better assess the often sparse scientific evidence that is typically available.

This idea, however, will do almost nothing to help remedy the enormous scientific ignorance about the universe of chemical substances that are currently used in commerce, with more continuously being added. Consequently, courts may need to take additional steps within their authority to address the woeful ignorance about the chemical universe. This may necessitate changes in the liability rules.

If scientific knowledge about the toxicity of a substance for humans could be produced quickly, there would not be the concern that science delayed or incomplete was justice denied. If diseases could be identified at an early stage, left their signatures, or did not have long latency periods, there might be a lesser need for various kinds of nonhuman evidence. Scientists would not then need to piece together animal, mechanistic, genetic, structure-activity, and other inferential evidence to identify harms. However, given the nature of biology and the fact that science in its current stage of development does not have

---

[102] Berger, "Eliminating General Causation," 2152.

such capabilities, courts must recognize this and utilize scientifically reliable patterns of evidence that will permit plaintiffs to receive just treatment in tort cases. If this is not done or it is not adequate, more fundamental solutions to these issues will need to be found.

In 1993 when the Supreme Court heightened court review of scientific testimony and its foundation, it lowered a science veil over civil litigation. The law, dense and esoteric as it is, has become much more so because many cases of alleged wrongful injuries are being decided as if they were the outcome of scientific seminars. Tort law has become increasingly cloaked behind the arcana of scientific evidence and legally subtle discussions of admissibility and pre-trial hearings. Many of the issues about legal relationships between parties, the distribution of risks in society, and recent changes in admissibility rules that might concern us as citizens have not been well discussed. Indeed, they have rarely been raised. Even if there has been some discussion of them, the issues are sufficiently arcane, opaque, and open to demagogic presentation that it is difficult to have good public discussions of them. In short, our legal system has become less comprehensible to ordinary citizens than it was previously. In addition, citizens' realistic rights to the law have been reduced but they are likely unaware of the changes.

I have sought to lift some of the scientific and procedural veils from these issues. This involved identifying what is at stake, articulating some of the prag-matic difficulties that preclude scientific evidence from being easily utilized in legal cases and showing how courts could improve the application of *Daubert* while remaining faithful to the science needed in such cases. As citizens, we need to understand our institutions and how they affect us, even when this is difficult to do. Otherwise, we will be in a poor position to contribute intelligently to discussions concerning them and in a poor position to protect ourselves from institutional consequences that lie hidden. Without a better understanding of these issues, citizens risk being manipulated by vested interests who do not necessarily have their interests at stake. Some participants in the institution may also not be fully aware of the consequences that views about the science can have.

At the most superficial level, lifting this veil reveals that judges are reviewing expert testimony more stringently than before *Daubert*. Fewer scientists are being admitted. As a consequence this reduces access to some who have been wrongly injured, but it is difficult to know how many meritorious cases are not filed for these reasons. However, the aim was not merely to preclude more experts or legitimate cases (or at least one hopes this was not its aim). Rather, it was to infuse appropriate and reliable science into the law. On this, *Daubert* appears to have had some success, but because of counterproductive effects, the net balance of consequences is more mixed.

In screening scientific testimony, some trial judges and some appellate courts are now regrettably, but mistakenly, constraining expert testimony. They are utilizing simplified heuristics with asymmetrical adverse effects on plaintiffs that frustrate the Supreme Court's aim. This keeps good scientific evidence and expert testimony from court, denies some meritorious victims the possibility of public trials and precludes their opportunities to redress wrongs done.

There are correctives to some of these issues. In order to conduct fair admissibility reviews and avoid being manipulated by litigants, judges need to be sensitive to a wider range of errors to which experts and scientific studies are subject. They should fully recognize the complexity of scientific evidence, consider expert testimony based on all an expert's integrated evidence, and then rule on admissibility based on whether he or she proposes to testify within the range where reasonable experts would disagree. However, to do this courts must recognize the variety of explanatory paths to causal conclusions and the varied patterns of evidence that support reasonable causal inferences. Such approaches would move courts closer to the goal that seems to underlie the *Daubert* trilogy: ensuring that legal decisions were reasonably supported by the science pertinent to the issues of the case while also ensuring the possibility of justice between parties. If courts admit testimony within the range where reasonable experts disagree, litigants can hardly ask for more within the context of the adversary system. Ideas from *Kumho Tire* and the Third Circuit Court of Appeals suggest how courts could avoid some of the simplified heuristics. I provided numerous examples of scientific judgments to exemplify various explanatory paths to the conclusion that substances cause human harm.

However, after all this, addressing the science needed for social decisions largely at the end of a series of social events – leading from the creation of products to production to commercialization to distribution – is likely too little, too late. Too little health (and environmental) research is produced in the social lives of substances early on. This results in considerable ignorance about the thousands of substances introduced into commerce. Often it is too late to prevent harm to the public or workforce. It creates counterproductive incentives for companies to avoid testing in the future, multiplying mistakes and harm. The workforce, the larger public and the environment become guinea pigs for the productive capacities of commerce.

Moreover, *Daubert* appears to frustrate a larger goal of having social and legal decisions supported by the relevant technical evidence. Asking smart, but scientifically untrained judges to review scientific studies and inferences gives them a complex and difficult task to assess the substantive merits of science. Poorly implemented reviews of expert testimony reinforce legal incentives for firms not to test and not to monitor the safety of their products. This tends to reduce scientific information needed for social decisions. In fact, both testing and monitoring only seem to invite legal trouble for defendants, so they are not likely to conduct them. In addition, they invite misleading defensive science and possible corruption of the scientific literature.

Recall also that the tort law can serve as a backup to shortcomings of the regulatory law. Or it can catch and repair as best corrective justice can hope to do so unanticipated errors in identifying the toxicity of products (some of this is bound to occur). Both functions of torts are hampered by mistaken admissibility reviews.

Even reviews of expert testimony implemented well in accordance with suggestions made in this book are not a panacea. Up-front scientific and legal costs for those who have been injured will remain comparatively higher than they were in 1993. On an absolute scale, the costs of pursuing corrective justice for injuries wrongly inflicted are probably quite high, and thus, higher yet subsequent to the *Daubert* decison. Such costs almost certainly decrease plaintiffs' access to the legal system and put the possibility of justice beyond the reach of too many. Higher costs and reduced legal access lessen the uncertain deterrent effects of torts.

Solutions to these problems are not easy. It would be best for there to be greater social concern about the safety of products before they enter commerce; to produce better and more reliable scientific evidence contemporaneous with the development of products and to monitor them for health effects when they were in commerce. This would result in fewer surprises after commercialization and less need for tort law compensation for wrongfully injured parties. Failing that, courts have some alternatives. They could revert to or continue to use the *Frye* rule as Illinois and a number of the larger states have done. They could take some steps to develop liability rules within torts to encourage greater testing and monitoring of products, but will they do so?

The *Daubert* trilogy addressed only a part of a much larger problem faced by our technological society: ensuring that science better inform our legal institutions and social decisions consistent with preventing harm and ensuring just compensation to those wrongfully injured. The essentially small step taken in pursuit of those aims and late in the life of a typical product appears to aggravate the much larger issue of too little scientific evidence too late in support of social aims. It also likely increases the risks to public health and the environment in postmarket contexts because it inadvertently increases incentives for firms not to test and not to monitor for the health effects of their products.

Much more scientific and institutional work remains to be done in order to provide the protections to public and workplace health of an advanced industrial society concerned to protect its citizenry from harm. Until that is achieved, the populace will continue to be injured by poorly tested products. Unfortunately, their chances of redress for harms wrongly inflicted have decreased as a consequence of *Daubert* and its implementation. Until there are improvements in how science is used in toxic tort law, the possibility of justice for wrongly injured citizens will not be fully realized.

Bibliography

Addington v. Texas, 441 U.S. 418 (1979).

Advisory Committee on Evidence Rules. (2000, December). Proposed Amendment: Rule 702.

Ahlbom, A., and Feychting, M. (1993). Studies of Electromagnetic Fields and Cancer: How Inconsistent? *Environmental Science and Technology*, 27, 1018–1020.

Allen v. Pennsylvania Engineering Corp., 102 F.3d 194 (5th Cir. 1996).

Alonso-Zaldivar, R., and Maharaj, D. (2000, September 21). Tests Show Firestone 'Had to Know,' Probers Say: Congress Cites New Evidence Against Tire Maker as Sentiment Swings in Favor of Criminal Penalties in Such Cases. *Los Angeles Times*, C1.

Ambrosini v. Labarraque, 101 F.3d 129 (D.C. Cir. 1996).

Amdur, M. O., Doull, J., and Klaassen, C. D. (Eds.). (1991). *Casarett and Doull's Toxicology* (4th ed.). New York: Pergamon Press.

American and Foreign Ins. Co. v. General Elec. Co., 45 F.3d 13f5 (6th Cir. 1995).

American Federation of Labor and Congress of Indus. Organizations v. Occupational Safety and Health Admin., U.S. Dept. of Labor, 965 F.2d 962 (11th Cir. 1992).

American Law Institute. (2005). *Restatement of the Law: Torts: Liability for Physical Harm* (Proposed Final Draft).

American Petroleum Institute. (2003). Shanghai Studies: Internal Documents (unveiled in litigation), 1–163.

Ames, B. N. (1989). What Are the Major Carcinogens in the Etiology of Human Cancer? Environmental Pollution, Natural Carcinogens, and Causes of Human Cancer: Six Errors. In V. T. Devita, Jr., S. Hellman, and S. A. Rosenberg (Eds.), *Important Advances in Oncology* (pp. 237–247). Philadelphia: Lippincott.

Amici Curiae of the Lymphona Foundation of America, Carl F. Cranor, Devra Davis, Peter I. Defur, Brian G. Durie, Alan H. Lockwood, David Ozonoff, Arnold J. Schecter, and David Wallinga in Support of Respondents, U.S. Supreme Court, Dow Chemical Co., Monsanto Co., et al. v. Stephenson and Issacson. (2003). ["Agent Orange" Litigation].

Amicus Brief of Professor Alvan R. Feinstein in Support of Respondent at 4–8, *Daubert v. Merrell Dow Pharm., Inc.*, 509 U.S. 579 (1993).

Amicus Brief of Professor Kenneth Rothman, et al. In Support of Petitioners at 3–7, *Daubert v. Merrell Dow Pharm., Inc.*, 509 U.S. 579 (1993).

Amorgianos v. National Railway Passenger Corp., 303 F.3d 256 (2d Cir. 2002).

Anderson, L. M., Ward, J. M., Fox, S. D., Isaaq, H. J., and Riggs, C. W. (1986). Effects of a Single Dose of Polycholorinated Biphenyls to Infant Mice on N-Nitrosodimethylamine-Initiated Lung and Liver Tumors. *International Journal of Cancer*, 38(1), 109–116.

Anderson v. Bessemer City, 470 U.S. 564 (1985).

Andrews, L. S., and Snyder, R. (1991). Toxic Effects of Solvents and Vapors. In M. O. Amdur, J. Doull, C. D. Klaassen (Eds.), *Casarett and Doull's Toxicology* (4th ed., pp. 681–722). New York: Pergamon Press.

Aristotle. (1985). *Nicomachean Ethics* (T. Irwin, Trans.). Indianapolis: Hackett.

Ashby, J., and Tennant, R. W. (1988). Chemical Structure, Salmonella Mutagenicity and Extent of Carcinogenicity as Indicators of Genotoxic Carcinogensesis among 222 Chemicals Tested in Rodents by the U.S. NCI/NTP. *Mutation Research, 204,* 17–115.

Baer, K., and Shudtz, M. (2005, May 6). *Data Gaps White Paper.* Presented at the *Ward, Kershaw Environmental Law Symposium: The Data Gaps Dilemma: Why Toxic Ignorance Threatens Public Health* sponsored by the University of Maryland School of Law. Washington, DC.

Bailey, L. A., Gordis, L., and Green, M. D. (1994). Reference Guide on Epidemiology. In *Reference Manual on Scientific Evidence* (1st ed., pp. 121–180). Washington, DC: Federal Judicial Center.

Barefoot v. Estelle, 463 U.S. 880 (1983).

Benedi v. McNeil-P.P.C., Inc., 66 F.3d 1378 (4th Cir. 1995).

Benigni, R., and Giuliani, A. (1999). Tumor Profiles and Carcinogenic Potency in Rodents and Humans: Value for Cancer Risk Assessment. *Journal of Environmental Science and Health. Part C, Environmental Carcinogenesis and Ecotoxicology Reviews, 17*(1), 45–67.

Berenson, A. (2003, May 18). Trial Lawyers Are Now Focusing on Lawsuits Against Drug Makers. *New York Times.* Retrieved from http://www.nytimes.com.

Berenson, A. (2005, July 11). First Vioxx Suit: Entryway into a Legal Labyrinth? *New York Times.* Retrieved from http://www.nytimes.com.

Berenson, A. (2005, August 20). Jury Calls Merck Liable in Death of Man on Vioxx. *New York Times.* Retrieved from http://www.nytimes.com.

Berenson, A. (2005, August 21). For Merck, Vioxx Paper Trail Won't Go Away. *New York Times.* Retrieved from http://www.nytimes.com.

Berger, M. A. (1994a). Evidentiary Framework. In *Reference Manual on Scientific Evidence* (pp. 37–117). Washington, DC: Federal Judicial Center.

Berger, M. A. (1994b). Procedural Paradigms for Applying the Daubert Test. *Minnesota Law Review, 78,* 1345–1386.

Berger, M. A. (1997). Eliminating General Causation: Notes Towards a New Theory of Justice and Toxic Torts. *Columbia Law Review, 97,* 2117–2152.

Berger, M. A. (2000). The Supreme Court's Trilogy on the Admissibility of Expert Testimony. In *Reference Manual on Scientific Evidence* (2nd ed., pp. 9–38). Washington, DC: Federal Judicial Center.

Berger, M. A. (2001, Summer). Upsetting the Balance between Interests: The Impact of Supreme Court's Trilogy on Expert Testimony in Toxic Tort Litigation. *Law and Contemporary Problems, 64,* 289–326.

Berger, M. A. (2005). What Has a Decade of *Daubert* Wrought? *American Journal of Public Health, 95*(Suppl. 1), S59–S65.

Bernstein, D. E. (1994). The Admissibility of Scientific Evidence after *Daubert v. Merrell Dow Pharmaceuticals Inc. Cardozo Law Review 15,* 2137–2181.

Black, B., and Lilienfeld, D. E. (1984). Epidemiologic Proof in Toxic Tort Litigation. *Fordham Law Review, 52,* 732–785.

Black v. Food Lion, Inc., 171 F.3d 308 (5th Cir. 1998).

Black v. Food Lion, Case No. 97–11404 (1999).

Black's Law Dictionary. (1968). (4th ed.). St. Paul: West.

Black's Law Dictionary. (2004). (8th ed.). St. Paul: West.

Blanchard v. Eli Lilly and Company, 207 F. Supp. 2d 308 (D. Vt. 2002).

Boguski, M. S. (2002). Comparative Genomics: The Mouse that Roared. *Nature, 420,* 515–516.

Bond, J. A., et al. (1995). Epidemiological and Mechanistic Data Suggest that 1,3-Butadiene Will Not Be Carcinogenic to Humans at Exposures Likely to Be Encountered in the Environment or Workplace. *Carcinogenesis, 16,* 165–171.

Bradley v. Brown, 42 F.3d 434 (7th Cir. 1994).

Brasher v. Sandoz Pharmaceuticals Corp., and *Quinn v. Sandoz Pharmaceuticals Corp.*, 160 F. Supp. 2d 1291 (2001).

Braun v. Lorillard, Inc., 84 F.3d 230 (7th Cir.), *cert. denied*, 117 S.Ct. 480 (1996).

Breyer, S. S. (2000). Introduction. In *Reference Manual on Scientific Evidence* (2nd ed., pp. 1–8). Washington, DC: Federal Judicial Center.

Brock v. Merrell Dow Pharmaceuticals, Inc., 884 F.2d 166 (5th Cir. 1989), *modified*, 884 F.2d 166 (5th Cir. 1989), *cert. denied*, 494 U.S. 1046 (1990).

Brock v. Merrell Dow Pharmaceuticals, Inc., 874 F.2d 307 (5th Cir. 1989), *cert. denied*, 494 U.S. 1046 (1990).

Brodeur, P. (1985). *Outrageous Misconduct.* New York: Pantheon Books.

Brunner, M. J., Sullivan, T. M., Singer, A. W., Ryan, M. J., Toft, R. S., II, Menton, S. W., et al. (1996). *An Assessment of the Chronic Toxicity and Oncogenicity of Aroclor-1016, Aroclor-1242, Aroclor-1254 and Aroclor-1260 Administered in Diet to Rats.* Columbus, OH: Batelle Study No. SC920192, Chronic Toxicity and Oncogenicity Report.

Bunting v. Jamieson, 984 P.2d 467 (Wyo. 1999).

Calabrese, E. J. (1993, April 13). Did Occupational Exposure to ETO Cause Mr. Walter Allen's Brain Tumor? [Report].

Cancer BACUP, Non-Hodgkin's Lymphoma Information Centre. (2004, June 1). *What Are Non-Hodgkin's Lymphomas?* Retrieved September 22, 2004 from http://www.cancerbacup.org.uk/ Cancertype/Lymphomanon-Hodgkins/General/ WhatareNHLs.

Capiello, D. (2005). Oil Industry Funding Study to Contradict Cancer Claims. *Houston Chronicle*, April 29, 2005, AD: A1.

Capra, D. J. (1998). The Daubert Puzzle. *Georgia Law Review, 32*, 699–782.

Carbone, M., Klein, G., Gruber, J., and Wong, M. (2004, August 1). Modern Criteria to Establish Human Cancer Etiology. *Cancer Research, 64*, 5518–5524.

The Carcinogenic Potency Project. (n.d.). *Summary of Carcinogenic Potency Database by Chemical: Nonhuman Primates and Dogs.* Retrieved February 2, 2001 from ftp://potency.berkeley. edu/pub/tables/chemicalsummary.other.text.

Carmichael v. Samyang Tire, Inc., 131 F.3d 1433 (1997).

Carroll v. Litton Sys., Inc., No. B-C-88–253, 1990 WL 312969 (W.D.N.C. Oct.. 29, 1990).

Carruth, R. S., and Goldstein, B. D. (2001). Relative Risk Greater than Two in Proof of Causation in Toxic Tort Litigation. *Jurimetrics Journal, 41*, 195–209.

Casey v. Ohio Medical Products, Inc., 877 F. Supp. 1380 (N.D. Cal 1995).

Castleman, B. (1981). Regulations Affecting Use of Carcinogens. In N. I. Sax (Ed.), *Cancer Causing Chemicals* (pp. 78–98). New York: Van Nostrand Reinhold.

Cavallo v. Star Enter., 892 F. Supp. 756 (E.D. Va. 1995).

Cella v. United States, 998 F2d 419 (C.A. 7 (Ind.) 1993).

Chambers v. Exxon Corp., 81 F. Supp. 2d 661 (M.D. La. 2000).

Chan, P. K., and Hayes, A. W. (1989). Principles and Methods for Acute Toxicity and Eye Irritancy. In A. W. Hayes (Ed.), *Principles and Methods of Toxicology* (2nd ed., pp. 169–220). New York: Raven Press.

Chen, B., Zhao, W.-L., Jin, J., Xue, Y.-Q, Cheng, X., Chen, X.-T., Cui1, J., Chen, Z.-M., Cao, Q., Yang, G., Yao, Y., Xia, H.-L, Tong, J.-H., Li, J.-M. Chen, J., Xiong, S.-M., Shen, Z.-X., Waxman, S., Chen, Z. and Chen, S.-J. (2005). Clinical and Cytogenetic Features of 508 Chinese Patients with Myelodysplastic Syndrome and Comparison with Those in Western Countries. *Leukemia* 19, 767–775

Chen, J., Stampfer, M. J., Hough, H. L., Garcia-Closas, M., Willett, W. C., Hennekens, C. H., et al. (1998). A Prospective Study of N-Acetyltransferase Fenotype, Red Meat Intake, and Risk of Colorectal Cancer. *Cancer Research, 58*, 3307–3311.

Chengelis, C. P., and Gad, S. C. (1992). Introduction. In C. P. Chengelis and S. C. Gad (Eds.), *Animal Models in Toxicology* (pp. 1–17). New York: Marcel Dekker.

Christoffel, T., and Teret, S. P. (1991). Epidemiology and the Law: Courts and Confidence Intervals. *American Journal of Public Health, 81*, 1661–1666.

Claar v. Burlington N.R.R., 29 F.3d 499 (9th Cir. 1994).

Clayson, D. B. (2001). *Toxicological Carcinogenesis.* New York: Lewis.

Clayson, D. B., Krewski, D., and Munro, I. (Eds.). (1985). *Toxicological Risk Assessment, Vol. I: Biological and Statistical Criteria.* Boca Raton, FL: CRC Press.

Cleary, E. W., et al. (Eds.). (1979). *McCormick on Evidence.* (2nd ed.). St. Paul: West.

Cleary, E. W., et al. (Eds.). (1984). *McCormick on Evidence.* (3rd ed.). St. Paul: West.

Clermont, K. M., and Eisenberg, T. (2000). Anti-Plaintiff Bias in the Federal Appellate Courts. *Judicature, 84,* 128–134.

Coghlan, L. G., Gimenez-Conti, I., Kleiner, H. E., Fischer, S. M., Runhaug, J. E., Conti, C. J., et al. (2000). Development and Initial Characterization of Several New Inbred Strains of SENCAR Mice for Studies of Multistage Skin Carcinogenesis. *Carcinogenesis, 21*(4), 641–646.

Cogliano, V. J., Baan, R. A., Straif, K., Grosse, Y., Secretan, M. B., El Ghissassi, F., and Kleihues, P. (2004). The Science and Practice of Carcinogen Identification and Evaluation. *Environmental Health Perspectives, 112,* 1269–1274.

Cohen, S. M. (2001). Alternative Models for Carcinogenicity Testing: Weight of Evidence Evaluations across Models. *Toxicologic Pathology, 29*(Suppl.), 183–190.

Cohrssen, J. J., and Covello, V. T. (1989). Risk Analysis: A Guide to Principles and Methods for Analyzing Health and Environmental Risks. Washington, DC: White House Council on Environmental Quality.

Collet, J. P., Macdonald, N., Cashman, N., Pless, R., and the Advisory Committee on Causality Assessment. (2000). Monitoring Signals for Vaccine Safety: The Assessment of Individual Adverse Event Reports by an Expert Advisory Committee. *Bulletin of the World Health Organization, 78,* 178–185.

Cone, M. (2003, April 20). Cause for Alarm over Chemicals. *Los Angeles Times*, A1.

Conney, A. H. (1982). Induction of Microsomal Enzymes by Foreign Chemicals and Carcinogenesis by Polycyclic Aromatic Hydrocarbons: G.H.A. Clowes Memorial Lecture. *Cancer Research, 42,* 3875–4917.

Cooter and Gell v. Hartmarx Corp., 496 U.S. 384 (1989).

Craighead, J. (Ed.). (1995). *Pathology of Environmental and Occupational Disease.* St. Louis: Mosby.

Cranor, C. F. (1993). *Regulating Toxic Substances.* New York: Oxford University Press.

Cranor, C. F. (1997). Eggshell Skulls and Loss of Hair from Fright: Some Moral and Legal Principles that Protect Susceptible Subpopulations. *Environmental Toxicology and Pharmacology, 4,* 239–245.

Cranor, C. F. (2003, Fall). *Daubert* and the Acceptability of Legal Decisions. *Law and Philosophy Newsletter,* 127–131.

Cranor, C. F. (2004). Some Legal Implications of the Precautionary Principle: Improving Information Generation and Legal Protections. *European Journal of Oncology, Library Vol. 2,* 31–51.

Cranor, C. F. (2005). Scientific Reasoning in the Laboratory and the Law. *American Journal of Public Health, 95* (Suppl. 1), S121–S128.

Cranor, C. F., and Eastmond, D. A. (2001). Scientific Ignorance and Reliable Patterns of Evidence in Toxic Tort Causation: Is There a Need for Liability Reform? *Law and Contemporary Problems, 64,* 5–48.

Cranor, C. F., Fischer, J. G., and Eastmond, D. A. (1996). Judicial Boundary-Drawing and the Need for Context-Sensitive Science in Toxic Torts after *Daubert v. Merrell Dow Pharmaceuticals, Inc. Virginia Environmental Law Journal, 16,* 1–77.

Cranor, C. F., and Strauss, D. (2005). Case Studies in Science and the Law. Article submitted for publication.

Cullen, M. R., Rosenstock, L., and Brooks, S. M. (1995). Clinical Approach and Establishing a Diagnosis of an Environmental Medical Disorder. In S. M. Brooks (Ed.), *Environmental Medicine* (pp. 217–231). St. Louis: Mosby.

Curfman, C. D., Morrissey, S., and Drazen, J. M. (2005). Expression of Concern: Bombardier, et al., Comparison of Upper Gastrointestinal Toxicity of Rofecoxib and Naproxen in Patients with Rheumatoid Arthritis. *New England Journal of Medicine*, 343, 2813–2814. Located at www.NEJM.org. December 20, 2005.

Daubert v. Merrell Dow Pharm., Inc., 509 U.S. 579 (1993).

Daubert v. Merrell Dow Pharm., Inc., 727 F. Supp. 570 (S.D. Cal. 1989), *aff'd*, 951 F.2d 1128 (9th Cir. 1991), *vacated*, 509 U.S. 579 (1993).

Daubert v. Merrell Dow Pharm., Inc., 951 F.2d 1128 (9th Cir. 1991), *vacated*, 509 U.S. 579 (1993).

Daubert v. Merrell Dow Pharm., Inc., 43 F.3d 1311 (9th Cir. 1995), *on remand from* 509 U.S. 579 (1993).

Dawson, B., and Berenson, A. (2005, August 20). Working Through a Decision Cut in Shades of Deep Gray. *New York Times*. Retrieved from http://www.nytimes.com.

Deitz, C. C., Zheng, W., Leff, M. A., Gross, M., Wen, W. Q., Doll, M. A., et al. (2000). N-Acetyltransferase-2 Genetic Polymorphism, Well-Done Meat Intake, and Breast Cancer Risk among Postmenopausal Women. *Cancer Epidemiology Biomarkers and Prevention, 9*, 905–910.

Denmark, H. (1987). Improving Litigation Against Drug Manufacturers for Failure to Warn Against Possible Side Effects: Keeping Dubious Lawsuits from Driving Good Drugs Off the Market. *Case Western Reserve Law Review, 40*, 413–428.

Denninson, Richard. (2005, May 6). *U.S. HPV Challenge and Beyond*. Presented at the *Ward, Kershaw Environmental Law Symposium: The Data Gaps Dilemma: Why Toxic Ignorance Threatens Public Health* sponsored by the University of Maryland School of Law. Washington, DC.

Development in the Law – Confronting the New Challenges of Scientific Evidence. (1995). *Harvard Law Review, 108*, 1481–1605.

Dixon, L., and Gill, B. (2002). *Changes in the Standards for Admitting Expert Evidence in Federal Cases Since the* Daubert *Decision*. Santa Monica, CA: RAND Institute for Civil Justice.

Dixon, R. (1986). Toxic Responses of the Reproductive System. In C. D. Klaassen, M. O. Amdur, and J. Doull (Eds.), *Casarett and Doull's Toxicology* (3rd ed., pp. 432–477). New York: Macmillan.

Donaldson v. Central Illinois Public Service Company, 199 Ill. 2d 63 (2002).

Dow Chemical Company, Monsanto Company v. Stephenson, and Isaacson (Supreme Court of the United States, 2002).

Ealy v. Richardson-Merrell, Inc., 897 F.2d 159 (D.C. Cir.), *cert. denied*, 498 U.S. 950 (1990).

Eco, U. (1983). *The Name of the Rose*. New York: Harcourt Brace Jovanovich.

Editorial: For Honest Reports of Drug Trials. (2004, September 11). *New York Times*, A14.

Edmond, G., and Mercer, D. (1996). Recognizing Daubert: What Judges Should Know About Falsificationism. *Expert Evidence, 5*, 28–40.

Egilman, D. S., and Rankin Bohme, S. (Eds.). (2005). Corporate Corruption of Science [Special Issue]. *International Journal of Occupational and Environmental Health*, II(4), available at http://www.ijoel.com

EPA, EDF, CMA Agree on Testing Program Targeting 2,800 Chemicals. (1998, October). *Environmental Health Newsletter, 37*, 193.

Epstein, S. S. (1990). Corporate Crime: Why We Cannot Trust Industry-Derived Safety Studies. *International Journal of Health Services, 20*, 433–455.

European Environmental Agency. (2000). *Late Lessons from Early Warnings: The Precautionary Principle 1896–2000*. Copenhagen, Denmark: European Environmental Community.

Eysenck, H. J. (1991). Were We Really Wrong? *American Journal of Public Health, 133*, 429–432.

Faigman, D. L., Kaye, D. H., Saks, M. J., and Sanders, J. (2002). *Modern Scientific Evidence: The Law and Science of Expert Testimony*. St. Paul: West.

Falk, H., Creech, J. L., Jr., Heath, C. W., Jr., Johnson, M. N., and Key, M. M. (1974, October 7). Hepatic Disease among Workers at a Vinyl Chloride Polymerization Plant. *Journal of the American Medical Association, 230*, 59–68.

Faustman, E. M., and Omenn, G. S. (2001). Risk Assessment. In C. D. Klaassen (Ed.), *Casarett and Doull's Toxicology* (6th ed., pp. 83–104). New York: McGraw-Hill.

Federal Judicial Center. (Ed.). (2000). *Reference Manual on Scientific Evidence* (2nd ed.). Washington, DC: Federal Judicial Center.

Federal Judicial Center. (Ed.). (2004). *Manual for Complex Litigation* (4th ed.). Washington, DC: Federal Judicial Center.

Feldman v. Lederle Labs., 479 A.2d 374 (N.J. 1984).

Fenichel, G. M., Lane, D. A., Livengood, J. R., Horwitz, S. J., Menkes, J. H., and Schwarrtz, J. F. (1989). Adverse Events Following Immunization: Assessing Probability of Causation. *Pediatric Neurology*, 5, 287–290.

Ferebee v. Chevron Chemical, Inc., 736 F.2d 1529 (D.C. Cir. 1984).

Finley, L. M. (1999). Guarding the Gate to the Courthouse: How Trial Judges are Using Their Evidentiary Screening Role to Remake Tort Causation Rules. *DePaul Law Review*, 49, 335–375.

Fisk, M. C. (1999, November 10). Chicago Hope: A $28M Verdict. *National Law Journal*, A10.

Fiss, O. M. (1984). Against Settlement. *Yale Law Journal*, 93, 1073–1090.

Fleiss, J. L. (1986). Significance Tests Have a Role in Epidemiologic Research: Reactions to A.M. Walker. *American Journal of Public Health*, 76, 559–560.

Foster, K. R., and Huber, P. W. (1997). *Judging Science: Scientific Knowledge and the Federal Court*. Cambridge, MA: MIT Press.

Fox and Goldsworthy. (1993). Molecular Analysis of the H-*ras* Gene: An Understanding of Mouse Liver Tumor Development. *CIIT Activities*, 13(7), 1–6.

Freiman, J. A., Chalmers, T. C., Smith, H., et al. (1978). The Importance of Beta, the Type II Error and Sample Size in the Design and Interpretation of the Randomized Control Trial: Survey of 71 'Negative' Trials. *New England Journal of Medicine*, 299, 690–694.

Freireich, E. J., Gehan, E. A., Rall, D. P., Schmidt, L. H., and Skipper, H. E. (1990). Quantitative Comparison of Toxicity of Anticancer Agents in Mouse, Rat, Hamster, Dog, Monkey and Man. *Cancer Chemotherapy Reports*, 50, 199–244.

Friedman, L. C., Daynard, R. A., and Banthin, C. N. (2005). How Tobacco-Friendly Science Escapes Scrutiny in the Courtroom. *American Journal of Public Health*, 95(Suppl. 1), S16–S19.

Frye v. U.S., 293 F.2d 1013 (D.C. Cir. 1923).

Fung, V. A., et al. (1995). The Carcinogenesis Bioassay in Perspective: Application in Identifying Human Cancer Hazards. *Environmental Health Perspectives*, 103, 680–683.

Furst, A. (1990). Yes, But Is It a Human Carcinogen? *Journal of the American College of Toxicology*, 9, 1–18.

Furuya, I., and Watanabe, S. (1993). Discriminative Stimulus Properties of Ephedra Herb (*Ephedra sinica*) in Rats. *Yakubutsu Seishin Kodo*, 13, 33–38.

Gad, S. C. (1992). Model Selection and Scaling. In C. P. Chengelis and S. C. Gad (Eds.), *Animal Models in Toxicology* (pp. 813–839). New York: Marcel Dekker.

Gallo, M. A. (2001). History and Scope of Toxicology. In C. D. Klaassen (Ed.), *Casarett and Doull's Toxicology* (6th ed., pp. 3–10). New York: McGraw-Hill.

Garlinger v. Hardee's Food Systems, Inc., 16 Fed. Appx 232 2001 929767 (4th Cir. 2001).

General Electric Company v. Joiner, 113 S.Ct. 512 (1997).

General Electric Company v. Joiner, 522 U.S. 136 (1997).

Gerrard, M. (Ed.). (1999). *The Law of Environmental Justice: Theories and Procedures to Address Disproportionate Risks*. Chicago: Section of Environment, Energy, and Resources, The American Bar Association.

Gillette, C. P., and Krier, J. E. (1999). Risk, Courts and Agencies. *University of Pennsylvania Law Review*, 38, 1077–1109.

Gitlin, J. N., Cook, L. L., Linton, O. W., Garrett-Mayer, E. (2004). Comparison of "B" Readers' Interpretations of Chest Radiographs for Asbestos Related Changes. *Academic Radiology*, 11, 843–856.

Glaser v. Thompson Med. Co., 32 F.3d 969 (6th Cir. 1994).

Glastetter v. Novartis Pharmaceuticals Corp., 252 F.3d 986 (8th Cir. 2001).

Globetti v. Sandoz Pharmaceuticals, Corp., 111 F. Supp. 2d 1174 (N.D. Ala. 2000).

Gold, L., et al. (1989). Interspecies Extrapolation in Carcinogenesis: Prediction between Rats and Mice. *Environmental Health Perspectives*, 81, 211–219.

Goldman, A. I. (1999). *Knowledge in a Social World*. New York: Oxford University Press.

Goldstein, B. D., and Henifin, M. S. (2000). Reference Guide on Toxicology. In Federal Judicial Center (Ed.), *Reference Manual on Scientific Evidence* (2nd ed., pp. 401–438). Washington, DC: Federal Judicial Center.

Goodman, S. N., and Royall, R. (1988). Evidence and Scientific Research. *American Journal of Public Health, 78,* 1568–1574.

Goodstein, D. (2000). How Science Works. In Federal Judicial Center (Ed.), *Reference Manual on Scientific Evidence* (2nd ed., pp. 67–82). Washington, DC: Federal Judicial Center.

Gordon, A. E., and Shaughnessy, A. F. (2003). Saw Palmetto for Prostate Disorders. *American Family Physician, 67,* 1281–1283.

Gottesman, M. H. (1998). From *Barefoot* to *Daubert* to *Joiner*: Triple Play or Double Error. *Arizona Law Review, 40,* 753–780.

Gottesman, M. H. (2003, February 27). Paper presented at *Science, the Courts, and Protective Justice* sponsored by the Science and Environmental Health Network and Georgetown Environmental Law and Policy Institute. Washington, DC

Goyer, R. A., and Clarkson, T. W. (2001). Toxic Effects of Metals. In C. D. Klaassen (Ed.), *Casarett and Doull's Toxicology* (6th ed., pp. 818–821). New York: McGraw-Hill.

Graham, M. H. (2000). The Expert Witness Predicament: Determining 'Reliable' under the Gate-keeping Test of Daubert, Kumho and Proposed Amended Rule 702 of the Federal Rules of Evidence. *Miami Law Review, 54,* 317–357.

Graham v. Playtex Prod., Inc., 993 F. Supp. 127 (N.D.N.Y. 1998).

Gray, George M., Li, P., Shlykhter, I., and Wilson, R. (1995). An Empirical Examination of Factors Influencing Prediction of Carcinogenic Hazard across Species. *Regulatory Toxicology and Pharmacology, 22,* 283–291.

Green, M. D. (1992). Legal Theory: Expert Witnesses and Sufficiency of Evidence in Toxic Substances Litigation. *Northwestern University Law Review, 86,* 643–699.

Green, M. D. (1996). *Bendectin and Birth Defects: The Challenges of Mass Toxic Substances Litigation.* Philadelphia: University of Pennsylvania Press.

Green, M. D. (1999). The Road Less Well Traveled (and Seen): Contemporary Lawmaking in Products Liability. *DePaul Law Review, 49,* 377–403.

Greene, G. (1999). *The Woman Who Knew Too Much: Alice Stewart and the Secrets of Radiation.* Ann Arbor: University of Michigan Press.

Greenland, S. (Ed.). (1987). *Evolution of Epidemiologic Ideas: Annotated Readings on Concepts and Methods.* Newton Lower Falls, MA: Epidemiology Resources.

Greenland, S. (1991). Invited Commentary: Science Versus Public Health Actions: Those Who Were Wrong Are Still Wrong. *American Journal of Public Health, 133,* 435–436.

Greenland, S. (1999). Relation of Probability of Causation to Relative Risk and Doubling Dose: A Methodologic Error That Has Become a Social Problem. *American Journal of Public Health, 89,* 1166–1169.

Greenland, S., and Robins, J. M. (1988). Conceptual Problems in the Definition and Interpretation of Attributable Fractions. *American Journal of Epidemiology, 128,* 1185–1196.

Greenland, S., and Robins, J. M. (2000). Epidemiology, Justice, and the Probability of Causation. *Jurimetrics Journal, 40,* 321–340.

Gregus, Z., and Klaassen, C. D. (2001). Mechanisms of Toxicity. In C. D. Klaassen (Ed.), *Casarett and Doull's Toxicology* (6th ed., pp. 35–82). New York: McGraw-Hill.

Gross, S. R. (1991). Expert Evidence. *Wisconsin Law Review, 1991,* 1113–1232.

Gulf South Insulation v. Consumer Product Safety Commission, 701 F.2d 1137 (5th Cir. 1983).

Haack, S. (1999). An Epistemologist in the Bramble-Bush: At the Supreme Court with Mr. Joiner. *Journal of Health Politics, Policy and Law, 26,* 217–237.

Haack, S. (2005). Trial and Error: The Supreme Court's Philosophy of Science. *American Journal of Public Health, 95*(Suppl. 1), S66–S74.

Haar, J. (1995). *A Civil Action.* New York: Random House, Inc.

Hagen v. Richardson-Merrell, 697 F. Supp. 334 (N.D. Ill. 1988).

Hagerty v. LandL Marine Services, Inc, 788 F.2d 315 (1986).

Halpern, A. C., and Altman, J. F. (1999). Genetic Predisposition to Skin Cancer. *Current Opinion in Oncology, 11*, 132–138.

Harman, G. (1994). The Inference to the Best Explanation. *Philosophical Review, 74*, 89–90.

Hartzema, A. G., Porta, M., and Tilson, H. H. (Eds.). (1998). *Pharmacoepidemiology: An Introduction* (3rd ed.). Cincinnati, OH: Harvey Whitney Books.

Hattis, D. (1997). Variability in Susceptibility: How Big, How Often, For What Responses to What Agents? *Environmental Toxicology and Pharmacology, 4*, 195–208.

Hattis, D., Banati, P., and Goble, R. (1999, December). Distributions of Individual Susceptibility among Humans for Toxic Effects − For What Fraction of Which Kinds of Chemicals and Effects Does the Traditional 10-Fold Factor Provide How Much Protection? *Annals of the New York Academy of Sciences, 895*, 286–316.

Hattis, D., and Barlow, K. (1996). Human Interindividual Variability in Cancer Risks. Technical and Management Challenges. *Health and Ecological Risk Assessment, 2*, 194–220.

Heath, C. W., Jr., Falk, H., and Creech, L., Jr. (1975). Characteristics of Cases of Angiosarcoma of the Liver among Vinyl Chloride Workers in the United States. *Annals of the New York Academy of Sciences*, 231–248.

Heikkila, R. E., et al. (1984). Dopaminergic Neurotoxicity of 1-Methyl-4-Phenyl-1,2,5,6-Tetrahydropyridine in Mice. *Science, 224*, 1451–1453.

Heller v. Shaw Industries, 167 F.3d 146 (3d Cir. 1999).

Hileman, B. (1994). Findings Point to Complexity of Health Effects of Electric, Magnetic Fields. *Chemical Engineering News, 72*, 27.

Hill, A. B. (1987). The Environment and Disease: Association or Causation? In S. Greenland (Ed.), *Evolution of Epidemiologic Ideas: Annotated Readings on Concepts and Methods* (pp. 15–20). Newton Lower Falls, MA: Epidemiology Resources. (Reprinted from *Proceedings of the Royal Society of Medicine*, 1965, *58*, 295–300.)

Hilts, P. J. (2003). *Protecting America's Health: The FDA, Business, and One Hundred Years of Regulation*. New York: Alfred K. Knopf.

Hines v. Consolidated Rail Corp., 926 F.2d 262 (3d Cir. 1991).

Holbrook v. Lykes, 80 F.3d 777 (1996).

Hollingworth, J. G., and Lasker, E. G. (2004, Winter). The Case Against Differential Diagnosis: *Daubert*, Medical Causation Testimony and the Scientific Method. *Journal of Health Law, 37*(1), 85–112.

Honoré, T. (1995). The Morality of Tort Law − Questions and Answers. In D. G. Owen (Ed.), *Philosophical Foundations of Tort Law* (pp. 73–95). Oxford: Clarendon Press.

Hooper, K., and McDonald, T. A. (2000). The PBDE's: An Emerging Environmental Challenge and Another Reason for Breast-Milk Monitoring Programs. *Environmental Health Perspectives, 108*(5), 387–392.

Hooper, L. L., Cecil, J. S., and Willging, T. E. (2001). Assessing Causation in Breast Implant Litigation: The Role of Science Panels. *Law and Contemporary Problems, 64*(4), 139–189.

Hopkins v. Dow Corning Corp., 33 F.3d 1116 (9th Cir. 1994).

Howerton v. Arai Helmet, Ltd., 348 N.C. 440, 697 S.E.2d 674 (2004).

Huber, P. (1991). *Galileo's Revenge: Junk Science in the Courtroom*. New York: Basic Books.

Huff, J. (1992). Applicability to Humans of Rodent-Specific Sites of Chemical Carcinogenicity: Tumors of the Forestomach and of the Harderian, Preputial, and Zymbal Glands Induced by Benzene. *Journal of Occupational Medicine and Toxicology, 1*, 109–141.

Huff, J. (1993). Chemicals and Cancer in Humans: First Evidence in Experimental Animals. *Environmental Health Perspectives, 100*, 201–210.

Huff, J. (1996, December). Alpha-2u-Globulin Nephropathy, Posed Mechanisms, and White Ravens. *Environmental Health Perspectives, 104*, 1264–1267.

Huff, J. (1999). Long-term Chemical Carcinogenesis Bioassays Predict Human Cancer Hazard: Issues, Controversies and Uncertainties. *Annals of the New York Academy of Sciences, 895*, 56–79.

Huff, J., and Hoel, D. (1992). Perspective and Overview of the Concepts and Value of Hazard Identification as the Initial Phase of Risk Assessment for Cancer and Human Health. *Scandinavian Journal of Work Environment and Health*, *18*, 83–89.

Huff, J., and Melnick, R. (2002, October 23–24). *Chemical Carcinogenesis Bioassays: Critical for the Sensible Application of the Precautionary Principle for Protecting Public Health*. Presentation to the Collegium Ramazzini. Bologna, Italy.

Huff, J., and Rall, D. P. (1992). Relevance to Humans of Carcinogenesis Results from Laboratory Animal Toxicology Studies. In J. M. Last and R. B. Wallace (Eds.), *Maxcy-Rosenau-Last Public Health and Preventive Medicine* (13th ed., pp. 433–452). Norwalk, CT: Appleton and Lange.

Hutchinson, T. A., and Lane, D. A. (1989). Standardized Methods of Causality Assessment of Suspected Adverse Drug Reactions. *Journal of Clinical Epidemiology*, *42*, 5–16.

Hyland, K. (1997). *Hedging in Scientific Research Articles*. Amsterdam: John Benjamins.

In re: Agent Orange product liability litigation, 611 F. Supp. 1223 (E.D.N.Y. 1985).

In re: Bendectin Prod. Liab. Litig., 732 F. Supp. 744 (E.D. Mich. 1990).

In re: Breast Implant Litigation, 11 F. Supp. 2d 1217 (2000).

In re: Ephedra Products Liability Litigation, 393 F. Supp. 2d 181 (2005).

In re: Hanford Nuclear Reservation Litigation 292 F.3d 1124 (C.A.9 (Wash. 2002)).

In re: Joint E. and S. Dist. Asbestos Litig., 827 F. Supp. 1014 (S.D.N.Y. 1993).

In re: Joint E. and S. Dist. Asbestos Litig., 758 F. Supp. 199 (S.D.N.Y. 1991), *aff'd*, 52 F.3d 1124 (2d Cir. 1995).

In re: MeridiaProds. Liab. Litig., 328 F. Supp. 2d 791 (N.D. Ohio 2004).

In re: Paoli R.R. Yard PCB Litig., 706 F. Supp. 358 (E.D. Pa. 1988), *rev'd*, 916 F.2d 829 (3d Cir. 1990), *cert. denied*, 499 U.S. 961 (1991).

In re: Paoli R.R. Yard PCB Litigation, 916 F.2d 829 (3d Cir. 1990).

In re: Paoli R.R. Yard PCB Litigation, 35 F.3d 717 (3d Cir. 1994), *cert. denied*, 115 S.Ct. 1253 (1995).

In re: Phenylpropanolamine (PPA) Products Liability Litigation, 289 F. Supp. 2d 1230 (2003)(W.D. Washington).

In re: Redlands Tort Litigation (2001), referenced in *Lockheed Martin Co. v. Superior Court*, 109 Cal. App.4th 24 (2003).

In re: TMI Litigation, 193 F.3d 613 (3d Cir. 1999).

In re: Winship, 397 U.S. 358 (1970).

Infante, P. F. (1992). Benzene and Leukemia: The 0.1 ppm ACGIH Proposed Threshold Limit Value for Benzene. *Applied Occupational Environmental Hygiene*, *7*, 253–262.

Infante, P. F. (1995, May-August). Benzene and Leukemia: Cell Types, Latency and Amount of Exposure Associated with Leukemia. *Advances in Occupational Medicine and Rehabilitation*, *Q*(2), 107–120.

Institute of Medicine. (1994). *Adverse Events Associated with Childhood Vaccines: Evidence Bearing on Causality*. (A. G. Hartzema, M. Porta, and H. H. Tilson, Eds.). Washington, DC: National Academy Press.

Institute of Medicine and National Research Council, Committee on the Framework for Evaluating the Safety of Dietary Supplements. (2005). *Dietary Supplements: A Framework for Evaluating Safety*. Washington, DC: National Academy Press.

Institute of Medicine, Committee to Review the Health Effects in Vietnam Veterans of Exposure to Herbicides. (1996). *Veterans and Agent Orange*. Washington DC: National Academy Press.

International Agency for Research on Cancer (IARC). (n.d.). Lists of IARC Evaluations. *Monograph Series*. Revised July 22, 2004. Retrieved from http://www-cie.iarc.fr/monoeval/grlist.html.

International Agency for Research on Cancer (IARC). (n.d.). Overall Evaluations of Carcinogenicity to Humans, Group 1: Carcinogenic to Humans. *Monograph Series*. Revised July 7, 2004. Retrieved from http://www-cie.iarc.fr/Monoeval/crthgr01.html.

International Agency for Research on Cancer (IARC). (n.d.). Overall Evaluations of Carcinogenicity to Humans, Group 2A: Probably Carcinogenic to Humans. *Monograph Series.* Revised
July 7, 2004. Retrieved from http://www-cie. iarc.fr/monoeval/crthgr02a.html.

International Agency for Research on Cancer (IARC). (n.d.). Preamble. *Monograph Series.* Revised
August 18, 2004. Retrieved from http://www-cie.iarc.fr/monoeval/preamble.html.

International Agency for Research on Cancer (IARC). (n.d.). Preamble, Section 8: Studies of
Cancer in Humans. *Monograph Series.* Revised December 17, 1998. Retrieved from http://www-
cie.iarc.fr/monoeval/studieshumans.html.

International Agency for Research on Cancer (IARC). (n.d.). Preamble, Section 9: Studies of
Cancer in Experimental Animals. *Monograph Series.* Revised January 5, 1999. Retrieved from
http://www-cie.iarc.fr/monoeval/studiesanimals.html.

International Agency for Research on Cancer (IARC). (n.d.). Preamble, Section 12: Evaluation.
Monograph Series. Revised January 5, 1999. Retrieved from http://www-cie.iarc.fr/monoeval/
eval.html.

International Agency for Research on Cancer (IARC). (n.d.). Preamble, Section 2: Objective
and Scope. *Monograph Series.* Revised December 7, 1999. Retrieved from http://www-cie.
iarc.fr/monoeval/objectives.html.

International Agency for Research on Cancer (IARC). (1974). Benzene. *Monograph Series, 7,*
203. Revised March 19, 1998. Retrieved from http://www-cie.iarc.fr/htdocs/monographs/
vol07/benzene.html.

International Agency for Research on Cancer (IARC). (1976). Safrole, Isosafrole, and Dihydrosafrole. *Monograph Series, 10,* 231. Revised March 22, 1998. Retrieved from http://www-cie.iarc.fr/
htdocs/monographs/vol10/ safrole.html.

International Agency for Research on Cancer (IARC). (1982a). Benzene. *Monograph Series,*
29, 93. Revised April 9, 1998. Retrieved from http://www-cie.iarc.fr/htdocs/monographs/
vol29/benzene.html.

International Agency for Research on Cancer (IARC). (1982b). Benzidine and Its Sulphate,
Hydrochloride and Dihydrochloride. *Monograph Series, 29,* 149. Revised April 9, 1998.
Retrieved from http://wwwcie.iarc.fr/htdocs/monographs/vol29/benzidine.html.

International Agency for Research on Cancer (IARC). (1987a). Benzene (Group 1). *Monograph
Series, Supplement 7,* 120. Revised February 6, 1998. Retrieved from http://www.cie.iarc.fr/
htdocs/monographs/suppl7/benzene.html.

International Agency for Research on Cancer (IARC). (1987b). Benzidine-Based Dyes (Group 2A).
Monograph Series, Supplement 7, 125. Revised February 11, 1998. Retrieved from http://www-
cie.iarc.fr/htdocs/monographs/suppl17/benzidinedyes.html.

International Agency for Research on Cancer (IARC). (1987c). Chloroethyl Nitrosoureas. *Monograph Series, Supplement 7,* 150. Revised February 6, 1998. Retrieved from http://www-cie.
iarc.fr/htdocs/monographs/suppl7/chloroethylnitrosoureas.html.

International Agency for Research on Cancer (IARC). (1987d). Polychlorinated Biphenyls. *Monograph Series, Supplement 7,* 322. Revised February 11, 1998. Retrieved from http://www-
cie.iarc.fr/htdocs/monographs/suppl7/polychlorinated biphenyls.html.

International Agency for Research on Cancer (IARC). (1987e). Vinyl Chloride (Group 1). *Monograph Series, Supplement 7,* 373. Revised February 10, 1998. Retrieved from http://www-
cie.iarc.fr/htdocs/monographs/suppl7/vinylchloride.html.

International Agency for Research on Cancer (IARC). (1993). Occupational Exposures of
Hairdressers and Barbers and Personal Use of Hair Colourants; Some Hair Dyes, Cosmetic Colourants, Industrial Dyestuffs and Aromatic Amines." *Monograph Series, 57,* n.p.
Revised August 22, 1997. Retrieved from http://www-cie.iarc.fr/htdocs/indexes/vol57index.
html.

International Agency for Research on Cancer (IARC). (1994). Ethylene Oxide (Group 1).
Monograph Series, 60, 73. Revised August 26, 1997. Retrieved from http://www-cie.iarc.
fr/htdocs/monographs/vol60/m60-02.htm.

International Agency for Research on Cancer (IARC). (1995a). Formaldehyde (Group 2A). *Monograph Series, 62,* 217. Revised August 13, 1997. Retrieved from http://www-cie.iarc. fr/htdocs/monographs/vol62/formal.html.

International Agency for Research on Cancer (IARC). (1995b). Tetrachloroethylene. *Monograph Series, 63,* 159. Revised May 20, 1997. Retrieved from http://www-cie.iarc.fr/htdocs/monographs/vol63/tetrachloroethylene.htm.

International Agency for Research on Cancer (IARC). (1995c). Trichloroethylene. *Monograph Series, 63,* 75. Revised May 20, 1997. Retrieved from http://www-cie.iarc.fr/htdocs/monographs/vol63/trichloroethylene.htm.

International Agency for Research on Cancer (IARC). (1997). Polychlorinated Dibenzo-*para*-Dioxins. *Monograph Series, 69,* 33. Revised August 12, 1997. Retrieved from http://www-cie.iarc.fr/htdocs/monographs/vol69/dioxin.html.

International Agency for Research on Cancer (IARC). (1999a). Consensus Report: The Use of Short- and Medium-term Tests for Carcinogens and Data on Genetic Effects in Carcinogenic Hazard Evaluation." *IARC Scientific Publications No. 146* (D. B. McGregor, J. M. Rice, and S. Venitt, Eds.). Rev. April 29, 1999. Retrieved from http://www-cie.iarc.fr/htdocs/iarcpubs/pub146/pub146consensus.html.

International Agency for Research on Cancer (IARC). (1999b). 1,3-Butadiene (Group 2A). *Monograph Series, 71,* 109. Revised April 12, 1999. Retrieved from http://www-cie.iarc.fr/htdocs/monographs/vol71/002-butadiene.html.

International Agency for Research on Cancer (IARC). (2000). Neutrons. *Monograph Series, 75,* n.p. Revised April 19, 2000. Retrieved from http://www-cie.iarc.fr/htdocs/monographs/vol75/neutrons.html.

James, F., Jr., and Hazard, G. C., Jr. (1977). *Civil Procedure* (2nd ed.). Boston: Little, Brown and Company.

James, R. C. (1985). General Principles of Toxicology. In P. L. Williams and J. L. Burson (Eds.), *Industrial Toxicology: Safety and Health Applications in the Workplace* (pp. 7–26). New York: Lifetime Learning Publications.

Jasanoff, S. (1995). *Science at the Bar: Law, Science and Technology in America.* Cambridge, MA: Harvard University Press.

Jasanoff, S. (2005). Law's Knowledge: Science for Justice in Legal Settings. *American Journal of Public Health, 95*(Suppl. 1), S49–S58.

Joiner v. General Electric Co., 864 F. Supp. 1310 (N. D. Georgia 1994).

Joiner v. General Electric Co., 78 F.3d 524 (11th Cir. 1996).

Joyce, C. (1990, April 14). Public Being 'Misled' over Asbestos Dangers: Science Magazine Publishes Paper Claiming Public Health Risk. *New Scientist,* 16.

Kalaria, R. N., Mitchell, M. J., and Harik, S. L. (1987). Correlation of 1-Methyl-4-Phenyl-1,2,3,6-Tetrahydropyridine Neurotoxicity with Blood-Brain Barrier Monoamine Oxidase Activity. *Proceedings Natl. Acad. Sci. U.S.A., 84*(10), 3521–3525.

Kannankeril v. Terminix International Inc., 128 F.3d 802 (3d Cir. 1997).

Kassirer, J. P. (1989). Diagnostic Reasoning. *Annals of Internal Medicine, 110,* 893–900.

Kassirer, J. P., and Cecil, J. S. (2002, September 13). Inconsistency in Evidentiary Standards for Medical Testimony: Disorder in the Courts. *Journal of the American Medical Association, 28*(11), 1382–1387.

Kassirer, J. P., and Kopelman, R. I. (1991). *Learning Clinical Reasoning.* Baltimore: Williams and Wilkins.

Keeton, W. P., Dobbs, D. B., Keeton, R. E., and Owen, D. G. (1984). *Prosser and Keeton on Torts* (5th ed.). St. Paul, MN: West.

Kelsey, K. T., and LaMontagne, A. D. (1992, October 13). Plaintiff's Expert Opinion Affidavit [Letter].

Kennedy, D. (2004, July). Science, Law and the IBM Case. *Science, 305*(16), 309.

Kennedy v. Collagen Corp., 974 F.2d 1342 (9th Cir. 1992).

Kimbrough, R. D. (1982). Pathological Changes in Human Beings Acutely Poisoned by Dimethyl-nitrosamine. In P. N. Magee (Ed.), *Nitrosamines and Human Cancer* (pp. 25–34). Cold Spring Harbor, NY: Cold Spring Harbor Laboratory.

Kimbrough, R. D. (1985). Case Studies. In P. L. Williams and J. L. Burson (Eds.), *Industrial Toxicology: Safety and Health Applications in the Workplace* (pp. 414–431). New York: Lifetime Learning Publications.

Kitcher, P. (1993). *The Advancement of Science: Science without Legend, Objectivity without Illusions.* New York: Oxford University Press.

Klaassen, C. D. (Ed.). (2001). *Casarett and Doull's Toxicology* (6th ed.). New York: McGraw-Hill.

Klaassen, C. D., Amdur, M. O., and Doull, J. (Eds.). (1996). *Casarett and Doull's Toxicology* (5th ed.). New York: McGraw-Hill.

Klatskin, G., and Kimberg, D. V. (1969). Recurrent Hepatitis Attributable to Halothane Sensitization in an Anesthetist. *The New England Journal of Medicine, 280,* 515–522.

Kogevinas, M., and Boffetta, P. (1991). Letter to the editor. *British Journal of Industrial Medicine, 48,* 575–576.

Kolata, G. (2000, September 26). Controversial Drug Makes a Comeback. *New York Times,* F1.

Kramer, M. S., and Lane, D. A. (1992). Causal Propositions in Clinical Research and Practice. *Journal of Clinical Epidemiology, 45,* 639–649.

Kuhn, T. S. (1977). *The Essential Tension.* Chicago: University of Chicago Press.

Kumho Tire Co. v. Carmichael, 526 U.S. 137 (1999).

Lake, C. R., and Quirk, R. S. (1984). CNS Stimulants and the Look-Alike Drugs. *Psychiatry Cin. North American, 7,* 689–701.

Lakie v. Smithkline Beecham, 965 F. Supp. 49 (D.D.C. 1997).

Lan, Q., et al. (2004). Hematoxtoxicity in Workers Exposed to Low Levels of Benzene. *Science, 306,* 1774–1776.

Lilienfeld, D. E. (1991). The Silence: The Asbestos Industry and Early Occupational Cancer Research – A Case Study. *American Journal of Public Health, 81,* 791–798.

Lockheed Martin Co. v. Superior Court, 109 Cal. App.4th 24 (2003).

Logerquist v. McVey, 196 Ariz. 470, 1 P.3d 113 (2000).

Lynch v. Merrell-National Lab., Div. of Richardson-Merrell, Inc., 830 F.2d 1190 (1st Cir. 1987).

MacMahon, B., and Pugh, T. F. (1987). Causes and Entities of Disease. In S. Greenland (Ed.), *Evolution of Epidemiologic Ideas: Annotated Readings on Concepts and Methods* (pp. 26–34). Newton Lower Falls, MA: Epidemiology Resources. (Reprinted from *Methods of Preventive Medicine,* pp. 11–18, by D. W. Clark and B. MacMahon, Eds., 1967, Boston: Little, Brown and Company)

Magistrini v. One Hour Martinizing, 180 F. Supp. 2d 584 (2002).

Maguire, J. M. (1947). *Evidence, Common Sense and Common Law.* Chicago: Foundation Press.

Manson, J., and Wise, L. D. (1991). Teratogens. In M. O. Amdur, C. D. Klaassen, and J. Doull (Eds.), *Casarett and Doull's Toxicology* (4th ed., pp. 226–254). New York: Pergamon Press.

Marder v. G.D. Searle and Co., 630 F. Supp. 1087 (D. Md. 1986).

Markowitz, G., and Rosner, D. (2002). *Deceit and Denial: The Deadly Politics of Industrial Pollution.* Berkeley: University of California Press.

Marx, J. (1990). Animal Carcinogen Testing Challenged. *Science, 250,* 743.

Mattison, D. R., and Craighead, J. E. (1995). Reproductive System. In J. E. Craighead (Ed.), *Pathology of Environmental and Occupational Disease* (pp. 559–572). St. Louis: Mosby.

Maurer v. United States, 668 F.2d 98 (2d Cir. 1981).

McClain, R. M., Keller, D., Casciano, D., Fu, P., MacDonald, J., Popp, J., et al. (2001). Neonatal Mouse Model: Review of Methods and Results. *Toxicologic Pathology, 29* (Suppl.), 128–137.

McClain v. Metabolife International, Inc., 2005 WL 477861 (11th Cir. (Ala)).

McCullock v. H. B. Fuller Co., 61 F.3d 1038 (2d Cir. 1995).

McElveen, J. C., and Amantea, C. (1995). Risk Symposium: Legislating Risk Assessment. *University of Cincinnati Law Review, 63,* 1553–1598.

McGarity, T. O. (1997). Some Throughts on the 'Deossifying' the Rule-Making Process. *Duke Law Journal 41*, 1335–1462.

McGarity, T. O. (2005). *Daubert* and the Proper Role for the Courts in Health, Safety, and Environmental Regulation. *American Journal of Public Health, 95*(Suppl. 1), S92–S98.

McGarity, T. O. and Shapiro, S. A. (1993). *Workers at Risk: The Failed Promise of the Occupational Safety and Health Administration.* Westport, CT: Praeger.

McKee v. Moore, 648 P.2d 21 (Okla. 1982).

Meier, B. (2004, September 8). Medical Editors Likely to Call for Registration of Drug Tests at Outset. *New York Times.* Retrieved from http://www.nytimes.com.

Melnick, R. L., and Kohn, M. C. (1995). Mechanistic Data Indicate that 1, 3-Butadiene Is a Human Carcinogen. *Carcinogenesis, 16,* 157–163.

Melnick, R. L., Kohn, M. C., and Huff, J. (1997, September). Weight of Evidence Versus Weight of Speculation to Evaluate the Alpha2u-Globulin Hypothesis. *Environmental Health Perspectives, 105,* 904–906.

Mendes-Silva v. United States, 980 F.2d 1482 (D.C. Cir. 1993).

Merrell Dow Pharmaceuticals, Inc. v. Havner, 953 S.W.2d 706 (1997).

Merrill, R. (2004). FDA Regulatory Requirements as Tort Standards. *Journal of Law and Policy, Science for Judges II: The Practice of Epidemiology and Administrative Agency Created Science, 12,* 549–558.

Metabolife International v. Wornick, 264 F.3d 832 (9th Cir. 2001).

Metzger, R. (3 June 2005). The Demise of *Daubert* in State Courts. Commentary for *LexisNexis MEALEY'S Emerging Toxic Torts, 14*(5). Available from http://www.mealeys.com.

Michaels, D. (1988). Waiting for the Body Count: Corporate Decision Making and Bladder Cancer in the U.S. Dye Industry. *Medical Anthropology Quarterly, 2,* 215–227.

Michaels, D. (Ed.). (2005). Scientific Evidence and Public Policy [Special issue]. *American Journal of Public Health, 95*(Suppl. 1).

Michaels, D. (2005, June). Doubt Is Their Product. *Scientific American, 96,* 96–101.

Michaels, D., and Monforton, C. (2005). Manufacturing Uncertainty: Contested Science and the Protection of the Public's Health and Environment. *American Journal of Public Health, 95*(Suppl. 1), S39–S48.

Micklethwait, J., and Wooldridge, A. (2004). *The Right Nation: Conservative Power in America.* New York: Penguin Press.

Mill, J. S. (1941). *A System of Logic: Ratiocinative and Inductive.* London: Longmany, Green and Company.

*Mitchell v. Gencorp Inc.,*165 F.3d 778 (10th Cir. 1999).

Moore v. Ashland Chemical Inc., 151 F.3d 269 (5th Cir. (Tex.) 1998).

Mossman, B. T., et al. (1990). Asbestos: Scientific Developments and Implications for Public Policy. *Science, 247,* 294–301.

The Mouse Genome Sequencing Consortium, MacAndrew, A. (2002, December 5). Comparison of Mouse and Human Coding Genes. *Nature, 420,* 520–562.

The Mouse Genome Sequencing Consortium, Waterston, R., et al. (2002, December 5). Initial Sequencing and Comparative Analysis of the Mouse Genome. *Nature, 420,* 520–562.

National Institute of Environmental Health Sciences of the National Institutes of Health. (1998). *Assessment of Health Effects from Exposure to Power-line Frequency Electric and Magnetic Field.* (C. J. Portier and M. S. Wolfe, Eds.). Research Triangle Park, NC: NIH Publication No. 98–3981.

National Research Council. (1983). *Risk Assessment in the Federal Government: Managing the Process.* Washington, DC: U.S. Government Printing Office.

National Research Council. (1984). *Toxicity Testing: Strategies to Determine Needs and Priorities.* Washington, DC: U.S. Government Printing Office.

National Research Council. (1999). *Arsenic in Drinking Water.* Washington, DC: National Academy Press. Also at http://www.nap.edu/books/0309076293/html/

Nesson, C. (1985). The Evidence or the Event? On Judicial Proof and the Acceptability of Verdicts. *Harvard Law Review, 98,* 1357–1392.

Neutra, R. R., DelPizzo, V., and Lee, G. M. (2002). *An Evaluation of the Possible Risks from Electric and Magnetic Fields (EMFs) from Power Lines, Internal Wiring, Electrical Occupations, and Appliances.* Oakland: California Department of Health Services.

Nicholson, W. J. (1988). IARC Evaluations in the Light of Limitations of Human Epidemiologic Data. *Annals of the New York Academy of Sciences, 534,* 44–54.

Occupational Safety and Health Act of 1970. 29 U.S.C. § 655(b)(5) (1976).

Occupational Safety and Health Administration (OSHA). Occupational Exposure to Benzene; Proposed Rule and Notice Hearing. 50 Fed. Reg. 50512 (Dec. 10, 1985) (to be codified at 29 C.F.R. pt. 1910).

Oddi v. Ford Motor Co., 234 F.3d 143 (3d Cir. 2000).

O'Leary v. Secretary of HHS, No. 90-1729V, 1997 WL 254217.

Ominsky v. Chas. Weinhagen and Co. (1911), 129 N.W. Rptr. 845–846.

Ong, E. K., and Glantz, S. A. (2000, April 8). Tobacco Industry Efforts Subverting International Agency for Research on Cancer's Second-Hand Smoke Study. *Lancet, 355,* 1253–1259.

Oppel, R. A., Jr. (2000, September 22). Environmental Tests 'Falsified,' U.S. Says. *New York Times,* A14.

Ozonoff, D. (2005). Epistemology in the Courtroom: A Little 'Knowledge' Is a Dangerous Thing. *American Journal of Public Health, 95*(Suppl. 1), S13–S15.

Ozonoff, D., and Boden, L. I. (1987). Truth and Consequences: Health Agency Responses to Environmental Health Problems. *Science Technology and Human Values, 12,* 70–77.

Page, T. (1978). A Generic View of Toxic Chemicals and Similar Risks. *Ecology Law Quarterly, 7,* 207–244.

Palca, J. (1992). Lead Researcher Confronts Accusers in Public Hearing. *Science, 256,* 437–438.

Paoli RR. Yard PCB Litigation, 35 F.3d 717 (1994).

Parkinson, A. (2001). Biotransformation of Xenobiotics. In C. D. Klaassen (Ed.), *Casarett and Doull's Toxicology* (6th ed., pp. 133–224). New York: McGraw-Hill.

Peer Review Committee to Review Perchlorate. (2004, June). *Perchlorate in Drinking Water: A Science and Policy Review.* Irvine: University of California, Irvine.

Peer Review of Defendants' Expert's Report by Anonymous Reviewer. (2004, January 12).

Peer Review of Plaintiffs' Expert's Report by Anonymous Reviewer. (2004, January 12).

Peer Review of Plaintiffs' Expert's Report by Anonymous Reviewer. (2004, April 14).

People v. O'Neill, Film Recovery Systems, et al., 550 N.E. 2d 1090 (1990).

Perera, F. (1996). Molecular Epidemiology: Insights into Cancer Susceptibility, Risk Assessment, and Prevention. *Journal of the National Cancer Institute, 88,* 496–509.

Perera, F. P., Boffetta, P., and Nisbet, I. C. T. (1989). What Are The Major Carcinogens in the Etiology of Human Cancer? Industrial Carcinogens. In V. T. Devita, Jr., S. Hellman, and S. A. Rosenberg (Eds.), *Important Advances in Oncology* (pp. 249–265). Philadelphia: Lippincott.

Petersen, M. (2000, August 29). Settlement Is Approved in Diet Drug Case. *New York Times,* C2.

Pitot, H. C., III, and Dragan, Y. P. (2001). Chemical Carcinogensesis. In C. D. Klaassen (Ed.), *Casarett and Doull's Toxicology.* (6th ed., pp. 241–320). New York: McGraw-Hill.

Poirier, M. C. (2001). In Memoriam: James A. Miller (1915–2000). *Carcinogenesis, 22*(4), 681–683.

Poole, C. (1987). Beyond the Confidence Interval. *American Journal of Public Health, 77,* 195–199.

Preston, R. J., and Hoffmann, G. R. (2001). Genetic Toxicology. In C. D. Klaassen (Ed.), *Casarett and Doull's Toxicology* (6th ed., pp. 321–350). New York: McGraw-Hill.

Quine, W. V. O. (1960). *Word and Object.* Cambridge, MA: MIT Press.

Rall, D. P., Hogan, M. D., Huff, J. E., Schwetz, B. A., and Tennant, R. W. (1987). Alternatives to Using Human Experience in Assessing Health Risks. *Annual Review of Public Health, 8,* 355–385.

Raloff, J. (1995). Physicists Offer Reassurances on EMF: Electromagnetic Fields and Their Link to Cancer Might Be Tenuous. *Science News, 47,* 308.

Rawls, J. (1971). *A Theory of Justice.* Cambridge, MA: Belknap Press of Harvard University Press.

Rawls, J. (1993). *Political Liberalism.* Cambridge, MA: Harvard University Press.

Renaud v. Martin Marietta Corp., 749 F. Supp. 1545 (D. Colo. 1990).

Rice, J. M. (1999). Editorial: On the Application of Data on Mode of Action to Carcinogenesis. *Toxicological Sciences, 49,* 175–177.

Rice, J. M., et al. (1999). Rodent Tumors of Urinary Bladder, Renal Cortex, and Thyroid Gland. *Toxicological Sciences, 49,* 166.

Richardson v. Richardson-Merrell, Inc., 857 F.2d 823 (D.C. Cir. 1988), *cert. denied,* 493 U.S. 882 (1989).

Rinsky, R. A., Hornung, R. W., Silver, S. R., and Tseng, C. Y. (2002). Benzene Exposure and Hematopoietic Mortality: A Long-Term Epidemiological Risk Assessment. *American Journal of Industrial Medicine, 42,* 474–480.

Roberti v. Andy's Termite and Pest Control, Inc., 6 Cal. Rptr. 3d 827 (2003).

Robins, J. M., and Greenland, S. (1989a). Estimability and Estimation of Excess and Etiologic Fractions. *Statistics in Medicine, 8,* 845–859.

Robins, J. M., and Greenland, S. (1989b). The Probability of Causation under a Stochastic Model for Individual Risk. *Biometrics, 46,* 1125–1138.

Robins, J. M., and Greenland, S. (1991). Estimability and Estimation of Expected Years of Life Lost Due to a Hazardous Exposure. *Statistics in Medicine, 10,* 79–93.

Rosen v. Ciba-Geigy Corp., 78 F.3d 316 (7th Cir.), *cert. denied,* 519 U.S. 819 (1996).

Rothman, K. (1986). *Modern Epidemiology.* Boston: Little, Brown and Company.

Rothman, K. J. (1987). Causes. In S. Greenland (Ed.), *Evolution of Epidemiologic Ideas: Annotated Readings on Concepts and Methods* (pp. 40–45). Chestnut Hill, MA: Epidemiology Resources.

Rothman K. J., and Greenland, S. (2005). Causation and Causal Inference in Epidemiology. *American Journal of Public Health, 95* (Suppl. 1), S144–S150.

Roueché, B. (1982, May/June). The Lemonade Mystery. *The Saturday Evening Post, 59,* 120.

Ruden, C. (2001). Interpretations of Primary Carcinogenicity Data in 29 Trichloroethylene Risk Assessments. *Toxicology, 169,* 209–225.

Saakbo Rubanick v. Witco Chem. Corp., 242 N.J. Super. 36, 576 A.2d 4 (1990).

Safety: Congress Cites New Evidence Against Tire Maker as Sentiment Swings in Favor of Criminal Penalties in Such Cases (2000, September 21). *Los Angeles Times,* C1.

Saks, M. J. (1992). Do We Really Know Anything About the Behavior of the Tort Litigation System – And Why Not? *Pennsylvania Law Review, 140,* 1147–1289.

Saks, M. J. (2000). The Aftermath of Daubert: An Evolving Jurisprudence of Expert Evidence. *Jurimetrics Journal, 40,* 229–241.

Sanders, J. (1994). Scientific Validity, Admissibility and Mass Torts after *Daubert. Minnesota Law Review, 38,* 1387–1441.

Sanders, J. (2001). *Bendectin on Trial: A Study of Mass Tort Litigation.* Ann Arbor: University of Michigan Press.

Sanders, J., and Machal-Faulks, J. (2001). The Admissibility of Differential Diagnosis Testimony to Prove Causation in Toxic Tort Cases: The Interplay of Adjective and Substantive Law. *Law and Contemporary Problems, 64,* 107–138.

Santone, K. S., and Powis, G. (1991). Mechanism of and Tests for Injuries. In W. J. Hayes, Jr. and E. R. Laws, Jr. (Eds.), *Handbook of Pesticide Toxicology* (pp. 169–214). New York: Harcourt Brace Jovanovich.

Santosky v. Kramer, 455 U.S. 745 (1982).

Savitz, D. A. (1993). Health Effects of Low-Frequency Electric and Magnetic Fields, Special Report Commentary. *Environmental Science and Technology, 27,* 52–54.

Savitz, D. A. (2001, September 31). Report to Court Concerning Federal Rule of Evidence 706.

Savitz, D. A., and Andrews, K. W. (1996). Risk of Myelogenous Leukaemia and Multiple Myeloma in Workers Exposed to Benzene. *Occupational and Environmental Medicine, 33,* 357–358.

Savitz, D. A., and Andrews, K. W. (1997). Review of Epidemiological Evidence on Benzene and Lymphatic and Hematopoietic Cancers. *American Journal of Industrial Medicine, 31,* 287–295.

Schlesselman, J. J. (1974). Sample Size Requirements in Cohort and Case-Control Studies of Disease. *American Journal of Epidemiology, 99,* 381–384.

Schottenfeld, D., and Haas, J. F. (1979). Carcinogens in the Workplace. *CA – Cancer Journal for Clinicians, 29,* 144–159.

Schuck, P. (1992). Legal Complexity: Some Causes, Consequences, and Cures. *Duke Law Journal, 42,* 1–52.

Schuck, P. H. (1993). Multi-Culturalism Redux: Science, Law, and Politics. *Yale Law and Policy Review, 11,* 1–46.

Shank, R. C., and Herron, D. C. (1982). Methylation of Human Liver DNA after Probable Dimethylnitrosamine Poisoning. In P. N. Magee (Ed.), *Nitrosamines and Human Cancer* (pp. 153–159). Cold Spring Harbor, NY: Cold Spring Harbor Laboratory.

Sheehan v. Daily Racing Form, Inc., 104 F.3d 940 (7th Cir. 1997).

Silbergeld, E. K. (1991). The Role of Toxicology in Causation: A Scientific Perspective. *Courts, Health Science and the Law, 1*(3), 374–385.

Silver, S. R., Rinsky, R. A., Cooper, S. P., Hornung, R. W., and Lai, D. (2002). Effect of Follow-up Time on Risk Estimates: Longitudinal Examination of the Relative Risks of Leukemia and Multiple Myeloma in a Rubber Hydrochloride Cohort. *American Journal of Industrial Medicine, 42,* 481–489.

Sindell v. Abbott Laboratories et al., 26 Cal.3d 588, 607 P.2d 924 (1980).

Skill v. Martinez, 91 F.R.D. 498 (D.N.J. 1981), *aff'd on other grounds,* 677 F.2d 368 (3d Cir. 1982).

Skyrms, B. (1966). *Choice and Chance: An Introduction to Inductive Logic.* Belmont, CA: Dickenson.

Smith, M. A., Rubenstein, L., and Ungerleider, R. S. (1994). Therapy-Related Acute Myeloid Leukemia Following Treatment with Epipodophyllotoxins: Estimating the Risks. *Medical and Podiatric Oncology, 23,* 86–98.

Snyder, R. (1984). The Benzene Problem in Perspective. *Fundamental and Applied Toxicology, 4,* 692–699.

Snyder v. Secretary of Health and Human Services, 2002 WL 31965742 (Fed. CI 2002).

Soldo v. Sandoz Pharmaceuticals Corporation, Civil Action No. 98-1712 (January 16, 2002).

Soldo v. Sandoz Pharmaceuticals Corp., 244 F. Supp. 2d 434 (W.D. Pa., January 13, 2003).

Soldo v. Sandoz Pharmaceuticals Corporation, 2003 WL 355931 (W.D. Pa.).

Speiser v. Randall, 357 U.S. 513 (1958).

Steenland, K., Bertazzi, P., Baccarelli, A., and Kogevinas, M. (2004). Dioxin Revisited: Developments Since the 1997 IARC Classification of Dioxin as a Human Carcinogen. *Environmental Health Perspectives 112*(13), 1265–1268.

Stephenson v. Dow Chemical Co., 273 F.3d 249 C.A.2 (N.Y.), 2001.

Stevens v. the Secretary of Health and Human Services, 2001 WL 387418 (Fed. CI).

Strong, J. W., et al. (1992). *McCormick on Evidence* (4th ed.). St. Paul, MN: West.

Sullivan, A. K. (1993). Classification, Pathogenesis, and Etiology of Neoplastic Diseases of the Hematopoietic System. In G. R. Lee, et al. (Eds.), *Wintrobe's Clinical Hematology* (Vol. 2, 9th ed., pp. 1725–1791). Philadelphia: Lea and Febiger.

Susser, M. (1987). Judgment and Causal Inferences Criteria in Epidemiologic Studies. In S. Greenland (Ed.), *Evolution of Epidemiologic Ideas: Annotated Readings on Concepts and Methods* (pp. 69–83). Newton Lower Falls, MA: Epidemiology Resources. (Reprinted from *American Journal of Epidemiology,* 1977, *105,* 1–15)

Swift, M., Morrell, D., Massey, R. B., and Chase, C. L. (1991). Incidence of Cancer in 161 Families Affected by Ataxia-telangiectasia. *New England Journal of Medicine, 325,* 1831–1836.

Tanner v. Westbrook, 174 F.3d 542 (5th Cir. 1999).

Temple, R. (1979). Meta-Analysis and Epidemiologic Studies in Drug Development and Post-marketing Surveillance. *Journal of the American Medical Association, 281,* 841–844.

Thagard, P. (1999). *How Scientists Explain Disease.* Princeton: Princeton University Press.

Thomas v. Hoffman-La-Roche, Inc., 731 F. Supp. 224 (N.D. Miss. 1989), *aff'd on other grounds,* 949 F.2d 806 (5th Cir. 1992).

Thompson, W. D. (1987). Statistical Criteria in the Interpretation of Epidemiologic Data. *American Journal of Public Health, 77*, 191–194.

Thornton, J. (2001). *Pandora's Poison: Chlorine, Health and a New Environmental Strategy.* Cambridge, MA: MIT Press.

Timbrell, J. (2000). *Principles of Biochemical Toxicology* (3rd ed.). London: Taylor and Francis.

Tizon, T. A. (2005, May 16). Cases Against Nuclear Plant Finally Heard: After 15 Years of Delays, 2300 Plaintiffs Who Say Radioactive Releases at the Hanford Site Made Them Seriously Ill Wait for a Jury's Decision. *Los Angeles Times*, A2.

Tomatis, L., Huff, J., Hertz-Picciotto, I., Sandler, D. P., Bucher, J., Boffetta, P., et al. (1997). Avoided and Avoidable Risks of Cancer. *Carcinogenesis, 18*, 97–105.

Toole v. Richardson-Merrell, Inc., 251 Cal. App. 2d 689 (1967).

Travis, C. C. (1993). Interspecies Extrapolation of Toxic Data. In R. G. M. Wang, J. B. Knaak, and H. I. Maibach (Eds.), *Health Risk Assessment: Dermal and Inhalation Exposure and Absorption of Toxicants* (pp. 387–410). Boca Raton, FL: CRC Press.

Travis, C. C., and Hester, S. T. (1991). Global Chemical Pollution. *Environmental Science and Technology, 25*, 814–819.

Turpin v. Merrell Dow Pharm., Inc., 959 F.2d 1349 (6th Cir. 1992).

United States. (2000). *Federal Rules of Evidence.* Washington, DC: U.S. Government Printing Office.

U.S. Congress, Office of Technology Assessment. (1983). *The Information Content of Premanufacture Notices.* Washington, DC: U.S. Government Printing Office.

U.S. Congress, Office of Technology Assessment. (1987). *Identifying and Regulating Carcinogens.* Washington, DC: U.S. Government Printing Office.

U.S. Congress, Office of Technology Assessment. (1995). *Screening and Testing Chemicals in Commerce.* Washington, DC: U.S. Government Printing Office.

U.S. Department of Health and Human Services. (1995). *Toxicological Profile for Asbestos.*

U.S. Department of Health and Human Services, Food and Drug Administration. Notice on Opportunity for a Hearing on a Proposal to Withdraw Approval of the Indication of Bromocriptine Mesylate (Parlodel) for the Prevention of Physiological Lactation. 59 Fed. Reg. 43347 (Aug. 23, 1994).

U.S. Department of Health and Human Services, National Toxicology Program. (n.d.). Report on Carcinogens. Retrieved June 1, 1999 from http://ntp.niehs.nih.gov/ntpweb/index.cfm?objectid=72016262-BDB7-CEBA-FA60E922B18C2540.

U.S. Department of Health and Human Services, National Toxicology Program (1996, September 26). Listing Criteria. Retrieved May 28, 1999 from http://ntp.niehs.nih.gov/ntpweb/index.cfm?objectid=03C9CE38-E5CD-EE56-D21B94351DBC8FC3.

U.S. Department of Health and Human Services, National Toxicology Program. (2000, October 20). *Ninth Annual Report on Carcinogens.* Retrieved from http://ehis.niehs.nih.gov/roc/ninth/known.pdf.

U.S. Department of Health and Human Services, National Toxicology Program. (2002a). Safrole: Cas. No. 94-59-7. *Tenth Report on Carcinogens.*

U.S. Department of Health and Human Services, National Toxicology Program. (2002b). Polychlorinated Biphenyls (PCBs): Cas. No. 1336-36-3. *Tenth Report on Carcinogens.*

U.S. Department of Health and Human Services, National Toxicology Program. (2005). Benzidine and Dyes Metabolized to Benzidine. In *Eleventh Annual Report on Carcinogens.* Research Triangle Park, NC: U.S. Department of Health and Human Services, Public Health Service, National Toxicology Program. Retrieved from http://ntp.niehs.nih.gov/ntp/roc/eleventh/profiles/s020benz.pdf.

U.S. Department of Health and Human Services, Public Health Service, National Institutes of Health, National Toxicology Program. (1996, February). Comparative Initiation/Promotion Skin Pain Studies of B6C3F1 Mice, Swiss (CD-1) Mice, and SENCAR Mice. *Technical Report Series*, No. 441.

U.S. Department of Health and Human Services, Taskforce on Health Risk Assessment. (1986). *Determining Risks to Health: Federal Policy and Practice.* Dover, MA: Auburn House.

U.S. Environmental Protection Agency. Perchlorate. Retrieved from http://www.epa.gov/swerffrr/documents/perchlorate.htm.

U.S. Environmental Protection Agency. Proposed Guidelines for Carcinogen Risk Assessment. 61 Fed. Reg. 17960 (April 23, 1996).

U.S. Environmental Protection Agency. (1996, September). PCBs: Cancer Dose-Response Assessment and Application to Environmental Mixtures. Washington, DC: EPA/600/P-96/001F.

U.S. Environmental Protection Agency. (2005, February 23). Arsenic in Drinking Water. Retrieved from http://www.epa.gov/safewater/arsenic.html.

U.S. Food and Drug Administration. Final Rule Declaring Dietary Supplements Containing Ephedrine Alkaloids Adulterated Because They Present an Unreasonable Risk. 69 Fed. Reg. 6787 (Feb. 11, 2004).

U.S. Supreme Court. (2003). *Federal Rules of Civil Procedure.* Retrieved from the Legal Information Institute (Cornell University Law School) at http://www.law.cornell.edu/rules/frcp/.

United States v. Dorsey, 45 F.3d 809 (4th Cir. 1995).

United States v. 14.38 Acres of Land Situated in Leflore County, Mississippi, 80 F.3d 1074 (5th Cir. 1996).

Van Raalte, H. G. S., and Grasso, P. (1982). Hematological, Myelotoxic, Clastogenic, Carcinogenic, and Leukemogenic Effects of Benzene. *Regulatory Toxicology and Pharmacology, 2,* 153–176.

Venitt, S. (1994). Mechanisms of Carcinogenesis and Individual Susceptibility to 40 Cancers. *Clinical Chemistry, 40,* 1421–1425.

Vidmar, N. (2005). Expert Evidence, the Adversary System, and the Jury. *American Journal of Public Health, Supplement 1,* 95, S137–143.

Villari v. Terminix Int. Inc., 692 F. Supp. 568 (E.D. Pa. 1988).

Viterbo v. Down Chemical Co., 826 F.2d 420 (5th Cir. 1987).

Waalkes, M. P., et al. (1994). The Scientific Fallacy of Route Specificity of Carcinogenesis with Particular Reference to Cadmium. *Regulatory Toxicology and Pharmacology, 20,* 119–121.

Wade-Greaux v. Whitehall Lab., Inc., 874 F. Supp. 1441 (D.V.I.), *aff'd,* 46 F.3d 1120 (3d Cir. 1994).

Wade-Greaux v. Whitehall Lab., Inc., 46 F.3d 1120 (3d Cir. 1994).

Wagner, W., and Steinzor, R. (Eds.). (2006). *Rescuing Science from Politics.* New York: Cambridge University Press.

Wald, M. L. (2000, January 29). U.S. Acknowledges Radiation Killed Weapons Workers. *New York Times,* A1.

Walker, A. M. (1986). Reporting the Results of Epidemiologic Studies. *American Journal of Public Health, 76,* 556–558.

Walker, V. R. (1996). Preponderance, Probability and Warranted Fact Finding. *Brooklyn Law Review, 62,* 1075–1136.

Walker, V. R. (2006). Transforming Science into Law: Transparency and Default Reasoning in International Trade Disputes. In W. Wagner and R. Steinzor (Eds.), *Rescuing Science from Politics.* New York: Cambridge University Press.

Ward, E., Smith, A. B., and Halperin, W. (1987). 4,4′-Methylenebis (2-Chloraniline): An Unregulated Carcinogen. *American Journal of Industrial Medicine, 12,* 537–549.

Weed, D. (1997). Underdetermination and Incommensurability in Contemporary Epidemiology. *Kennedy Institute of Ethics Journal, 7,* 107–114.

Wells v. Ortho Pharmaceutical Corp., 615 F. Supp. 262 (N.D. Ga. 1985).

Wells v. Ortho Pharm. Corp., 788 F.2d 741 (11th Cir. 1986).

Westberry v. Gislaved Gummi AB, 178 F.3d 257 (4th Cir. 1999).

Willman, D. (2000, June 4). The Rise and Fall of the Killer Drug Rezulin; People Were Dying as Specialists Waged War Against Their FDA Superiors. *Los Angeles Times,* A1.

Willman, D. (2001, March 11). Risk Was Known as FDA Ok'd Fatal Drug. *Los Angeles Times,* A1.

Willman, D. (2002, June 30). Hidden Risks, Lethal Truth. *Los Angeles Times*, 1. Retrieved from http://www.latimes.com.

Witschi, H., and Last, J. (2001). Toxic Regulation of the Respiratory System. In C. D. Klaassen (Ed.), *Casarett and Doull's Toxicology* (6th ed., pp. 515–534). New York: McGraw-Hill.

Wong, O. (1990). A Cohort Mortality Study and a Case Control Study of Workers Potentially Exposed to Styrene in Reinforced Plastics and Composite Industry. *British Journal of Industrial Medicine*, 47, 753–762.

Woodward, J., and Goodstein, D. (1996). Conduct, Misconduct and the Structure of Science. *American Scientist*, 84, 479–490.

World Health Organization. (1994). *Brominated Diphenyl Ethers, IPCS Environmental Health Criteria 163*. Geneva: Author.

Wright, L. (1989). *Practical Reasoning*. New York: Harcourt Brace Jovanovich.

Wright, L. (2001). *Critical Thinking: An Introduction to Analytical Reading and Reasoning*. New York: Oxford University Press.

Wright and Miller Treatise, 29 Fed. Prac. and Proc. Evid. §6266.

Wright v. Willamette Industries, Inc., 91 F.3d 1105 (8th Cir. 1996).

Written Direct Testimony of Sander Greenland, Dr. P.H., in Opposition to Baxter Healthcare Corporation's Petition for Declaratory Judgment. (1999, April 30).

Zuchowicz v. United States, 140 F.3d 381 (2d Cir. 1998).

Index

Italicized page numbers indicate a more significant entry on a topic.